COMICS
for
CHOICE

**ILLUSTRATED ABORTION STORIES,
HISTORY, AND POLITICS**

Comics for Choice: Illustrated Abortion Stories, History, and Politics
First Printing, Summer 2017
ISBN 978-1-68148-598-0

Edited by Hazel Newlevant, Whit Taylor, and Ø.K. Fox
Cover illustration by Sophia Foster-Dimino
Book design by Jasmine Silver

Crickx, *DLF*, and *Logisoso* fonts by Open Source Publishing (OSP)
osp.kitchen

Printed in the United States.

Comics for Choice was sparked by my outrage at the clinic closures and suffocating restrictions on abortion rights in states like Texas. It is not enough for abortion to remain technically legal; it is a moral imperative for abortion care to be accessible to all who need and want it. The right to abortion is the right to bodily autonomy, and to determine one's own life path. When our 45th president was elected, and the future of abortion rights seemed more uncertain than ever, I couldn't wait any longer. The very next morning, my co-editors and I set the wheels in motion to create the book you now read.

Our aim with Comics for Choice was to create a book that would educate readers about many facets of the history of abortion in America, the incredible diversity of reasons people choose it, and what we can do to protect this crucial right. We wanted to make a book that would help our many readers who've had abortions feel understood and supported.

It was vitally important to us to include the voices of activists, healthcare professionals, and reproductive justice experts in Comics for Choice, not just people who've devoted their lives to drawing comics. Comic artists volunteered to team up with these writers, so we could include as many perspectives and knowledge bases as possible, shared in comics form. Helping to connect these collaborations was one of the most exciting parts of editing this anthology.

Comics for Choice was initially published through a Generosity campaign that raised over $30,000 for the National Network of Abortion Funds. Future sales of the book benefit the editors and contributors.

Working with the writers and artists in this anthology to bring their stories to print has been my great honor. There's something simple and powerful about seeing a drawing of someone's experience, not just reading it. I believe comics are perfectly suited to communicating memorably and encouraging empathy, and that's exactly what we need when it comes to reproductive justice.

Hazel Newlevant, Co-Editor and Publisher

I was really happy to be involved with this project. It helped me transform some shame I couldn't seem to shake. I was never ashamed of having an abortion, but I was hard on myself for making mistakes with my birth control, because I felt I knew better. I had excellent sex education, I volunteered at local Planned Parenthood benefits my whole life, and my godmother is a nurse who I had always turned to for sample packs when I was un- or underinsured and couldn't afford birth control. How did I manage to wind up needing an abortion in my mid-twenties? One answer is birth control was making me feel dysphoric, and I was tired of juggling different types to find the magical one that'd keep my PCOS in check and not make me terribly moody. The real answer is it doesn't matter, mistakes happen, and an abortion is a totally normal procedure.

I am really happy this anthology includes stories from non-binary folks. I am someone who was born with an abnormally high level of testosterone for someone with a uterus and ovaries, and that has given me health problems my whole life. It has taken me over a decade to realize the solution for me is a shot of progestin and daily testosterone. I thank Medicaid, and finally seeing a doctor versed in trans issues. Medicaid for all!

Thank you all for your stories. I am proud of all of us for surviving under patriarchal capitalism.

Ø.K. Fox, Co-Editor

When Hazel proposed the idea of co-editing an anthology about abortion with Ø.K. Fox, I jumped at the offer. As a public health professional and a cartoonist, I have come to understand the power that the comics medium has in relaying important personal stories as well as educational and journalistic ones. I knew that that the

c̶ the perfect choice

abortion, because it

ct with readers,

increase

tigma.

nto the

ring

a clinical

worked

ho needed

looking to

ded options

ave pregnancy

nuing the pregnancy,

adop ion. This experience opened my eyes to the diversity of experiences, values, and beliefs that people hold around abortion. Providing non-judgmental counseling and education has been my goal, and it is really no different with this anthology. I am excited by the breadth and depth of this book and the openness and talent of our creators and contributors. I am pleased to support NNAF and I hope that this book will challenge readers as they explore the historical, scientific, legal, and personal aspects of abortion.

Whit Taylor, Co-Editor

Table of Contents

ENCOUNTERING ABORTION RESTRICTIONS, FROM KENYA TO TEXAS

STORY BY: MJ FLORES ART BY: KAT FAJARDO

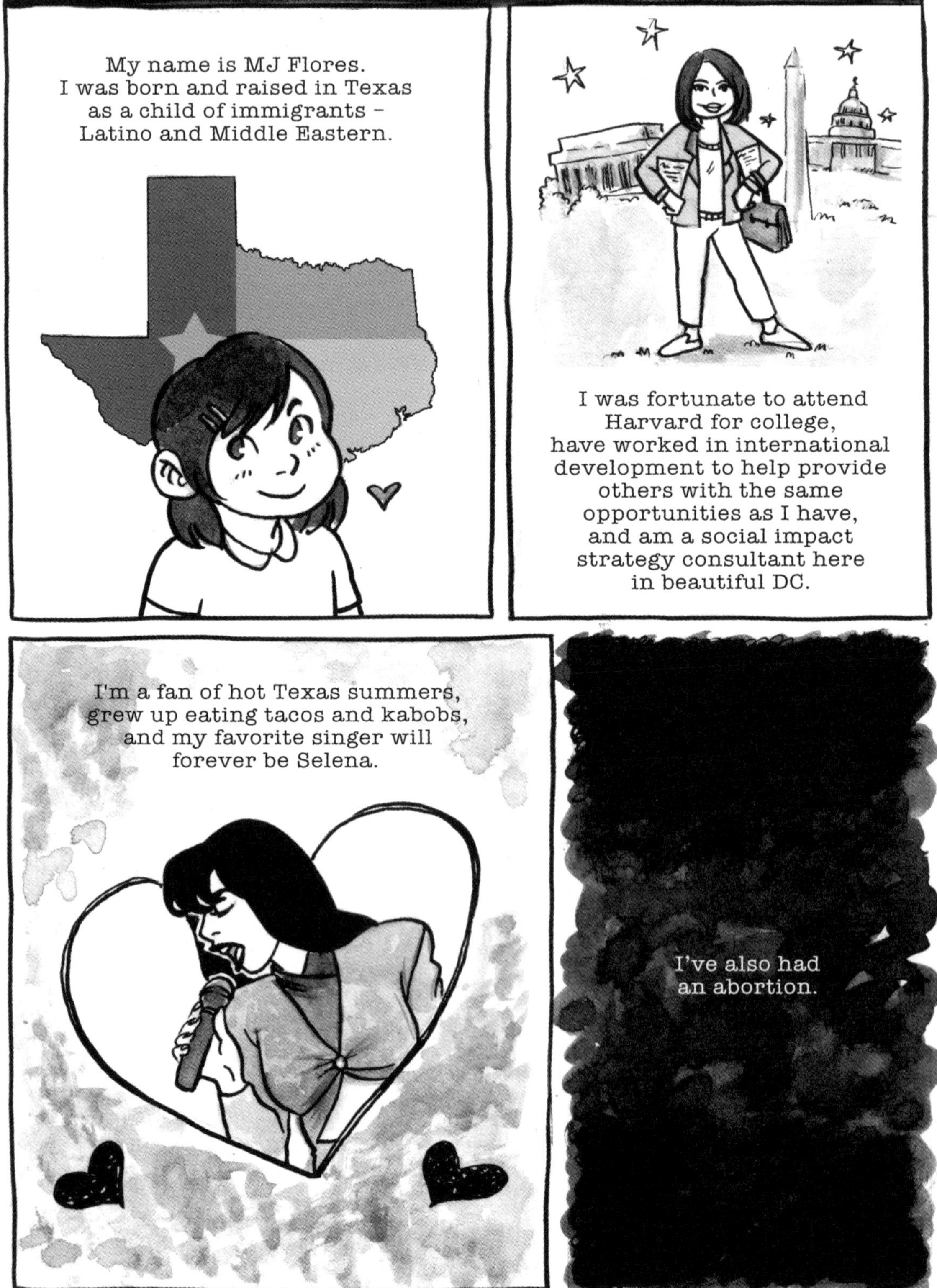
My name is MJ Flores.
I was born and raised in Texas
as a child of immigrants –
Latino and Middle Eastern.
I was fortunate to attend
Harvard for college,
have worked in international
development to help provide
others with the same
opportunities as I have,
and am a social impact
strategy consultant here
in beautiful DC.
I'm a fan of hot Texas summers,
grew up eating tacos and kabobs,
and my favorite singer will
forever be Selena.
I've also had
an abortion.

After college, I chose to work in rural Kenya to help coordinate health and education programs.

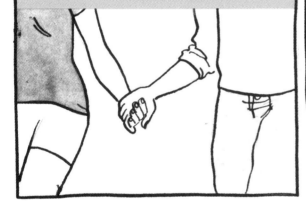

I was dating a guy at the time, and my birth control failed. Multiple forms of birth control failed – the condom broke, the morning after pill did not work.

I never thought I would ever experience an unplanned pregnancy – most of us never do – and, despite being supportive of abortion access, I never imagined I would get an abortion if I did get pregnant.

I was wrong.

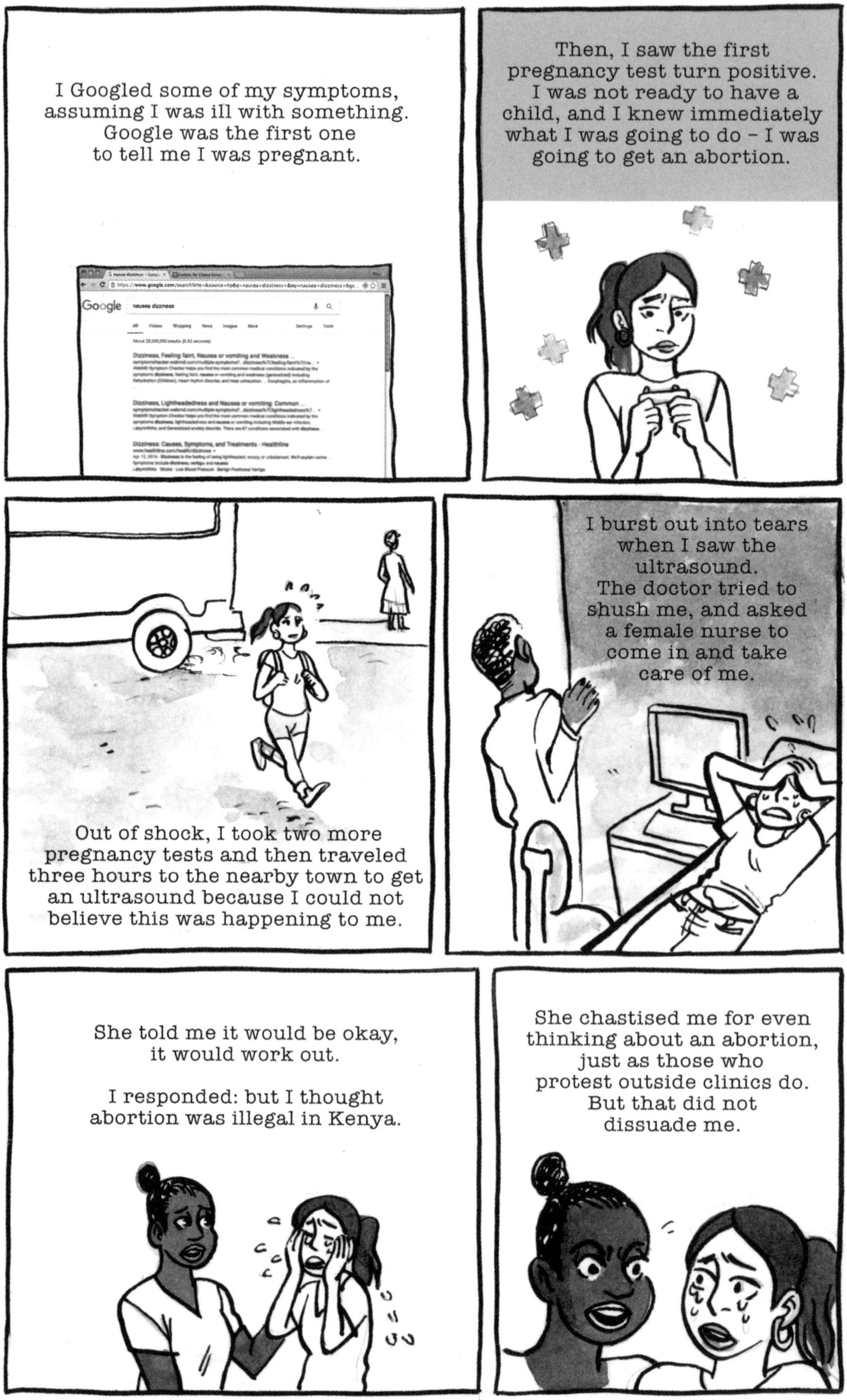
I Googled some of my symptoms, assuming I was ill with something. Google was the first one to tell me I was pregnant.
Google
nausea dizziness
Then, I saw the first pregnancy test turn positive. I was not ready to have a child, and I knew immediately what I was going to do – I was going to get an abortion.
Out of shock, I took two more pregnancy tests and then traveled three hours to the nearby town to get an ultrasound because I could not believe this was happening to me.
I burst out into tears when I saw the ultrasound. The doctor tried to shush me, and asked a female nurse to come in and take care of me.
She told me it would be okay, it would work out.
I responded: but I thought abortion was illegal in Kenya.
She chastised me for even thinking about an abortion, just as those who protest outside clinics do. But that did not dissuade me.

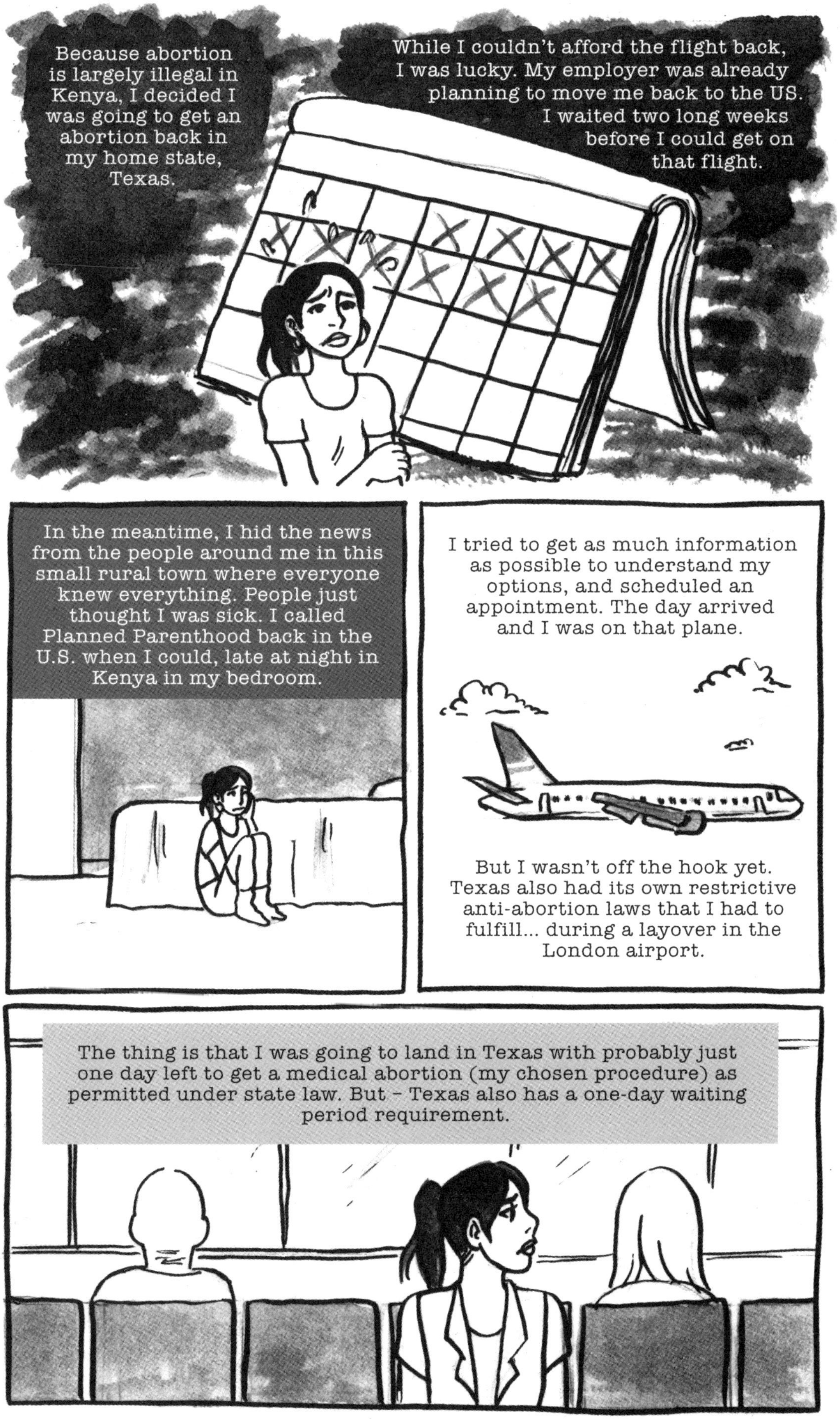
Because abortion is largely illegal in Kenya, I decided I was going to get an abortion back in my home state, Texas.
While I couldn't afford the flight back, I was lucky. My employer was already planning to move me back to the US. I waited two long weeks before I could get on that flight.
In the meantime, I hid the news from the people around me in this small rural town where everyone knew everything. People just thought I was sick. I called Planned Parenthood back in the U.S. when I could, late at night in Kenya in my bedroom.
I tried to get as much information as possible to understand my options, and scheduled an appointment. The day arrived and I was on that plane.
But I wasn't off the hook yet. Texas also had its own restrictive anti-abortion laws that I had to fulfill... during a layover in the London airport.
The thing is that I was going to land in Texas with probably just one day left to get a medical abortion (my chosen procedure) as permitted under state law. But – Texas also has a one-day waiting period requirement.

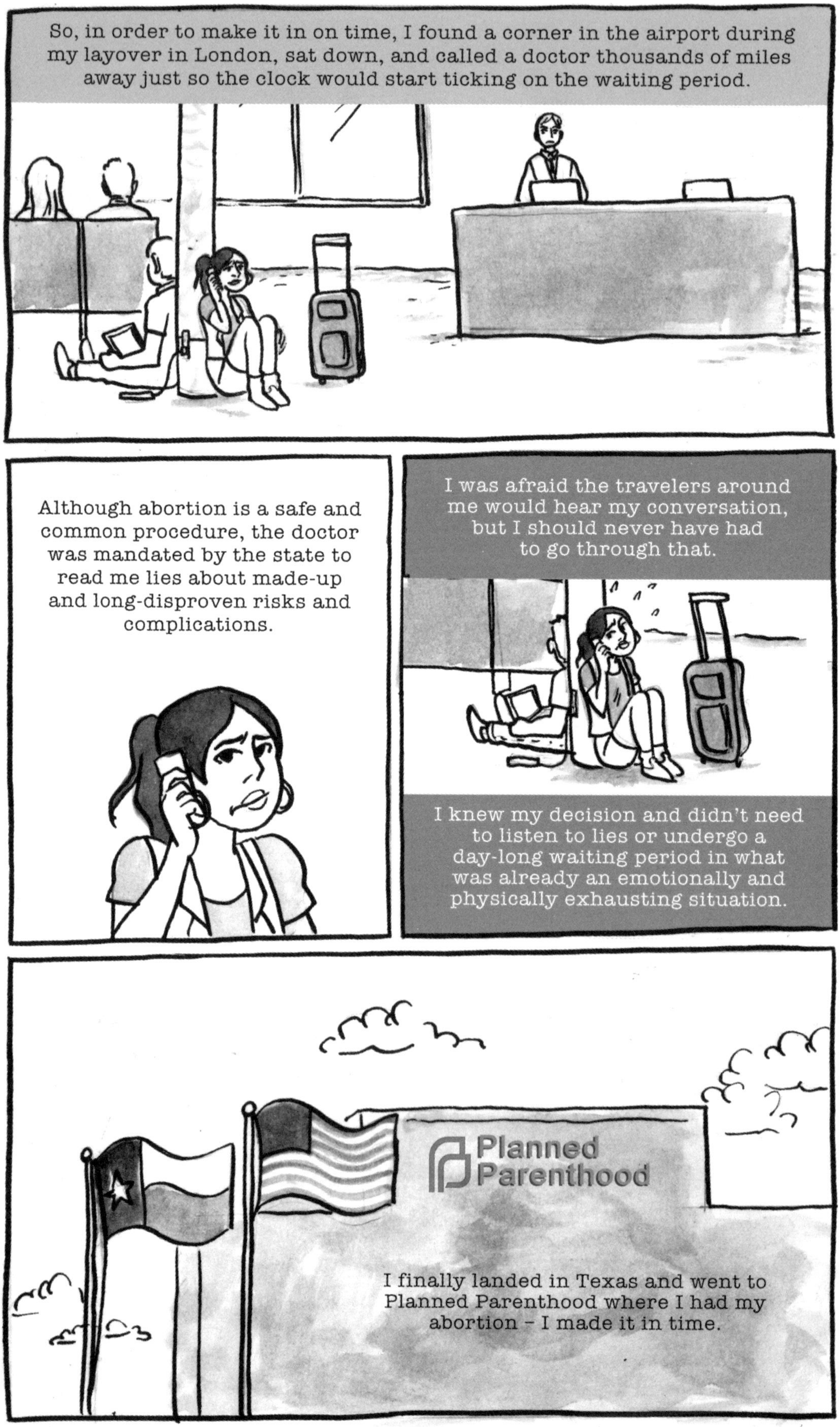
So, in order to make it in on time, I found a corner in the airport during my layover in London, sat down, and called a doctor thousands of miles away just so the clock would start ticking on the waiting period.
Although abortion is a safe and common procedure, the doctor was mandated by the state to read me lies about made-up and long-disproven risks and complications.
I was afraid the travelers around me would hear my conversation, but I should never have had to go through that.
I knew my decision and didn't need to listen to lies or undergo a day-long waiting period in what was already an emotionally and physically exhausting situation.
Planned Parenthood
I finally landed in Texas and went to Planned Parenthood where I had my abortion – I made it in time.

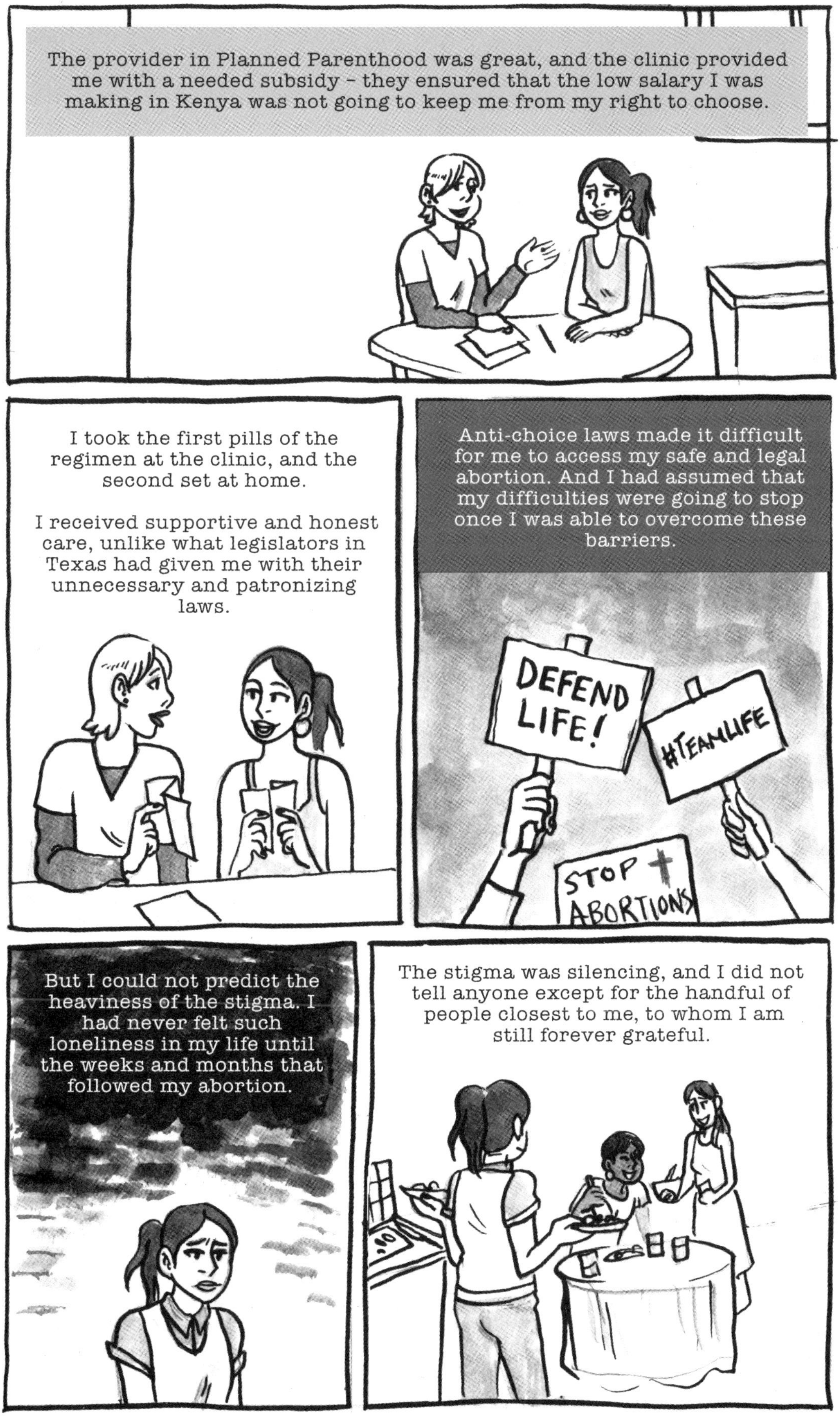

The provider in Planned Parenthood was great, and the clinic provided me with a needed subsidy - they ensured that the low salary I was making in Kenya was not going to keep me from my right to choose.
I took the first pills of the regimen at the clinic, and the second set at home.
I received supportive and honest care, unlike what legislators in Texas had given me with their unnecessary and patronizing laws.
Anti-choice laws made it difficult for me to access my safe and legal abortion. And I had assumed that my difficulties were going to stop once I was able to overcome these barriers.
DEFEND LIFE!
#TEAMLIFE
STOP ABORTIONS
But I could not predict the heaviness of the stigma. I had never felt such loneliness in my life until the weeks and months that followed my abortion.
The stigma was silencing, and I did not tell anyone except for the handful of people closest to me, to whom I am still forever grateful.

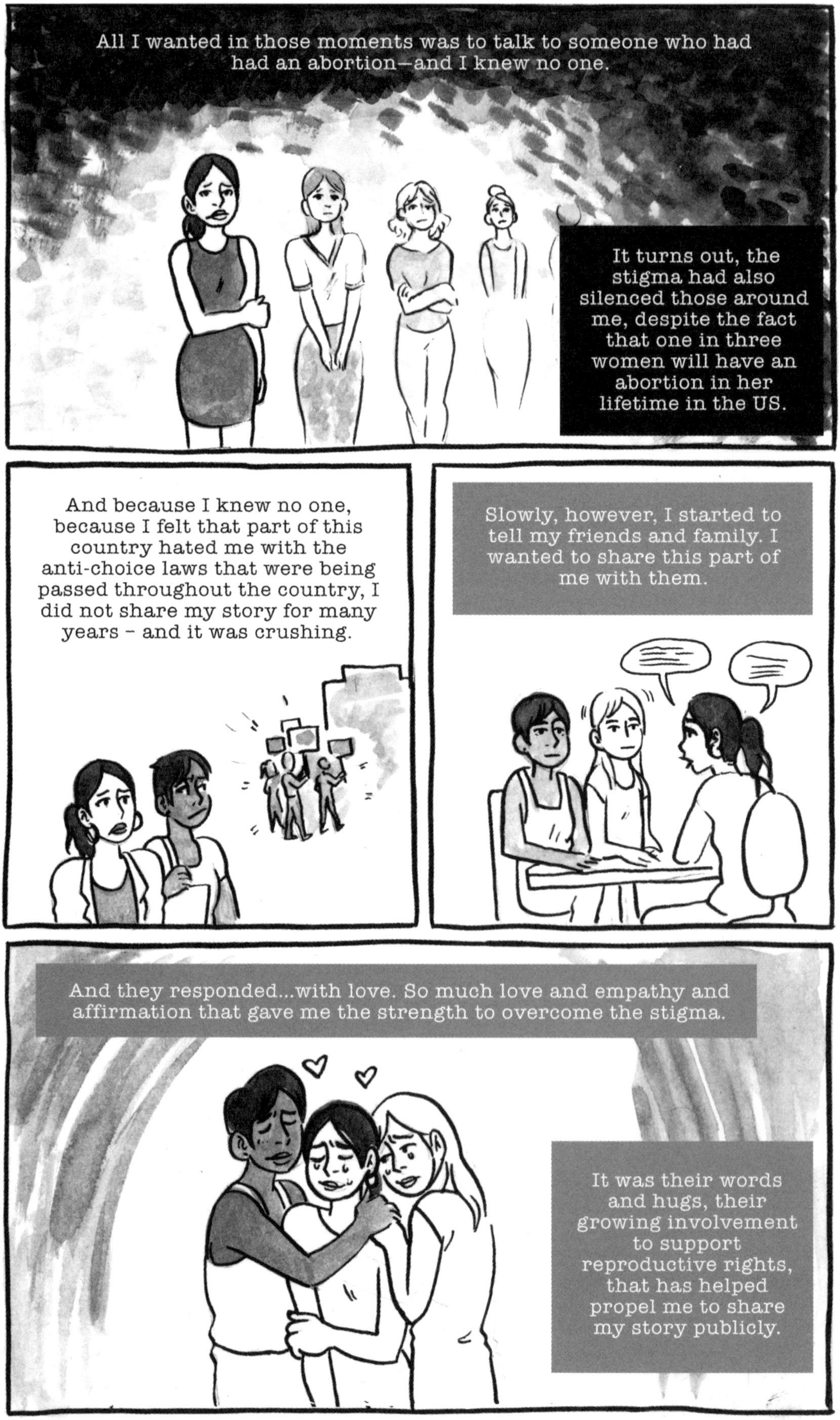
All I wanted in those moments was to talk to someone who had had an abortion—and I knew no one.
It turns out, the stigma had also silenced those around me, despite the fact that one in three women will have an abortion in her lifetime in the US.
And because I knew no one, because I felt that part of this country hated me with the anti-choice laws that were being passed throughout the country, I did not share my story for many years - and it was crushing.
Slowly, however, I started to tell my friends and family. I wanted to share this part of me with them.
And they responded...with love. So much love and empathy and affirmation that gave me the strength to overcome the stigma.
It was their words and hugs, their growing involvement to support reproductive rights, that has helped propel me to share my story publicly.

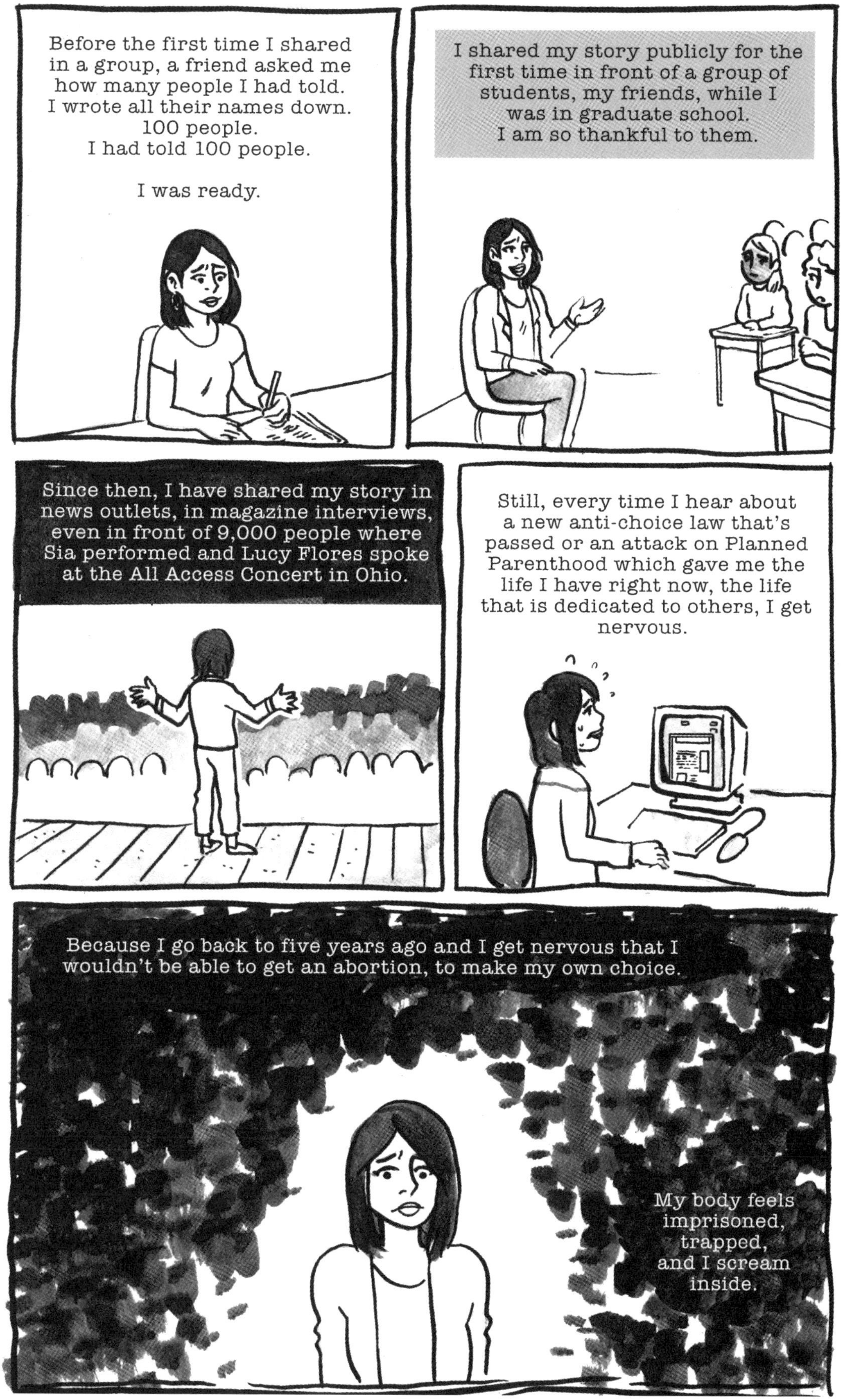
Before the first time I shared in a group, a friend asked me how many people I had told. I wrote all their names down. 100 people. I had told 100 people.
I was ready.
I shared my story publicly for the first time in front of a group of students, my friends, while I was in graduate school. I am so thankful to them.
Since then, I have shared my story in news outlets, in magazine interviews, even in front of 9,000 people where Sia performed and Lucy Flores spoke at the All Access Concert in Ohio.
Still, every time I hear about a new anti-choice law that's passed or an attack on Planned Parenthood which gave me the life I have right now, the life that is dedicated to others, I get nervous.
Because I go back to five years ago and I get nervous that I wouldn't be able to get an abortion, to make my own choice.
My body feels imprisoned, trapped, and I scream inside.

I know an unintended pregnancy can happen again, to me and to anyone else, and I am made worried by the onslaught of these attacks on our rights and our retrogression to that harder, more unforgiving, less understanding country we used to be...and as we still see in other parts of the world.

So I urge everyone, to remember that it can happen to them, or their sister, their wife, their friend, and speak up in support of abortion access to your friends and family,

sign the petitions,

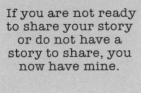

call your Representatives,

and donate to clinics, abortion funds, and advocacy organizations if you can.

DONATE

If you are not ready to share your story or do not have a story to share, you now have mine.

Please share it – let's remind people that choices around abortion happen to real people who should have autonomy over their bodies and lives.

The stigma silenced me for too long. But I no longer will be silenced, and together, we can silence the stigma.

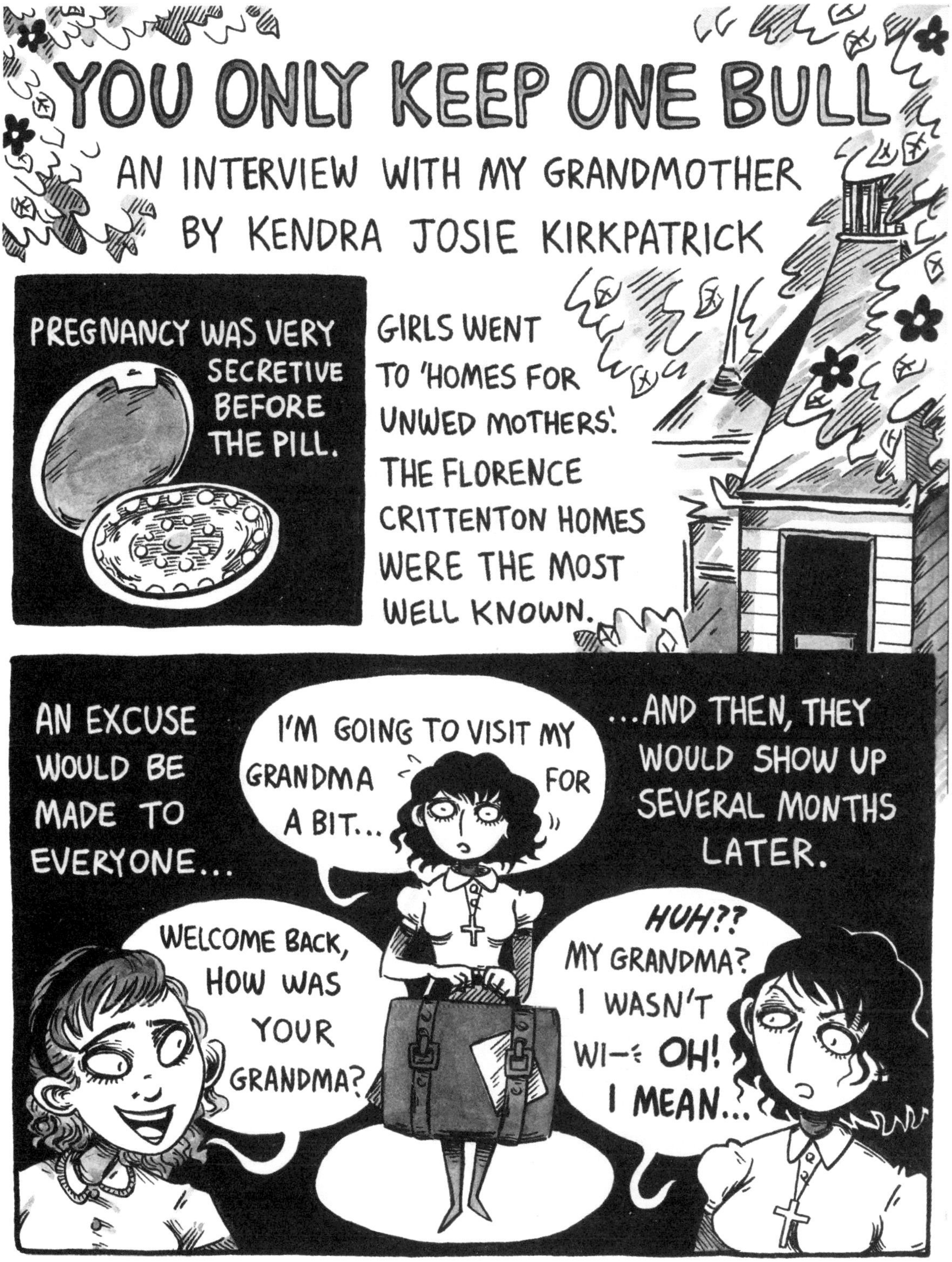
YOU ONLY KEEP ONE BULL
AN INTERVIEW WITH MY GRANDMOTHER
BY KENDRA JOSIE KIRKPATRICK
PREGNANCY WAS VERY SECRETIVE BEFORE THE PILL.
GIRLS WENT TO 'HOMES FOR UNWED MOTHERS'. THE FLORENCE CRITTENTON HOMES WERE THE MOST WELL KNOWN.
AN EXCUSE WOULD BE MADE TO EVERYONE...
I'M GOING TO VISIT MY GRANDMA FOR A BIT...
...AND THEN, THEY WOULD SHOW UP SEVERAL MONTHS LATER.
WELCOME BACK, HOW WAS YOUR GRANDMA?
HUH?? MY GRANDMA? I WASN'T WI- OH! I MEAN...

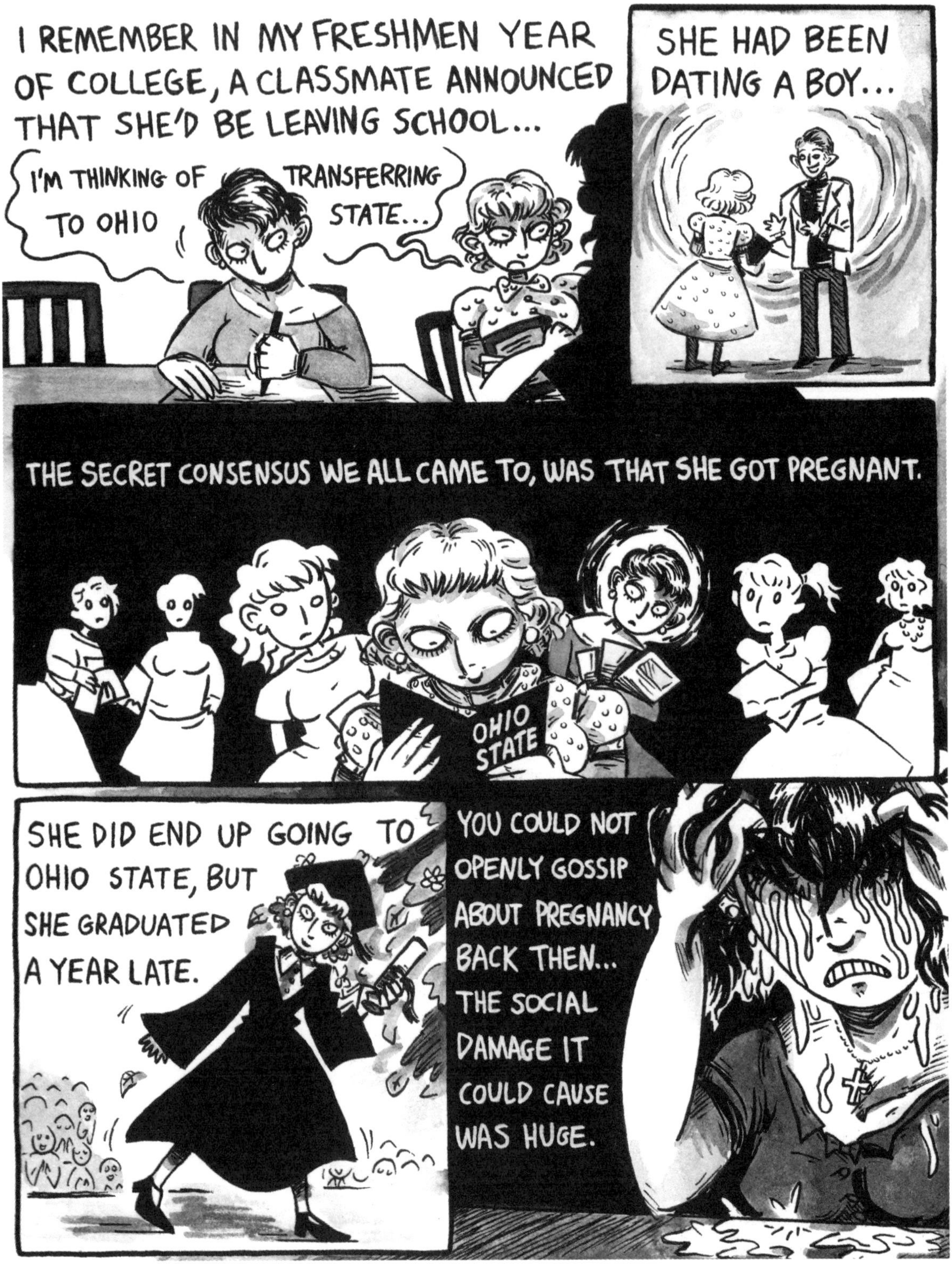
I REMEMBER IN MY FRESHMEN YEAR OF COLLEGE, A CLASSMATE ANNOUNCED THAT SHE'D BE LEAVING SCHOOL...
I'M THINKING OF TRANSFERRING TO OHIO STATE...
SHE HAD BEEN DATING A BOY...
THE SECRET CONSENSUS WE ALL CAME TO, WAS THAT SHE GOT PREGNANT.
OHIO STATE
SHE DID END UP GOING TO OHIO STATE, BUT SHE GRADUATED A YEAR LATE.
YOU COULD NOT OPENLY GOSSIP ABOUT PREGNANCY BACK THEN... THE SOCIAL DAMAGE IT COULD CAUSE WAS HUGE.

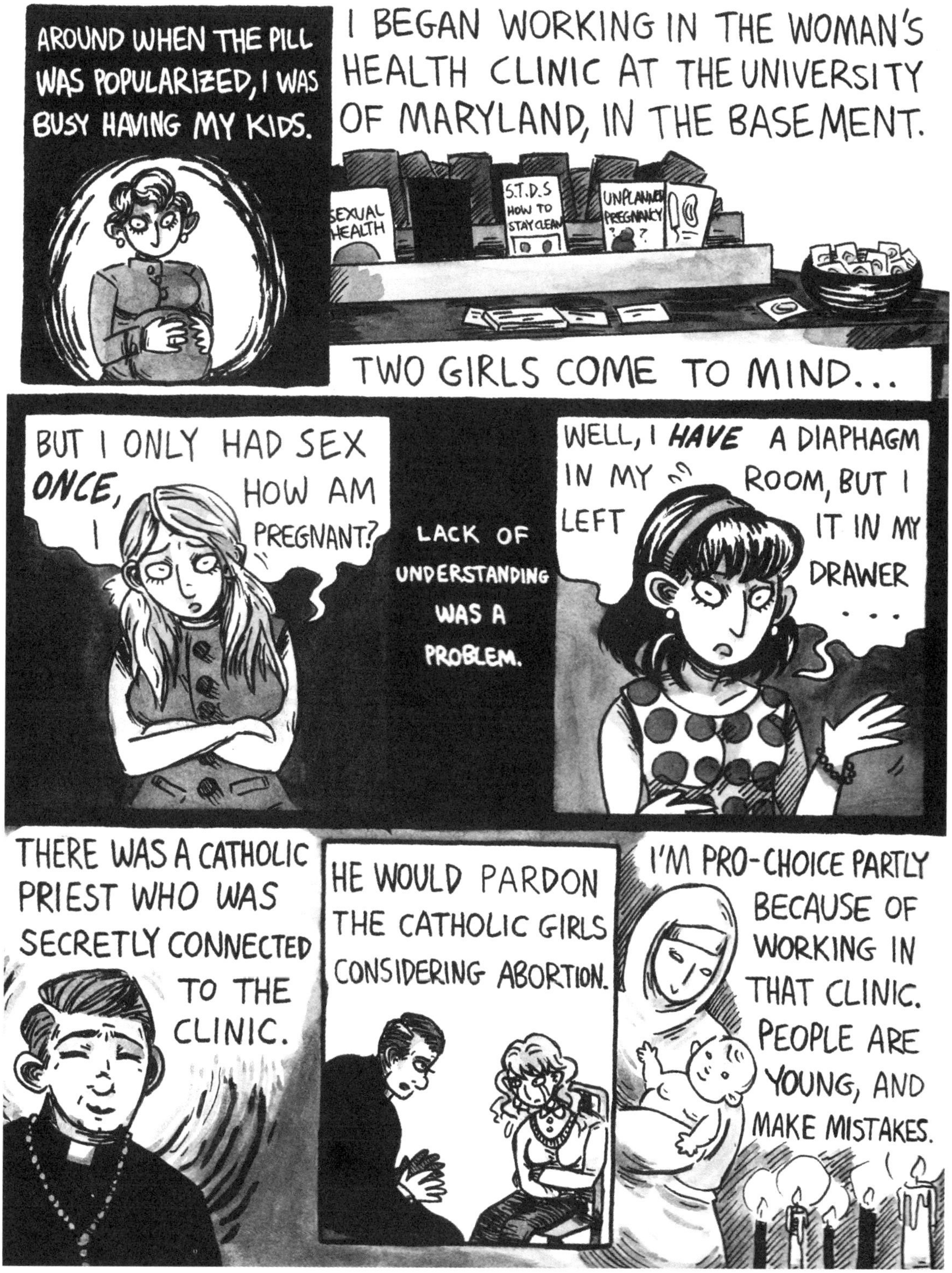
AROUND WHEN THE PILL WAS POPULARIZED, I WAS BUSY HAVING MY KIDS.
I BEGAN WORKING IN THE WOMAN'S HEALTH CLINIC AT THE UNIVERSITY OF MARYLAND, IN THE BASEMENT.
SEXUAL HEALTH
S.T.D.S HOW TO STAY CLEAN
UNPLANNED PREGNANCY
TWO GIRLS COME TO MIND...
BUT I ONLY HAD SEX ONCE, HOW AM I PREGNANT?
LACK OF UNDERSTANDING WAS A PROBLEM.
WELL, I HAVE A DIAPHAGM IN MY ROOM, BUT I LEFT IT IN MY DRAWER...
THERE WAS A CATHOLIC PRIEST WHO WAS SECRETLY CONNECTED TO THE CLINIC.
HE WOULD PARDON THE CATHOLIC GIRLS CONSIDERING ABORTION.
I'M PRO-CHOICE PARTLY BECAUSE OF WORKING IN THAT CLINIC. PEOPLE ARE YOUNG, AND MAKE MISTAKES.

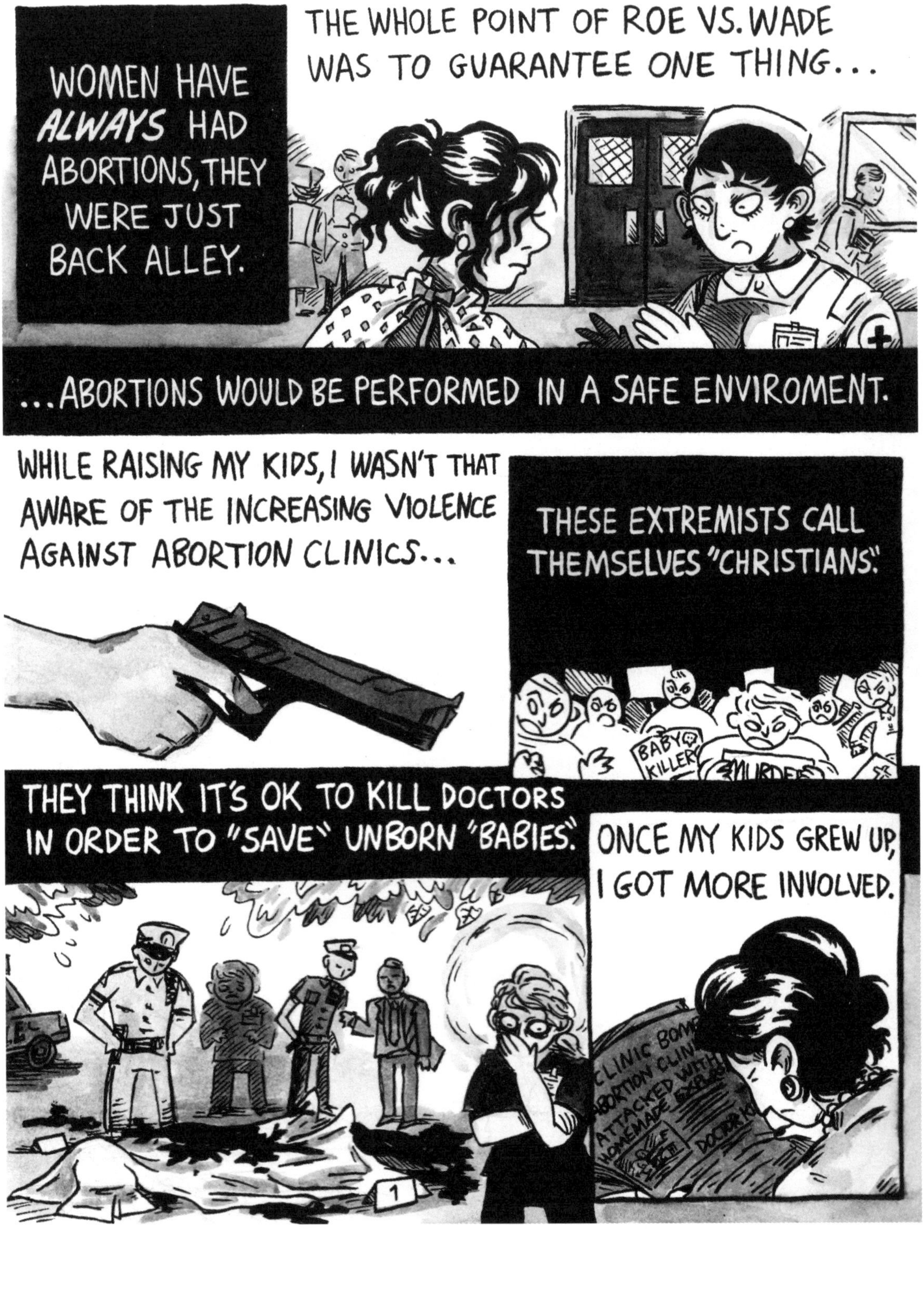
WOMEN HAVE *ALWAYS* HAD ABORTIONS, THEY WERE JUST BACK ALLEY.
THE WHOLE POINT OF ROE VS. WADE WAS TO GUARANTEE ONE THING...
...ABORTIONS WOULD BE PERFORMED IN A SAFE ENVIROMENT.
WHILE RAISING MY KIDS, I WASN'T THAT AWARE OF THE INCREASING VIOLENCE AGAINST ABORTION CLINICS...
THESE EXTREMISTS CALL THEMSELVES "CHRISTIANS."
BABY KILLER
THEY THINK IT'S OK TO KILL DOCTORS IN ORDER TO "SAVE" UNBORN "BABIES."
1
ONCE MY KIDS GREW UP, I GOT MORE INVOLVED.

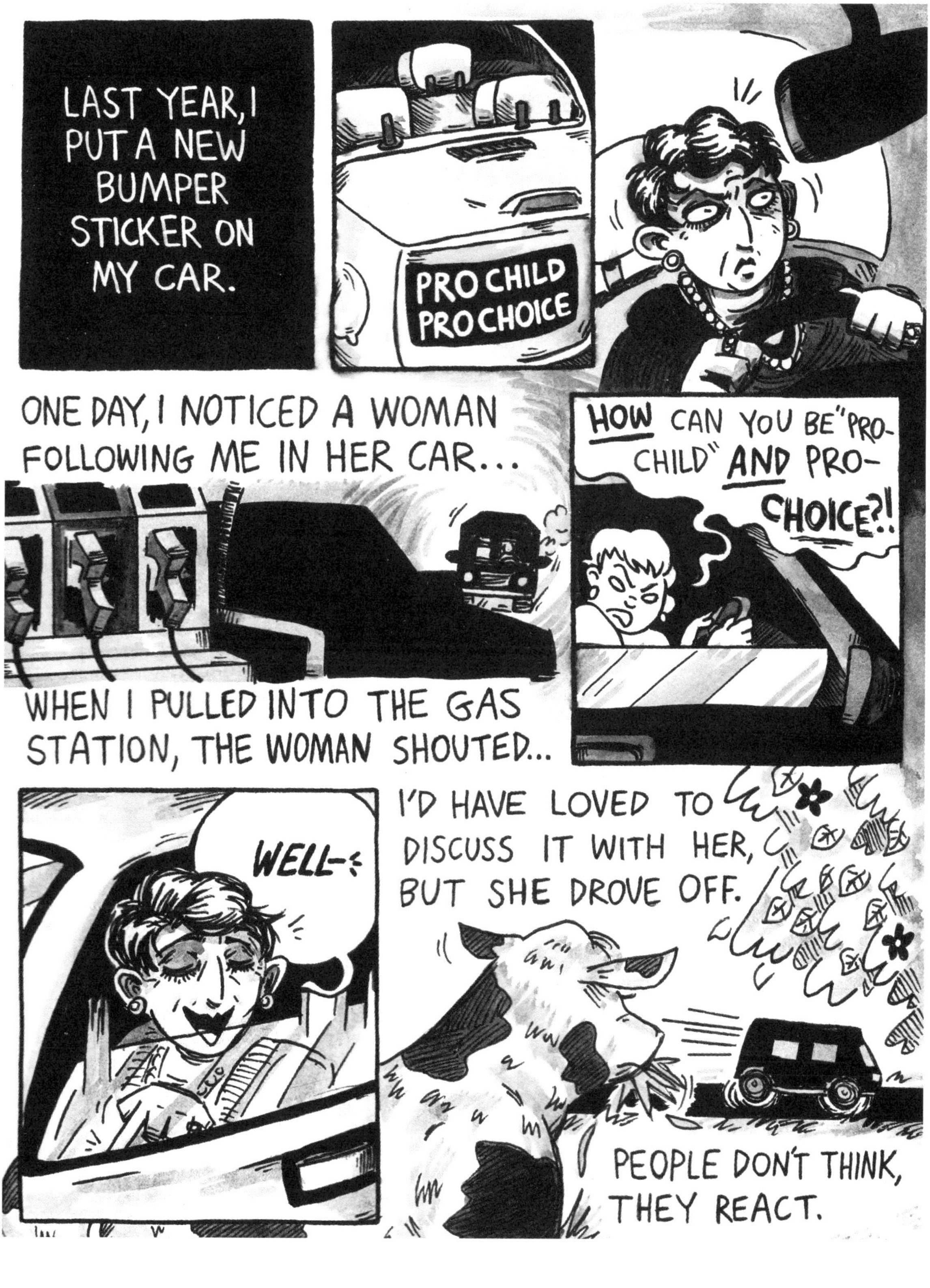
LAST YEAR, I PUT A NEW BUMPER STICKER ON MY CAR.
PRO CHILD PRO CHOICE
ONE DAY, I NOTICED A WOMAN FOLLOWING ME IN HER CAR...
WHEN I PULLED INTO THE GAS STATION, THE WOMAN SHOUTED...
HOW CAN YOU BE "PRO-CHILD" AND PRO-CHOICE?!
WELL-
I'D HAVE LOVED TO DISCUSS IT WITH HER, BUT SHE DROVE OFF.
PEOPLE DON'T THINK, THEY REACT.

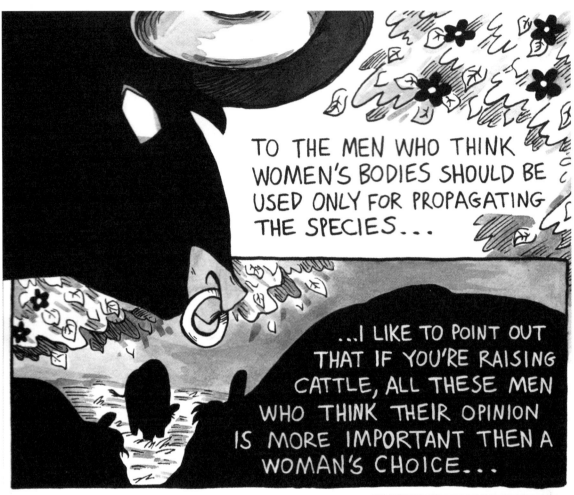

TO THE MEN WHO THINK WOMEN'S BODIES SHOULD BE USED ONLY FOR PROPAGATING THE SPECIES...

...I LIKE TO POINT OUT THAT IF YOU'RE RAISING CATTLE, ALL THESE MEN WHO THINK THEIR OPINION IS MORE IMPORTANT THEN A WOMAN'S CHOICE...

...THEY'D ALL BE IRRELEVANT...

...BECAUSE YOU ONLY KEEP ONE BULL AROUND.

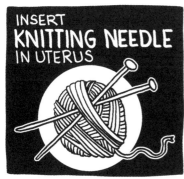
INSERT KNITTING NEEDLE IN UTERUS

DRINK DETERGENT
SUDSO

BEAT STOMACH WITH BASEBALL BAT

SPEND THE NIGHT IN THE SNOW

DO IT YOURSELF ABORTION
HORROR STORIES
METHODS WOMEN HAVE USED WHEN MEDICAL ABORTION IS UNAVAILABLE.
JENNIFER CAMPER

SQUIRT SOAP AND TURPENTINE IN UTERUS
SOAP
TURP

DRINK BLEACH
BLEACH

INSERT CHILI PEPPERS IN VAGINA

FALL DOWN STAIRS

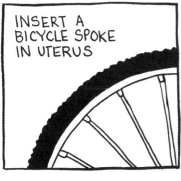
INSERT A BICYCLE SPOKE IN UTERUS

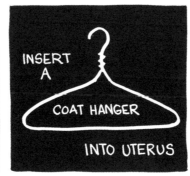
INSERT A COAT HANGER INTO UTERUS

DRINK LYE
LYE

TAKE A BATH IN BOILING WATER

STARVE

FALL OFF ROOF

They Called Her Dr. D:

Tennessee's first Black woman legislator and abortion reform.

Writer: Dr. Cynthia Greenlee
Artist: Jaz Malone

Dorothy Brown
born: circa 1919
died: 2004

Just an infant, Dorothy Brown was placed in a New York orphanage.

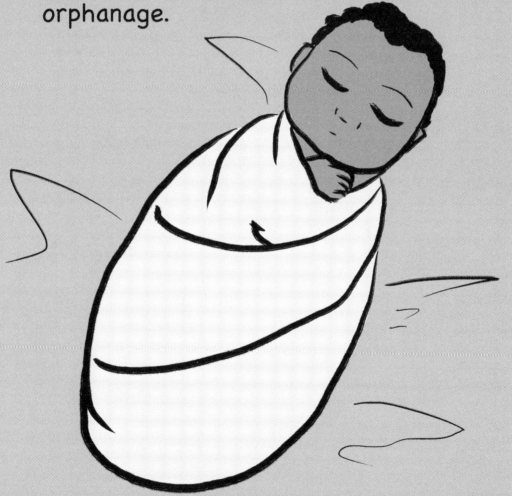

Her mother couldn't take care of her.

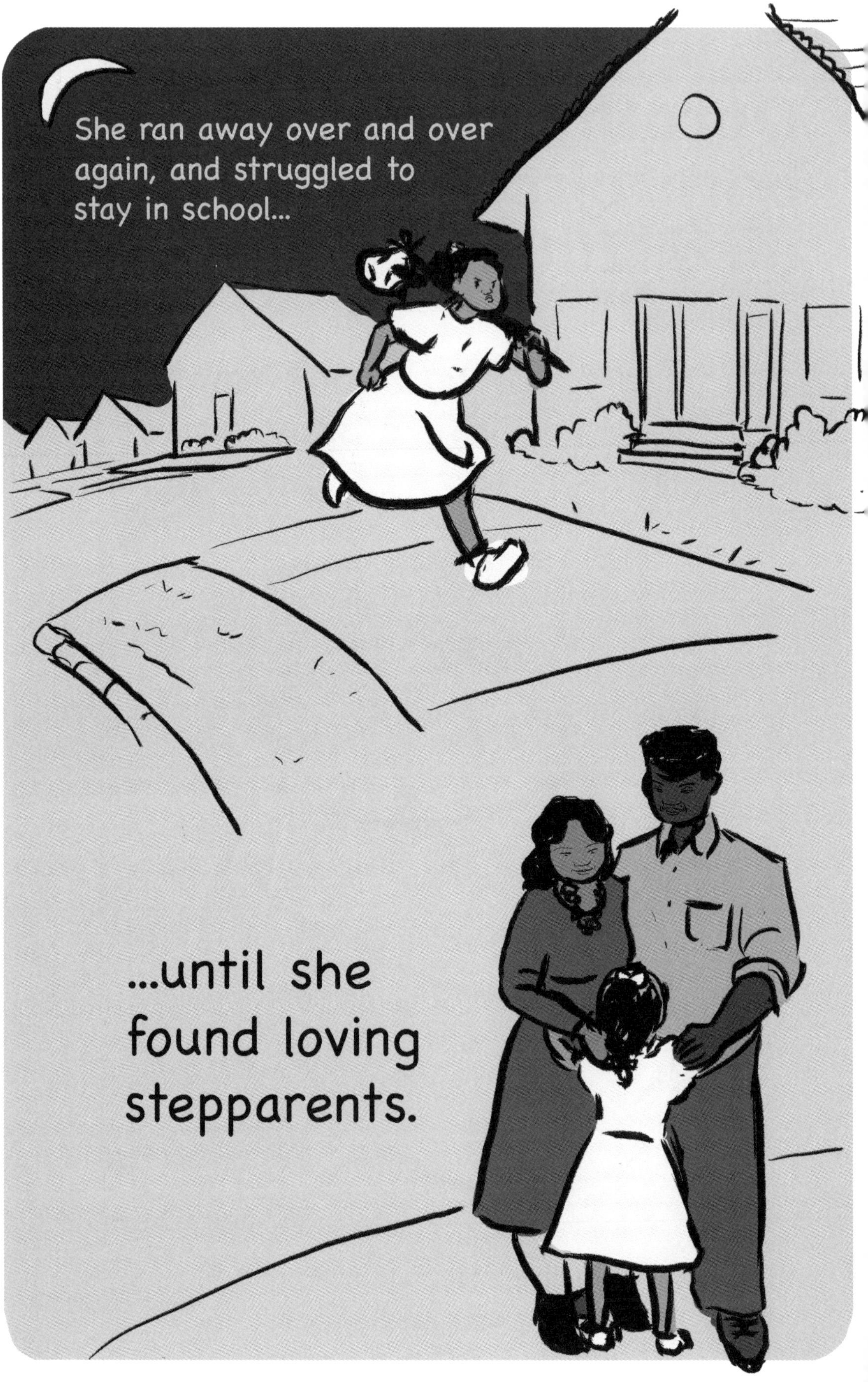

She ran away over and over again, and struggled to stay in school...
...until she found loving stepparents.

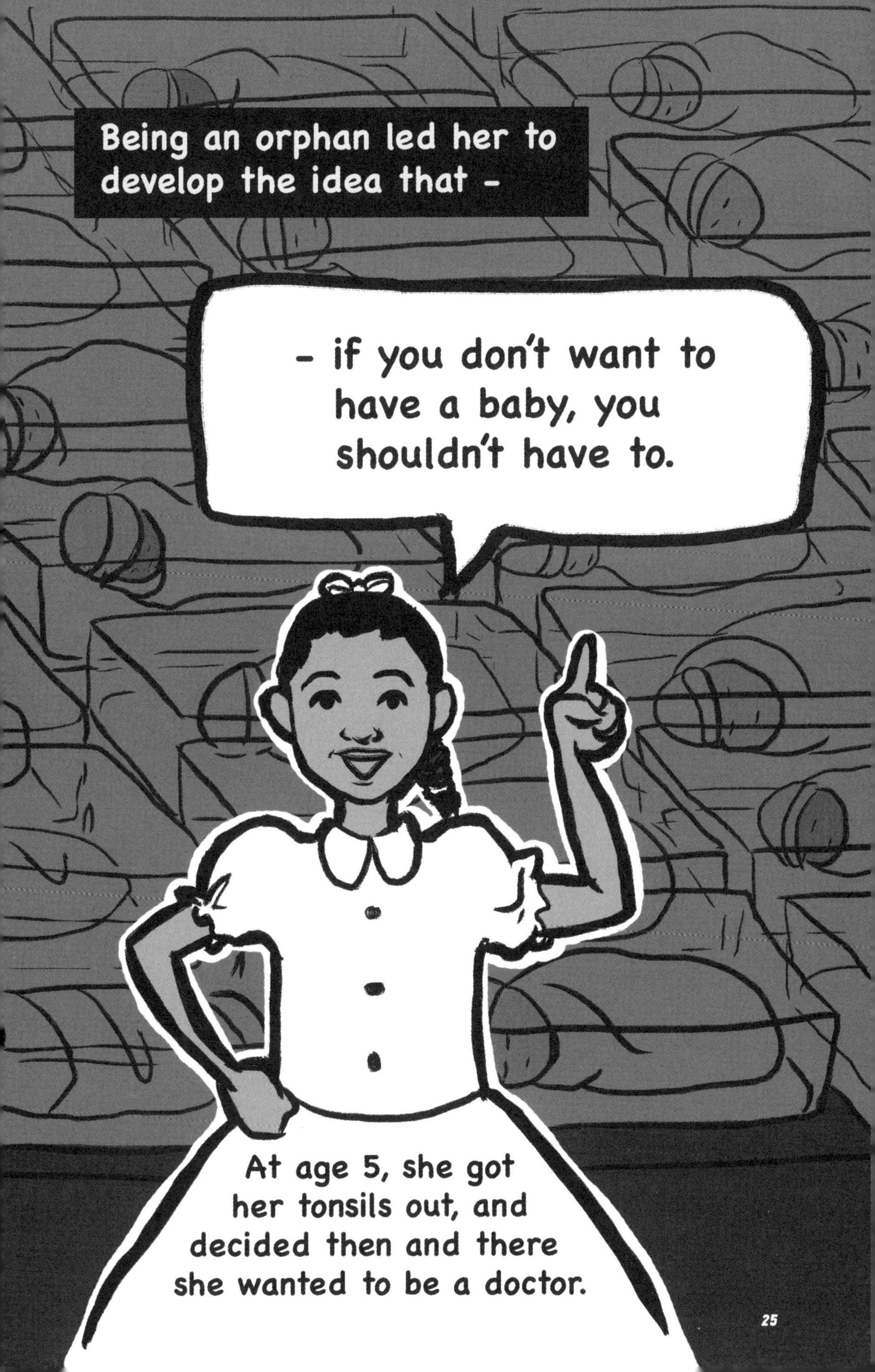
Being an orphan led her to develop the idea that -
- if you don't want to have a baby, you shouldn't have to.
At age 5, she got her tonsils out, and decided then and there she wanted to be a doctor.

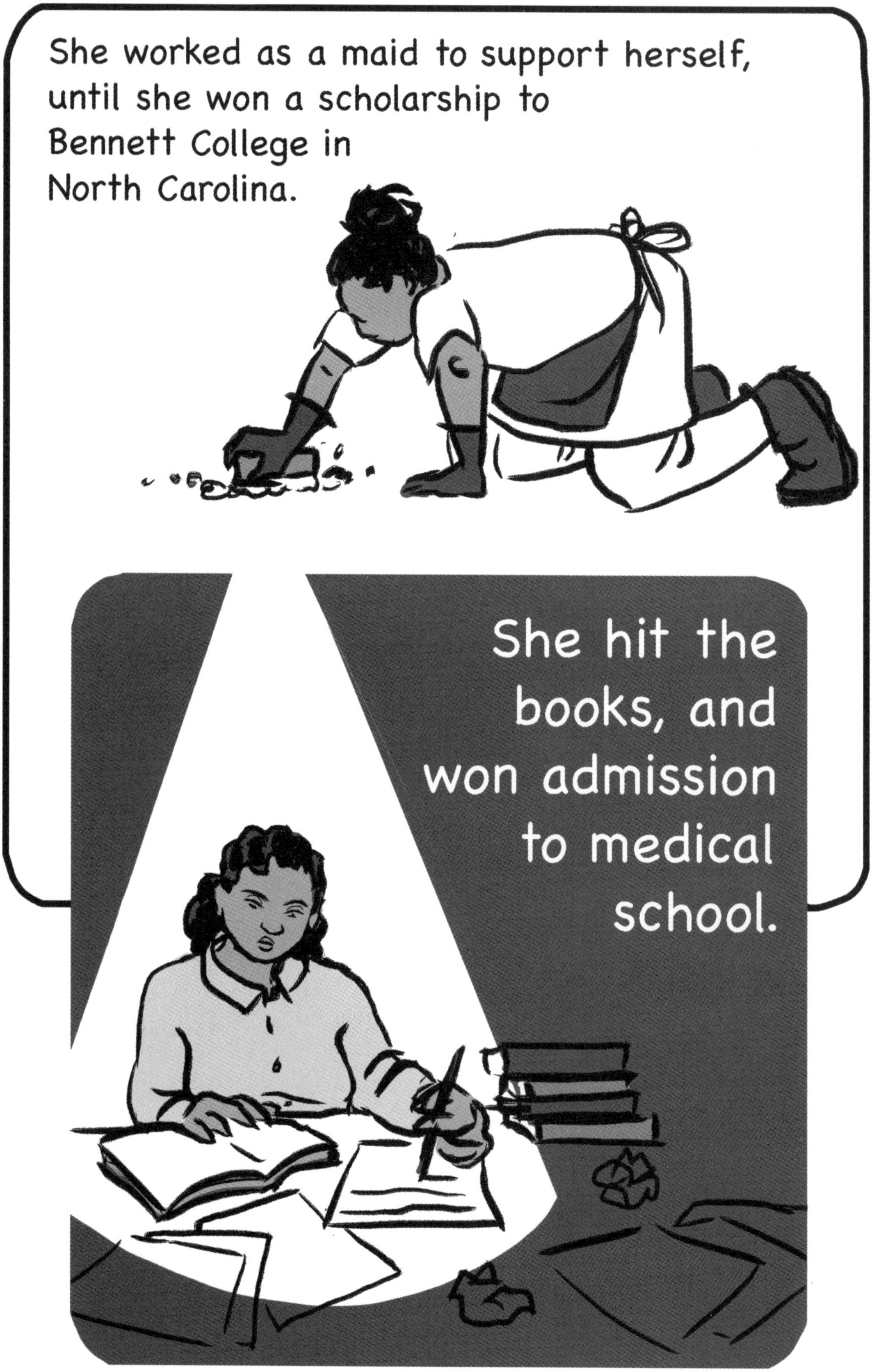
She worked as a maid to support herself, until she won a scholarship to Bennett College in North Carolina.
She hit the books, and won admission to medical school.

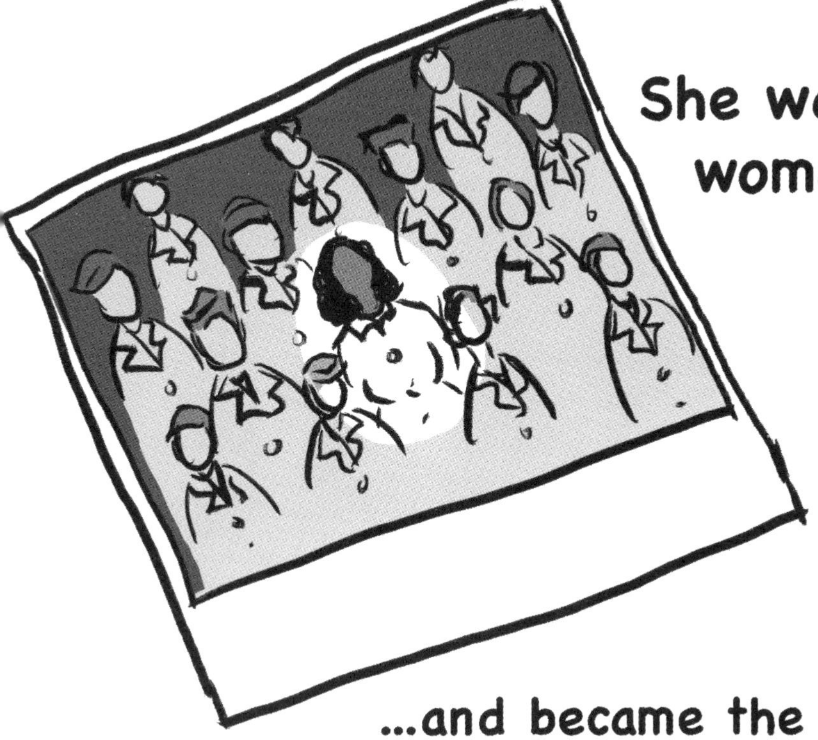

She was the only woman in a sea of male residents...

...and became the first female surgeon from Meharry, a Black medical school in Tennessee.

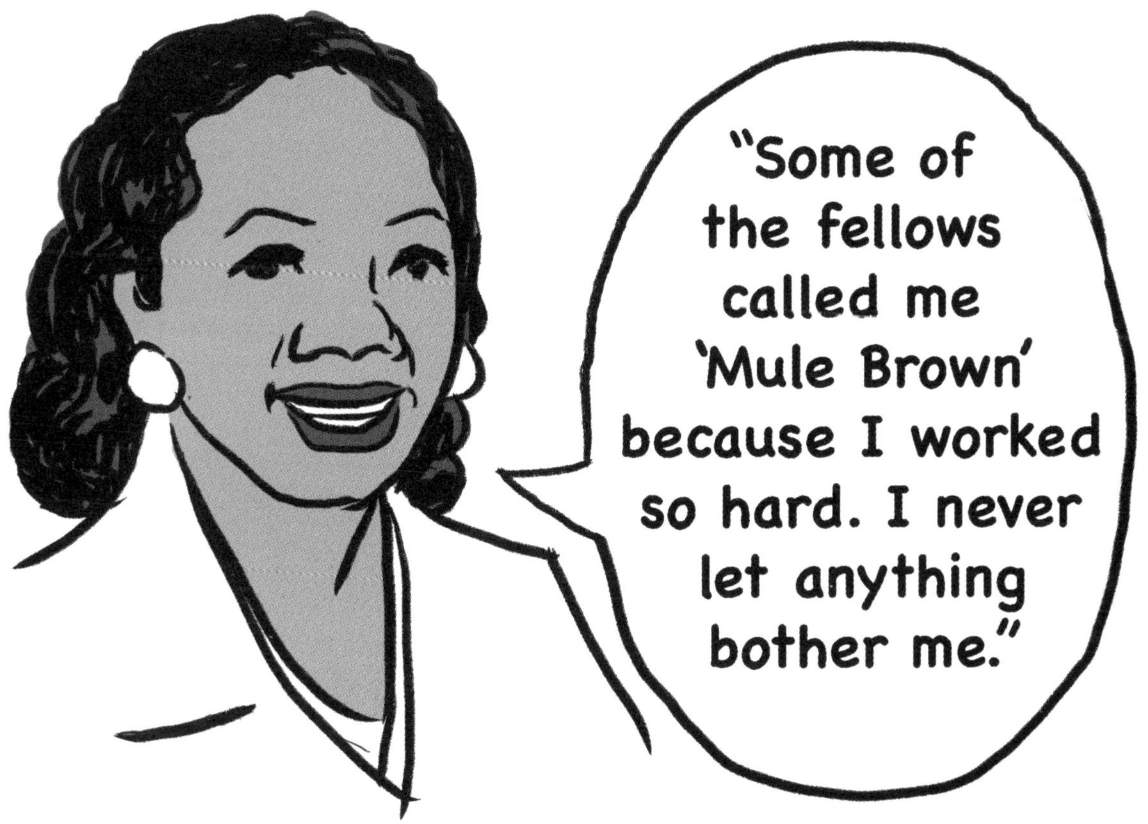
"Some of the fellows called me 'Mule Brown' because I worked so hard. I never let anything bother me."

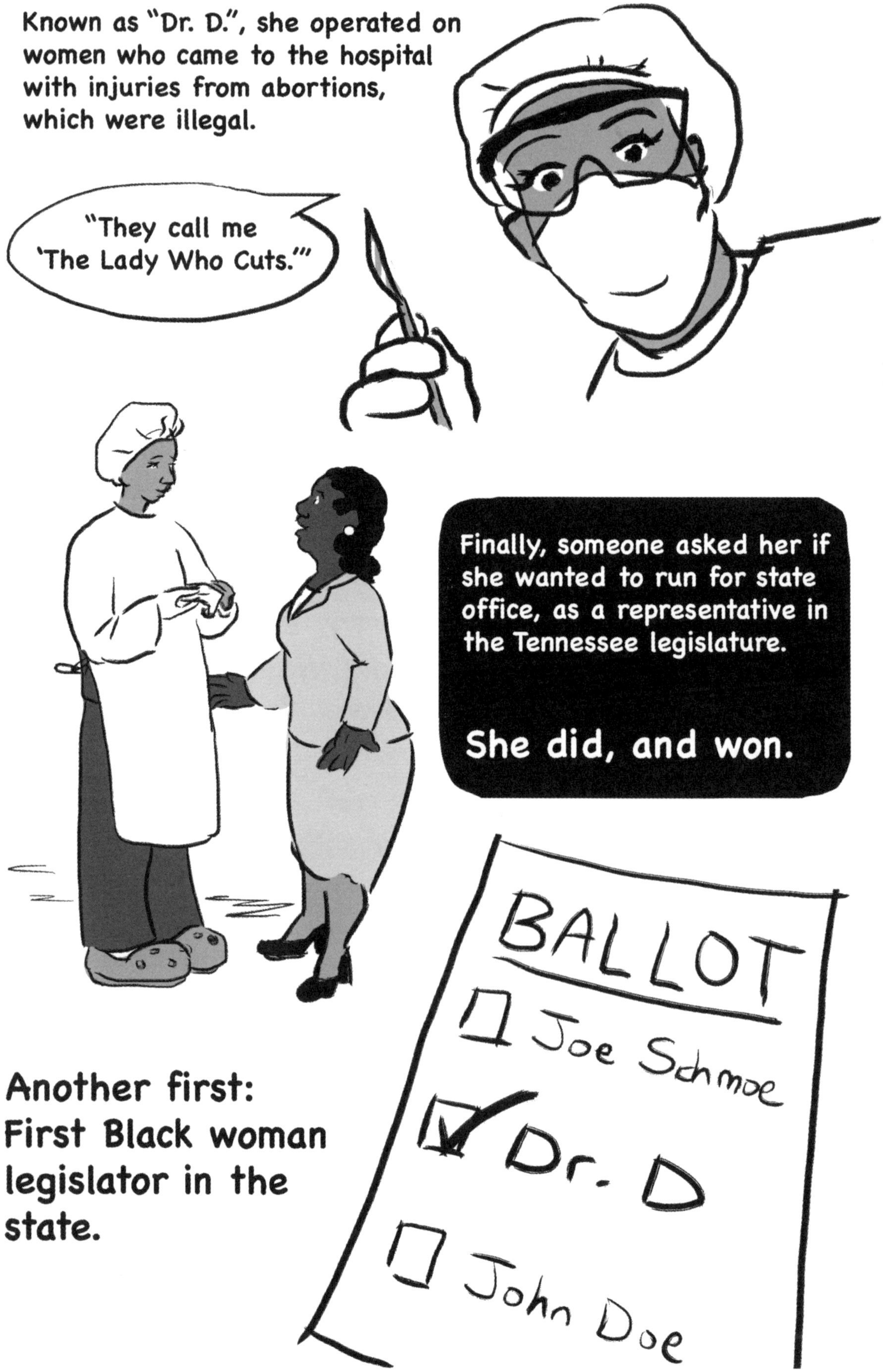
Known as "Dr. D.", she operated on women who came to the hospital with injuries from abortions, which were illegal.
"They call me 'The Lady Who Cuts.'"
Finally, someone asked her if she wanted to run for state office, as a representative in the Tennessee legislature.
She did, and won.
BALLOT
Joe Schmoe
Dr. D
John Doe
Another first: First Black woman legislator in the state.

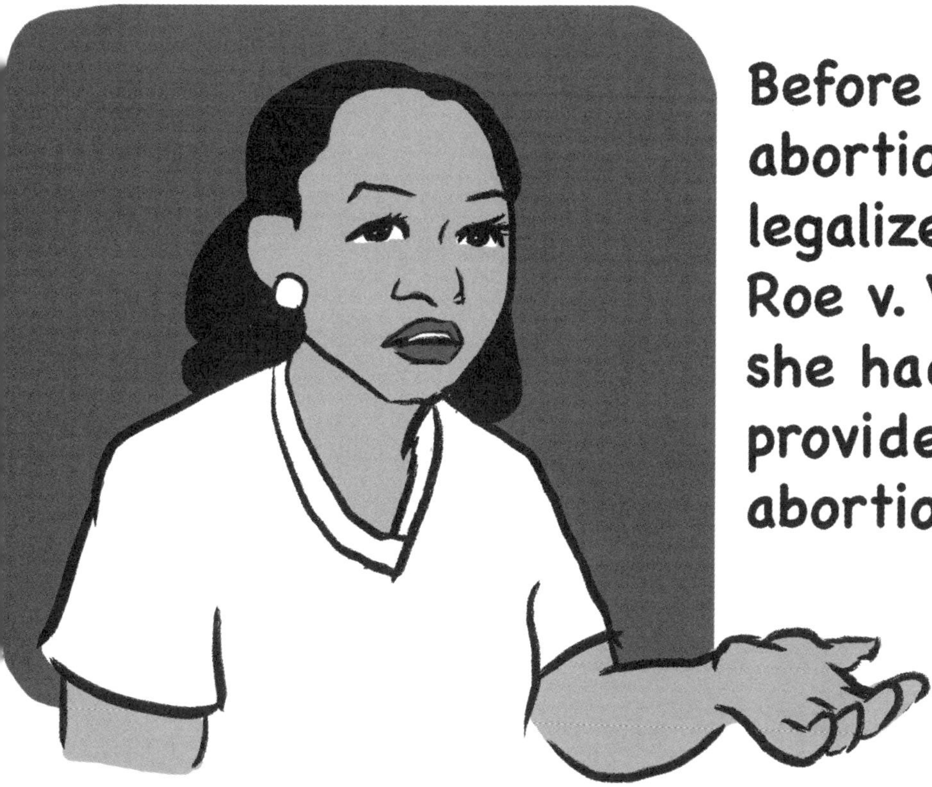

Before abortion was legalized in Roe v. Wade, she had provided abortions.

"I don't think I broke the law. What was in the book of statutes was that a woman could have a termination if it would spare the mother."

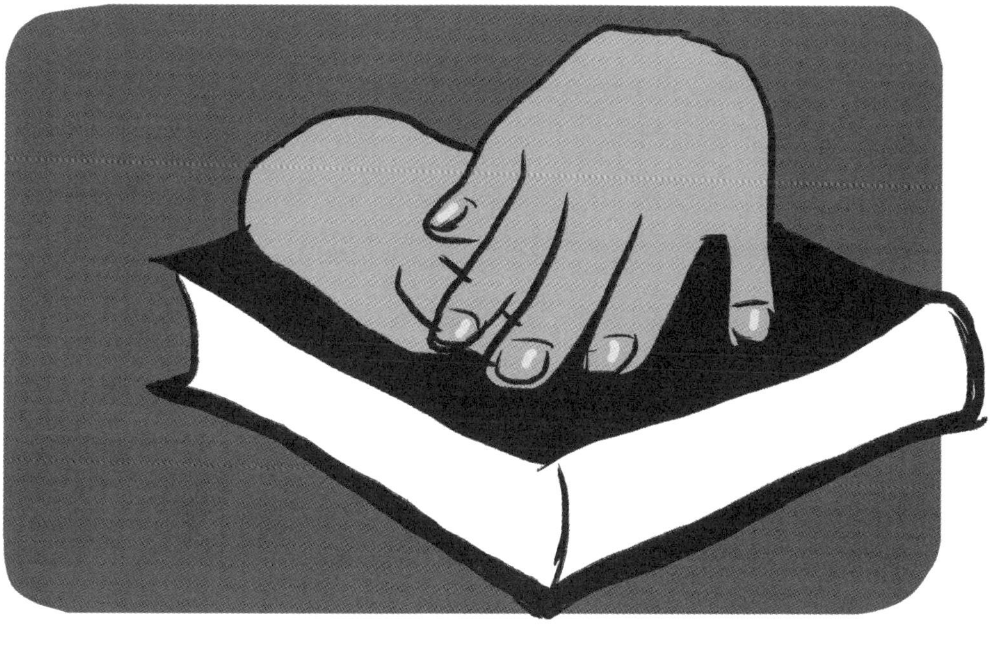

She would run from the Capitol to the hospital to see patients.

And finally, she decided to -

"- do something for my profession."

Bill No. 931

In 1967, she introduced a bill to change the state's abortion law, which only allowed women to have abortions if they were going to die from the pregnancy.

The bill proposed allowing abortion in cases of rape and incest.

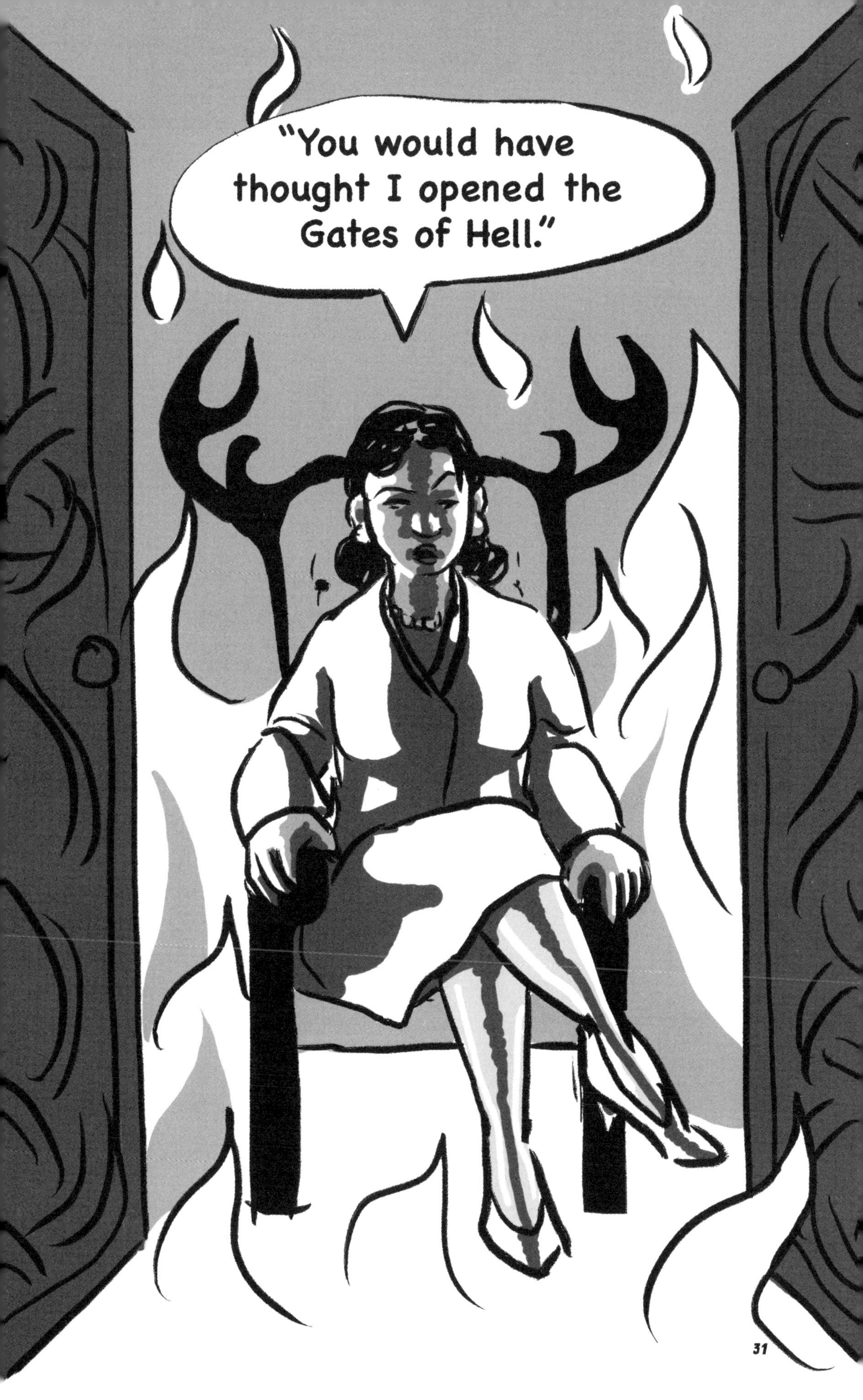
"You would have thought I opened the Gates of Hell."

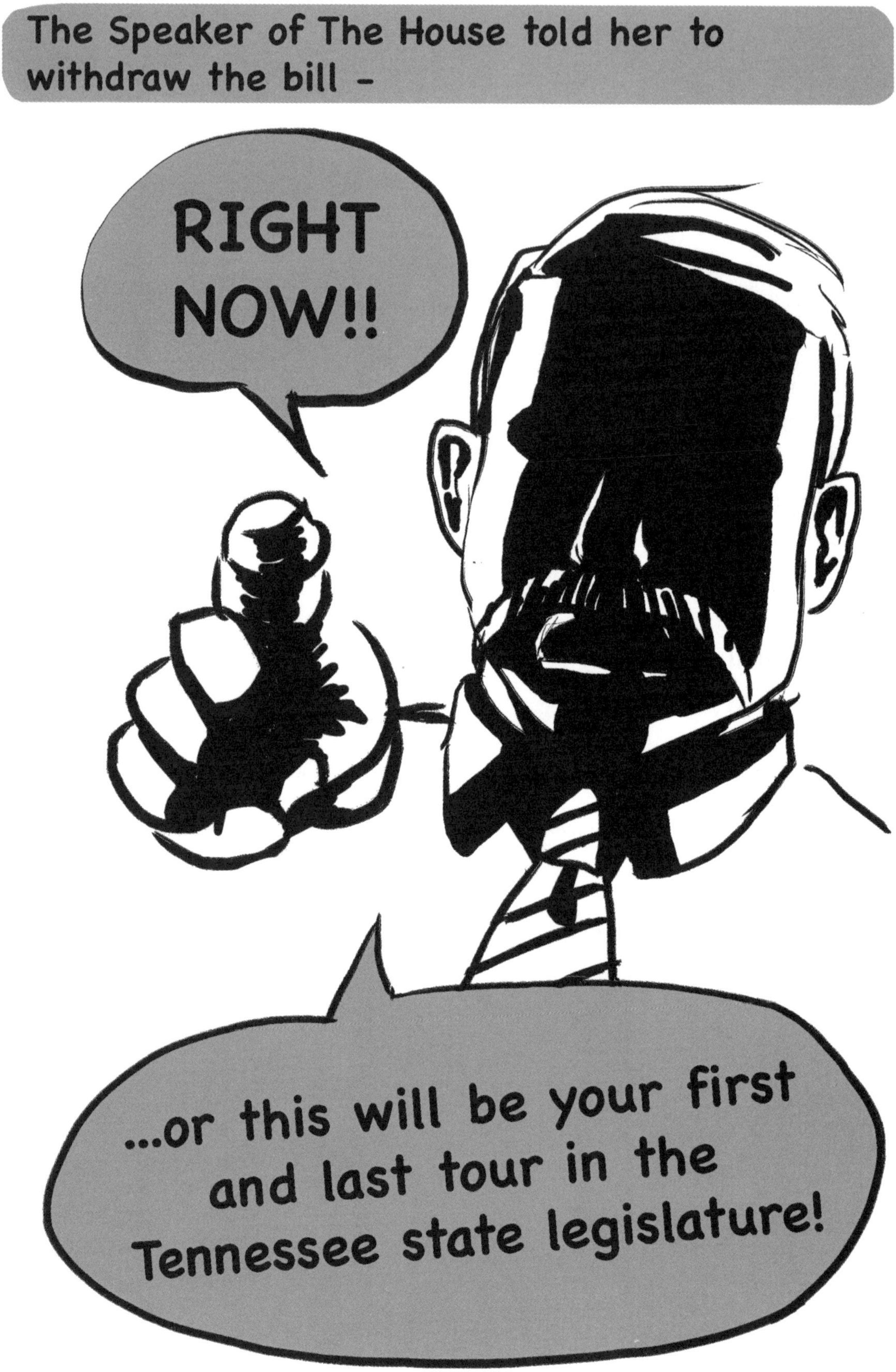
The Speaker of The House told her to withdraw the bill -
RIGHT NOW!!
...or this will be your first and last tour in the Tennessee state legislature!

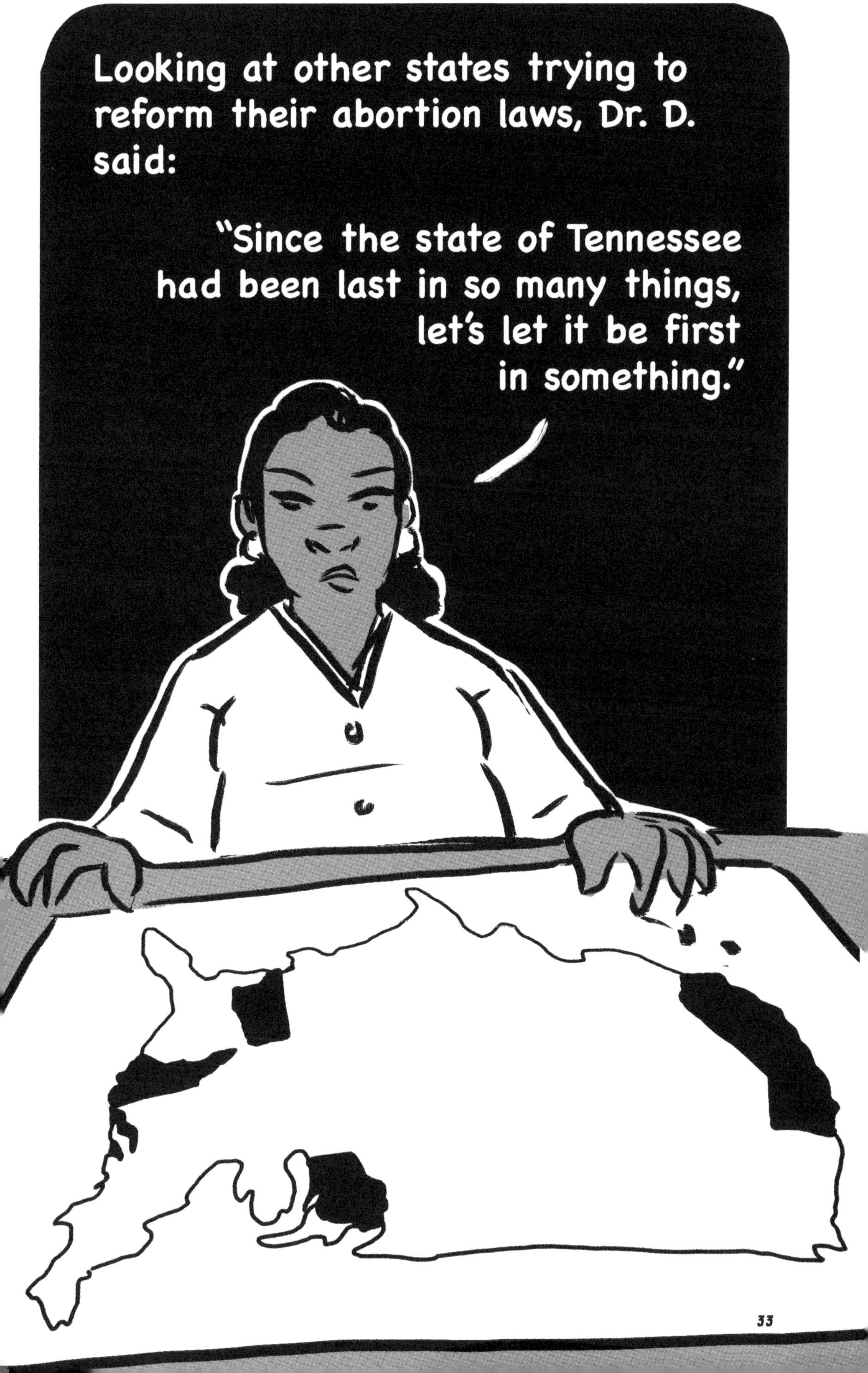
Looking at other states trying to reform their abortion laws, Dr. D. said:
"Since the state of Tennessee had been last in so many things, let's let it be first in something."

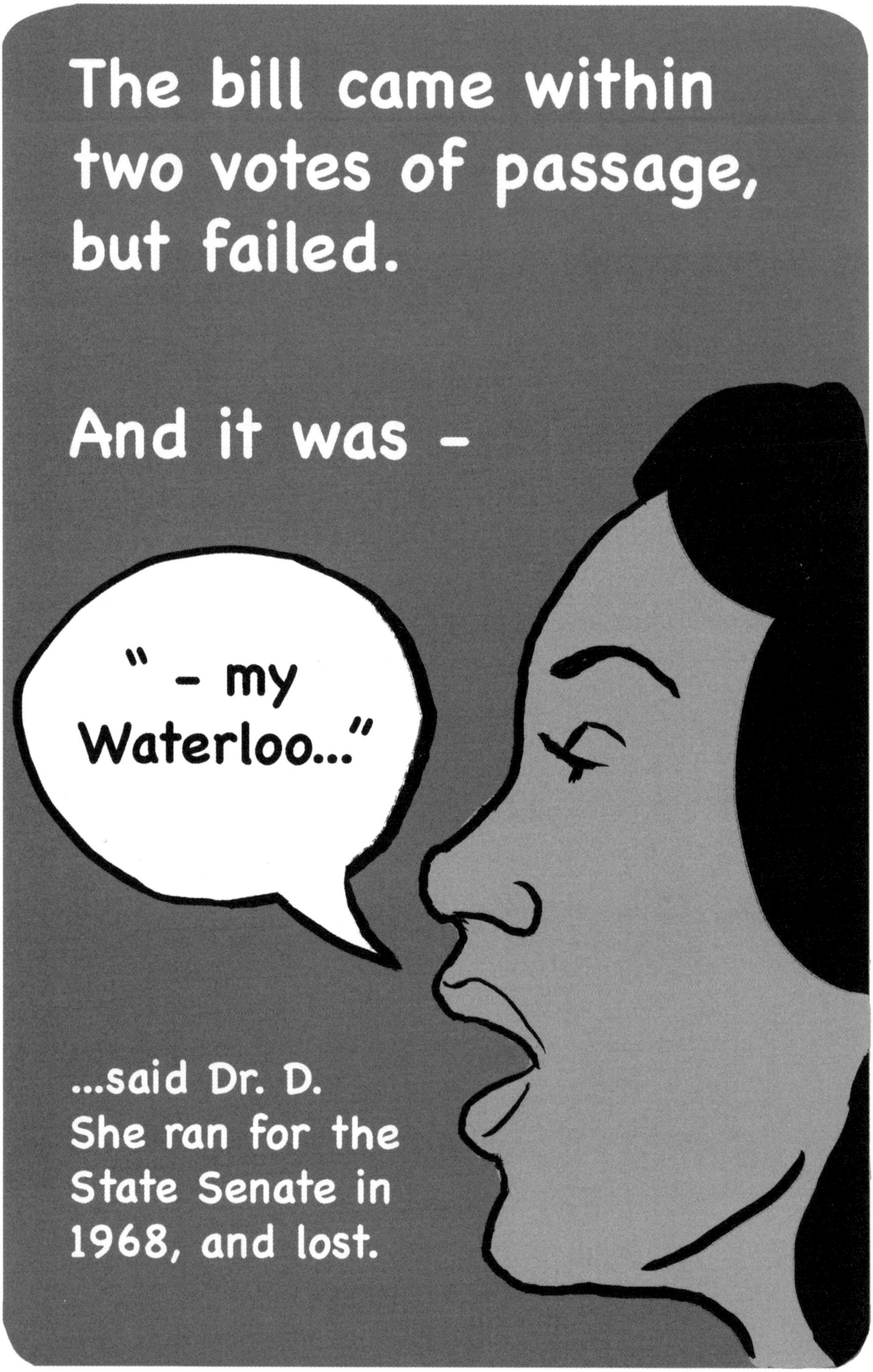
The bill came within two votes of passage, but failed.
And it was -
" - my Waterloo..."
...said Dr. D. She ran for the State Senate in 1968, and lost.

Dr. D. kept on moving.

Throughout her political and medical careers, she:

 Lobbied for "Negro History Month"

☑ Established a human relations commission

☑ Became one of the first single women to adopt in her state

☑ Battled the idea that abortion was an anti-Black racial conspiracy.

In 1973, she told a health conference:

"Now first, let's dispense with 'genocide!'

There's been genocide in this country since 1619."

Dorothy Brown always said what she meant and meant what she said.

THE END

ABORTION TRIALS

Story by Rickie Solinger

Art by Rachel Merrill

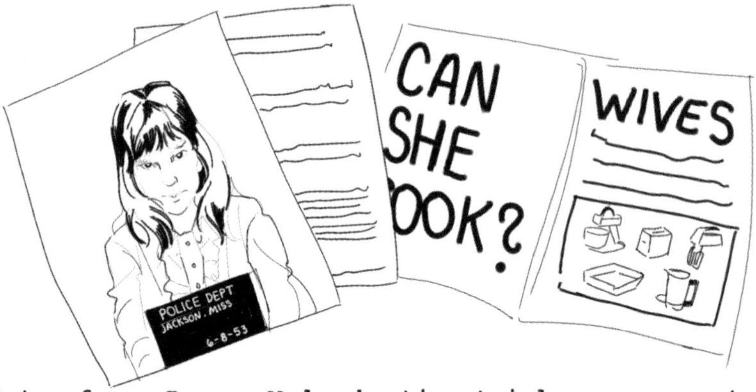
POLICE DEPT
JACKSON, MISS
6-8-53
CAN
SHE
OOK?
WIVES

Transcripts of pre-Roe v. Wade abortion trials are scary to read. And not because they tell grisly tales about back-alley butchers and death. Public health records show far fewer incompetent practitioners than popular history has claimed. The trials make such difficult reading because they show how in St. Louis, Los Angeles, Sacramento, Trenton, New York – all over the country – girls and women were pulled into courtrooms to testify not about their decisions to murder their own unborn child, but about how they had the temerity to murder motherhood, the only true destiny for real women.

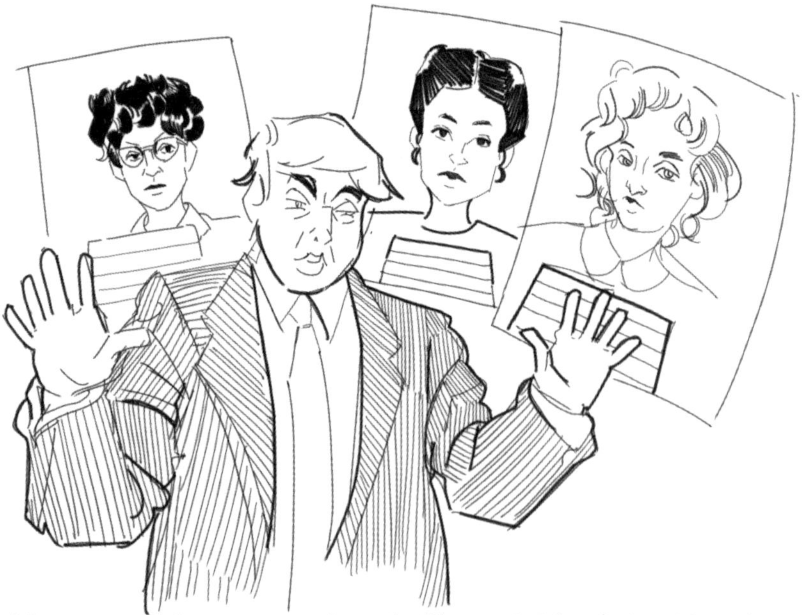

Since President Donald J. Trump has indicated his intention to send the matter of abortion "back to the states," many of which will surely re-criminalize abortion, it is reasonable to think about the immediate, concrete consequences for girls and women who will surely continue to terminate their pregnancies no matter what the law says, as they always have. When criminal abortion trials were at their peak after World War II, public health experts estimated that up to one million criminal procedures were performed every year in the United States.
If abortion is recriminalized, there will, once again, be abortions, arrests, trials, and convictions.

As frightening as it was to sneak off for an illegal abortion in the decades preceding Roe, before feminists had defined reproductive health as a human right, the courtroom could be even more frightening, even a house of horrors. Attorneys defending the practitioner aimed to undermine the credibility of the prosecution's witnesses by describing girls and women who terminated their pregnancies as immoral, dishonest and willing to do anything for their own welfare. The typical girl, one lawyer said in court, tells her boyfriend that she needs $250 or $500 and then she goes off to buy some pretty new clothes. How, he asked the jury, can you take the testimony of that kind of girl against my client? A popular defense tactic was to get the girl to admit that she had slept with a man not her husband,or that she was just plain promiscuous. The lawyer for the defense asked one young woman if she had been pregnant before, and if she were, indeed, not married, and how many men she had had sex with, all questions that the judge forced responses to.

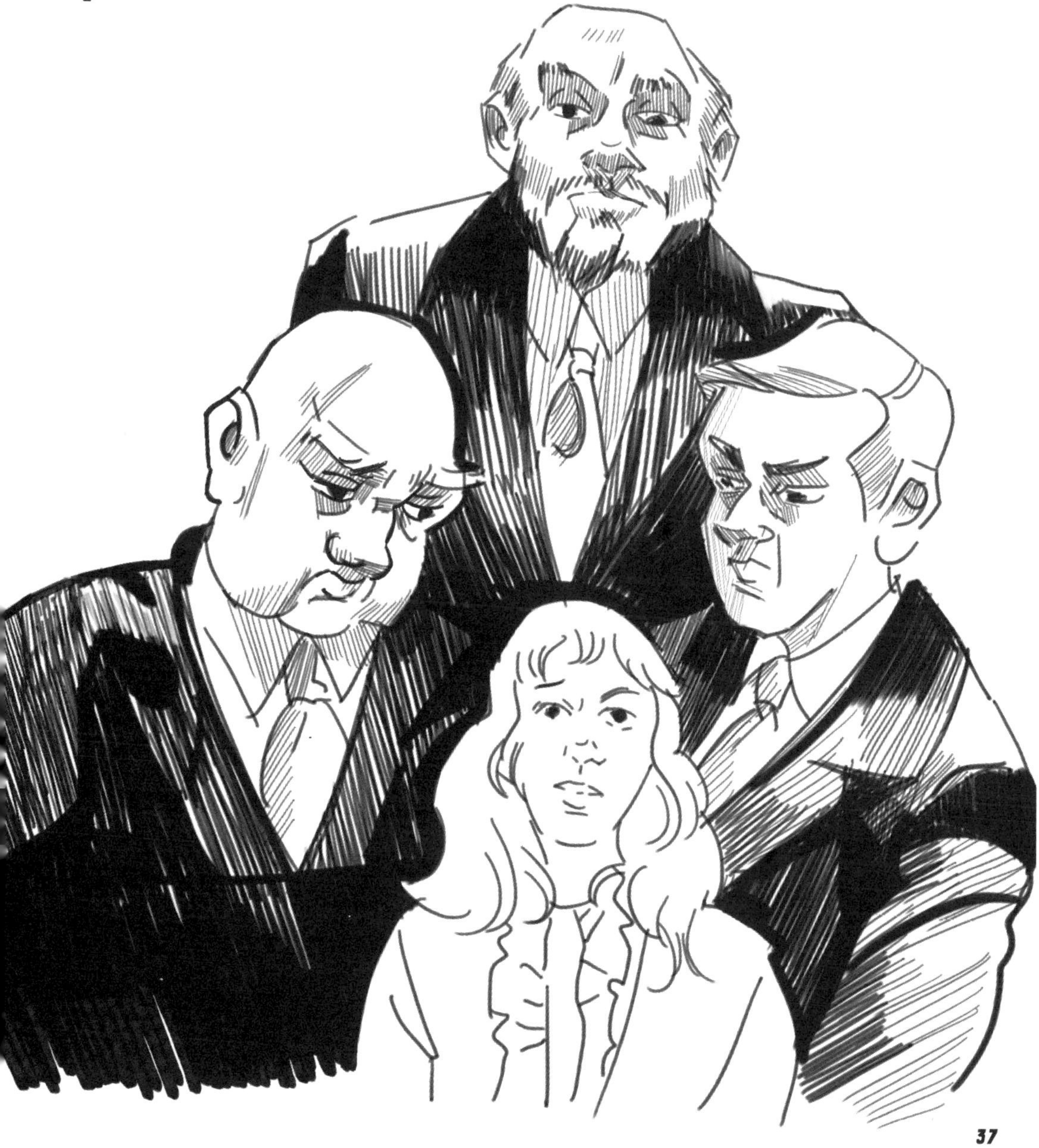

Prosecutors called for making pregnancy "reportable," and for bringing criminal charges against girls and women who terminated their pregnancies.

Quite often, prosecuting lawyers seemed to act on the theory that the more sexual references and sexual innuendo they could spread around in the courtroom, the more perverse the case and the more perverted and culpable the accused.

Over and over in these trials, women were forced to describe how they undressed in the practitioner's office. They were forced to describe whether and how the practitioner put a hand or a finger into their privates parts. In many of these postwar trials, girls and women had pictures of their bodies drawn on courtroom chalkboards for the edification of the audience. They sat in the witness box as the abortion table was wheeled into the courtroom and placed in front of them.

The trial transcripts and the newspaper coverage of the trials show that the lawyers and the judges running these trials, along with the journalists covering them and the doctors and others who testified, and even the interested citizens who filled up the courtrooms, did not seem to find the eroticization of the court inappropriate or unseemly.

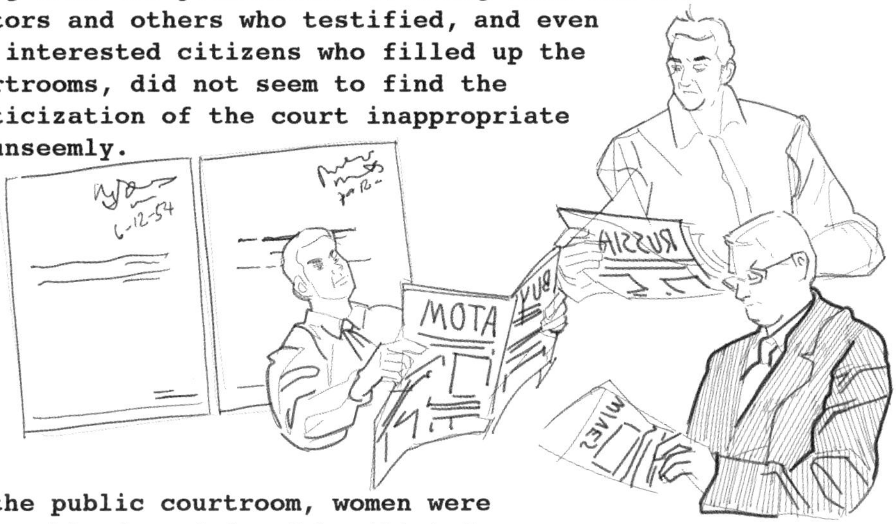
6-12-54
MOTA
BUY

In the public courtroom, women were thoroughly degraded and humiliated, the most private facts of their lives publicly revealed and reviled: their bodies, their sexuality, their wombs, the intimate sources of their personal dignity. The doctors, lawyers, judges, journalist, and myriad expert witnesses spoke up, one by one, to reaffirm their prerogatives over women's bodies and their lives. And their leverage extended beyond the courtroom because the displays in the morning papers after an abortion raid and the theatrics in the courtrooms carried power cultural messages.

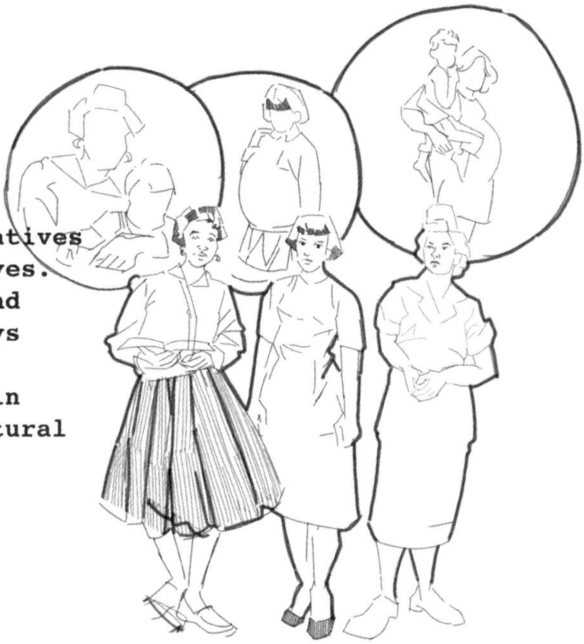

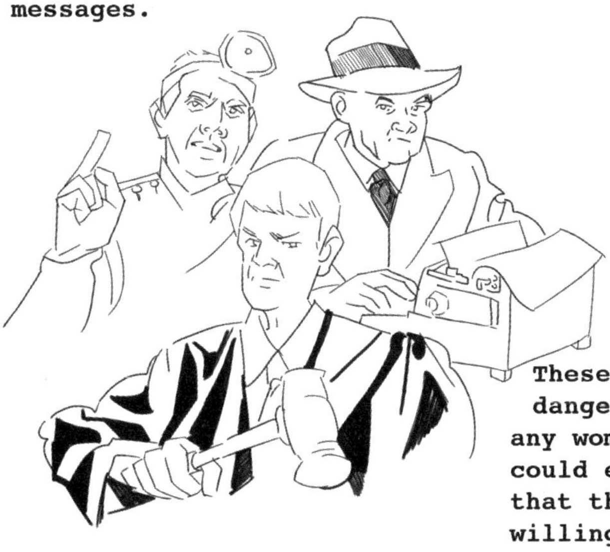

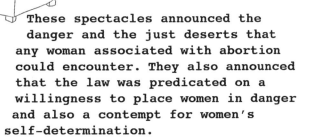

These spectacles announced the danger and the just deserts that any woman associated with abortion could encounter. They also announced that the law was predicated on a willingness to place women in danger and also a contempt for women's self-determination.

Anyone could see that enforcing anti-abortion laws involved the degradation of women. In this way, the mid-twentieth-century prosecution of women associated with abortion embodied the message that every woman, whether or not she ever had or ever would climb up on the abortion table, was endangered by the statutes that criminalized abortion.

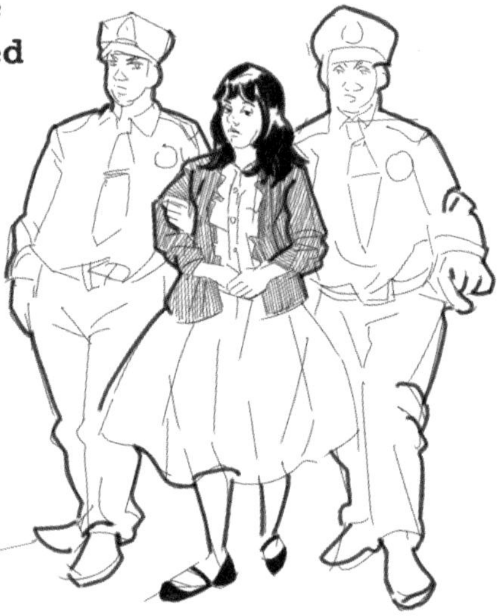

As the law evolves under the presidency of Donald J. Trump, women may be similarly endangered, depending on the state where they live.

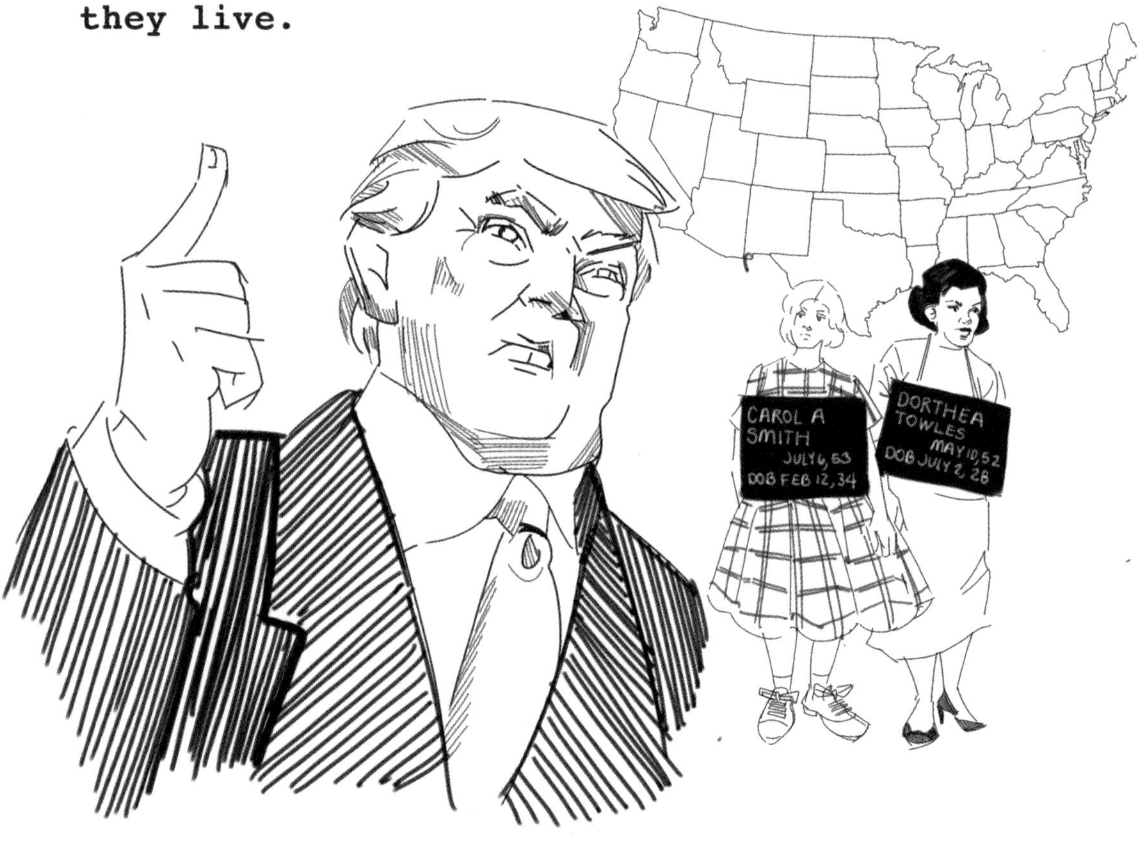
CAROL A SMITH
JULY 6, 53
DOB FEB 12, 34
DORTHEA TOWLES
MAY 10, 52
DOB JULY 2, 28

JANE

RACHEL WILSON
ALLY SHWED

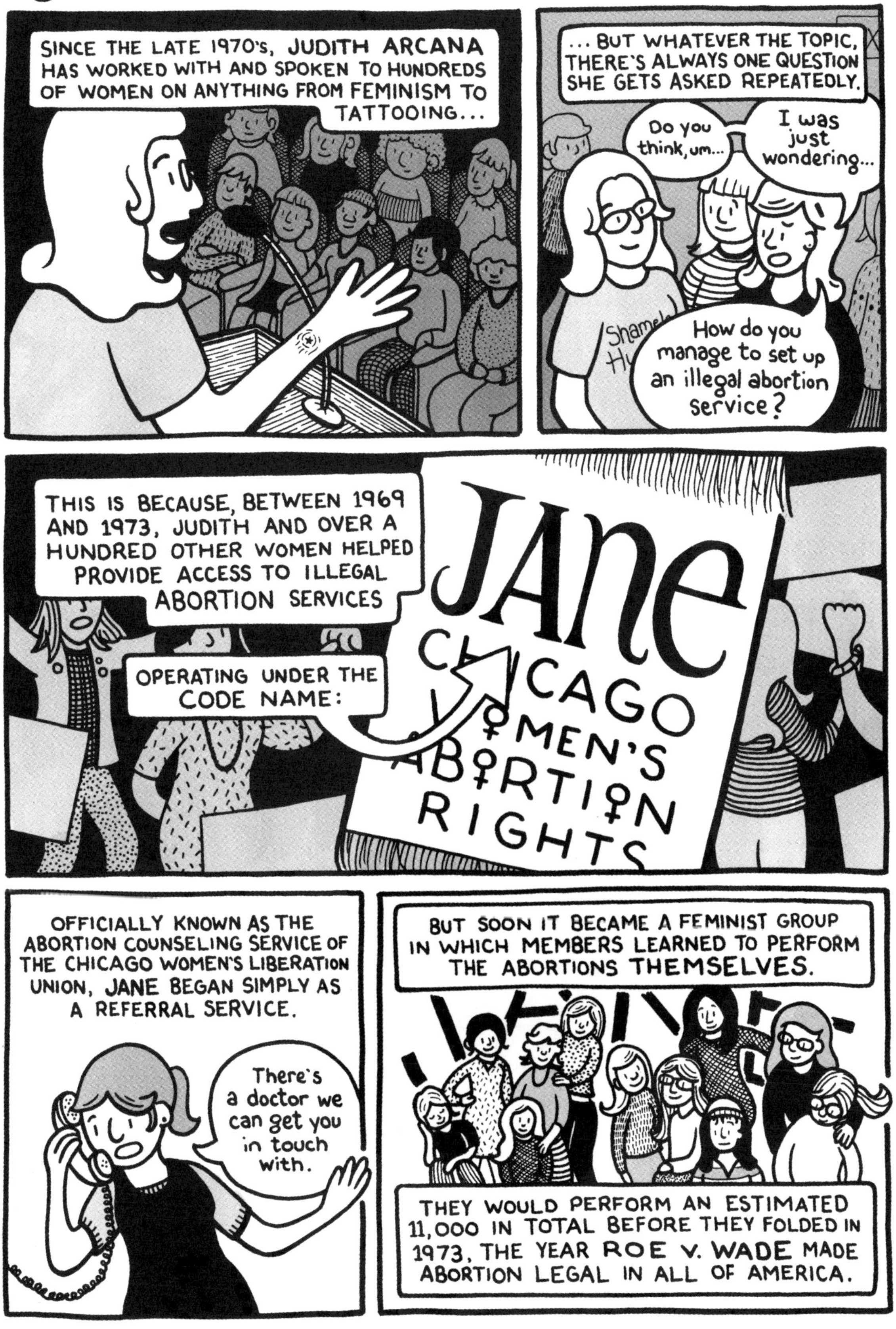

SINCE THE LATE 1970's, JUDITH ARCANA HAS WORKED WITH AND SPOKEN TO HUNDREDS OF WOMEN ON ANYTHING FROM FEMINISM TO TATTOOING...
... BUT WHATEVER THE TOPIC, THERE'S ALWAYS ONE QUESTION SHE GETS ASKED REPEATEDLY.
Do you think, um...
I was just wondering...
How do you manage to set up an illegal abortion service?
THIS IS BECAUSE, BETWEEN 1969 AND 1973, JUDITH AND OVER A HUNDRED OTHER WOMEN HELPED PROVIDE ACCESS TO ILLEGAL ABORTION SERVICES
OPERATING UNDER THE CODE NAME:
JANE
RIGHTS
OFFICIALLY KNOWN AS THE ABORTION COUNSELING SERVICE OF THE CHICAGO WOMEN'S LIBERATION UNION, JANE BEGAN SIMPLY AS A REFERRAL SERVICE.
There's a doctor we can get you in touch with.
BUT SOON IT BECAME A FEMINIST GROUP IN WHICH MEMBERS LEARNED TO PERFORM THE ABORTIONS THEMSELVES.
THEY WOULD PERFORM AN ESTIMATED 11,000 IN TOTAL BEFORE THEY FOLDED IN 1973, THE YEAR ROE V. WADE MADE ABORTION LEGAL IN ALL OF AMERICA.

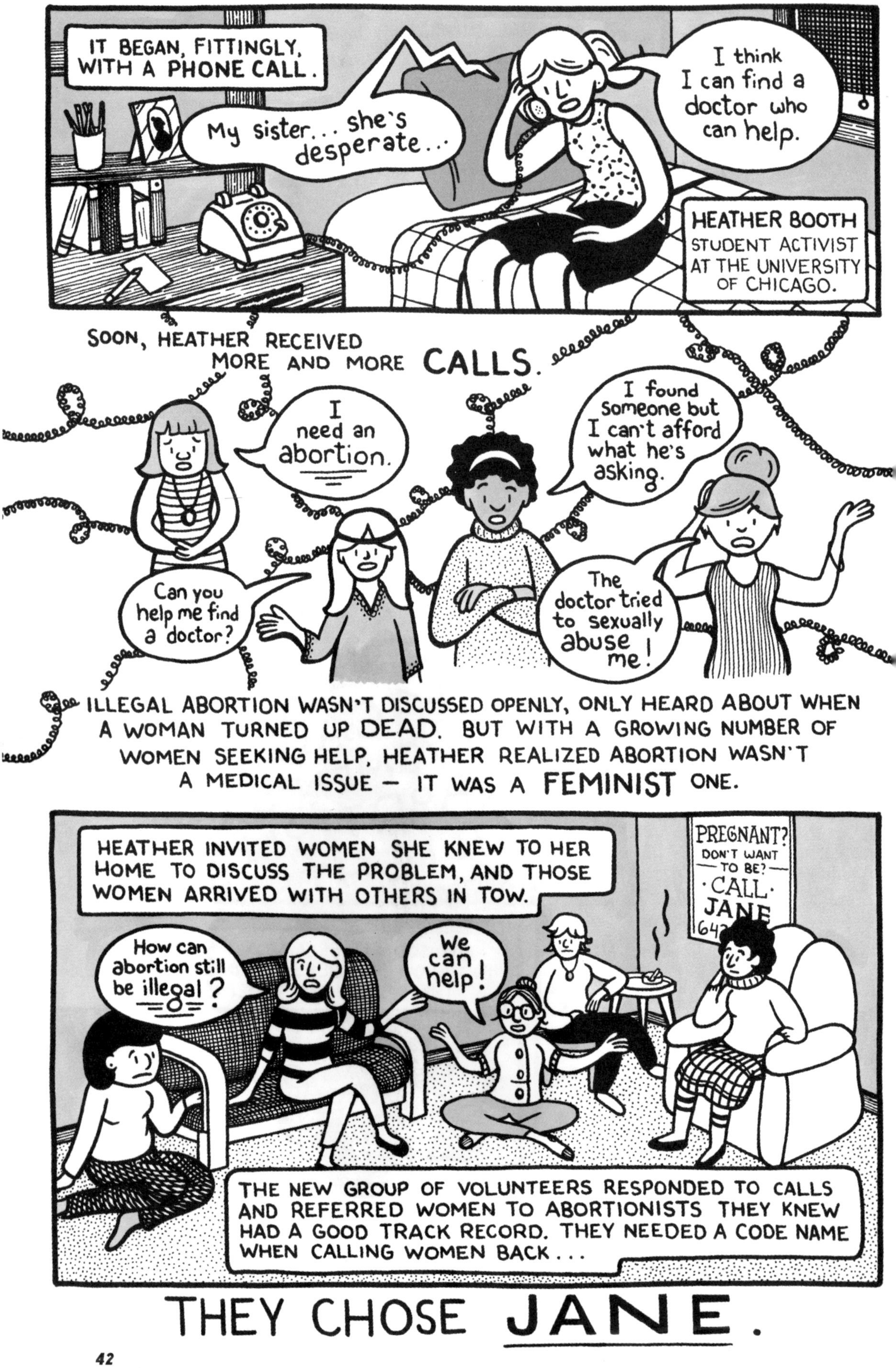

IT BEGAN, FITTINGLY, WITH A PHONE CALL.
My sister... she's desperate...
I think I can find a doctor who can help.
HEATHER BOOTH STUDENT ACTIVIST AT THE UNIVERSITY OF CHICAGO.
SOON, HEATHER RECEIVED MORE AND MORE CALLS.
I need an abortion.
I found someone but I can't afford what he's asking.
Can you help me find a doctor?
The doctor tried to sexually abuse me!
ILLEGAL ABORTION WASN'T DISCUSSED OPENLY, ONLY HEARD ABOUT WHEN A WOMAN TURNED UP DEAD. BUT WITH A GROWING NUMBER OF WOMEN SEEKING HELP, HEATHER REALIZED ABORTION WASN'T A MEDICAL ISSUE – IT WAS A FEMINIST ONE.
HEATHER INVITED WOMEN SHE KNEW TO HER HOME TO DISCUSS THE PROBLEM, AND THOSE WOMEN ARRIVED WITH OTHERS IN TOW.
PREGNANT? DON'T WANT TO BE? ·CALL· JANE
How can abortion still be illegal?
We can help!
THE NEW GROUP OF VOLUNTEERS RESPONDED TO CALLS AND REFERRED WOMEN TO ABORTIONISTS THEY KNEW HAD A GOOD TRACK RECORD. THEY NEEDED A CODE NAME WHEN CALLING WOMEN BACK...
THEY CHOSE JANE.

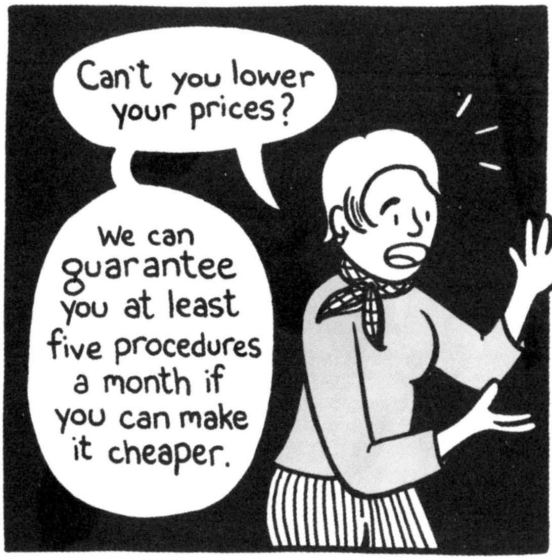
Can't you lower your prices?
We can guarantee you at least five procedures a month if you can make it cheaper.

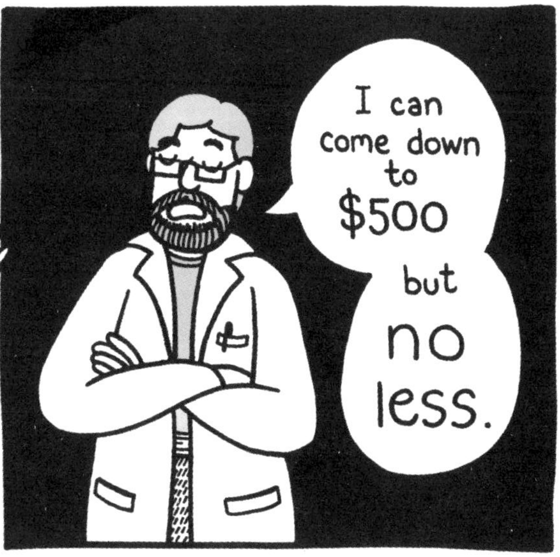
I can come down to $500
but no less.

THE JANES WERE UNHAPPY WITH HOW LITTLE CONTROL THEY HAD OVER THE PROCESS. ABORTIONISTS CHARGED BETWEEN

$500 *to* $1000

AND WOULDN'T ALLOW WOMEN TO BE ACCOMPANIED. ALL THE JANES COULD DO WAS CHECK ON THEM AFTER THE PROCEDURE.

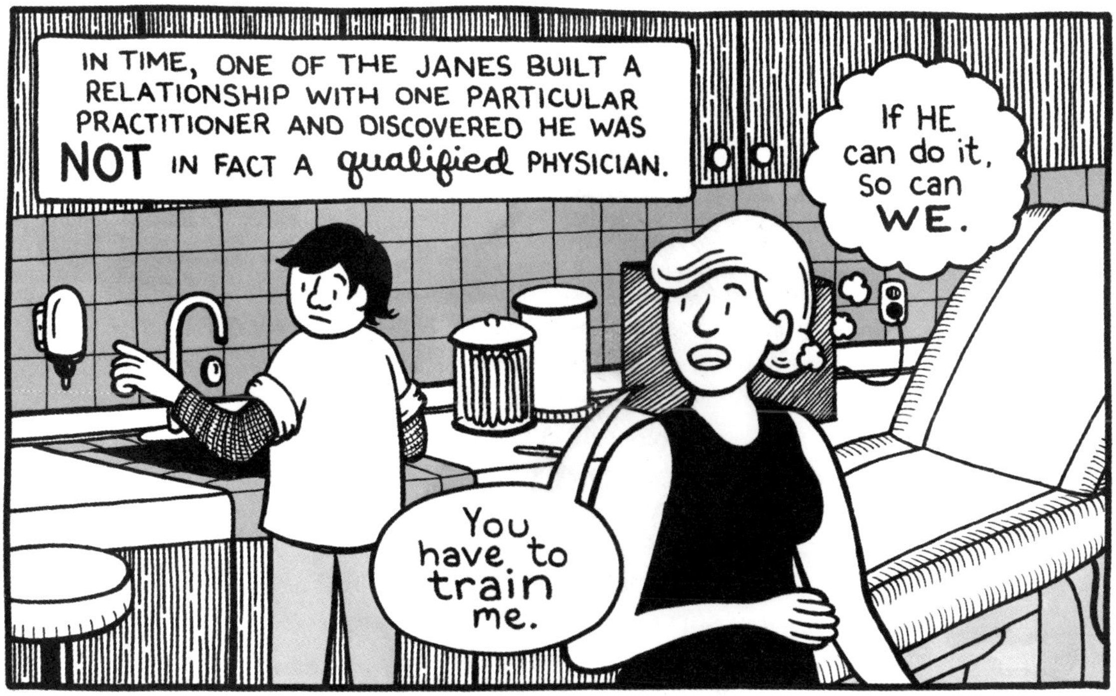
IN TIME, ONE OF THE JANES BUILT A RELATIONSHIP WITH ONE PARTICULAR PRACTITIONER AND DISCOVERED HE WAS **NOT** IN FACT A *qualified* PHYSICIAN.
If HE can do it, so can WE.
You have to train me.

THUS, THE GROUP WAS ABLE TO REGULATE THE PROCESS FROM *start* TO *finish*, KNOWING WOMEN WOULD BE **SAFE** IN THEIR HANDS AND SUPPORTED ALL THE WAY THROUGH.

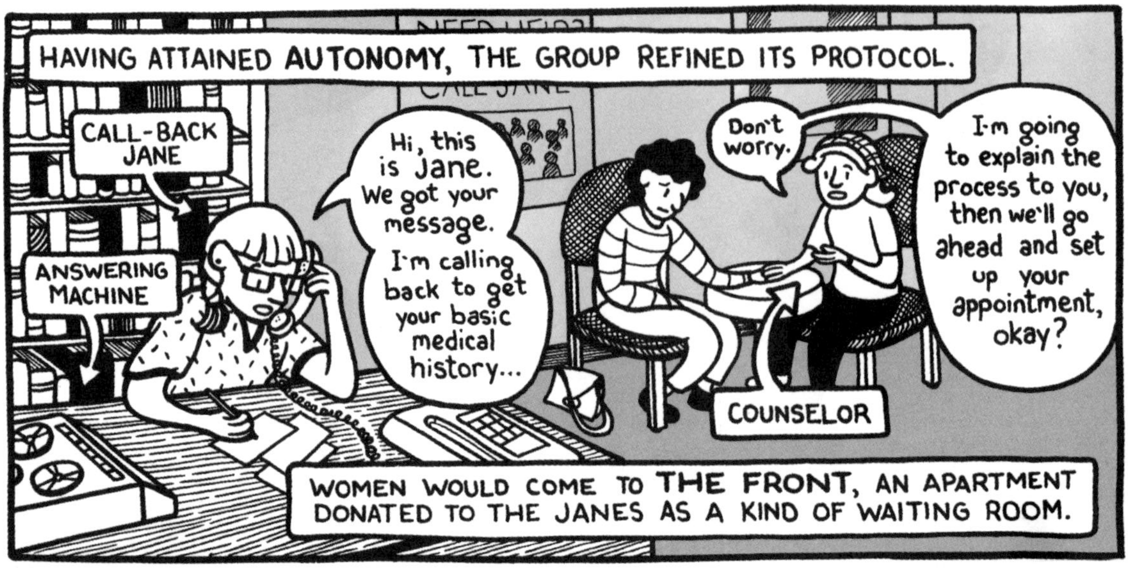
HAVING ATTAINED AUTONOMY, THE GROUP REFINED ITS PROTOCOL.
CALL-BACK JANE
ANSWERING MACHINE
Hi, this is Jane. We got your message.
I'm calling back to get your basic medical history...
Don't worry.
I'm going to explain the process to you, then we'll go ahead and set up your appointment, okay?
COUNSELOR
WOMEN WOULD COME TO THE FRONT, AN APARTMENT DONATED TO THE JANES AS A KIND OF WAITING ROOM.

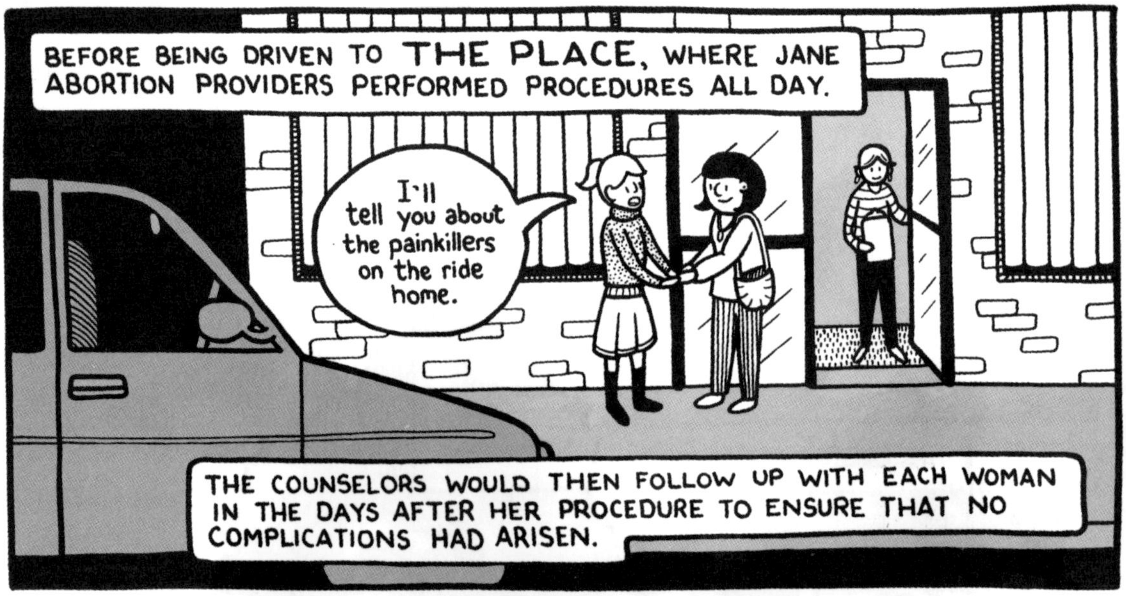
BEFORE BEING DRIVEN TO THE PLACE, WHERE JANE ABORTION PROVIDERS PERFORMED PROCEDURES ALL DAY.
I'll tell you about the painkillers on the ride home.
THE COUNSELORS WOULD THEN FOLLOW UP WITH EACH WOMAN IN THE DAYS AFTER HER PROCEDURE TO ENSURE THAT NO COMPLICATIONS HAD ARISEN.

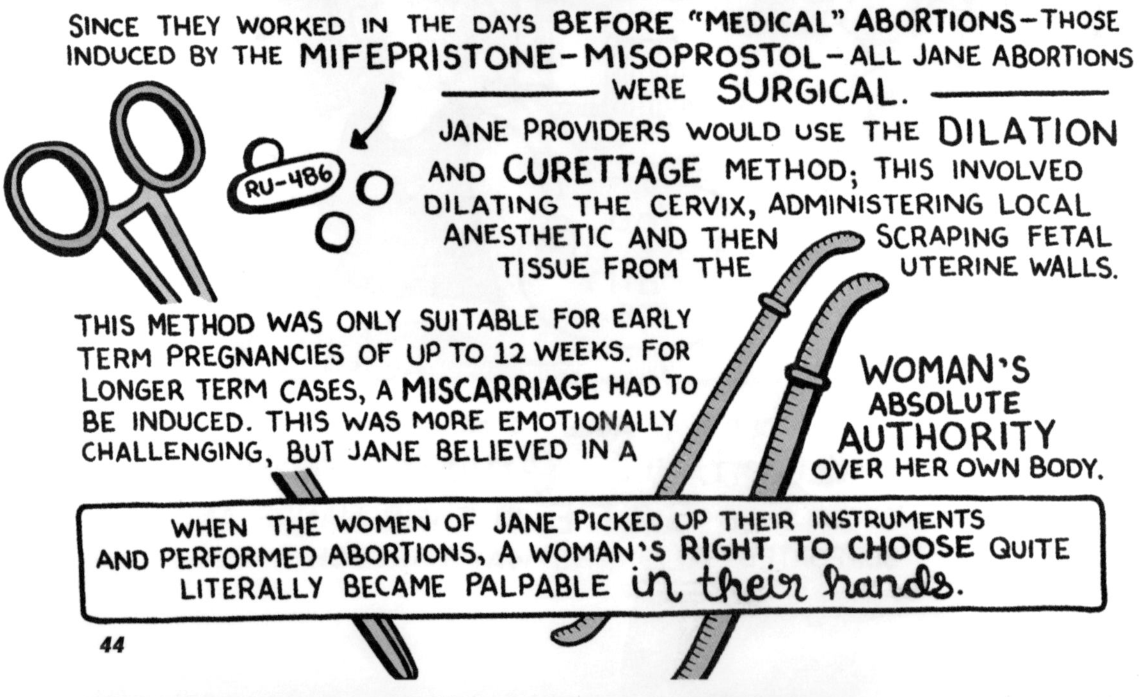
SINCE THEY WORKED IN THE DAYS BEFORE "MEDICAL" ABORTIONS—THOSE INDUCED BY THE MIFEPRISTONE-MISOPROSTOL—ALL JANE ABORTIONS WERE SURGICAL.
RU-486
JANE PROVIDERS WOULD USE THE DILATION AND CURETTAGE METHOD; THIS INVOLVED DILATING THE CERVIX, ADMINISTERING LOCAL ANESTHETIC AND THEN SCRAPING FETAL TISSUE FROM THE UTERINE WALLS.
THIS METHOD WAS ONLY SUITABLE FOR EARLY TERM PREGNANCIES OF UP TO 12 WEEKS. FOR LONGER TERM CASES, A MISCARRIAGE HAD TO BE INDUCED. THIS WAS MORE EMOTIONALLY CHALLENGING, BUT JANE BELIEVED IN A WOMAN'S ABSOLUTE AUTHORITY OVER HER OWN BODY.
WHEN THE WOMEN OF JANE PICKED UP THEIR INSTRUMENTS AND PERFORMED ABORTIONS, A WOMAN'S RIGHT TO CHOOSE QUITE LITERALLY BECAME PALPABLE in their hands.

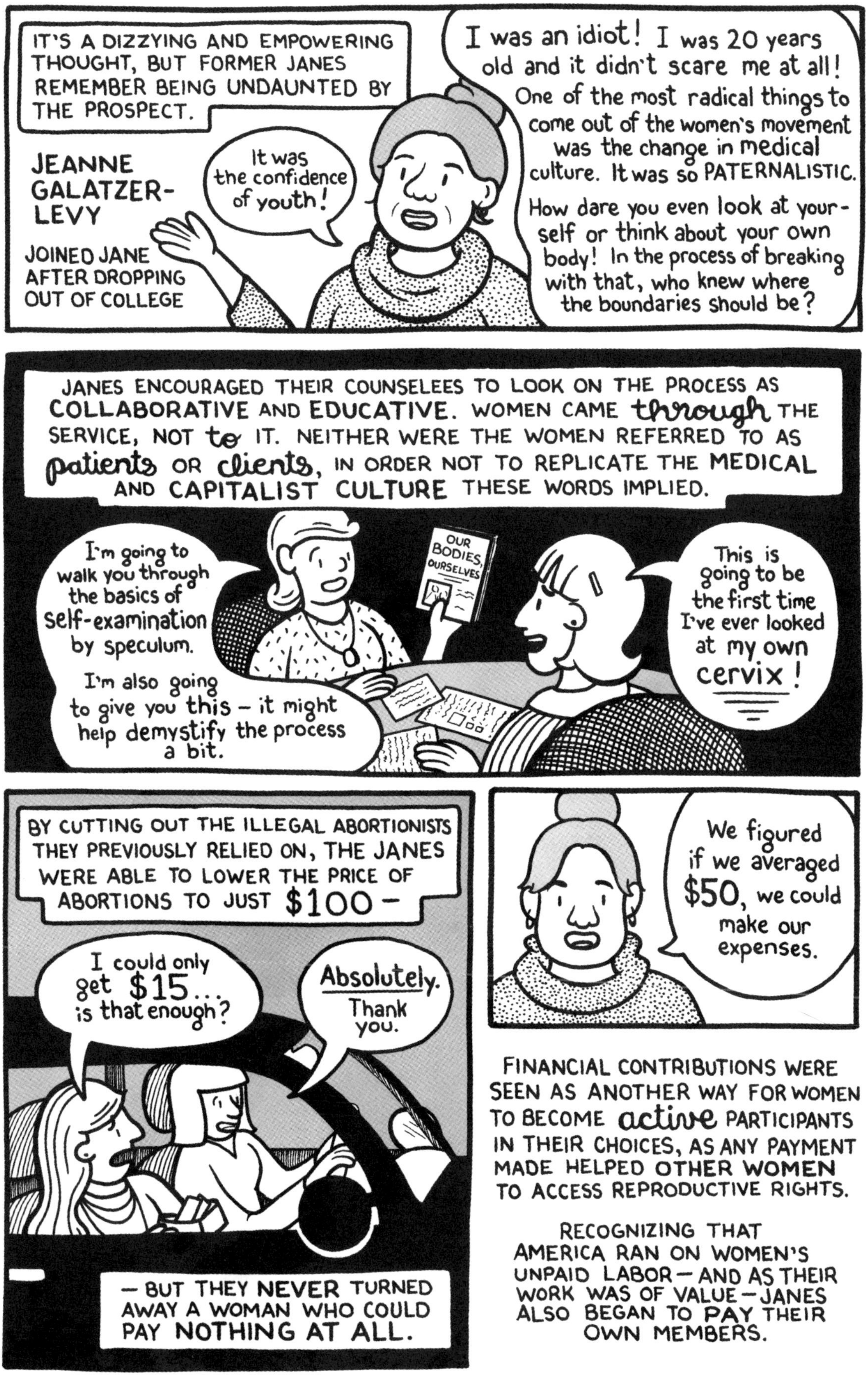

IT'S A DIZZYING AND EMPOWERING THOUGHT, BUT FORMER JANES REMEMBER BEING UNDAUNTED BY THE PROSPECT.
JEANNE GALATZER-LEVY
JOINED JANE AFTER DROPPING OUT OF COLLEGE
It was the confidence of youth!
I was an idiot! I was 20 years old and it didn't scare me at all! One of the most radical things to come out of the women's movement was the change in medical culture. It was so PATERNALISTIC.
How dare you even look at yourself or think about your own body! In the process of breaking with that, who knew where the boundaries should be?
JANES ENCOURAGED THEIR COUNSELEES TO LOOK ON THE PROCESS AS COLLABORATIVE AND EDUCATIVE. WOMEN CAME *through* THE SERVICE, NOT *to* IT. NEITHER WERE THE WOMEN REFERRED TO AS *patients* OR *clients*, IN ORDER NOT TO REPLICATE THE MEDICAL AND CAPITALIST CULTURE THESE WORDS IMPLIED.
I'm going to walk you through the basics of self-examination by speculum.
I'm also going to give you this – it might help demystify the process a bit.
OUR BODIES, OURSELVES
This is going to be the first time I've ever looked at my own cervix!
BY CUTTING OUT THE ILLEGAL ABORTIONISTS THEY PREVIOUSLY RELIED ON, THE JANES WERE ABLE TO LOWER THE PRICE OF ABORTIONS TO JUST $100 –
I could only get $15... is that enough?
Absolutely. Thank you.
– BUT THEY NEVER TURNED AWAY A WOMAN WHO COULD PAY NOTHING AT ALL.
We figured if we averaged $50, we could make our expenses.
FINANCIAL CONTRIBUTIONS WERE SEEN AS ANOTHER WAY FOR WOMEN TO BECOME *active* PARTICIPANTS IN THEIR CHOICES, AS ANY PAYMENT MADE HELPED OTHER WOMEN TO ACCESS REPRODUCTIVE RIGHTS.
RECOGNIZING THAT AMERICA RAN ON WOMEN'S UNPAID LABOR – AND AS THEIR WORK WAS OF VALUE – JANES ALSO BEGAN TO PAY THEIR OWN MEMBERS.

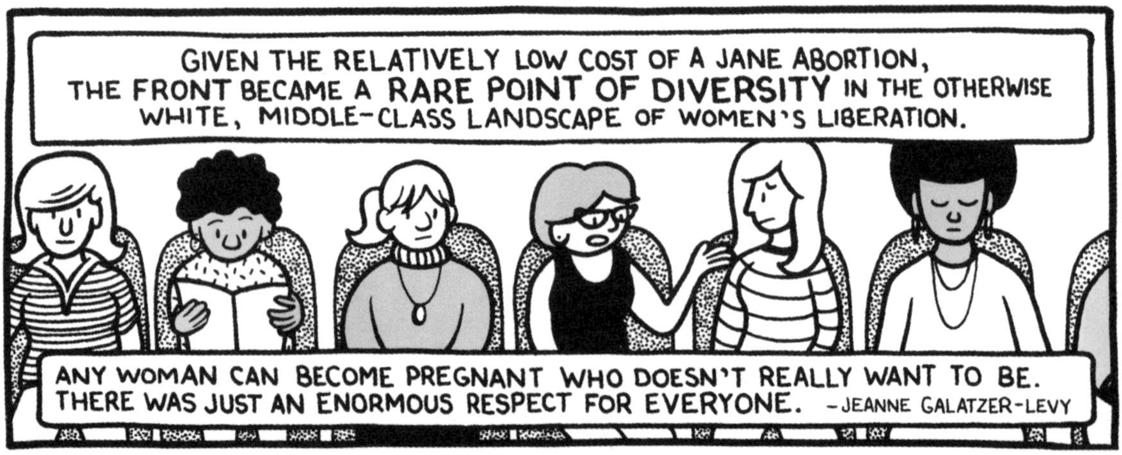
GIVEN THE RELATIVELY LOW COST OF A JANE ABORTION, THE FRONT BECAME A RARE POINT OF DIVERSITY IN THE OTHERWISE WHITE, MIDDLE-CLASS LANDSCAPE OF WOMEN'S LIBERATION.
ANY WOMAN CAN BECOME PREGNANT WHO DOESN'T REALLY WANT TO BE. THERE WAS JUST AN ENORMOUS RESPECT FOR EVERYONE. -JEANNE GALATZER-LEVY

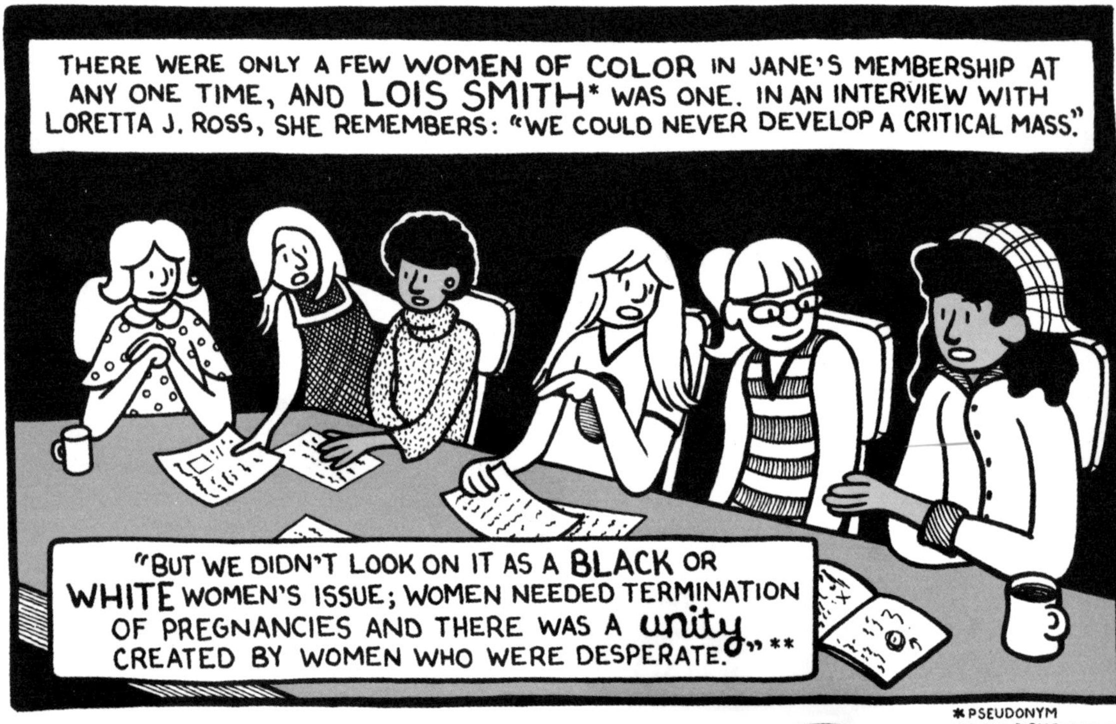
THERE WERE ONLY A FEW WOMEN OF COLOR IN JANE'S MEMBERSHIP AT ANY ONE TIME, AND LOIS SMITH* WAS ONE. IN AN INTERVIEW WITH LORETTA J. ROSS, SHE REMEMBERS: "WE COULD NEVER DEVELOP A CRITICAL MASS."
"BUT WE DIDN'T LOOK ON IT AS A BLACK OR WHITE WOMEN'S ISSUE; WOMEN NEEDED TERMINATION OF PREGNANCIES AND THERE WAS A unity CREATED BY WOMEN WHO WERE DESPERATE." **

*PSEUDONYM
**SEE BIBLIOGRAPHY

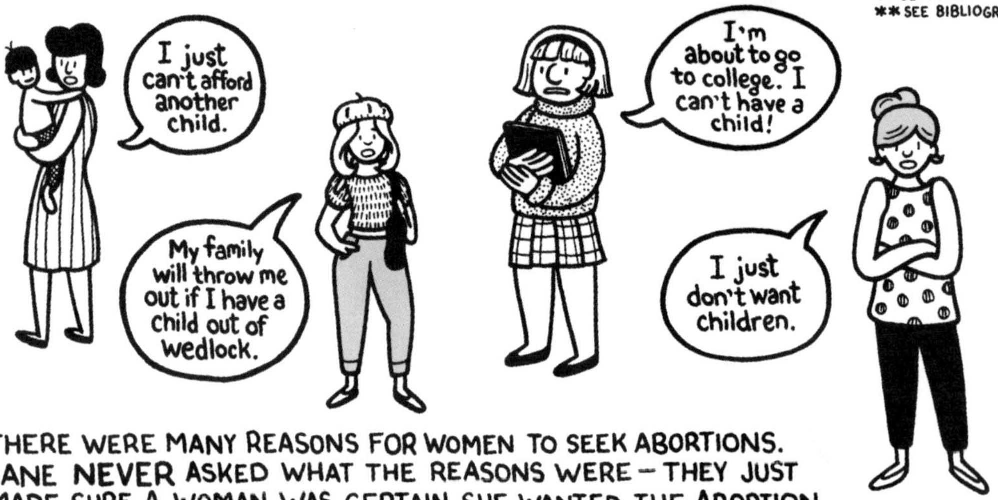
I just can't afford another child.
My family will throw me out if I have a child out of wedlock.
I'm about to go to college. I can't have a child!
I just don't want children.

THERE WERE MANY REASONS FOR WOMEN TO SEEK ABORTIONS. JANE NEVER ASKED WHAT THE REASONS WERE – THEY JUST MADE SURE A WOMAN WAS CERTAIN SHE WANTED THE ABORTION AND WASN'T BEING FORCED INTO IT BY HER FAMILY OR PARTNER.

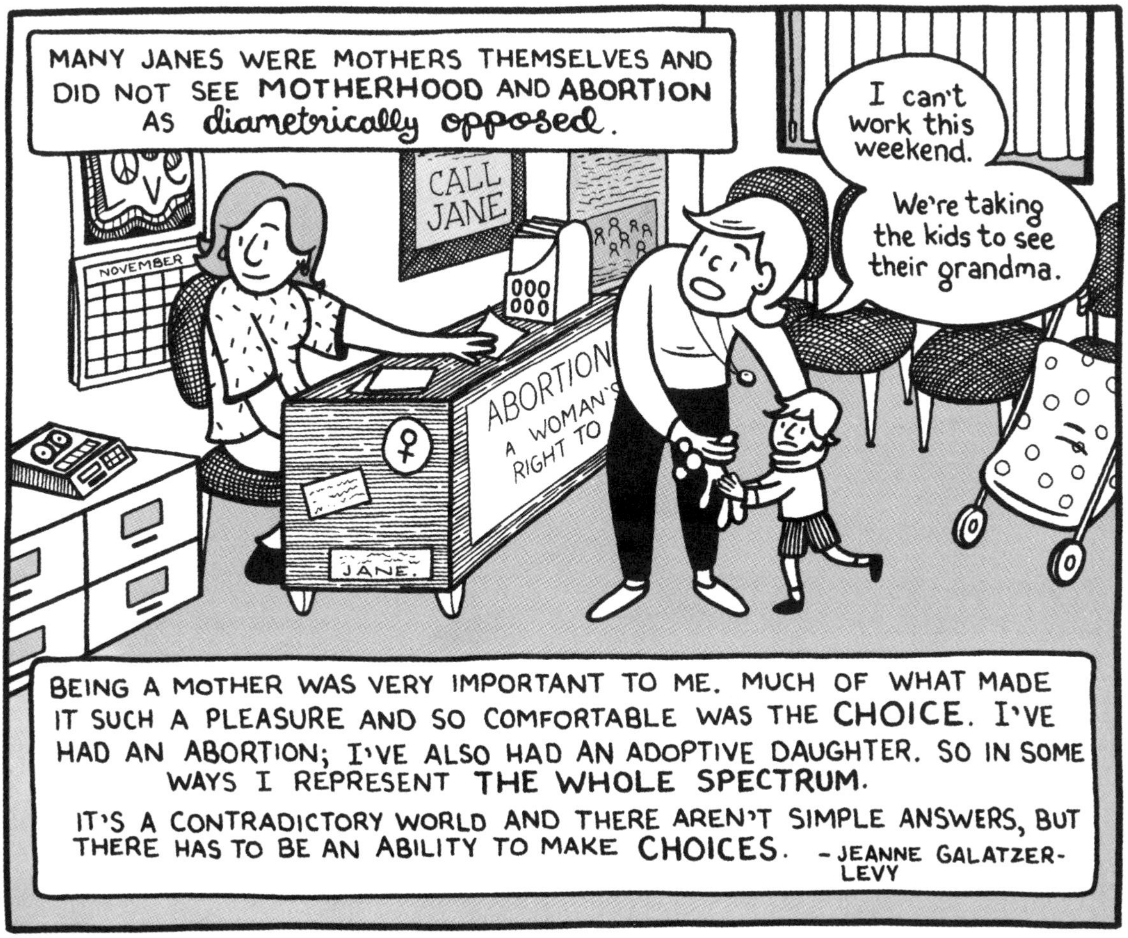
MANY JANES WERE MOTHERS THEMSELVES AND DID NOT SEE MOTHERHOOD AND ABORTION AS diametrically opposed.
I can't work this weekend.
We're taking the kids to see their grandma.
NOVEMBER
CALL JANE
ABORTION A WOMAN'S RIGHT TO
JANE.
BEING A MOTHER WAS VERY IMPORTANT TO ME. MUCH OF WHAT MADE IT SUCH A PLEASURE AND SO COMFORTABLE WAS THE CHOICE. I'VE HAD AN ABORTION; I'VE ALSO HAD AN ADOPTIVE DAUGHTER. SO IN SOME WAYS I REPRESENT THE WHOLE SPECTRUM.
IT'S A CONTRADICTORY WORLD AND THERE AREN'T SIMPLE ANSWERS, BUT THERE HAS TO BE AN ABILITY TO MAKE CHOICES. - JEANNE GALATZER-LEVY

IT'S TEMPTING TO VIEW JANE AS A *legend* OF THE WOMEN'S LIBERATION MOVEMENT, BUT FORMER JANES REFUSE THE IDEA THAT THE GROUP WAS SOME SPECIAL PRODUCT OF HISTORY.

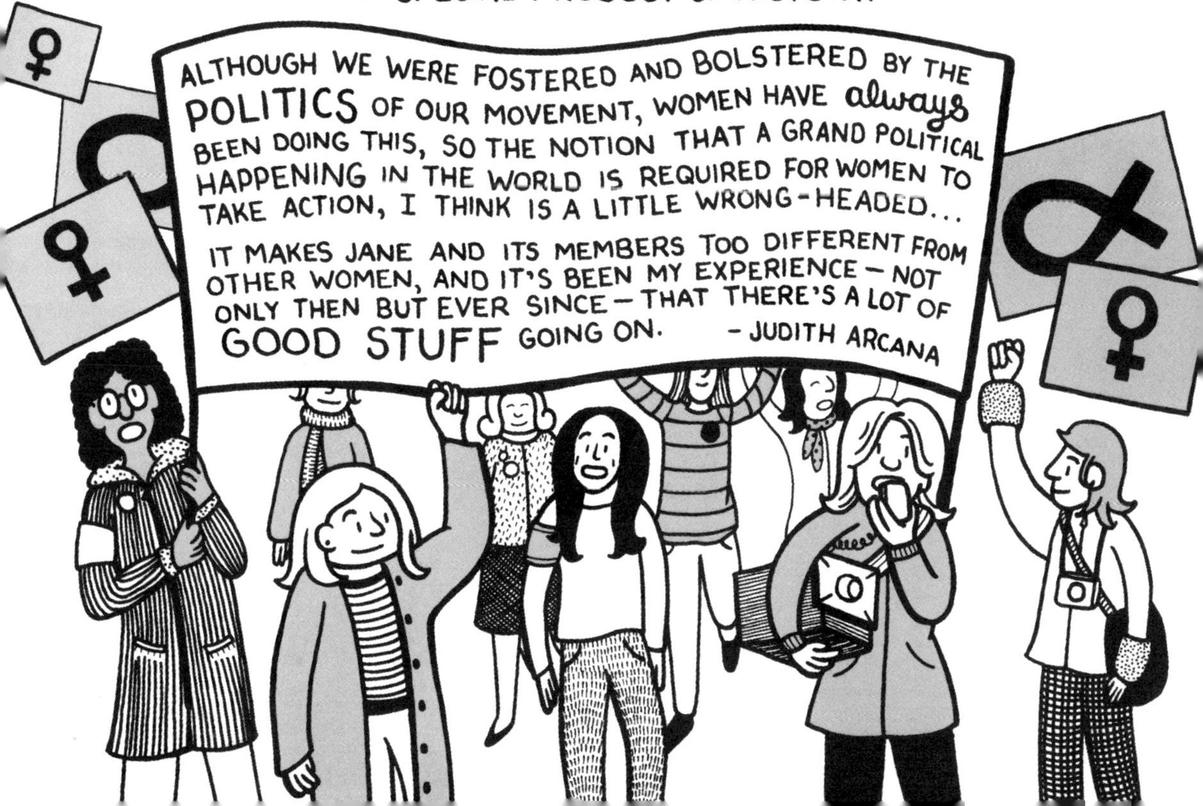
ALTHOUGH WE WERE FOSTERED AND BOLSTERED BY THE POLITICS OF OUR MOVEMENT, WOMEN HAVE always BEEN DOING THIS, SO THE NOTION THAT A GRAND POLITICAL HAPPENING IN THE WORLD IS REQUIRED FOR WOMEN TO TAKE ACTION, I THINK IS A LITTLE WRONG-HEADED...
IT MAKES JANE AND ITS MEMBERS TOO DIFFERENT FROM OTHER WOMEN, AND IT'S BEEN MY EXPERIENCE — NOT ONLY THEN BUT EVER SINCE — THAT THERE'S A LOT OF GOOD STUFF GOING ON. - JUDITH ARCANA

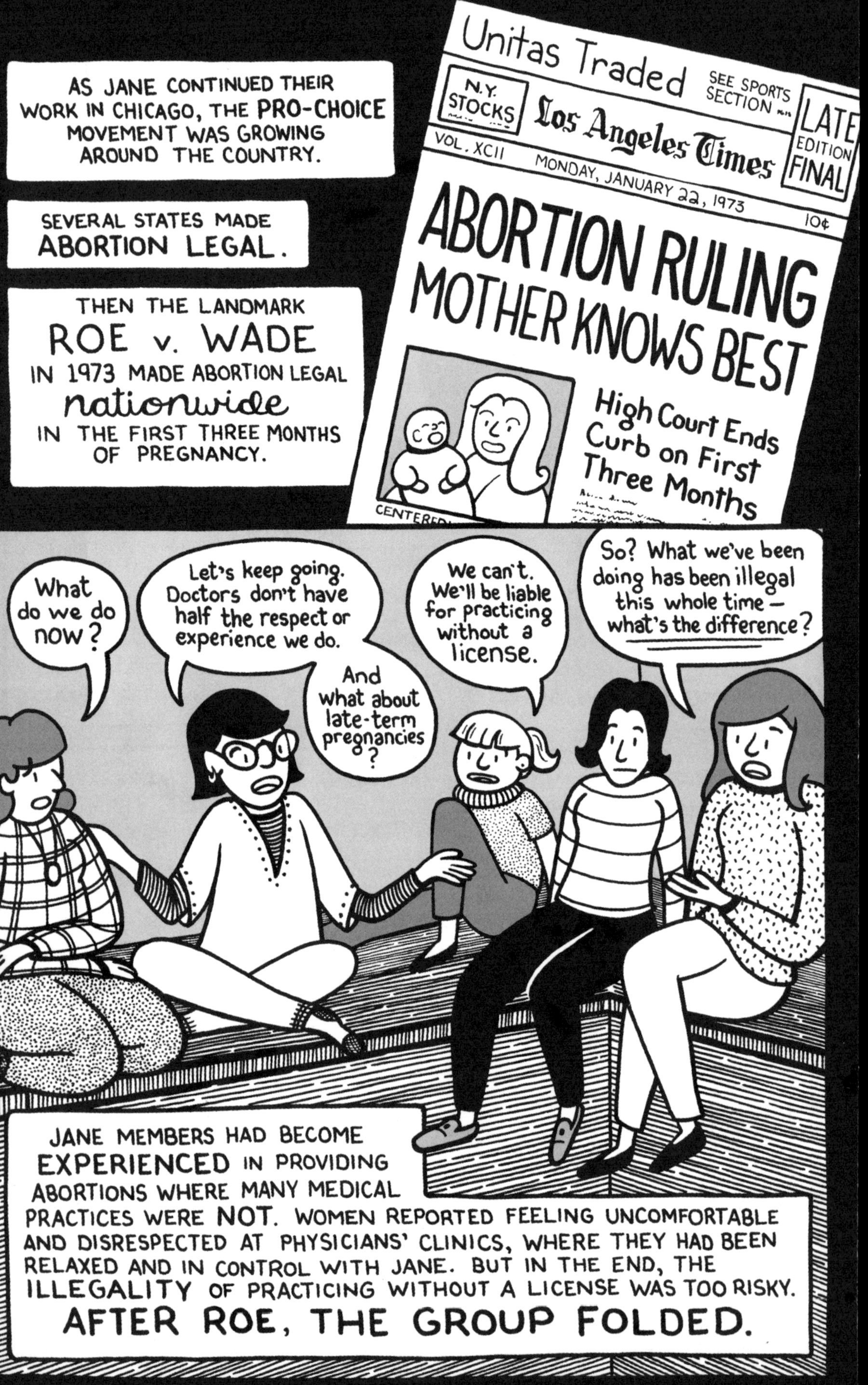
AS JANE CONTINUED THEIR WORK IN CHICAGO, THE PRO-CHOICE MOVEMENT WAS GROWING AROUND THE COUNTRY.
SEVERAL STATES MADE ABORTION LEGAL.
THEN THE LANDMARK ROE v. WADE IN 1973 MADE ABORTION LEGAL nationwide IN THE FIRST THREE MONTHS OF PREGNANCY.
Unitas Traded
SEE SPORTS SECTION
N.Y. STOCKS
Los Angeles Times
LATE EDITION FINAL
VOL. XCII
MONDAY, JANUARY 22, 1973
10¢
ABORTION RULING MOTHER KNOWS BEST
High Court Ends Curb on First Three Months
What do we do now?
Let's keep going. Doctors don't have half the respect or experience we do.
And what about late-term pregnancies?
We can't. We'll be liable for practicing without a license.
So? What we've been doing has been illegal this whole time — what's the difference?
JANE MEMBERS HAD BECOME EXPERIENCED IN PROVIDING ABORTIONS WHERE MANY MEDICAL PRACTICES WERE NOT. WOMEN REPORTED FEELING UNCOMFORTABLE AND DISRESPECTED AT PHYSICIANS' CLINICS, WHERE THEY HAD BEEN RELAXED AND IN CONTROL WITH JANE. BUT IN THE END, THE ILLEGALITY OF PRACTICING WITHOUT A LICENSE WAS TOO RISKY.
AFTER ROE, THE GROUP FOLDED.

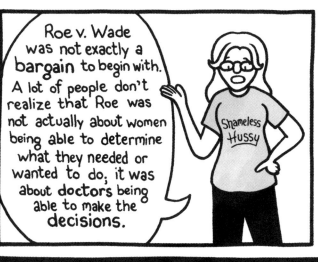

"Roe v. Wade was not exactly a **bargain** to begin with. A lot of people don't realize that Roe was not actually about women being able to determine what they needed or wanted to do; it was about **doctors** being able to make the **decisions.**"

SINCE THE RULING, **ATTITUDES** TOWARD ABORTION HAVE CHANGED.

JANE WANTED TO *demystify* THE PROCEDURE.

BUT IN MANY PARTS OF SOCIETY, ABORTION IS STILL CONSIDERED **TABOO** AND WOMEN ARE LEFT **UNSUPPORTED.**

THIS *wasn't* THE FUTURE OF REPRODUCTIVE CARE THAT THE JANES HAD WORKED SO HARD TO CREATE.

NOW, OPPOSITION FROM A FORCEFUL **ANTI-ABORTION** MOVEMENT HAS CHANGED THE WAY ABORTION IS SPOKEN ABOUT, INFLUENCING WOMEN'S **FEELINGS,** TRESPASSING ON THEIR RIGHT TO **PRIVACY.** AND EXERTING PRESSURE ON POLITICIANS TO **INFRINGE** ON WOMEN'S HEALTHCARE IN ORDER TO WIN VOTES.

STOP — PROTECT LIFE — A CHILD — MURDER HERE — CHOOSE LIFE — BABIES ARE MURDERED INSIDE — Pro Life — LET YOUR BABY LIVE — DEVELOPING — PROTESTS AT HEALTH CLINIC — NEWS

"In many states, it is as difficult to get an abortion **NOW** as it was **BEFORE** Roe v. Wade."

"Women now have **feelings** about the fetus that I do **NOT** share."

"The anti-abortion movement has managed in the past four decades, quite brilliantly, to change the culture, the mindset, the thinking, and even the feelings:"

"the **emotional** response to **abortion, motherhood, pregnancy.**"

THE DENVER POST

INSIDE THE COLORADO SPRINGS PLANNED PARENTHOOD ATTACK

3 DEAD, 9 WOUNDED

"Their radically violent wing is very active and **EXTREMELY DANGEROUS,** so the danger to women who are attempting to do the *good work* now comes not only from the officials— the cops and the politicians— but also from the **serious bad guys.**"

I'M REALLY VERY *encouraged*, DESPITE EVERYTHING. THERE'S AN ENORMOUS AMOUNT OF ANGER AND PUSHBACK– THERE'S A LOT OF UPPITY WOMEN OUT THERE! I'M SEEING THEM MOVING US FORWARD. I'M FINDING IT A VERY *exciting* TIME FOR WOMEN.

THE THING ABOUT THE WOMEN IN JANE IS WE WERE PERFECTLY ORDINARY PEOPLE; IT'S A MATTER OF, YOU *PUSH* ORDINARY PEOPLE FAR ENOUGH AND ORDINARY PEOPLE DO

EXTRAORDINARY THINGS.

–JEANNE GALATZER-LEVY

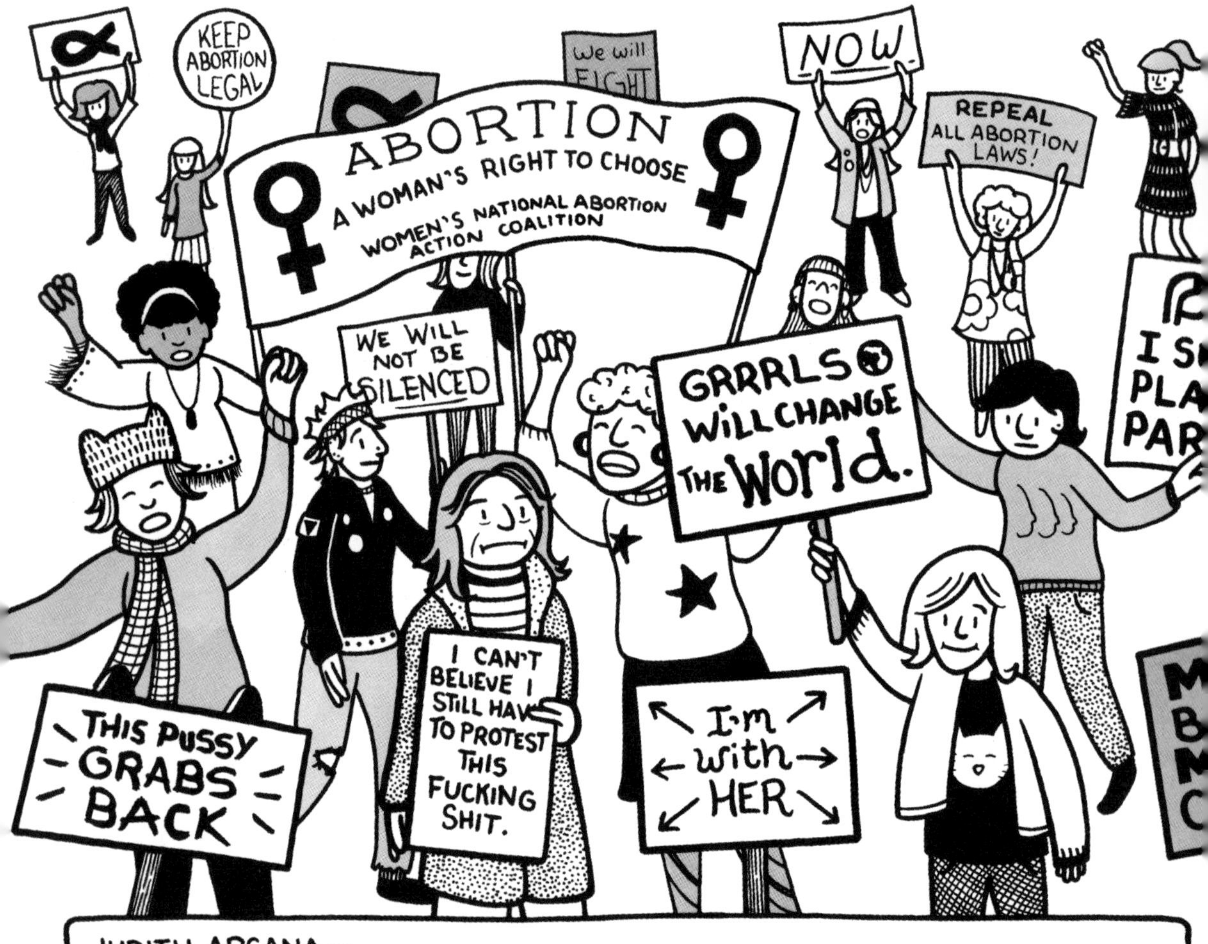

KEEP ABORTION LEGAL
We will
ABORTION A WOMAN'S RIGHT TO CHOOSE
WOMEN'S NATIONAL ABORTION ACTION COALITION
NOW
REPEAL ALL ABORTION LAWS!
WE WILL NOT BE SILENCED
GRRRLS WILL CHANGE THE World.
THIS PUSSY GRABS BACK
I CAN'T BELIEVE I STILL HAV TO PROTEST THIS FUCKING SHIT.
I'm with HER

JUDITH ARCANA –

I'M ACTUALLY *hopeful*, IF YOU CAN BELIEVE IT, BECAUSE THE YOUNG ONES ARE SO SMART. THEY'RE TOUGH AND THEY REALLY REALLY ARE PISSED OFF. THERE AREN'T MILLIONS OF THEM YET, BUT THERE ARE THOUSANDS AND THOUSANDS ALL OVER THE COUNTRY, AND *THEY'RE DOING IT!* AND I JUST THINK:

→ OKAY! ←

Let's get going here!

UNDUE BURDENS

How U.S. reproductive rights law fails poor people

by Hallie Jay Pope

When we talk about abortion and the law in the U.S., most people probably think of <u>Roe v. Wade</u>.

In that landmark case, the Supreme Court decided that the 14th Amendment protects the right to have an abortion.

What someone does with their uterus is a private choice between them and their doctor!

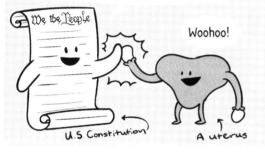

Woohoo!

U.S Constitution

A uterus

But this right has **limits**...

"The right of personal privacy includes the abortion decision, but this right is **not** unqualified and must be considered against important state interests in regulation."

Justice Harry Blackmun

The <u>Roe</u> Court set up a test for evaluating abortion restrictions based on the trimesters of a pregnancy, weighing the pregnant person's* interests against the interests of the state.

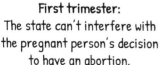

First trimester:
The state can't interfere with the pregnant person's decision to have an abortion.

Second trimester on:
The state can impose regulations that reasonably relate to the pregnant person's health.

Viability:
The state can ban abortions not needed for health reasons in order to protect "potential life."

*Why am I saying "person" instead of "woman"? Transgender men and gender-non-conforming people can get pregnant too! And they often face additional hurdles to accessing reproductive care.

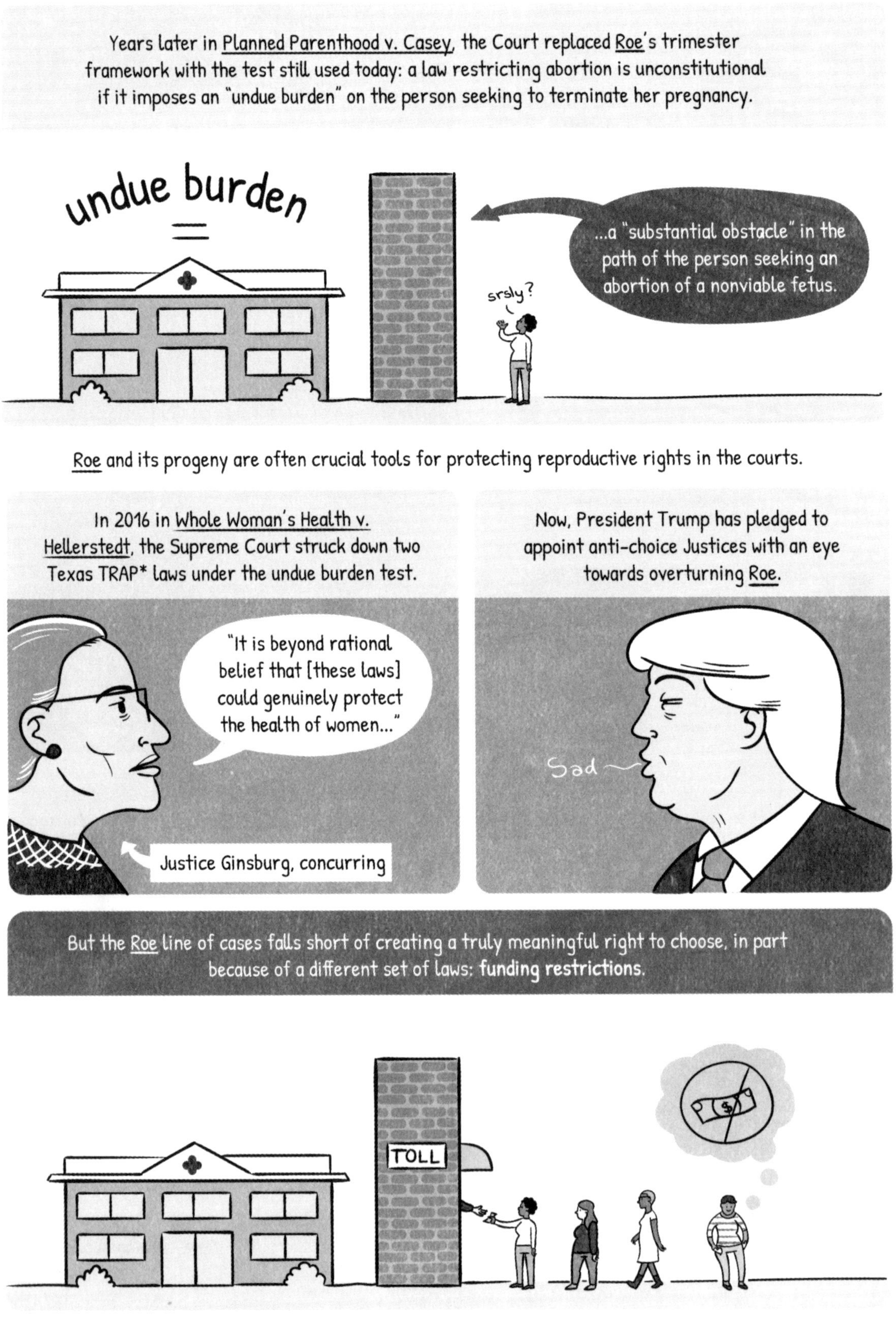
Years later in Planned Parenthood v. Casey, the Court replaced Roe's trimester framework with the test still used today: a law restricting abortion is unconstitutional if it imposes an "undue burden" on the person seeking to terminate her pregnancy.
undue burden
=
...a "substantial obstacle" in the path of the person seeking an abortion of a nonviable fetus.
srsly?
Roe and its progeny are often crucial tools for protecting reproductive rights in the courts.
In 2016 in Whole Woman's Health v. Hellerstedt, the Supreme Court struck down two Texas TRAP* laws under the undue burden test.
"It is beyond rational belief that [these laws] could genuinely protect the health of women..."
Justice Ginsburg, concurring
Now, President Trump has pledged to appoint anti-choice Justices with an eye towards overturning Roe.
Sad
But the Roe line of cases falls short of creating a truly meaningful right to choose, in part because of a different set of laws: funding restrictions.
TOLL
$

*TRAP = targeted regulation of abortion providers

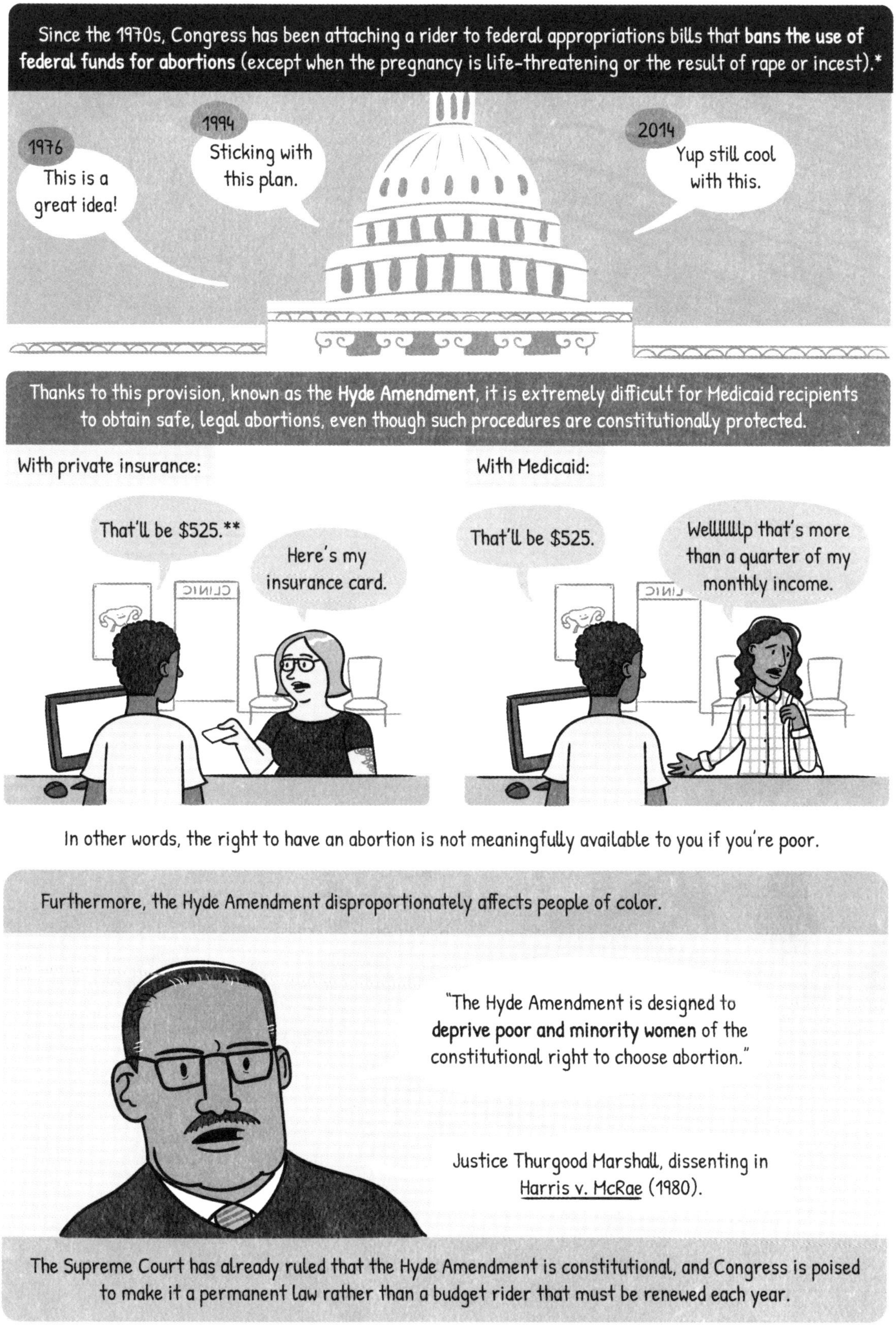
Since the 1970s, Congress has been attaching a rider to federal appropriations bills that **bans the use of federal funds for abortions** (except when the pregnancy is life-threatening or the result of rape or incest).*
1976
This is a great idea!
1994
Sticking with this plan.
2014
Yup still cool with this.
Thanks to this provision, known as the **Hyde Amendment**, it is extremely difficult for Medicaid recipients to obtain safe, legal abortions, even though such procedures are constitutionally protected.
With private insurance:
That'll be $525.**
Here's my insurance card.
CLINIC
With Medicaid:
That'll be $525.
Welllllp that's more than a quarter of my monthly income.
CLINIC
In other words, the right to have an abortion is not meaningfully available to you if you're poor.
Furthermore, the Hyde Amendment disproportionately affects people of color.
"The Hyde Amendment is designed to **deprive poor and minority women** of the constitutional right to choose abortion."
Justice Thurgood Marshall, dissenting in Harris v. McRae (1980).
The Supreme Court has already ruled that the Hyde Amendment is constitutional, and Congress is poised to make it a permanent law rather than a budget rider that must be renewed each year.

*Some versions haven't even included the rape or incest exceptions, but the most recent one does.
**A first trimester abortion costs $300-$850.

While the Hyde Amendment makes <u>Roe</u> an empty promise for poor people in the U.S., the Mexico City Policy demeans it abroad.

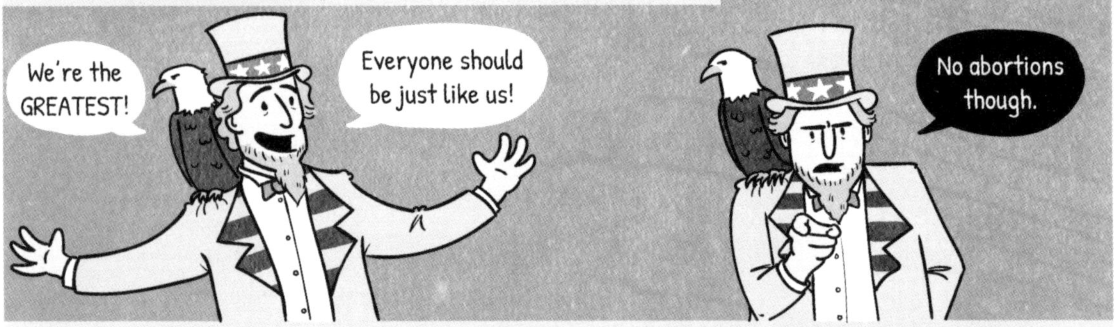
We're the GREATEST!
Everyone should be just like us!
No abortions though.

You might think that the U.S. government would want to encourage the international provision of a right it supposedly guarantees to its own citizens. But the Mexico City Policy does exactly the opposite.

This policy, also known as the Global Gag Rule, has existed under every Republican president since Reagan.

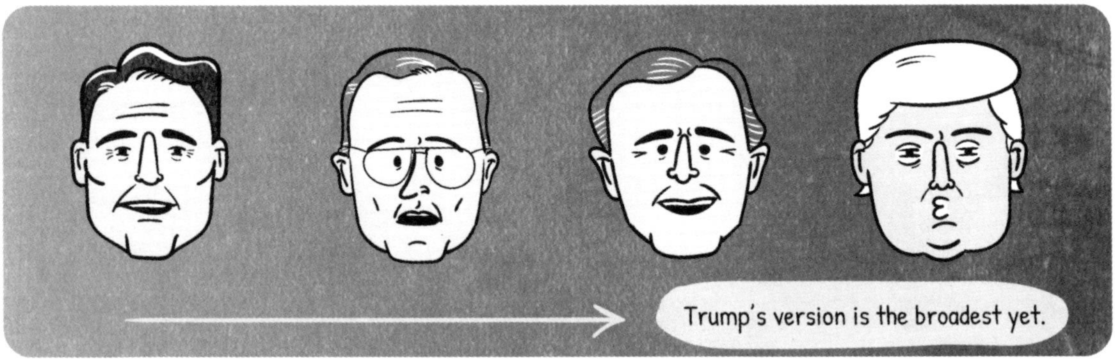
Trump's version is the broadest yet.

Under the current rule, the U.S. will not give **any** international health funds* to NGOs that "perform or actively promote abortion as a method of family planning in other nations."

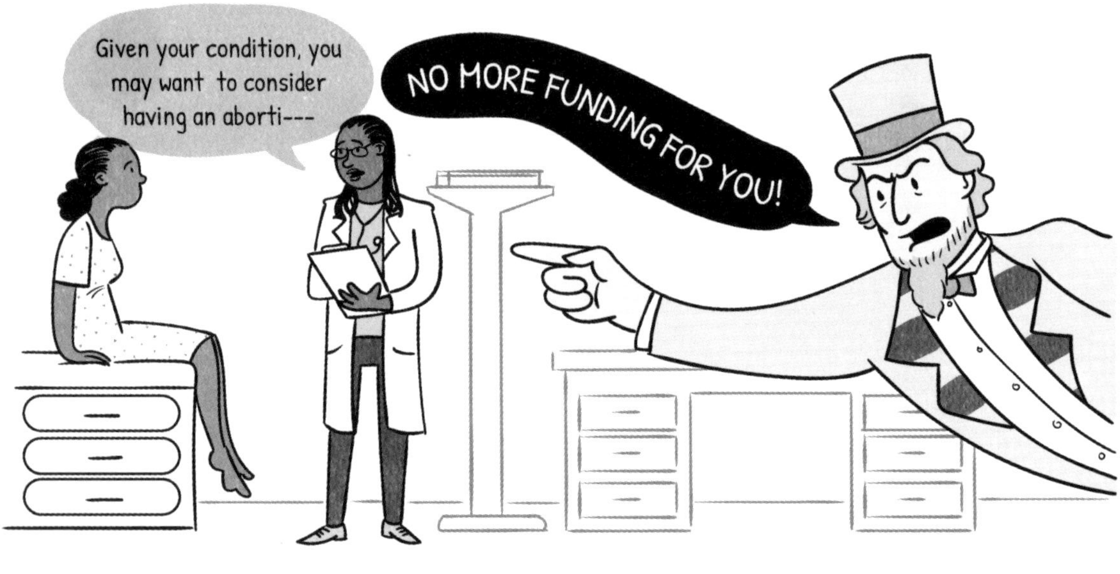
Given your condition, you may want to consider having an aborti---
NO MORE FUNDING FOR YOU!

*Past versions applied only to international family planning funds.

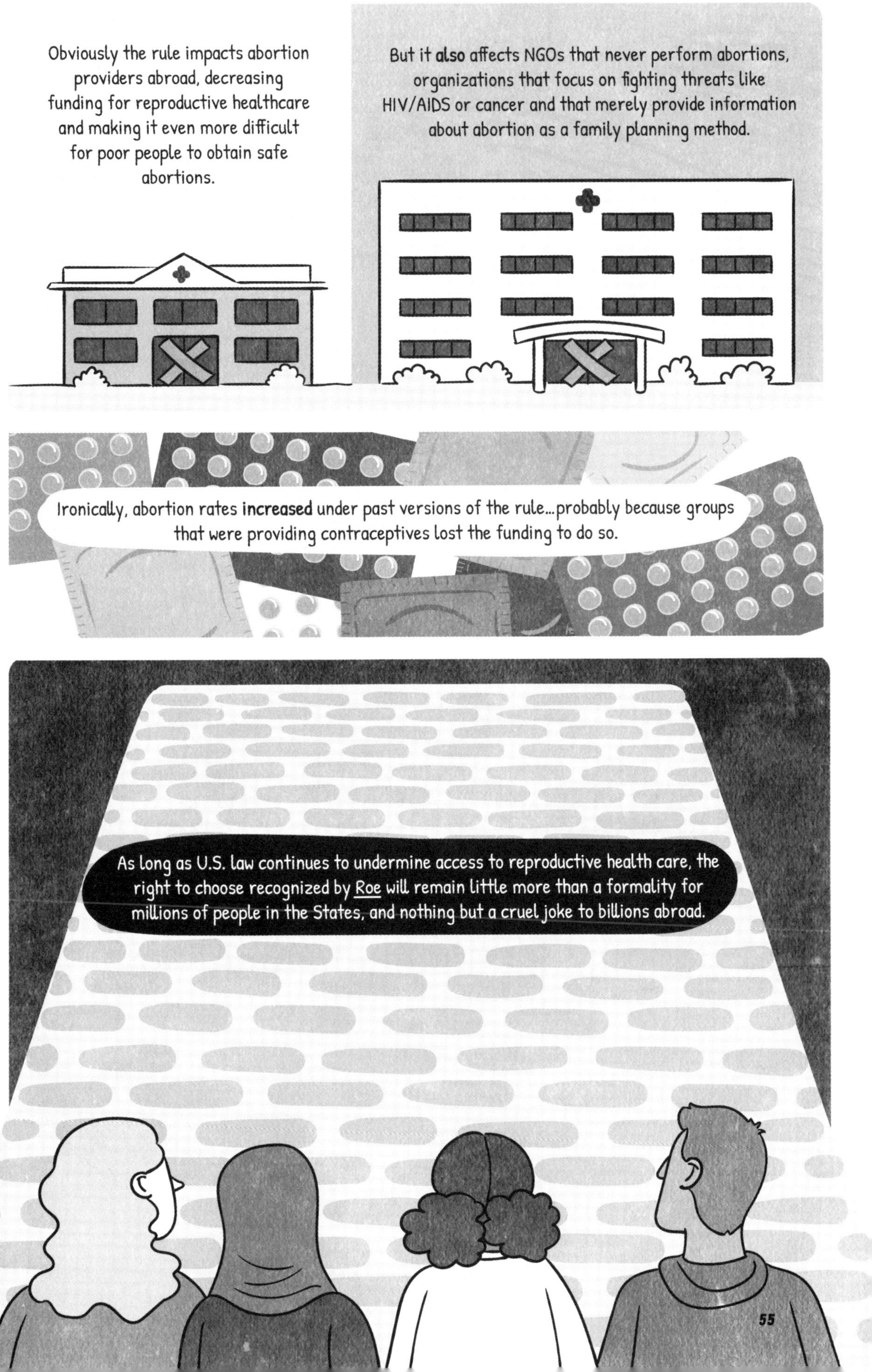
Obviously the rule impacts abortion providers abroad, decreasing funding for reproductive healthcare and making it even more difficult for poor people to obtain safe abortions.
But it also affects NGOs that never perform abortions, organizations that focus on fighting threats like HIV/AIDS or cancer and that merely provide information about abortion as a family planning method.
Ironically, abortion rates increased under past versions of the rule...probably because groups that were providing contraceptives lost the funding to do so.
As long as U.S. law continues to undermine access to reproductive health care, the right to choose recognized by Roe will remain little more than a formality for millions of people in the States, and nothing but a cruel joke to billions abroad.

Okay, this is **Anna Sellheim** and this is MY MOTHER'S STORY.

Now?

Yeah, go!

 So I guess this all started with your father in the 70s. We had just moved in together.

Dad & I always used contraceptives. I had used an IUD that tore my body apart and the pill was too much.

So I used a diaphragm.

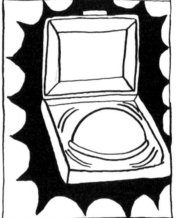

And one morning I woke up and knew I was pregnant.

For every pregnancy I have been aware, almost immediately, that I had a baby inside me.

I had never thought about having children and Dad didn't want any because he had lost contact with his daughter from a previous marriage and it had been very painful.

It was a life, I could feel it. But I didn't think through the ramifications.

Dad said: You have to have an abortion. We haven't been together that long. We don't know where we're going and we haven't settled down.

So, with little thought I had one, but it was emotionally devastating.

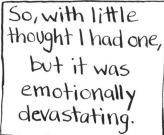

WAITING ROOM POLICY

We continued our relationship and committed to each other without even saying it.

I got pregnant again and had a miscarriage.

You have to understand, no one talked to me about anything. I didn't even know what a miscarriage was, I had to look it up. And not on the internet.

And I told Dad: If I get pregnant again I'm having the baby.

And he didn't say anything.

HAHAHA Okay!

I don't know what he thought!

God knows, I thought every time I looked at him I got pregnant. Even though I used the diaphragm.

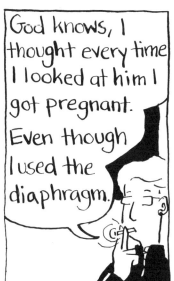

So I got pregnant again.

It was wonderful. It was everything I thought it would be, I loved it.

So we had your brother and Dad loved it. He was ecstatic.

We were living in Maine but Dad wanted to leave so he moved to DC to start a company with a friend.

MOM
DAD

I moved to NYC and only saw him on weekends.

Why did you move to NYC instead of DC?

I got a job there. I wouldn't go anywhere without a job. I was an executive in NYC.

I got pregnant again. It didn't make sense to have the baby because I was, essentially, living as a single mother.

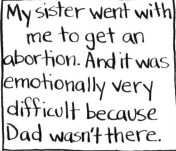

My sister went with me to get an abortion. And it was emotionally very difficult because Dad wasn't there.

TING
POLICY

Soon after that I moved to DC to be with Dad, and I told him:

I am having the next child. You know I'll get pregnant again

So I'm telling you now, if you don't do something I'm having another baby!

And we did!

HAHAHA!

And you were impossible. You were definitely IT.

But you were adorable and wonderful too.

58

So dad had a vasectomy. He didn't want 3 children. He originally didn't want any!

And I've told you this story:

Hey Terry! How ya doin?

I'll tell you how I'm doing—

I just got clipped!

Yeah, I've told many of my friends that story because it's hilarious!

That was your father!

So why are you pro-choice?

I'm a feminist.

I know but... I guess I'm just surprised by the language you're using.

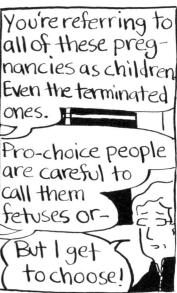

You're referring to all of these pregnancies as children. Even the terminated ones.

Pro-choice people are careful to call them fetuses or—

But I get to choose!

I made my choices with and without my husband. It's my body, I get to do whatever I want with it!

Lawmakers get the hell out of my life!

And that's why I took you and your brother to pro-choice rallies, so I could show that you could have children and still be pro-choice.

Women get to choose. It's nobody else's business.

59

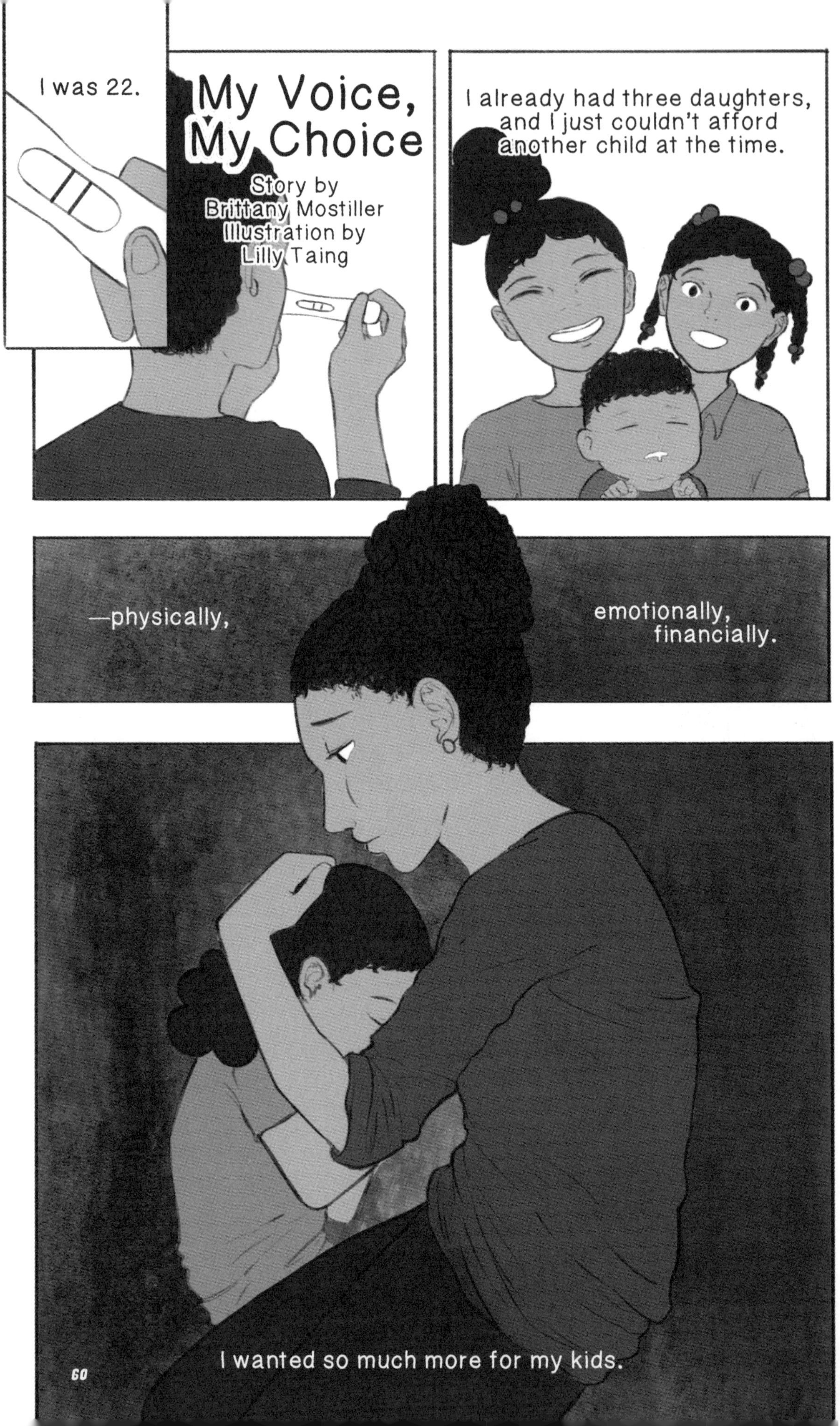
I was 22.
My Voice, My Choice
Story by Brittany Mostiller
Illustration by Lilly Taing
I already had three daughters, and I just couldn't afford another child at the time.
—physically,
emotionally, financially.
I wanted so much more for my kids.

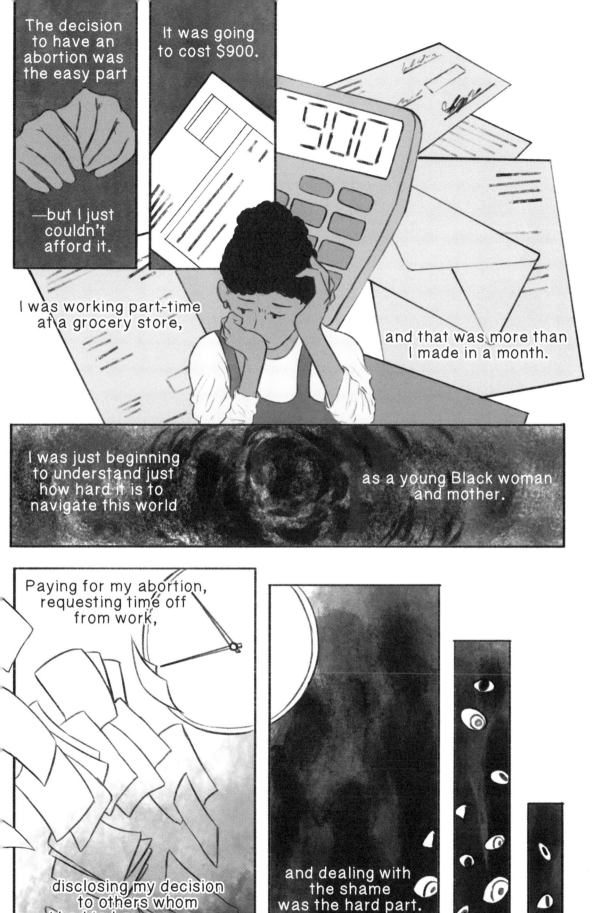

The decision to have an abortion was the easy part

It was going to cost $900.

—but I just couldn't afford it.

I was working part-time at a grocery store,

and that was more than I made in a month.

I was just beginning to understand just how hard it is to navigate this world

as a young Black woman and mother.

Paying for my abortion, requesting time off from work,

disclosing my decision to others whom I had to borrow money,

and dealing with the shame was the hard part.

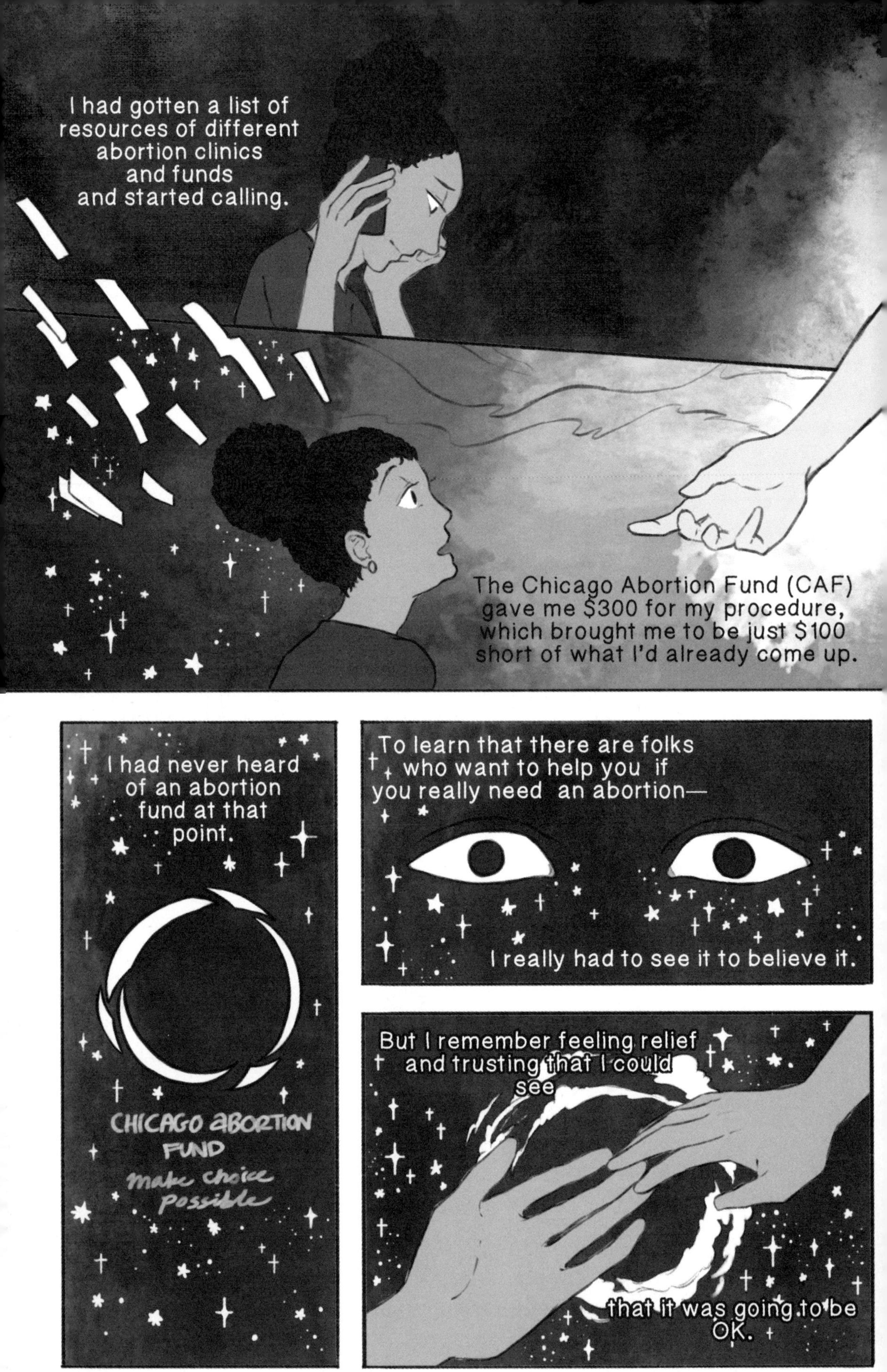
I had gotten a list of resources of different abortion clinics and funds and started calling.
The Chicago Abortion Fund (CAF) gave me $300 for my procedure, which brought me to be just $100 short of what I'd already come up.
I had never heard of an abortion fund at that point.
CHICAGO ABORTION FUND
make choice possible
To learn that there are folks who want to help you if you really need an abortion—
I really had to see it to believe it.
But I remember feeling relief and trusting that I could see
that it was going to be OK.

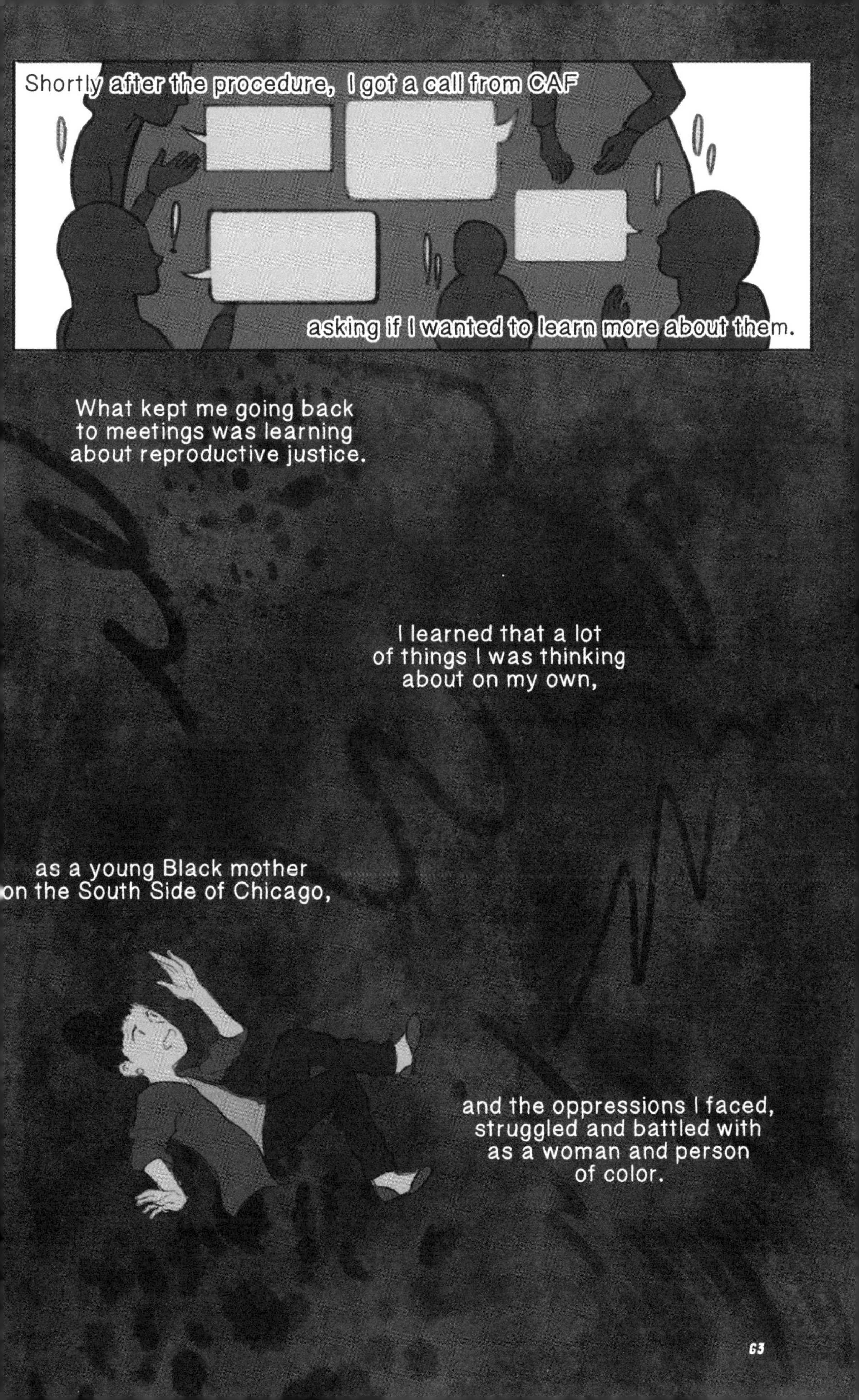
Shortly after the procedure, I got a call from CAF
asking if I wanted to learn more about them.
What kept me going back to meetings was learning about reproductive justice.
I learned that a lot of things I was thinking about on my own,
as a young Black mother on the South Side of Chicago,
and the oppressions I faced, struggled and battled with as a woman and person of color.

Abortion care, poverty, education— all these social justice issues are intertwined.

I saw all these systems of oppression,

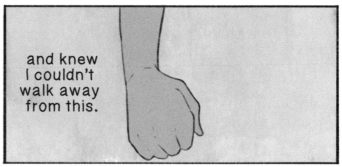

and knew I couldn't walk away from this.

You have to be secure in knowing what you need to be healthy and well.

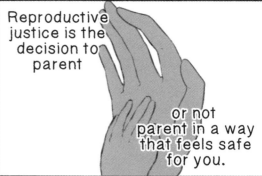

Reproductive justice is the decision to parent

or not parent in a way that feels safe for you.

It will always be tied to feeling safe in your surroundings.

We have to do our part, big or small, but we have to do something and we have to fight for justice.

These aren't difficult conversations, they are necessary conversations.

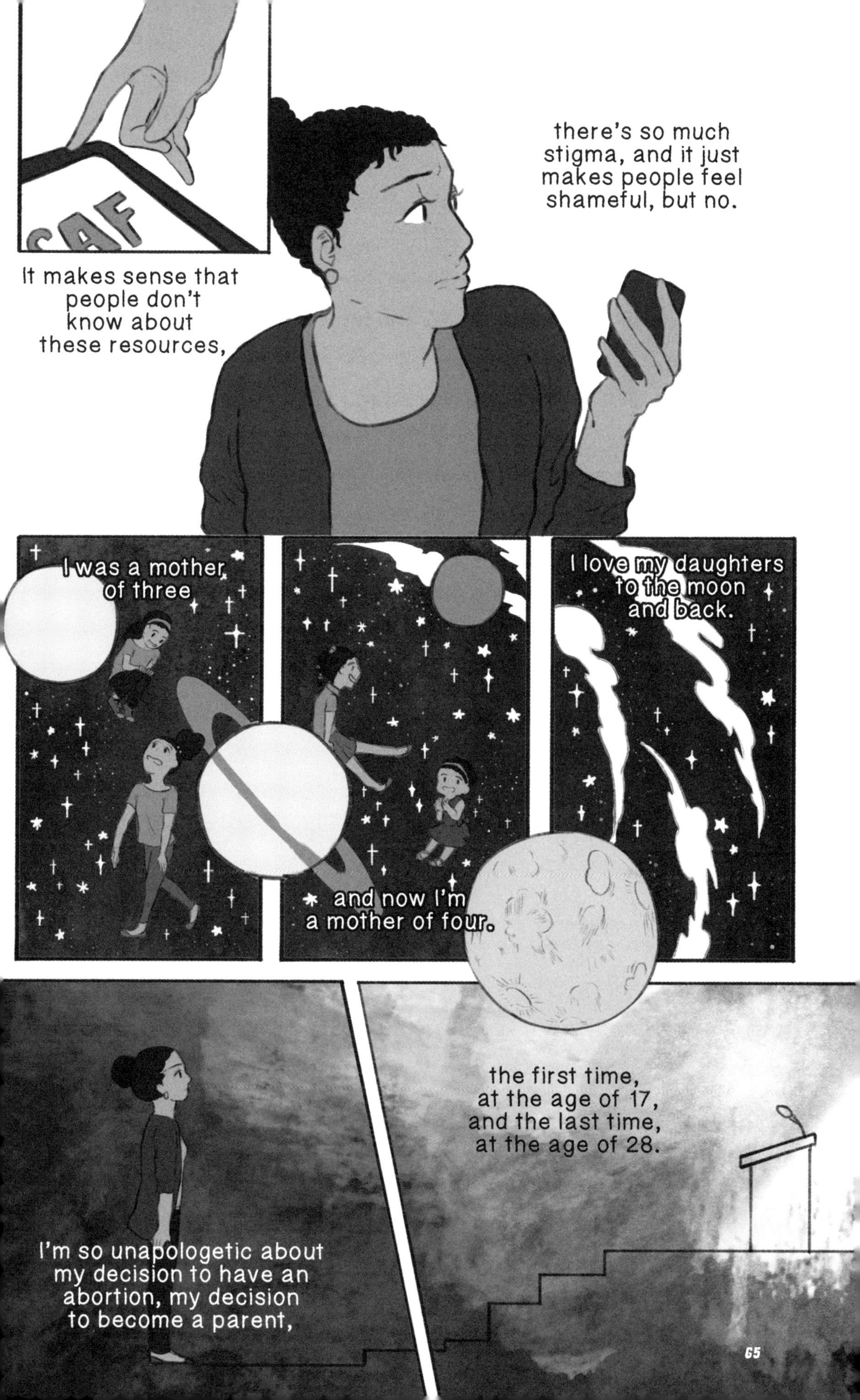
CAF
It makes sense that people don't know about these resources,
there's so much stigma, and it just makes people feel shameful, but no.
I was a mother of three
and now I'm a mother of four.
I love my daughters to the moon and back.
I'm so unapologetic about my decision to have an abortion, my decision to become a parent,
the first time, at the age of 17, and the last time, at the age of 28.

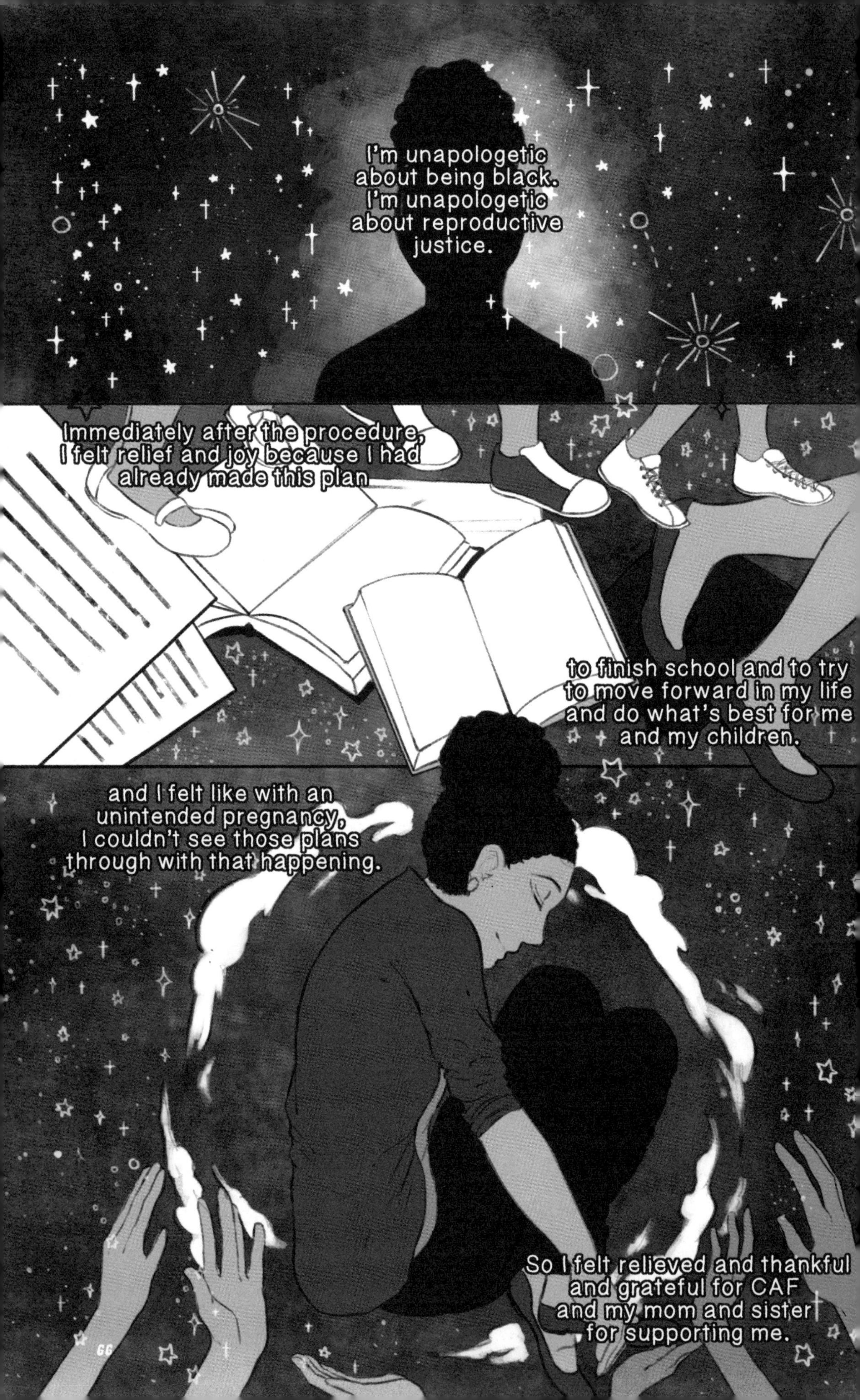
I'm unapologetic about being black. I'm unapologetic about reproductive justice.
Immediately after the procedure, I felt relief and joy because I had already made this plan
to finish school and to try to move forward in my life and do what's best for me and my children.
and I felt like with an unintended pregnancy, I couldn't see those plans through with that happening.
So I felt relieved and thankful and grateful for CAF and my mom and sister for supporting me.
66

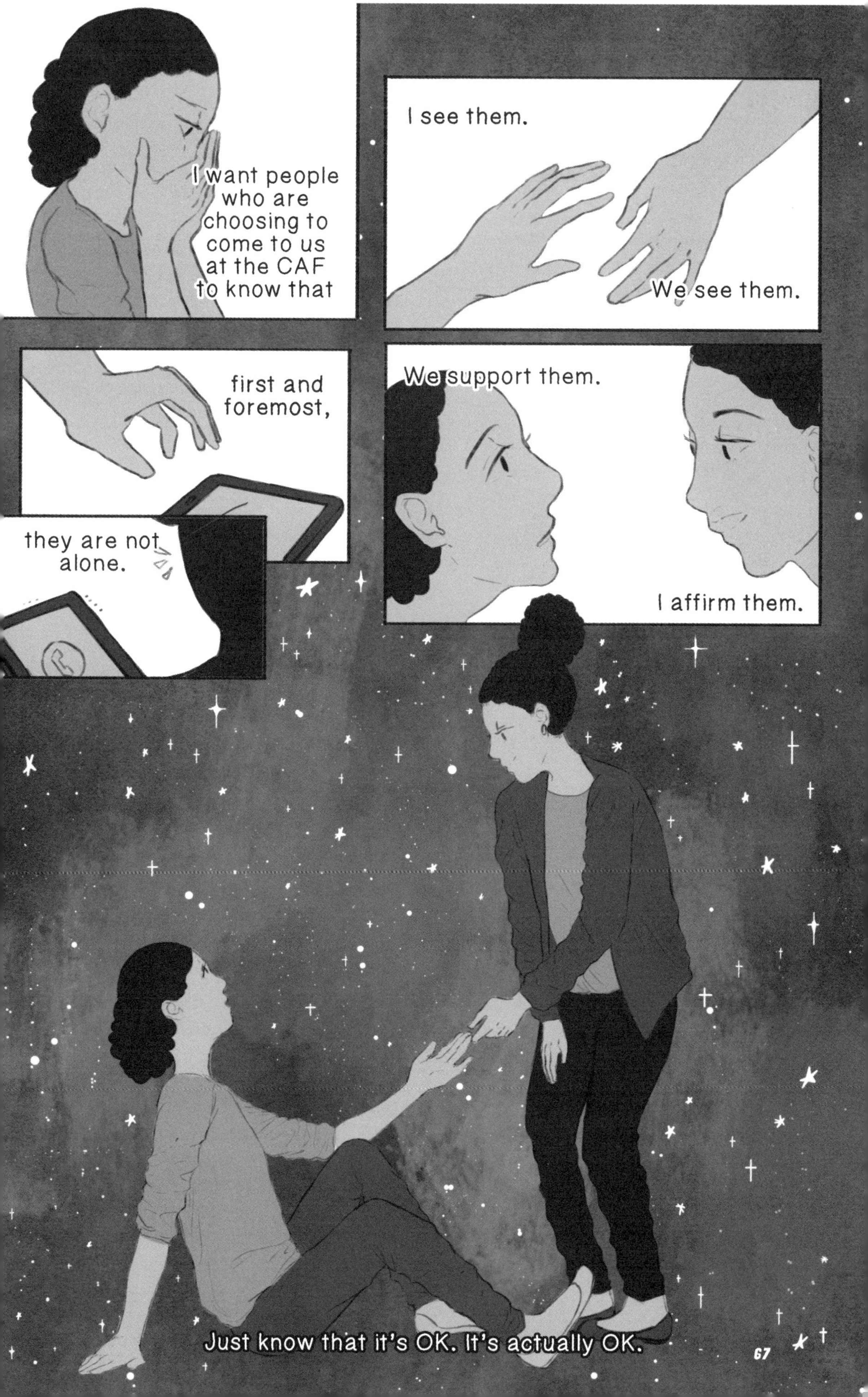
I want people who are choosing to come to us at the CAF to know that
I see them.
We see them.
first and foremost,
We support them.
they are not alone.
I affirm them.
Just know that it's OK. It's actually OK.

The Unruly Mob

Written by Lindsay Rodriguez
Illustrated by Lucy Haslam

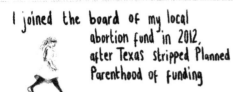

I joined the board of my local abortion fund in 2012, after Texas stripped Planned Parenthood of funding

I felt incredibly frustrated and alone watching the people in my majority Latinx community

 have their

ABORTION ACCESS

continually attacked

and knowing it was the people with the least amount of money and power who got stuck with the worst deal.

I almost

APPLICATION

APPLICATION

never applied.

But I was learning more about the important work funds do to make access available, regardless of where you live or how much you earn.

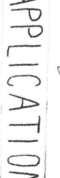

APPLICATION

And ended up becoming the first Lilith Fund board member in

SAN ANTONIO

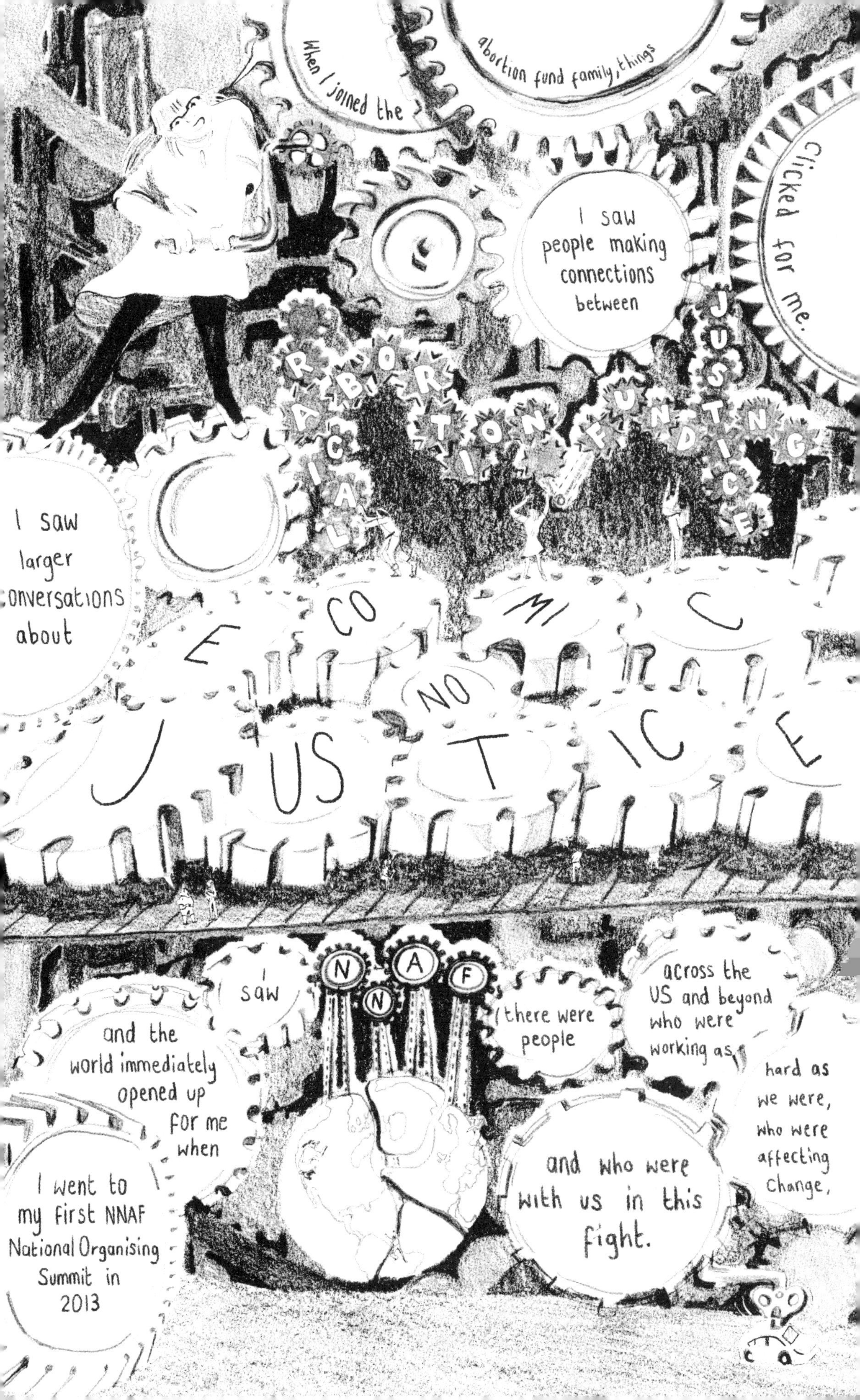

When I joined the
abortion fund family, things
clicked for me.
I saw people making connections between
RACIAL
ABORTION
FUNDING
JUSTICE
I saw larger conversations about
ECONOMIC
JUSTICE
and the world immediately opened up for me when
I went to my first NNAF National Organising Summit in 2013
I saw
NNAF
there were people
across the US and beyond who were working as
hard as we were, who were affecting change,
and who were with us in this fight.

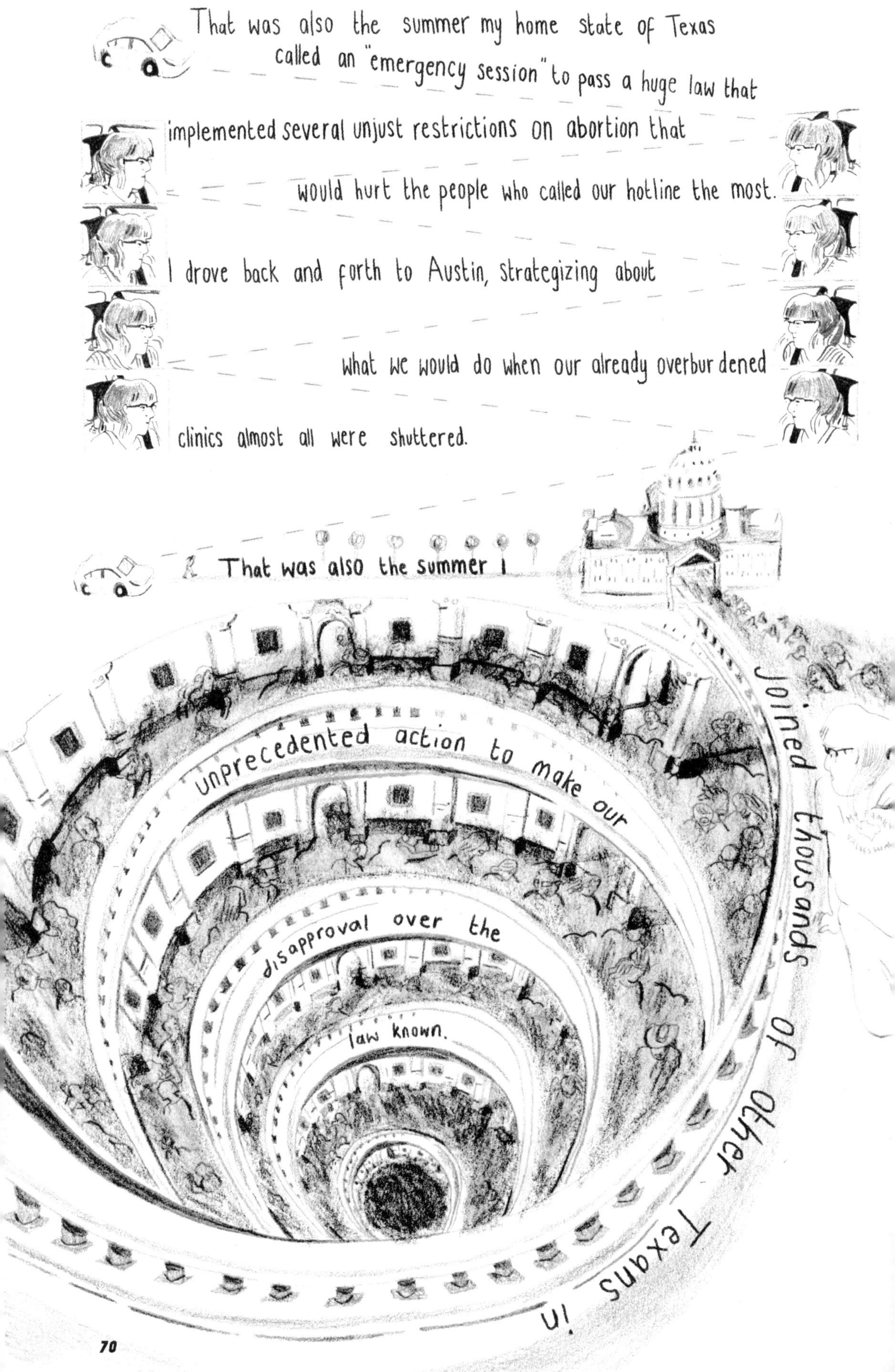
That was also the summer my home state of Texas called an "emergency session" to pass a huge law that implemented several unjust restrictions on abortion that would hurt the people who called our hotline the most.
I drove back and forth to Austin, strategizing about what we would do when our already overburdened clinics almost all were shuttered.
That was also the summer I joined thousands of other Texans in unprecedented action to make our disapproval over the law known.

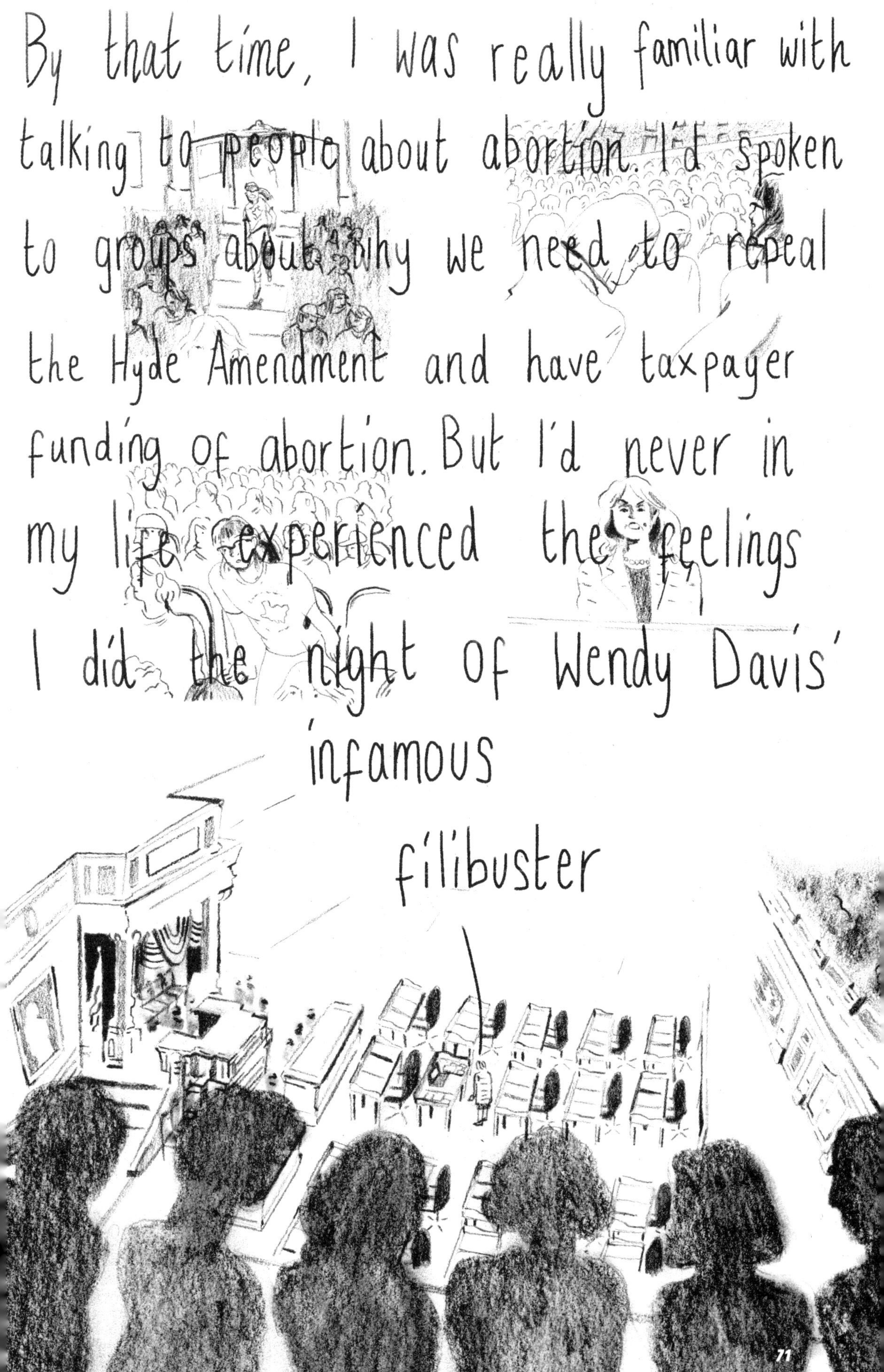
By that time, I was really familiar with talking to people about abortion. I'd spoken to groups about why we need to repeal the Hyde Amendment and have taxpayer funding of abortion. But I'd never in my life experienced the feelings I did the night of Wendy Davis' infamous
filibuster

STOP STOP STOP STOP STOP
The whole day was like something out of a movie
with clear cut
STOP
STOP STOP STOP STOP STOP STOP STOP
heroes
and
STOP
d-v-i-l-l-a-i-n-s
BOO BOO BOO BOO

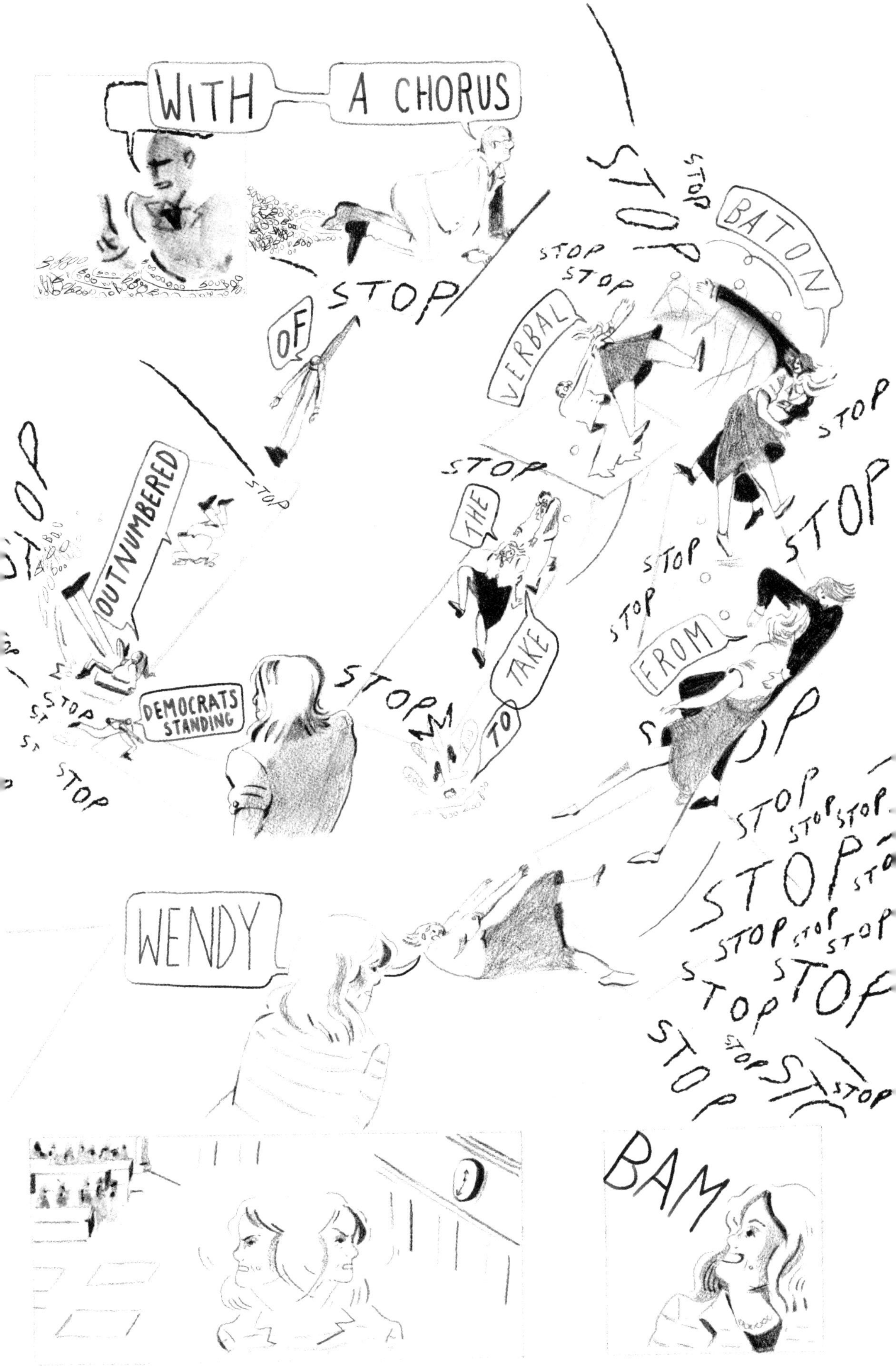
WITH
A CHORUS
OF
STOP
OUTNUMBERED
DEMOCRATS STANDING
THE
TAKE
TO
VERBAL
BATON
FROM
WENDY
BAM

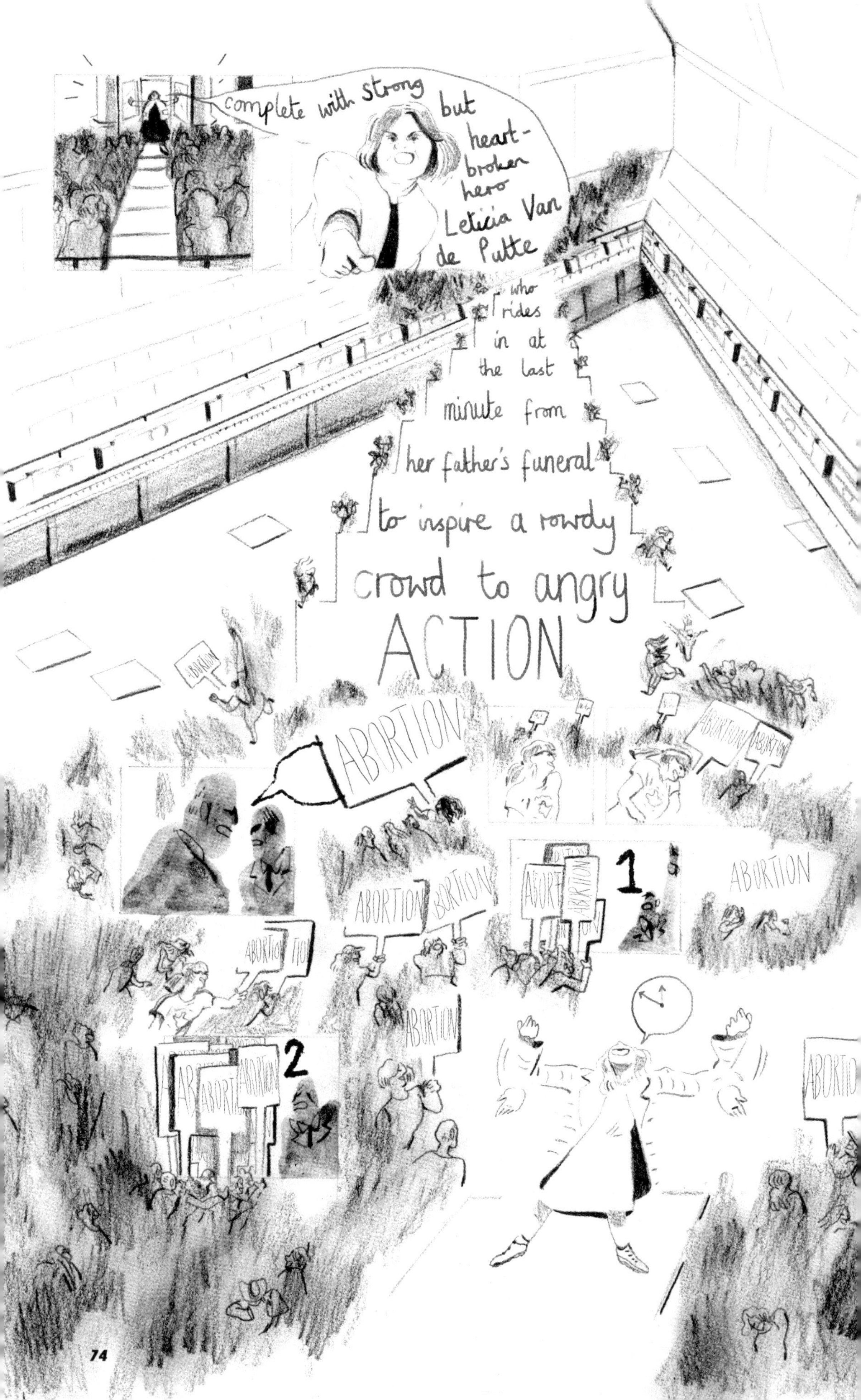
complete with strong but heart-broken hero Leticia Van de Putte
who rides in at the last minute from her father's funeral to inspire a rowdy crowd to angry ACTION
ABORTION
ABORTION
ABORTION
ABORTION
ABORTION
ABORTION
1
2
ABORTION
ABORTION

Of course the Republicans called another session and jammed the law through anyway. It was fucked up and ended up at the Supreme Court, where it famously was overturned.

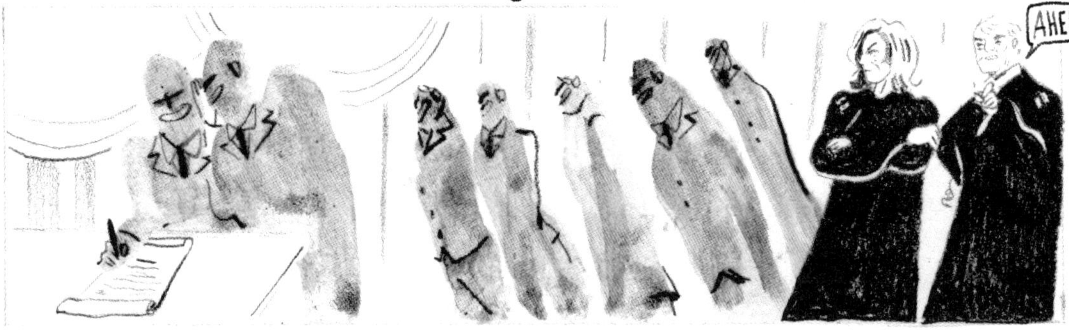
AHEM

I often say those who are involved in abortion funds end up being part of this movement forever.

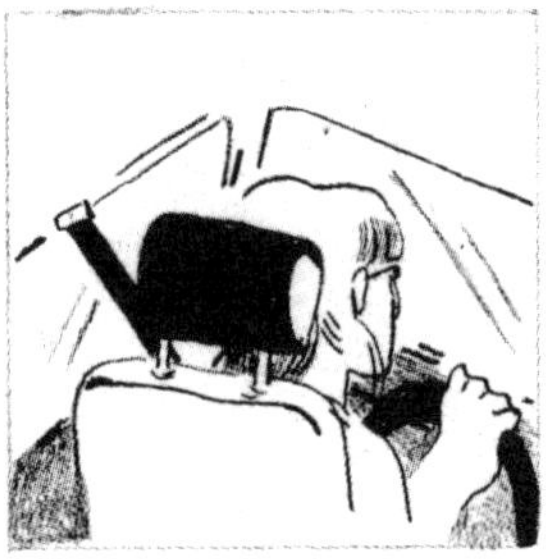

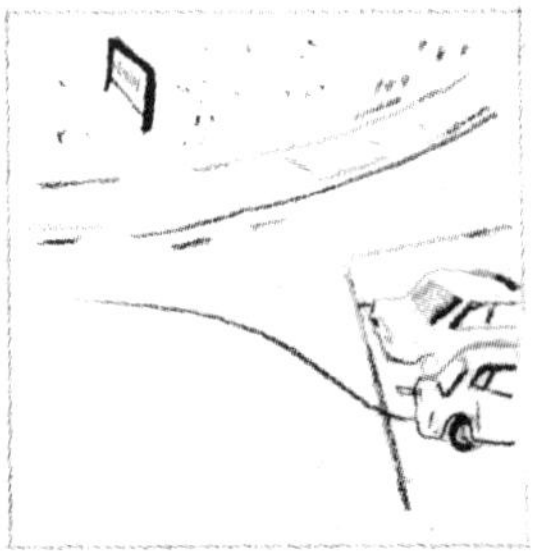

Once you've opened the door to understanding the intricate way abortion...

is a flashpoint to so many of the biggest injustices in our world

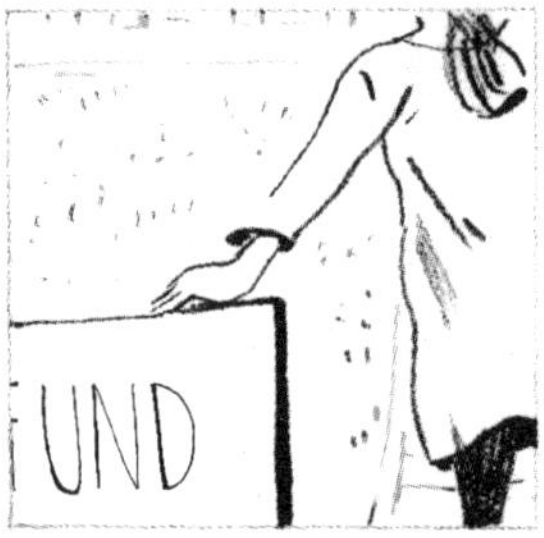
UND

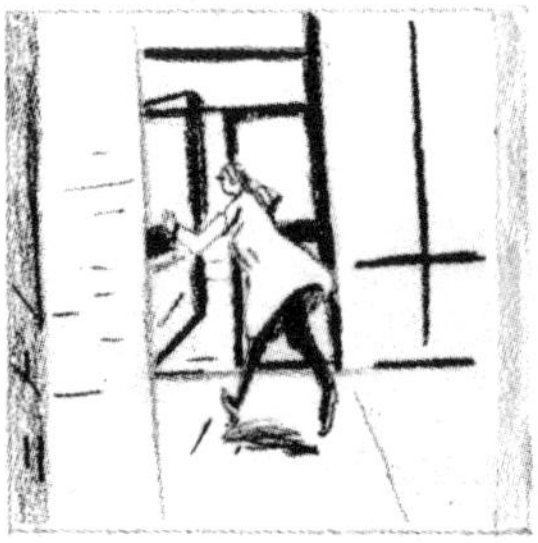

to racism, poverty, gender injustices, immigration and disability issues, community resources

– it's pretty impossible to close that door again.

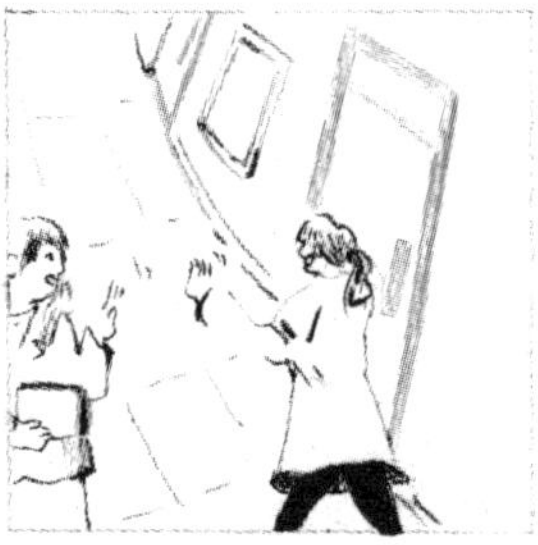

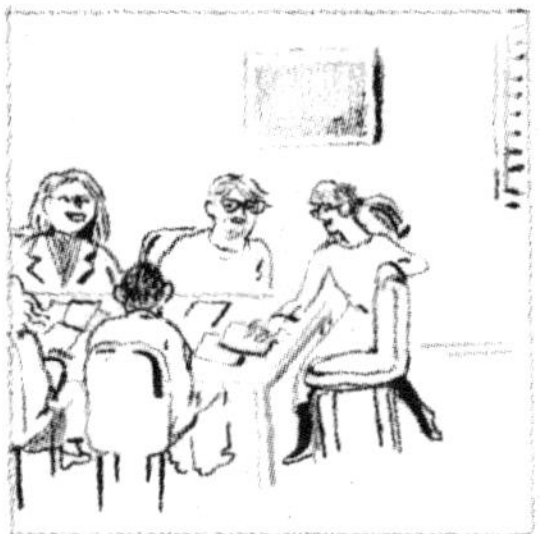

The cruelty and repression in Texas has spread, and to be honest: I'm scared.

But one thing I don't worry about anymore is being alone.

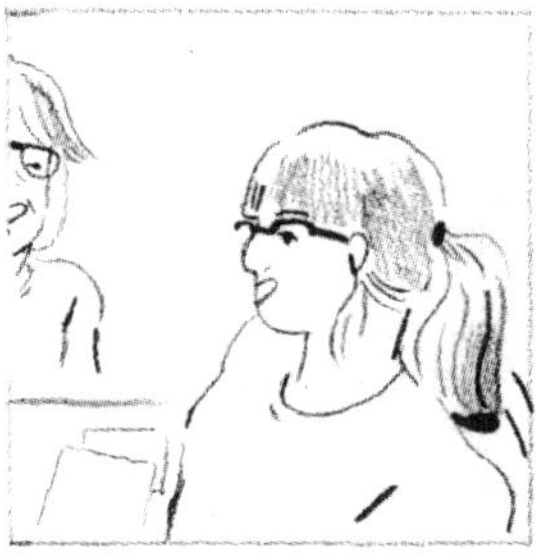

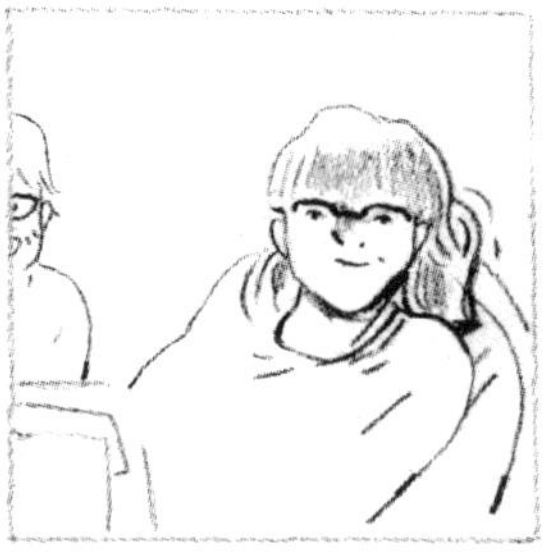

COMING OUT

A TEXAS ABORTION STORY

BY SAM ROMERO
AND ERIN LUX

TEXAS IS A HUGE STATE

WE HAVE EVERYTHING FROM DESERT TO WETLANDS

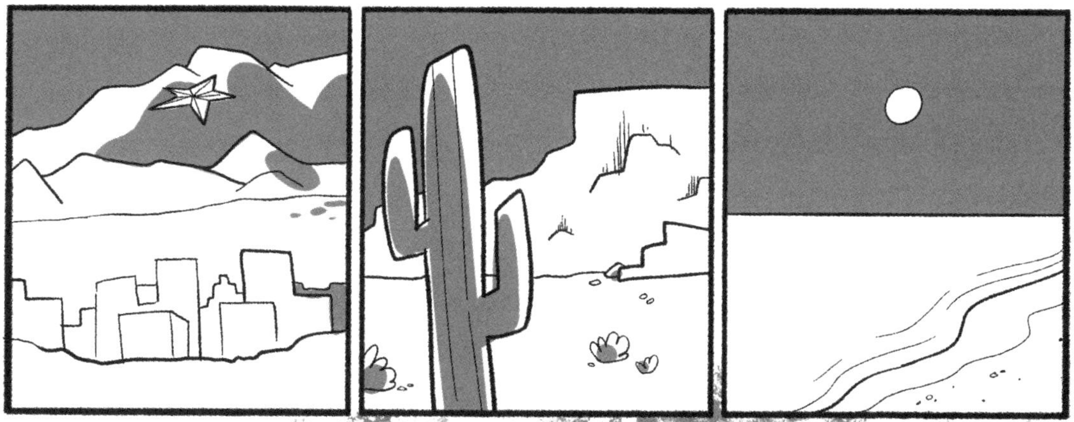

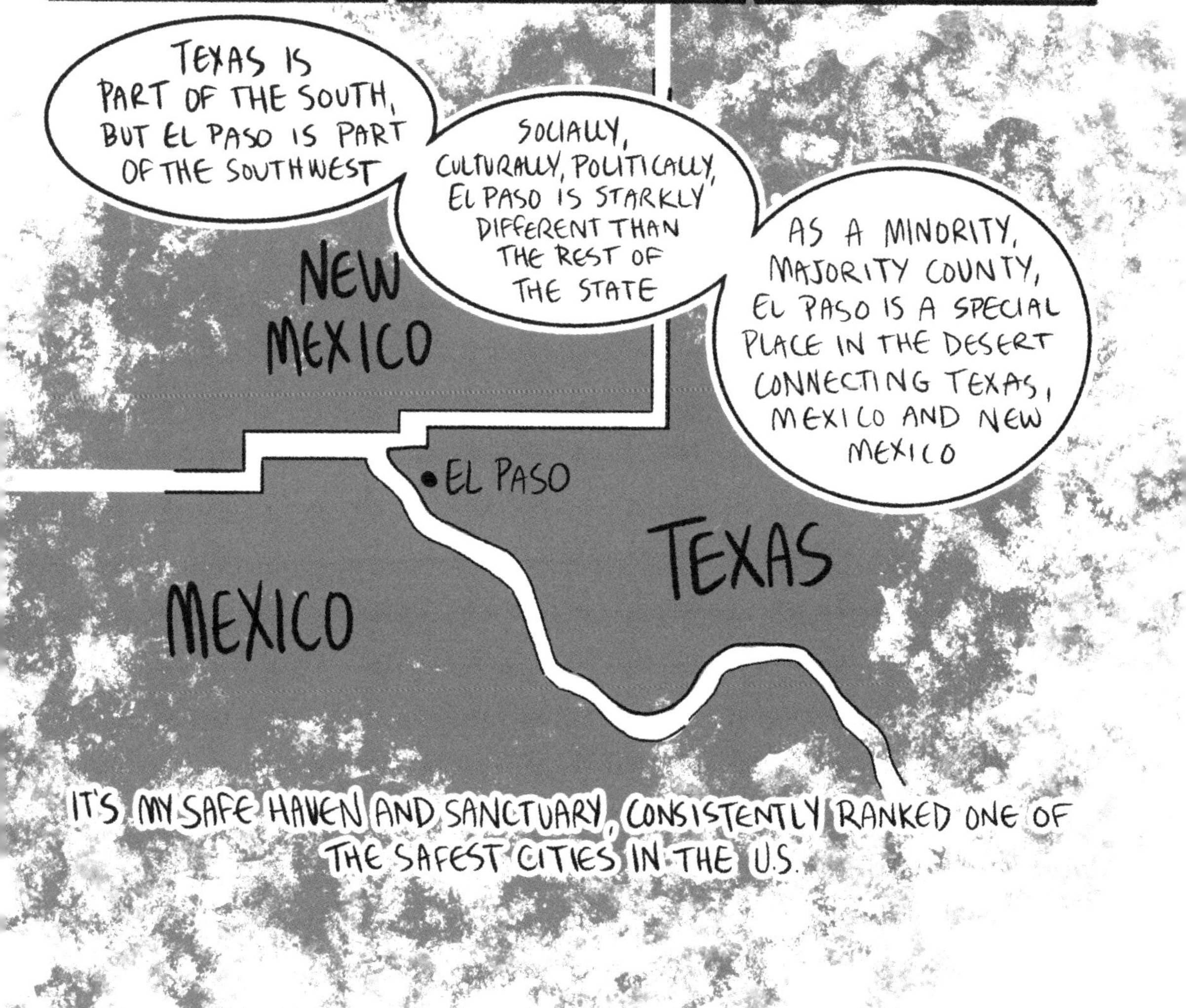
TEXAS IS PART OF THE SOUTH, BUT EL PASO IS PART OF THE SOUTHWEST
SOCIALLY, CULTURALLY, POLITICALLY, EL PASO IS STARKLY DIFFERENT THAN THE REST OF THE STATE
AS A MINORITY, MAJORITY COUNTY, EL PASO IS A SPECIAL PLACE IN THE DESERT CONNECTING TEXAS, MEXICO AND NEW MEXICO
NEW MEXICO
EL PASO
TEXAS
MEXICO
IT'S MY SAFE HAVEN AND SANCTUARY, CONSISTENTLY RANKED ONE OF THE SAFEST CITIES IN THE U.S.

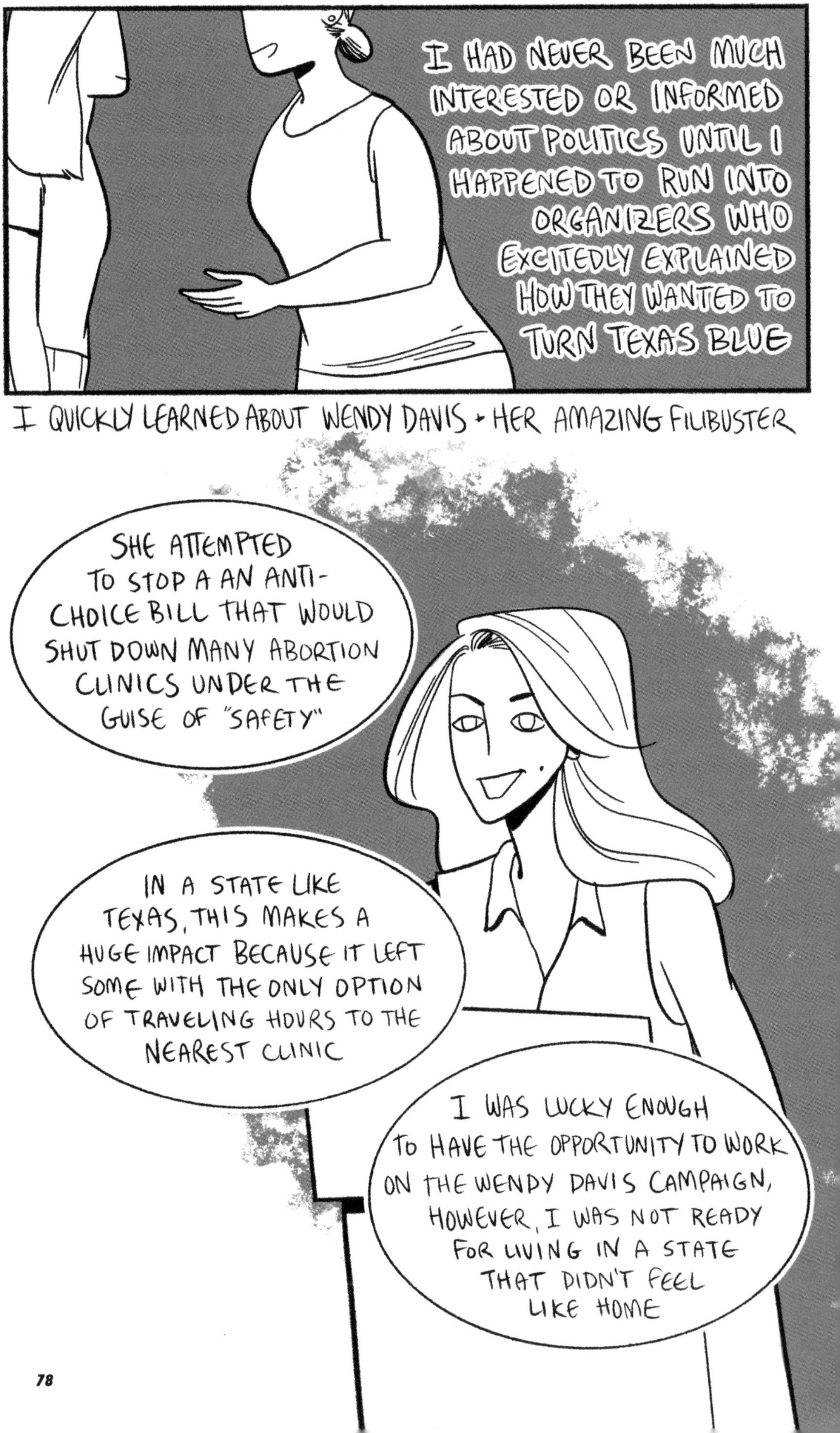
I HAD NEVER BEEN MUCH INTERESTED OR INFORMED ABOUT POLITICS UNTIL I HAPPENED TO RUN INTO ORGANIZERS WHO EXCITEDLY EXPLAINED HOW THEY WANTED TO TURN TEXAS BLUE
I QUICKLY LEARNED ABOUT WENDY DAVIS + HER AMAZING FILIBUSTER
SHE ATTEMPTED TO STOP A AN ANTI-CHOICE BILL THAT WOULD SHUT DOWN MANY ABORTION CLINICS UNDER THE GUISE OF "SAFETY"
IN A STATE LIKE TEXAS, THIS MAKES A HUGE IMPACT BECAUSE IT LEFT SOME WITH THE ONLY OPTION OF TRAVELING HOURS TO THE NEAREST CLINIC
I WAS LUCKY ENOUGH TO HAVE THE OPPORTUNITY TO WORK ON THE WENDY DAVIS CAMPAIGN, HOWEVER, I WAS NOT READY FOR LIVING IN A STATE THAT DIDN'T FEEL LIKE HOME

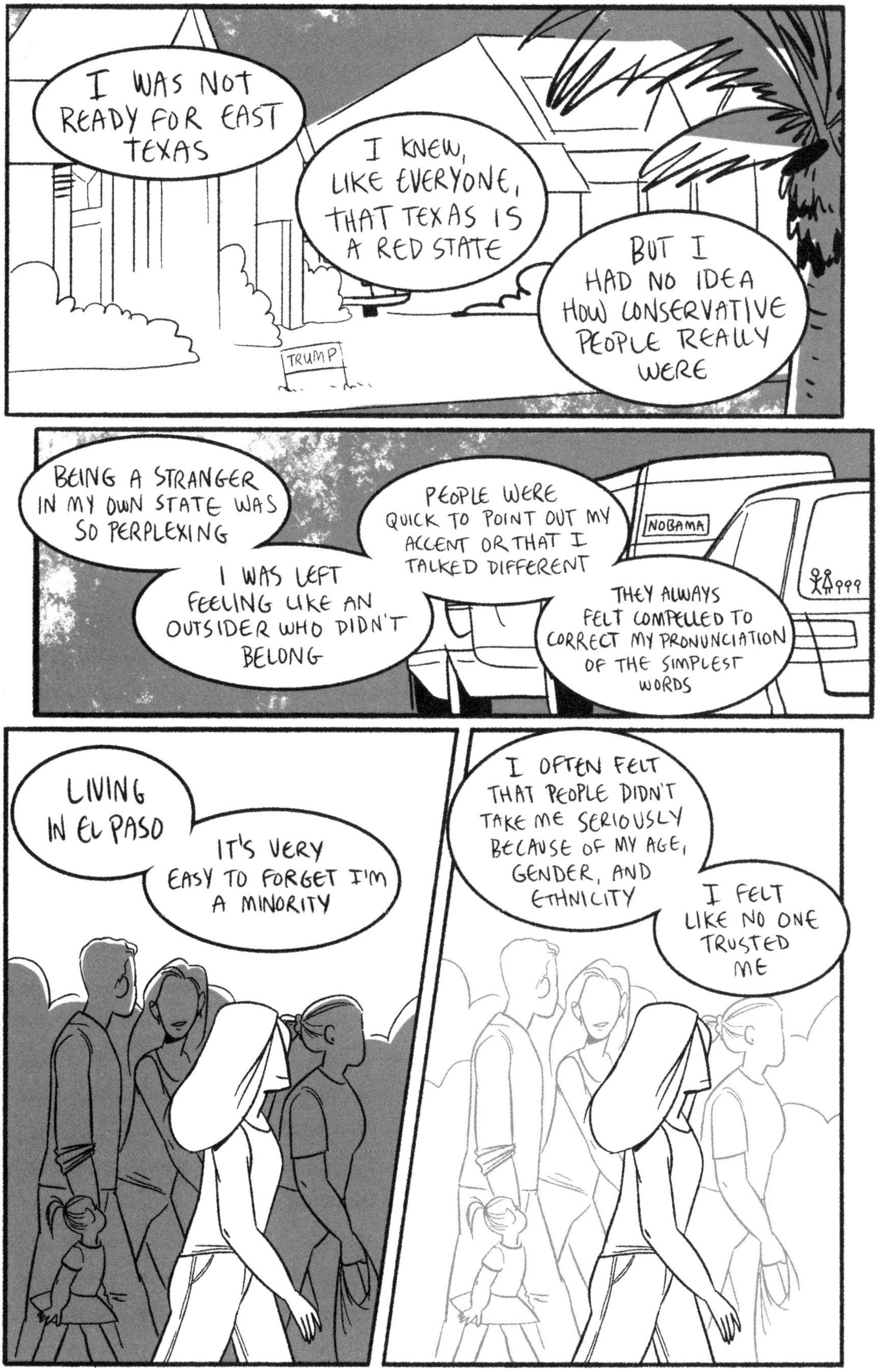
I WAS NOT READY FOR EAST TEXAS
I KNEW, LIKE EVERYONE, THAT TEXAS IS A RED STATE
BUT I HAD NO IDEA HOW CONSERVATIVE PEOPLE REALLY WERE
TRUMP
BEING A STRANGER IN MY OWN STATE WAS SO PERPLEXING
I WAS LEFT FEELING LIKE AN OUTSIDER WHO DIDN'T BELONG
PEOPLE WERE QUICK TO POINT OUT MY ACCENT OR THAT I TALKED DIFFERENT
NOBAMA
THEY ALWAYS FELT COMPELLED TO CORRECT MY PRONUNCIATION OF THE SIMPLEST WORDS
LIVING IN EL PASO
IT'S VERY EASY TO FORGET I'M A MINORITY
I OFTEN FELT THAT PEOPLE DIDN'T TAKE ME SERIOUSLY BECAUSE OF MY AGE, GENDER, AND ETHNICITY
I FELT LIKE NO ONE TRUSTED ME

ON TOP OF EVERYTHING, I FELT SAD

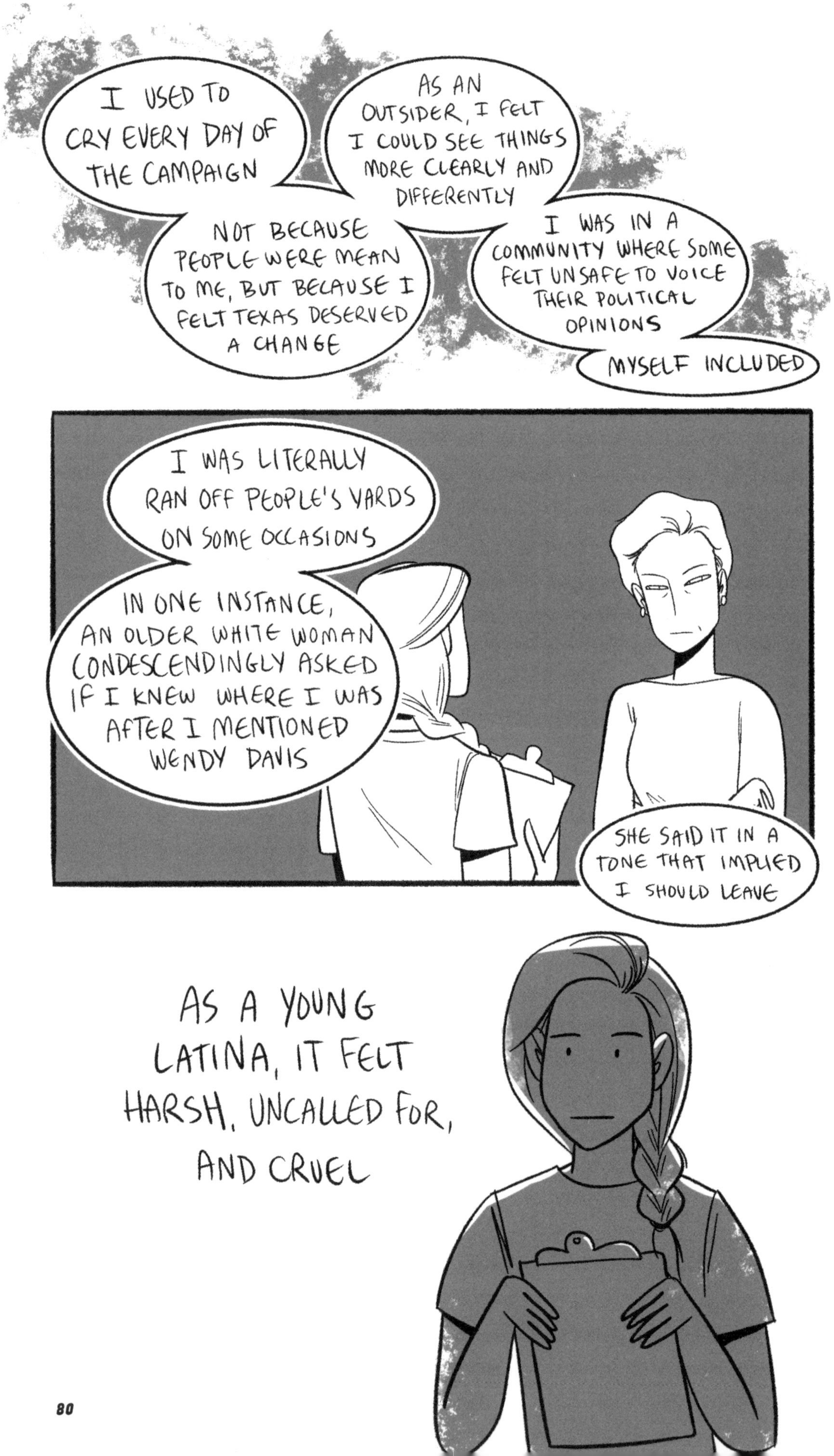
I USED TO CRY EVERY DAY OF THE CAMPAIGN
NOT BECAUSE PEOPLE WERE MEAN TO ME, BUT BECAUSE I FELT TEXAS DESERVED A CHANGE
AS AN OUTSIDER, I FELT I COULD SEE THINGS MORE CLEARLY AND DIFFERENTLY
I WAS IN A COMMUNITY WHERE SOME FELT UNSAFE TO VOICE THEIR POLITICAL OPINIONS
MYSELF INCLUDED
I WAS LITERALLY RAN OFF PEOPLE'S YARDS ON SOME OCCASIONS
IN ONE INSTANCE, AN OLDER WHITE WOMAN CONDESCENDINGLY ASKED IF I KNEW WHERE I WAS AFTER I MENTIONED WENDY DAVIS
SHE SAID IT IN A TONE THAT IMPLIED I SHOULD LEAVE
AS A YOUNG LATINA, IT FELT HARSH, UNCALLED FOR, AND CRUEL

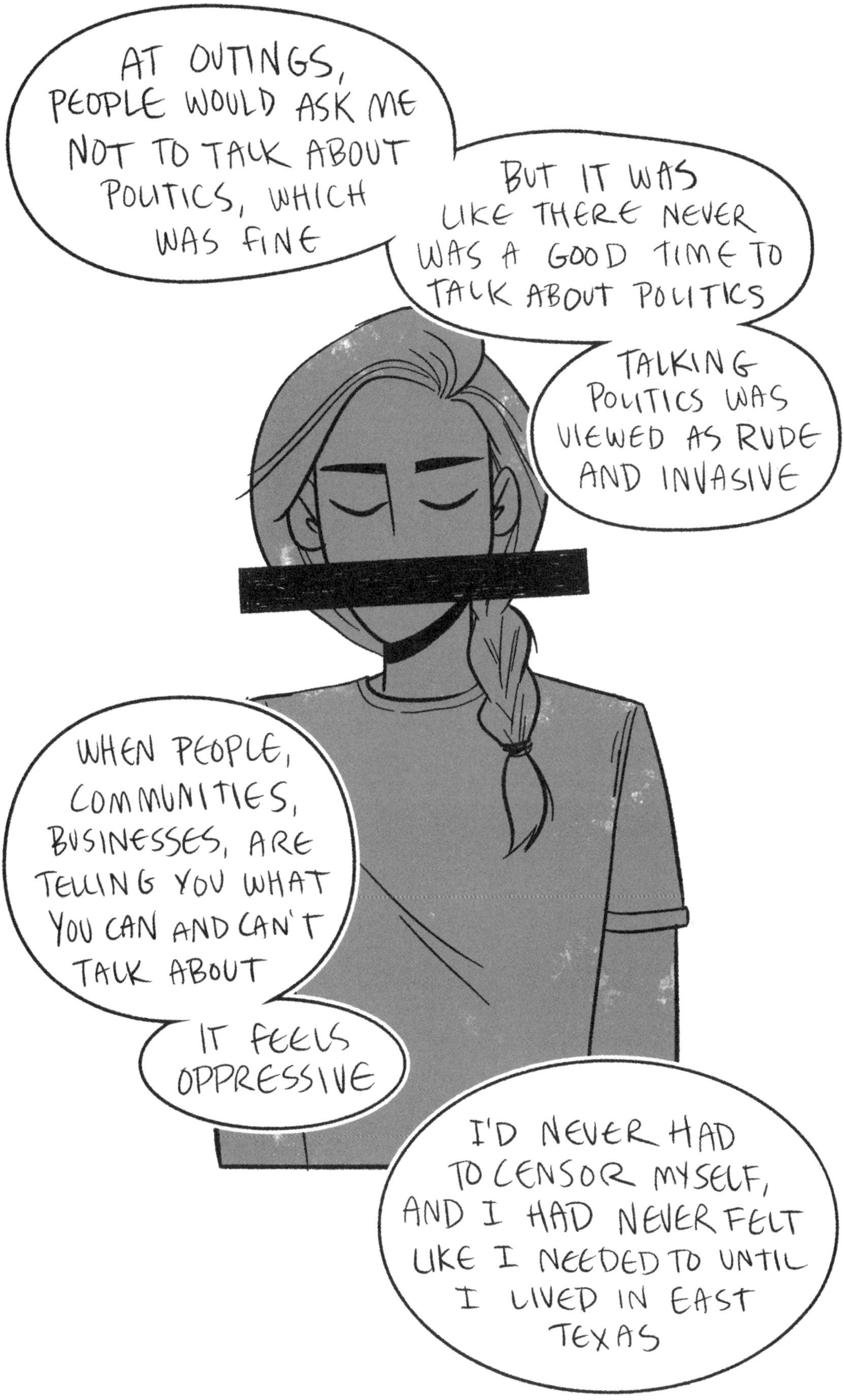
AT OUTINGS, PEOPLE WOULD ASK ME NOT TO TALK ABOUT POLITICS, WHICH WAS FINE
BUT IT WAS LIKE THERE NEVER WAS A GOOD TIME TO TALK ABOUT POLITICS
TALKING POLITICS WAS VIEWED AS RUDE AND INVASIVE
WHEN PEOPLE, COMMUNITIES, BUSINESSES, ARE TELLING YOU WHAT YOU CAN AND CAN'T TALK ABOUT
IT FEELS OPPRESSIVE
I'D NEVER HAD TO CENSOR MYSELF, AND I HAD NEVER FELT LIKE I NEEDED TO UNTIL I LIVED IN EAST TEXAS

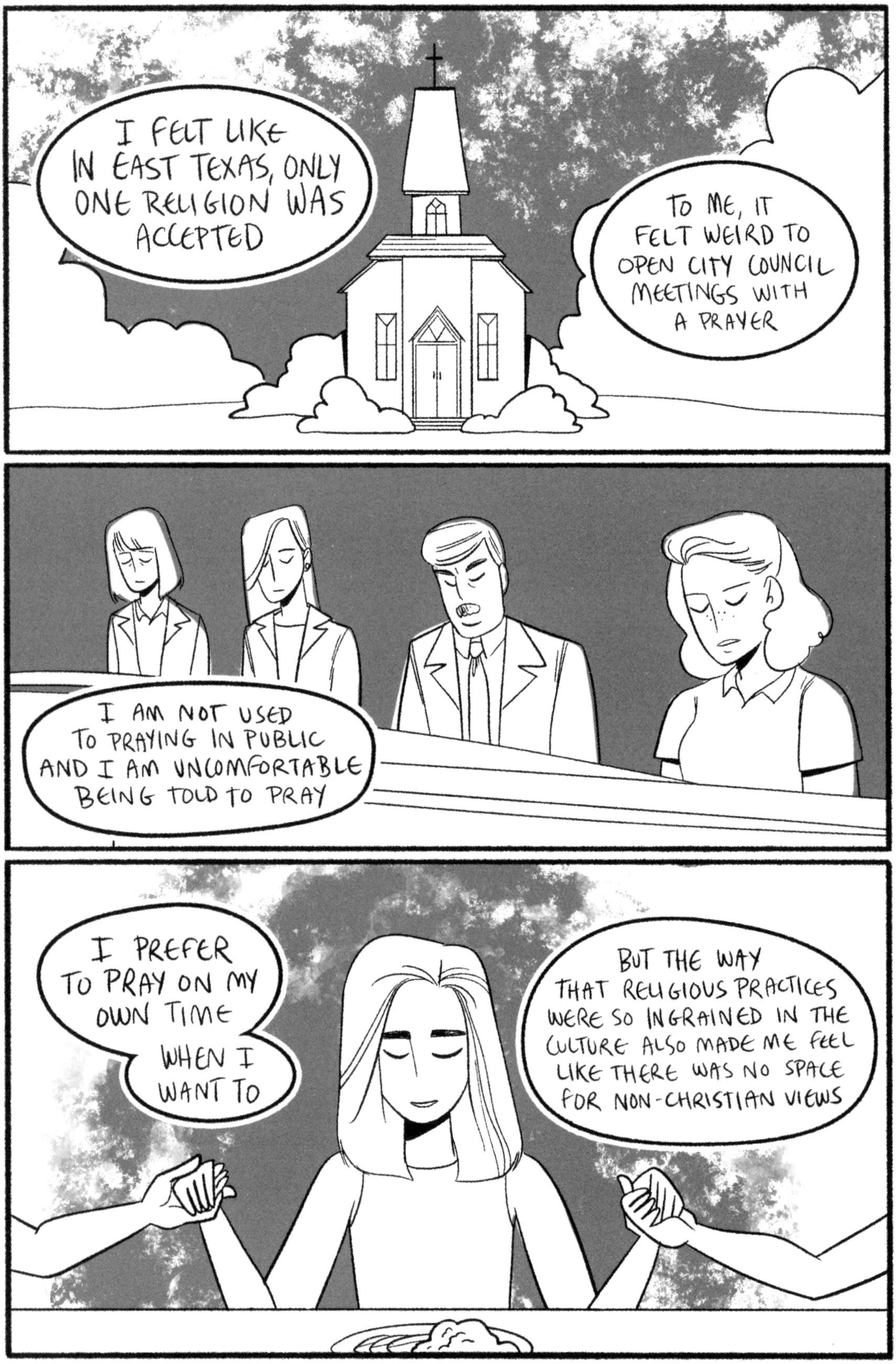
I FELT LIKE IN EAST TEXAS, ONLY ONE RELIGION WAS ACCEPTED
TO ME, IT FELT WEIRD TO OPEN CITY COUNCIL MEETINGS WITH A PRAYER
I AM NOT USED TO PRAYING IN PUBLIC AND I AM UNCOMFORTABLE BEING TOLD TO PRAY
I PREFER TO PRAY ON MY OWN TIME
WHEN I WANT TO
BUT THE WAY THAT RELIGIOUS PRACTICES WERE SO INGRAINED IN THE CULTURE ALSO MADE ME FEEL LIKE THERE WAS NO SPACE FOR NON-CHRISTIAN VIEWS

IT'S A WEIRD THING TO FEEL LIKE EVEN YOUR SPIRITUALITY IS BEING POLICED

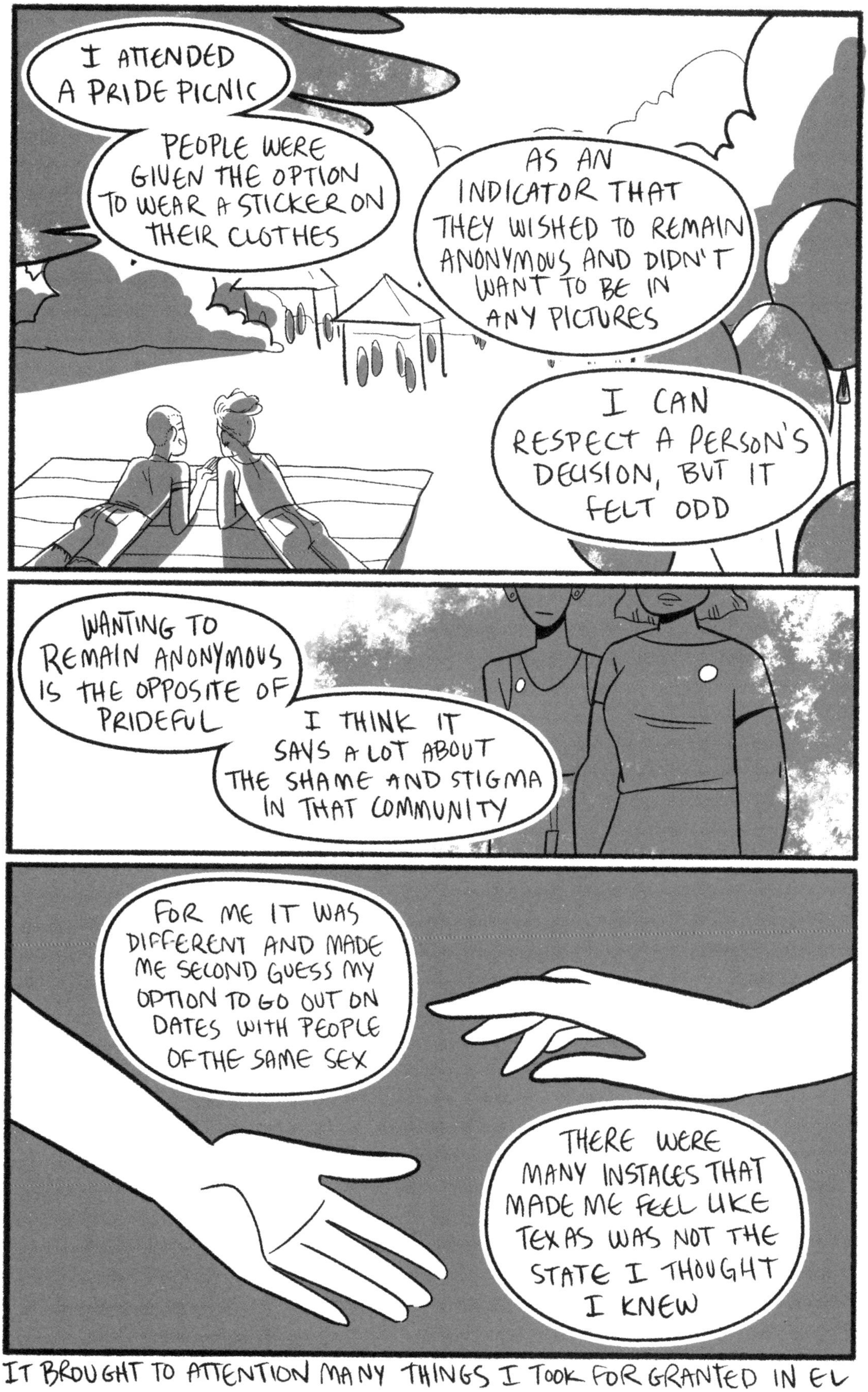
I ATTENDED A PRIDE PICNIC
PEOPLE WERE GIVEN THE OPTION TO WEAR A STICKER ON THEIR CLOTHES
AS AN INDICATOR THAT THEY WISHED TO REMAIN ANONYMOUS AND DIDN'T WANT TO BE IN ANY PICTURES
I CAN RESPECT A PERSON'S DECISION, BUT IT FELT ODD
WANTING TO REMAIN ANONYMOUS IS THE OPPOSITE OF PRIDEFUL
I THINK IT SAYS A LOT ABOUT THE SHAME AND STIGMA IN THAT COMMUNITY
FOR ME IT WAS DIFFERENT AND MADE ME SECOND GUESS MY OPTION TO GO OUT ON DATES WITH PEOPLE OF THE SAME SEX
THERE WERE MANY INSTACES THAT MADE ME FEEL LIKE TEXAS WAS NOT THE STATE I THOUGHT I KNEW

IT BROUGHT TO ATTENTION MANY THINGS I TOOK FOR GRANTED IN EL PASO, SUCH AS MY FREEDOM OF SPEECH, RELIGION + OVERALL SAFETY

WHEN IT CAME TO ABORTION, IT WAS ALWAYS A GENDERED CONVERSATION

IN TEXAS, EVEN THE DEMOCRATS ARE MODERATE

I MET A LOT OF SINGLE ISSUE VOTERS (THE SINGLE ISSUE BEING ABORTION)

PEOPLE WHO REFUSED TO HAVE A RATIONAL CONVERSATION

PRAY TO END ABORTION

STOP ABORTION

BODIES ARE ...ERED

Defund

FOR SOME, IT'S ABOUT WOMEN WHO NEED TO KEEP THEIR LEGS SHUT

OR THE WOMAN'S JOB TO PRACTICE SAFE SEX

IT WAS AS IF MEN WERE COMPLETELY ABSOLVED FROM THE PROCESS

SOME PEOPLE THOUGHT IT WOULD BE HELPFUL TO DECIDE IF THERE WAS A WAY TO FILTER AND JUDGE WHO SHOULD HAVE AN ABORTION ON A CASE-BY-CASE BASIS

AS IF ONLY SOME PEOPLE "DESERVED" ABORTIONS

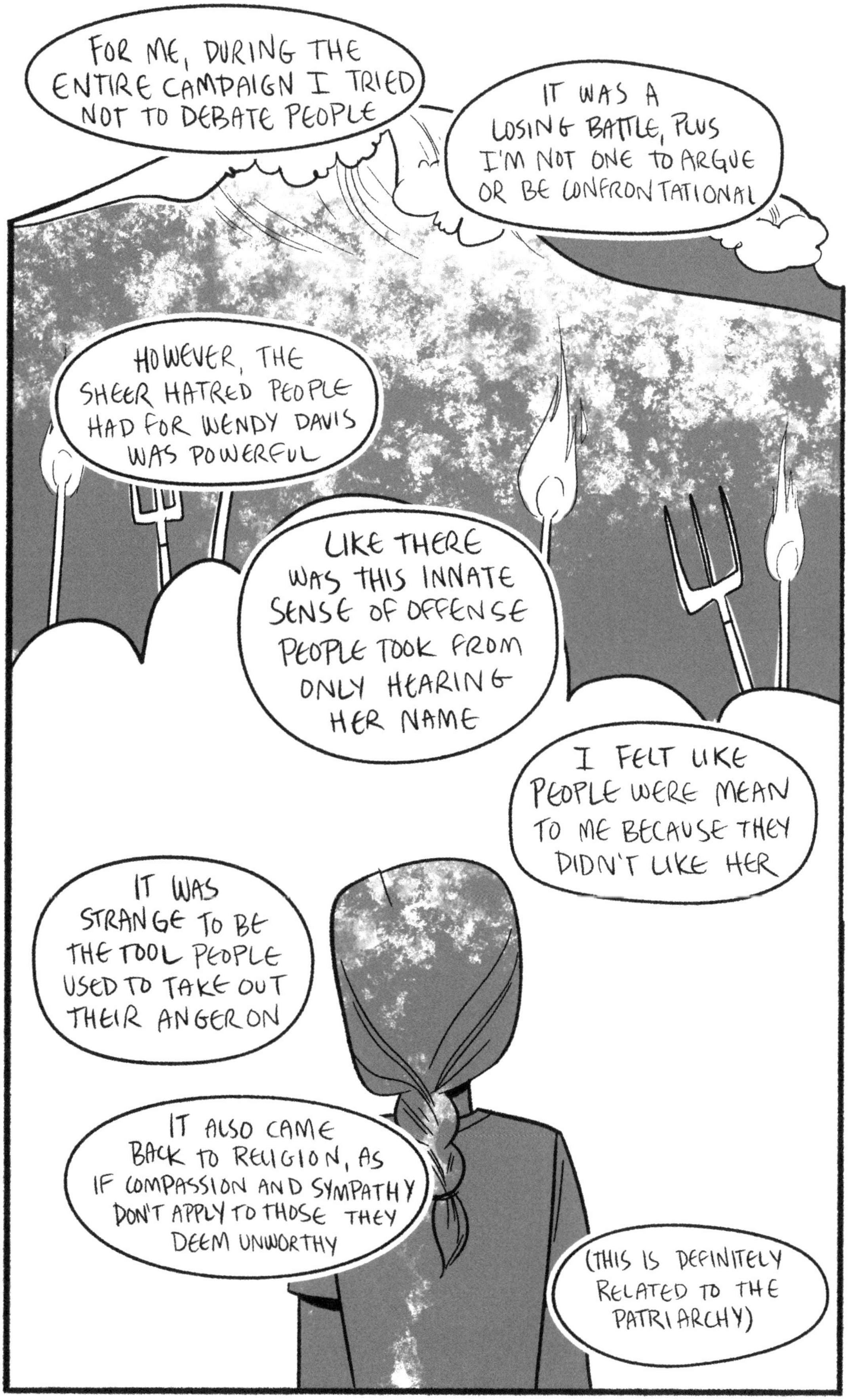
FOR ME, DURING THE ENTIRE CAMPAIGN I TRIED NOT TO DEBATE PEOPLE
IT WAS A LOSING BATTLE, PLUS I'M NOT ONE TO ARGUE OR BE CONFRONTATIONAL
HOWEVER, THE SHEER HATRED PEOPLE HAD FOR WENDY DAVIS WAS POWERFUL
LIKE THERE WAS THIS INNATE SENSE OF OFFENSE PEOPLE TOOK FROM ONLY HEARING HER NAME
I FELT LIKE PEOPLE WERE MEAN TO ME BECAUSE THEY DIDN'T LIKE HER
IT WAS STRANGE TO BE THE TOOL PEOPLE USED TO TAKE OUT THEIR ANGER ON
IT ALSO CAME BACK TO RELIGION, AS IF COMPASSION AND SYMPATHY DON'T APPLY TO THOSE THEY DEEM UNWORTHY
(THIS IS DEFINITELY RELATED TO THE PATRIARCHY)

WHEN WENDY LOST, I FELT HEARTBROKEN AND MAD AT MYSELF FOR BEING SO NAÏVE

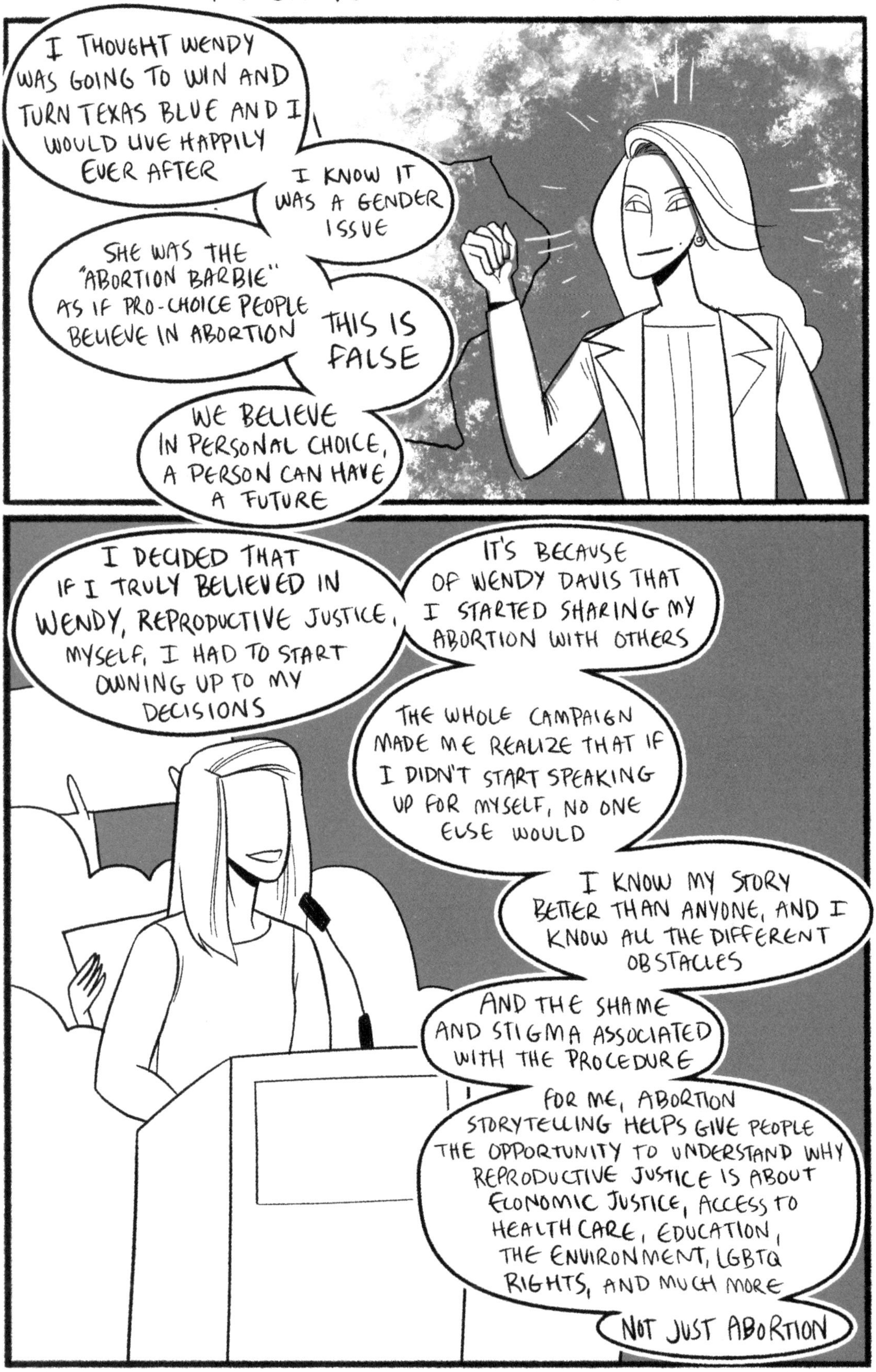

I THOUGHT WENDY WAS GOING TO WIN AND TURN TEXAS BLUE AND I WOULD LIVE HAPPILY EVER AFTER
I KNOW IT WAS A GENDER ISSUE
SHE WAS THE "ABORTION BARBIE" AS IF PRO-CHOICE PEOPLE BELIEVE IN ABORTION
THIS IS FALSE
WE BELIEVE IN PERSONAL CHOICE, A PERSON CAN HAVE A FUTURE
I DECIDED THAT IF I TRULY BELIEVED IN WENDY, REPRODUCTIVE JUSTICE, MYSELF, I HAD TO START OWNING UP TO MY DECISIONS
IT'S BECAUSE OF WENDY DAVIS THAT I STARTED SHARING MY ABORTION WITH OTHERS
THE WHOLE CAMPAIGN MADE ME REALIZE THAT IF I DIDN'T START SPEAKING UP FOR MYSELF, NO ONE ELSE WOULD
I KNOW MY STORY BETTER THAN ANYONE, AND I KNOW ALL THE DIFFERENT OBSTACLES
AND THE SHAME AND STIGMA ASSOCIATED WITH THE PROCEDURE
FOR ME, ABORTION STORYTELLING HELPS GIVE PEOPLE THE OPPORTUNITY TO UNDERSTAND WHY REPRODUCTIVE JUSTICE IS ABOUT ECONOMIC JUSTICE, ACCESS TO HEALTH CARE, EDUCATION, THE ENVIRONMENT, LGBTQ RIGHTS, AND MUCH MORE
NOT JUST ABORTION

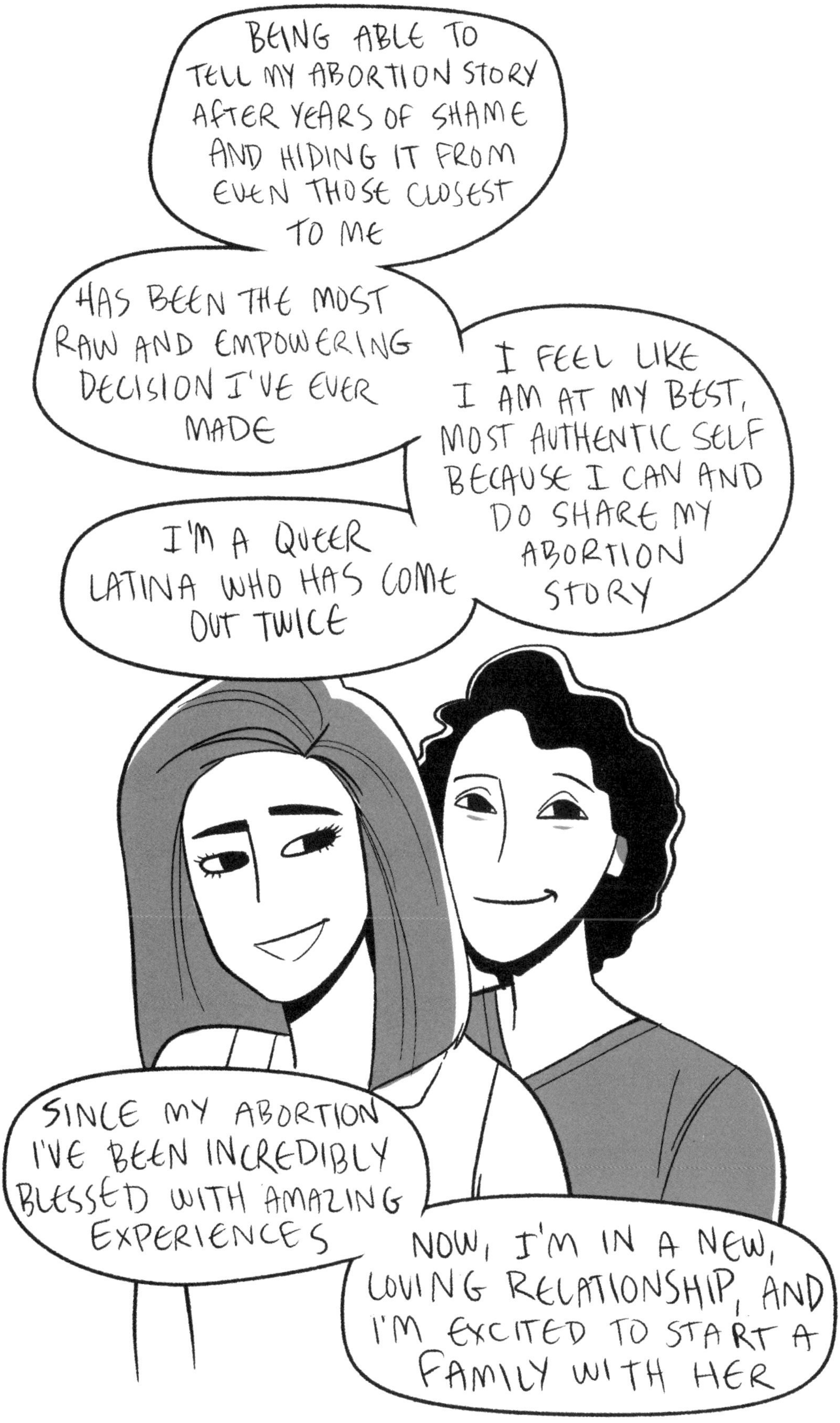
BEING ABLE TO TELL MY ABORTION STORY AFTER YEARS OF SHAME AND HIDING IT FROM EVEN THOSE CLOSEST TO ME
HAS BEEN THE MOST RAW AND EMPOWERING DECISION I'VE EVER MADE
I'M A QUEER LATINA WHO HAS COME OUT TWICE
I FEEL LIKE I AM AT MY BEST, MOST AUTHENTIC SELF BECAUSE I CAN AND DO SHARE MY ABORTION STORY
SINCE MY ABORTION I'VE BEEN INCREDIBLY BLESSED WITH AMAZING EXPERIENCES
NOW, I'M IN A NEW, LOVING RELATIONSHIP, AND I'M EXCITED TO START A FAMILY WITH HER

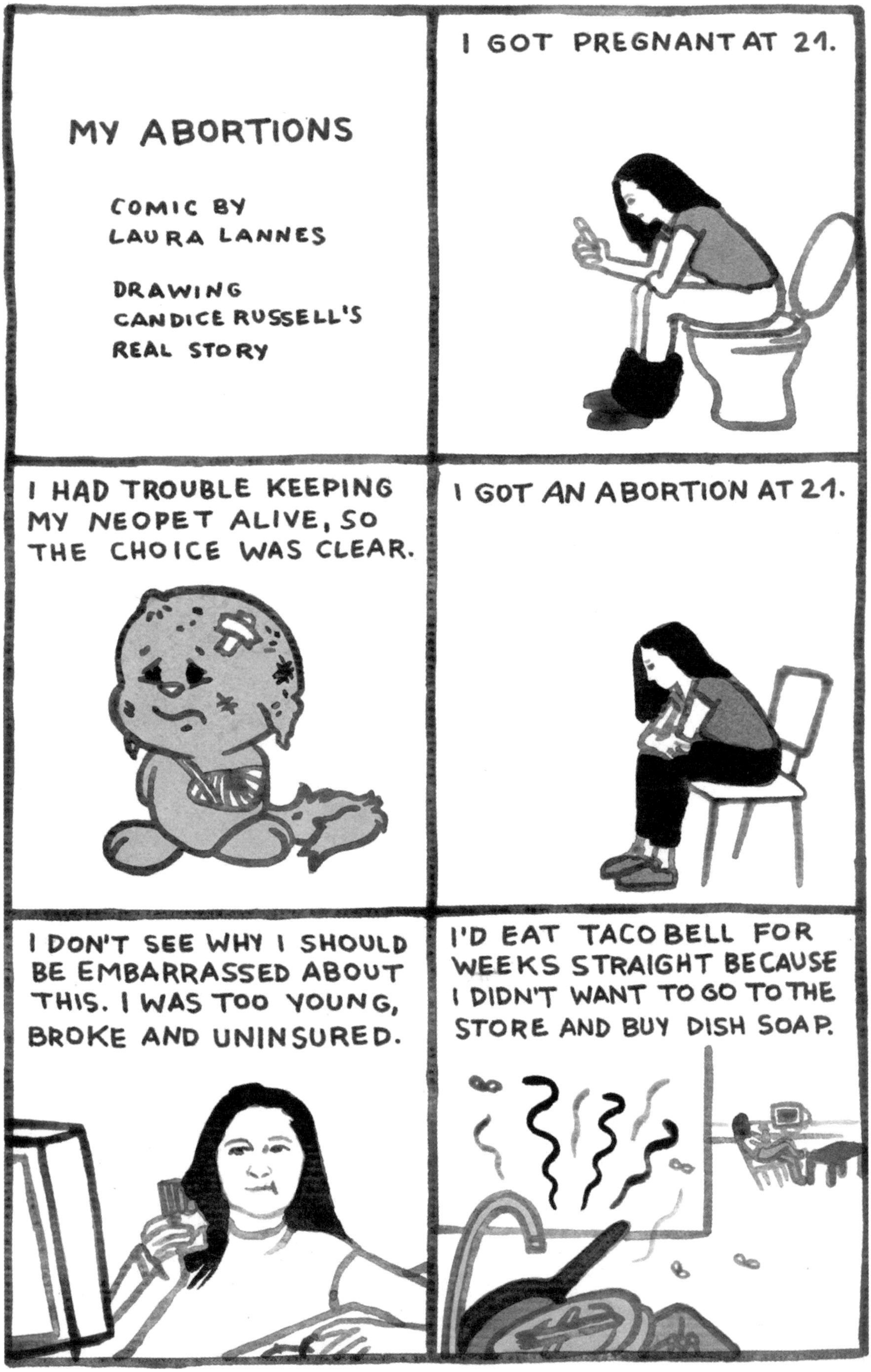
MY ABORTIONS
COMIC BY LAURA LANNES
DRAWING CANDICE RUSSELL'S REAL STORY
I GOT PREGNANT AT 21.
I HAD TROUBLE KEEPING MY NEOPET ALIVE, SO THE CHOICE WAS CLEAR.
I GOT AN ABORTION AT 21.
I DON'T SEE WHY I SHOULD BE EMBARRASSED ABOUT THIS. I WAS TOO YOUNG, BROKE AND UNINSURED.
I'D EAT TACO BELL FOR WEEKS STRAIGHT BECAUSE I DIDN'T WANT TO GO TO THE STORE AND BUY DISH SOAP.

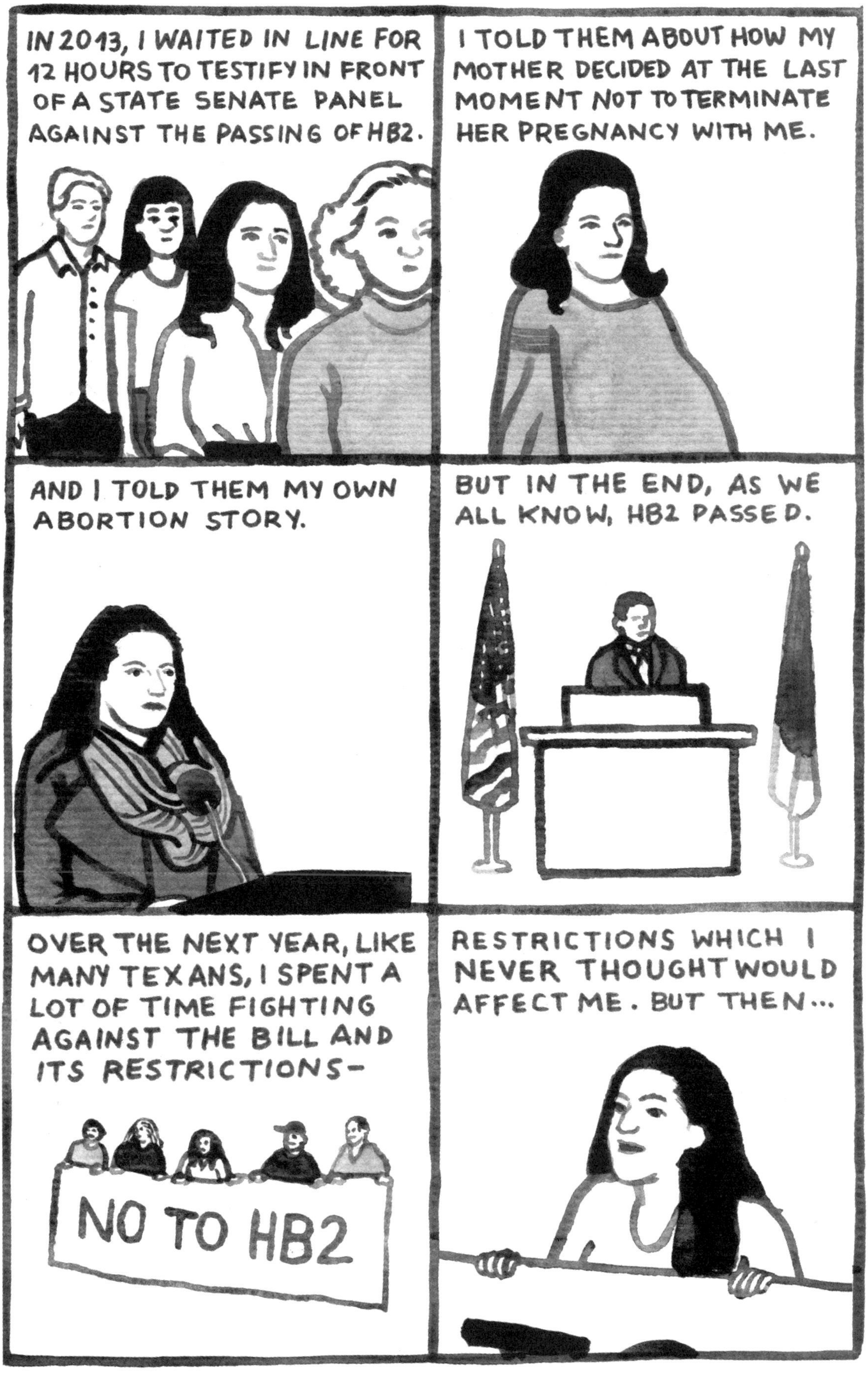
IN 2013, I WAITED IN LINE FOR 12 HOURS TO TESTIFY IN FRONT OF A STATE SENATE PANEL AGAINST THE PASSING OF HB2.
I TOLD THEM ABOUT HOW MY MOTHER DECIDED AT THE LAST MOMENT NOT TO TERMINATE HER PREGNANCY WITH ME.
AND I TOLD THEM MY OWN ABORTION STORY.
BUT IN THE END, AS WE ALL KNOW, HB2 PASSED.
OVER THE NEXT YEAR, LIKE MANY TEXANS, I SPENT A LOT OF TIME FIGHTING AGAINST THE BILL AND ITS RESTRICTIONS—
NO TO HB2
RESTRICTIONS WHICH I NEVER THOUGHT WOULD AFFECT ME. BUT THEN...

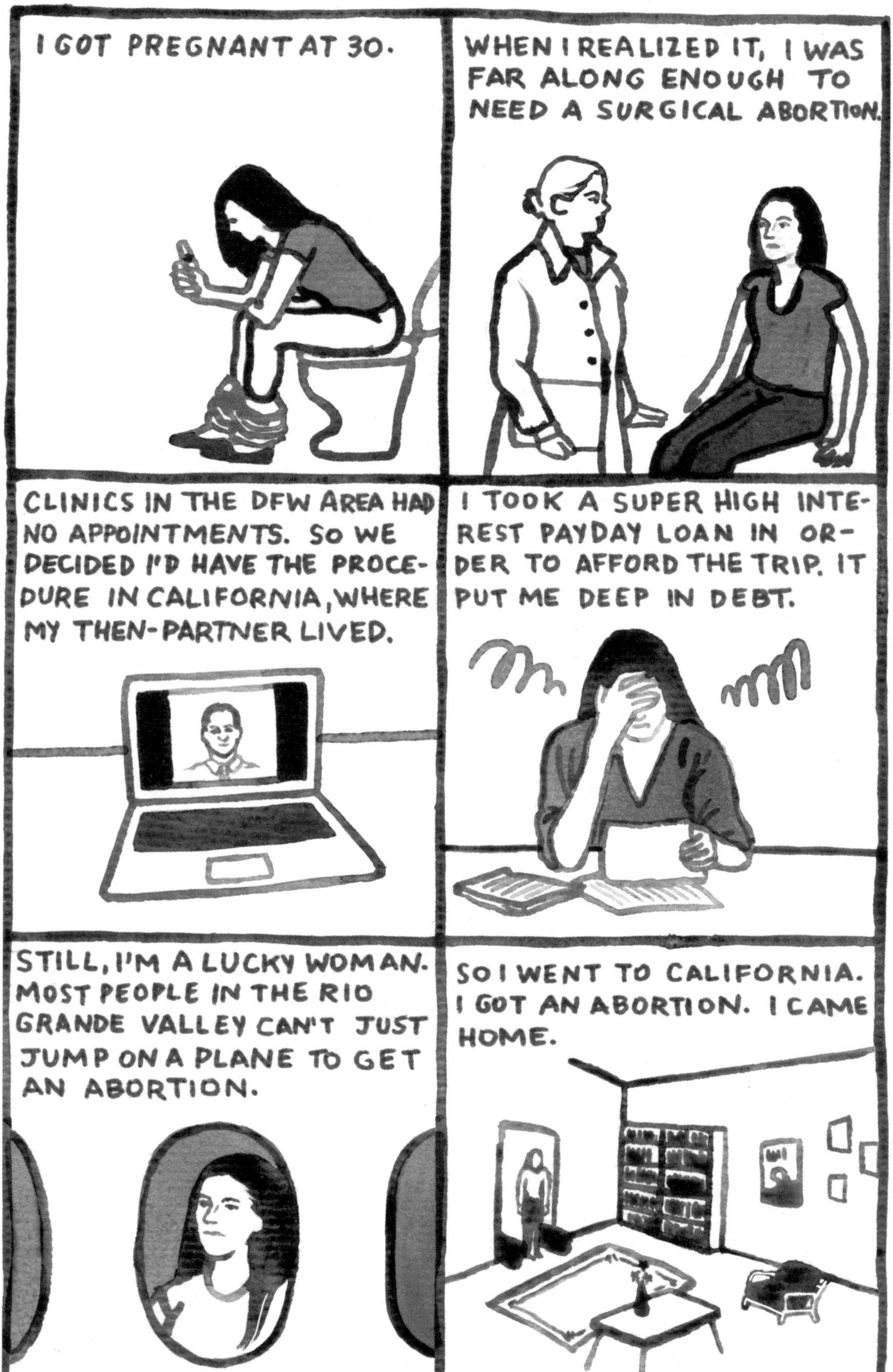
I GOT PREGNANT AT 30.
WHEN I REALIZED IT, I WAS FAR ALONG ENOUGH TO NEED A SURGICAL ABORTION.
CLINICS IN THE DFW AREA HAD NO APPOINTMENTS. SO WE DECIDED I'D HAVE THE PROCEDURE IN CALIFORNIA, WHERE MY THEN-PARTNER LIVED.
I TOOK A SUPER HIGH INTEREST PAYDAY LOAN IN ORDER TO AFFORD THE TRIP. IT PUT ME DEEP IN DEBT.
STILL, I'M A LUCKY WOMAN. MOST PEOPLE IN THE RIO GRANDE VALLEY CAN'T JUST JUMP ON A PLANE TO GET AN ABORTION.
SO I WENT TO CALIFORNIA. I GOT AN ABORTION. I CAME HOME.

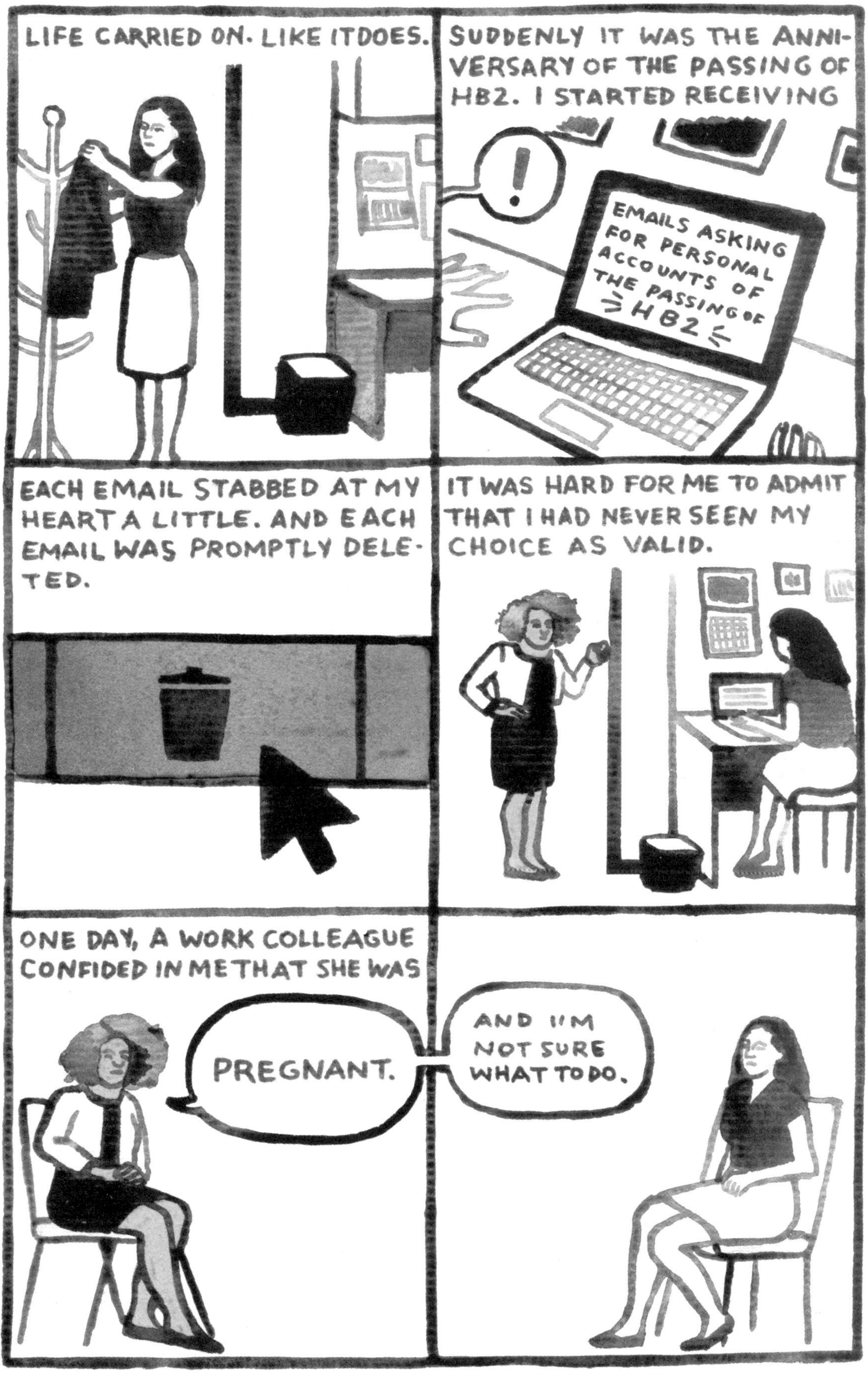
LIFE CARRIED ON. LIKE IT DOES.
SUDDENLY IT WAS THE ANNIVERSARY OF THE PASSING OF HB2. I STARTED RECEIVING
!
EMAILS ASKING FOR PERSONAL ACCOUNTS OF THE PASSING OF HB2
EACH EMAIL STABBED AT MY HEART A LITTLE. AND EACH EMAIL WAS PROMPTLY DELETED.
IT WAS HARD FOR ME TO ADMIT THAT I HAD NEVER SEEN MY CHOICE AS VALID.
ONE DAY, A WORK COLLEAGUE CONFIDED IN ME THAT SHE WAS
PREGNANT.
AND I'M NOT SURE WHAT TO DO.

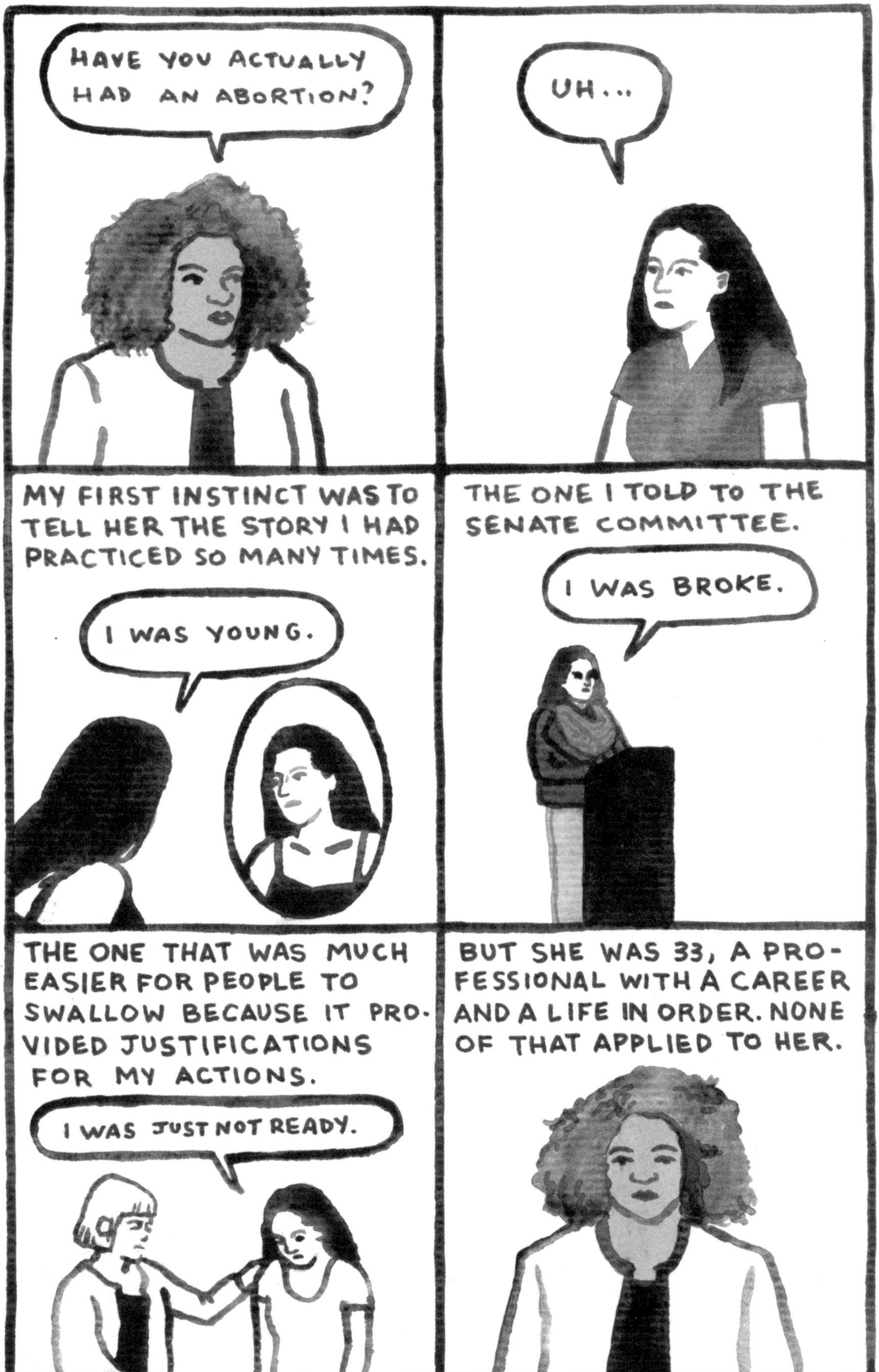
HAVE YOU ACTUALLY HAD AN ABORTION?
UH...
MY FIRST INSTINCT WAS TO TELL HER THE STORY I HAD PRACTICED SO MANY TIMES.
I WAS YOUNG.
THE ONE I TOLD TO THE SENATE COMMITTEE.
I WAS BROKE.
THE ONE THAT WAS MUCH EASIER FOR PEOPLE TO SWALLOW BECAUSE IT PROVIDED JUSTIFICATIONS FOR MY ACTIONS.
I WAS JUST NOT READY.
BUT SHE WAS 33, A PROFESSIONAL WITH A CAREER AND A LIFE IN ORDER. NONE OF THAT APPLIED TO HER.

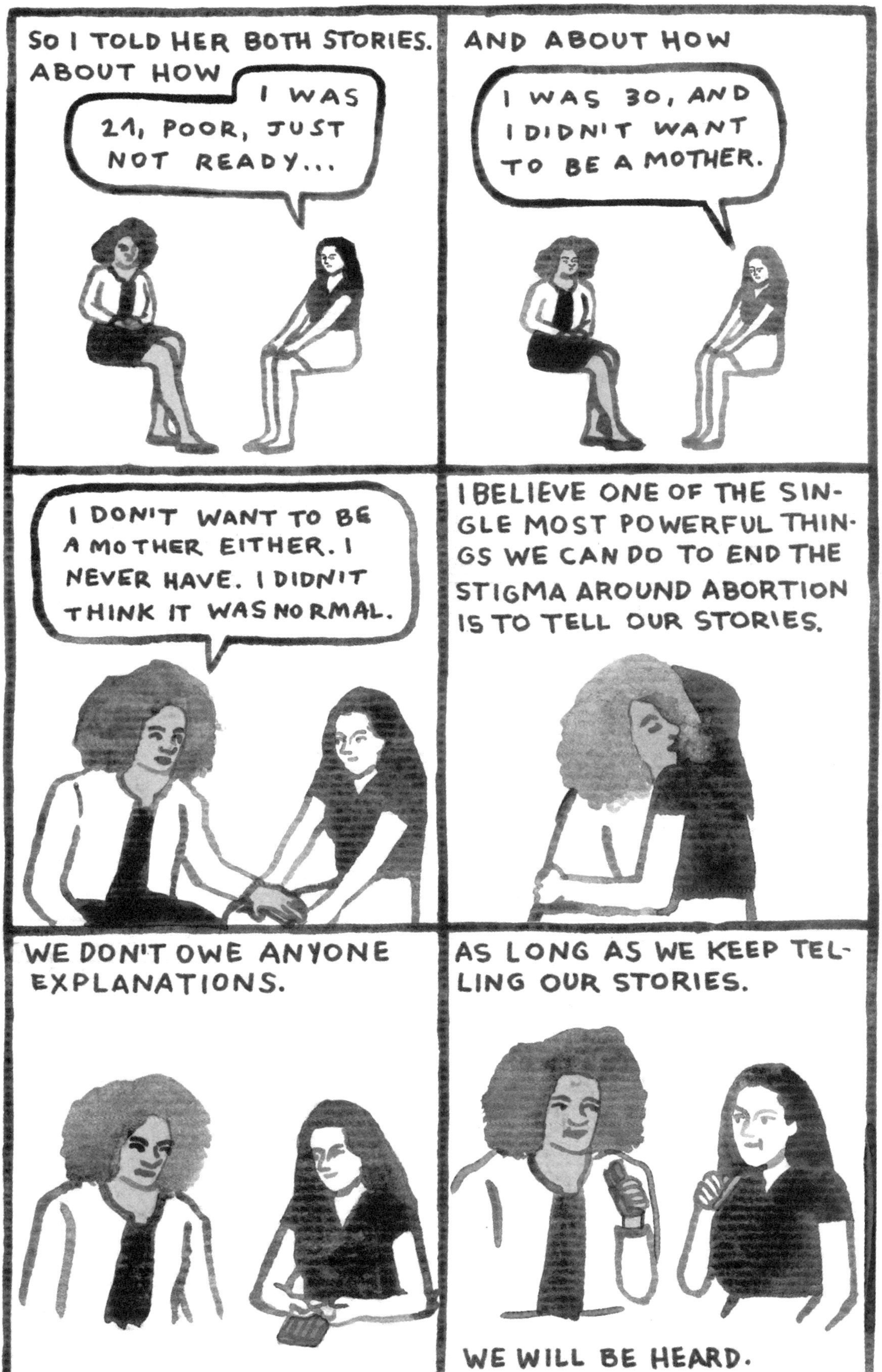
SO I TOLD HER BOTH STORIES. ABOUT HOW
I WAS 21, POOR, JUST NOT READY...
AND ABOUT HOW
I WAS 30, AND I DIDN'T WANT TO BE A MOTHER.
I DON'T WANT TO BE A MOTHER EITHER. I NEVER HAVE. I DIDN'T THINK IT WAS NORMAL.
I BELIEVE ONE OF THE SINGLE MOST POWERFUL THINGS WE CAN DO TO END THE STIGMA AROUND ABORTION IS TO TELL OUR STORIES.
WE DON'T OWE ANYONE EXPLANATIONS.
AS LONG AS WE KEEP TELLING OUR STORIES.
WE WILL BE HEARD.

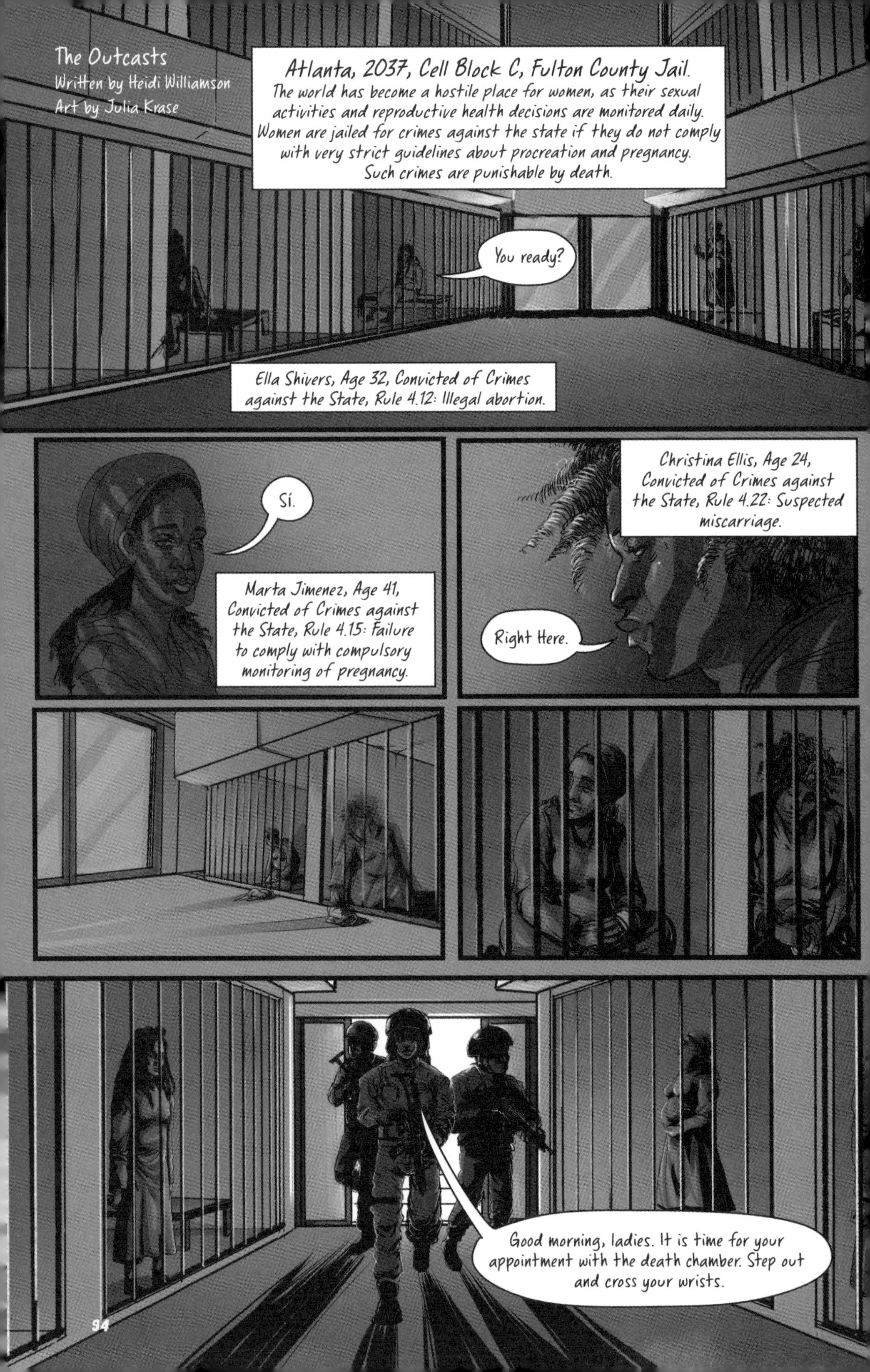
The Outcasts
Written by Heidi Williamson
Art by Julia Krase
Atlanta, 2037, Cell Block C, Fulton County Jail.
The world has become a hostile place for women, as their sexual activities and reproductive health decisions are monitored daily. Women are jailed for crimes against the state if they do not comply with very strict guidelines about procreation and pregnancy. Such crimes are punishable by death.
You ready?
Ella Shivers, Age 32, Convicted of Crimes against the State, Rule 4.12: Illegal abortion.
Sí.
Marta Jimenez, Age 41, Convicted of Crimes against the State, Rule 4.15: Failure to comply with compulsory monitoring of pregnancy.
Christina Ellis, Age 24, Convicted of Crimes against the State, Rule 4.22: Suspected miscarriage.
Right Here.
Good morning, ladies. It is time for your appointment with the death chamber. Step out and cross your wrists.

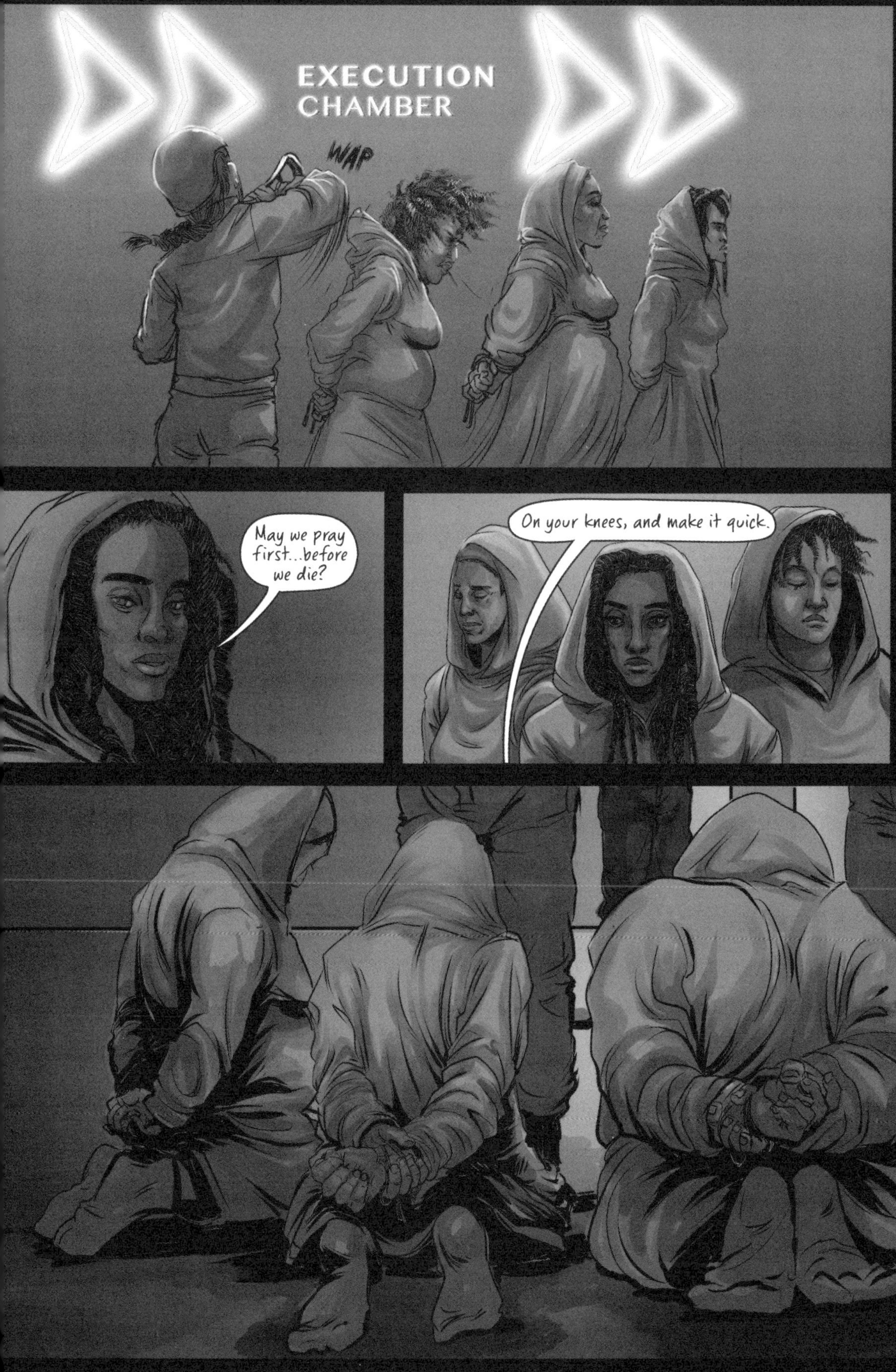
EXECUTION
CHAMBER
WAP
May we pray first...before we die?
On your knees, and make it quick.

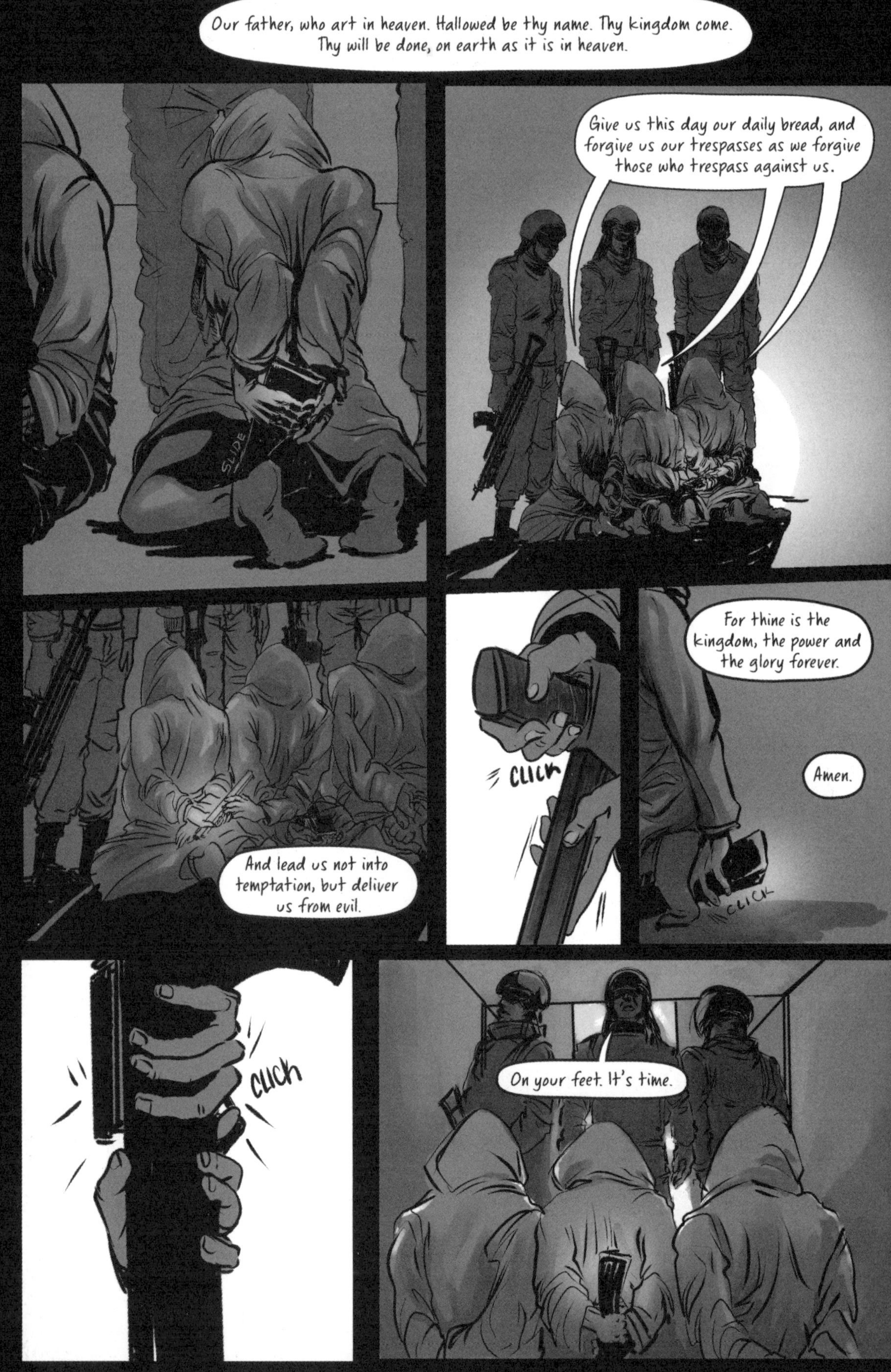
Our father, who art in heaven. Hallowed be thy name. Thy kingdom come. Thy will be done, on earth as it is in heaven.
SLIDE
Give us this day our daily bread, and forgive us our trespasses as we forgive those who trespass against us.
And lead us not into temptation, but deliver us from evil.
CLICK
For thine is the kingdom, the power and the glory forever.
Amen.
CLICK
CLICK
On your feet. It's time.

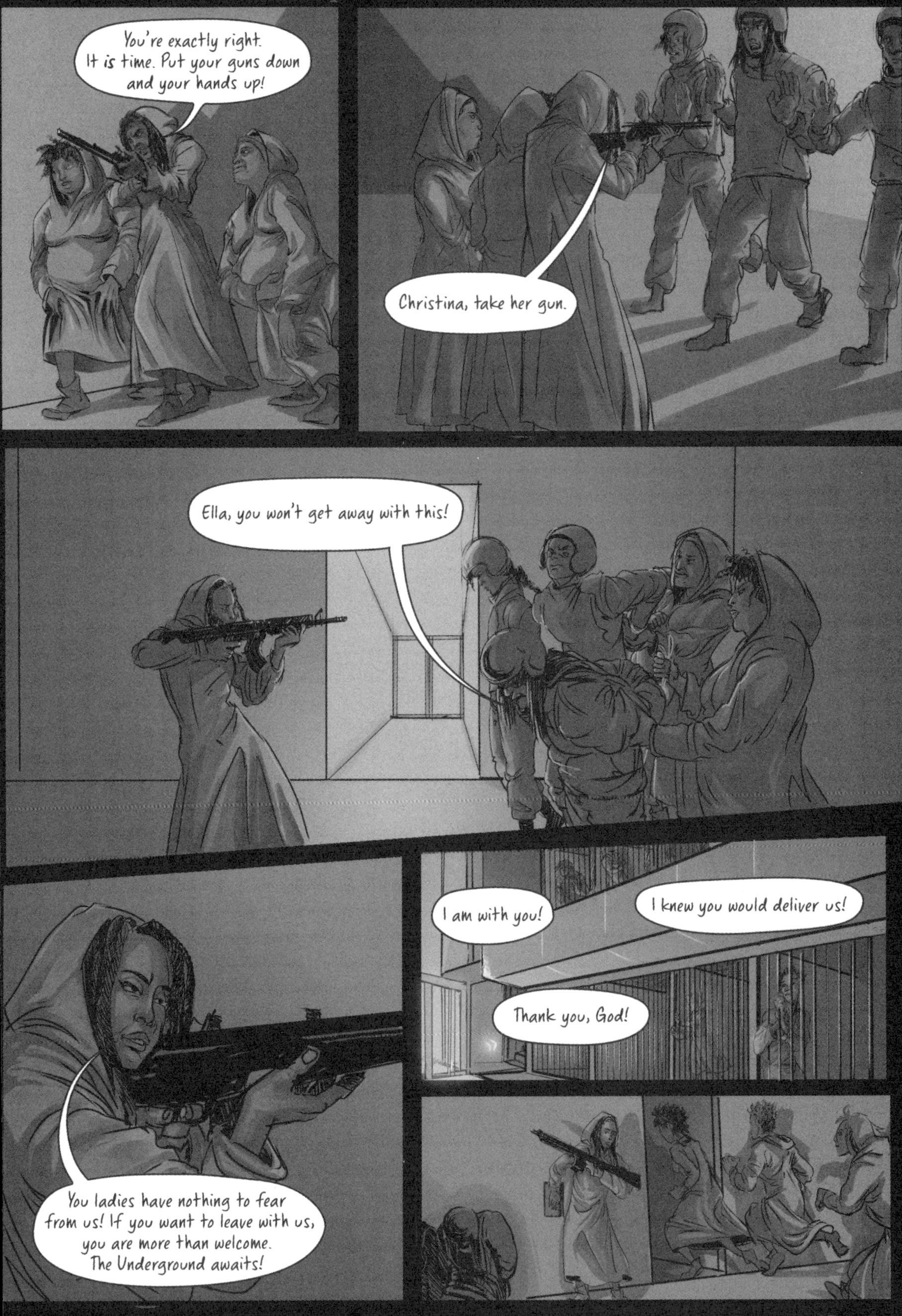
You're exactly right. It is time. Put your guns down and your hands up!
Christina, take her gun.
Ella, you won't get away with this!
You ladies have nothing to fear from us! If you want to leave with us, you are more than welcome. The Underground awaits!
I am with you!
I knew you would deliver us!
Thank you, God!

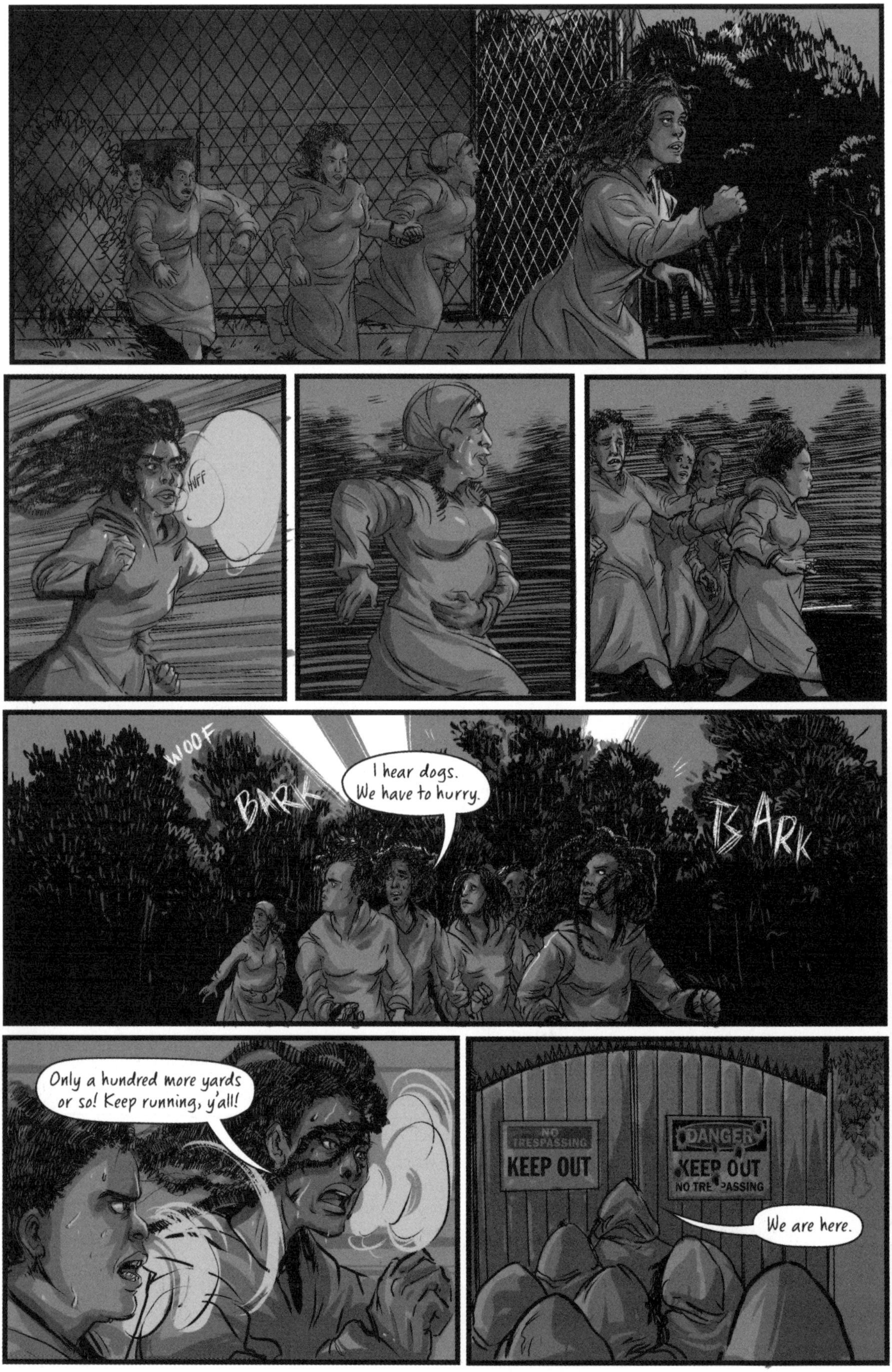
HUFF
WOOF
BARK
I hear dogs. We have to hurry.
BARK
Only a hundred more yards or so! Keep running, y'all!
NO TRESPASSING
KEEP OUT
DANGER
KEEP OUT
NO TRESPASSING
We are here.

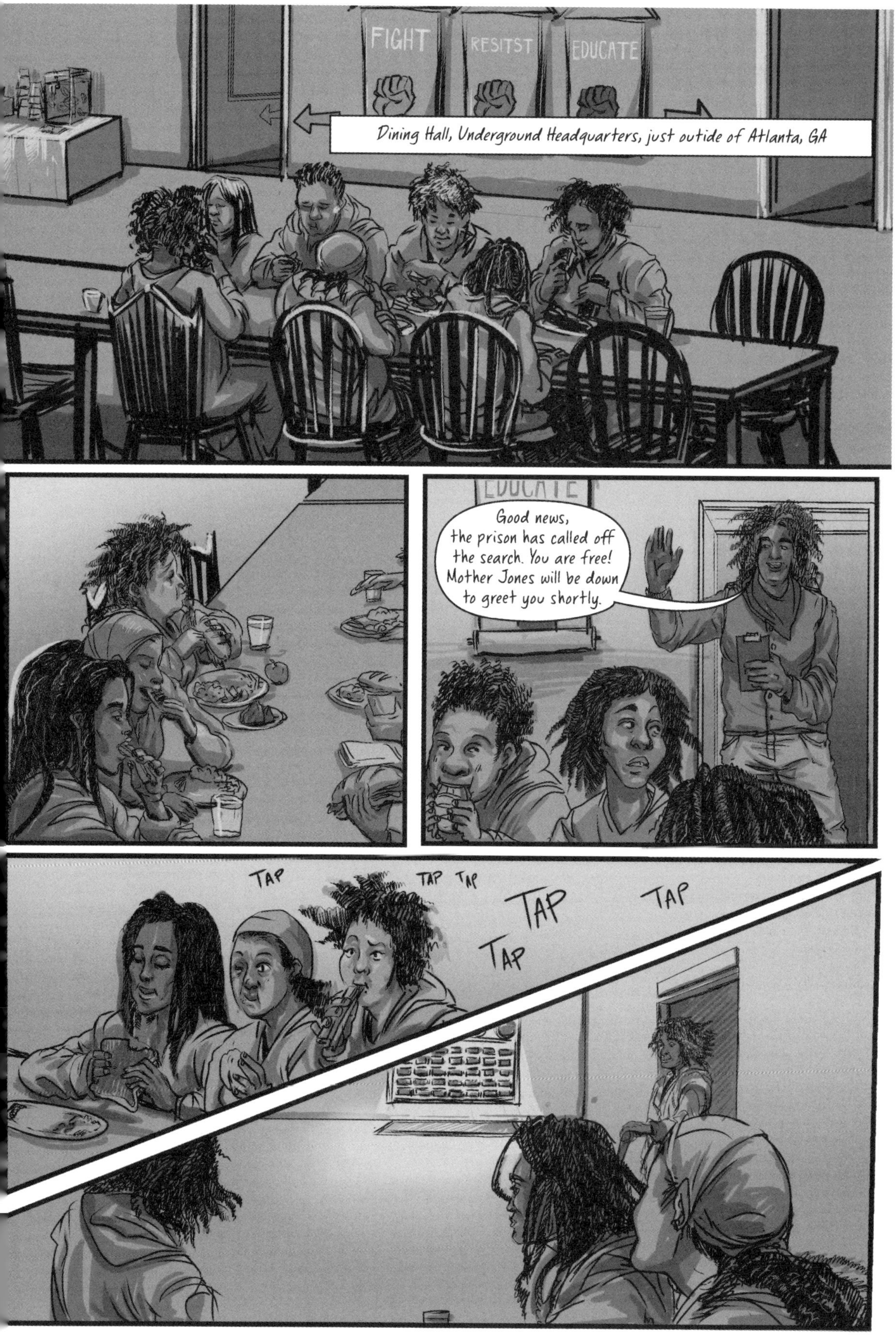
FIGHT
RESITST
EDUCATE
Dining Hall, Underground Headquarters, just outide of Atlanta, GA
Good news, the prison has called off the search. You are free! Mother Jones will be down to greet you shortly.
TAP
TAP TAP
TAP
TAP
TAP

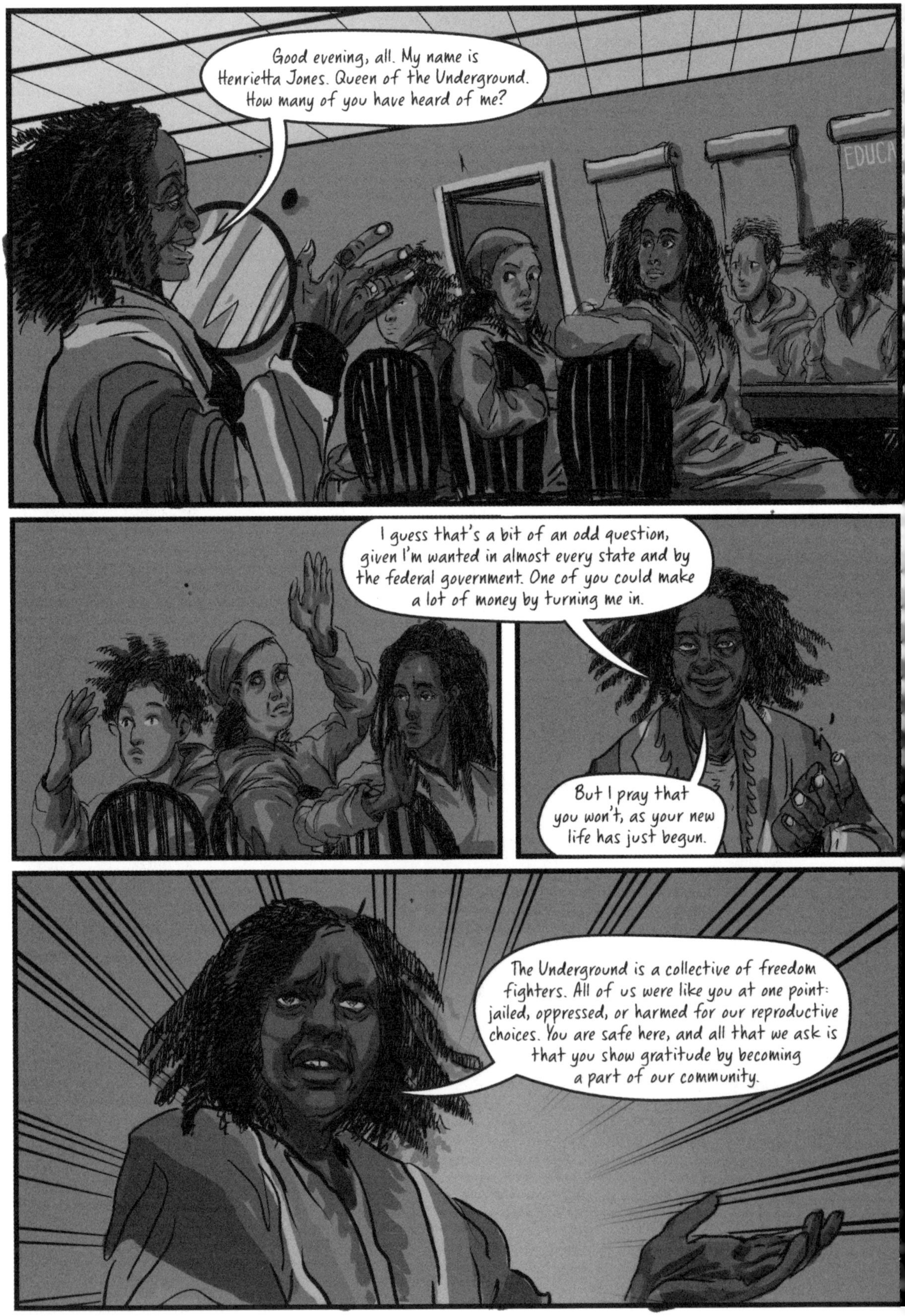
Good evening, all. My name is Henrietta Jones. Queen of the Underground. How many of you have heard of me?
EDUCA
I guess that's a bit of an odd question, given I'm wanted in almost every state and by the federal government. One of you could make a lot of money by turning me in.
But I pray that you won't, as your new life has just begun.
The Underground is a collective of freedom fighters. All of us were like you at one point: jailed, oppressed, or harmed for our reproductive choices. You are safe here, and all that we ask is that you show gratitude by becoming a part of our community.

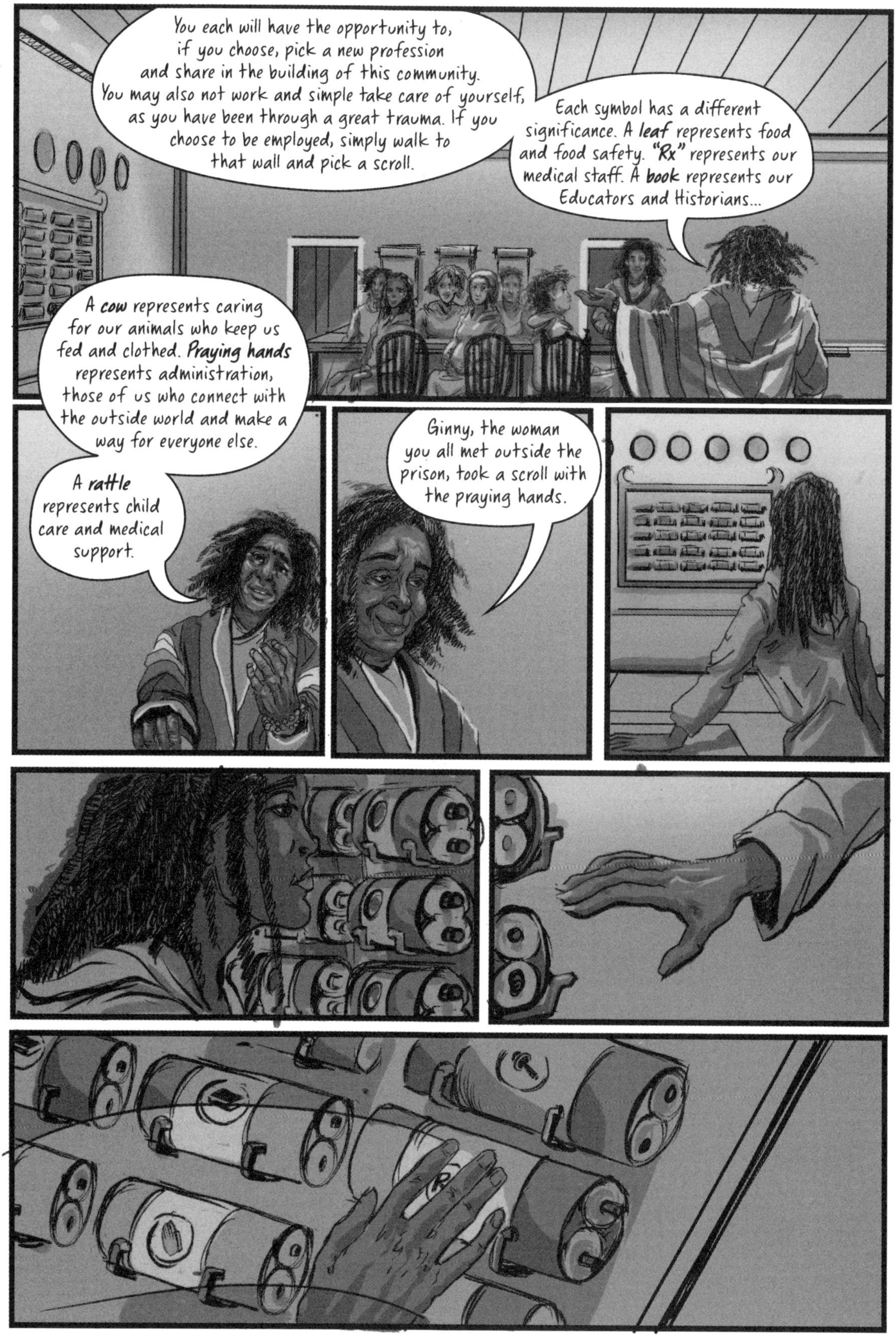
You each will have the opportunity to, if you choose, pick a new profession and share in the building of this community. You may also not work and simple take care of yourself, as you have been through a great trauma. If you choose to be employed, simply walk to that wall and pick a scroll.
Each symbol has a different significance. A **leaf** represents food and food safety. **"Rx"** represents our medical staff. A **book** represents our Educators and Historians...
A **cow** represents caring for our animals who keep us fed and clothed. **Praying hands** represents administration, those of us who connect with the outside world and make a way for everyone else.
A **rattle** represents child care and medical support.
Ginny, the woman you all met outside the prison, took a scroll with the praying hands.

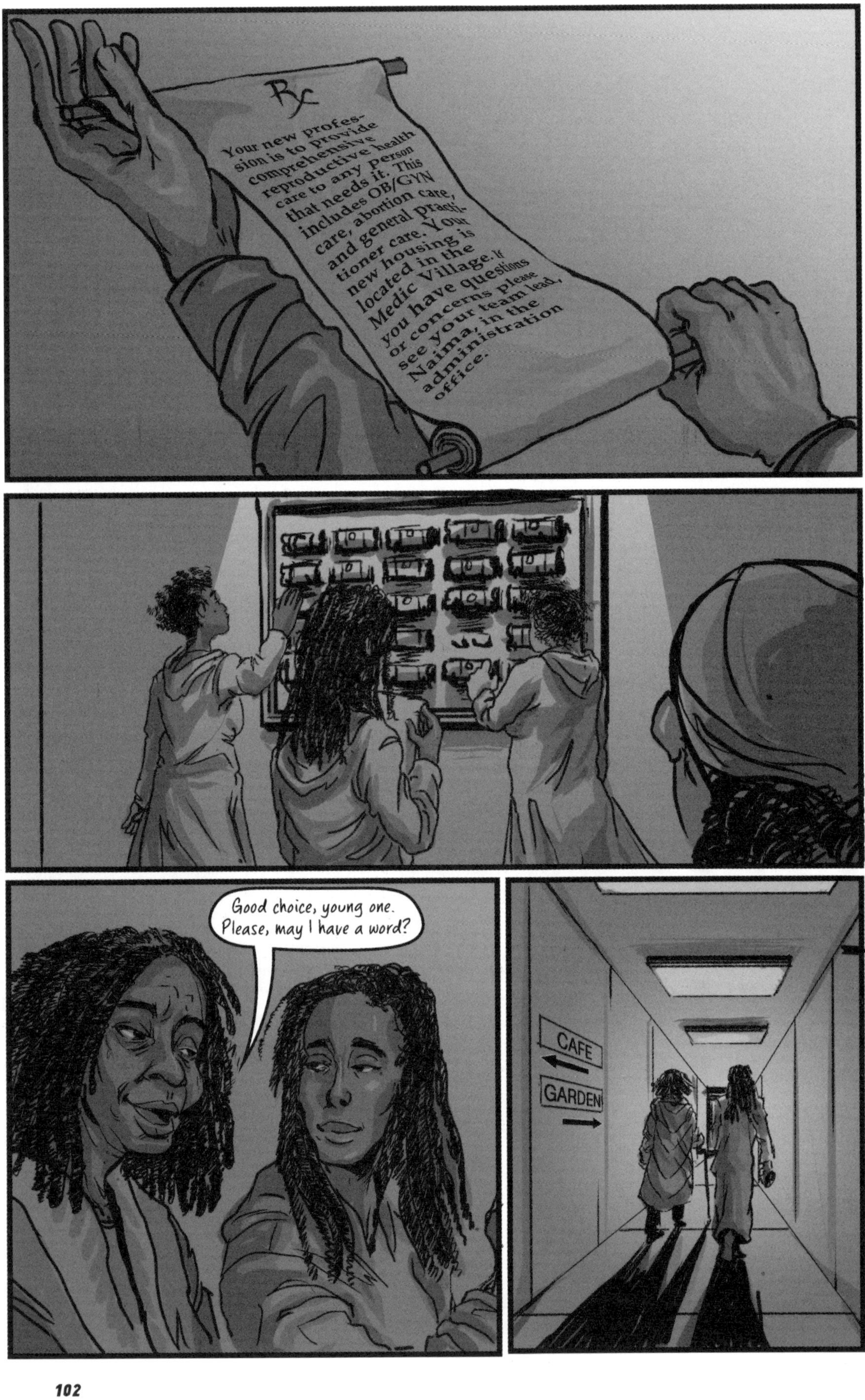
Rx
Your new profes-
sion is to provide
comprehensive
reproductive health
care to any person
that needs it. This
includes OB/GYN
care, abortion care,
and general practi-
tioner care. Your
new housing is
located in the
Medic Village. If
you have questions
or concerns please
see your team lead,
Naima, in the
administration
office.
Good choice, young one. Please, may I have a word?
CAFE
GARDEN

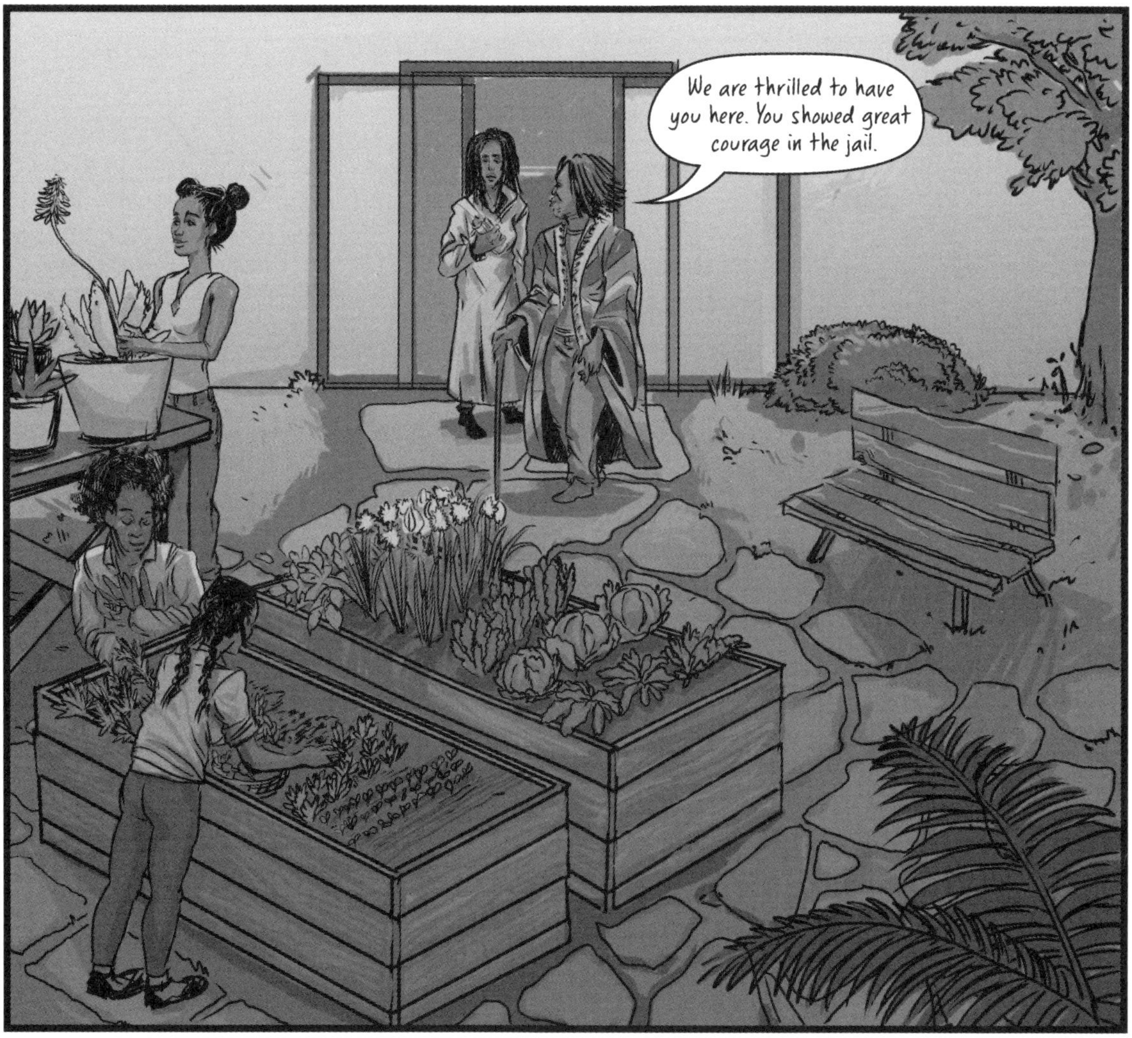
We are thrilled to have you here. You showed great courage in the jail.

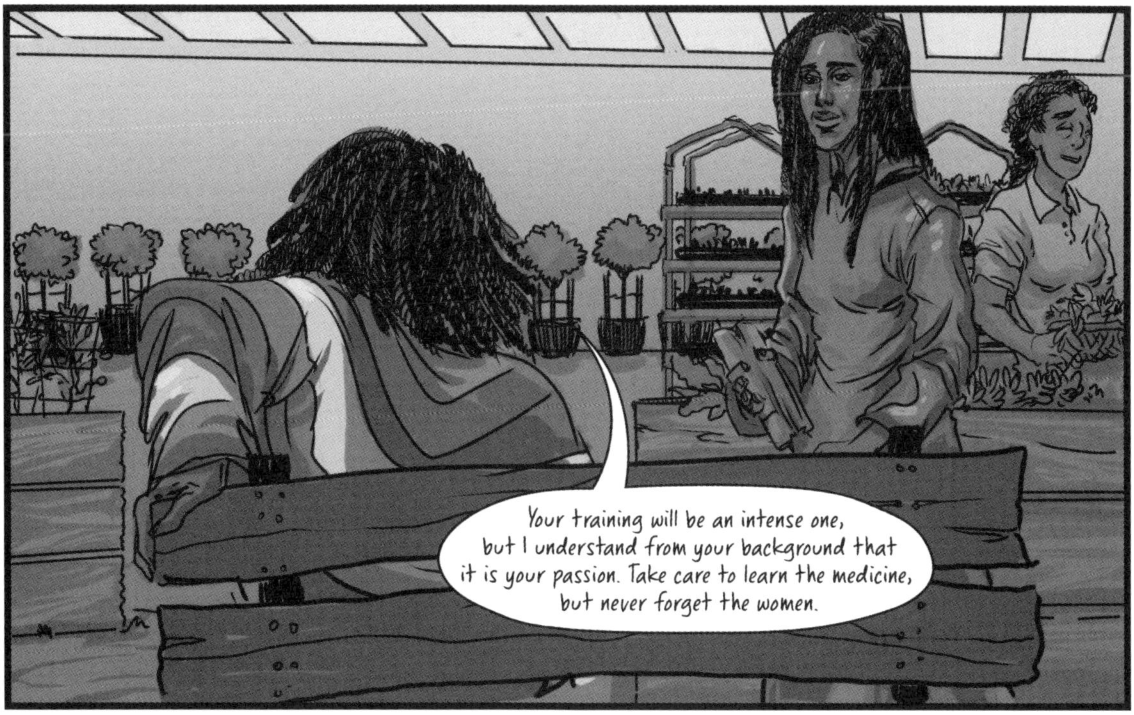
Your training will be an intense one, but I understand from your background that it is your passion. Take care to learn the medicine, but never forget the women.

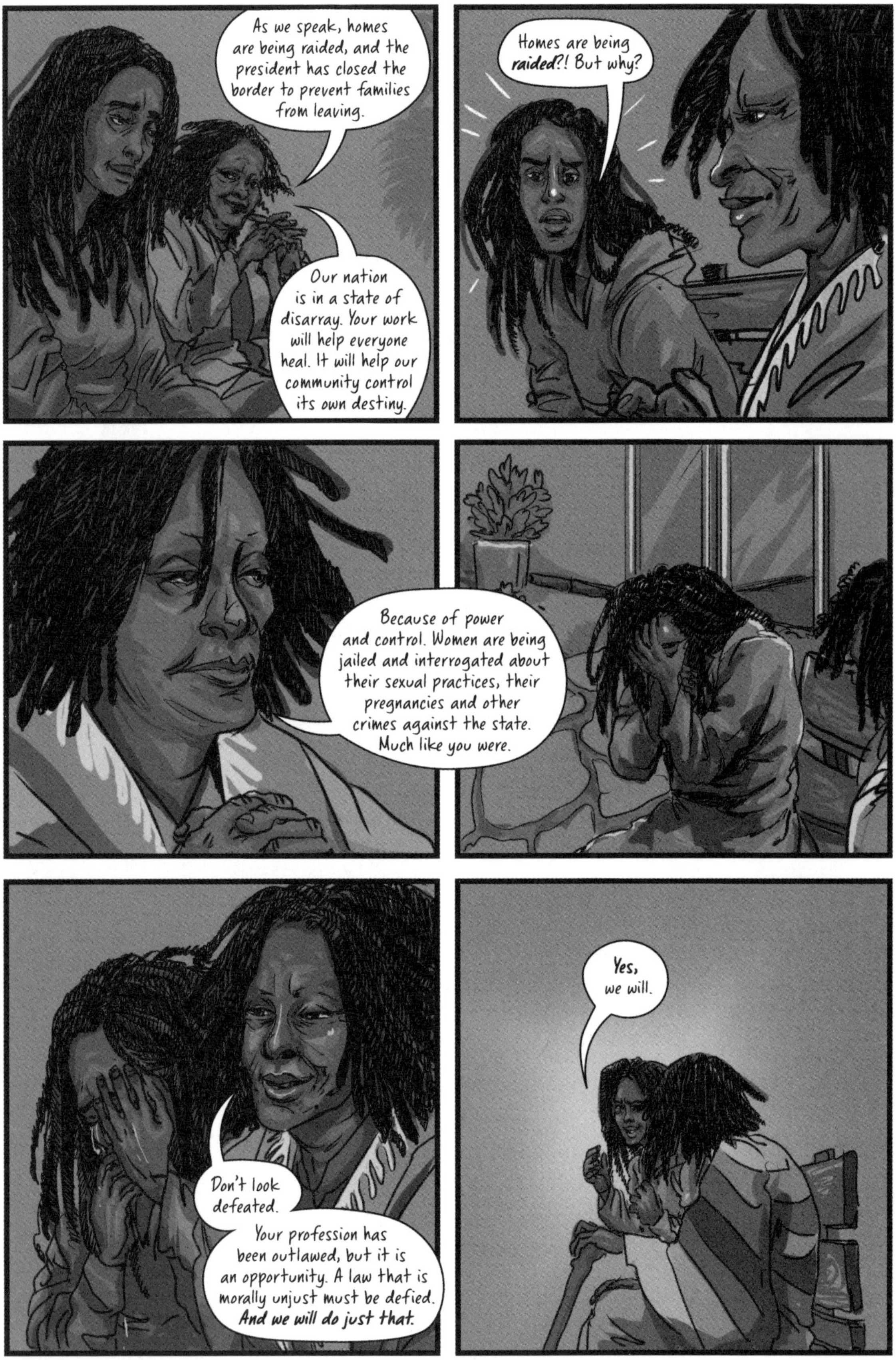

As we speak, homes are being raided, and the president has closed the border to prevent families from leaving.
Our nation is in a state of disarray. Your work will help everyone heal. It will help our community control its own destiny.
Homes are being **raided**?! But why?
Because of power and control. Women are being jailed and interrogated about their sexual practices, their pregnancies and other crimes against the state. Much like you were.
Don't look defeated.
Your profession has been outlawed, but it is an opportunity. A law that is morally unjust must be defied. **And we will do just that.**
Yes, we will.

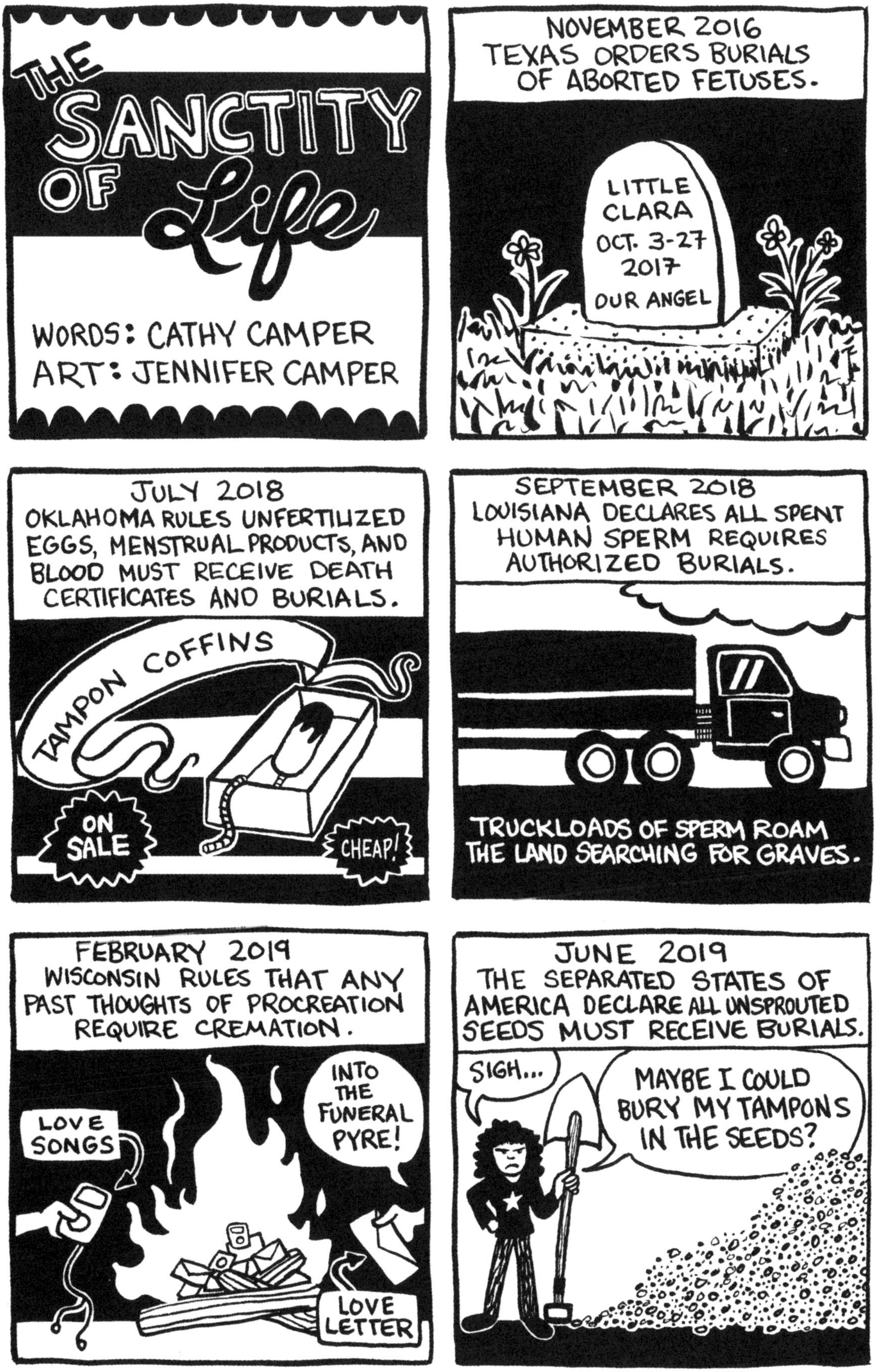
THE SANCTITY OF Life
WORDS: CATHY CAMPER
ART: JENNIFER CAMPER
NOVEMBER 2016
TEXAS ORDERS BURIALS OF ABORTED FETUSES.
LITTLE CLARA OCT. 3-27 2017 OUR ANGEL
JULY 2018
OKLAHOMA RULES UNFERTILIZED EGGS, MENSTRUAL PRODUCTS, AND BLOOD MUST RECEIVE DEATH CERTIFICATES AND BURIALS.
TAMPON COFFINS
ON SALE
CHEAP!
SEPTEMBER 2018
LOUISIANA DECLARES ALL SPENT HUMAN SPERM REQUIRES AUTHORIZED BURIALS.
TRUCKLOADS OF SPERM ROAM THE LAND SEARCHING FOR GRAVES.
FEBRUARY 2019
WISCONSIN RULES THAT ANY PAST THOUGHTS OF PROCREATION REQUIRE CREMATION.
LOVE SONGS
INTO THE FUNERAL PYRE!
LOVE LETTER
JUNE 2019
THE SEPARATED STATES OF AMERICA DECLARE ALL UNSPROUTED SEEDS MUST RECEIVE BURIALS.
SIGH...
MAYBE I COULD BURY MY TAMPONS IN THE SEEDS?

BODY & SOUL, SCIENCE & RELIGION:
ALL CROWDED INTO ONE UTERUS
PHYSICAL AND SPIRITUAL MILESTONES OF EMBRYOLOGICAL AND FETAL DEVELOPMENT.
BY KRIOTA WILLBERG

1ST TRIMESTER (WEEKS 0-12)

Conception/Fertilization occurs when a **sperm** fuses with an **egg**.

Woo hoo!

Rats!

A fertilized egg is called a **zygote**.

(Egg, sperm, zygote, and souls not drawn to scale.)

CONCEPTION/FERTILIZATION

Conception and **fertilization** are often used **synonymously**. We'll use them that way too.

Ensoulment is when the human-to-be gets a soul.

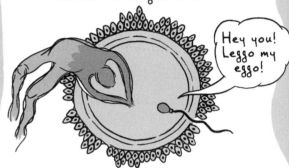

Hey you! Leggo my eggo!

Hindus, Sikhs, Christians, and Buddhists say the zygote is imbued with a soul **at the moment of conception**. But there is not unanimous agreement on this between all religions.

EMBRYONIC PERIOD
starts 3 WEEKS post conception

The embryo forms 3 types of tissues: **ectoderm, mesoderm,** and **endoderm**. They begin to fold around each other.

Starts out looking like this,

then this,

then this.

Magnified

Unmagnified*   •   •   •

4 WEEKS post conception

By DAY 22 the embryo has a heart tube (HT) that contracts and pushes blood around.

The tube is made from **mesoderm**. It will fold and loop to develop into a four-chambered heart.

22 Days

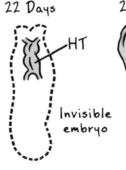

HT

Invisible embryo

24 Days

HT

25 Days

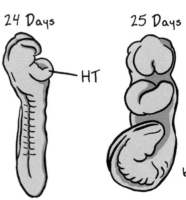

Un-magnified*

•

*Sizes are approximate because these embryos are TINY!

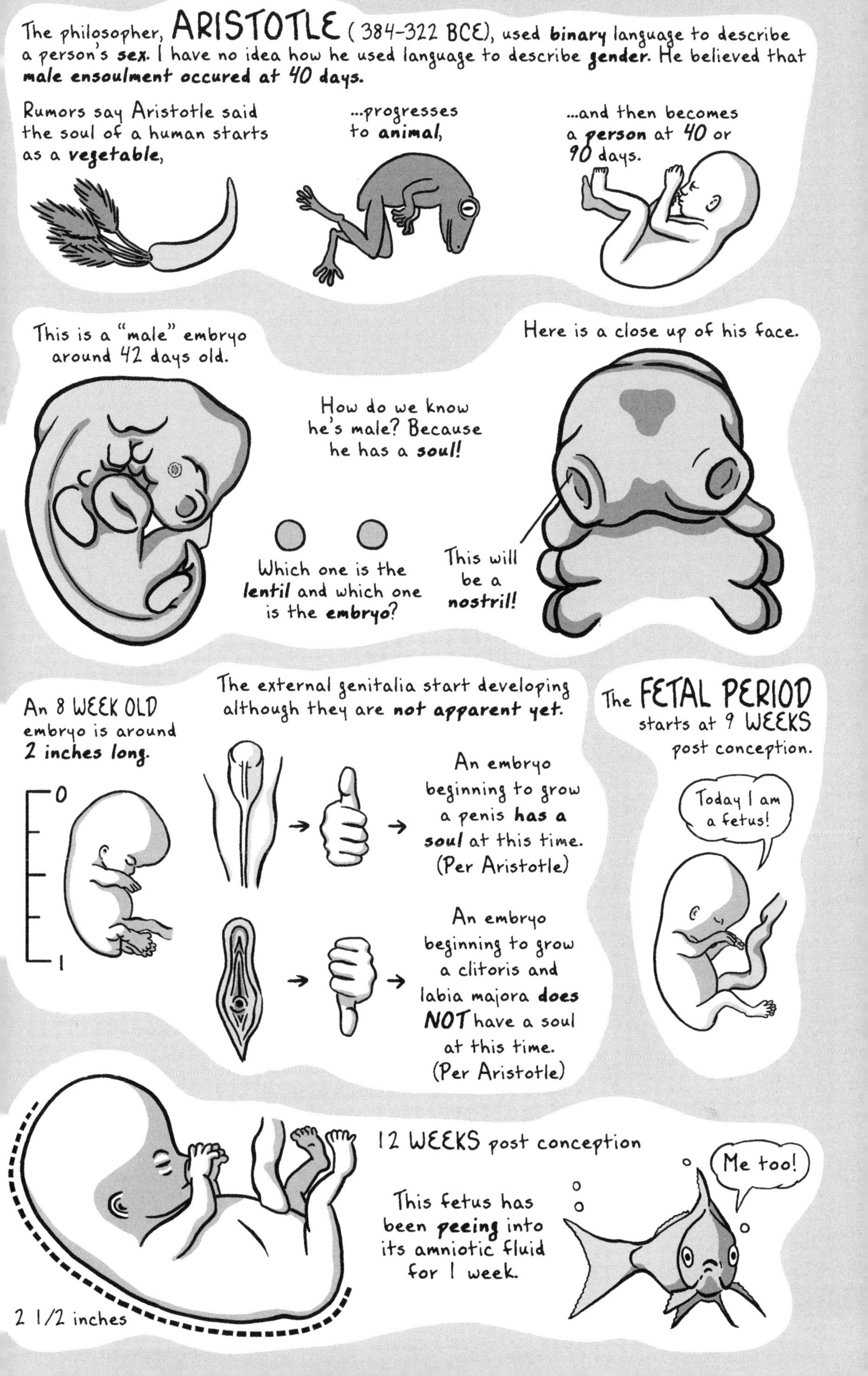

The philosopher, ARISTOTLE (384–322 BCE), used **binary** language to describe a person's **sex**. I have no idea how he used language to describe **gender**. He believed that **male ensoulment occured at 40 days.**

Rumors say Aristotle said the soul of a human starts as a **vegetable**,

...progresses to **animal**,

...and then becomes a **person** at **40** or **90** days.

This is a "male" embryo around 42 days old.

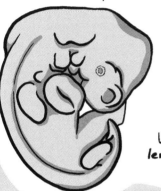

How do we know he's male? Because he has a **soul!**

Which one is the **lentil** and which one is the **embryo?**

Here is a close up of his face.

This will be a **nostril!**

An 8 WEEK OLD embryo is around **2 inches long.**

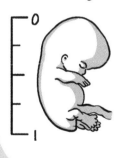

The external genitalia start developing although they are **not apparent yet.**

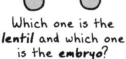

An embryo beginning to grow a penis **has a soul** at this time. (Per Aristotle)

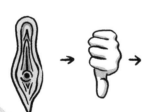

An embryo beginning to grow a clitoris and labia majora **does NOT** have a soul at this time. (Per Aristotle)

The **FETAL PERIOD** starts at 9 **WEEKS** post conception.

Today I am a fetus!

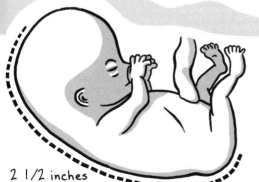

2 1/2 inches

12 WEEKS post conception

This fetus has been **peeing** into its amniotic fluid for 1 week.

Me too!

2ND TRIMESTER
WEEKS 13-28

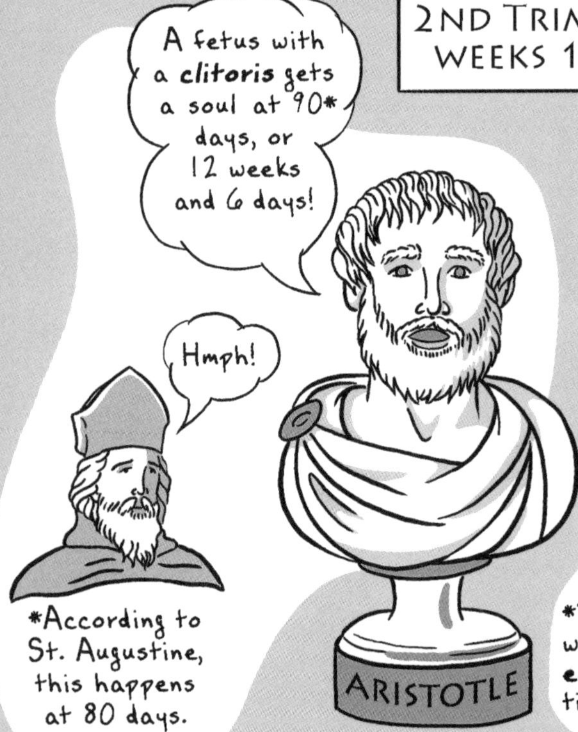
A fetus with a **clitoris** gets a soul at 90* days, or 12 weeks and 6 days!
Hmph!
ARISTOTLE

*According to St. Augustine, this happens at 80 days.

13 WEEKS
post conception

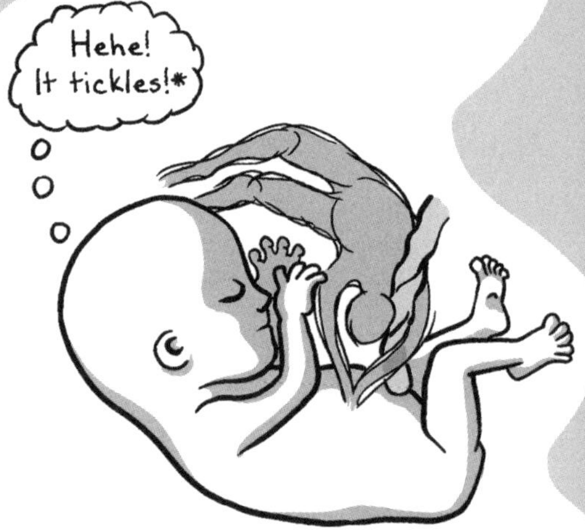
Hehe! It tickles!*

*This is a joke. It is not educational. At 13 weeks the nervous system (formed by the **ectoderm)** is **not** developed enough to feel tickled, that's why this is funny.

120 DAYS or 17 WEEKS PLUS 1 DAY post conception

From an ***Islamic perspective***, "the spirit is breathed in after 120 days."

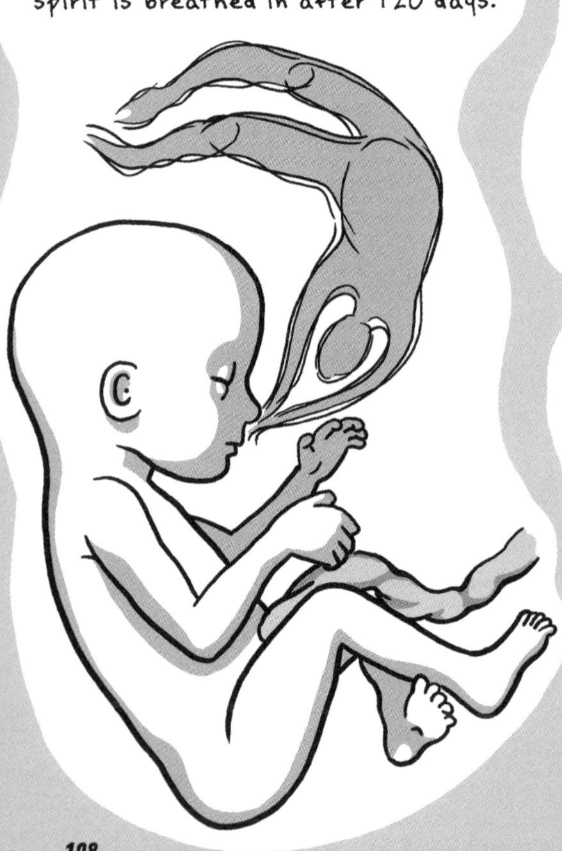

The lungs, formed from **endoderm**, are in the early stages of developing specific tubes and tissues for gas exchange. They **cannot function outside the womb** at this time.

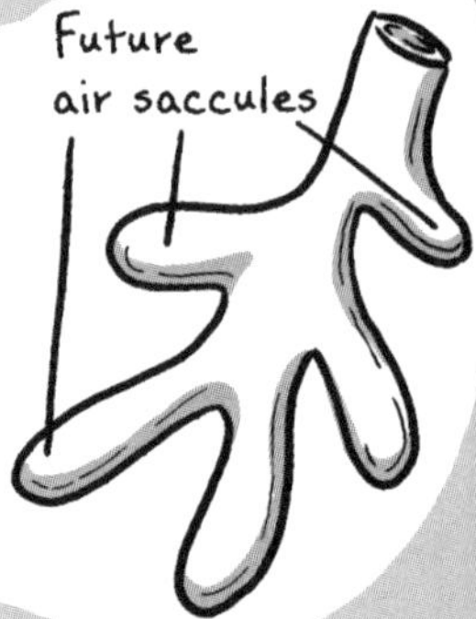
Future air saccules

In the ***last trimester*** the lungs develop air ***saccules.*** After birth they will mature into air sacs called ***alveoli***. In order for lungs to work, the saccules and alveoli need to have an internal coating of ***surfactant***. It ***keeps the saccules*** and alvioli **from collapsing** and sticking together after exhalation.

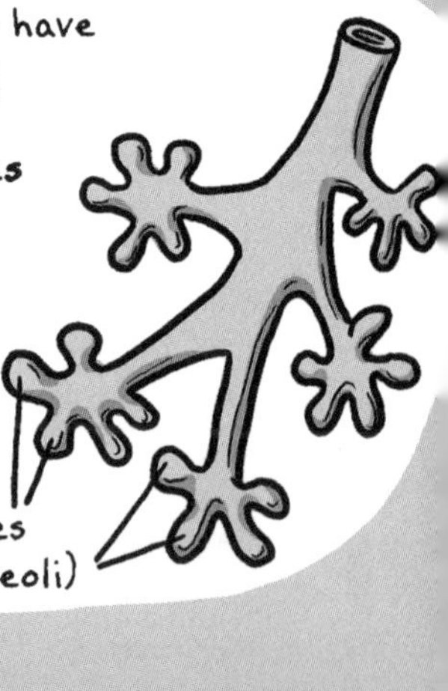
Air saccules (future alveoli)

The time at which a mother starts to feel her fetus move in her uterus is called

QUICKENING.

Note: In order to accommodate dramatic "action lines," the uteri on this page are missing structures vital to pregnancy (such as the placenta.)

Throughout history quickening has been sited as the **indication of ensoulment.**

Some people claimed to know the **gender** of the fetus based on aspects of quickening.

In the **United States** during the **19th century** abortion during the first trimester was generally **morally acceptable**

Woman's body.

There was not concensus on the **precise moment** of ensoulment, but it was generally agreed that **prior** to ensoulment the embryo was considered a part of the **mother's** body.

After ensoulment the embryo became a **person.**

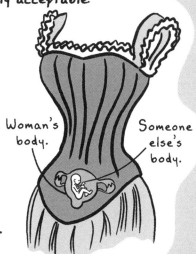

Woman's body.

Someone else's body.

At 20 WEEKS the fetus is around 7 1/2" long.

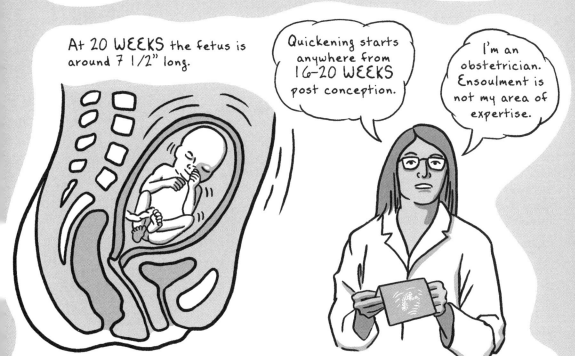

Quickening starts anywhere from 16–20 WEEKS post conception.

I'm an obstetrician. Ensoulment is not my area of expertise.

Contemporary medical sources write about ensoulment in the context of **bioethical** discussions about **pregnancy** and/or **abortion** from various religious perspectives.

VIABILITY

A fetus is **VIABLE** when it can **survive outside the womb.**

*I'm not viable unless I weigh **at least** as much as two cups of raw hamburger!*

*That's **500 grams**; just over 1 pound!*

With **intensive** medical technology, drugs, and care, some babies **might** survive out of the womb as early as 21 **WEEKS** post conception.

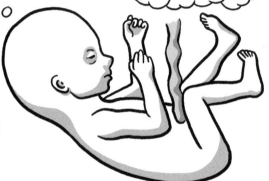

*I **can't breathe** on my own.*

*That means I am viable **only** if I have **access** to expensive machines.*

It can't be done now, but in the **future**, if a fetus is **conceived** and **gestated** in a laboratory, does that mean it's **viable from conception?**

Complications of **preterm birth** can include: respiratory distress; infections; poor neurological conditions such as cerebral palsy; and more. Some of these are **permanent.**

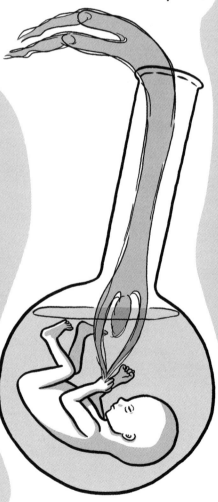

Healthy babies born 26 **WEEKS** after conception have a **90% chance** of surviving **without** impairment. Babies born at this time weigh almost 2 1/4 pounds, which equals 1,000 grams.

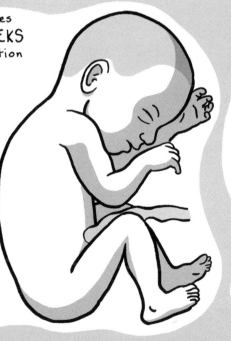

"Viability" becomes a **fluid term** as medical technology advances.

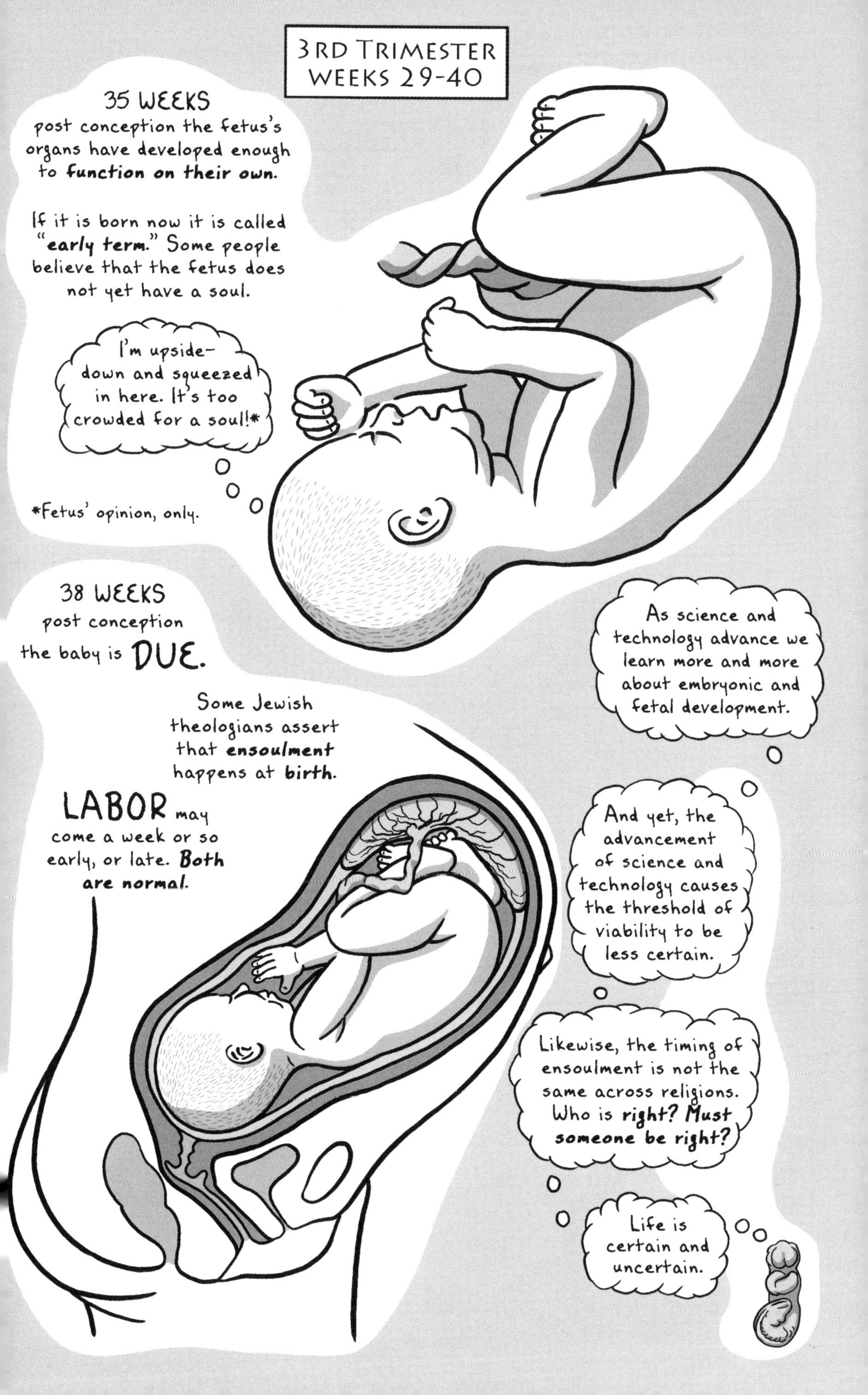
3RD TRIMESTER
WEEKS 29-40
35 WEEKS
post conception the fetus's organs have developed enough to **function on their own.**
If it is born now it is called "**early term.**" Some people believe that the fetus does not yet have a soul.
I'm upside-down and squeezed in here. It's too crowded for a soul!*
*Fetus' opinion, only.
38 WEEKS
post conception the baby is DUE.
Some Jewish theologians assert that **ensoulment** happens at **birth.**
LABOR may come a week or so early, or late. **Both are normal.**
As science and technology advance we learn more and more about embryonic and fetal development.
And yet, the advancement of science and technology causes the threshold of viability to be less certain.
Likewise, the timing of ensoulment is not the same across religions. Who is **right? Must someone be right?**
Life is certain and uncertain.

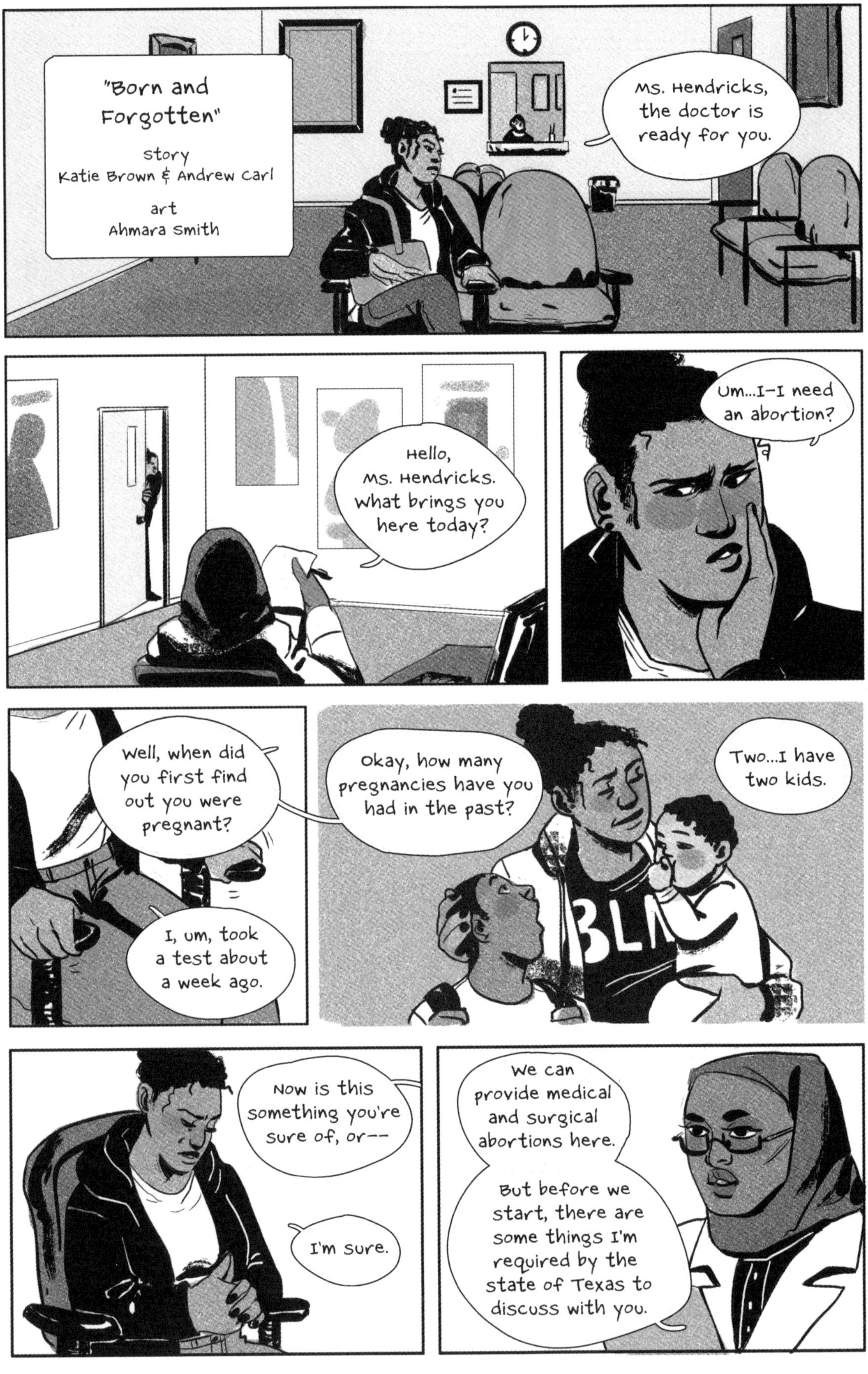
"Born and Forgotten"
story
Katie Brown & Andrew Carl
art
Ahmara Smith
Ms. Hendricks, the doctor is ready for you.
Hello, Ms. Hendricks. What brings you here today?
Um...I-I need an abortion?
Well, when did you first find out you were pregnant?
I, um, took a test about a week ago.
Okay, how many pregnancies have you had in the past?
Two...I have two kids.
Now is this something you're sure of, or--
I'm sure.
We can provide medical and surgical abortions here.
But before we start, there are some things I'm required by the state of Texas to discuss with you.

These pamphlets have been prepared by the state to provide "medical information" and contact resources for "options" counseling.

What's in there is dictated by anti-choice legislation.

I'm required to tell you about some of their contents...

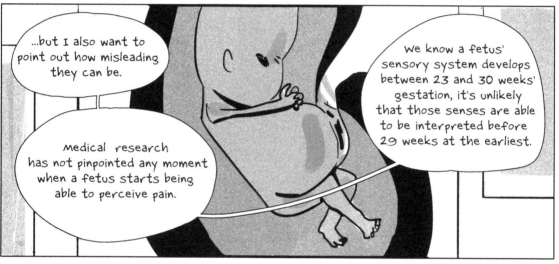

...but I also want to point out how misleading they can be.

Medical research has not pinpointed any moment when a fetus starts being able to perceive pain.

We know a fetus' sensory system develops between 23 and 30 weeks' gestation, it's unlikely that those senses are able to be interpreted before 29 weeks at the earliest.

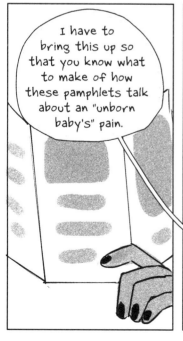

I have to bring this up so that you know what to make of how these pamphlets talk about an "unborn baby's" pain.

I want to assure you, these warnings come from anti-choice proponents without concern for medical fact.

Dang, I wish people tried this hard to protect living children...

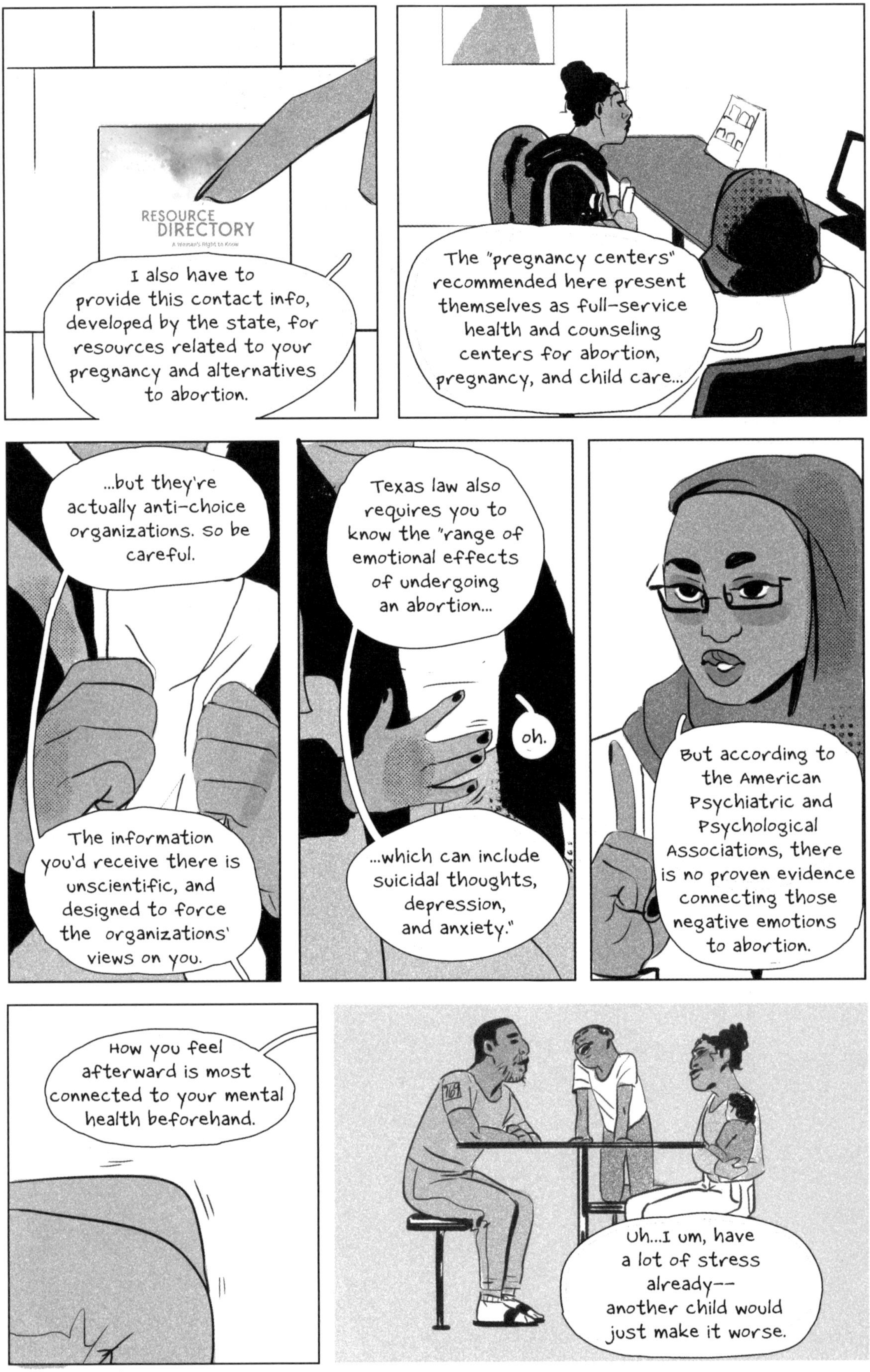
RESOURCE DIRECTORY
I also have to provide this contact info, developed by the state, for resources related to your pregnancy and alternatives to abortion.
The "pregnancy centers" recommended here present themselves as full-service health and counseling centers for abortion, pregnancy, and child care...
...but they're actually anti-choice organizations. so be careful.
The information you'd receive there is unscientific, and designed to force the organizations' views on you.
Texas law also requires you to know the "range of emotional effects of undergoing an abortion...
oh.
...which can include suicidal thoughts, depression, and anxiety."
But according to the American Psychiatric and Psychological Associations, there is no proven evidence connecting those negative emotions to abortion.
How you feel afterward is most connected to your mental health beforehand.
Uh...I um, have a lot of stress already--
another child would just make it worse.

Just like every medical procedure, abortion has risks, but it's safer than these materials make it seem. In fact, carrying a fetus to term is actually over 20 times more likely to result in death. These numbers are both very low. We'll go through all the potential risks before your procedure...

nod nod

...but right now. I just want to make sure you aren't misled.

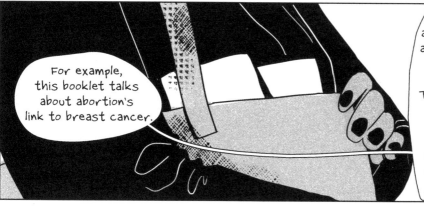

For example, this booklet talks about abortion's link to breast cancer.

But there is absolutely no proven association between abortion and risk of breast cancer. The National Cancer Institute and experts around the world have come to the same conclusion: there's just no connection.

If those politicians cared so much about breast cancer, maybe they could stop making it so hard to prevent it...

That will be $120 for your mammogram.

What?!

sorry, without the ACA...

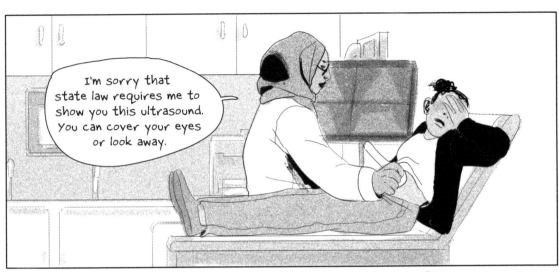

I'm sorry that state law requires me to show you this ultrasound. You can cover your eyes or look away.

So...it looks like you're at about 12 weeks.

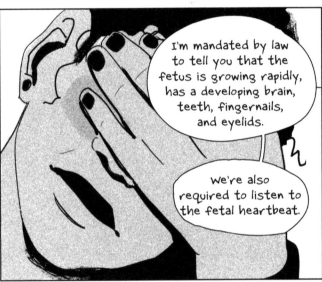

I'm mandated by law to tell you that the fetus is growing rapidly, has a developing brain, teeth, fingernails, and eyelids.

We're also required to listen to the fetal heartbeat.

I wonder why they're so mad.

People making me feel like I'm the one trying to hurt innocent babies.

Flint's water crisis continues to endanger its mainly minority and poor community. Children with elevated blood lead levels have exhibited developmental delay, weight loss, hearing loss, fatigue and seizures.

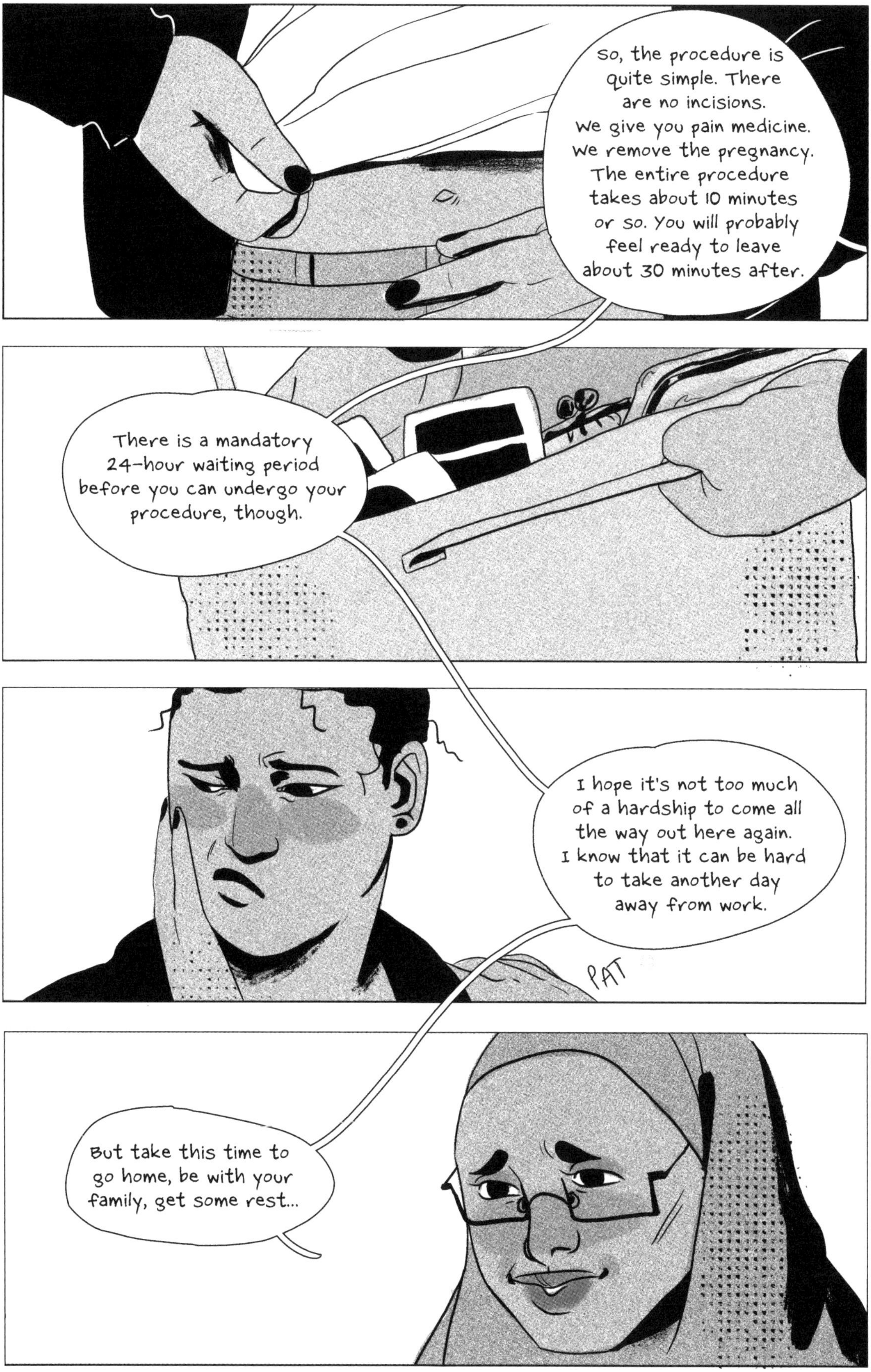
So, the procedure is quite simple. There are no incisions. We give you pain medicine. We remove the pregnancy. The entire procedure takes about 10 minutes or so. You will probably feel ready to leave about 30 minutes after.
There is a mandatory 24-hour waiting period before you can undergo your procedure, though.
I hope it's not too much of a hardship to come all the way out here again. I know that it can be hard to take another day away from work.
PAT
But take this time to go home, be with your family, get some rest...

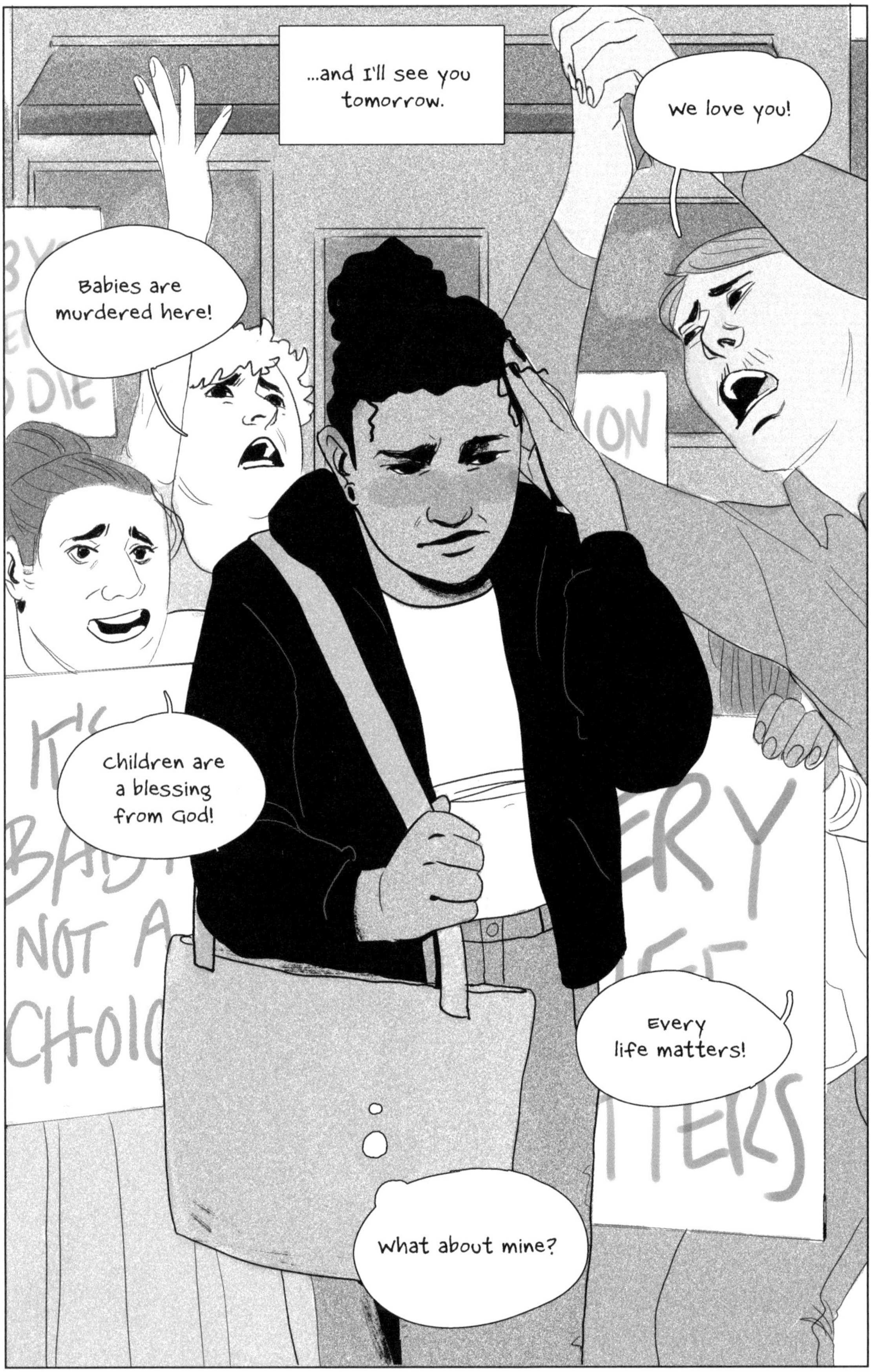
...and I'll see you tomorrow.
We love you!
Babies are murdered here!
Children are a blessing from God!
Every life matters!
What about mine?

SATURDAY MORNING

I REGRET MY ABORTION

GOD IS PRO LIFE

STOP KILLI BABI

ADOPTION IS AN OPTION

Author: Benita Ulisano
Artist: Laura Martin

sigh

Morning, Lynda.

Looks like we already have company.

Yeah, they got here at like 4AM. Anyway, here's your supplies—

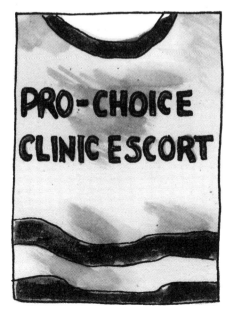

PRO-CHOICE CLINIC ESCORT

FPA FAMILY PLANNING ASSOCIATES

ABORTION IS WRONG.

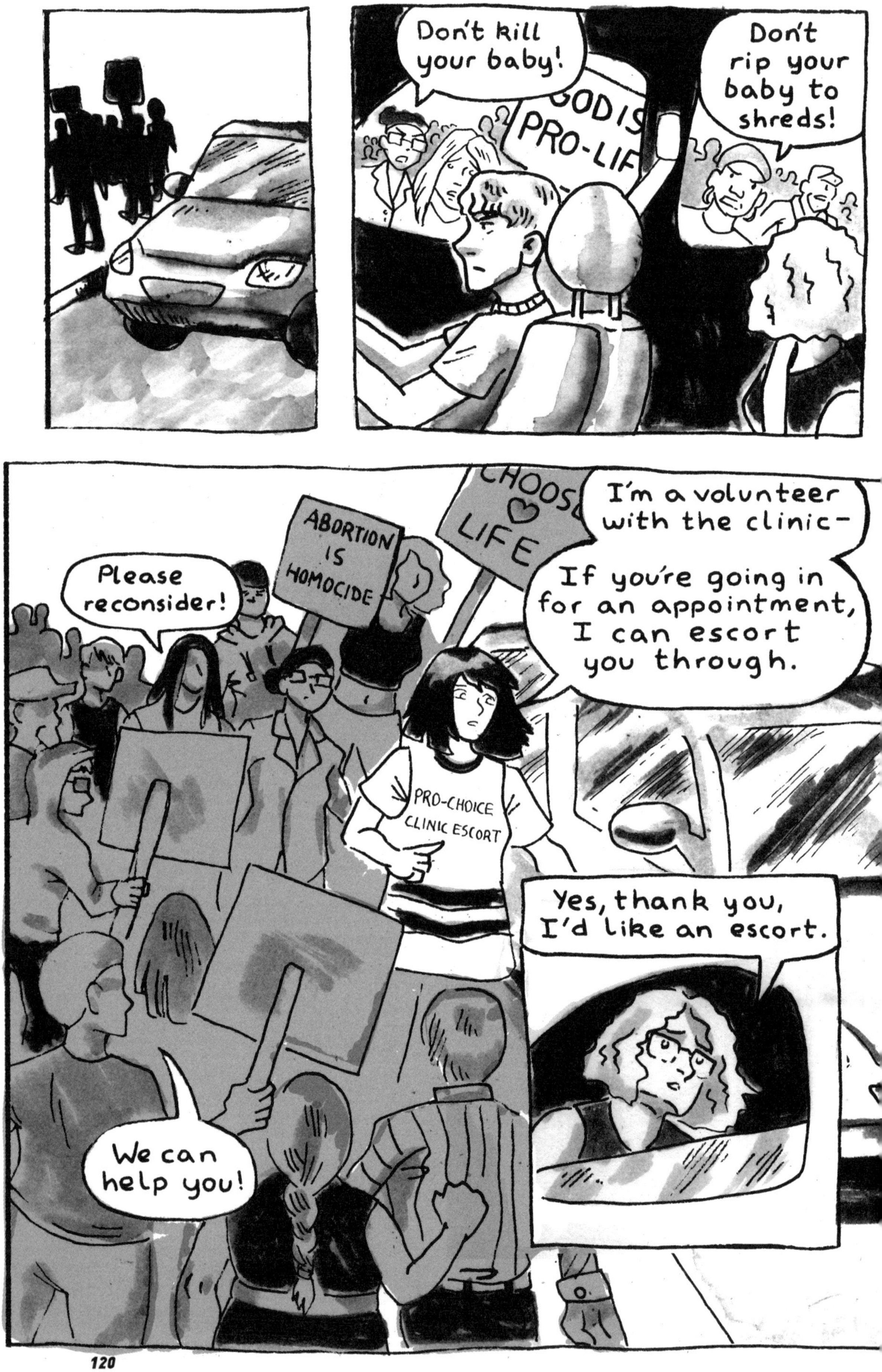

Don't kill your baby!
GOD IS PRO-LIF
Don't rip your baby to shreds!
ABORTION IS HOMOCIDE
Please reconsider!
I'm a volunteer with the clinic–
If you're going in for an appointment, I can escort you through.
PRO-CHOICE CLINIC ESCORT
Yes, thank you, I'd like an escort.
We can help you!

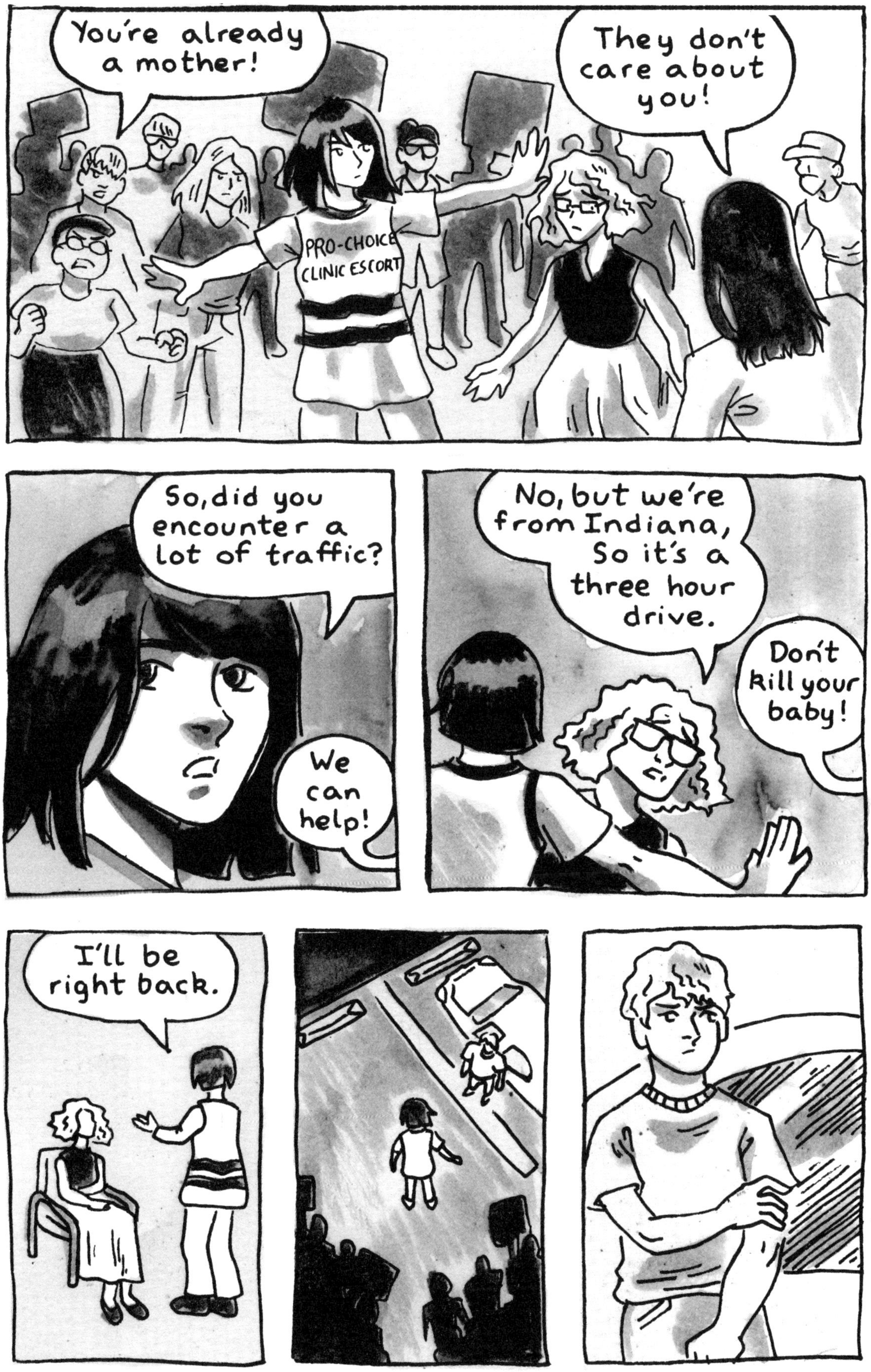
You're already a mother!
PRO-CHOICE CLINIC ESCORT
They don't care about you!
So, did you encounter a lot of traffic?
We can help!
No, but we're from Indiana, So it's a three hour drive.
Don't kill your baby!
I'll be right back.

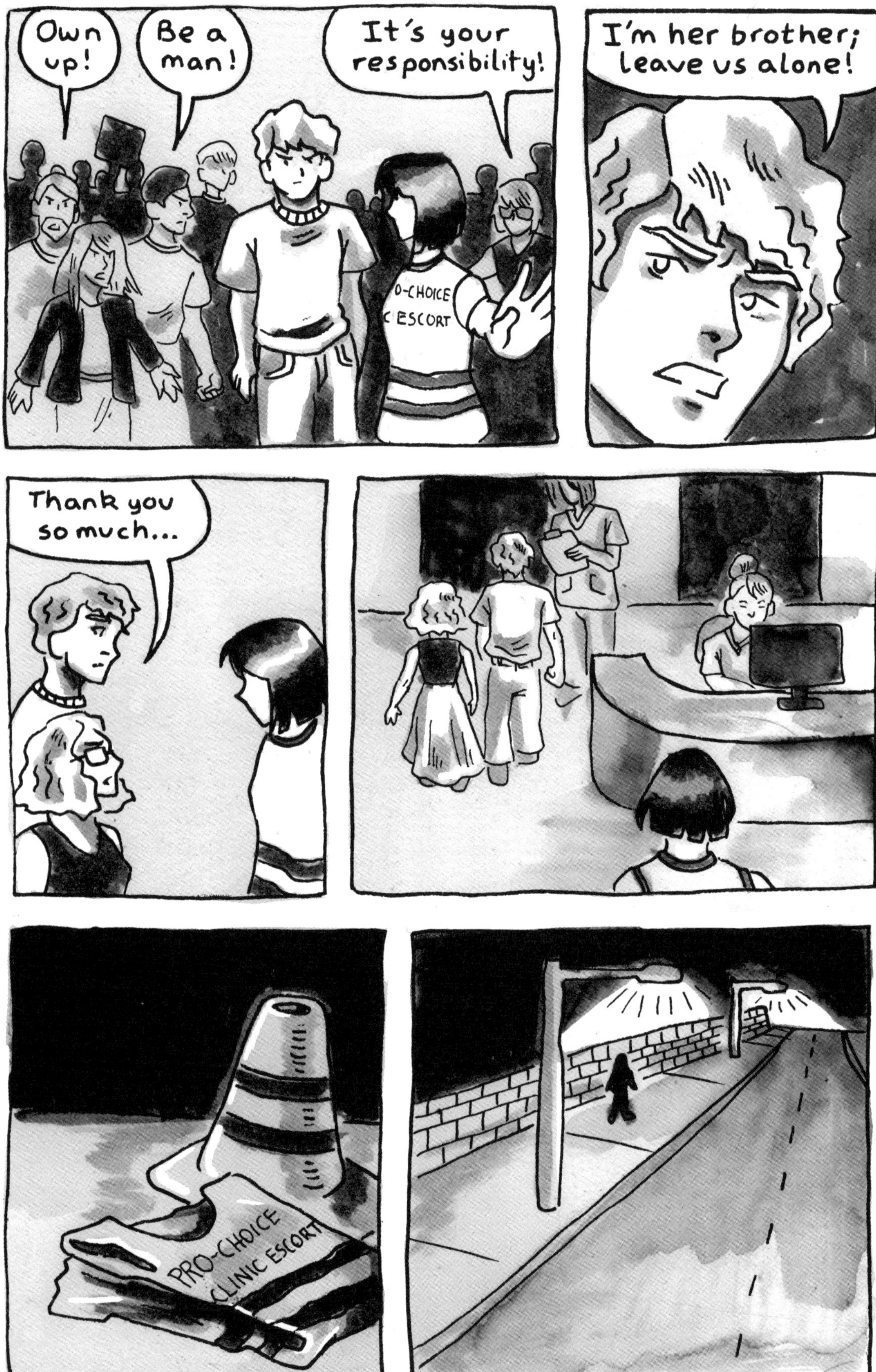
Own up!
Be a man!
It's your responsibility!
O-CHOICE
ESCORT
I'm her brother; leave us alone!
Thank you so much...
PRO-CHOICE
CLINIC ESCORT

They CAN'T GET That FROM US.

STEPH KRAFT SHELEY

IN THE UNITED STATES, ORGANIZATIONS THAT PROVIDE HEALTHCARE ARE RUN LIKE FOR-PROFIT BUSINESSES, AND MOST TAKE THE CORPORATE FORM. THE PRECISE STRUCTURE OF THESE BUSINESSES DIFFERS FROM ORGANIZATION TO ORGANIZATION, BUT MOST ARE ARRANGED IN A HIERARCHY WHEREIN EACH LEVEL MUST ACCOUNT TO THE NEXT LEVEL UP FOR ITS FINANCIAL BOTTOM LINE.

BOARD OF DIRECTORS
C-LEVEL OFFICERS (CEO, CFO, etc.)
MANAGERS
HOSPITALS
OUTPATIENT MEDICAL OFFICES
OUTPATIENT SERVICES
H
EMERGENCY/TRAUMA
CARDIOLOGY ASSOCIATES
OB/GYN
FAMILY CARE
IMAGING CENTER
URGENT CARE CENTER
SURGICAL CENTER

HEALTHCARE ORGANIZATIONS ARE INCREASINGLY MOVING TOWARD FULL INTEGRATION, WHICH ALLOWS PATIENTS WITH THE ABILITY TO PAY TO SEEK MOST OF THEIR CARE FROM THE SAME ORGANIZATION. THESE INTEGRATED ORGANIZATIONS ARE CALLED HEALTH SYSTEMS. MANY COMMUNITIES HAVE MULTIPLE HEALTH SYSTEMS, AND MANY HEALTH SYSTEMS OPERATE IN MULTIPLE COMMUNITIES.

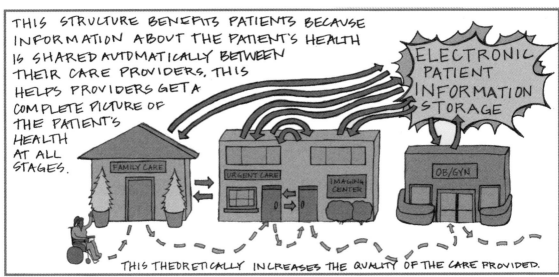

THIS STRUCTURE BENEFITS PATIENTS BECAUSE INFORMATION ABOUT THE PATIENT'S HEALTH IS SHARED AUTOMATICALLY BETWEEN THEIR CARE PROVIDERS. THIS HELPS PROVIDERS GET A COMPLETE PICTURE OF THE PATIENT'S HEALTH AT ALL STAGES.

ELECTRONIC PATIENT INFORMATION STORAGE

FAMILY CARE

URGENT CARE

IMAGING CENTER

OB/GYN

THIS THEORETICALLY INCREASES THE QUALITY OF THE CARE PROVIDED.

THIS STRUCTURE ALSO HEAVILY BENEFITS THE HEALTH SYSTEM BY KEEPING MONEY GENERATED BY ALL TYPES OF HEALTH SERVICES FLOWING BACK TO THE HEALTH SYSTEM. THIS INCENTIVIZES HEALTH SYSTEMS TO PROVIDE ALL THE CARE THAT PATIENTS REQUIRE.

HEALTH SYSTEM

CARDIOLOGY ASSO

AMBULATORY SURGICAL CENTER

LABORATORY

EMERGENCY

EXCEPT, FOR SOME REASON, ABORTION.

HEALTH SYSTEM

FAMILY CARE

OB/GYN

I NEED AN ABORTION.

ARE YOU ACTIVELY DYING?

NO.

WE CAN'T HELP YOU.

I NEED AN ABORTION
I DON'T DO THOSE

I NEED AN ABORTION
I CAN'T DO THAT

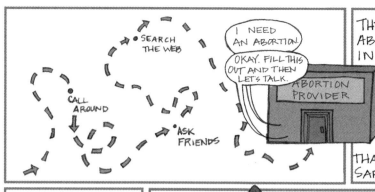

SEARCH THE WEB

CALL AROUND

ASK FRIENDS

I NEED AN ABORTION.

OKAY. FILL THIS OUT AND THEN LET'S TALK.

ABORTION PROVIDER

THE VAST MAJORITY OF ABORTIONS ARE PERFORMED IN DEDICATED REPRODUCTIVE HEALTH CLINICS RATHER THAN DOCTORS' OFFICES OR HOSPITALS.

THIS SEGREGATION PERSISTS DESPITE THE FACT THAT ABORTION IS EXTREMELY SAFE AND COMMON.

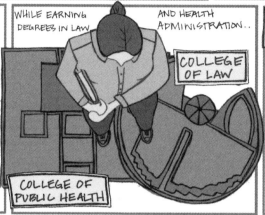

THE SEPARATION OF ABORTION AND ITS CONSEQUENCES BECAME CLEAR TO ME AS I PURSUED EDUCATIONAL AND PROFESSIONAL OPPORTUNITIES.

WHILE EARNING DEGREES IN LAW

AND HEALTH ADMINISTRATION...

COLLEGE OF LAW

COLLEGE OF PUBLIC HEALTH

BOARD ROOM
INDEPENDENT FEMINIST WOMEN'S HEALTH CLINIC

...I SPENT FREE TIME ON AN ABORTION PROVIDER'S BOARD

STUDYING LAW CONVINCED ME THAT THE RIGHT TO LEGAL ABORTION MUST BE PRESERVED.

WeThePe

HEALTH LAW and POLICY 4 med.

STUDYING HEALTH ADMINISTRATION, I LEARNED THE BUSINESS OF PROVIDING HEALTHCARE. BUT I FREQUENTLY ENCOUNTERED MESSAGES FROM PROFESSORS AND CLASSMATES SUGGESTING THAT ABORTION IS DEVIANT BEHAVIOR, AND SO UNCOMMON THAT WE NEED NOT DISCUSS IT IN DETAIL.

Strategic Planning & Marketing

ANALYTICS

Revenue Cycle Management

Professional Dress for the Workplace

Health Policy

Public Health

I KNEW, HOWEVER, THAT ABORTION IS A COMMON HEALTH NEED.

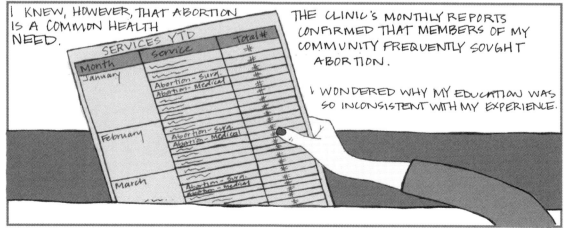

SERVICES YTD

Month	Service	Total #
January	Abortion - Surg.	
	Abortion - Medical	
February	Abortion - Surg.	
	Abortion - Medical	
March	Abortion - Surg.	
	Abortion - Medical	

THE CLINIC'S MONTHLY REPORTS CONFIRMED THAT MEMBERS OF MY COMMUNITY FREQUENTLY SOUGHT ABORTION.

I WONDERED WHY MY EDUCATION WAS SO INCONSISTENT WITH MY EXPERIENCE.

I DID SOME RESEARCH, AND STARTED RAISING THE ISSUE OF ABORTION IN MY CLASSES. THE RESPONSES THIS PROBING ELICITED FROM THOSE WITH EXPERTISE IN HEALTH CARE HELPED ME UNDERSTAND WHY AND HOW MAINSTREAM HEALTH CARE EXCLUDES ABORTION.

Stigma

ABORTION STIGMA STEMS FROM THE PERCEPTION THAT SOCIETY GENERALLY DISAPPROVES OF ABORTION.

me
...AND THAT'S WHY HEALTH ADMINS SHOULD BE KNOWLEDGE-ABLE ABOUT ABORTION.
THAT'S INTERESTING, BUT IT'S IMPORTANT TO NOTE THAT EVERY ABORTION HURTS SOMEONE, BE IT MOM, DAD OR BABY.
ME
PROFESSOR
I DON'T THINK EVERY ABORTION IS A TRAGEDY, BUT WE CAN AGREE TO DISAGREE ON THAT.
COMMUNITY HEALTH CENTER CEO
WE DO A LOT OF BIRTHS FOR THE LOW-INCOME POPULATION
WHAT DO YOU DO WHEN A PATIENT NEEDS AN ABORTION?
me
... YEAH, WELL... IF THAT'S WHAT SHE DECIDES TO DO, SHE CAN'T GET THAT FROM US.

I EXPERIENCED ABORTION STIGMA IN THE FORM OF PRESSURE NOT TO USE THE WORD "ABORTION." IT BECAME CLEAR THAT HEARING THE WORD SPOKEN ALOUD MADE STUDENTS AND PROFESSORS UNCOMFORTABLE. ON ONLY ONE OCCASION DID A PROFESSOR INITIATE A DISCUSSION OF ABORTION'S STATUS IN HEALTHCARE, BUT HE ENDED HIS TALK BY VOICING A PERSONAL OBJECTION TO ABORTION. THE RESULT IS THAT FUTURE HEALTH LEADERS LEARNED THAT IF ABORTION MAKES THEM UNCOMFORTABLE, THEY ARE FREE TO IGNORE IT ALTOGETHER.

Religious Directives

SOME HEALTH SYSTEMS ARE OWNED OR SPONSORED BY THE CATHOLIC CHURCH. THESE ORGANIZATIONS OPERATE SUBJECT TO A SET OF DIRECTIVES THAT EXPRESSLY PROHIBIT ABORTION CARE. CATHOLIC HOSPITALS AND HEALTH SYSTEMS ARE THEREFORE PROHIBITED FROM PERFORMING ABORTIONS, SAVE IN SOME CASES WHERE THE PATIENT'S LIFE IS THREATENED.

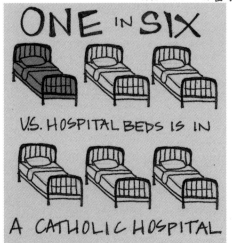

ONE IN SIX
U.S. HOSPITAL BEDS IS IN
A CATHOLIC HOSPITAL

NEW HEALTH SYSTEM
MERGER
CATHOLIC HEALTH SYSTEM
SECULAR HEALTH SYSTEM

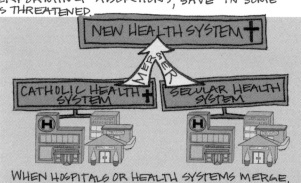

WHEN HOSPITALS OR HEALTH SYSTEMS MERGE, OR WHEN ONE ACQUIRES ANOTHER, THE RELIGIOUS DIRECTIVES OF ONE HOSPITAL MAY BE APPLIED TO ALL OF THE FACILITIES IN THE NEWLY-FORMED SYSTEM. WHEN THAT HAPPENS, THE NEW PARENT ORGANIZATION MAY FORBID PROVIDERS TO PROVIDE ABORTION CARE.

Unprofitability

BOTH FOR-PROFIT AND NONPROFIT HEALTH SYSTEMS ARE MOTIVATED BY PROFIT. "NO MARGIN NO MISSION" IS A COMMON PHRASE IN DISCUSSIONS ABOUT NONPROFIT HEALTHCARE, AND IT REFERS TO THE IDEA THAT IF AN ORGANIZATION DOESN'T EARN MORE THAN IT SPENDS, IT WILL GO OUT OF BUSINESS AND THUS UNABLE TO FULFILL ITS CHARITABLE DUTIES.* THEREFORE, HEALTHCARE PROVIDERS STRONGLY PREFER TO OFFER SERVICES THAT CAN GENERATE SUBSTANTIAL REIMBURSEMENTS FROM A PATIENT'S INSURER. PUBLIC AND PRIVATE INSURANCE COVERAGE VARIES AMONG THE STATES, WITH THE MAJORITY PLACING RESTRICTIONS ON ABORTION COVERAGE. THE MAJORITY OF ABORTIONS ARE PAID FOR OUT OF POCKET, AND MANY PATIENTS REQUIRE FINANCIAL ASSISTANCE TO HELP PAY FOR THEIR ABORTIONS.

*"NO MARGIN, NO MISSION" IS TOO OFTEN USED TO JUSTIFY PROFIT-DRIVEN ACTIVITIES THAT ARE INCONSISTENT WITH THE COMMUNITY'S NEEDS.

History

AFTER ROE V. WADE LEGALIZED ABORTION NATIONWIDE, HEALTH CARE PROVIDERS AND COMMUNITY ACTIVISTS HAD TO DECIDE HOW TO ESTABLISH ACCESS TO ABORTION CARE.

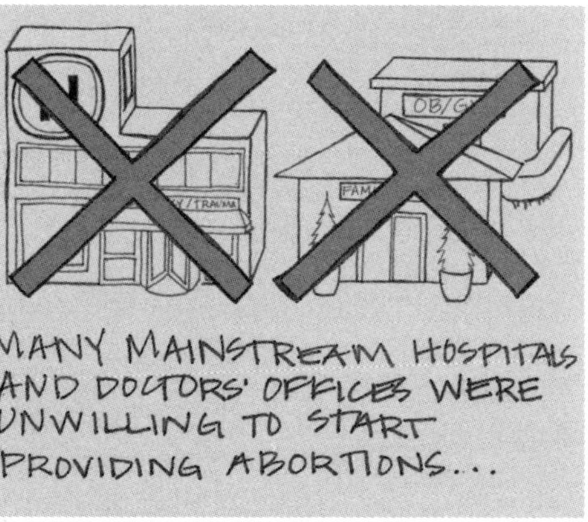

OB/GY
FAM

MANY MAINSTREAM HOSPITALS AND DOCTORS' OFFICES WERE UNWILLING TO START PROVIDING ABORTIONS...

...SO ADVOCATES AND SUPPORTIVE PHYSICIANS BEGAN SETTING UP SEPARATE CLINICS WHERE THEY COULD PROVIDE ABORTIONS.

THESE TYPICALLY TOOK ONE OF TWO FORMS:

FEMINIST CLINICS	MEDICAL ABORTION CLINICS
• REJECTION OF PATRIARCHY	• EMPHASIZED SAFE ABORTION BY TRAINED PHYSICIANS
• EMPHASIZED WOMAN-CENTERED CARE	• ENCOURAGED RESEARCH ON SAFE ABORTION PRACTICES
• WOMEN TOOK ON PROVIDER ROLES	
• PRIORITIZED PATIENT EDUCATION	

Schoen, J. (2013)

WHILE MAINSTREAM HEALTHCARE'S REJECTION OF ABORTION CARE WAS THE CAUSE OF ABORTION SEGREGATION, THE RISE OF STANDALONE CLINICS HAS NOT BEEN ENTIRELY NEGATIVE. STANDALONE CLINICS DEVELOPED AS PLACES FOR WOMEN TO ESCAPE THE MALE-DOMINATED AND PATRIARCHAL MEDICAL ESTABLISHMENT. TODAY, MANY STANDALONE CLINICS OPERATE UNDER THE SAME PHILOSOPHY.

THE VALUE OF THESE CLINICS IS SIGNIFICANT, AND WHILE ABORTION SHOULD BE MADE AVAILABLE FROM MAINSTREAM HEALTHCARE PROVIDERS, PATIENTS SHOULD ALWAYS HAVE THE OPTION TO OBTAIN THEIR REPRODUCTIVE HEALTH CARE FROM A STANDALONE CLINIC.

WHAT EFFECT DOES ABORTION SEGREGATION HAVE ON PATIENTS?

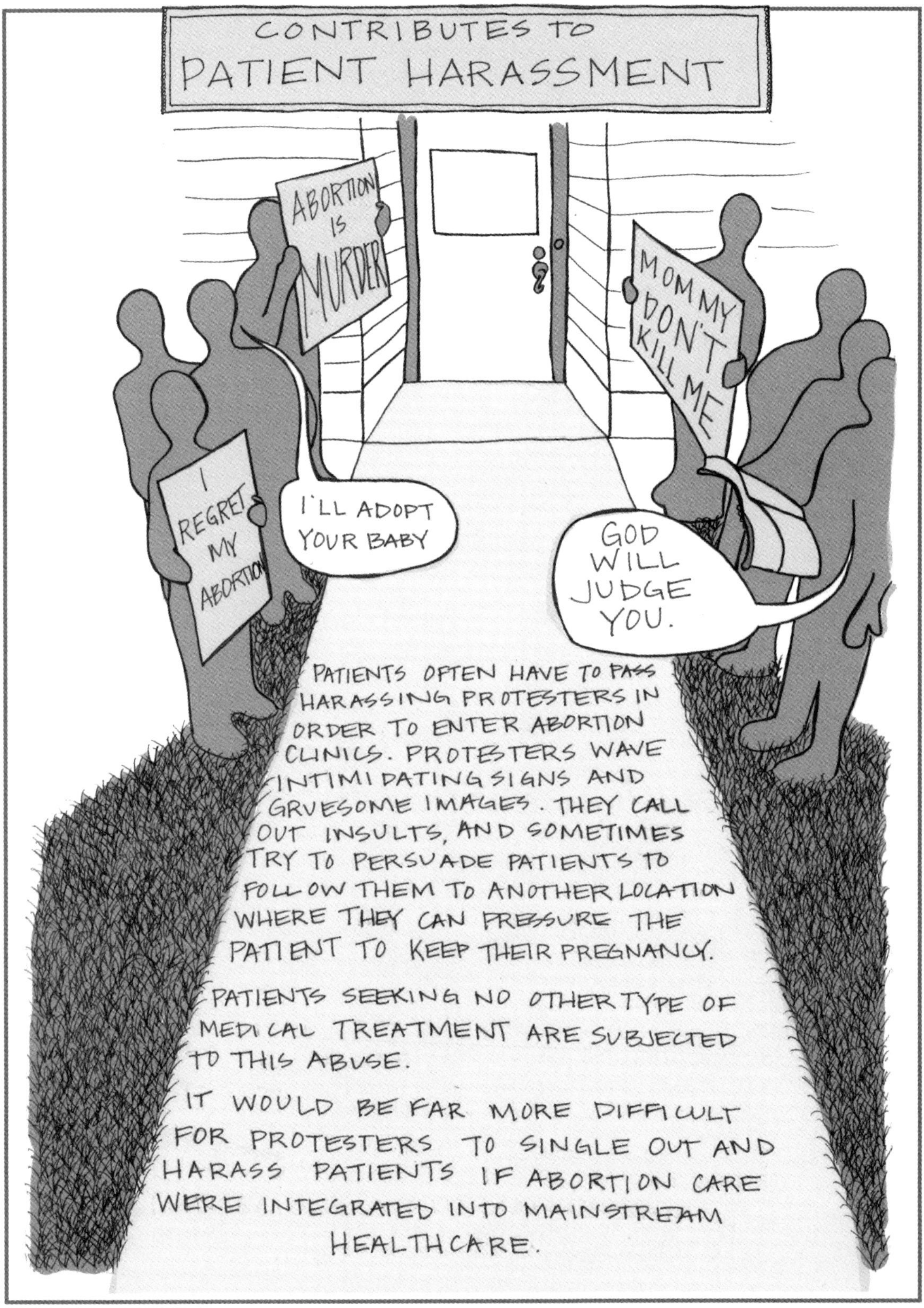
CONTRIBUTES TO PATIENT HARASSMENT
ABORTION IS MURDER
MOMMY DON'T KILL ME
I REGRET MY ABORTION
I'LL ADOPT YOUR BABY
GOD WILL JUDGE YOU.
PATIENTS OFTEN HAVE TO PASS HARASSING PROTESTERS IN ORDER TO ENTER ABORTION CLINICS. PROTESTERS WAVE INTIMIDATING SIGNS AND GRUESOME IMAGES. THEY CALL OUT INSULTS, AND SOMETIMES TRY TO PERSUADE PATIENTS TO FOLLOW THEM TO ANOTHER LOCATION WHERE THEY CAN PRESSURE THE PATIENT TO KEEP THEIR PREGNANCY.
PATIENTS SEEKING NO OTHER TYPE OF MEDICAL TREATMENT ARE SUBJECTED TO THIS ABUSE.
IT WOULD BE FAR MORE DIFFICULT FOR PROTESTERS TO SINGLE OUT AND HARASS PATIENTS IF ABORTION CARE WERE INTEGRATED INTO MAINSTREAM HEALTHCARE.

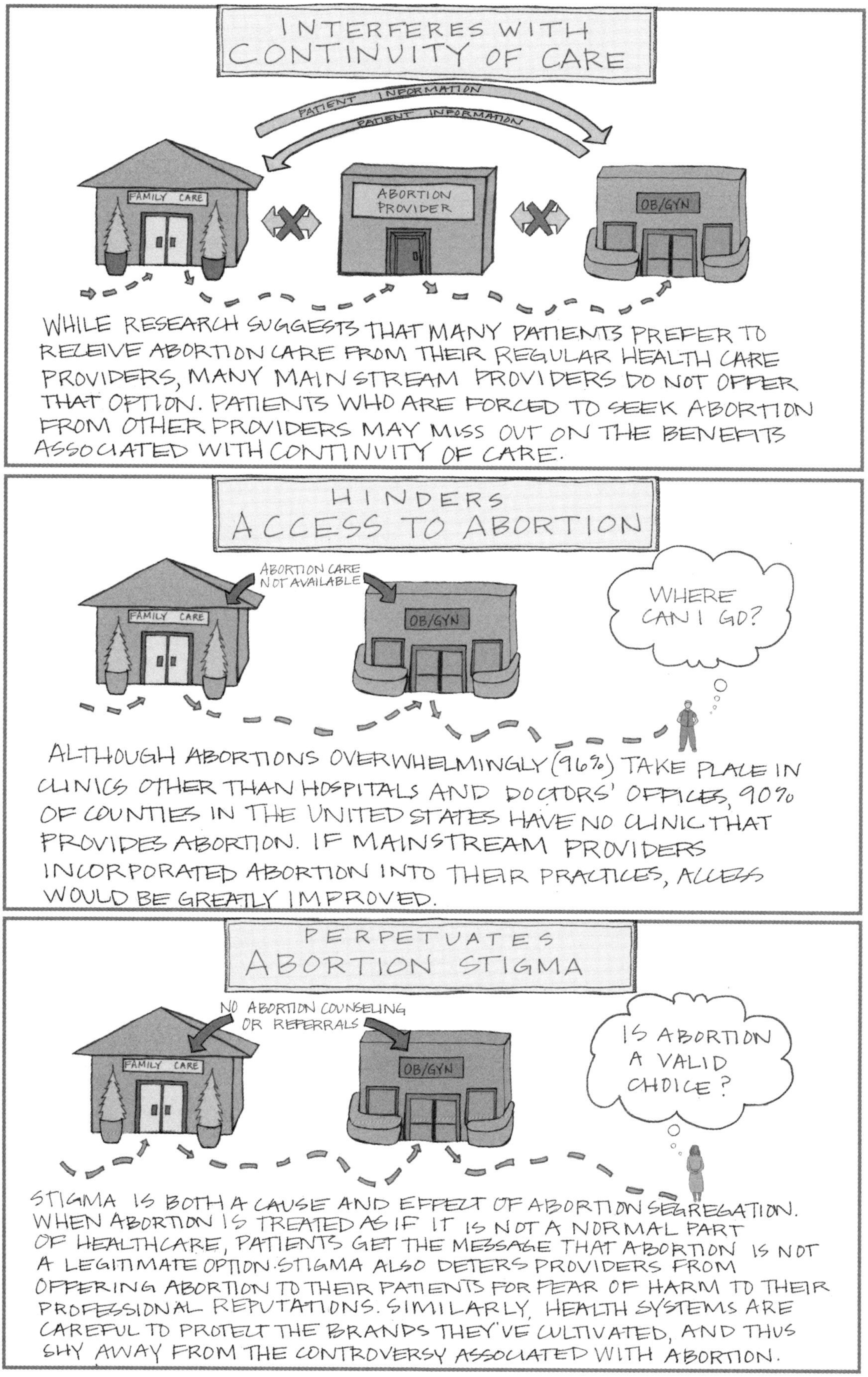
INTERFERES WITH CONTINUVITY OF CARE
PATIENT INFORMATION
PATIENT INFORMATION
FAMILY CARE
ABORTION PROVIDER
OB/GYN
WHILE RESEARCH SUGGESTS THAT MANY PATIENTS PREFER TO RECEIVE ABORTION CARE FROM THEIR REGULAR HEALTH CARE PROVIDERS, MANY MAINSTREAM PROVIDERS DO NOT OFFER THAT OPTION. PATIENTS WHO ARE FORCED TO SEEK ABORTION FROM OTHER PROVIDERS MAY MISS OUT ON THE BENEFITS ASSOCIATED WITH CONTINUVITY OF CARE.
HINDERS ACCESS TO ABORTION
ABORTION CARE NOT AVAILABLE
FAMILY CARE
OB/GYN
WHERE CAN I GO?
ALTHOUGH ABORTIONS OVERWHELMINGLY (96%) TAKE PLACE IN CLINICS OTHER THAN HOSPITALS AND DOCTORS' OFFICES, 90% OF COUNTIES IN THE UNITED STATES HAVE NO CLINIC THAT PROVIDES ABORTION. IF MAINSTREAM PROVIDERS INCORPORATED ABORTION INTO THEIR PRACTICES, ACCESS WOULD BE GREATLY IMPROVED.
PERPETUATES ABORTION STIGMA
NO ABORTION COUNSELING OR REFERRALS
FAMILY CARE
OB/GYN
IS ABORTION A VALID CHOICE?
STIGMA IS BOTH A CAUSE AND EFFECT OF ABORTION SEGREGATION. WHEN ABORTION IS TREATED AS IF IT IS NOT A NORMAL PART OF HEALTHCARE, PATIENTS GET THE MESSAGE THAT ABORTION IS NOT A LEGITIMATE OPTION. STIGMA ALSO DETERS PROVIDERS FROM OFFERING ABORTION TO THEIR PATIENTS FOR FEAR OF HARM TO THEIR PROFESSIONAL REPUTATIONS. SIMILARLY, HEALTH SYSTEMS ARE CAREFUL TO PROTECT THE BRANDS THEY'VE CULTIVATED, AND THUS SHY AWAY FROM THE CONTROVERSY ASSOCIATED WITH ABORTION.

WHY SHOULD HOSPITALS, HEALTH SYSTEMS AND OTHER HEALTHCARE ORGANIZATIONS TAKE RESPONSIBILITY FOR PROVIDING ABORTION CARE?

TAX-EXEMPT STATUS OBLIGATES NONPROFIT ORGANIZATIONS TO ADDRESS THE COMMUNITY'S NEEDS

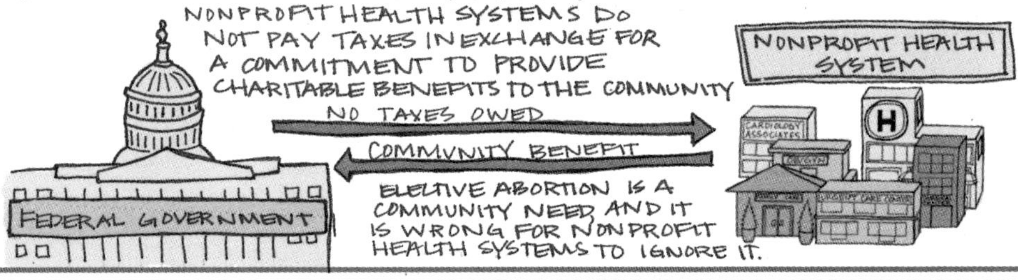

NONPROFIT HEALTH SYSTEMS DO NOT PAY TAXES IN EXCHANGE FOR A COMMITMENT TO PROVIDE CHARITABLE BENEFITS TO THE COMMUNITY
NONPROFIT HEALTH SYSTEM
NO TAXES OWED
COMMUNITY BENEFIT
FEDERAL GOVERNMENT
CARDIOLOGY ASSOCIATES
ELECTIVE ABORTION IS A COMMUNITY NEED AND IT IS WRONG FOR NONPROFIT HEALTH SYSTEMS TO IGNORE IT.

HEALTHCARE PROVIDERS HAVE UNIQUE RESPONSIBILITIES TO THEIR COMMUNITIES

WHETHER OPERATED FOR PROFIT OR NOT, HEALTHCARE ORGANIZATIONS ARE STEWARDS OF A COMMUNITY RESOURCE—HEALTH CARE—TO WHICH EVERY PERSON SHOULD BE AFFORDED EQUAL ACCESS. ABORTION CARE IS AN ESSENTIAL ELEMENT OF REPRODUCTIVE HEALTHCARE FOR PEOPLE CAPABLE OF BECOMING PREGNANT (JUST UNDER ½ OF THE POPULATION AT SOME POINT IN THEIR LIVES.)

HEALTHCARE ORGANIZATIONS CURRENTLY GET AWAY WITH PRETENDING THAT ABORTION ISN'T HEALTHCARE, OR THAT IT IS A CONVENIENCE RATHER THAN A BASIC NEED. THIS ATTITUDE PERSISTS DESPITE MOUNTING EVIDENCE THAT ABORTION ACCESS IS VITAL TO THE HEALTH AND WELFARE OF INDIVIDUALS AND COMMUNITIES.

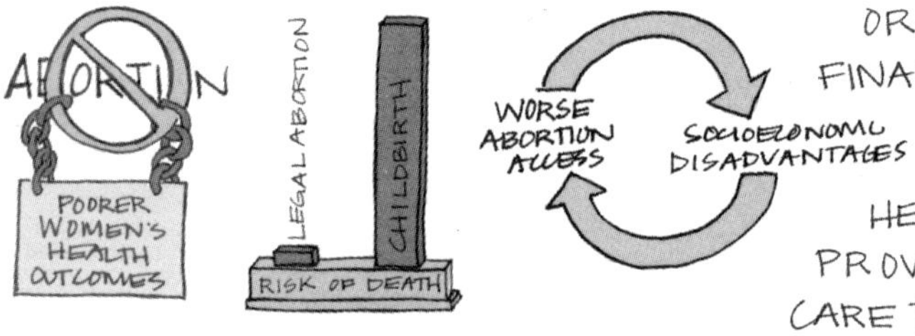

ABORTION
POORER WOMEN'S HEALTH OUTCOMES
LEGAL ABORTION
CHILDBIRTH
RISK OF DEATH
WORSE ABORTION ACCESS
SOCIOECONOMIC DISADVANTAGES

IT IS TIME FOR HEALTH ORGANIZATIONS THAT FINANCIALLY THRIVE ON COMMUNITIES' ILLNESSES TO BE HELD ACCOUNTABLE FOR PROVIDING ALL OF THE BASIC CARE THE COMMUNITY NEEDS.

WE CAN START BY:

- **ADVOCATING** FOR PUBLIC AND PRIVATE INSURANCE COVERAGE OF ABORTION
- **PROTESTING** RELIGIOUS INFLUENCE OVER HEALTH CARE
- **INSISTING** UPON EVIDENCE-BASED ABORTION EDUCATION IN HEALTH PROFESSIONS
- **DEMANDING** THAT HEALTHCARE ORGANIZATIONS ADDRESS ABORTION AS A COMMUNITY HEALTH NEED
- **DISCUSSING** ABORTION CARE WITH YOUR REGULAR HEALTHCARE PROVIDER

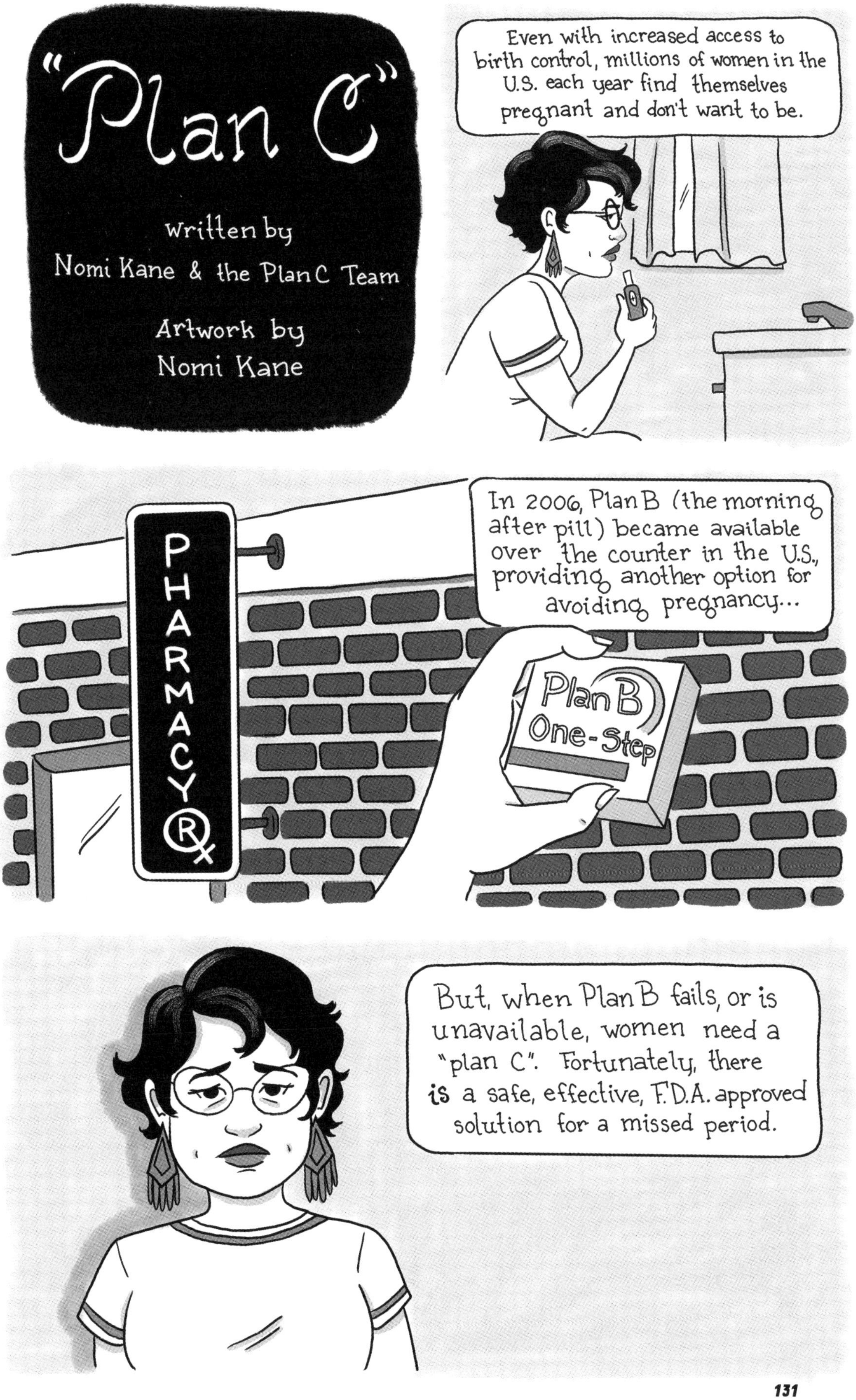
"Plan C"
Written by
Nomi Kane & the Plan C Team
Artwork by
Nomi Kane
Even with increased access to birth control, millions of women in the U.S. each year find themselves pregnant and don't want to be.
PHARMACY ℞
In 2006, Plan B (the morning after pill) became available over the counter in the U.S., providing another option for avoiding pregnancy...
Plan B One-Step
But, when Plan B fails, or is unavailable, women need a "plan C". Fortunately, there **is** a safe, effective, F.D.A. approved solution for a missed period.

This "Plan C" is a combination of medications called mifepristone and misoprostol. When taken as directed up to 10 weeks after a missed period the pills are safe and 95% effective.

MIFEPRISTONE

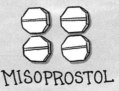

MISOPROSTOL

In the U.S., the most common way to get mifepristone and misoprostol is from health care providers who offer abortion services...

But there are many barriers to access in the U.S. Because mifepristone and misoprostol enable women to safely and effectively manage early abortion on their own, some women are obtaining and taking these pills independently.

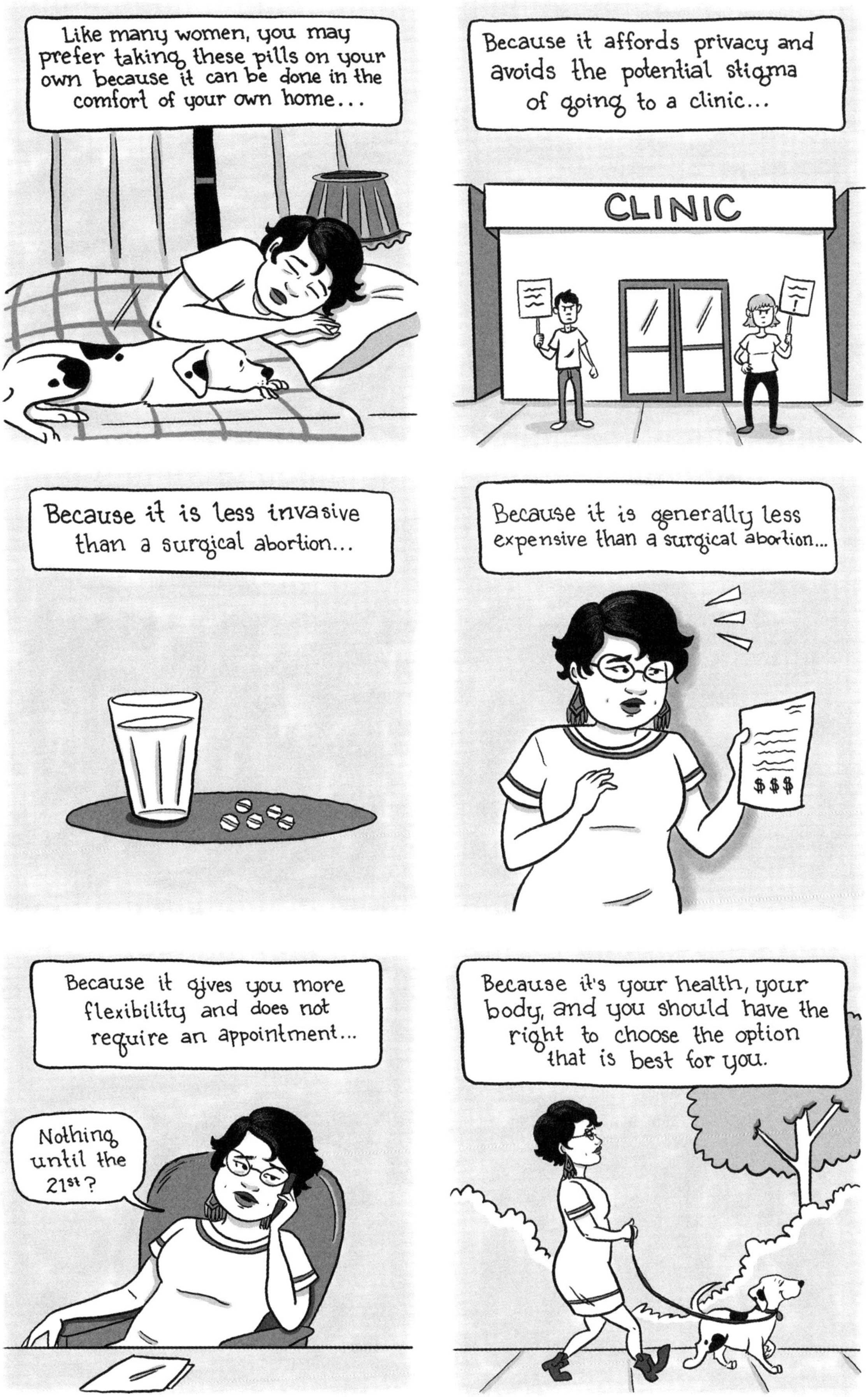

Like many women, you may prefer taking these pills on your own because it can be done in the comfort of your own home...
Because it affords privacy and avoids the potential stigma of going to a clinic...
CLINIC
Because it is less invasive than a surgical abortion...
Because it is generally less expensive than a surgical abortion...
$$$
Because it gives you more flexibility and does not require an appointment...
Nothing until the 21st?
Because it's your health, your body, and you should have the right to choose the option that is best for you.

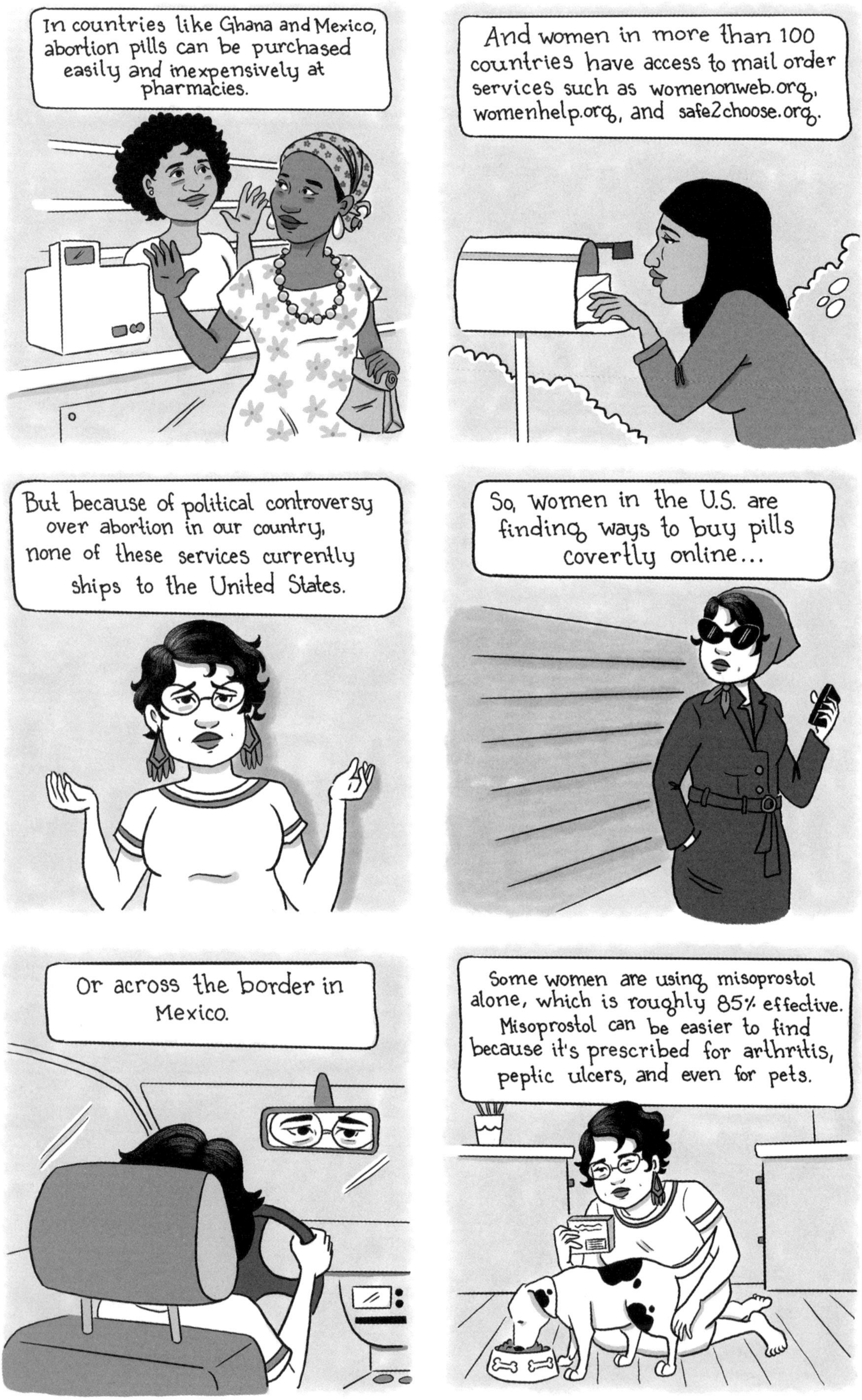
In countries like Ghana and Mexico, abortion pills can be purchased easily and inexpensively at pharmacies.
And women in more than 100 countries have access to mail order services such as womenonweb.org, womenhelp.org, and safe2choose.org.
But because of political controversy over abortion in our country, none of these services currently ships to the United States.
So, women in the U.S. are finding ways to buy pills covertly online...
Or across the border in Mexico.
Some women are using misoprostol alone, which is roughly 85% effective. Misoprostol can be easier to find because it's prescribed for arthritis, peptic ulcers, and even for pets.

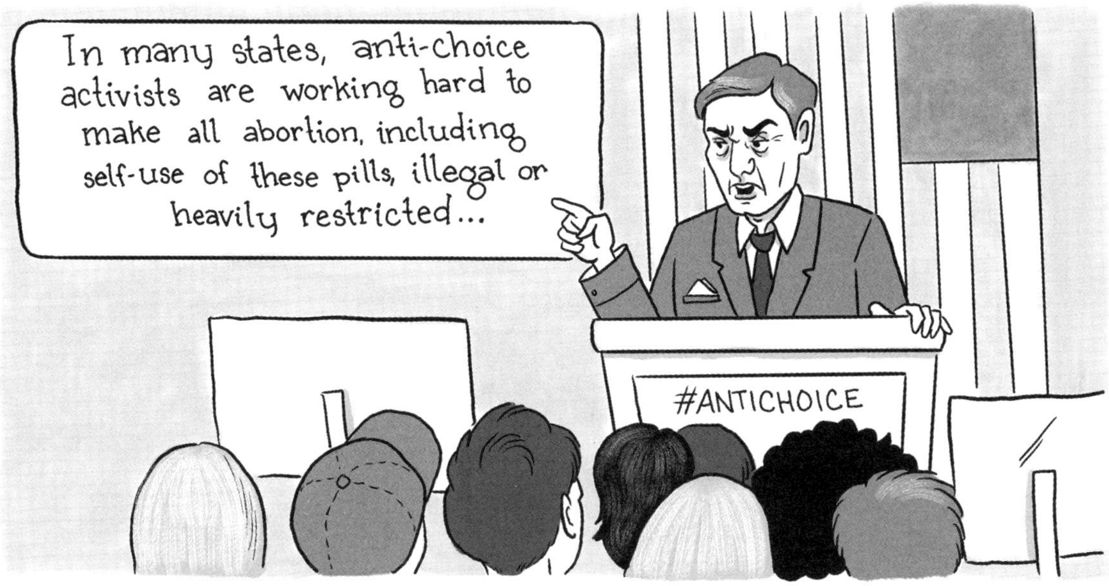
In many states, anti-choice activists are working hard to make all abortion, including self-use of these pills, illegal or heavily restricted...
#ANTICHOICE

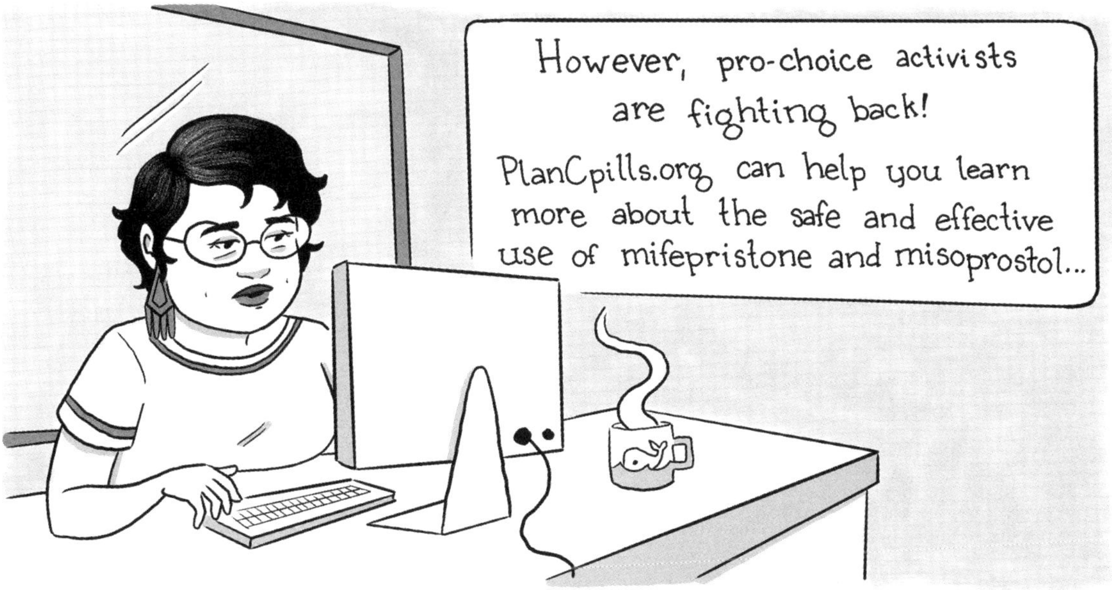
However, pro-choice activists are fighting back!
PlanCpills.org can help you learn more about the safe and effective use of mifepristone and misoprostol...

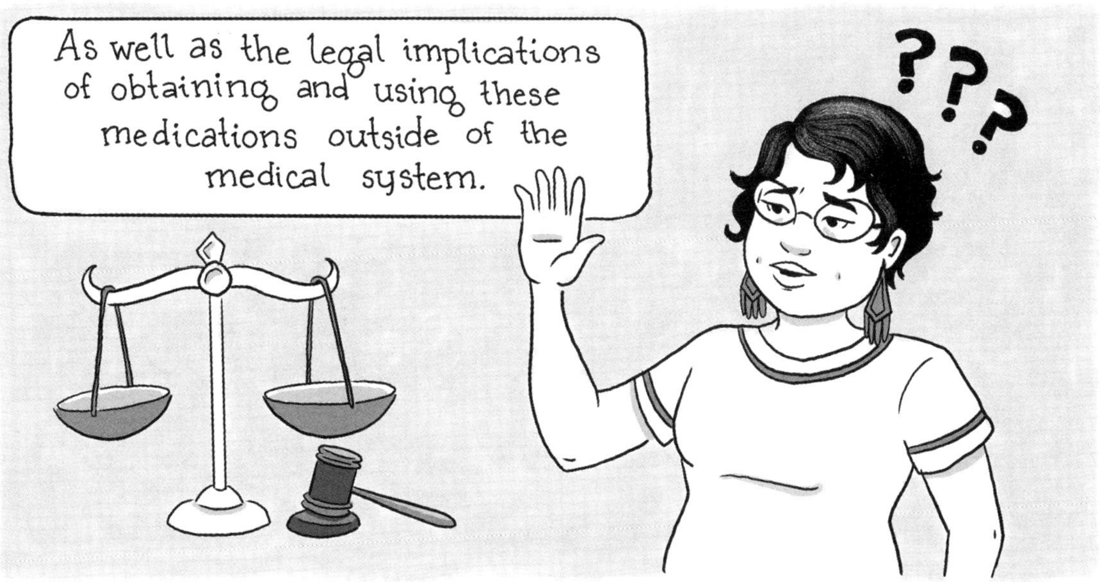
As well as the legal implications of obtaining and using these medications outside of the medical system.
???

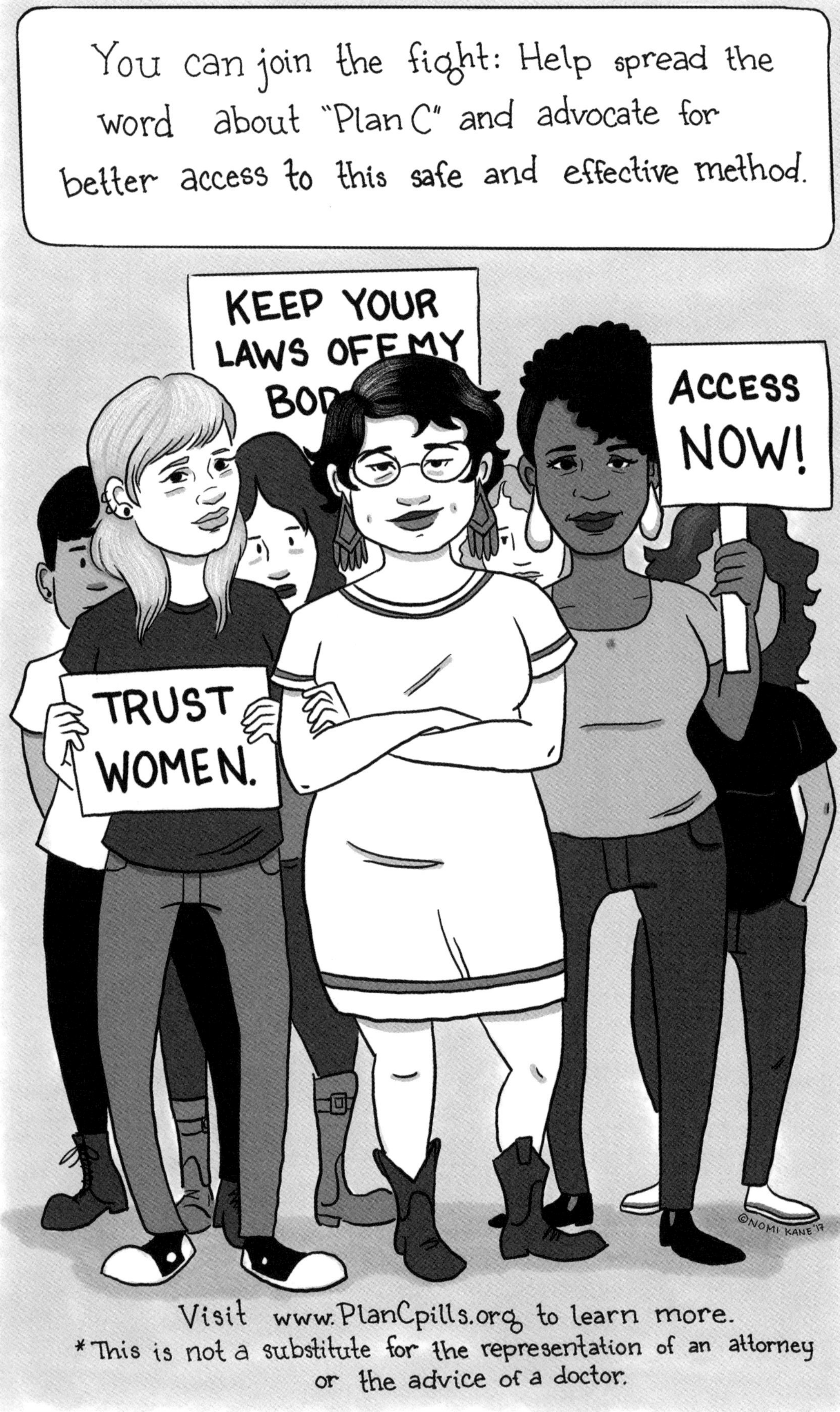
You can join the fight: Help spread the word about "Plan C" and advocate for better access to this safe and effective method.
KEEP YOUR LAWS OFF MY BOD
ACCESS NOW!
TRUST WOMEN.
©NOMI KANE '17

Visit www.PlanCpills.org to learn more.

*This is not a substitute for the representation of an attorney or the advice of a doctor.

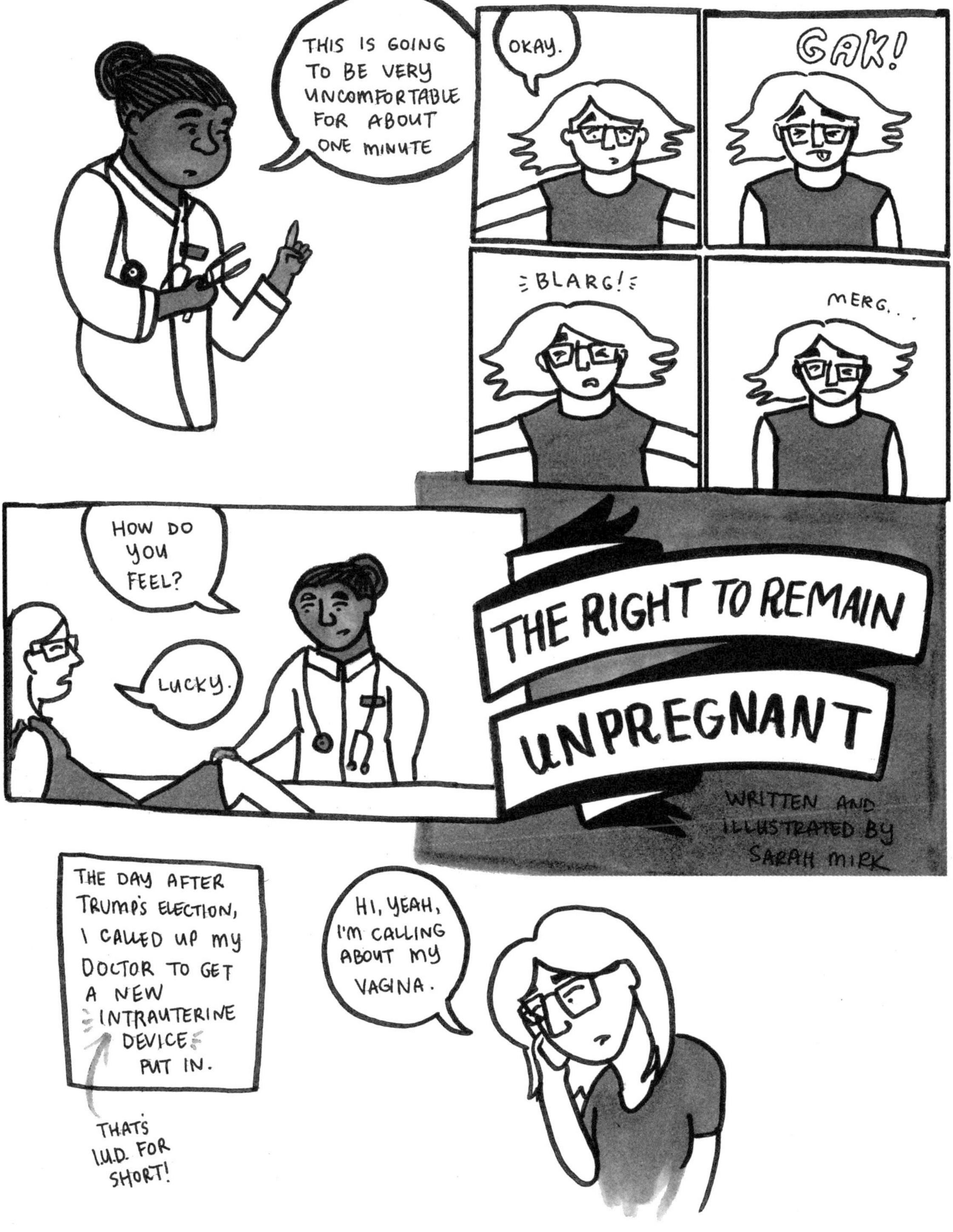
THIS IS GOING TO BE VERY UNCOMFORTABLE FOR ABOUT ONE MINUTE
OKAY.
GAK!
BLARG!
MERG...
HOW DO YOU FEEL?
LUCKY.
THE RIGHT TO REMAIN UNPREGNANT
WRITTEN AND ILLUSTRATED BY SARAH MIRK
THE DAY AFTER TRUMP'S ELECTION, I CALLED UP MY DOCTOR TO GET A NEW INTRAUTERINE DEVICE PUT IN.
THAT'S I.U.D. FOR SHORT!
HI, YEAH, I'M CALLING ABOUT MY VAGINA.

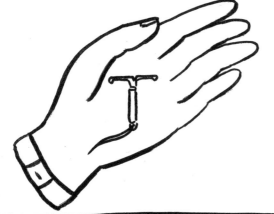

I WANT MY BIRTH CONTROL TO LAST FOR THE ENTIRE TRUMP ADMINISTRATION—
IF THEY REPEAL OBAMACARE, MY BIRTH CONTROL COVERAGE WILL DISAPPEAR.
IUDS LAST FIVE TO TEN YEARS— HOPEFULLY LONGER THAN THE PRESIDENT'S TERM.

I AM FAR FROM ALONE WITH THIS FEAR

IN THE MONTH AFTER THE ELECTION, SOME PLANNED PARENTHOODS SAW A 400% INCREASE IN IUD APPOINTMENTS

I'VE NEVER WANTED TO BE PREGNANT

BUT I'VE ONLY BEEN ABLE TO MAKE THAT CHOICE THANKS TO LUCK AND PRIVILEGE

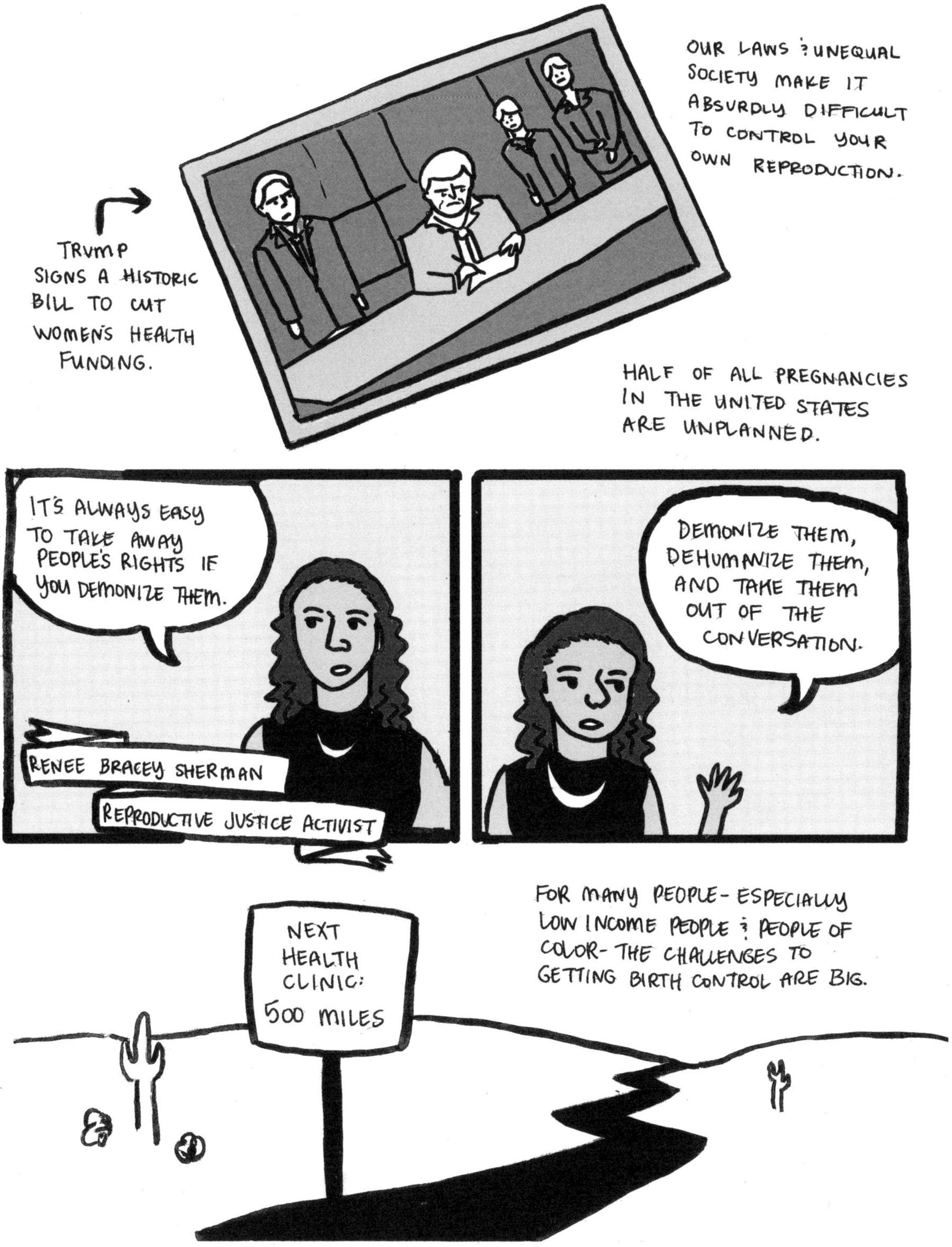
TRUMP SIGNS A HISTORIC BILL TO CUT WOMEN'S HEALTH FUNDING.
OUR LAWS & UNEQUAL SOCIETY MAKE IT ABSURDLY DIFFICULT TO CONTROL YOUR OWN REPRODUCTION.
HALF OF ALL PREGNANCIES IN THE UNITED STATES ARE UNPLANNED.
IT'S ALWAYS EASY TO TAKE AWAY PEOPLE'S RIGHTS IF YOU DEMONIZE THEM.
RENEE BRACEY SHERMAN
REPRODUCTIVE JUSTICE ACTIVIST
DEMONIZE THEM, DEHUMANIZE THEM, AND TAKE THEM OUT OF THE CONVERSATION.
NEXT HEALTH CLINIC: 500 MILES
FOR MANY PEOPLE- ESPECIALLY LOW INCOME PEOPLE & PEOPLE OF COLOR- THE CHALLENGES TO GETTING BIRTH CONTROL ARE BIG.

WITHOUT INSURANCE, GETTING AN IUD COSTS AN AVERAGE OF $1,600.

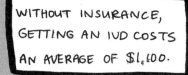

I THINK INVESTING IN FAMILY PLANNING IS THE SMARTEST INVESTMENT THE FEDERAL GOVERNMENT CAN MAKE.

CECILE RICHARDS
PRESIDENT OF THE PLANNED PARENTHOOD FEDERATION OF AMERICA

"I THINK THEY SHOULD BE JUST DROPPING IT OUT OF AIRPLANES AND IT SHOULD BE FREE FOR EVERY WOMAN."

IN 2009, COLORADO STARTED AN EXPERIMENT.

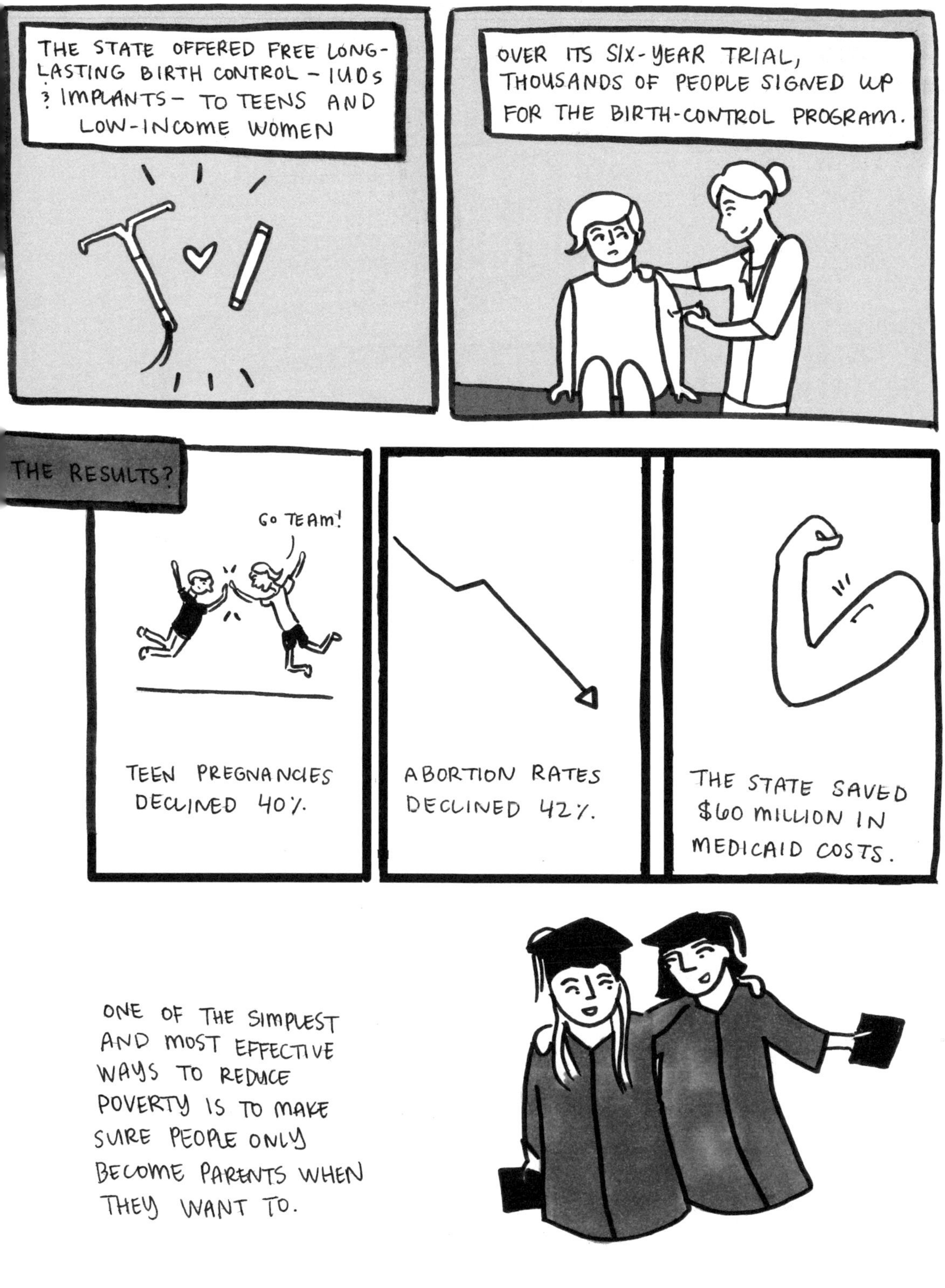
THE STATE OFFERED FREE LONG-LASTING BIRTH CONTROL – IUDS & IMPLANTS – TO TEENS AND LOW-INCOME WOMEN
OVER ITS SIX-YEAR TRIAL, THOUSANDS OF PEOPLE SIGNED UP FOR THE BIRTH-CONTROL PROGRAM.
THE RESULTS?
GO TEAM!
TEEN PREGNANCIES DECLINED 40%.
ABORTION RATES DECLINED 42%.
THE STATE SAVED $60 MILLION IN MEDICAID COSTS.
ONE OF THE SIMPLEST AND MOST EFFECTIVE WAYS TO REDUCE POVERTY IS TO MAKE SURE PEOPLE ONLY BECOME PARENTS WHEN THEY WANT TO.

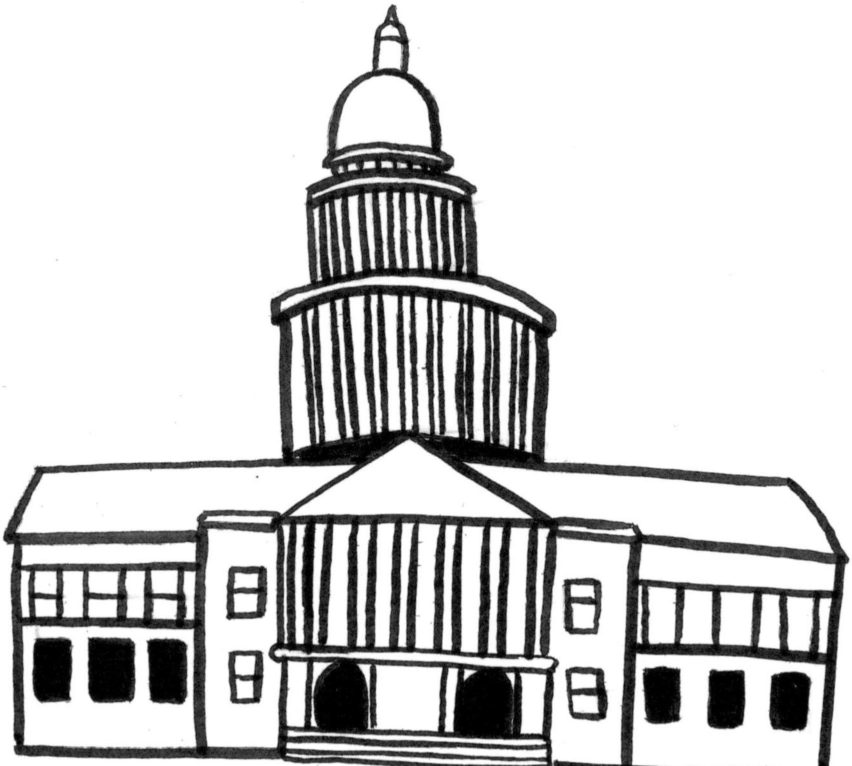

THEN IN 2015, REPUBLICANS IN THE STATE LEGISLATURE REFUSED TO FUND THE PROGRAM.

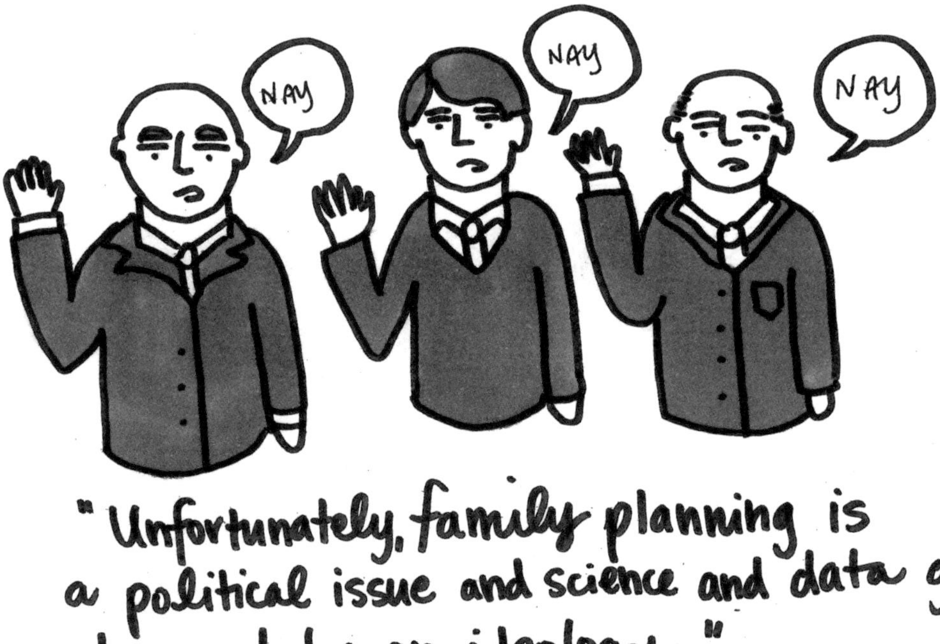
NAY
NAY
NAY

"Unfortunately, family planning is a political issue and science and data gets trumped by an ideology."

—GRETA KLINGLER, COLORADO DEPT. OF PUBLIC HEALTH

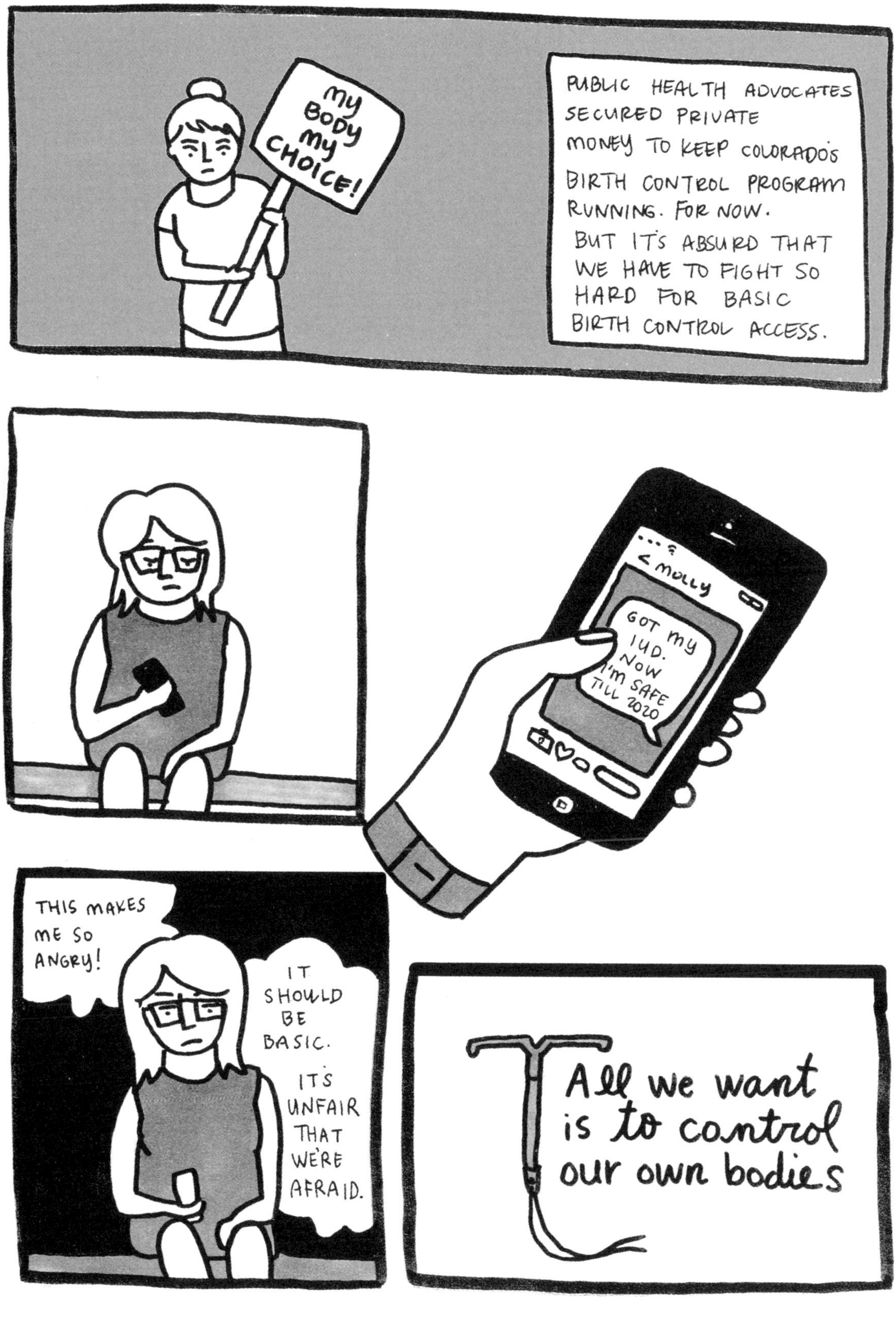

MY BODY MY CHOICE!
PUBLIC HEALTH ADVOCATES SECURED PRIVATE MONEY TO KEEP COLORADO'S BIRTH CONTROL PROGRAM RUNNING. FOR NOW.
BUT IT'S ABSURD THAT WE HAVE TO FIGHT SO HARD FOR BASIC BIRTH CONTROL ACCESS.
< MOLLY
GOT MY IUD. NOW I'M SAFE TILL 2020
THIS MAKES ME SO ANGRY!
IT SHOULD BE BASIC.
IT'S UNFAIR THAT WE'RE AFRAID.
All we want is to control our own bodies

"OCTOBER"

by kris louis

it was october 2012 when i found out that i was pregnant.

my boyfriend and i went to a convention, and the whole weekend i expected to get my period, but it never came.

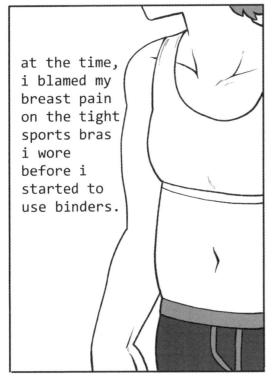

at the time, i blamed my breast pain on the tight sports bras i wore before i started to use binders.

but...

but i'm on the pill...

you never think it can happen to you.

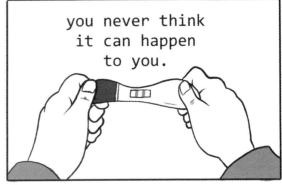

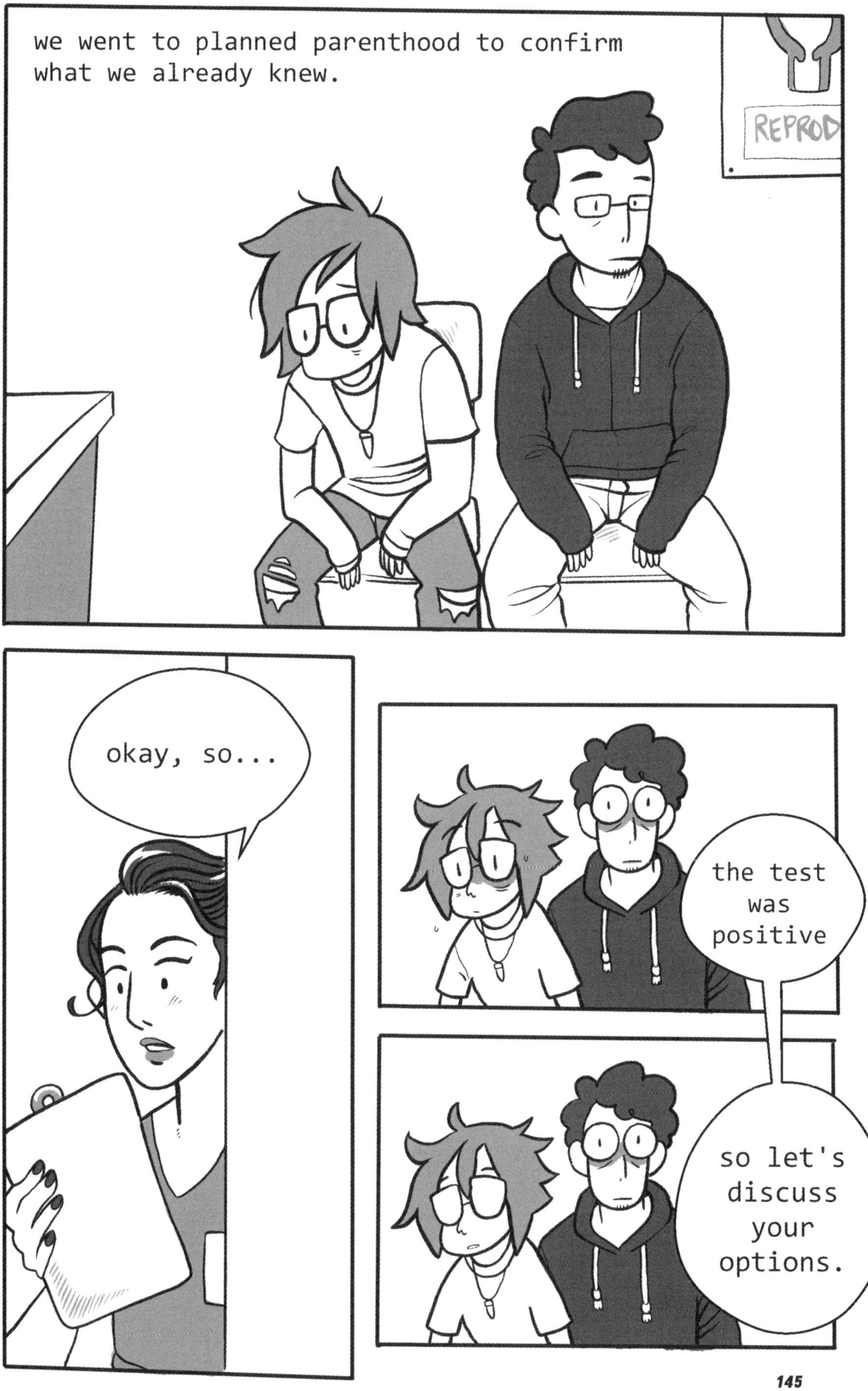
we went to planned parenthood to confirm what we already knew.
REPROD
okay, so...
the test was positive
so let's discuss your options.

HA! HAHA-

i'm getting an abortion. so tell me what i need to do next

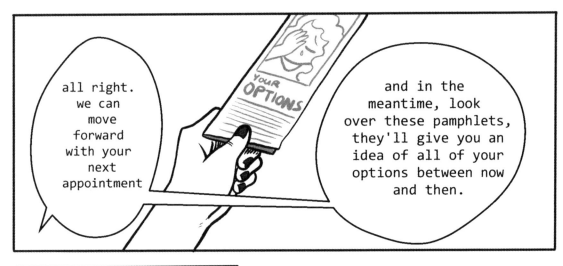

all right. we can move forward with your next appointment

YOUR OPTIONS

and in the meantime, look over these pamphlets, they'll give you an idea of all of your options between now and then.

thank you

i couldn't even consider a future where i had any other options.

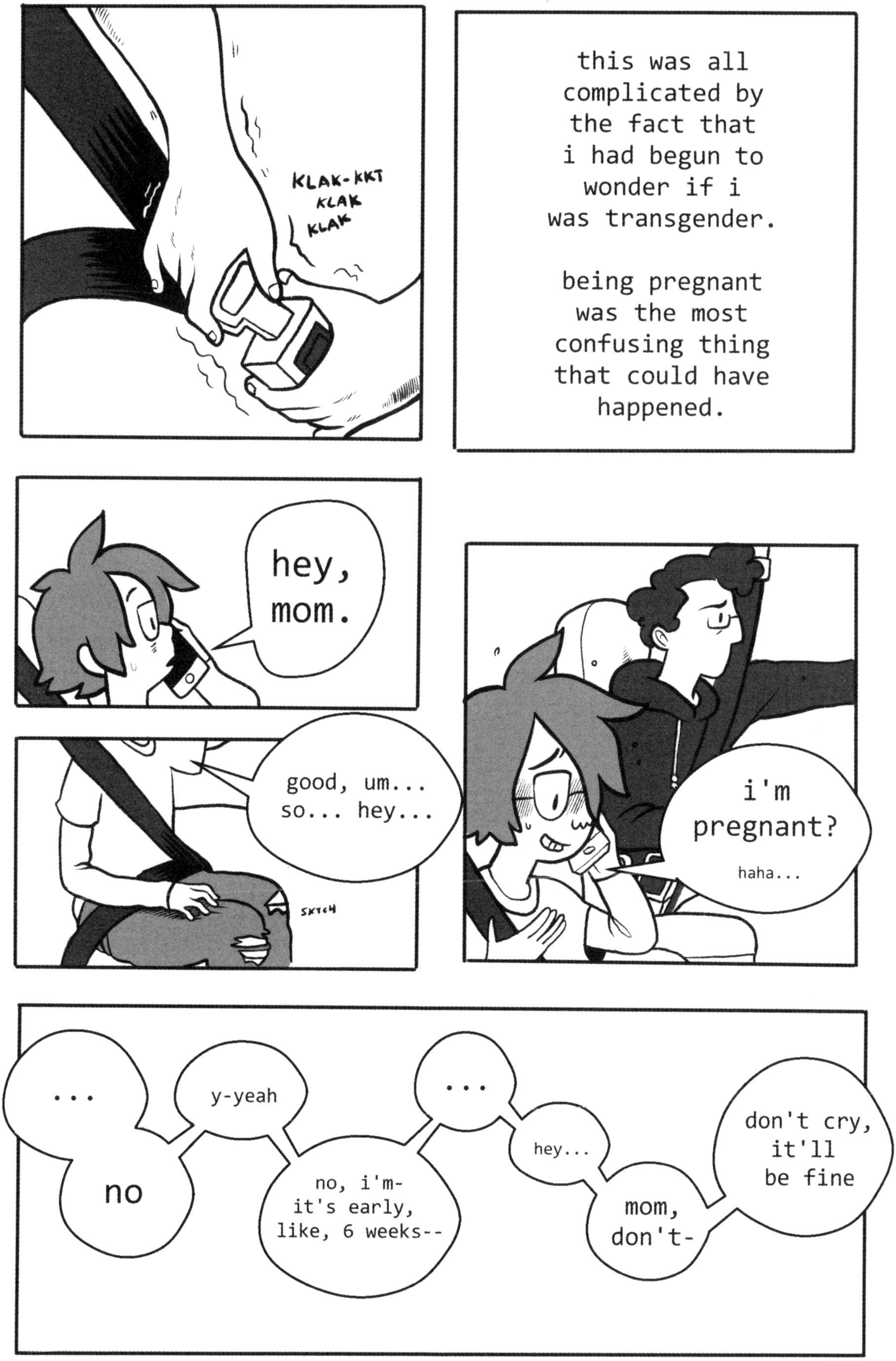
KLAK-KKT
KLAK
KLAK
this was all complicated by the fact that i had begun to wonder if i was transgender.
being pregnant was the most confusing thing that could have happened.
hey, mom.
good, um... so... hey...
SKTCH
i'm pregnant?
haha...
...
no
y-yeah
no, i'm- it's early, like, 6 weeks--
...
hey...
mom, don't-
don't cry, it'll be fine

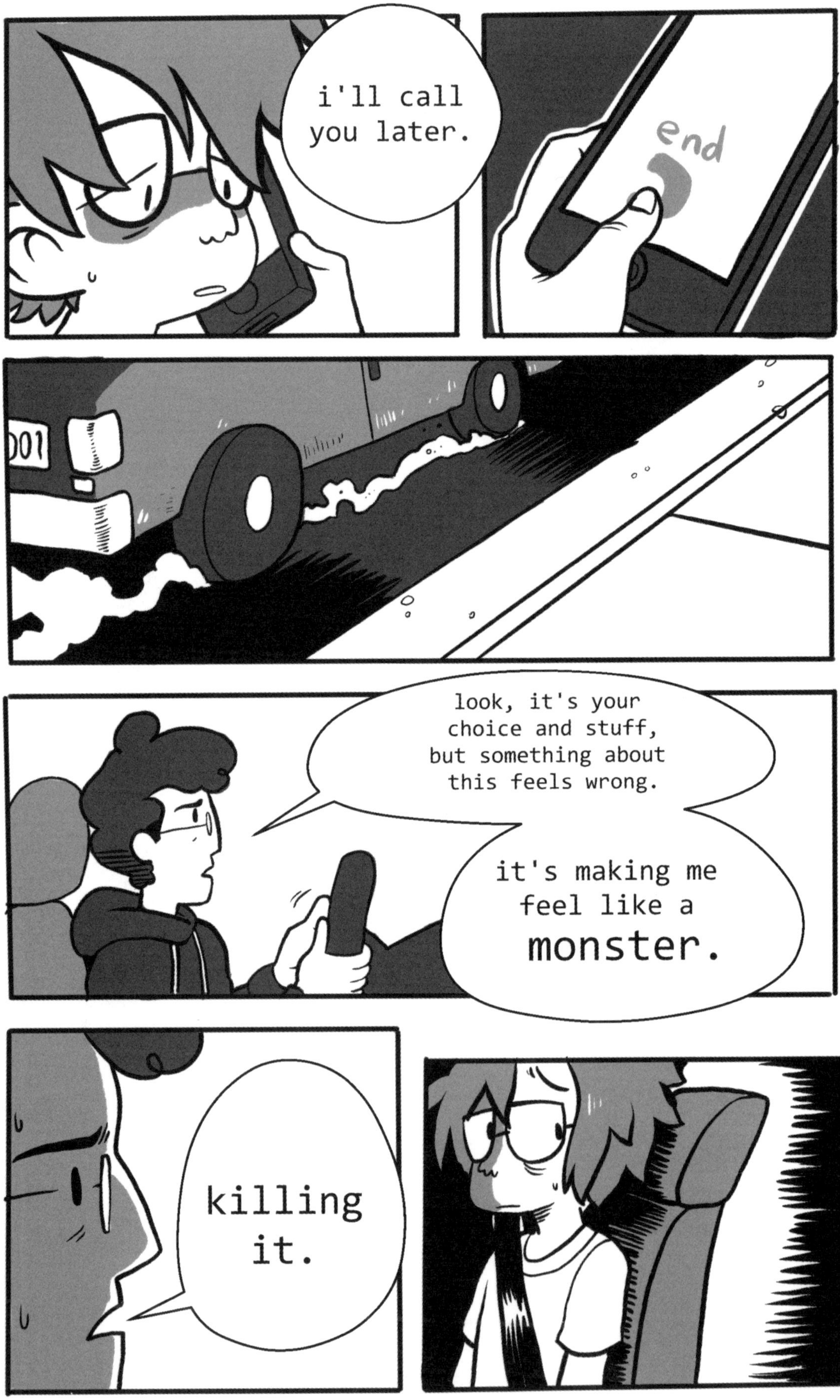
i'll call you later.
end
001
look, it's your choice and stuff, but something about this feels wrong.
it's making me feel like a monster.
killing it.

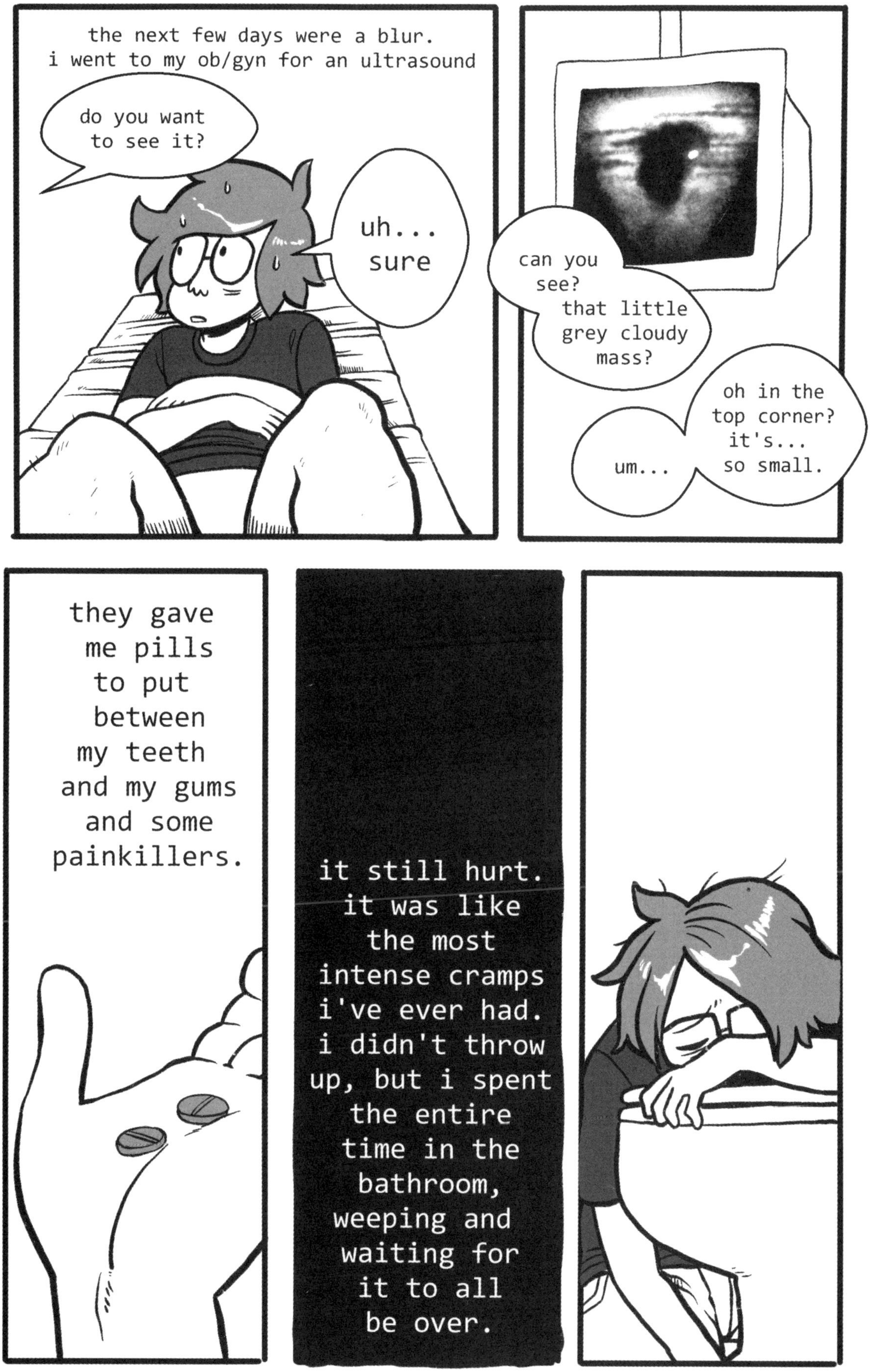
the next few days were a blur.
i went to my ob/gyn for an ultrasound
do you want to see it?
uh... sure
can you see?
that little grey cloudy mass?
oh in the top corner? it's... so small.
um...
they gave me pills to put between my teeth and my gums and some painkillers.
it still hurt. it was like the most intense cramps i've ever had. i didn't throw up, but i spent the entire time in the bathroom, weeping and waiting for it to all be over.

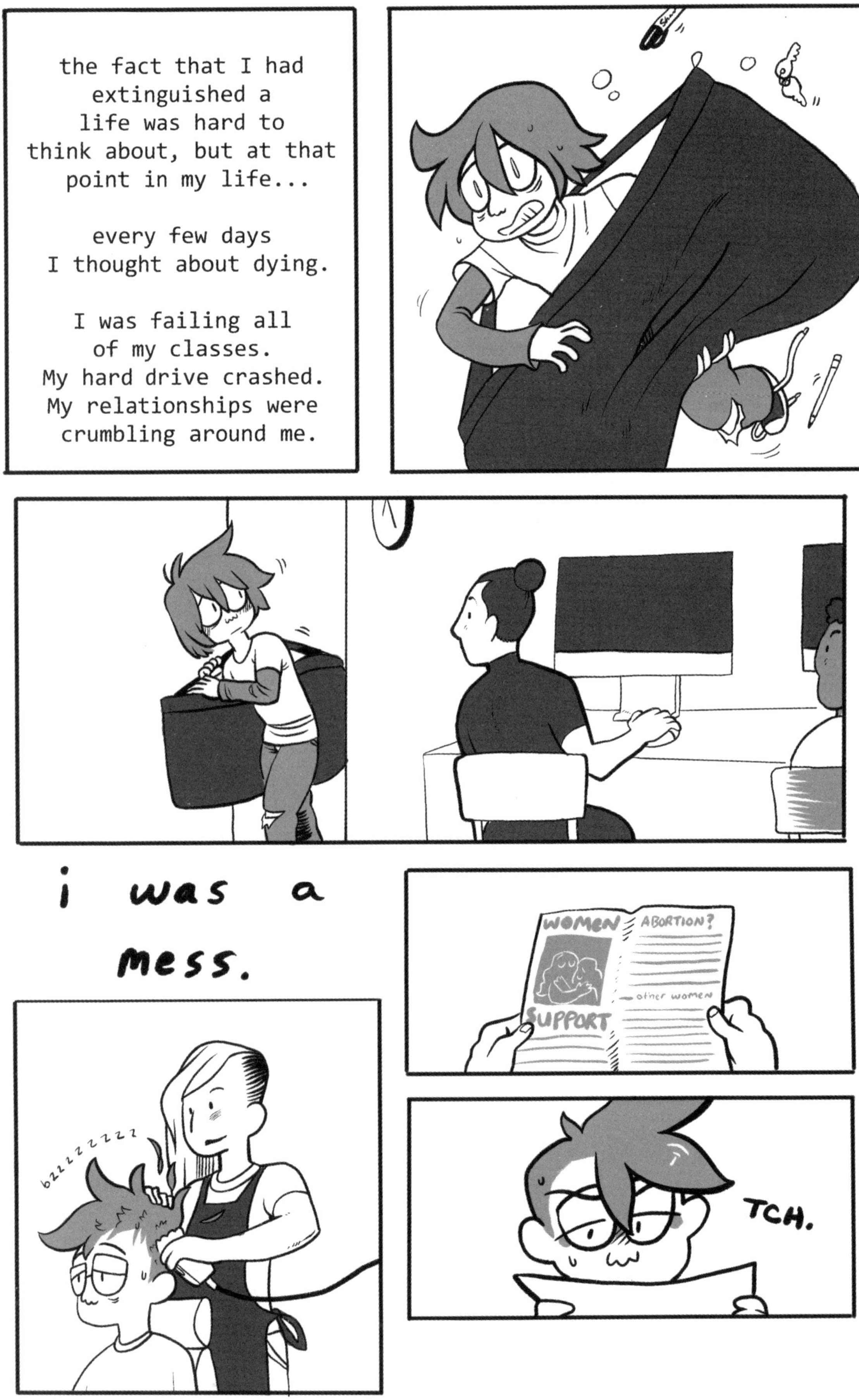
the fact that I had extinguished a life was hard to think about, but at that point in my life...
every few days I thought about dying.
I was failing all of my classes. My hard drive crashed. My relationships were crumbling around me.
i was a mess.
bzzzzzzzz
WOMEN
ABORTION?
other women
SUPPORT
TCH.

i don't want to sugarcoat it.
getting an abortion was one of
the hardest, loneliest
things i've ever done.
to pretend that it was easy or
convenient would be
a disservice to me
and others like me.

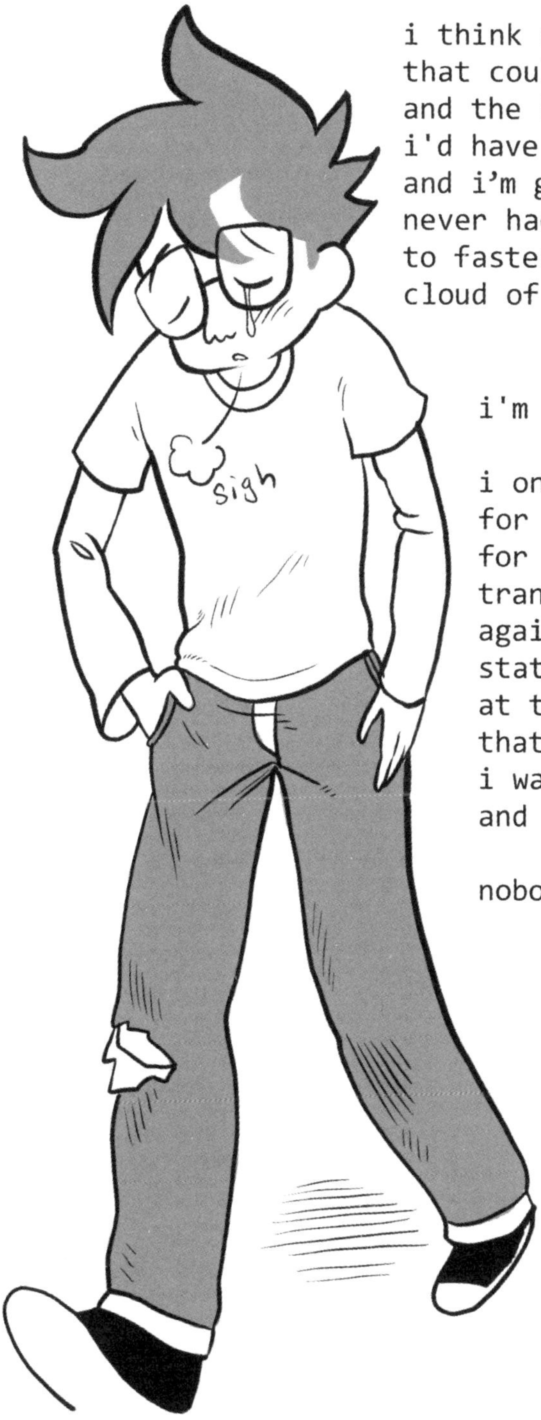
sigh

i think about the child
that could have been,
and the kind of life
i'd have given,
and i'm glad that their spirit
never had a chance
to fasten to that tiny
cloud of cells I couldn't quite see.

i'm glad i had the choice.

i only wish i wasn't so alone
for it all. there was no precedent
for me to draw on: as a young, confused
trans person, my own body had turned
against me. dysphoria was an under-
statement, i felt like an alien
at the whim of organs and blood
that had pinned me inside of them.
i was trapped under a wave of fate,
and when i chose to change it,

nobody was there to say

"it's ok."

"i see you."

"you're not alone."

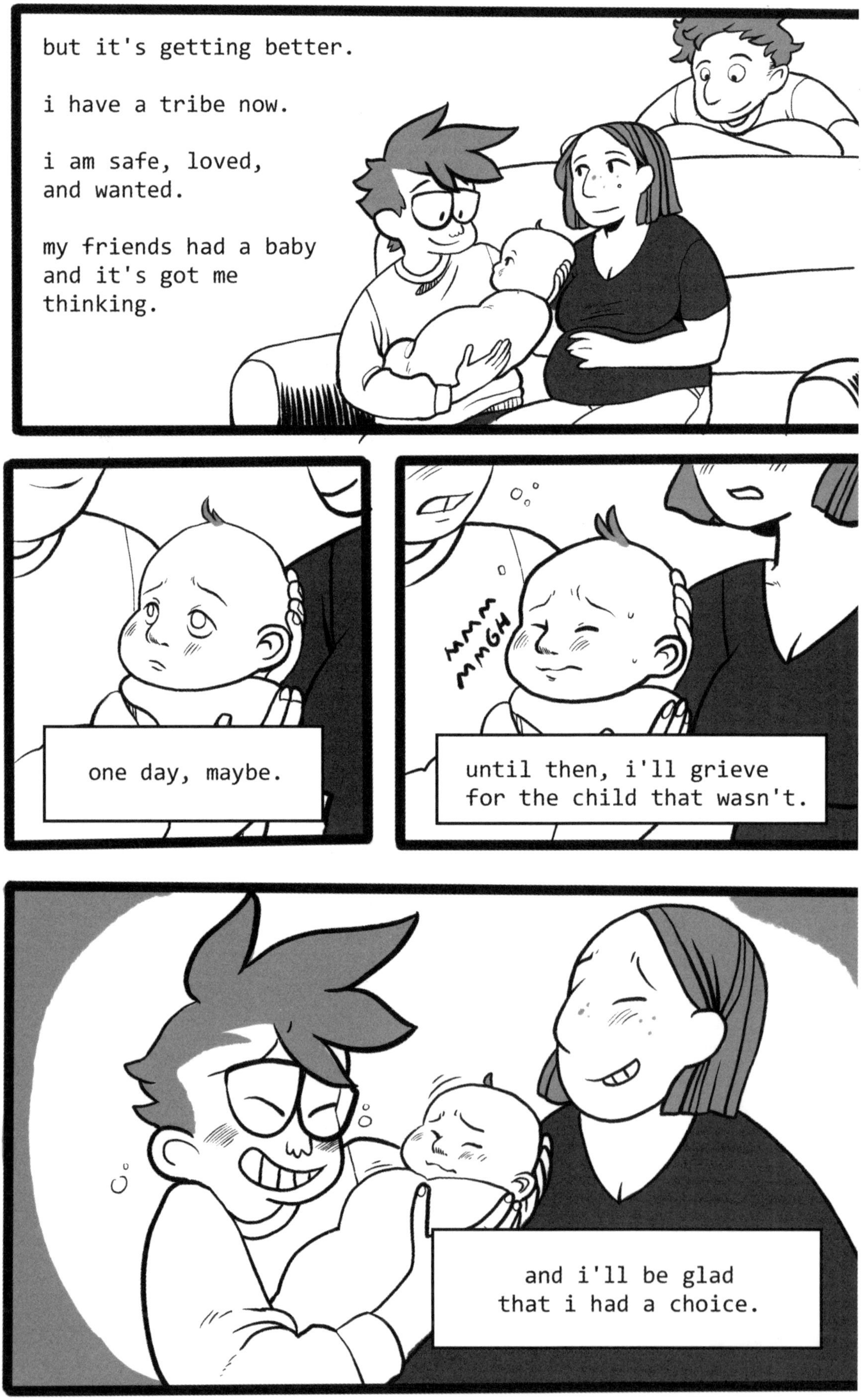
but it's getting better.
i have a tribe now.
i am safe, loved, and wanted.
my friends had a baby and it's got me thinking.
one day, maybe.
MMM MMGH
until then, i'll grieve for the child that wasn't.
and i'll be glad that i had a choice.

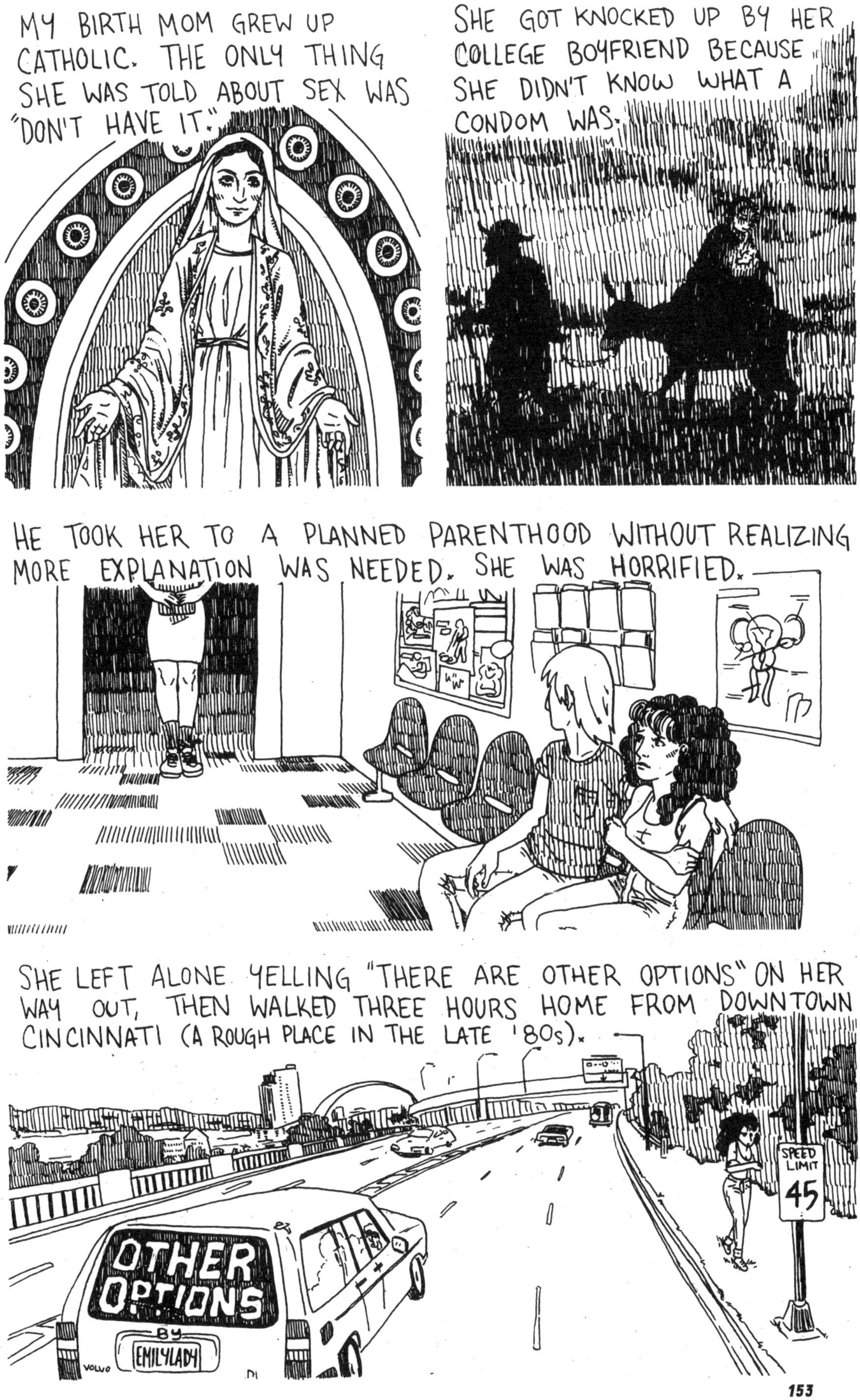
MY BIRTH MOM GREW UP CATHOLIC. THE ONLY THING SHE WAS TOLD ABOUT SEX WAS "DON'T HAVE IT."
SHE GOT KNOCKED UP BY HER COLLEGE BOYFRIEND BECAUSE SHE DIDN'T KNOW WHAT A CONDOM WAS.
HE TOOK HER TO A PLANNED PARENTHOOD WITHOUT REALIZING MORE EXPLANATION WAS NEEDED. SHE WAS HORRIFIED.
SHE LEFT ALONE YELLING "THERE ARE OTHER OPTIONS" ON HER WAY OUT, THEN WALKED THREE HOURS HOME FROM DOWNTOWN CINCINNATI (A ROUGH PLACE IN THE LATE '80s).
SPEED LIMIT 45
OTHER OPTIONS
BY
EMILYLADY
VOLVO

GROWING UP AS AN ADOPTED CHILD I HAD AN ACCUTE KNOWLEDGE THAT I HAD NEARLY BEEN ABORTED, AND IT GAVE ME AN UNEASY CLOSENESS TO THE SUBJECT.

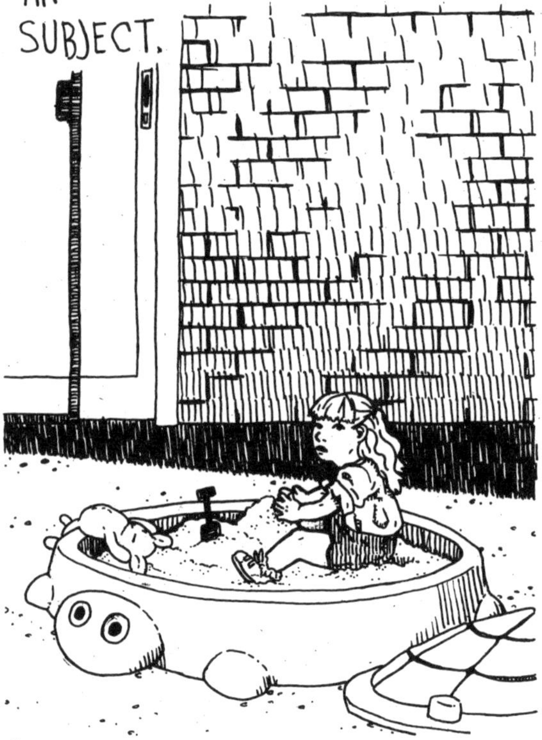

I WAS NEVER REALLY ANTI-CHOICE, BUT I DEFINITELY DIDN'T LIKE THE IDEA OF ABORTION.

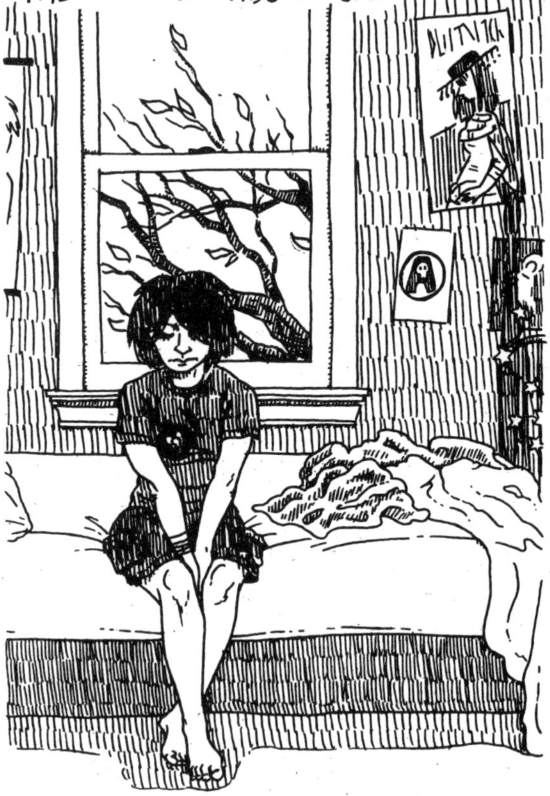

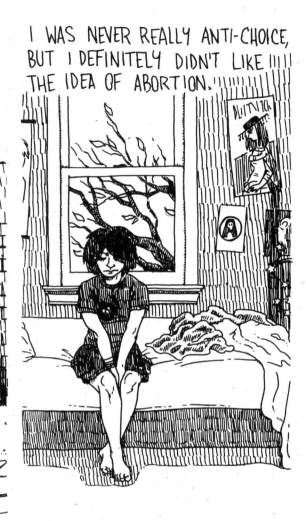

I HAD A PREGNANCY SCARE IN HIGH SCHOOL, AND MY MOM TOLD ME WE WERE GOING TO PLANNED PARENTHOOD FOR AN ABORTION, AND THAT I DIDN'T HAVE A CHOICE.

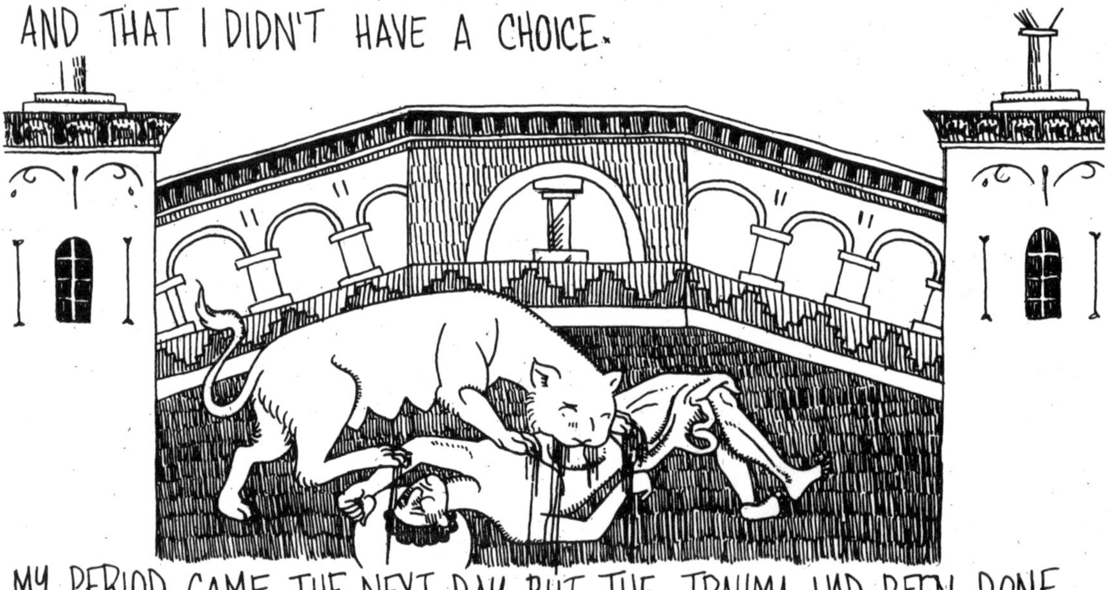

MY PERIOD CAME THE NEXT DAY, BUT THE TRAUMA HAD BEEN DONE.

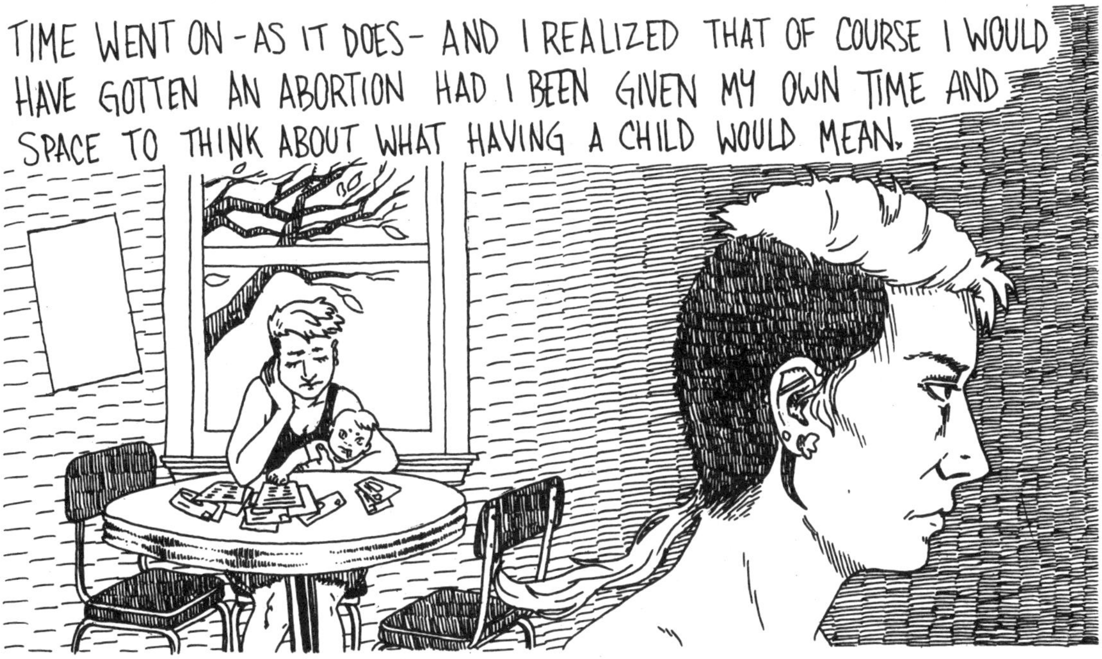
TIME WENT ON - AS IT DOES - AND I REALIZED THAT OF COURSE I WOULD HAVE GOTTEN AN ABORTION HAD I BEEN GIVEN MY OWN TIME AND SPACE TO THINK ABOUT WHAT HAVING A CHILD WOULD MEAN.

THIS WAS REINFORCED WHEN I MET MY BIRTH MOM AT EIGHTEEN. PEOPLE TALK ABOUT HOW AN ABORTION AFFECTS YOU, BUT HAVING TO GIVE UP A CHILD STATISTICALLY HAS MUCH LONGER-LASTING PSYCHOLOGICAL RAMIFICATIONS.

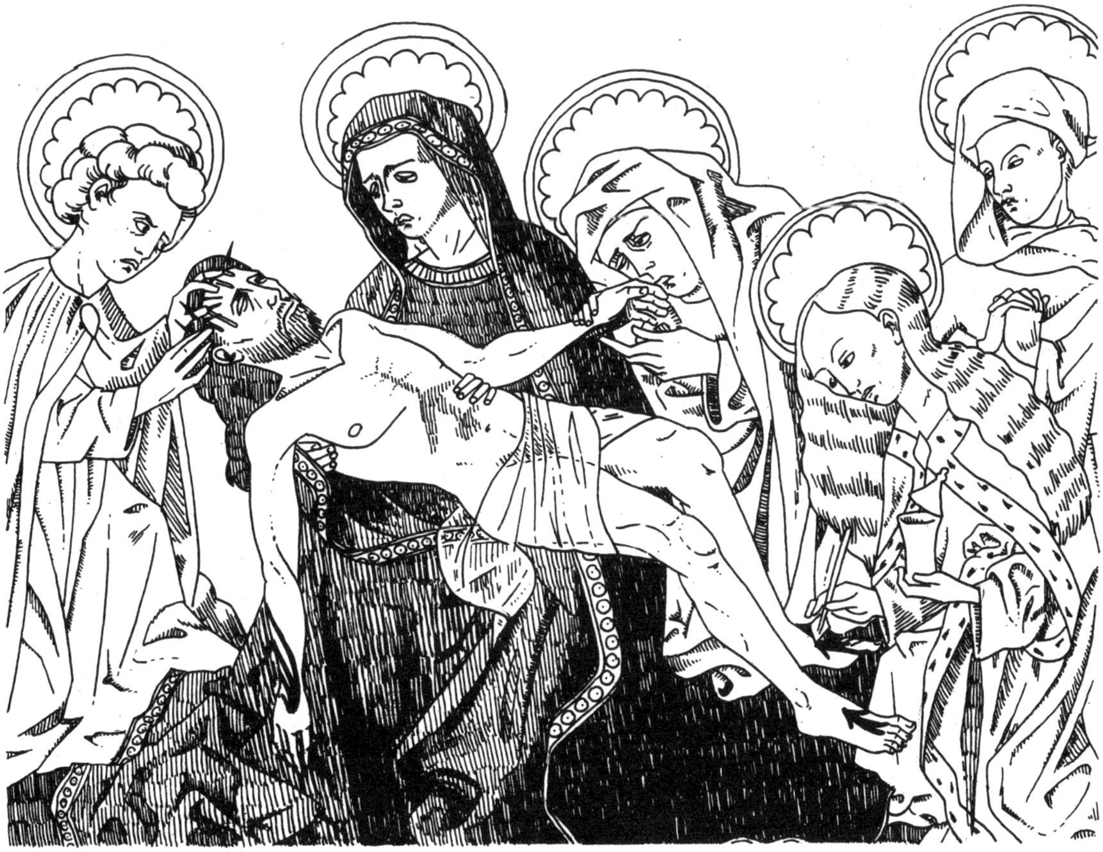

TODAY I'M A GENDERQUEER INDIVIDUAL WITH NO DESIRE FOR CHILDREN OF MY OWN, AND A STRONG BELIEF THAT PEOPLE SHOULD BE ALLOWED TO DECIDE WHAT SHAPE THEIR LIFE WILL TAKE. MAYBE I'LL EVEN DONATE MY EGGS TO A FRIEND WHO NEEDS THEM MORE THAN I DO.

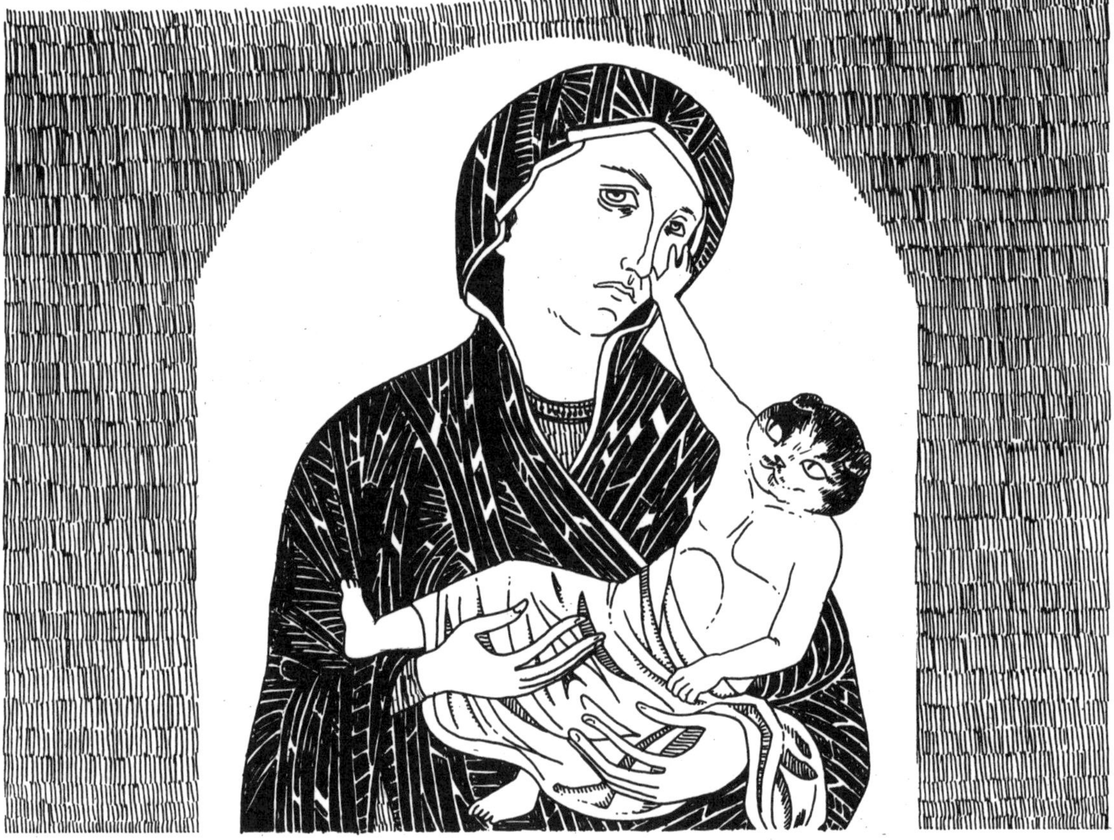

WE FORGET JUST HOW MANY OPTIONS THERE ARE.

EVERY ONE OF THEM IS VALID.

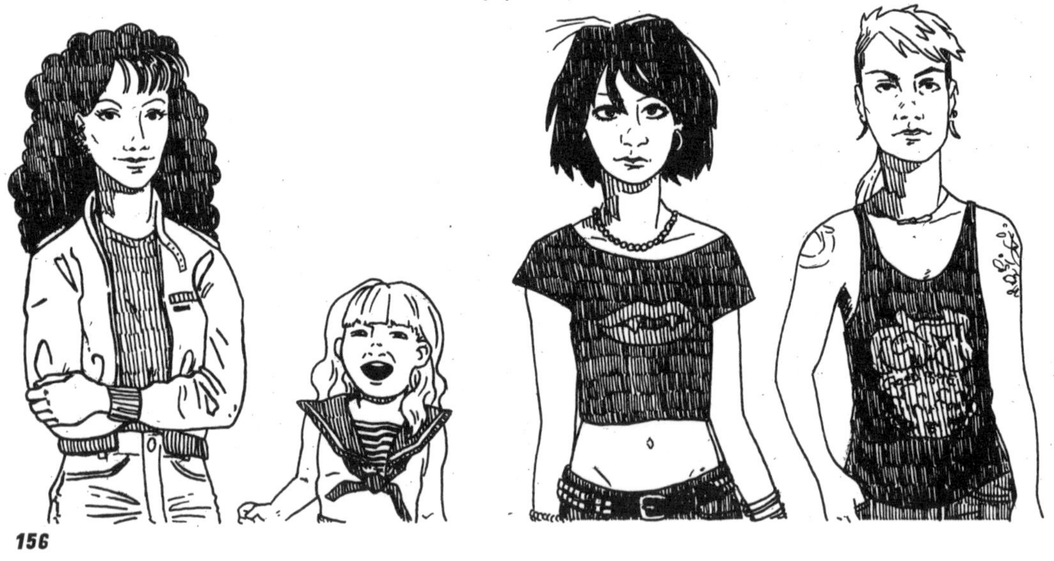

MY NAME IS SAGE COFFEY AND I HAD AN ABORTION.

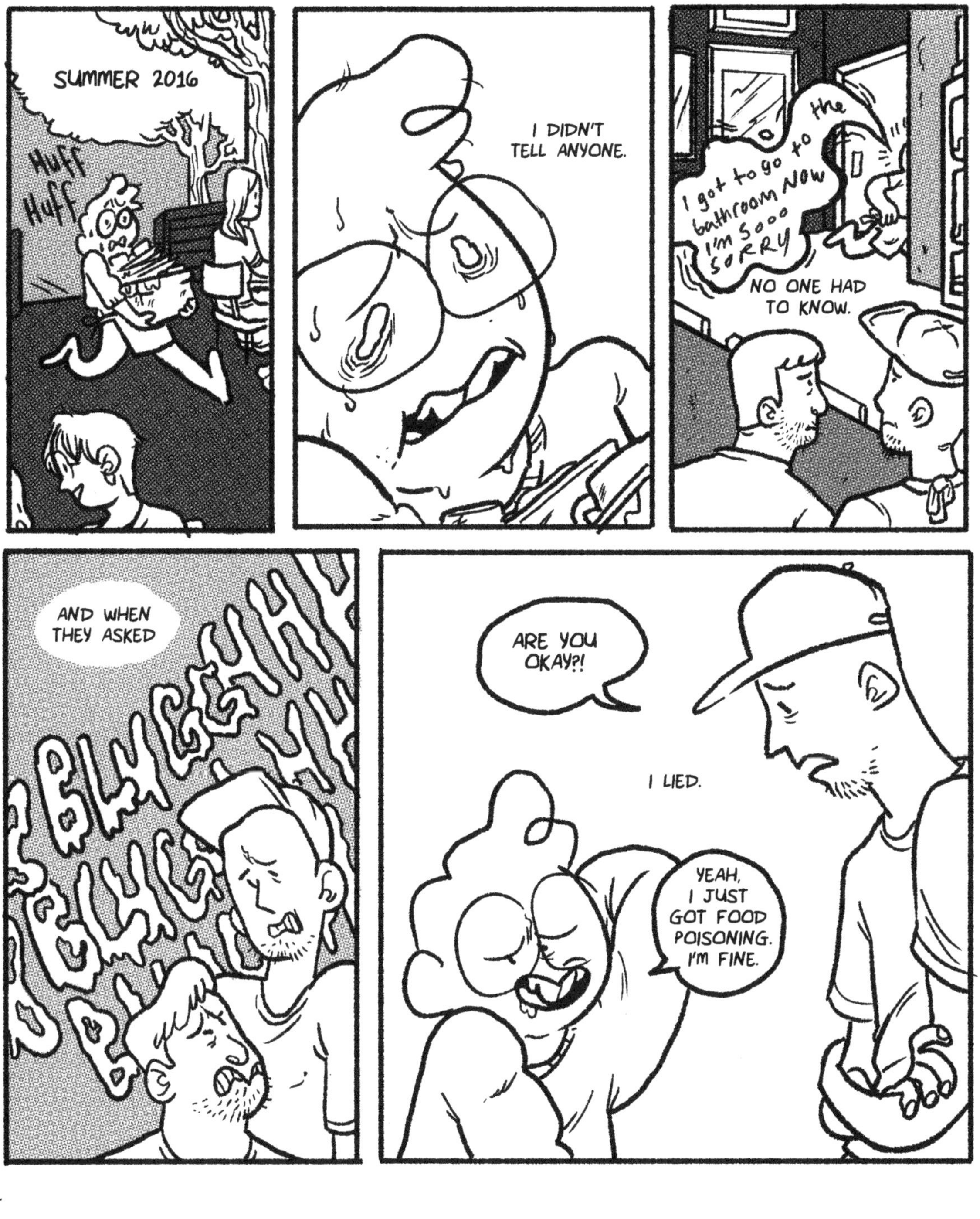
SUMMER 2016
Huff Huff
I DIDN'T TELL ANYONE.
I got to go to the bathroom NOW I'm Sooo SORRY
NO ONE HAD TO KNOW.
AND WHEN THEY ASKED
ARE YOU OKAY?!
I LIED.
YEAH, I JUST GOT FOOD POISONING. I'M FINE.

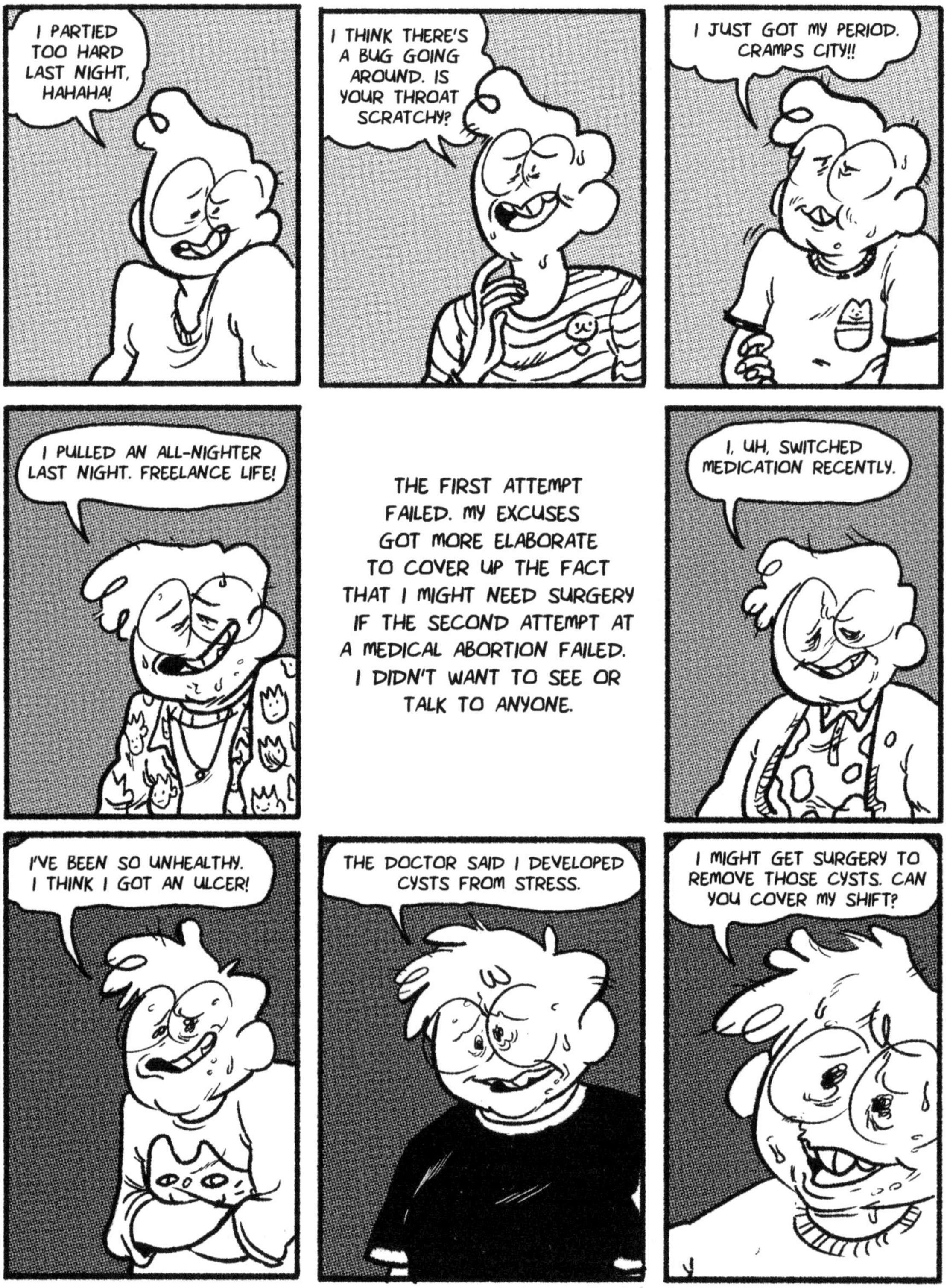
I PARTIED TOO HARD LAST NIGHT, HAHAHA!
I THINK THERE'S A BUG GOING AROUND. IS YOUR THROAT SCRATCHY?
I JUST GOT MY PERIOD. CRAMPS CITY!!
I PULLED AN ALL-NIGHTER LAST NIGHT. FREELANCE LIFE!
THE FIRST ATTEMPT FAILED. MY EXCUSES GOT MORE ELABORATE TO COVER UP THE FACT THAT I MIGHT NEED SURGERY IF THE SECOND ATTEMPT AT A MEDICAL ABORTION FAILED. I DIDN'T WANT TO SEE OR TALK TO ANYONE.
I, UH, SWITCHED MEDICATION RECENTLY.
I'VE BEEN SO UNHEALTHY. I THINK I GOT AN ULCER!
THE DOCTOR SAID I DEVELOPED CYSTS FROM STRESS.
I MIGHT GET SURGERY TO REMOVE THOSE CYSTS. CAN YOU COVER MY SHIFT?

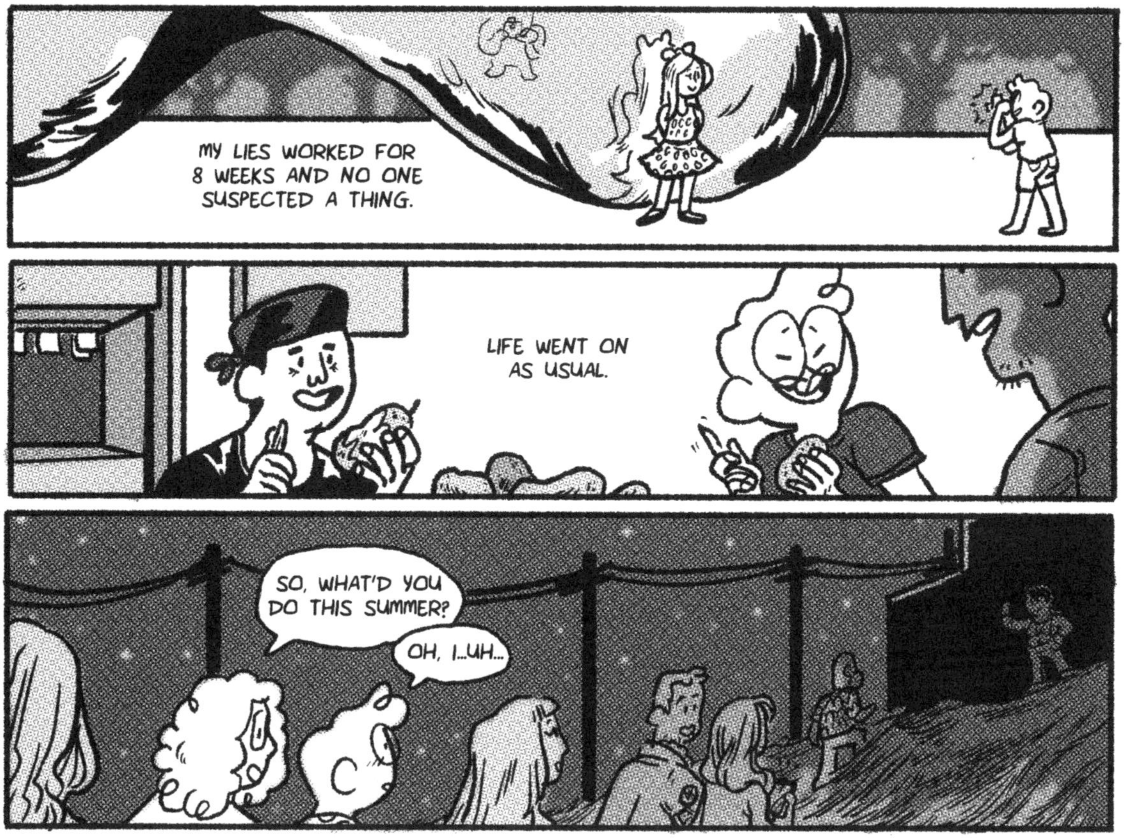
MY LIES WORKED FOR
8 WEEKS AND NO ONE
SUSPECTED A THING.
LIFE WENT ON
AS USUAL.
SO, WHAT'D YOU
DO THIS SUMMER?
OH, I...UH...

IF I HAD JUST TOLD SOMEONE

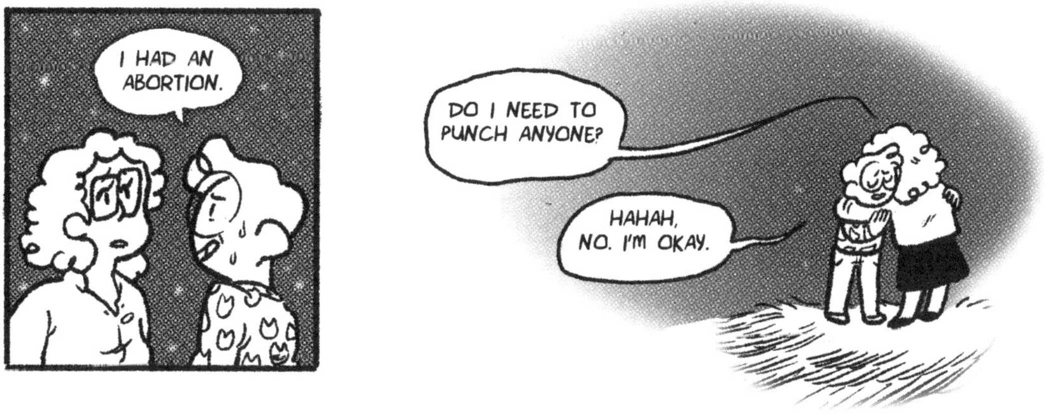
I HAD AN
ABORTION.
DO I NEED TO
PUNCH ANYONE?
HAHAH,
NO. I'M OKAY.

I WOULD'VE GOTTEN THE SUPPORT I DESPERATELY NEEDED.

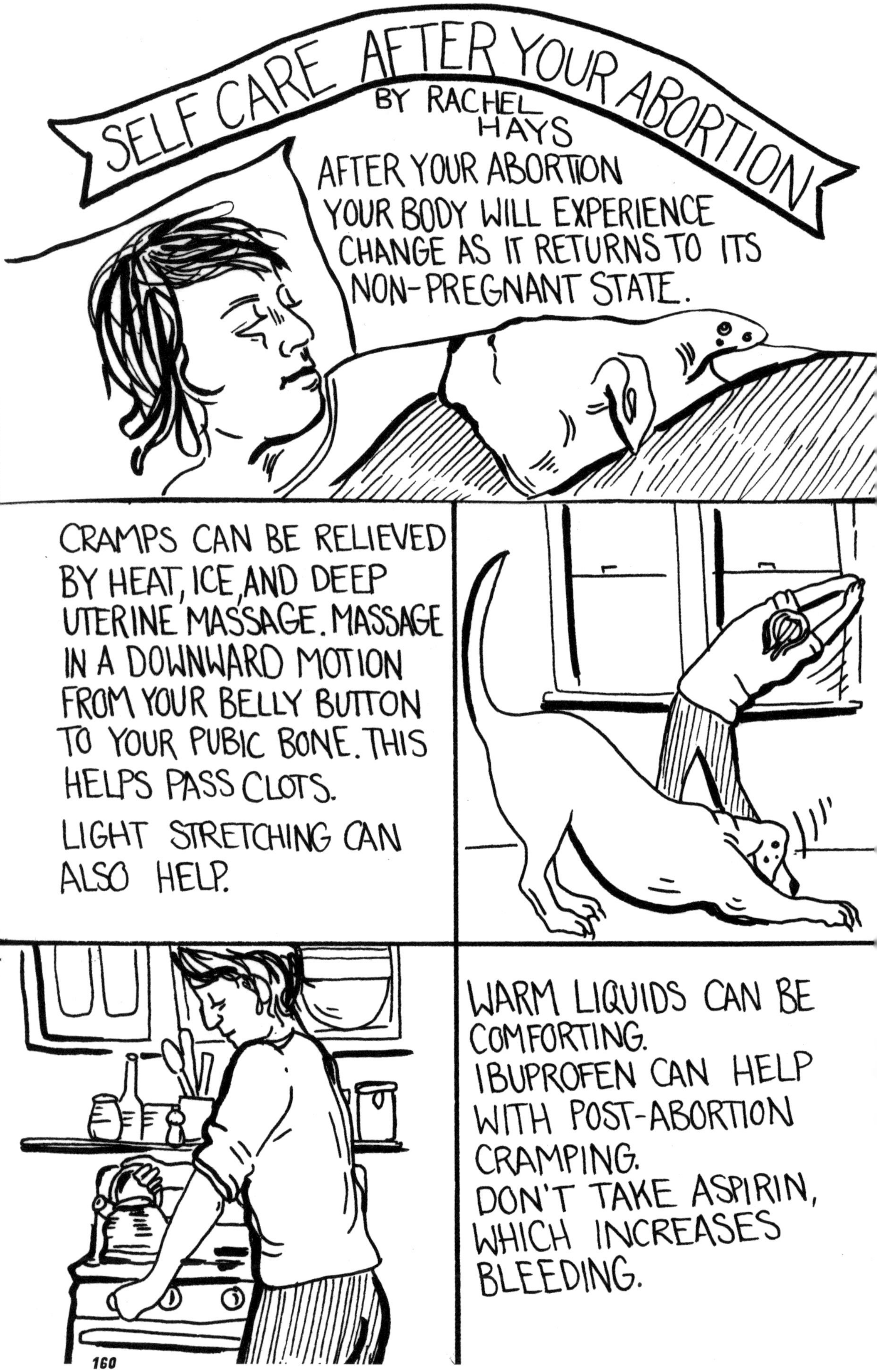
SELF CARE AFTER YOUR ABORTION
BY RACHEL HAYS
AFTER YOUR ABORTION YOUR BODY WILL EXPERIENCE CHANGE AS IT RETURNS TO ITS NON-PREGNANT STATE.
CRAMPS CAN BE RELIEVED BY HEAT, ICE, AND DEEP UTERINE MASSAGE. MASSAGE IN A DOWNWARD MOTION FROM YOUR BELLY BUTTON TO YOUR PUBIC BONE. THIS HELPS PASS CLOTS.
LIGHT STRETCHING CAN ALSO HELP.
WARM LIQUIDS CAN BE COMFORTING.
IBUPROFEN CAN HELP WITH POST-ABORTION CRAMPING.
DON'T TAKE ASPIRIN, WHICH INCREASES BLEEDING.

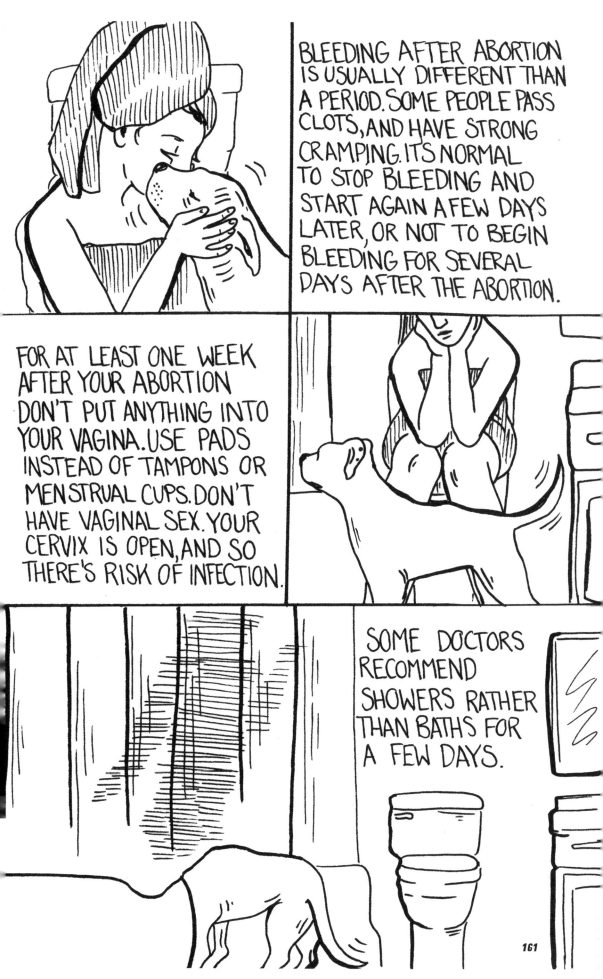

BLEEDING AFTER ABORTION IS USUALLY DIFFERENT THAN A PERIOD. SOME PEOPLE PASS CLOTS, AND HAVE STRONG CRAMPING. ITS NORMAL TO STOP BLEEDING AND START AGAIN A FEW DAYS LATER, OR NOT TO BEGIN BLEEDING FOR SEVERAL DAYS AFTER THE ABORTION.

FOR AT LEAST ONE WEEK AFTER YOUR ABORTION DON'T PUT ANYTHING INTO YOUR VAGINA. USE PADS INSTEAD OF TAMPONS OR MENSTRUAL CUPS. DON'T HAVE VAGINAL SEX. YOUR CERVIX IS OPEN, AND SO THERE'S RISK OF INFECTION.

SOME DOCTORS RECOMMEND SHOWERS RATHER THAN BATHS FOR A FEW DAYS.

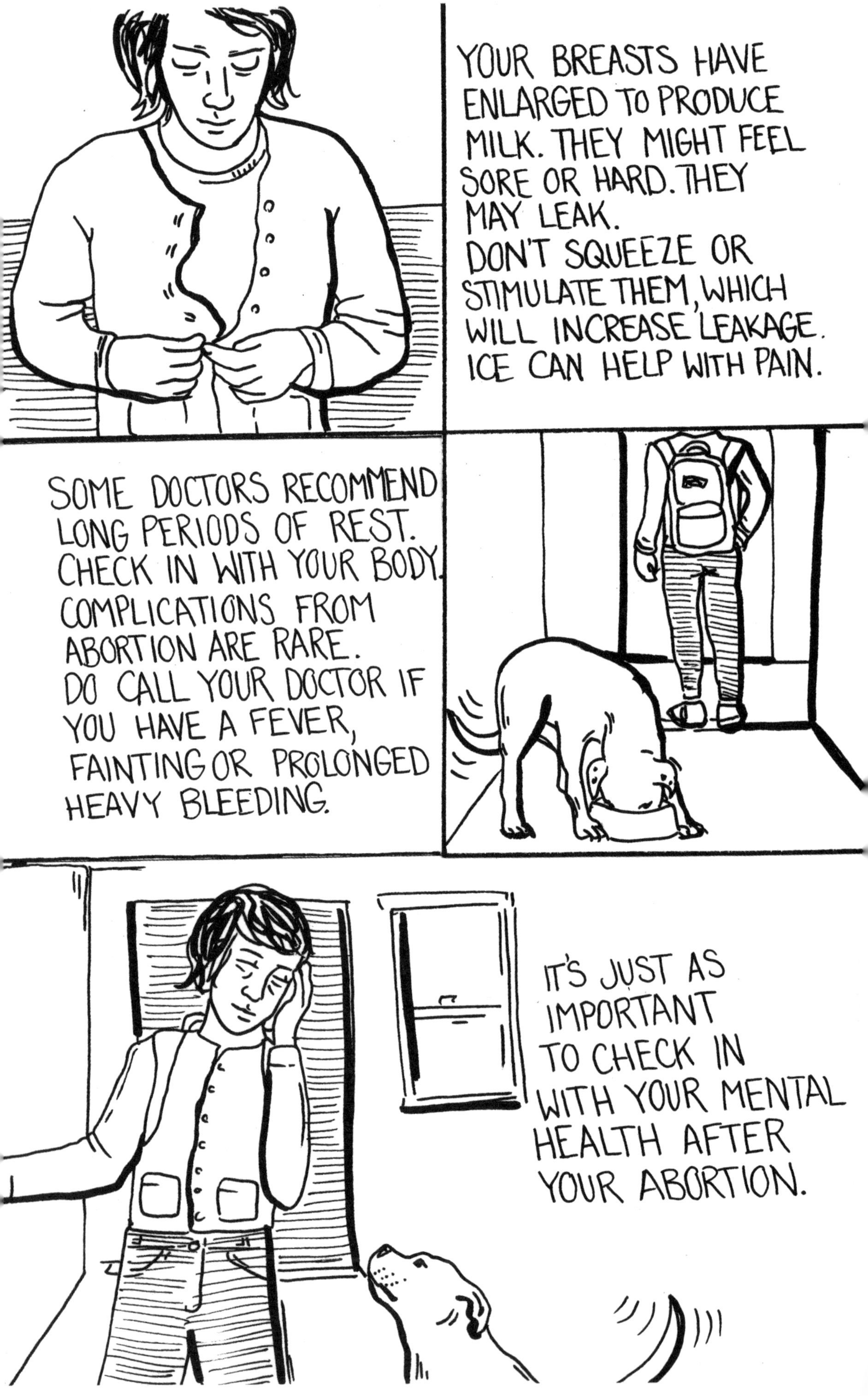
YOUR BREASTS HAVE ENLARGED TO PRODUCE MILK. THEY MIGHT FEEL SORE OR HARD. THEY MAY LEAK.
DON'T SQUEEZE OR STIMULATE THEM, WHICH WILL INCREASE LEAKAGE. ICE CAN HELP WITH PAIN.
SOME DOCTORS RECOMMEND LONG PERIODS OF REST. CHECK IN WITH YOUR BODY. COMPLICATIONS FROM ABORTION ARE RARE.
DO CALL YOUR DOCTOR IF YOU HAVE A FEVER, FAINTING OR PROLONGED HEAVY BLEEDING.
IT'S JUST AS IMPORTANT TO CHECK IN WITH YOUR MENTAL HEALTH AFTER YOUR ABORTION.

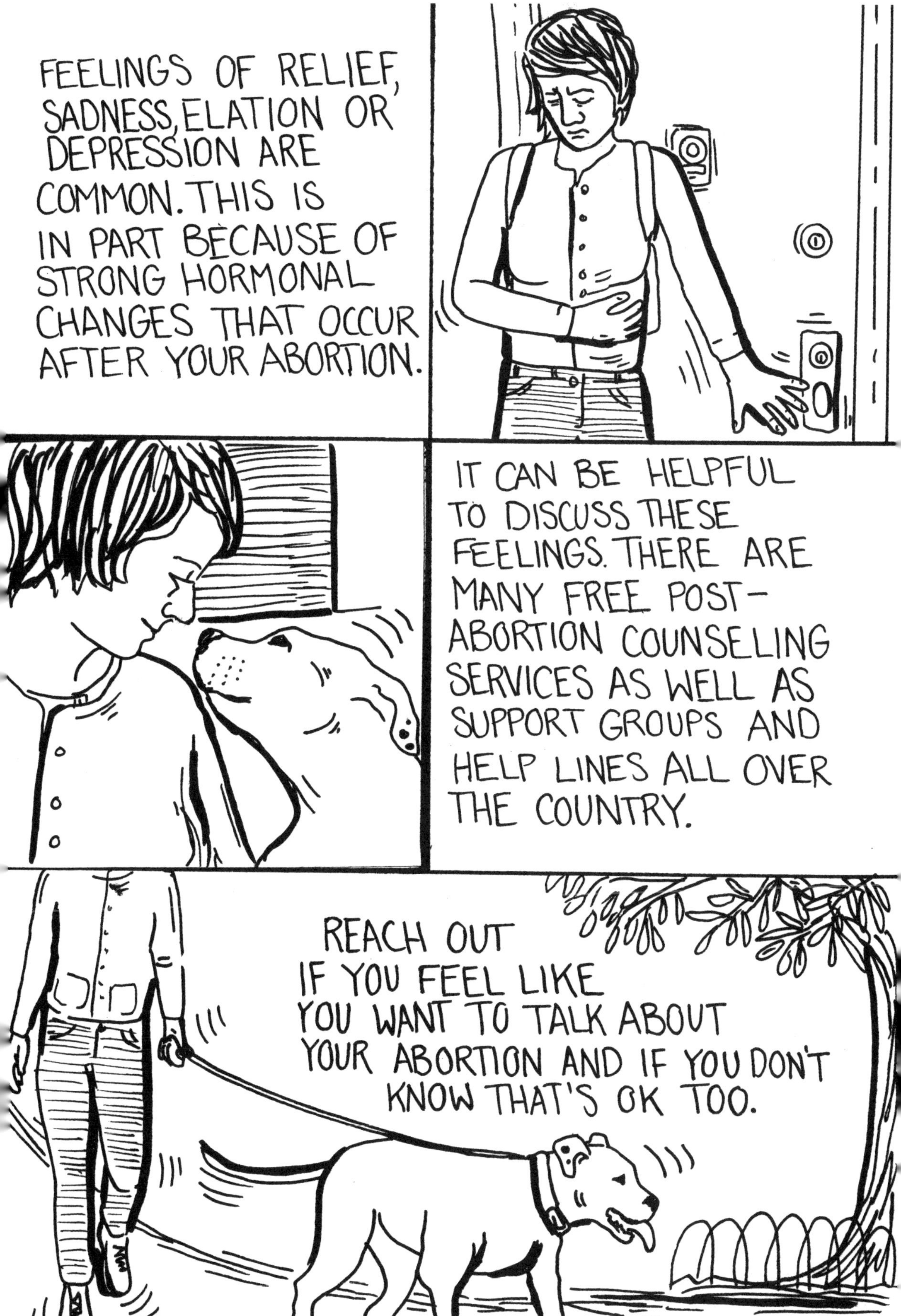
FEELINGS OF RELIEF, SADNESS, ELATION OR DEPRESSION ARE COMMON. THIS IS IN PART BECAUSE OF STRONG HORMONAL CHANGES THAT OCCUR AFTER YOUR ABORTION.
IT CAN BE HELPFUL TO DISCUSS THESE FEELINGS. THERE ARE MANY FREE POST-ABORTION COUNSELING SERVICES AS WELL AS SUPPORT GROUPS AND HELP LINES ALL OVER THE COUNTRY.
REACH OUT IF YOU FEEL LIKE YOU WANT TO TALK ABOUT YOUR ABORTION AND IF YOU DON'T KNOW THAT'S OK TOO.

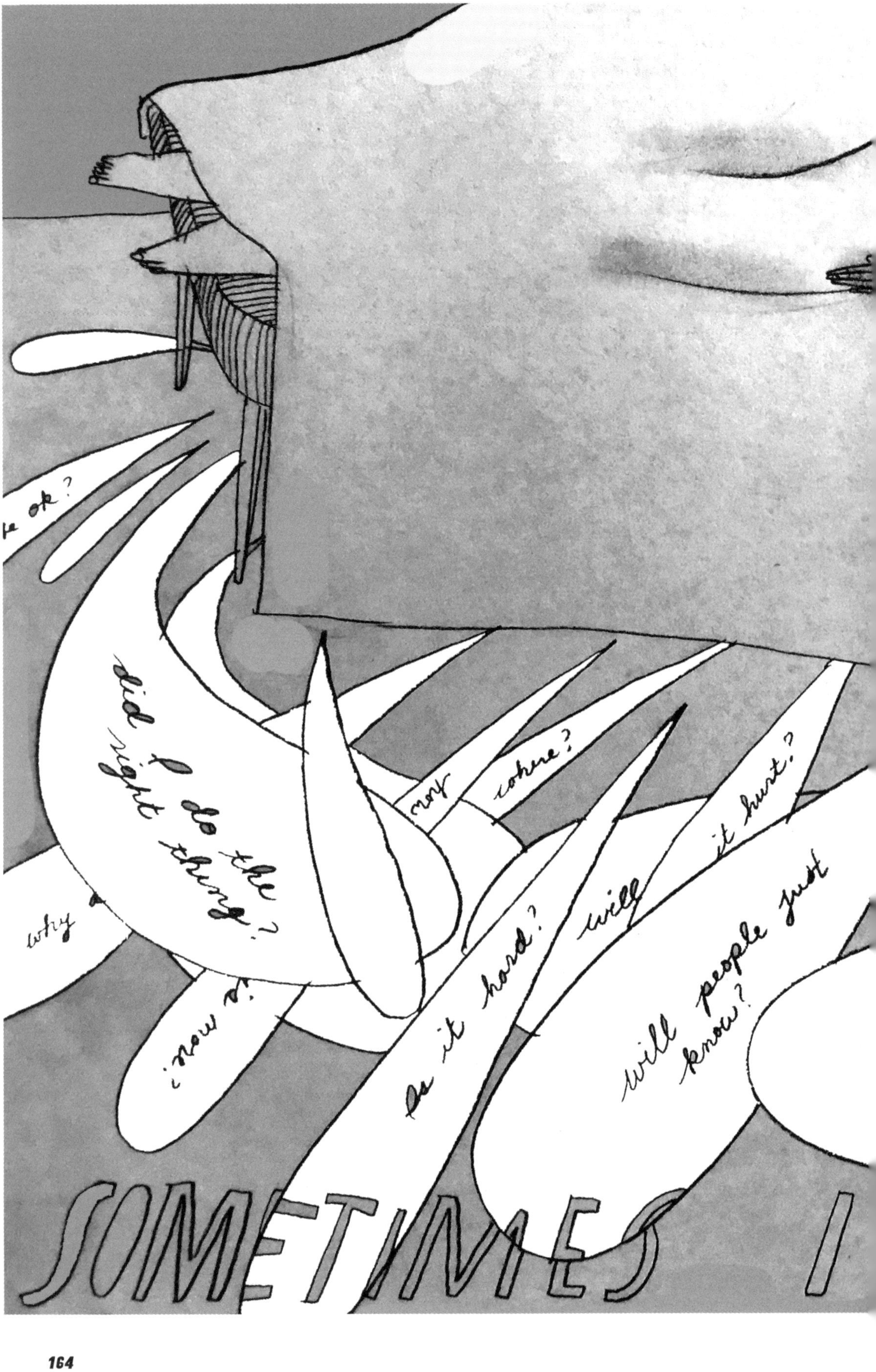
did I do the right thing?
why
is it hard?
will it hurt?
will people just know?
SOMETIMES I

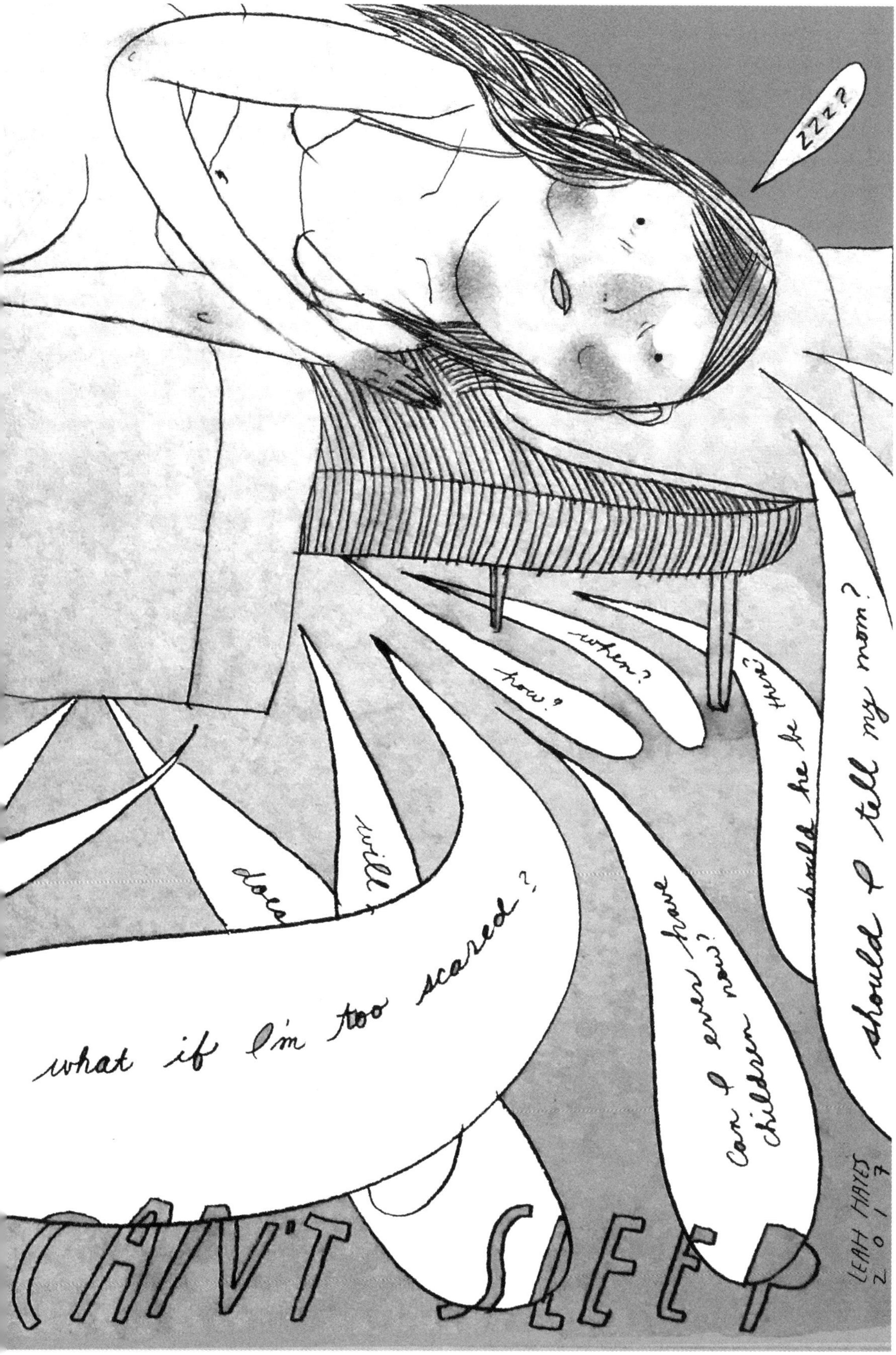
CAN'T SLEEP
LEAH HAYES 2017
zzz?
what if I'm too scared?
Can I ever have children now?
should he be there?
should I tell my mom?
how?
when?

PAST TENSE, FUTURE FORWARD

WRITTEN BY TANYA DEPASS
ART BY WREN CHAVERS

ARE YOU SURE?

YES, POSITIVE RESULT
I'M SORRY

THE LATE 1990S...

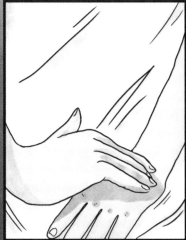

THANK YOU, I NEED A FEW MINUTES PLEASE

OF COURSE, I'LL HAVE INFORMATION FOR YOU WAITING AT THE DESK

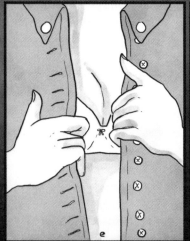

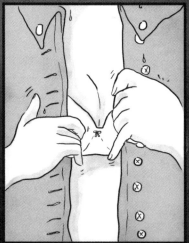

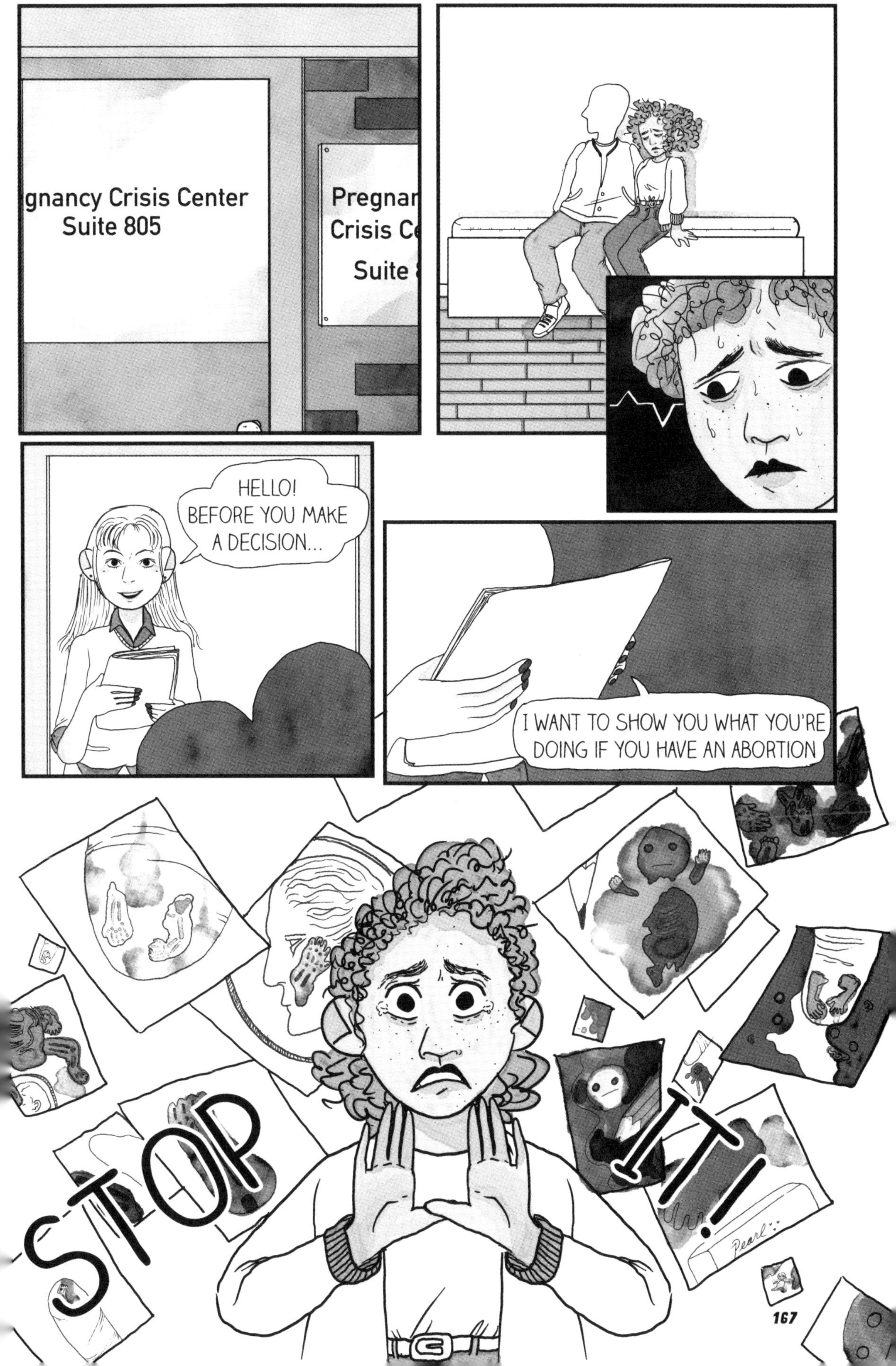
gnancy Crisis Center
Suite 805
Pregnar
Crisis Ce
Suite 8
HELLO! BEFORE YOU MAKE A DECISION...
I WANT TO SHOW YOU WHAT YOU'RE DOING IF YOU HAVE AN ABORTION
STOP IT!
Pearl

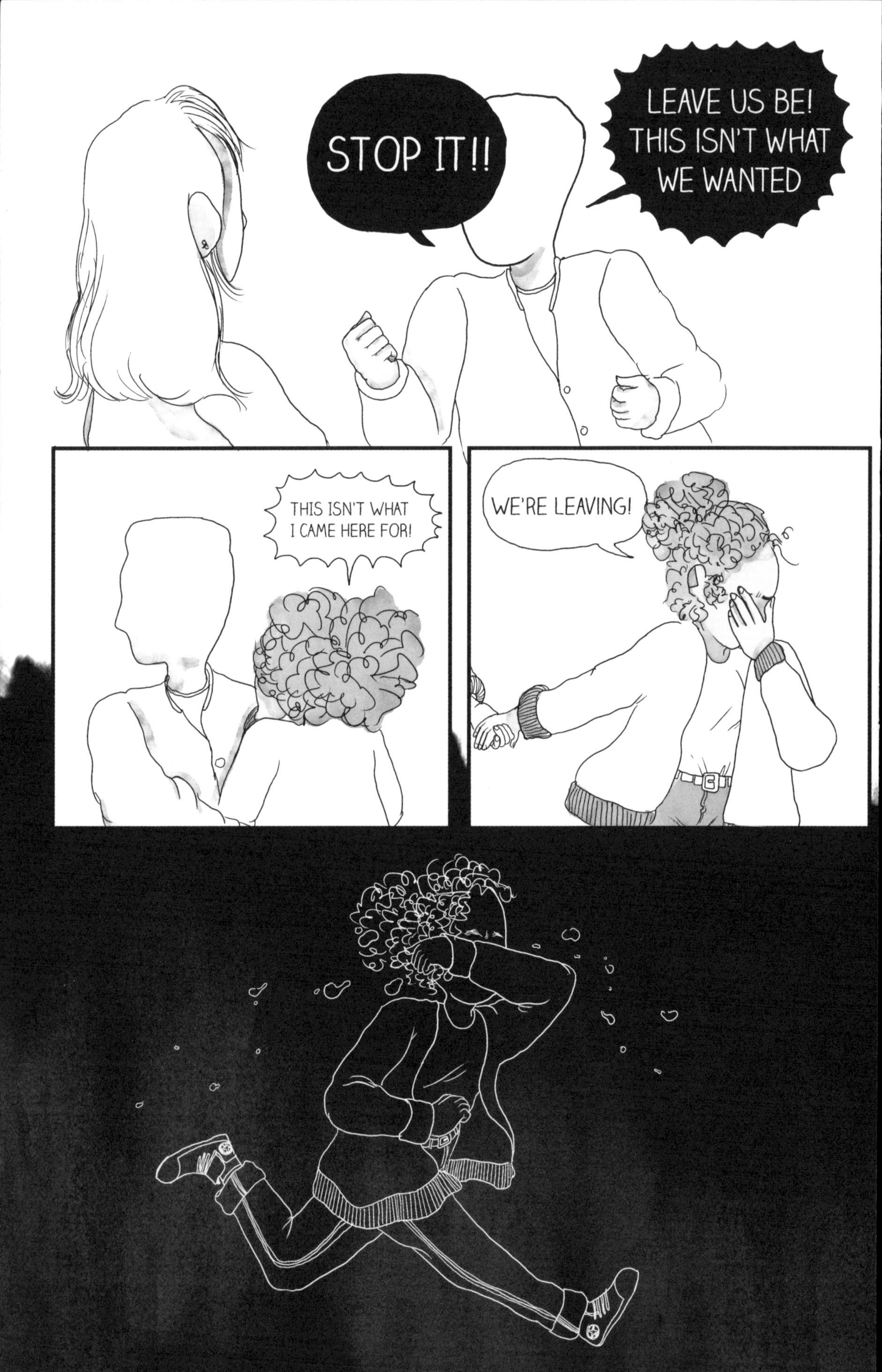
STOP IT!!
LEAVE US BE! THIS ISN'T WHAT WE WANTED
THIS ISN'T WHAT I CAME HERE FOR!
WE'RE LEAVING!

I SHOULD HAVE KNOWN BETTER...

THAT PLACE SEEMED TOO GOOD TO BE TRUE

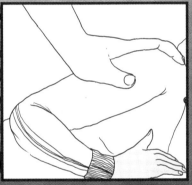

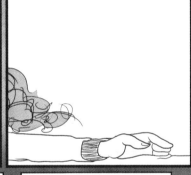

DON'T BLAME YOURSELF, LET'S TRY AGAIN TOMORROW

FOUND PLANNED PARENTHOOD

MIGHT AS WELL CALL FIRST TO BE SURE

...

THANK YOU

I'LL SEE YOU IN TWO WEEKS

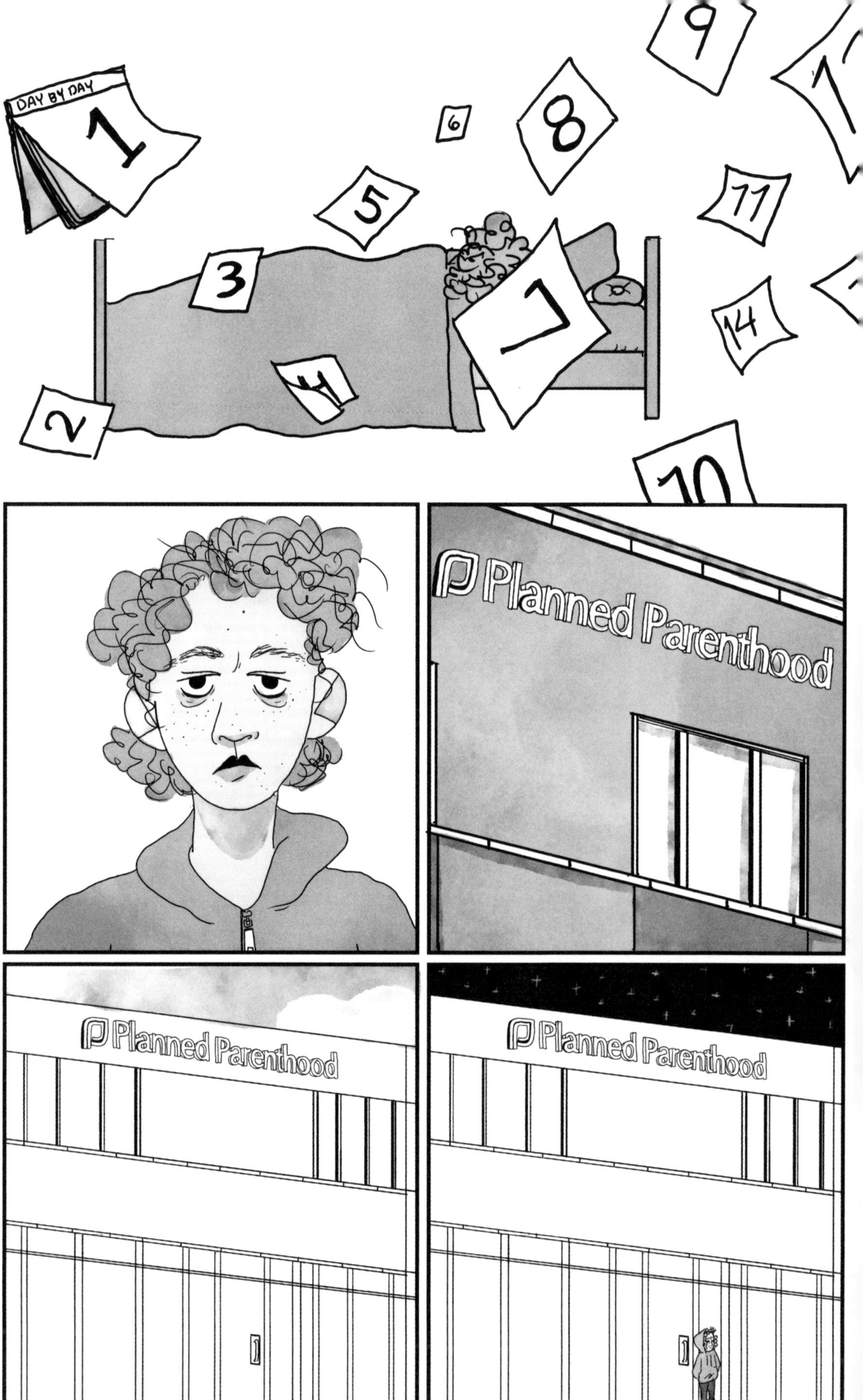
DAY BY DAY
Planned Parenthood
Planned Parenthood
Planned Parenthood

WHAT IF WE'RE WRONG?

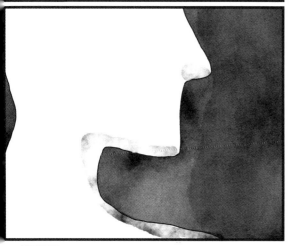

NOT WRONG,
WE MADE THE BEST DECISION
EVEN IF IT WASN'T AN EASY ONE.
REST UP, I'LL BE HERE

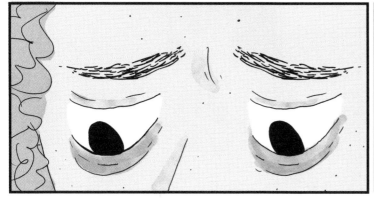

I...HOPE SO,
IT JUST REALLY
FUCKING HURTS.

WHY DO I FEEL SO BAD?

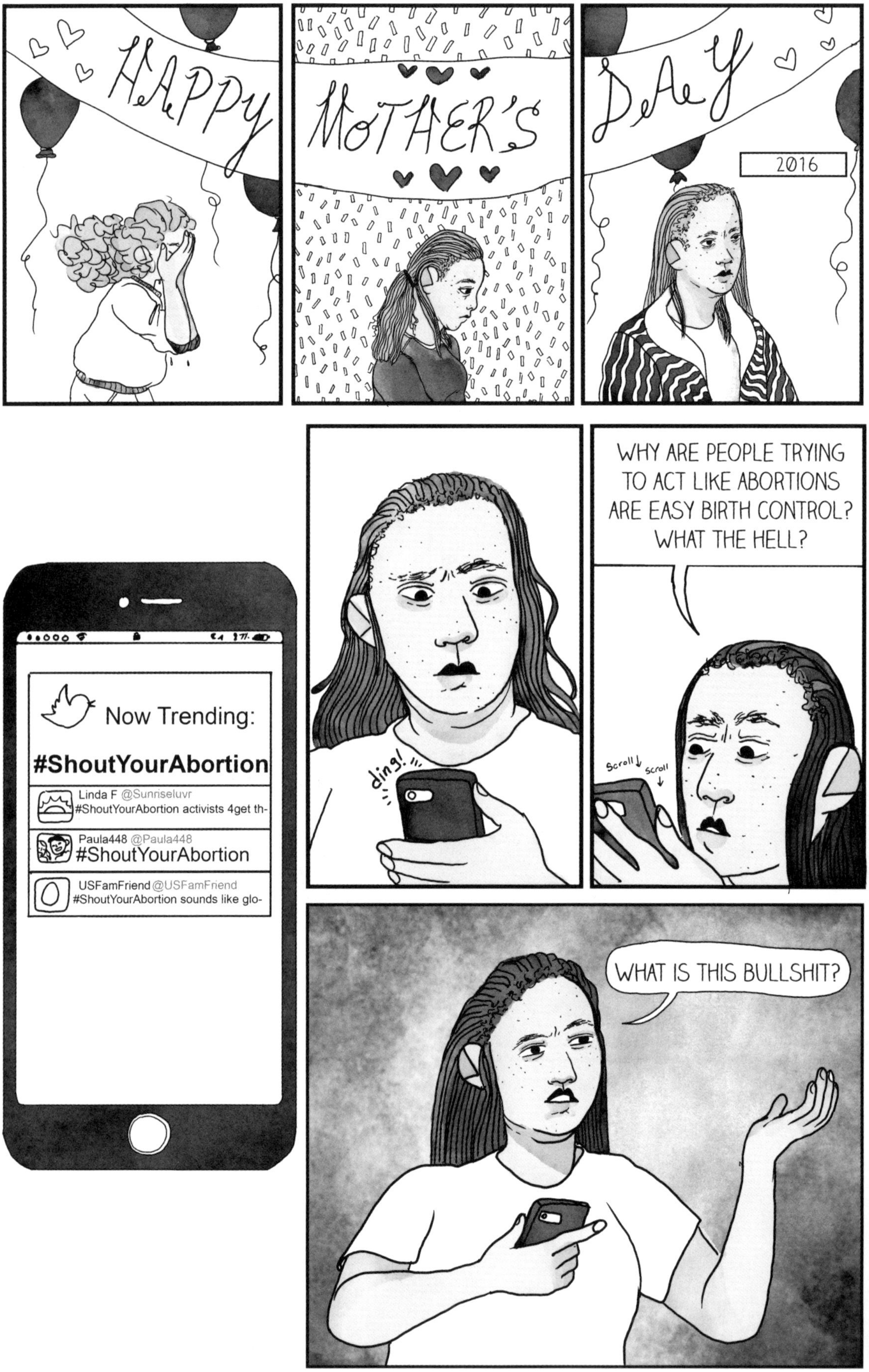

HAPPY
MOTHER'S
DAY
2016
Now Trending:
#ShoutYourAbortion
Linda F @Sunriseluvr
#ShoutYourAbortion activists 4get th-
Paula448 @Paula448
#ShoutYourAbortion
USFamFriend @USFamFriend
#ShoutYourAbortion sounds like glo-
ding!
WHY ARE PEOPLE TRYING TO ACT LIKE ABORTIONS ARE EASY BIRTH CONTROL? WHAT THE HELL?
Scroll
Scroll
WHAT IS THIS BULLSHIT?

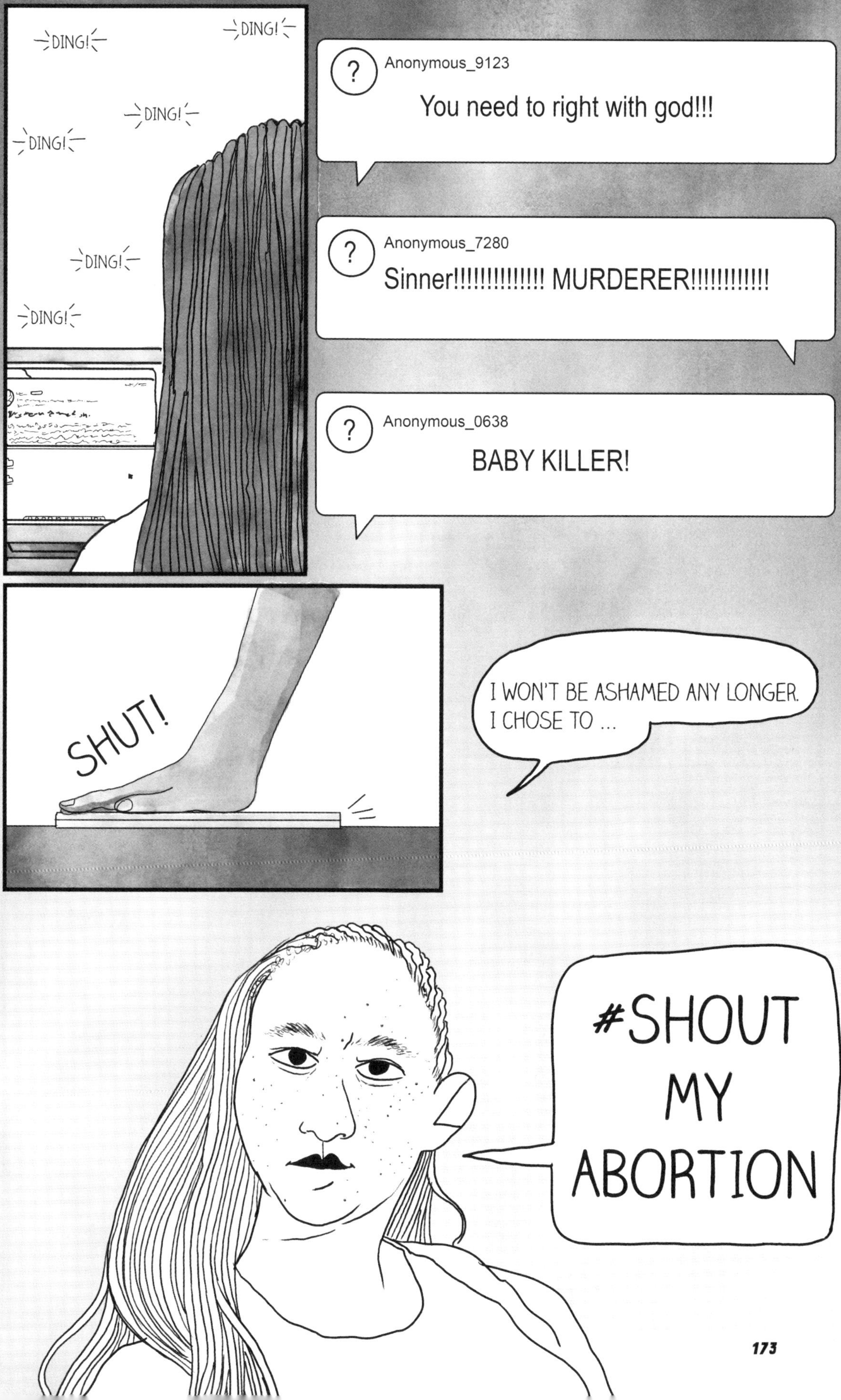
DING!
DING!
DING!
DING!
DING!
DING!
Anonymous_9123
You need to right with god!!!
Anonymous_7280
Sinner!!!!!!!!!!!!!! MURDERER!!!!!!!!!!!!
Anonymous_0638
BABY KILLER!
SHUT!
I WON'T BE ASHAMED ANY LONGER. I CHOSE TO ...
#SHOUT MY ABORTION

THE STORY OF MY ABORTION

BY TATIANA GILL

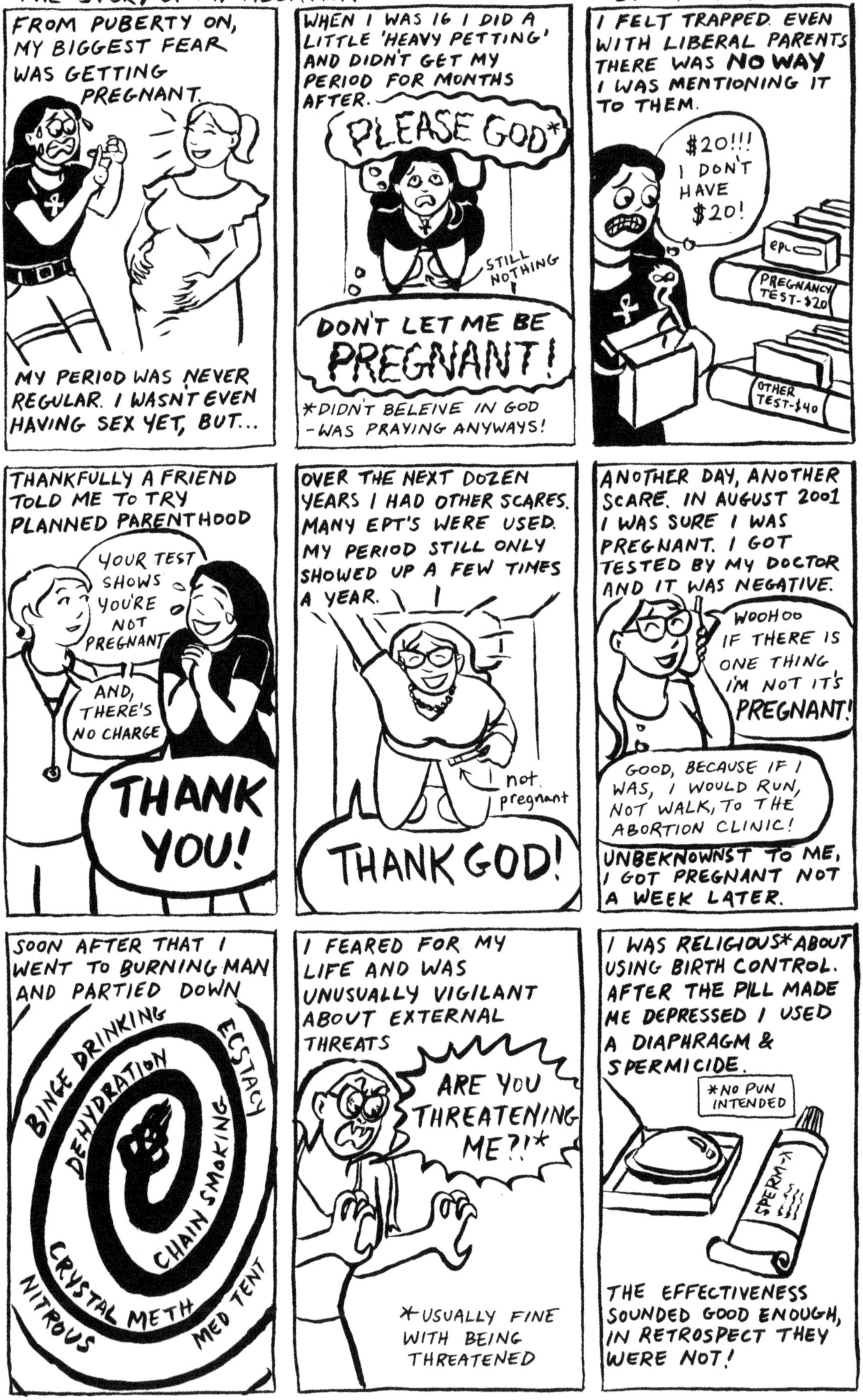

FROM PUBERTY ON, MY BIGGEST FEAR WAS GETTING PREGNANT.
MY PERIOD WAS NEVER REGULAR. I WASN'T EVEN HAVING SEX YET, BUT...
WHEN I WAS 16 I DID A LITTLE 'HEAVY PETTING' AND DIDN'T GET MY PERIOD FOR MONTHS AFTER.
PLEASE GOD*
STILL NOTHING
DON'T LET ME BE PREGNANT!
*DIDN'T BELEIVE IN GOD -WAS PRAYING ANYWAYS!
I FELT TRAPPED. EVEN WITH LIBERAL PARENTS THERE WAS NO WAY I WAS MENTIONING IT TO THEM.
$20!!! I DON'T HAVE $20!
EPT
PREGNANCY TEST-$20
OTHER TEST-$40
THANKFULLY A FRIEND TOLD ME TO TRY PLANNED PARENTHOOD
YOUR TEST SHOWS YOU'RE NOT PREGNANT
AND, THERE'S NO CHARGE
THANK YOU!
OVER THE NEXT DOZEN YEARS I HAD OTHER SCARES. MANY EPT'S WERE USED. MY PERIOD STILL ONLY SHOWED UP A FEW TIMES A YEAR.
not pregnant
THANK GOD!
ANOTHER DAY, ANOTHER SCARE. IN AUGUST 2001 I WAS SURE I WAS PREGNANT. I GOT TESTED BY MY DOCTOR AND IT WAS NEGATIVE.
WOOHOO IF THERE IS ONE THING I'M NOT IT'S PREGNANT!
GOOD, BECAUSE IF I WAS, I WOULD RUN, NOT WALK, TO THE ABORTION CLINIC!
UNBEKNOWNST TO ME, I GOT PREGNANT NOT A WEEK LATER.
SOON AFTER THAT I WENT TO BURNING MAN AND PARTIED DOWN
BINGE DRINKING
DEHYDRATION
ECSTACY
CHAIN SMOKING
CRYSTAL METH
NITROUS
MED TENT
I FEARED FOR MY LIFE AND WAS UNUSUALLY VIGILANT ABOUT EXTERNAL THREATS
ARE YOU THREATENING ME?!*
*USUALLY FINE WITH BEING THREATENED
I WAS RELIGIOUS* ABOUT USING BIRTH CONTROL. AFTER THE PILL MADE ME DEPRESSED I USED A DIAPHRAGM & SPERMICIDE.
*NO PUN INTENDED
SPERM-X
THE EFFECTIVENESS SOUNDED GOOD ENOUGH, IN RETROSPECT THEY WERE NOT!

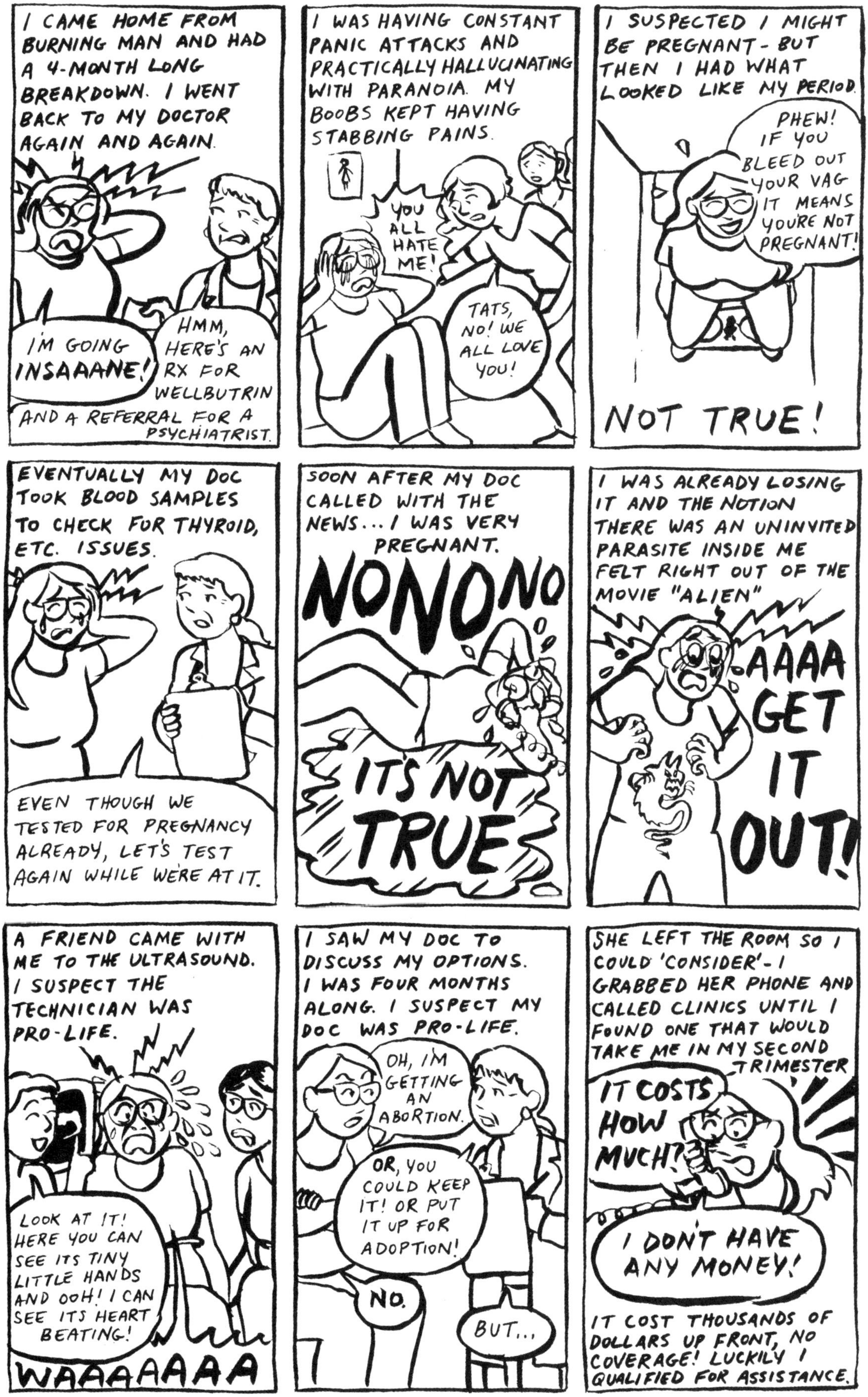
I CAME HOME FROM BURNING MAN AND HAD A 4-MONTH LONG BREAKDOWN. I WENT BACK TO MY DOCTOR AGAIN AND AGAIN.
I'M GOING INSAAANE!
HMM, HERE'S AN RX FOR WELLBUTRIN
AND A REFERRAL FOR A PSYCHIATRIST.
I WAS HAVING CONSTANT PANIC ATTACKS AND PRACTICALLY HALLUCINATING WITH PARANOIA. MY BOOBS KEPT HAVING STABBING PAINS.
YOU ALL HATE ME!
TATS, NO! WE ALL LOVE YOU!
I SUSPECTED I MIGHT BE PREGNANT - BUT THEN I HAD WHAT LOOKED LIKE MY PERIOD.
PHEW! IF YOU BLEED OUT YOUR VAG IT MEANS YOU'RE NOT PREGNANT!
NOT TRUE!
EVENTUALLY MY DOC TOOK BLOOD SAMPLES TO CHECK FOR THYROID, ETC. ISSUES.
EVEN THOUGH WE TESTED FOR PREGNANCY ALREADY, LET'S TEST AGAIN WHILE WE'RE AT IT.
SOON AFTER MY DOC CALLED WITH THE NEWS... I WAS VERY PREGNANT.
NONONO
IT'S NOT TRUE
I WAS ALREADY LOSING IT AND THE NOTION THERE WAS AN UNINVITED PARASITE INSIDE ME FELT RIGHT OUT OF THE MOVIE "ALIEN"
AAAA GET IT OUT!
A FRIEND CAME WITH ME TO THE ULTRASOUND. I SUSPECT THE TECHNICIAN WAS PRO-LIFE.
LOOK AT IT! HERE YOU CAN SEE ITS TINY LITTLE HANDS AND OOH! I CAN SEE ITS HEART BEATING!
WAAAAAAA
I SAW MY DOC TO DISCUSS MY OPTIONS. I WAS FOUR MONTHS ALONG. I SUSPECT MY DOC WAS PRO-LIFE.
OH, I'M GETTING AN ABORTION.
OR, YOU COULD KEEP IT! OR PUT IT UP FOR ADOPTION!
NO.
BUT...
SHE LEFT THE ROOM SO I COULD 'CONSIDER' - I GRABBED HER PHONE AND CALLED CLINICS UNTIL I FOUND ONE THAT WOULD TAKE ME IN MY SECOND TRIMESTER
IT COSTS HOW MUCH?
I DON'T HAVE ANY MONEY!
IT COST THOUSANDS OF DOLLARS UP FRONT, NO COVERAGE! LUCKILY I QUALIFIED FOR ASSISTANCE.

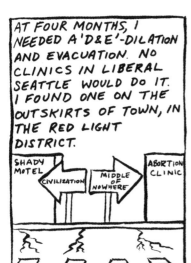

AT FOUR MONTHS, I NEEDED A 'D&E'-DILATION AND EVACUATION. NO CLINICS IN LIBERAL SEATTLE WOULD DO IT. I FOUND ONE ON THE OUTSKIRTS OF TOWN, IN THE RED LIGHT DISTRICT.

SHADY MOTEL
CIVILIZATION
MIDDLE OF NOWHERE
ABORTION CLINIC

THAT NIGHT, AS I WAS LOSING MY SHIT, MY BOYFRIEND AND I HAD A MATURE DISCUSSION ABOUT THE SITUATION.

THIS IS ALL YOUR FAULT!

WHAT?! THIS IS ALL YOUR FAULT!

THE NEXT FEW DAYS D R A G G E D PAST AS I WAITED FOR MY APPOINTMENTS. AT WORK MY BOSS SENT ME HOME - ONE LOOK AND HE KNEW I WASN'T WELL.

HOLE OF DESPAIR

A FRIEND DROVE ME OUT TO THE BOONIES FOR MY DIALATION APPOINTMENT. I HAD A MANDATORY COUNSELING TO MAKE SURE I WAS SURE.

NOW...
I'M SURE.
WELL...
I'M SURE

I WOULDN'T LIVE THROUGH 5 MORE MONTHS OF PREGNANCY AND I'M SURE I'D BRAIN DAMAGED THE FETUS.

IT WAS THE LONGEST WAIT OF MY LIFE

Highlights

DILATION=INSERTING OSMOTIC METAL RODS INTO MY CERVIX. THEY WOULD EXPAND OVERNIGHT TO DILATE MY CERVIX

AHHHHG

I WENT HOME AND WAITED AS THE RODS EXPANDED. FRIENDS CAME BY FOR MORAL SUPPORT. I TOOK PAINKILLERS BUT THEY BARELY MADE A DENT

AAGHKHH

THE NEXT DAY MY BOYFRIEND DROVE ME BACK OUT FOR MY EVACUATION. ANOTHER INFINITE WAIT.

Scraping & Sucking

IT WAS HORRIBLE BUT THE DRUGS WERE INCREDIBLE. I FLOATED IN THE CLOUDS PAINTED ON THE CEILING

A FEW DAYS LATER I CAME HOME FROM WORK AND REALIZED I'D BEEN LACTATING

AIEEEE

INTERNALIZED MISOGYNY
SEX ISSUES
MOMMY ISSUES
BODY ISSUES

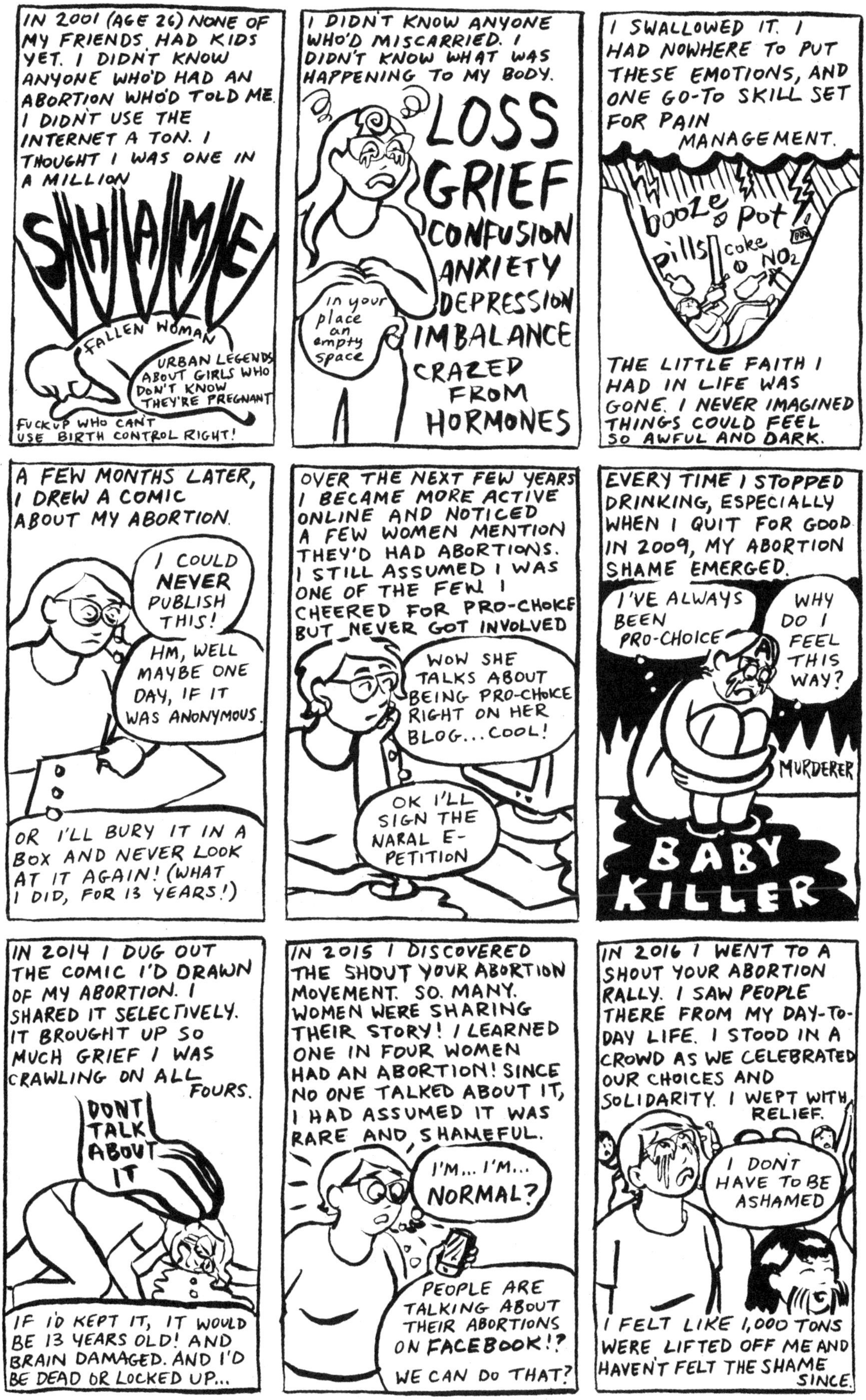
IN 2001 (AGE 26) NONE OF MY FRIENDS HAD KIDS YET. I DIDN'T KNOW ANYONE WHO'D HAD AN ABORTION WHO'D TOLD ME. I DIDN'T USE THE INTERNET A TON. I THOUGHT I WAS ONE IN A MILLION
SHAME
FALLEN WOMAN
URBAN LEGENDS ABOUT GIRLS WHO DON'T KNOW THEY'RE PREGNANT
FUCKUP WHO CAN'T USE BIRTH CONTROL RIGHT!
I DIDN'T KNOW ANYONE WHO'D MISCARRIED. I DIDN'T KNOW WHAT WAS HAPPENING TO MY BODY.
LOSS
GRIEF
CONFUSION
ANXIETY
DEPRESSION
IMBALANCE
CRAZED FROM HORMONES
in your place an empty space
I SWALLOWED IT. I HAD NOWHERE TO PUT THESE EMOTIONS, AND ONE GO-TO SKILL SET FOR PAIN MANAGEMENT.
booze
pot
pills
coke
NO2
THE LITTLE FAITH I HAD IN LIFE WAS GONE. I NEVER IMAGINED THINGS COULD FEEL SO AWFUL AND DARK.
A FEW MONTHS LATER, I DREW A COMIC ABOUT MY ABORTION.
I COULD NEVER PUBLISH THIS!
HM, WELL MAYBE ONE DAY, IF IT WAS ANONYMOUS.
OR I'LL BURY IT IN A BOX AND NEVER LOOK AT IT AGAIN! (WHAT I DID, FOR 13 YEARS!)
OVER THE NEXT FEW YEARS I BECAME MORE ACTIVE ONLINE AND NOTICED A FEW WOMEN MENTION THEY'D HAD ABORTIONS. I STILL ASSUMED I WAS ONE OF THE FEW. I CHEERED FOR PRO-CHOICE BUT NEVER GOT INVOLVED
WOW SHE TALKS ABOUT BEING PRO-CHOICE RIGHT ON HER BLOG... COOL!
OK I'LL SIGN THE NARAL E-PETITION
EVERY TIME I STOPPED DRINKING, ESPECIALLY WHEN I QUIT FOR GOOD IN 2009, MY ABORTION SHAME EMERGED.
I'VE ALWAYS BEEN PRO-CHOICE
WHY DO I FEEL THIS WAY?
MURDERER
BABY KILLER
IN 2014 I DUG OUT THE COMIC I'D DRAWN OF MY ABORTION. I SHARED IT SELECTIVELY. IT BROUGHT UP SO MUCH GRIEF I WAS CRAWLING ON ALL FOURS.
DONT TALK ABOUT IT
IF I'D KEPT IT, IT WOULD BE 13 YEARS OLD! AND BRAIN DAMAGED. AND I'D BE DEAD OR LOCKED UP...
IN 2015 I DISCOVERED THE SHOUT YOUR ABORTION MOVEMENT. SO. MANY. WOMEN WERE SHARING THEIR STORY! I LEARNED ONE IN FOUR WOMEN HAD AN ABORTION! SINCE NO ONE TALKED ABOUT IT, I HAD ASSUMED IT WAS RARE AND SHAMEFUL.
I'M... I'M... NORMAL?
PEOPLE ARE TALKING ABOUT THEIR ABORTIONS ON FACEBOOK!?
WE CAN DO THAT?
IN 2016 I WENT TO A SHOUT YOUR ABORTION RALLY. I SAW PEOPLE THERE FROM MY DAY-TO-DAY LIFE. I STOOD IN A CROWD AS WE CELEBRATED OUR CHOICES AND SOLIDARITY. I WEPT WITH RELIEF.
I DON'T HAVE TO BE ASHAMED
I FELT LIKE 1,000 TONS WERE LIFTED OFF ME AND HAVEN'T FELT THE SHAME SINCE.

I WEAR THE SHIRT I GOT AT THE S.Y.A. RALLY TO OTHER EVENTS AND MARCHES — WITH PRIDE.

EVERYONE KNOWS I HAD AN ABORTION

WOMEN HAVE RUN UP TO ME AND HUGGED ME FOR IT.

THANK YOU FOR WEARING THAT SHIRT!

I HAD ONE, TOO.

AW THANK YOU!

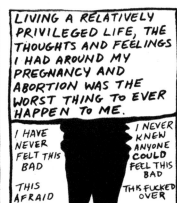

LIVING A RELATIVELY PRIVILEGED LIFE, THE THOUGHTS AND FEELINGS I HAD AROUND MY PREGNANCY AND ABORTION WAS THE WORST THING TO EVER HAPPEN TO ME.

I HAVE NEVER FELT THIS BAD

THIS AFRAID

THIS ASHAMED

THIS ROTTEN

MY SOUL

I NEVER KNEW ANYONE COULD FEEL THIS BAD

THIS FUCKED OVER

THIS WRONG

THIS DARK

I DIDN'T THINK ABORTION WAS WRONG, BUT I FELT SO BAD I REASONED I MUST BE BAD.

AS I GOT OLDER, MANY FRIENDS GOT PREGNANT AND FRIENDS LOST EMBRYOS FOR A VARIETY OF REASONS.

YOU MISCARRIED AND NOW YOU HAVE TO GET THE FETUS VACCUMED OUT? I'M SO SORRY! OH HON, THAT SOUNDS SO TRAUMATIC.

HUH... MAYBE WHAT I WENT THROUGH WAS TRAUMATIC*!

*I IMAGINE CHILDBIRTH AND RAISING KIDS CAN ALSO BE TRAUMATIC!

MY FRIEND HAS BEEN SO DEPRESSED AND DEVASTATED SINCE SHE MISCARRIED. IT MAKES SENSE BIOLOGICALLY!

EVEN THOUGH I CHOSE TO HAVE AN ABORTION, MY BODY MAY HAVE STILL BEEN REALLY UPSET THAT IT 'LOST' A PREGNANCY!

I NEVER PROCESSED MY GRIEF IN A HEALTHY, CATHARTIC WAY. I BEAT MYSELF UP FOR BEING A HUMAN!

I STARTED TO SEE FIRSTHAND HOW PREGNANCY CAN AFFECT SOMEONE.

ARE YOU FUCKING WITH ME?!

BRRR

I JUST NEED A FEW MORE NAPS

OHH... OF COURSE I WAS LOSING IT!

I AM STUNNED THAT DESPITE BEING RAISED IN LIBERAL SEATTLE AND IDENTIFYING AS PRO-CHOICE, I DID NOT FIND A COMMUNITY WILLING TO ADMIT TO AND DISCUSS THEIR ABORTIONS UNTIL I WAS 40 YEARS OLD!

I'M GLAD I MADE THE CHOICE I DID!

ME TOO!

LATELY I'VE SEEN ZINES, ARTICLES, COMICS AND BOOKS WHERE PEOPLE TALK ABOUT THEIR ABORTIONS. I NOW HAVE A COLLECTION!

Shrill

Dear Doctor

GREY AREA

SHOUT YOUR ABORTION NYC

LOUDER

I HAD AN ABORTION AND IT WAS FINE

MANY OF THEM SAY THAT IT WAS NOT HARD, SHAMEFUL OR REGRETTABLE — ESPECIALLY ONES THAT HAPPENED IN A POST-SECRETIVE WORLD.

HAPPY OR SAD, EASY OR HARD, EARLY OR LATE TERM, HAVING AN ABORTION IS OKAY.

IT IS YOUR ABORTION. YOU GET TO TALK ABOUT IT. THIS SHOUT YOUR ABORTION SLOGAN SUMS IT UP:

OUR STORIES ARE OURS TO TELL.

THIS IS MINE.

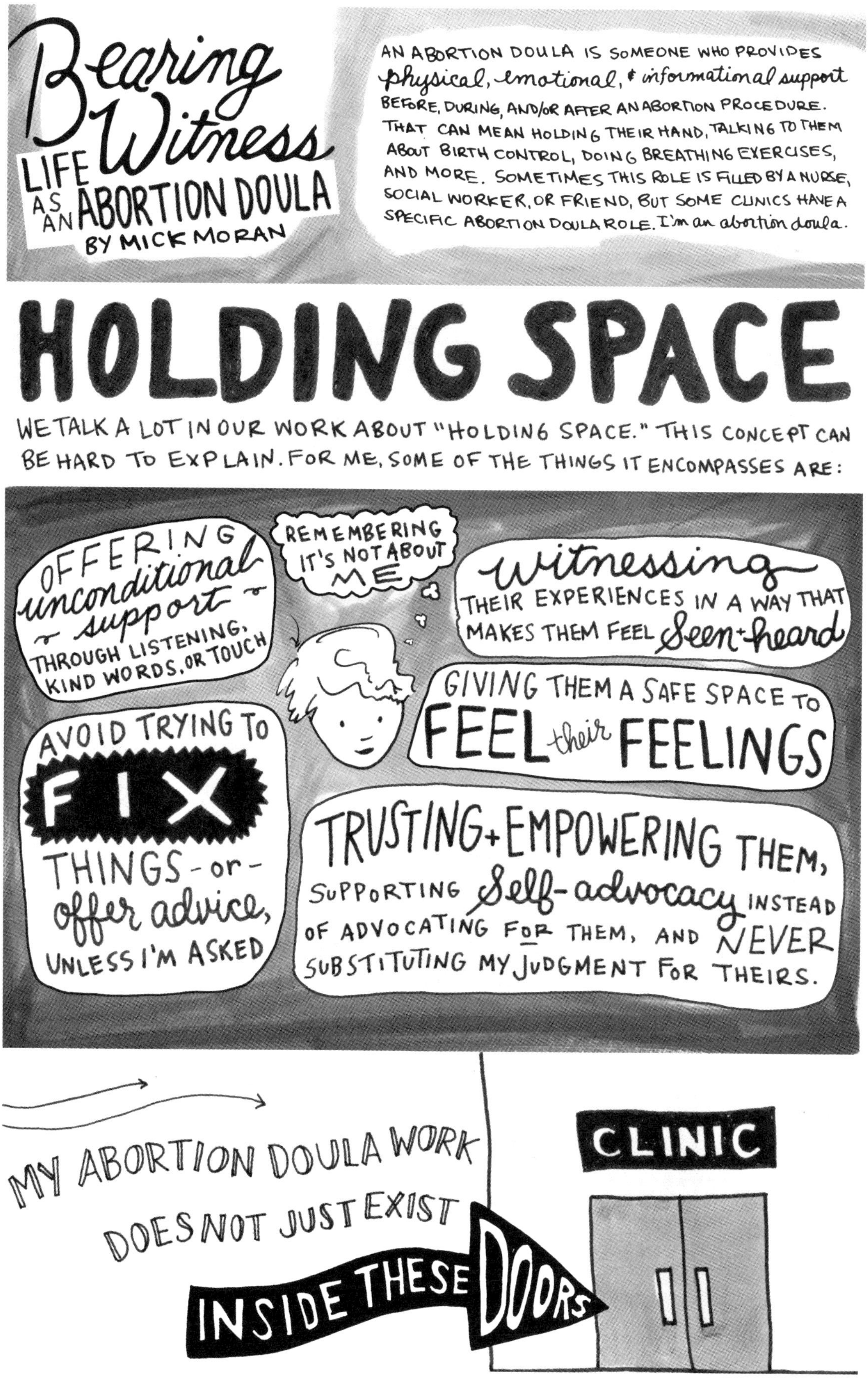

Bearing Witness
LIFE AS AN ABORTION DOULA
BY MICK MORAN
AN ABORTION DOULA IS SOMEONE WHO PROVIDES physical, emotional, & informational support BEFORE, DURING, AND/OR AFTER AN ABORTION PROCEDURE. THAT CAN MEAN HOLDING THEIR HAND, TALKING TO THEM ABOUT BIRTH CONTROL, DOING BREATHING EXERCISES, AND MORE. SOMETIMES THIS ROLE IS FILLED BY A NURSE, SOCIAL WORKER, OR FRIEND, BUT SOME CLINICS HAVE A SPECIFIC ABORTION DOULA ROLE. I'm an abortion doula.
HOLDING SPACE
WE TALK A LOT IN OUR WORK ABOUT "HOLDING SPACE." THIS CONCEPT CAN BE HARD TO EXPLAIN. FOR ME, SOME OF THE THINGS IT ENCOMPASSES ARE:
OFFERING unconditional ~ support ~ THROUGH LISTENING, KIND WORDS, OR TOUCH
REMEMBERING IT'S NOT ABOUT ME
witnessing THEIR EXPERIENCES IN A WAY THAT MAKES THEM FEEL seen + heard
GIVING THEM A SAFE SPACE TO FEEL their FEELINGS
AVOID TRYING TO FIX THINGS -or- offer advice, UNLESS I'M ASKED
TRUSTING + EMPOWERING THEM, SUPPORTING self-advocacy INSTEAD OF ADVOCATING FOR THEM, AND NEVER SUBSTITUTING MY JUDGMENT FOR THEIRS.
MY ABORTION DOULA WORK DOES NOT JUST EXIST INSIDE THESE DOORS
CLINIC

I TALK OPENLY ABOUT MY WORK AS AN ABORTION DOULA, AND I FIND MYSELF HOLDING SPACE FOR PEOPLE IN UNUSUAL PLACES. SOMEONE I MEET AT A PARTY MIGHT SHARE THEIR STORY OF BIRTH, ABORTION, OR LOSS. SOMETIMES THEY HAVE FELT SUCH STIGMA THAT THEY HAVE NEVER SHARED THE STORY BEFORE.

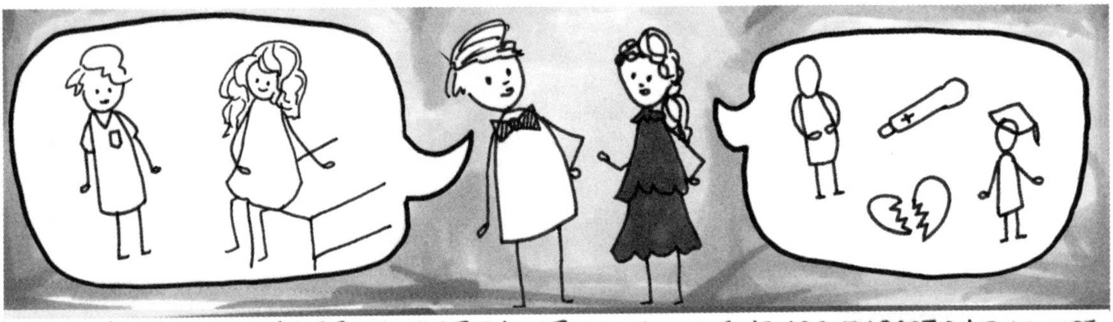

I ALSO HEAR MANY STORIES WHILE AT EVENTS WITH OUR ZINE ABOUT ABORTION SELF-CARE.

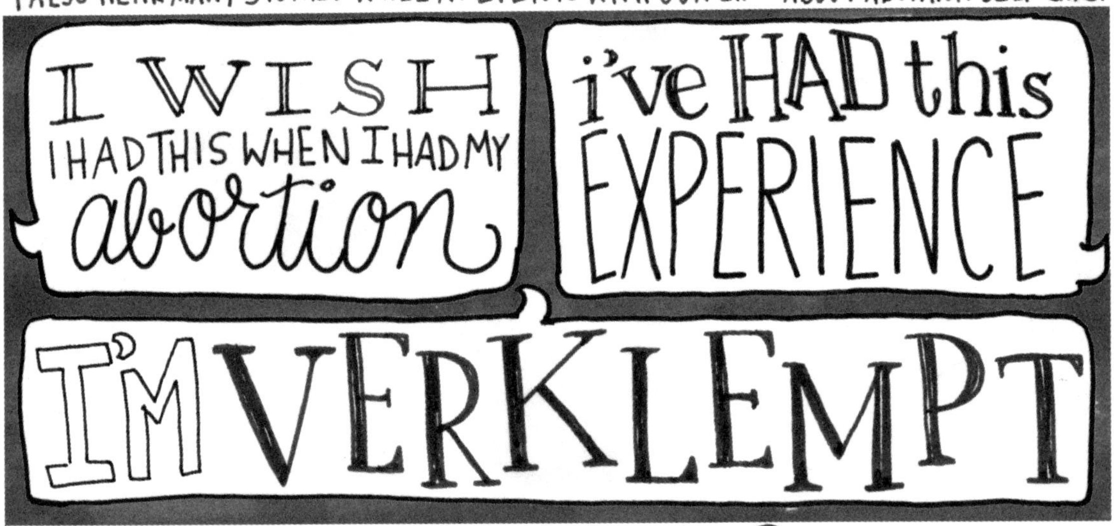
I WISH I HAD THIS WHEN I HAD MY abortion
i've HAD this EXPERIENCE
I'M VERKLEMPT

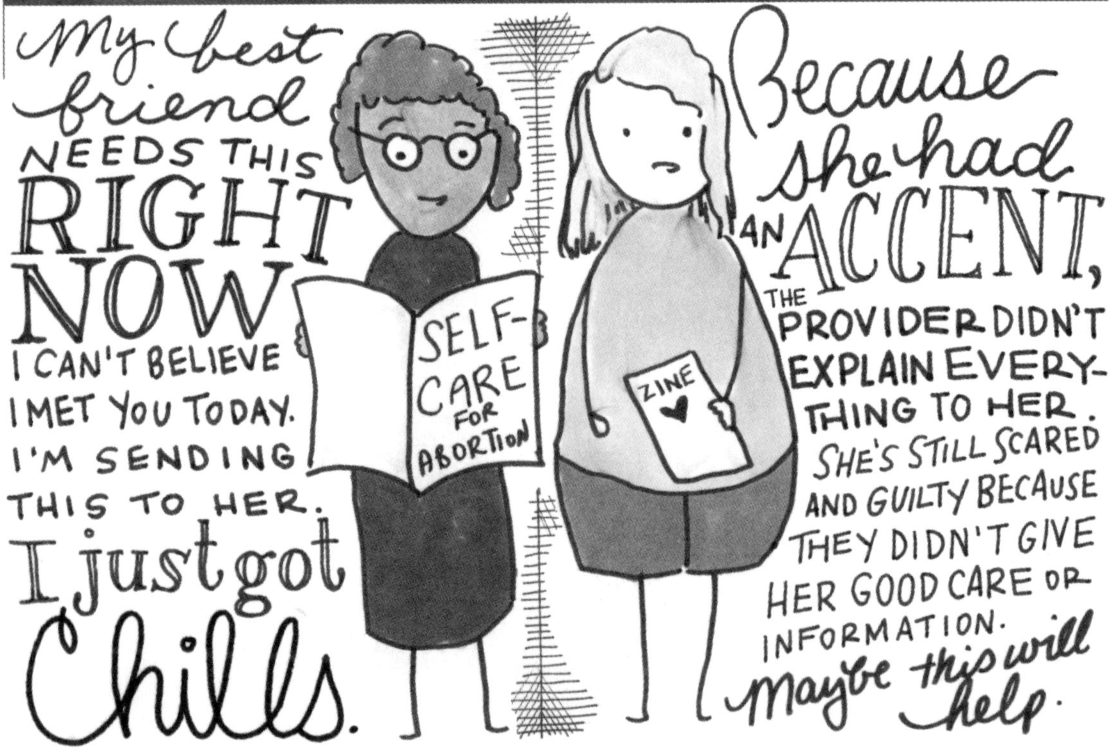
My best friend NEEDS THIS RIGHT NOW
I CAN'T BELIEVE I MET YOU TODAY.
I'M SENDING THIS TO HER.
I just got Chills.
SELF-CARE FOR ABORTION
ZINE
Because she had AN ACCENT, THE PROVIDER DIDN'T EXPLAIN EVERYTHING TO HER.
SHE'S STILL SCARED AND GUILTY BECAUSE THEY DIDN'T GIVE HER GOOD CARE OR INFORMATION.
maybe this will help.

BUT I HEAR FROM A LOT OF SUPPORT PEOPLE, TOO.

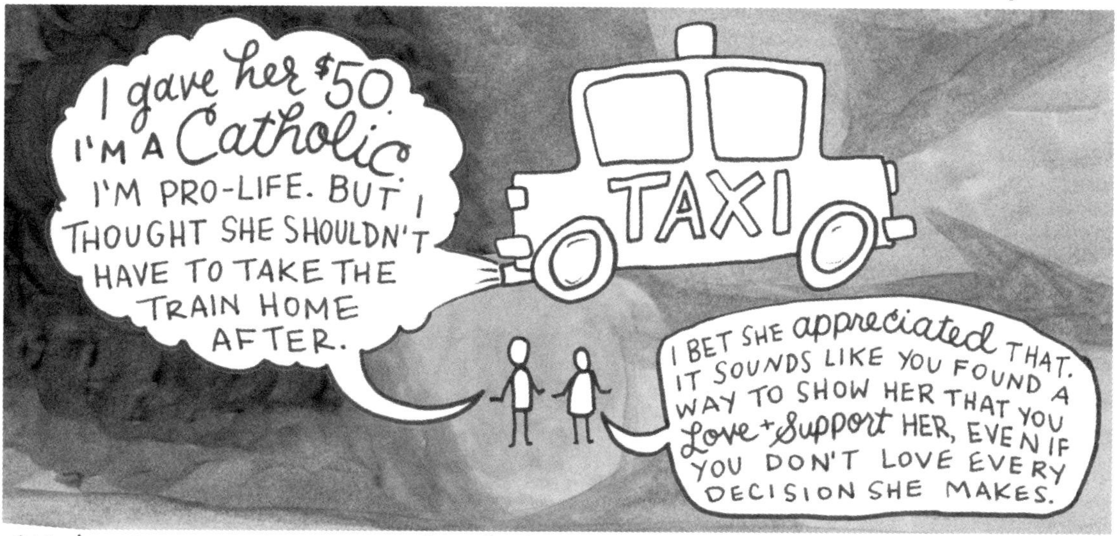
I gave her $50. I'M A Catholic. I'M PRO-LIFE. BUT I THOUGHT SHE SHOULDN'T HAVE TO TAKE THE TRAIN HOME AFTER.
TAXI
I BET SHE appreciated THAT. IT SOUNDS LIKE YOU FOUND A WAY TO SHOW HER THAT YOU Love + Support HER, EVEN IF YOU DON'T LOVE EVERY DECISION SHE MAKES.

I'M NOT ALWAYS SURE HOW PEOPLE WILL REACT WHEN I TELL THEM ABOUT MY WORK BECAUSE OF THE STIGMA SURROUNDING ABORTION...

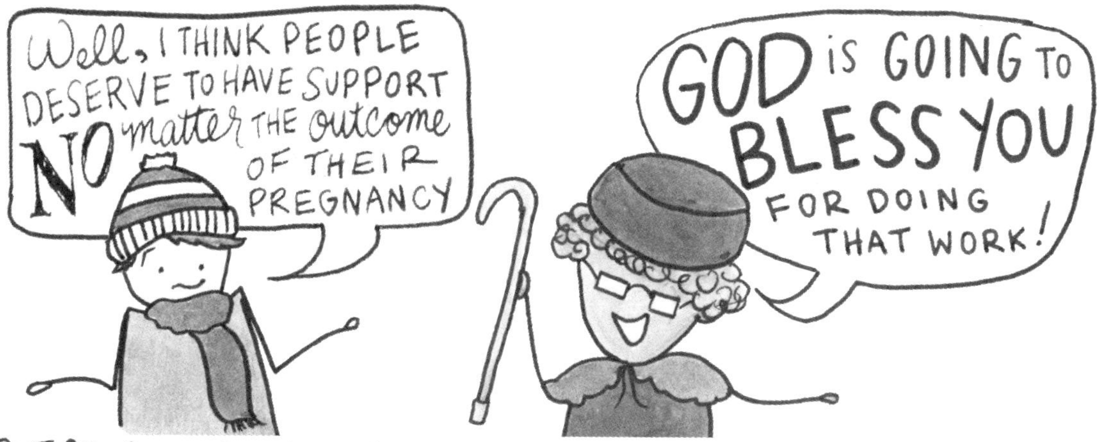
Well, I THINK PEOPLE DESERVE TO HAVE SUPPORT NO matter THE outcome OF THEIR PREGNANCY
GOD IS GOING TO BLESS YOU FOR DOING THAT WORK!

BUT PEOPLE OFTEN OVERWHELM ME WITH SUPPORT. THEIR REACTIONS, EVEN THE SILENT MOMENTS, CAN SHARE A STORY ABOUT ABORTION OR LOSS, SOMETIMES WITHOUT A SINGLE WORD BEING SPOKEN.

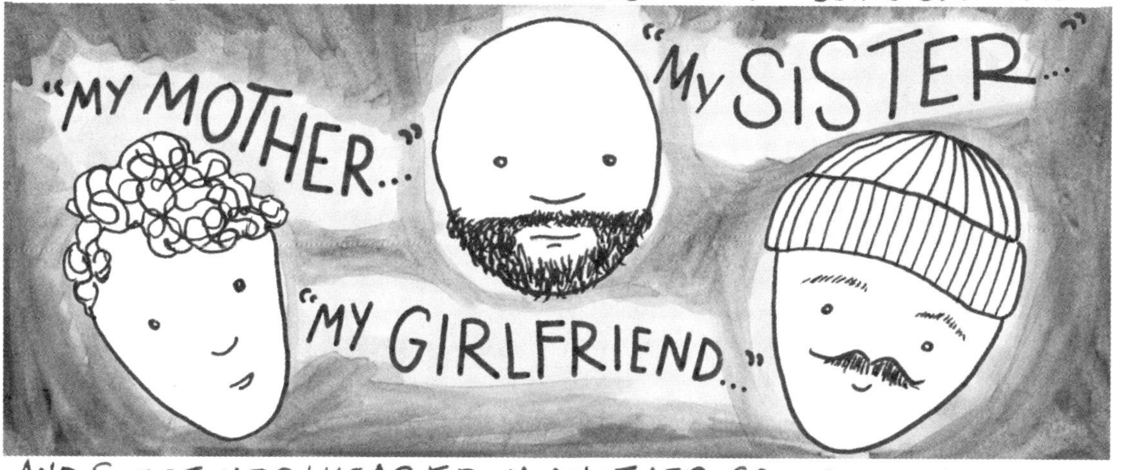
"MY MOTHER..."
"My SISTER..."
"MY GIRLFRIEND..."

AND SOMETIMES I HEAR FROM ANOTHER GROUP. THEY OFTEN SPEAK ABOUT ABORTION IN A MORE HESITANT, UNCERTAIN WAY.

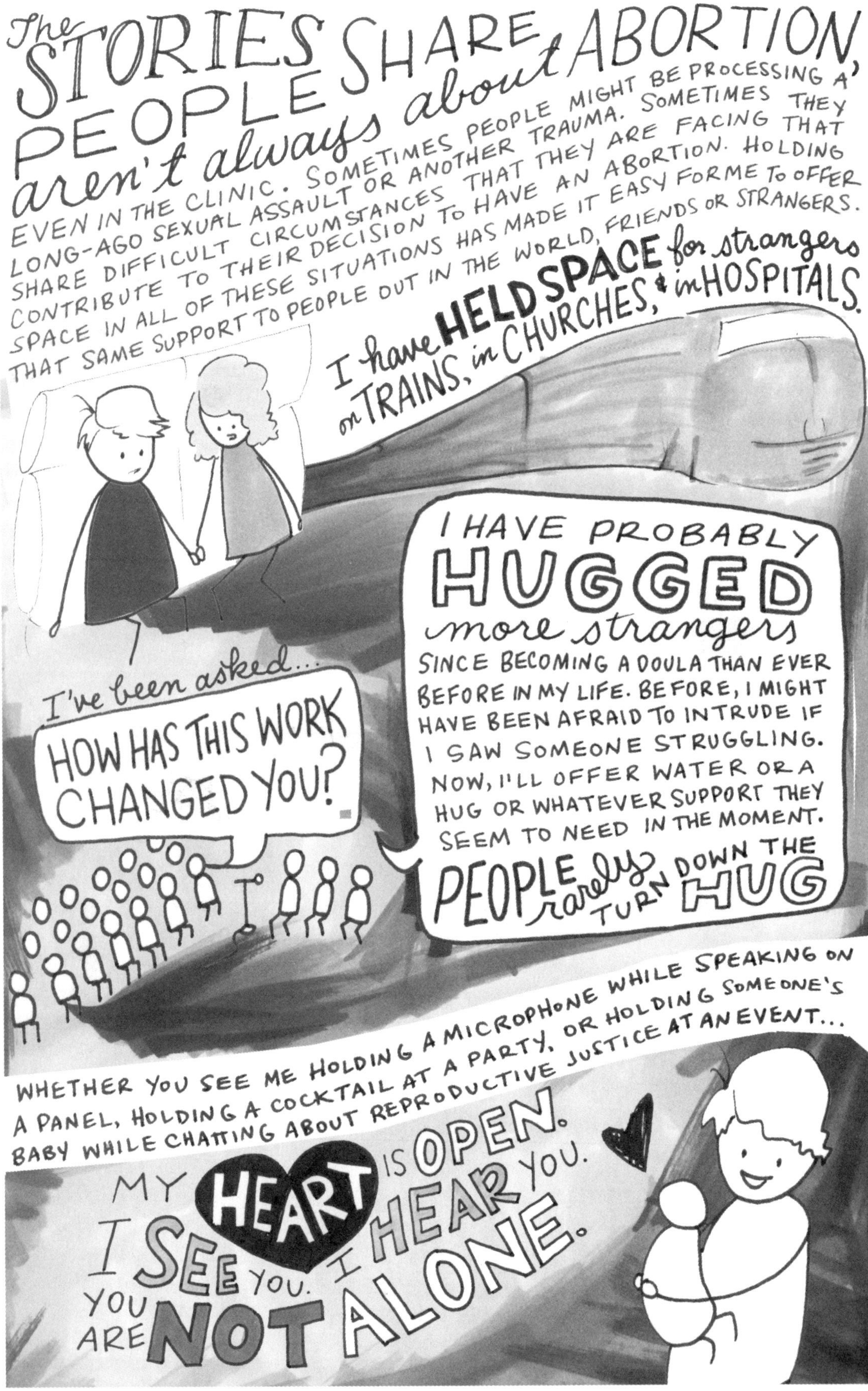
The STORIES PEOPLE SHARE aren't always about ABORTION,
EVEN IN THE CLINIC. SOMETIMES PEOPLE MIGHT BE PROCESSING A LONG-AGO SEXUAL ASSAULT OR ANOTHER TRAUMA. SOMETIMES THEY SHARE DIFFICULT CIRCUMSTANCES THAT THEY ARE FACING THAT CONTRIBUTE TO THEIR DECISION TO HAVE AN ABORTION. HOLDING SPACE IN ALL OF THESE SITUATIONS HAS MADE IT EASY FOR ME TO OFFER THAT SAME SUPPORT TO PEOPLE OUT IN THE WORLD, FRIENDS OR STRANGERS.
I have HELD SPACE for strangers on TRAINS, in CHURCHES, & in HOSPITALS.
I've been asked...
HOW HAS THIS WORK CHANGED YOU?
I HAVE PROBABLY HUGGED more strangers SINCE BECOMING A DOULA THAN EVER BEFORE IN MY LIFE. BEFORE, I MIGHT HAVE BEEN AFRAID TO INTRUDE IF I SAW SOMEONE STRUGGLING. NOW, I'LL OFFER WATER OR A HUG OR WHATEVER SUPPORT THEY SEEM TO NEED IN THE MOMENT.
PEOPLE rarely TURN DOWN THE HUG
WHETHER YOU SEE ME HOLDING A MICROPHONE WHILE SPEAKING ON A PANEL, HOLDING A COCKTAIL AT A PARTY, OR HOLDING SOMEONE'S BABY WHILE CHATTING ABOUT REPRODUCTIVE JUSTICE AT AN EVENT...
MY HEART IS OPEN.
I SEE YOU. I HEAR YOU.
YOU ARE NOT ALONE.

When It's Just A Job

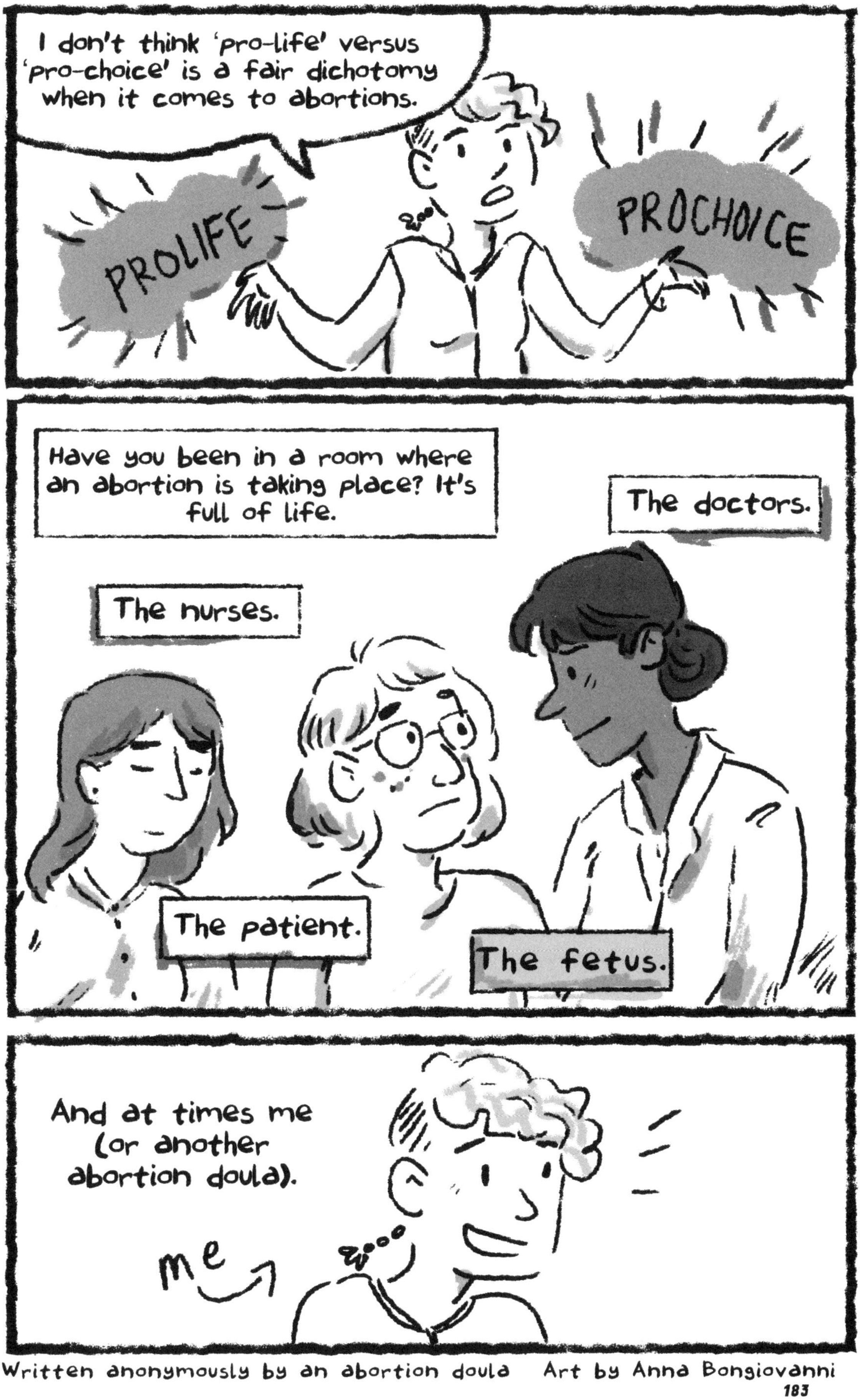
I don't think 'pro-life' versus 'pro-choice' is a fair dichotomy when it comes to abortions.
PROLIFE
PROCHOICE
Have you been in a room where an abortion is taking place? It's full of life.
The doctors.
The nurses.
The patient.
The fetus.
And at times me (or another abortion doula).
me

Written anonymously by an abortion doula Art by Anna Bongiovanni

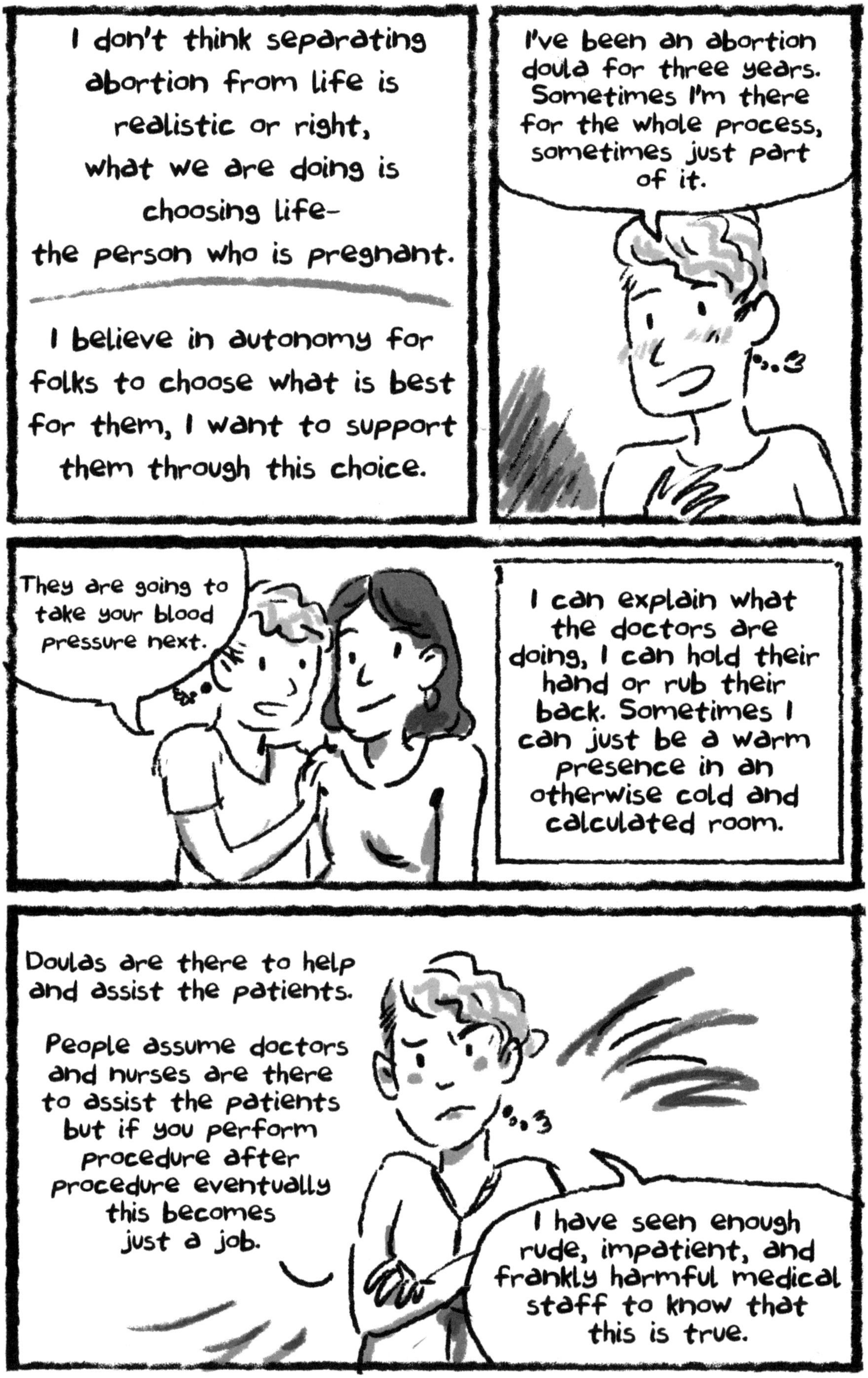
I don't think separating abortion from life is realistic or right, what we are doing is choosing life- the person who is pregnant.
I believe in autonomy for folks to choose what is best for them, I want to support them through this choice.
I've been an abortion doula for three years. Sometimes I'm there for the whole process, sometimes just part of it.
They are going to take your blood pressure next.
I can explain what the doctors are doing, I can hold their hand or rub their back. Sometimes I can just be a warm presence in an otherwise cold and calculated room.
Doulas are there to help and assist the patients.
People assume doctors and nurses are there to assist the patients but if you perform procedure after procedure eventually this becomes just a job.
I have seen enough rude, impatient, and frankly harmful medical staff to know that this is true.

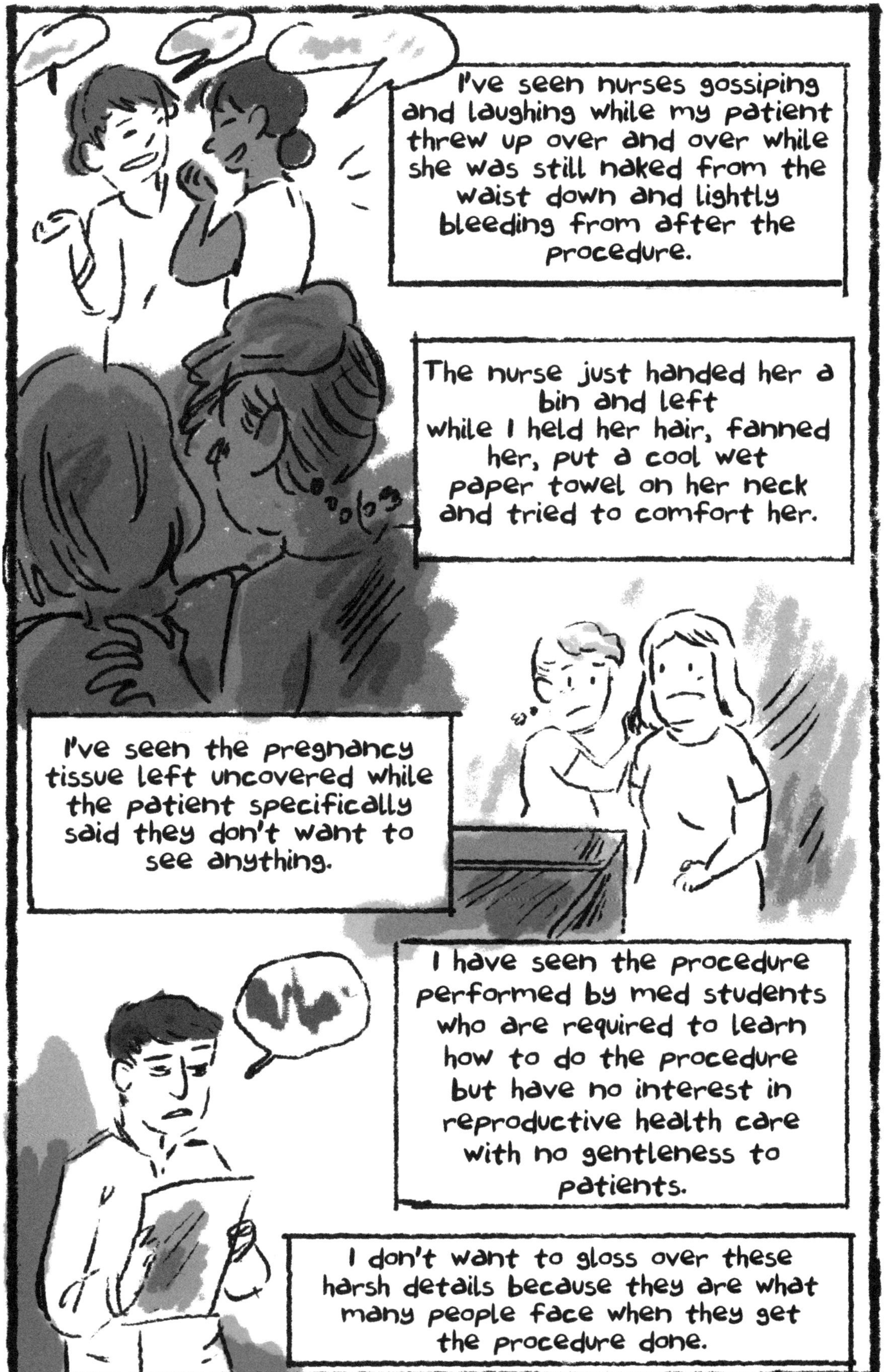
I've seen nurses gossiping and laughing while my patient threw up over and over while she was still naked from the waist down and lightly bleeding from after the procedure.
The nurse just handed her a bin and left while I held her hair, fanned her, put a cool wet paper towel on her neck and tried to comfort her.
I've seen the pregnancy tissue left uncovered while the patient specifically said they don't want to see anything.
I have seen the procedure performed by med students who are required to learn how to do the procedure but have no interest in reproductive health care with no gentleness to patients.
I don't want to gloss over these harsh details because they are what many people face when they get the procedure done.

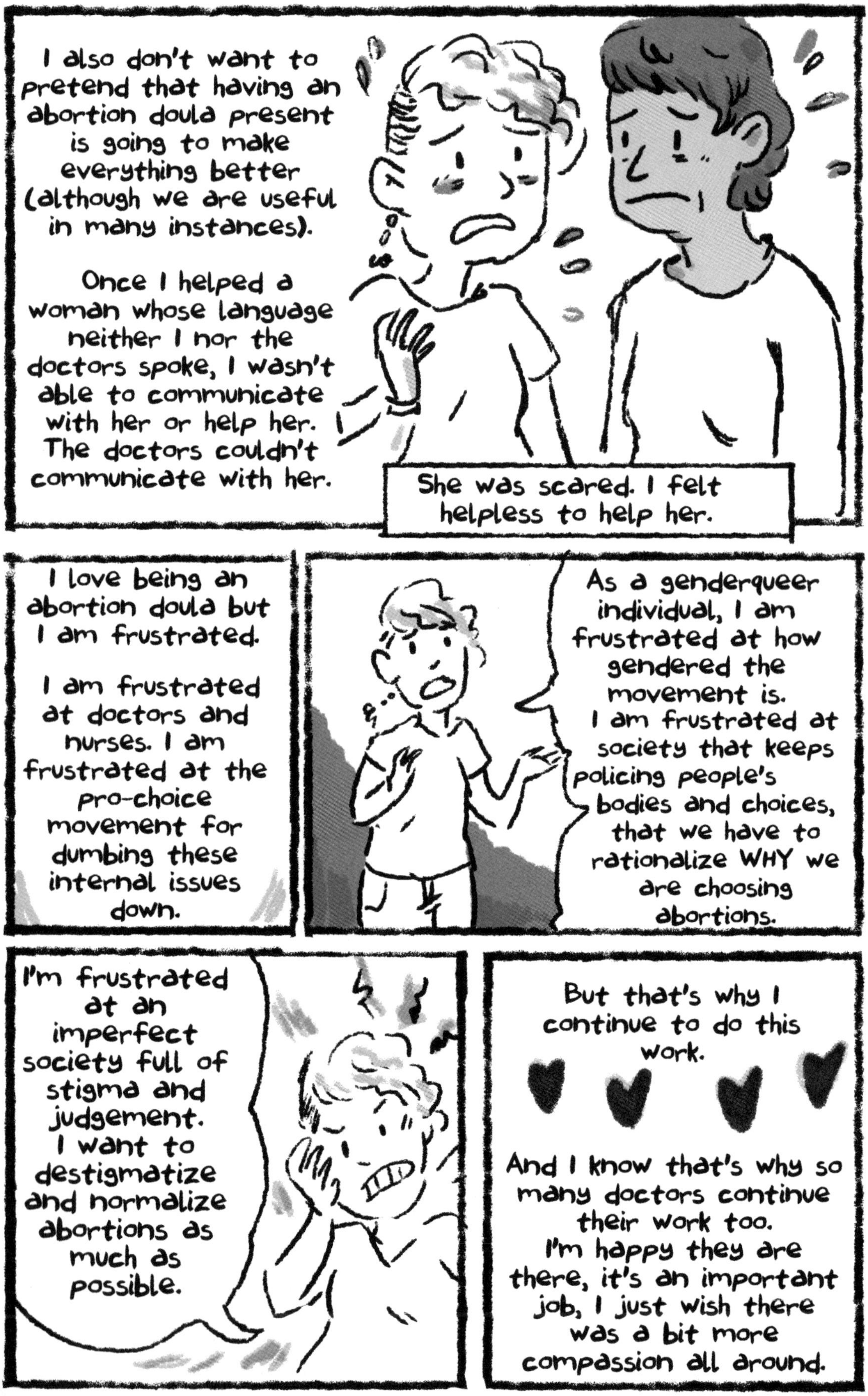
I also don't want to pretend that having an abortion doula present is going to make everything better (although we are useful in many instances).
Once I helped a woman whose language neither I nor the doctors spoke, I wasn't able to communicate with her or help her. The doctors couldn't communicate with her.
She was scared. I felt helpless to help her.
I love being an abortion doula but I am frustrated.
I am frustrated at doctors and nurses. I am frustrated at the pro-choice movement for dumbing these internal issues down.
As a genderqueer individual, I am frustrated at how gendered the movement is.
I am frustrated at society that keeps policing people's bodies and choices, that we have to rationalize WHY we are choosing abortions.
I'm frustrated at an imperfect society full of stigma and judgement.
I want to destigmatize and normalize abortions as much as possible.
But that's why I continue to do this work.
And I know that's why so many doctors continue their work too.
I'm happy they are there, it's an important job, I just wish there was a bit more compassion all around.

mundoferpecto

WRITTEN BY: DANIELA DIAZ   DRAWN BY: STEPHANIE RODRIGUEZ

AT 29 I MOVED FROM PENNSYLVANIA TO D.C. I LEFT TO WORK AT A WOMEN'S REPRODUCTIVE HEALTH ORGANIZATION

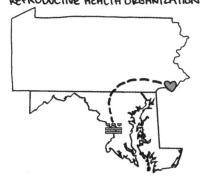

AT THE TIME I WAS USING THE NUVA RING. I LIKED IT BECAUSE I DIDN'T HAVE TO TAKE A PILL EVERY DAY

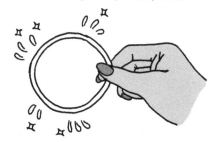

AFTER 3 WEEKS OF WEARING THE NUVA RING I REMOVED IT AND WAITED FOR MY PERIOD TO BEGIN; BUT IT NEVER CAME.

WEIRD THINGS STARTED HAPPENING

I WAS FALLING ASLEEP AT WORK

MY CRAVINGS WERE OUT OF CONTROL!

ALL I WANT IS FRUIT

AND I HAD NAUSEA, BUT AT THE TIME I THOUGHT IT WAS ACID REFLUX.

UGH

6 DAYS PASSED; THE ANXIETY OF WAITING FOR MY PERIOD DROVE ME TO BUY A PREGNANCY TEST.

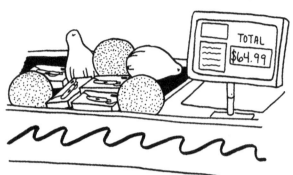

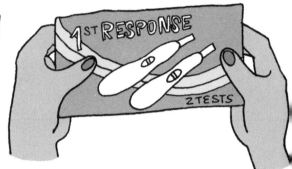

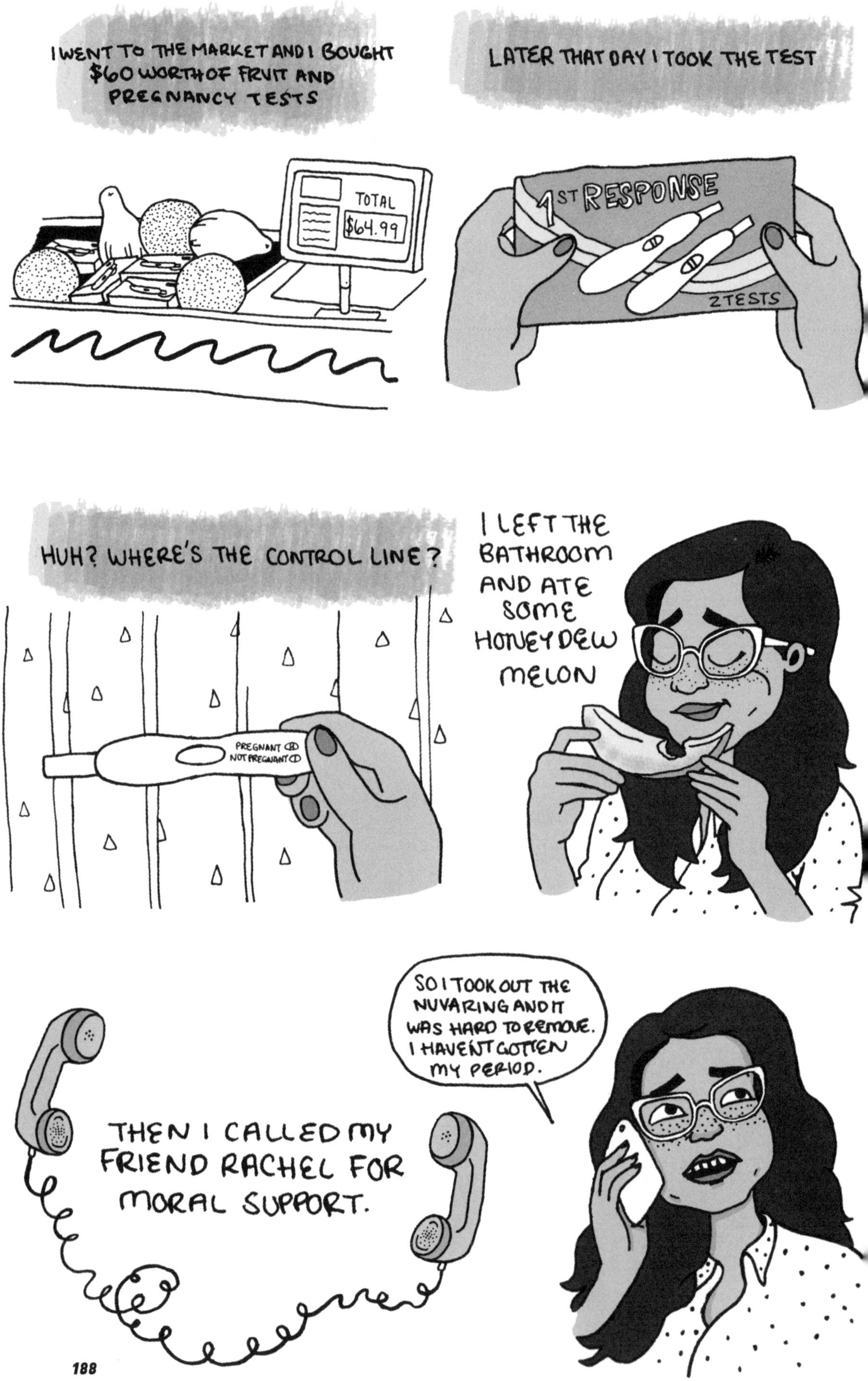

I WENT TO THE MARKET AND I BOUGHT $60 WORTH OF FRUIT AND PREGNANCY TESTS
TOTAL
$64.99
LATER THAT DAY I TOOK THE TEST
1ST RESPONSE
2 TESTS
HUH? WHERE'S THE CONTROL LINE?
PREGNANT
NOT PREGNANT
I LEFT THE BATHROOM AND ATE SOME HONEYDEW MELON
THEN I CALLED MY FRIEND RACHEL FOR MORAL SUPPORT.
SO I TOOK OUT THE NUVARING AND IT WAS HARD TO REMOVE. I HAVEN'T GOTTEN MY PERIOD.

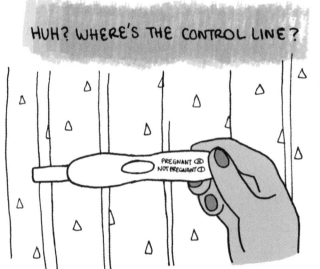

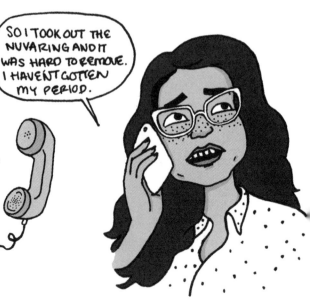

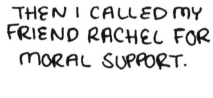

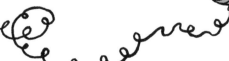

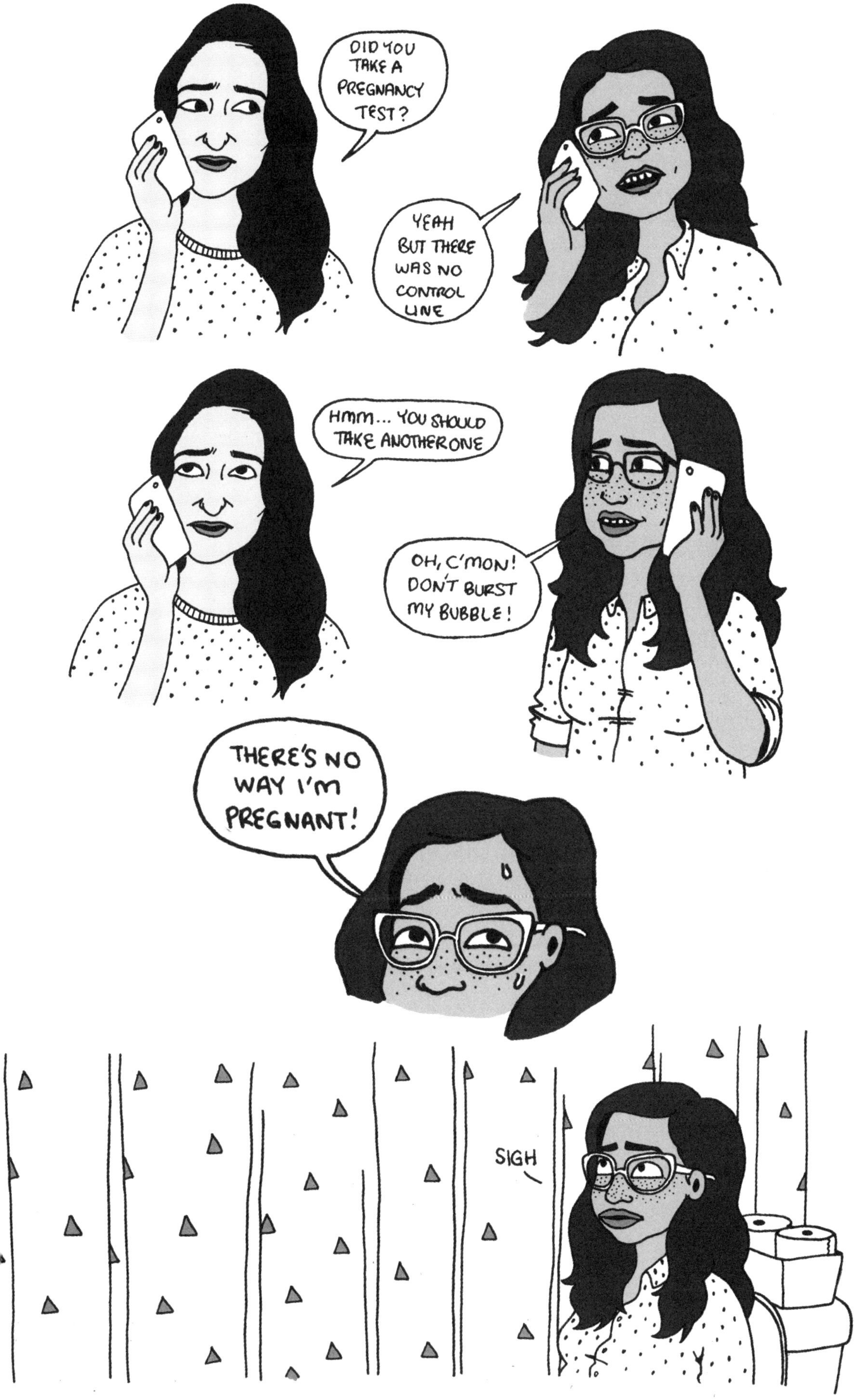
DID YOU TAKE A PREGNANCY TEST?
YEAH BUT THERE WAS NO CONTROL LINE
HMM... YOU SHOULD TAKE ANOTHER ONE
OH, C'MON! DON'T BURST MY BUBBLE!
THERE'S NO WAY I'M PREGNANT!
SIGH

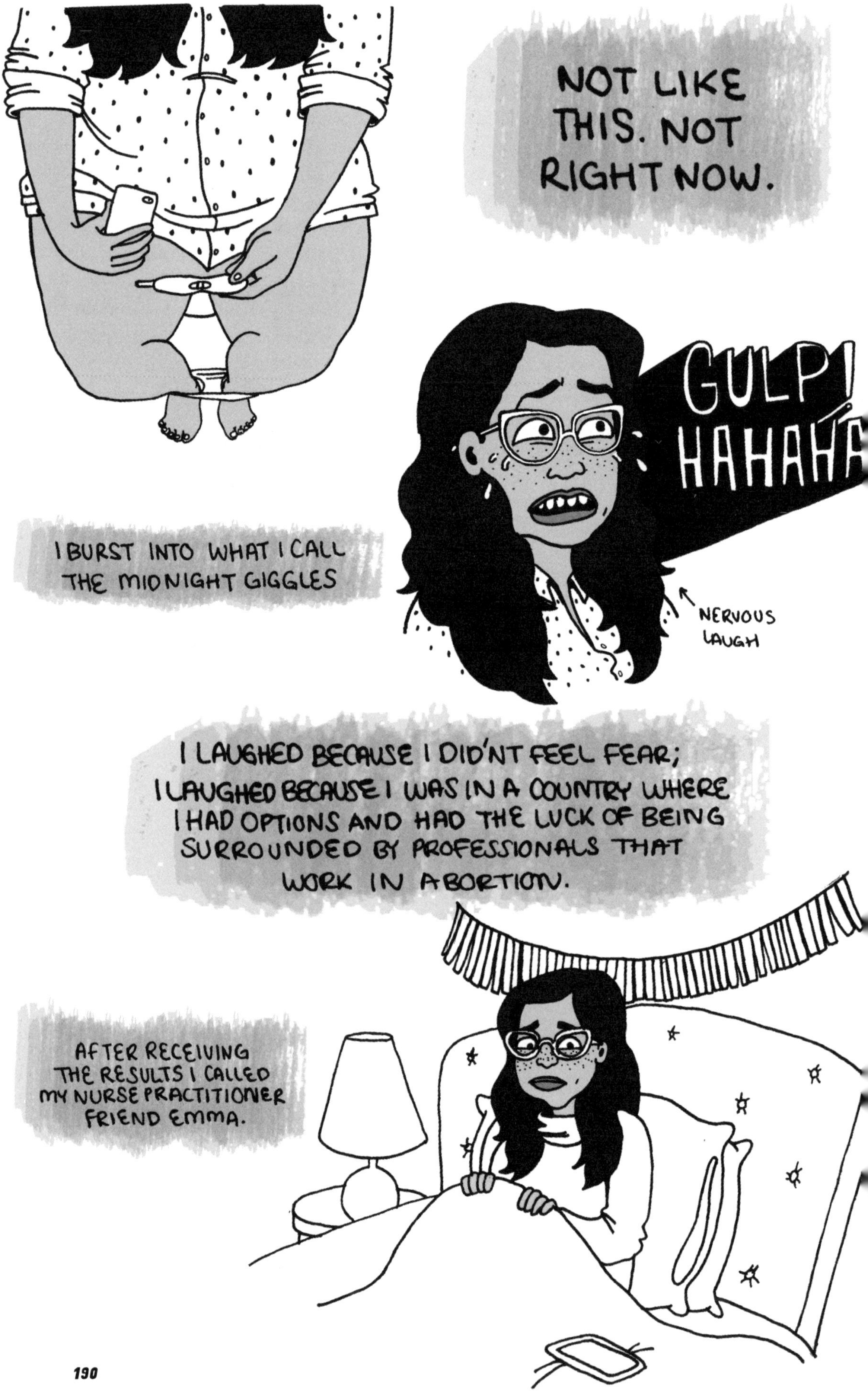

NOT LIKE THIS. NOT RIGHT NOW.
GULP! HAHAHA
I BURST INTO WHAT I CALL THE MIDNIGHT GIGGLES
NERVOUS LAUGH
I LAUGHED BECAUSE I DIDN'T FEEL FEAR; I LAUGHED BECAUSE I WAS IN A COUNTRY WHERE I HAD OPTIONS AND HAD THE LUCK OF BEING SURROUNDED BY PROFESSIONALS THAT WORK IN ABORTION.
AFTER RECEIVING THE RESULTS I CALLED MY NURSE PRACTITIONER FRIEND EMMA.

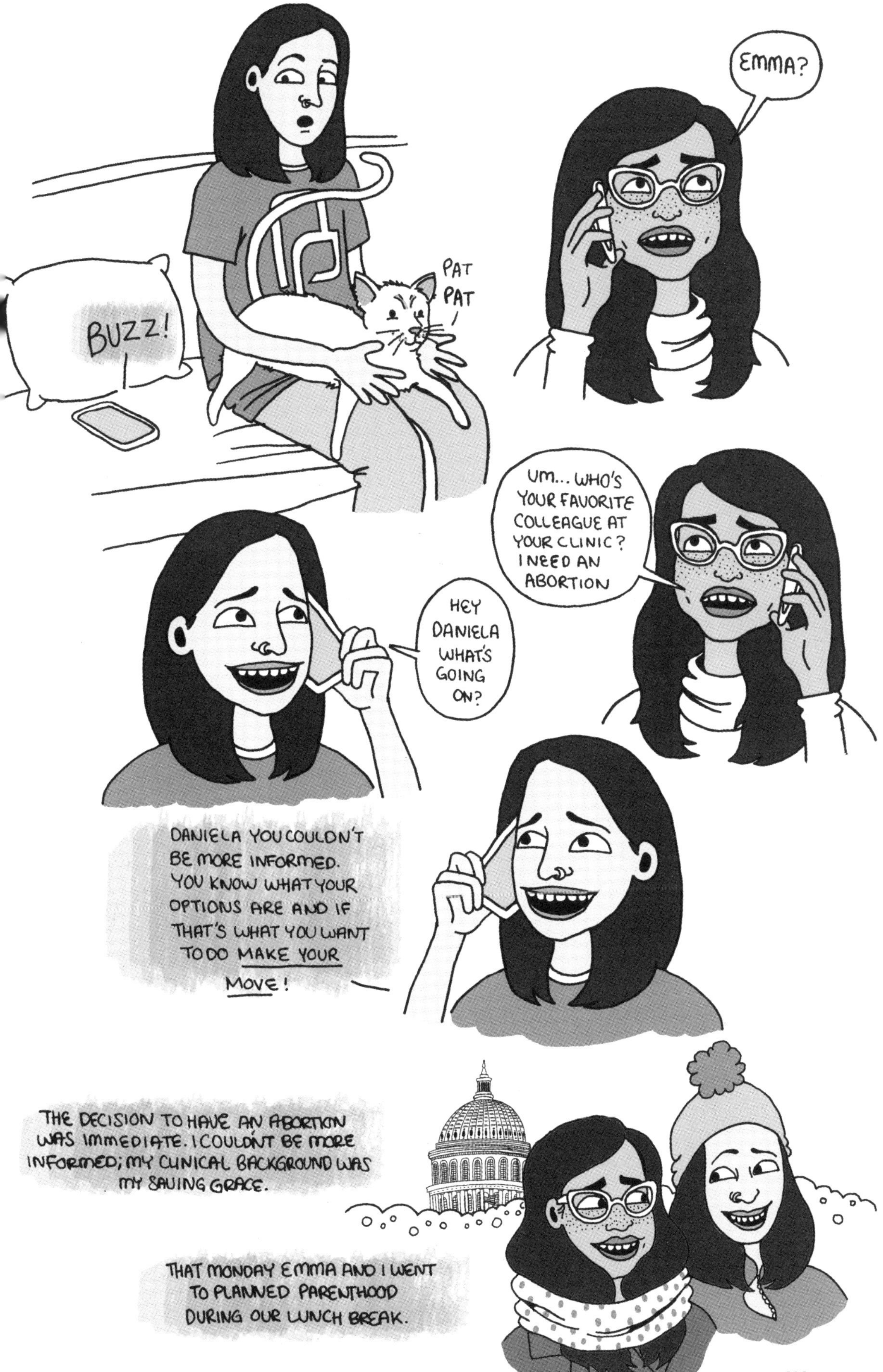
BUZZ!
PAT PAT
EMMA?
HEY DANIELA WHAT'S GOING ON?
UM... WHO'S YOUR FAVORITE COLLEAGUE AT YOUR CLINIC? I NEED AN ABORTION
DANIELA YOU COULDN'T BE MORE INFORMED. YOU KNOW WHAT YOUR OPTIONS ARE AND IF THAT'S WHAT YOU WANT TO DO MAKE YOUR MOVE!
THE DECISION TO HAVE AN ABORTION WAS IMMEDIATE. I COULDN'T BE MORE INFORMED; MY CLINICAL BACKGROUND WAS MY SAVING GRACE.
THAT MONDAY EMMA AND I WENT TO PLANNED PARENTHOOD DURING OUR LUNCH BREAK.

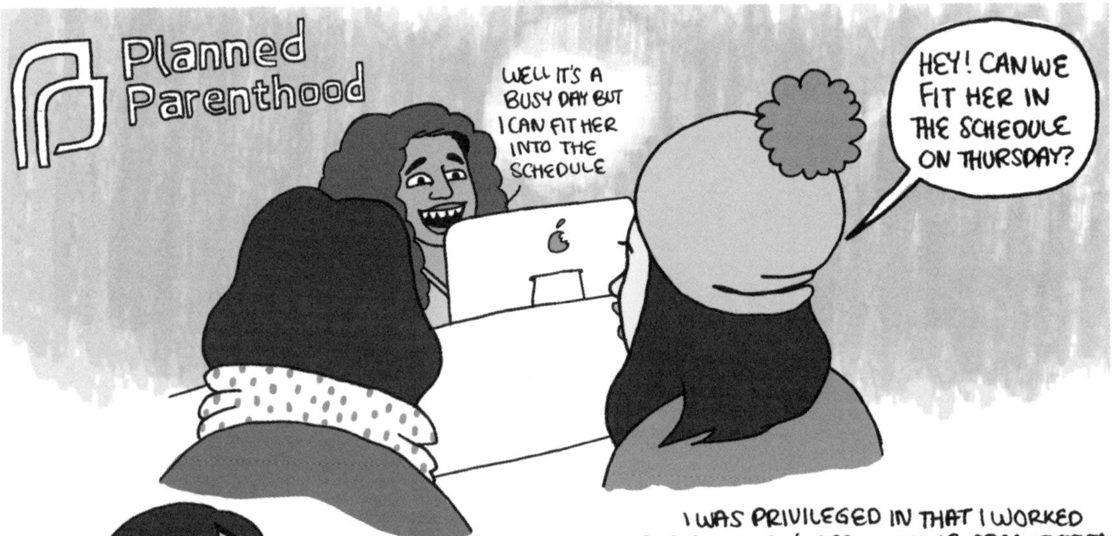
Planned Parenthood
WELL IT'S A BUSY DAY BUT I CAN FIT HER INTO THE SCHEDULE
HEY! CAN WE FIT HER IN THE SCHEDULE ON THURSDAY?

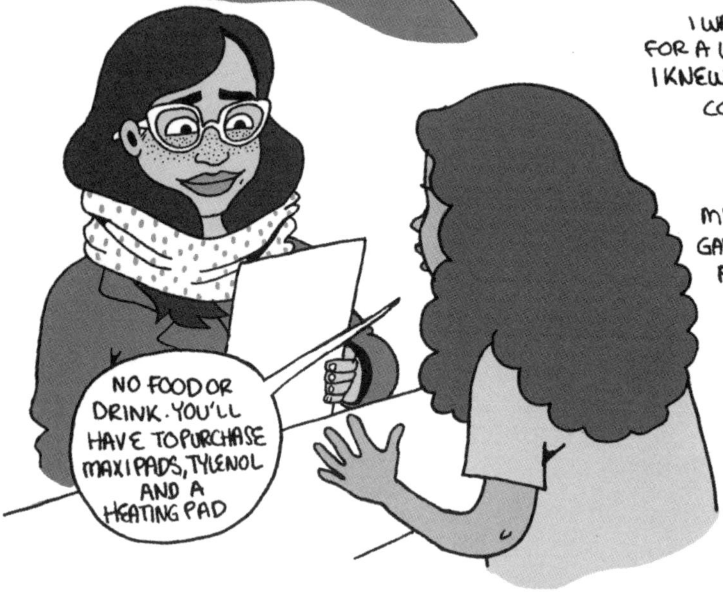
NO FOOD OR DRINK. YOU'LL HAVE TO PURCHASE MAXI PADS, TYLENOL AND A HEATING PAD

I WAS PRIVILEGED IN THAT I WORKED FOR A WOMEN'S REPRODUCTIVE ORGANIZATION. I KNEW MY RIGHTS, MY OPTIONS AND I COULD CONSULT WITH A PROFESSIONAL WORKING IN ABORTION.

MY EXPERIENCE IN THIS FIELD ALSO GAVE ME THE CONFIDENCE TO MAKE A POSITIVE DECISION WITHOUT ANY SHAME OR SELF BLAME.

BUT IT WASN'T ALL EASY.

A SNOWSTORM ROLLED INTO D.C. THE NIGHT BEFORE MY PROCEDURE.

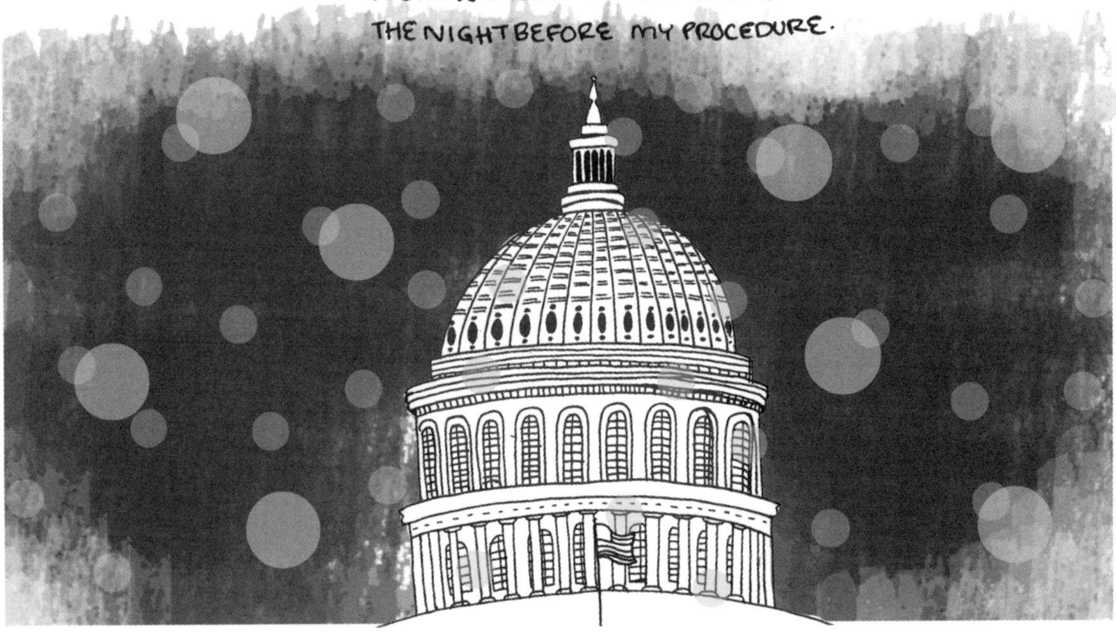

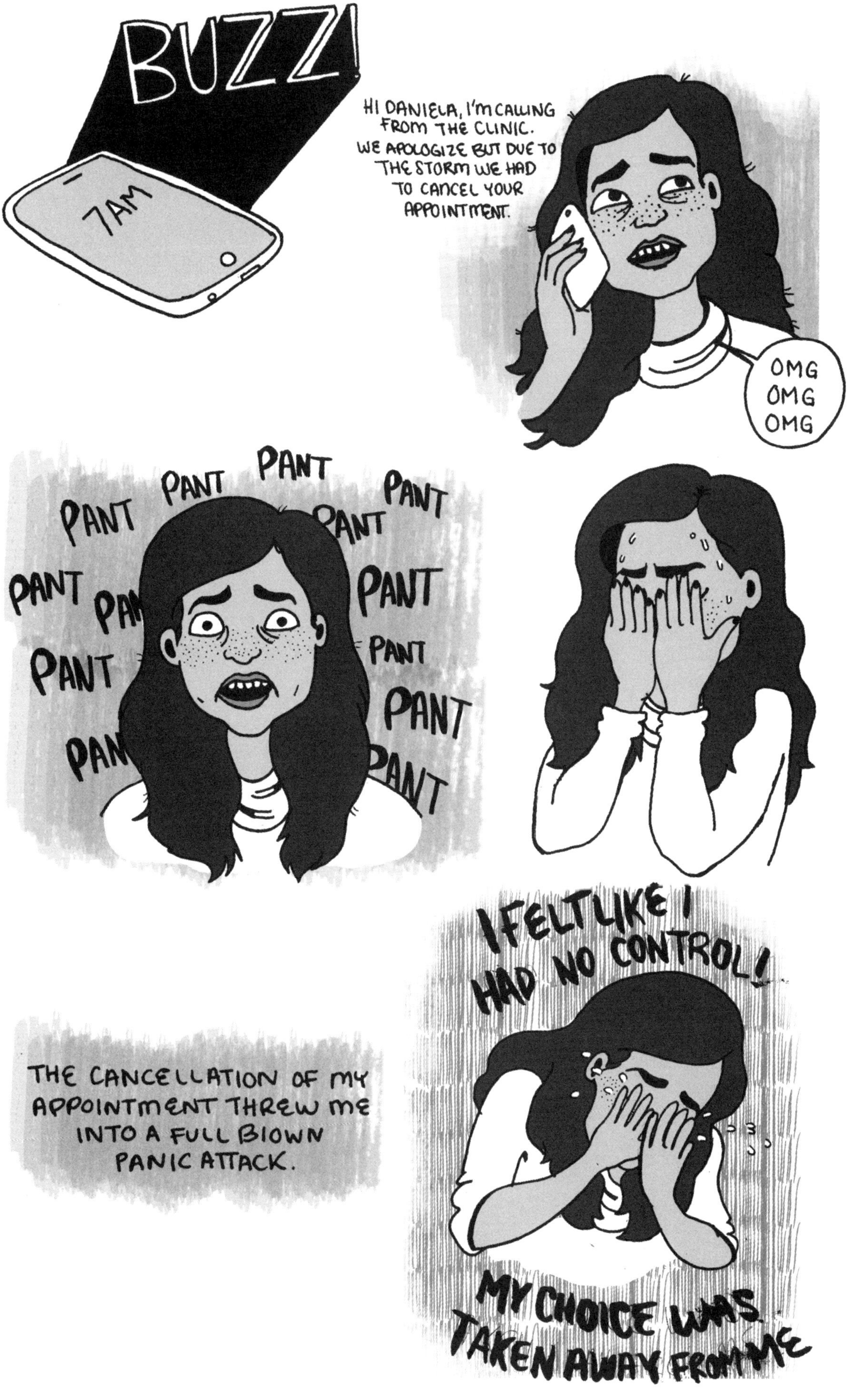
BUZZ!
7AM
HI DANIELA, I'M CALLING FROM THE CLINIC. WE APOLOGIZE BUT DUE TO THE STORM WE HAD TO CANCEL YOUR APPOINTMENT.
OMG OMG OMG
PANT PANT PANT PANT PANT PANT PANT PANT PANT PANT PANT PANT PANT PANT
THE CANCELLATION OF MY APPOINTMENT THREW ME INTO A FULL BLOWN PANIC ATTACK.
I FELT LIKE I HAD NO CONTROL!
MY CHOICE WAS TAKEN AWAY FROM ME

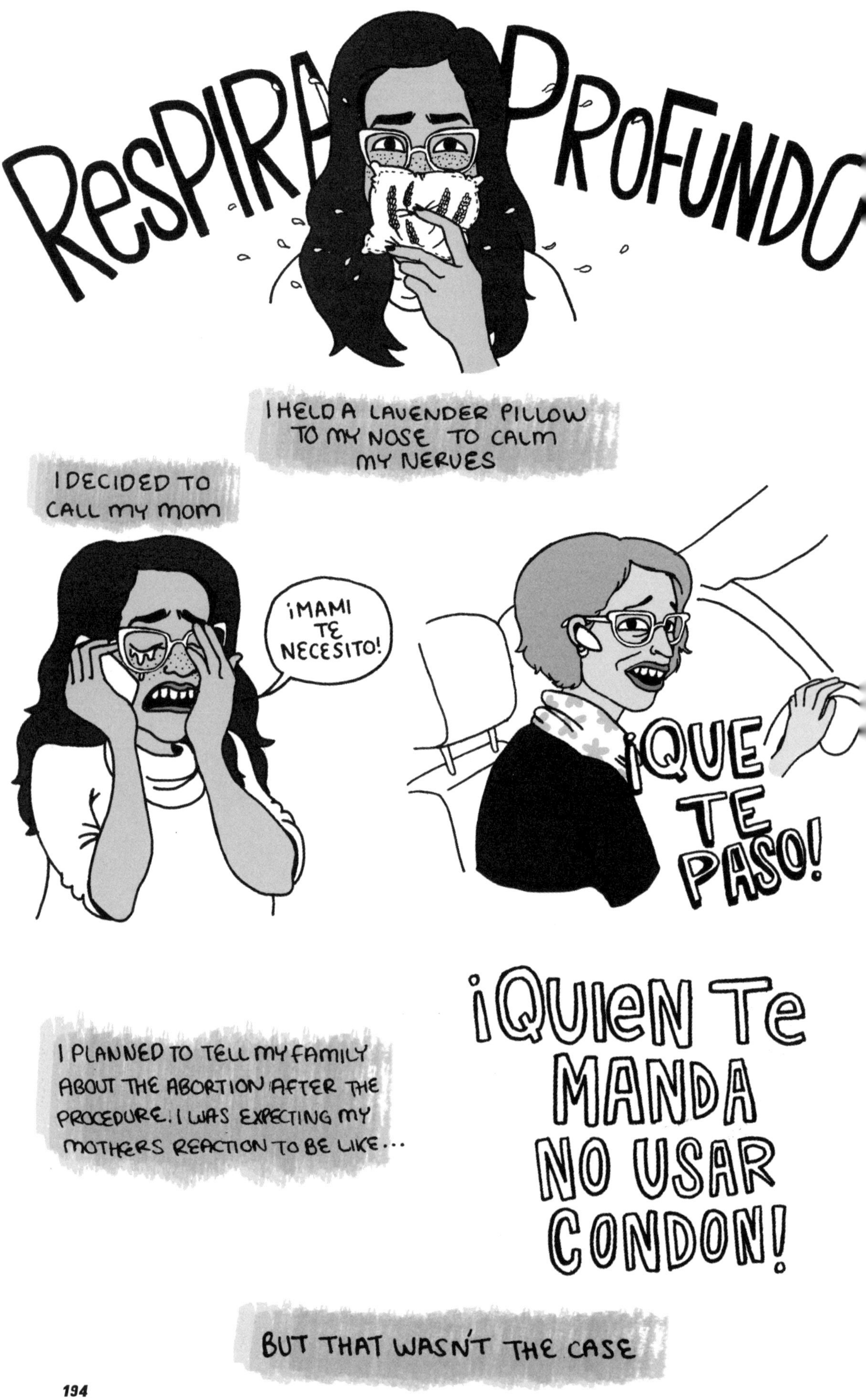
RESPIRA PROFUNDO
I HELD A LAVENDER PILLOW TO MY NOSE TO CALM MY NERVES
I DECIDED TO CALL MY MOM
¡MAMI TE NECESITO!
¡QUE TE PASO!
I PLANNED TO TELL MY FAMILY ABOUT THE ABORTION AFTER THE PROCEDURE. I WAS EXPECTING MY MOTHERS REACTION TO BE LIKE...
¡QUIEN TE MANDA NO USAR CONDON!
BUT THAT WASN'T THE CASE

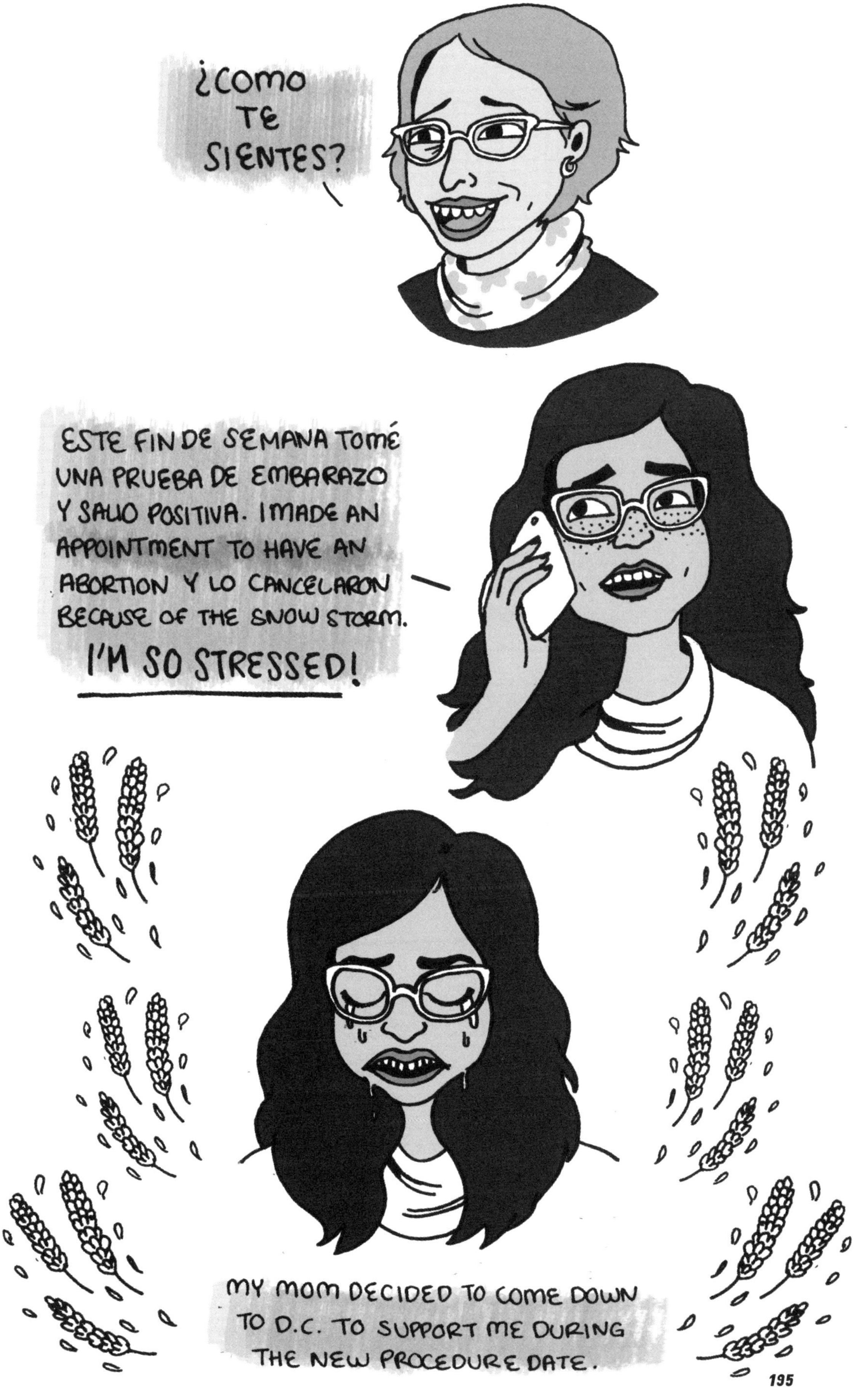
¿COMO TE SIENTES?
ESTE FIN DE SEMANA TOMÉ UNA PRUEBA DE EMBARAZO Y SALIO POSITIVA. I MADE AN APPOINTMENT TO HAVE AN ABORTION Y LO CANCELARON BECAUSE OF THE SNOW STORM.
I'M SO STRESSED!
MY MOM DECIDED TO COME DOWN TO D.C. TO SUPPORT ME DURING THE NEW PROCEDURE DATE.

PROCEDURE DAY

ON OUR WAY TO THE CLINIC I REALIZED THE CLINIC WAS BLOCKED BY PROTESTERS. I COULDN'T DEAL WITH THE STRESS OF THE PROCEDURE, PROTESTERS AND MY MOTHER'S NERVES.

I DECIDED IT WAS BEST FOR MY MOM NOT TO GO IN WITH ME.

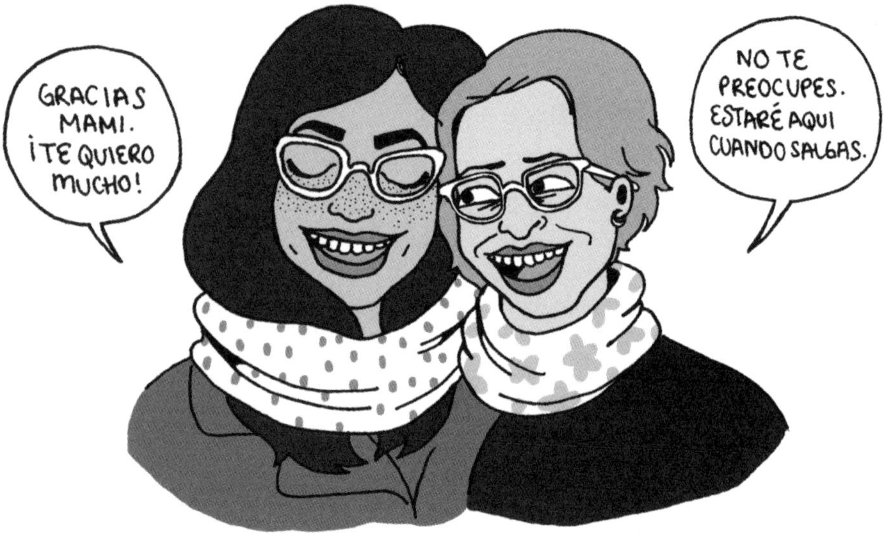
GRACIAS MAMI. ¡TE QUIERO MUCHO!
NO TE PREOCUPES. ESTARÉ AQUI CUANDO SALGAS.

AS I WALKED INTO THE CLINIC I THOUGHT TO MYSELF.

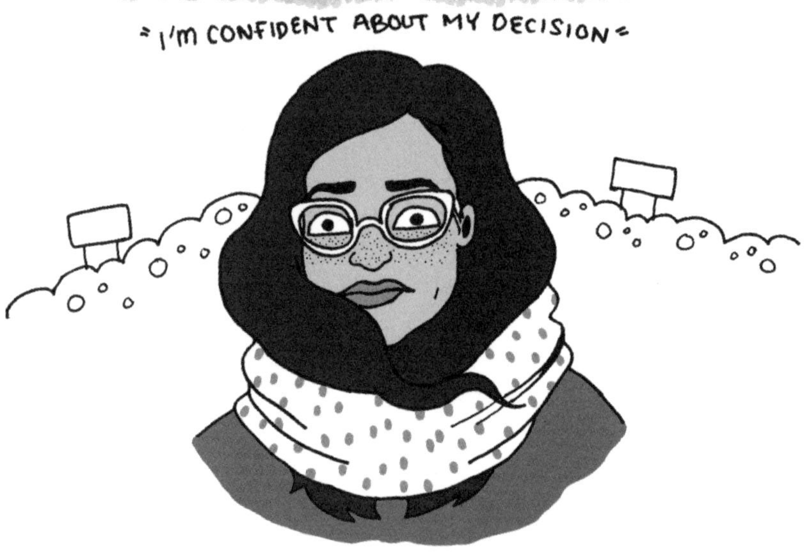
= I'M CONFIDENT ABOUT MY DECISION =

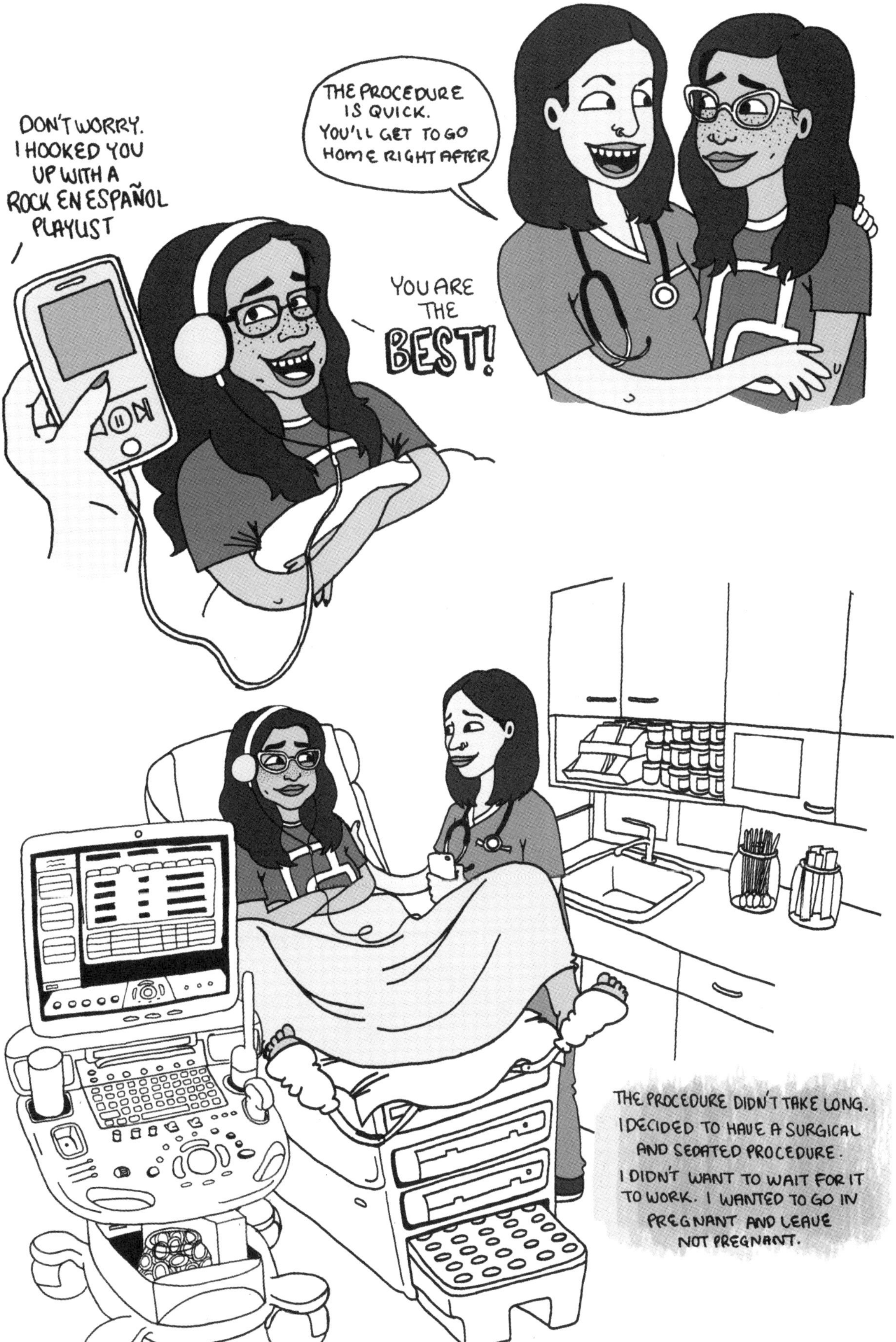
DON'T WORRY. I HOOKED YOU UP WITH A ROCK EN ESPAÑOL PLAYLIST
THE PROCEDURE IS QUICK. YOU'LL GET TO GO HOME RIGHT AFTER
YOU ARE THE BEST!
THE PROCEDURE DIDN'T TAKE LONG. I DECIDED TO HAVE A SURGICAL AND SEDATED PROCEDURE.
I DIDN'T WANT TO WAIT FOR IT TO WORK. I WANTED TO GO IN PREGNANT AND LEAVE NOT PREGNANT.

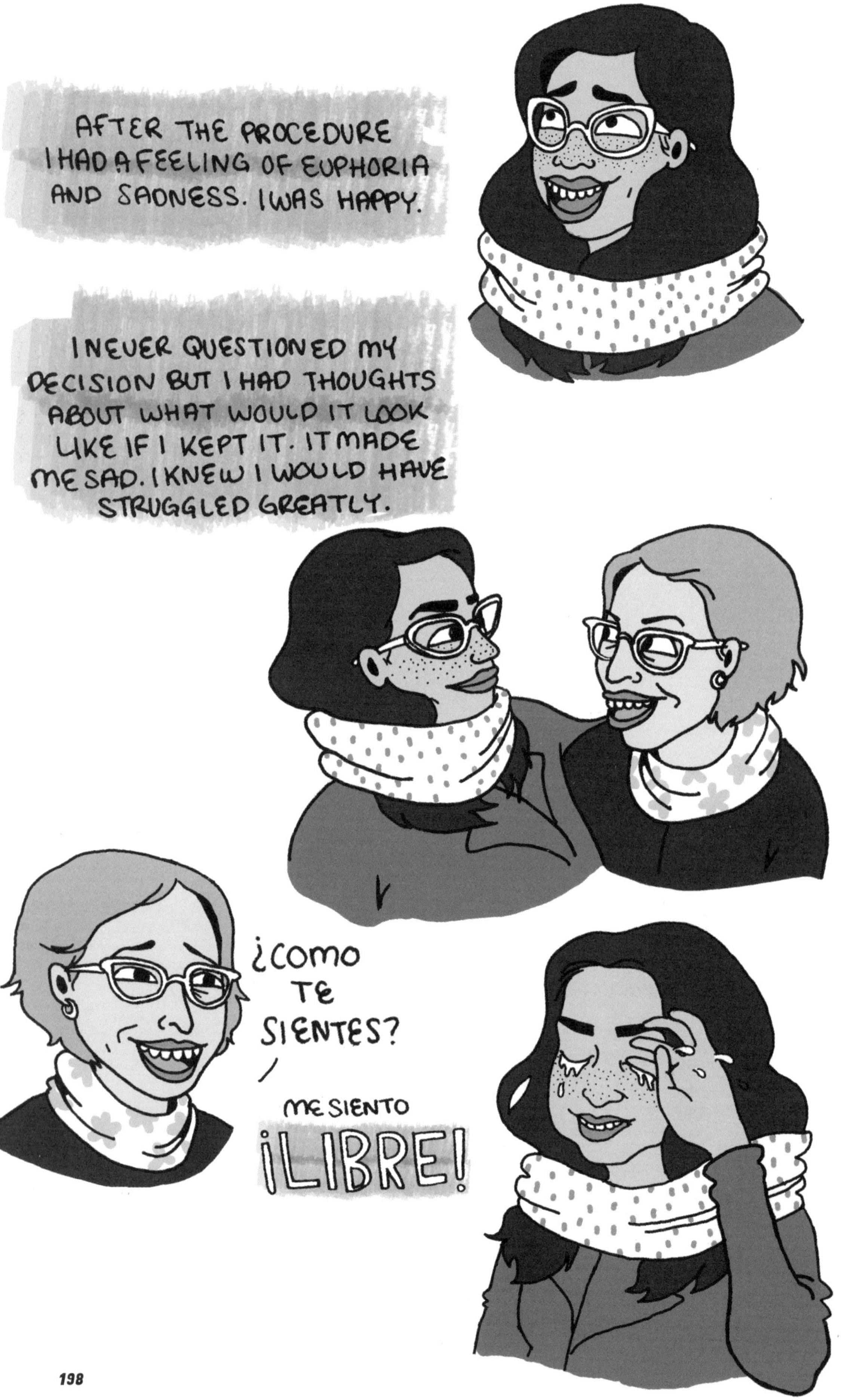
AFTER THE PROCEDURE I HAD A FEELING OF EUPHORIA AND SADNESS. I WAS HAPPY.
I NEVER QUESTIONED MY DECISION BUT I HAD THOUGHTS ABOUT WHAT WOULD IT LOOK LIKE IF I KEPT IT. IT MADE ME SAD. I KNEW I WOULD HAVE STRUGGLED GREATLY.
¿COMO TE SIENTES?
ME SIENTO ¡LIBRE!

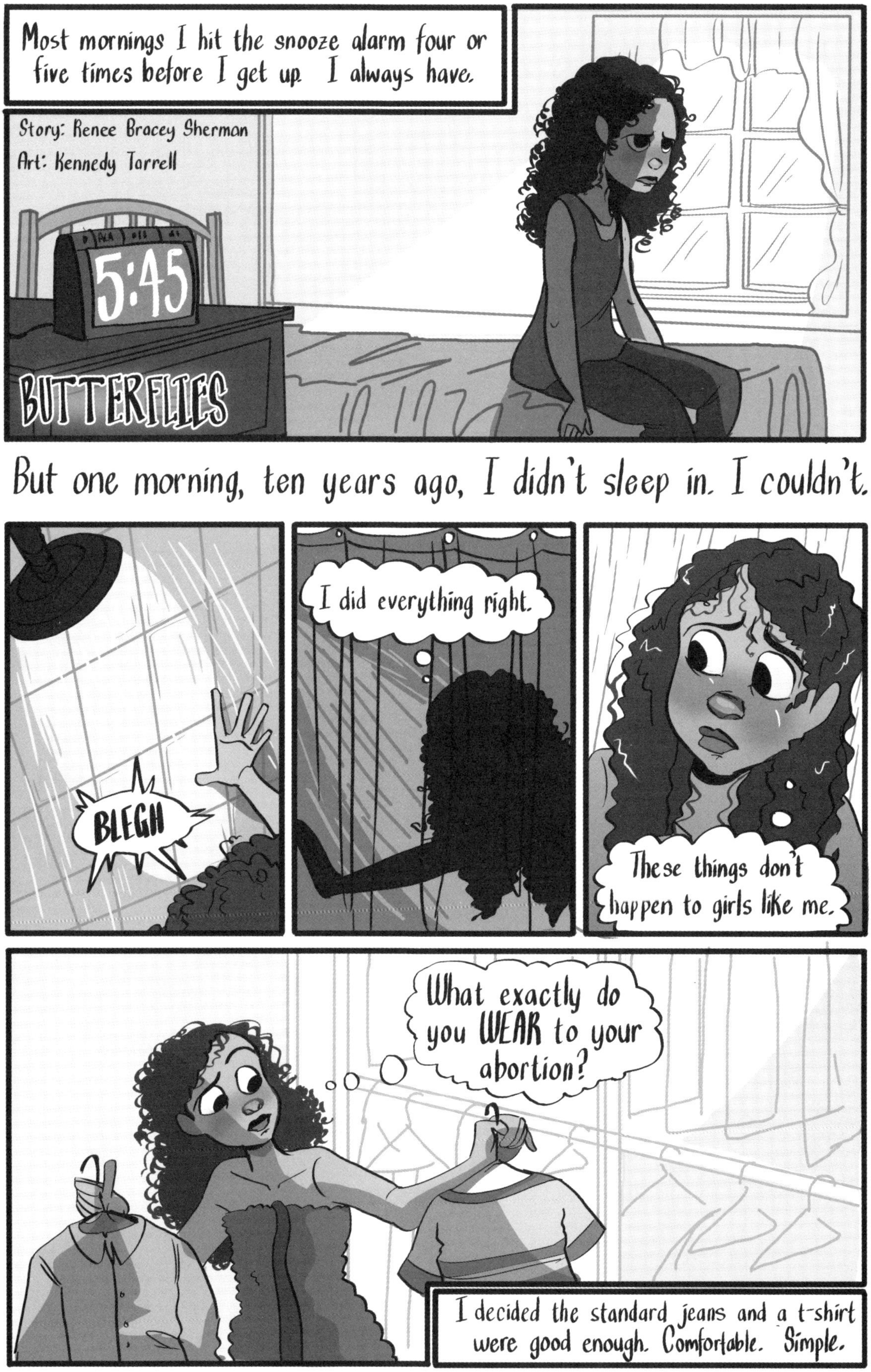

Most mornings I hit the snooze alarm four or five times before I get up. I always have.
Story: Renee Bracey Sherman
Art: Kennedy Tarrell
5:45
BUTTERFLIES
But one morning, ten years ago, I didn't sleep in. I couldn't.
BLEGH
I did everything right.
These things don't happen to girls like me.
What exactly do you WEAR to your abortion?
I decided the standard jeans and a t-shirt were good enough. Comfortable. Simple.

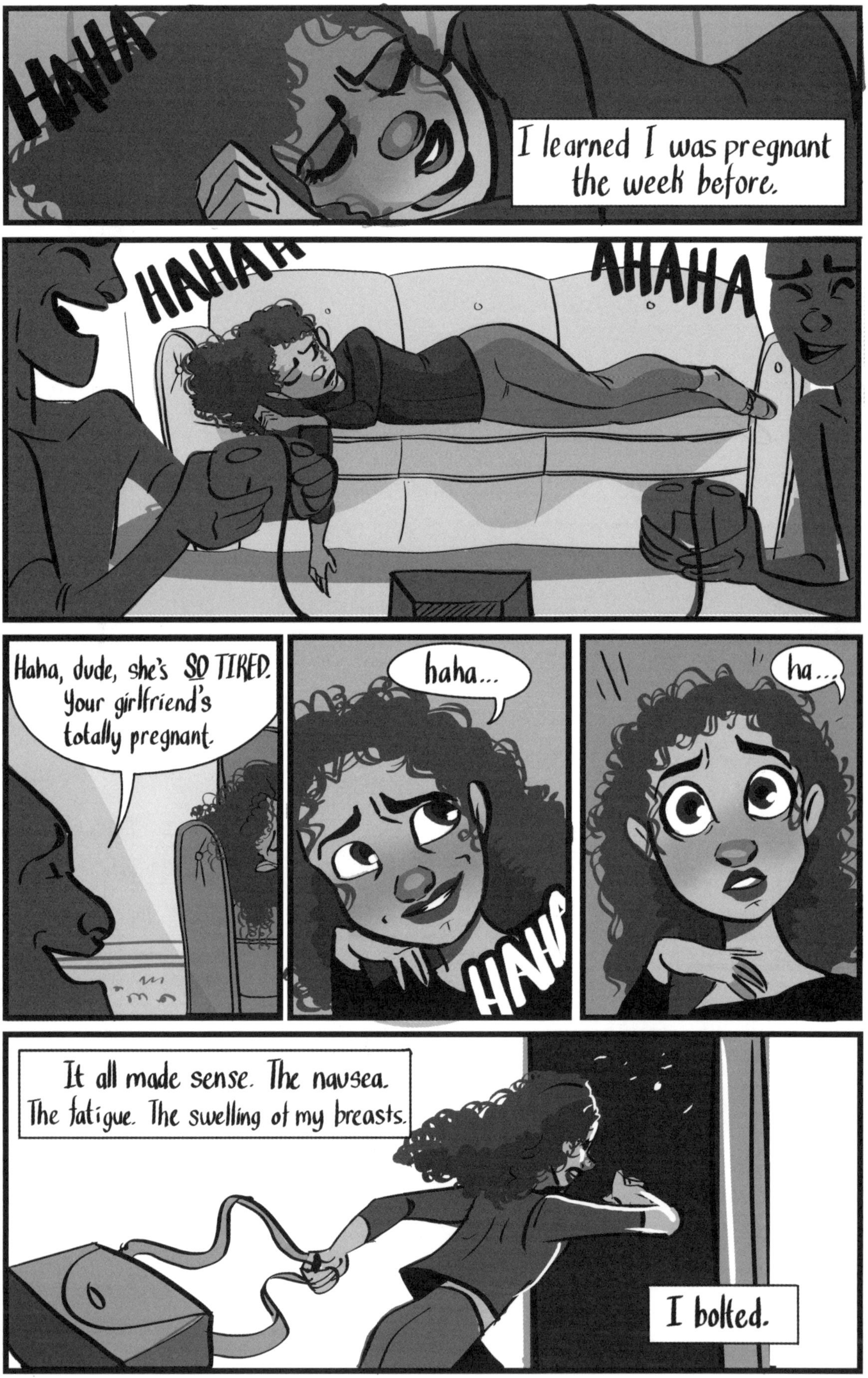
HAHA
I learned I was pregnant the week before.
HAHAH
AHAHA
Haha, dude, she's SO TIRED. Your girlfriend's totally pregnant.
haha...
HAH
ha...
It all made sense. The nausea. The fatigue. The swelling of my breasts.
I bolted.

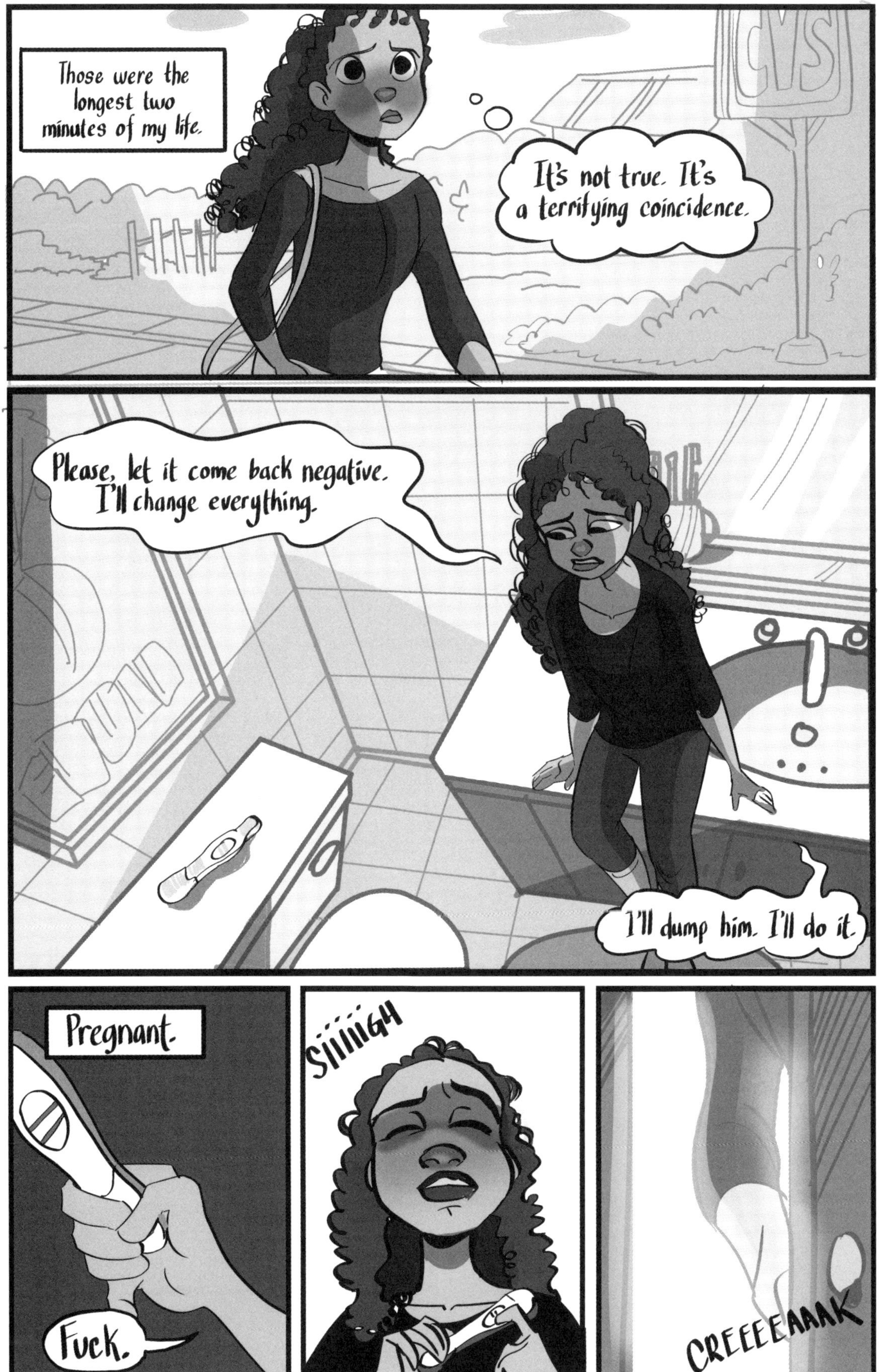
Those were the longest two minutes of my life.
It's not true. It's a terrifying coincidence.
Please, let it come back negative. I'll change everything.
I'll dump him. I'll do it.
Pregnant.
Fuck.
SIIIIIGH
CREEEEAAAK

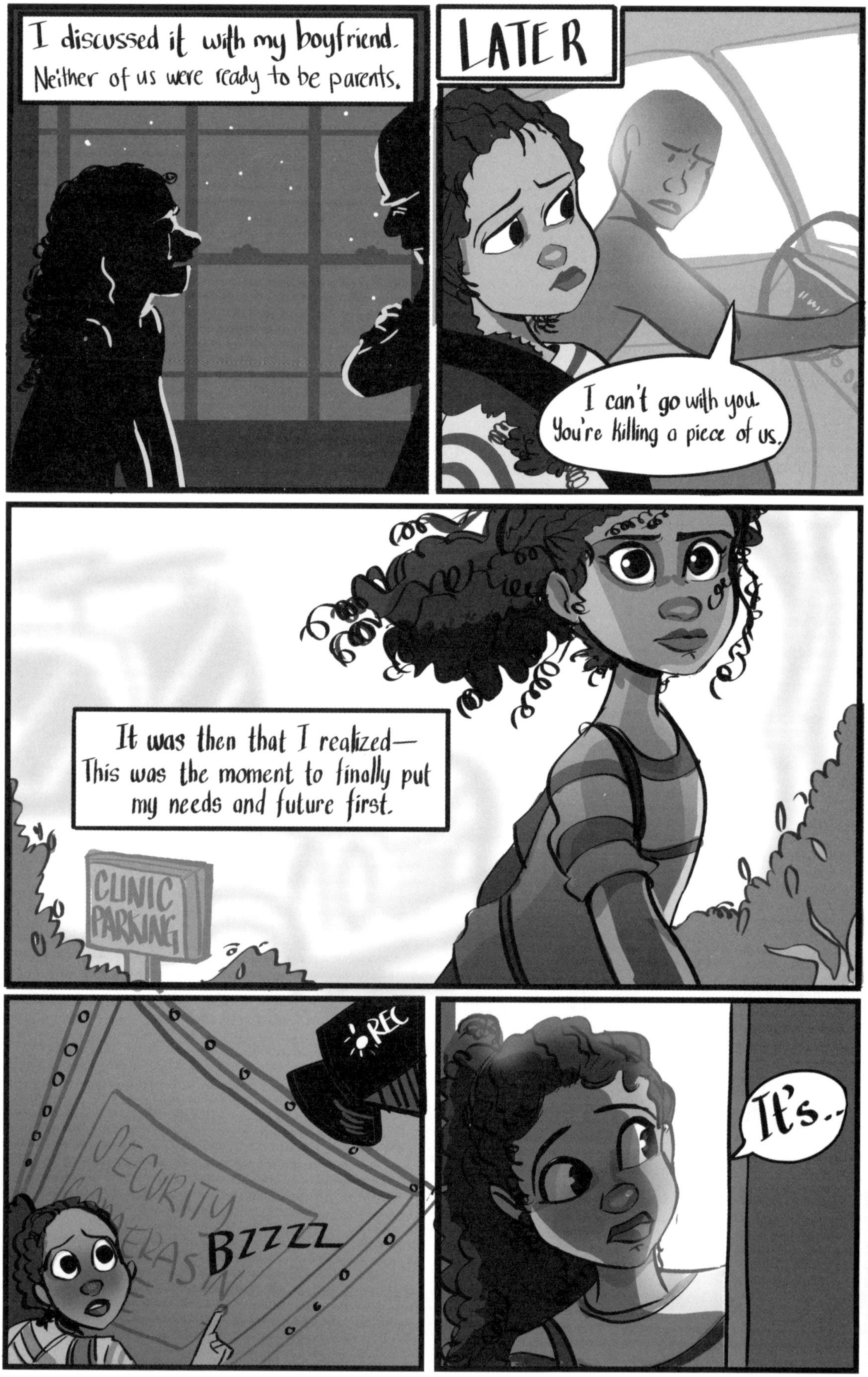
I discussed it with my boyfriend. Neither of us were ready to be parents.
LATER
I can't go with you. You're killing a piece of us.
It was then that I realized— This was the moment to finally put my needs and future first.
CLINIC PARKING
REC
SECURITY CAMERAS IN
BZZZZ
It's..

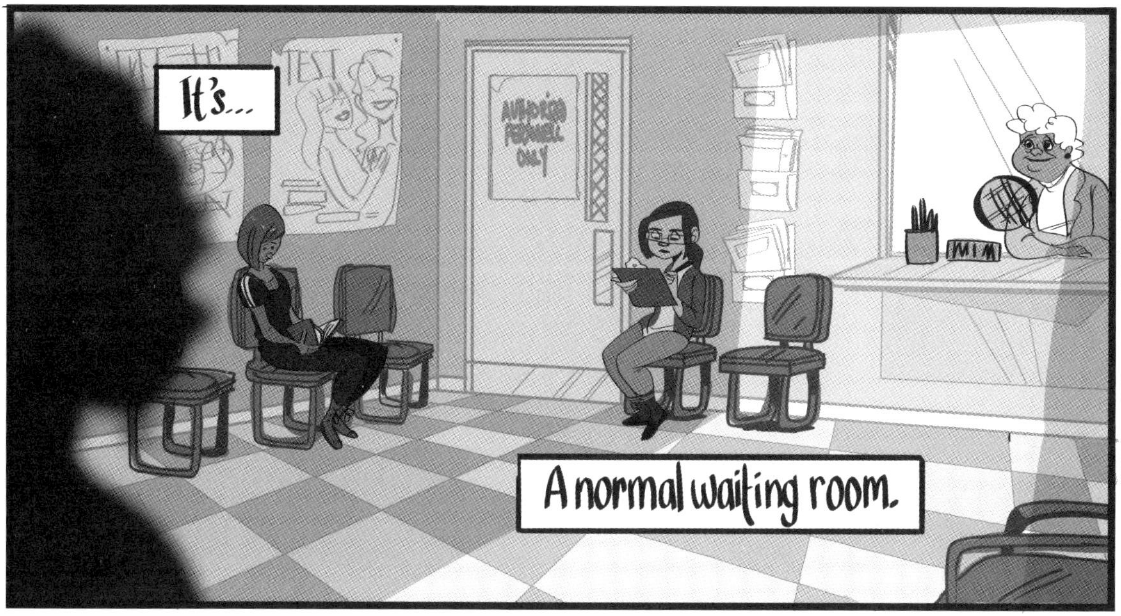
It's...
A normal waiting room.

$350. That's how much my abortion cost. I couldn't use my insurance because my parents would find out. I hadn't told them. I figured I would one day. Just not today.

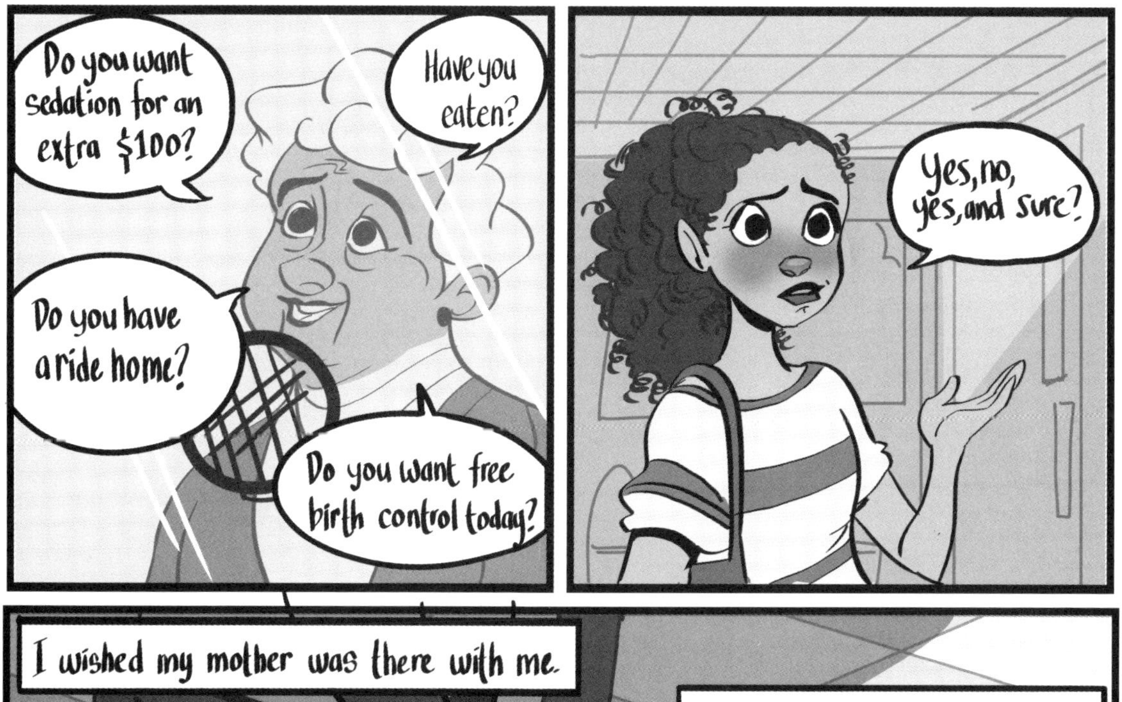
Do you want sedation for an extra $100?
Have you eaten?
Do you have a ride home?
Do you want free birth control today?
Yes, no, yes, and sure?

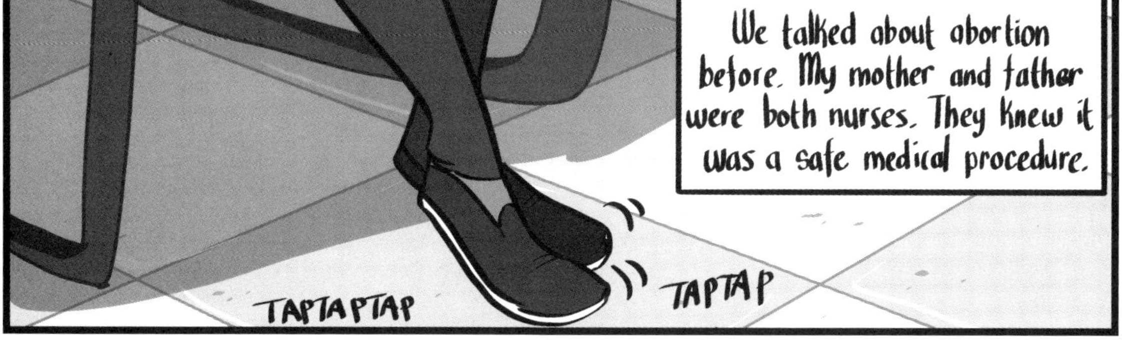
I wished my mother was there with me.
We talked about abortion before. My mother and father were both nurses. They knew it was a safe medical procedure.
TAPTAPTAP
TAPTAP

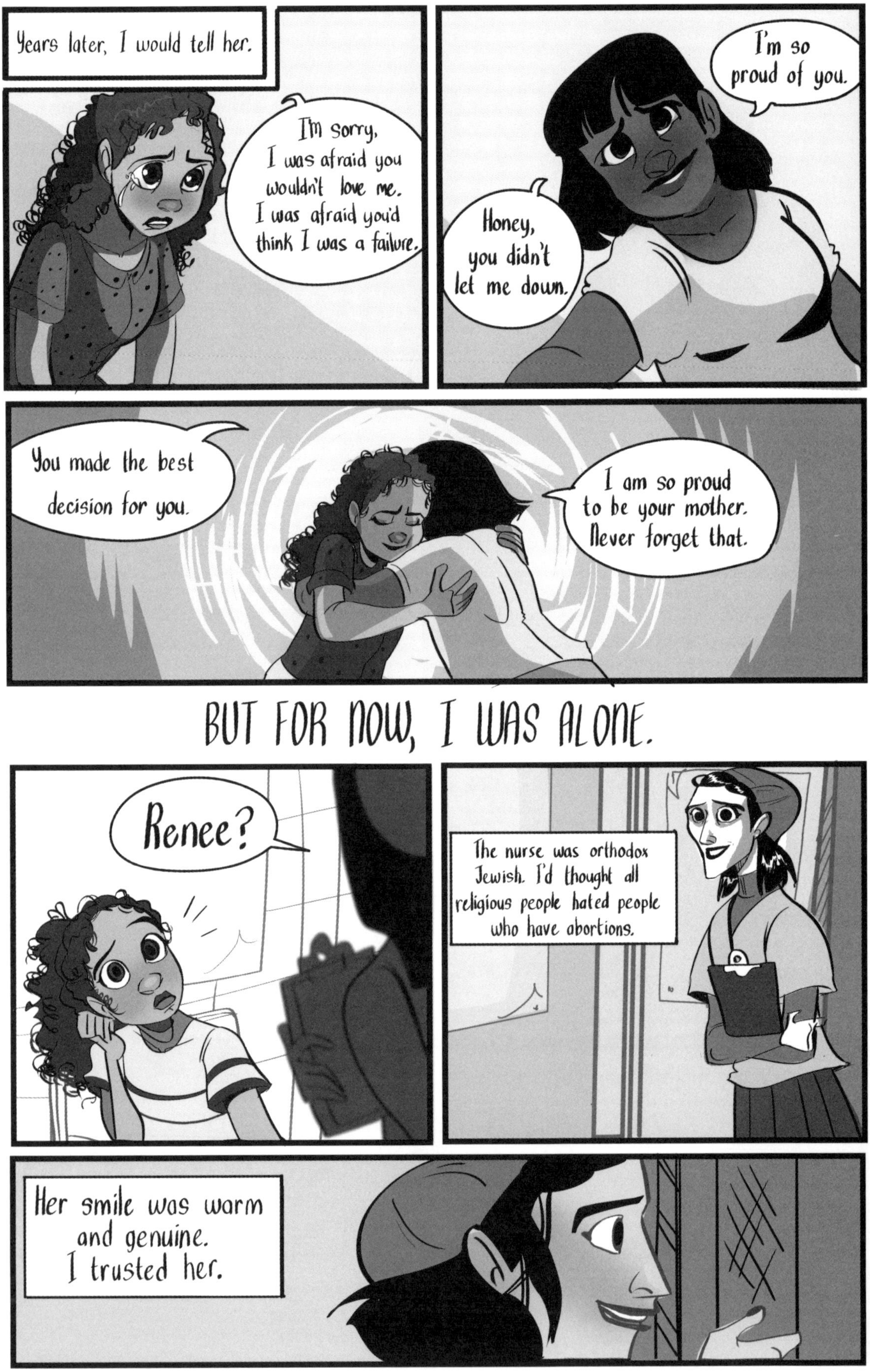
Years later, I would tell her.
I'm sorry, I was afraid you wouldn't love me. I was afraid you'd think I was a failure.
I'm so proud of you.
Honey, you didn't let me down.
You made the best decision for you.
I am so proud to be your mother. Never forget that.
BUT FOR NOW, I WAS ALONE.
Renee?
The nurse was orthodox Jewish. I'd thought all religious people hated people who have abortions.
Her smile was warm and genuine. I trusted her.

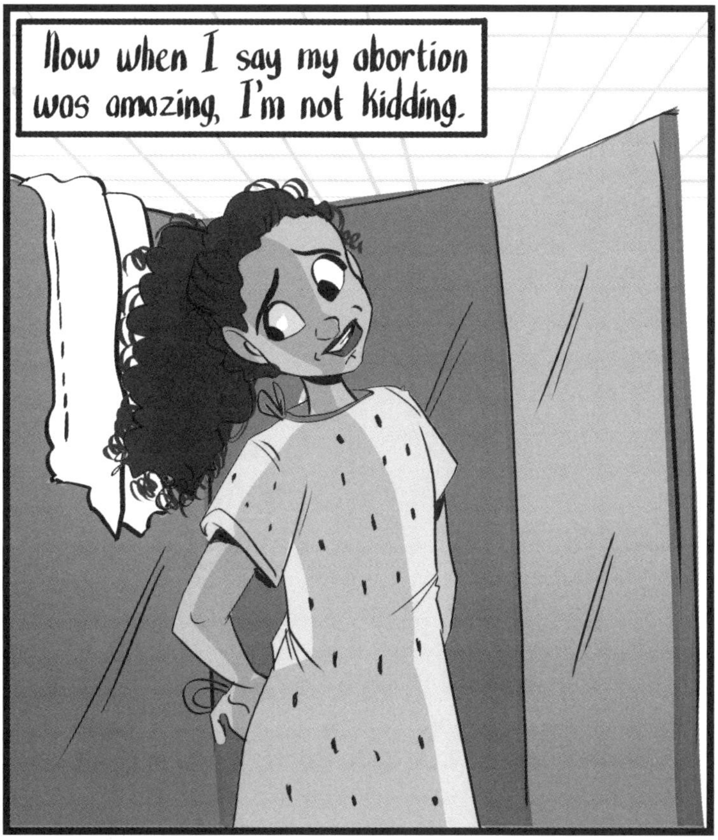
Now when I say my abortion was amazing, I'm not kidding.

In TV and media, they talk about abortion providers as if they're evil. But that's just propaganda. Mine wasn't like that at all.

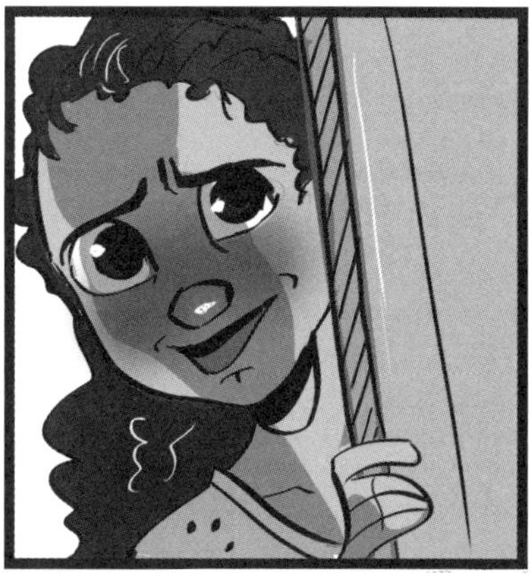

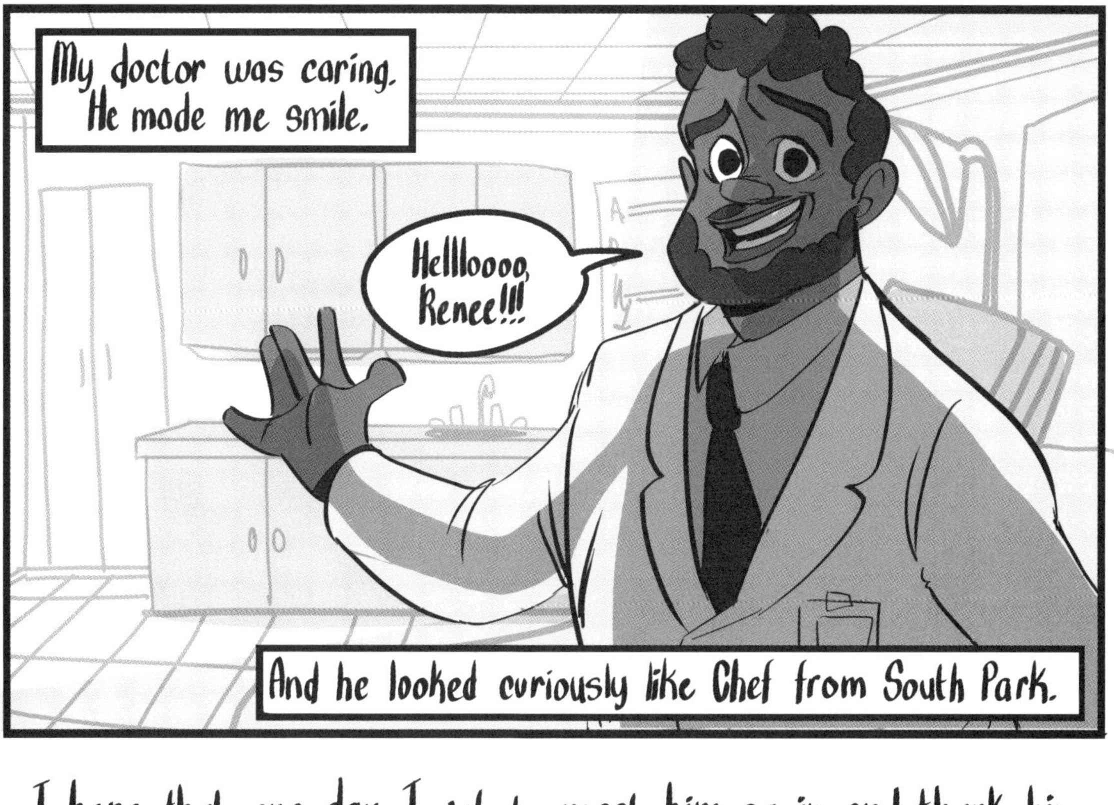
My doctor was caring. He made me smile.
Hellloooo, Renee!!!
And he looked curiously like Chef from South Park.

I hope that one day I get to meet him again and thank him.

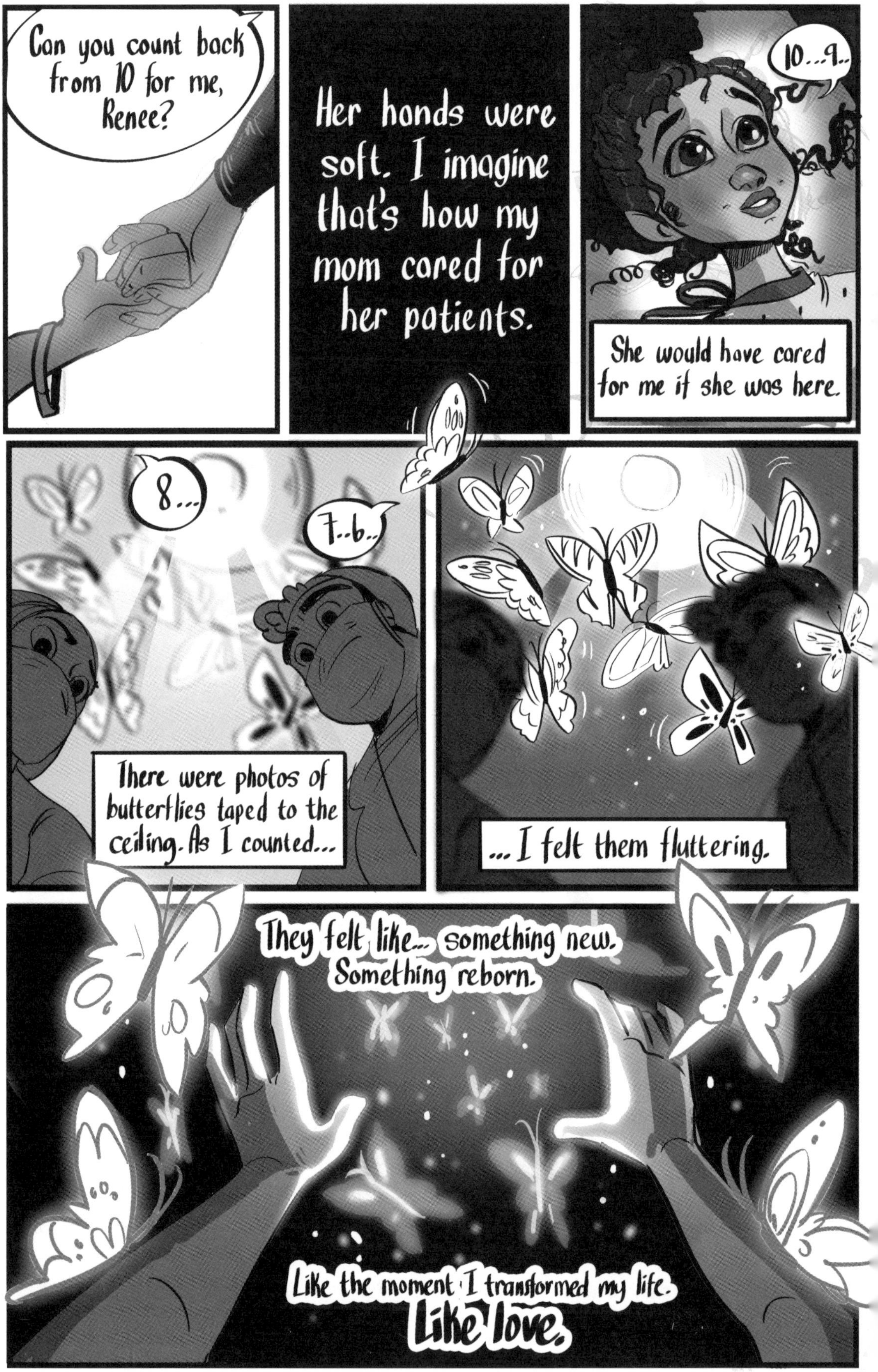

Can you count back from 10 for me, Renee?
Her hands were soft. I imagine that's how my mom cared for her patients.
10...9...
She would have cared for me if she was here.
8...
7...6...
There were photos of butterflies taped to the ceiling. As I counted...
...I felt them fluttering.
They felt like... something new. Something reborn.
Like the moment I transformed my life.
Like love.

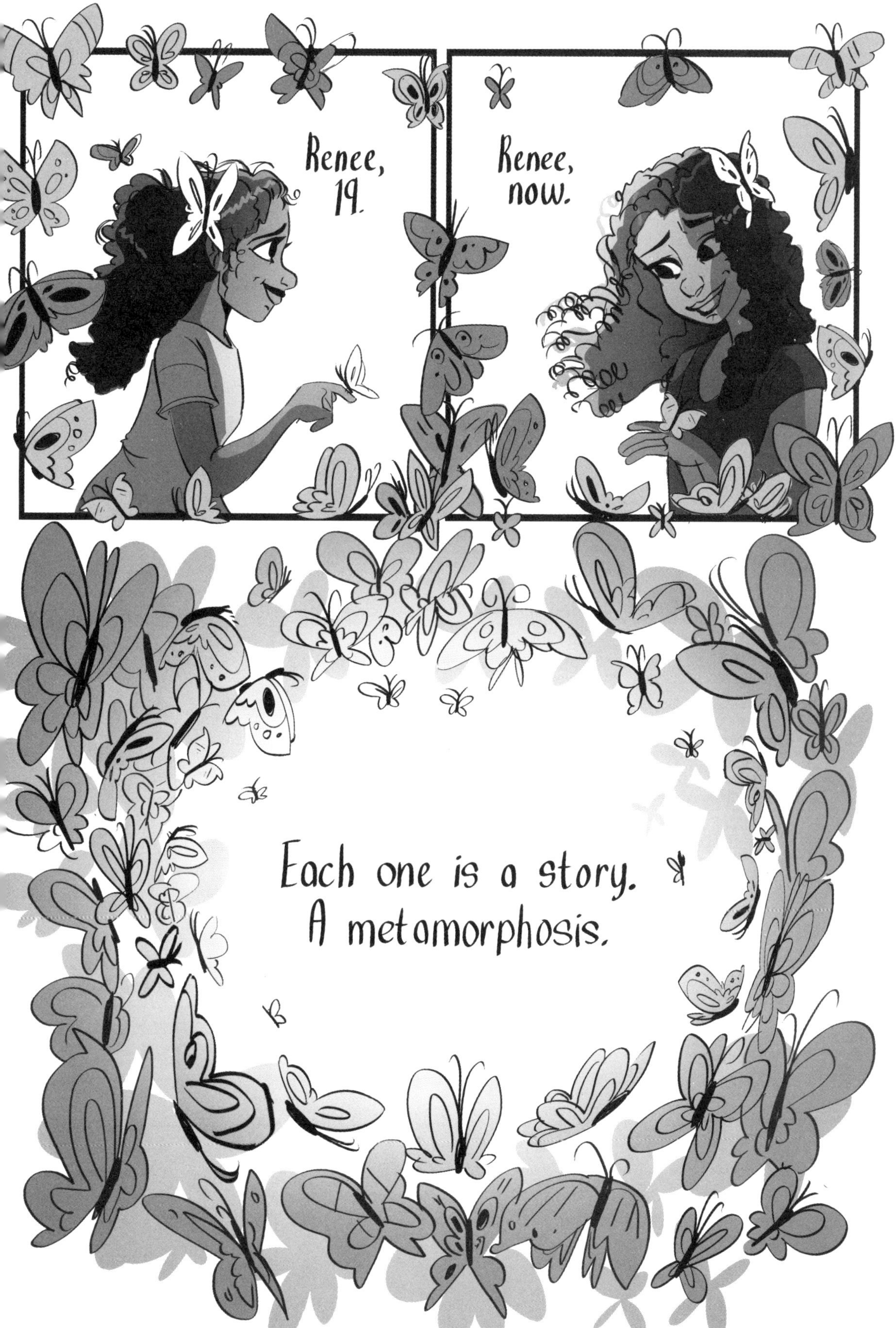
Renee, 19.
Renee, now.
Each one is a story.
A metamorphosis.

• STORY: RENEE BRACEY SHERMAN • ART: KENNEDY TARRELL •

ELEVEN

IN MEMORIAM

PEOPLE MURDERED
IN AMERICA
BY SO-CALLED
"PRO-LIFE" KILLERS

WORDS: JENNIFER CAMPER
ART: KATIE FRICAS

DAVID GUNN

DR. DAVID GUNN
NOVEMBER 16, 1945 –
MARCH 10, 1993

A DOCTOR WHO
PROVIDED ABORTIONS
AND WAS THREATENED
REPEATEDLY.
A DIVORCED FATHER
OF TWO. HIS DEATH
INSPIRED A MARILYN
MANSON SONG. SHOT
OUTSIDE THE CLINIC
IN PENSACOLA,
FLORIDA.

JOHN BAYARD BRITTON

DR. JOHN BAYARD
BRITTON
MAY 6, 1925 –
JULY 29, 1994

A DOCTOR WHO
PROVIDED ABORTIONS
AFTER DR. GUNN'S
DEATH. THOUGH HE
WAS AMBIVALENT
ABOUT THE
PROCEDURE, HE
NEEDED THE MONEY.
HE WAS THREATENED
OFTEN, WORE A
BULLET-PROOF
VEST, AND CARRIED
A GUN. SHOT IN HIS
TRUCK OUTSIDE THE
CLINIC IN PENSACOLA,
FLORIDA.

JAMES H. BARRETT

JAMES H. BARRETT
AUGUST 9, 1919 –
JULY 29, 1994

A RETIRED AIR FORCE
LT. COLONEL WHO
VOLUNTEERED AS A
SECURITY ESCORT
FOR DR. BRITTON. HE
WAS ACTIVE IN HIS
CHURCH AND MANY
COMMUNITY GROUPS.
HE WAS KILLED
WHILE ESCORTING
DR. BRITTON. HIS
WIFE, JUNE, ALSO
AN ESCORT, WAS
WOUNDED IN THE
SAME SHOOTING IN
PENSACOLA, FLORIDA.

SHANNON LOWNEY

SHANNON LOWNEY
JULY 7, 1969 –
DECEMBER 30, 1994

A RECEPTIONIST AT
PLANNED PARENTHOOD,
SHE HAD STUDIED IN
SPAIN AND WORKED
IN ECUADOR AS A
TRANSLATOR. SHE WAS
RAISED CATHOLIC,
BELIEVED STRONGLY IN
WOMEN'S HEALTH, AND
WAS PLANNING TO GET
HER MASTER'S DEGREE
IN SOCIAL WORK. SHOT
AT WORK IN BROOKLINE,
MASSACHUSETTS.

LEE ANN NICHOLS

LEE ANN NICHOLS
OCTOBER 27, 1956 –
DECEMBER 30, 1994

A RECEPTIONIST
AT PLANNED
PARENTHOOD,
ENGAGED TO BE
MARRIED. SHE WAS
RENOVATING HER
HOUSE WITH HER
FINANCÉ. SHE LOVED
NATURE AND HER
PETS. SHOT AT
WORK IN BROOKLINE,
MASSACHUSETTS.

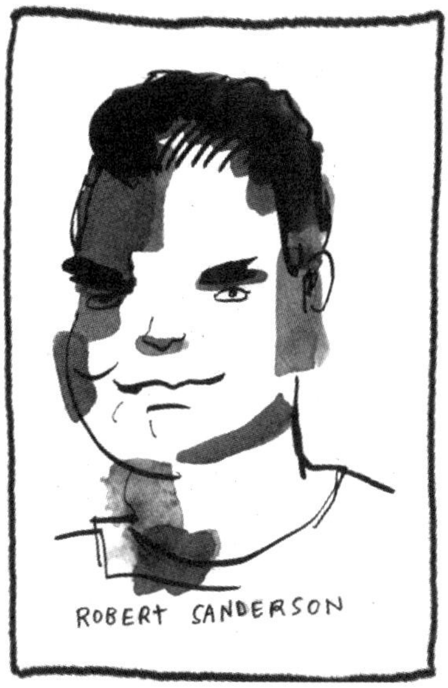
ROBERT SANDERSON

ROBERT SANDERSON
JUNE 19, 1963 – JANUARY 29, 1998

AN OFF-DUTY POLICE OFFICER WORKING AS A SECURITY GUARD AT A HEALTH CLINIC. MARRIED, WITH TWO STEP-CHILDREN, HE HAD SERVED IN THE AIR FORCE. HE WAS KILLED IN A BOMB EXPLOSION AT THE CLINIC IN BIRMINGHAM, ALABAMA. THE BOMB HAD BEEN SET BY THE SAME MAN WHO BOMBED THE ATLANTA CENTENNIAL OLYMPIC PARK AND A LESBIAN BAR.

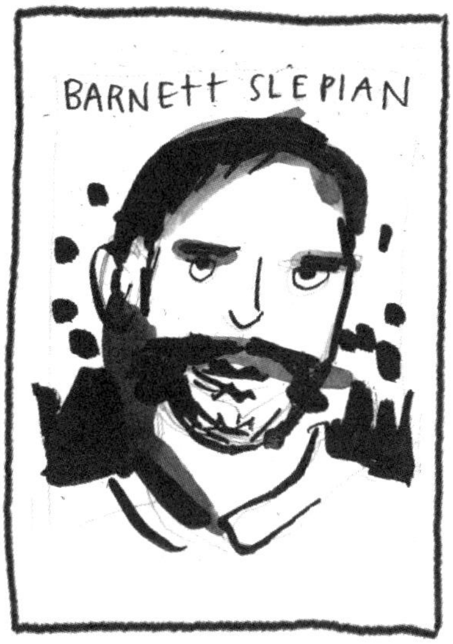
BARNETT SLEPIAN

DR. BARNETT SLEPIAN
APRIL 23, 1946 – OCTOBER 23, 1998

A DOCTOR WHO PROVIDED ABORTIONS, WAS SUBJECTED TO YEARS OF THREATS AND HARASSMENT. MARRIED AND A FATHER OF FOUR. AFTER ATTENDING SYNAGOGUE, HE WAS SHOT THROUGH HIS KITCHEN WINDOW AT HOME IN AMHERST, NEW YORK.

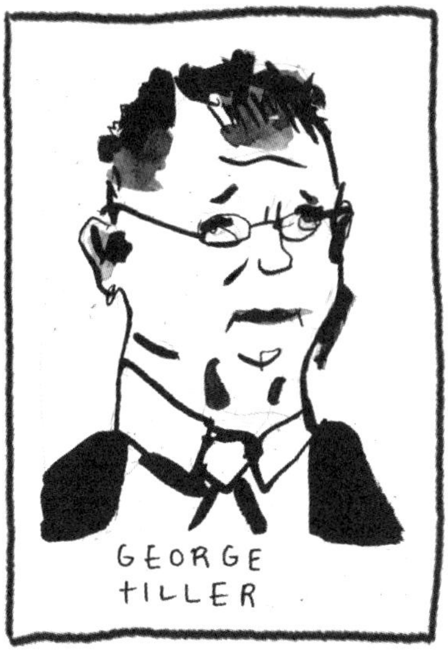
GEORGE TILLER

DR. GEORGE TILLER
AUGUST 8, 1941 – MAY 31, 2009

A DOCTOR WHO PROVIDED ABORTIONS AND WAS INVOLVED IN REPRODUCTIVE RIGHTS ACTIVISM. FREQUENTLY THREATENED, AND SURVIVED ONE ASSASSINATION ATTEMPT. HE WAS SHOT WHILE AT CHURCH, SERVING AS AN USHER DURING THE SUNDAY MORNING SERVICE, IN WICHITA, KANSAS.

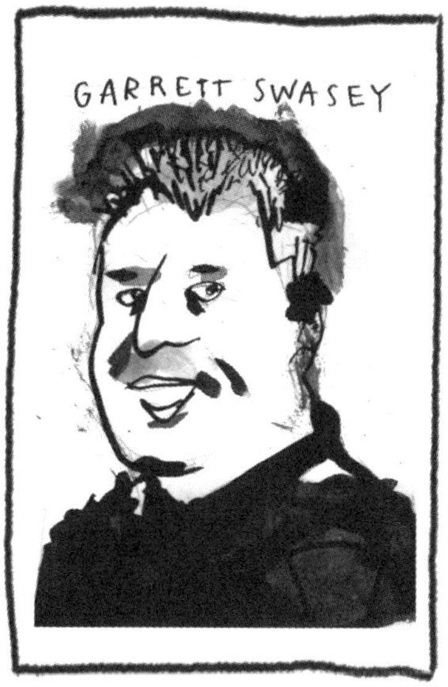
GARRETT SWASEY

GARRETT SWASEY
NOVEMBER 16, 1971 – NOVEMBER 27, 2015

AN AWARD-WINNING COMPETITIVE ICE SKATER, A FIGURE SKATING COACH, AND A POLICE OFFICER. HE WAS A CO-PASTOR AND ELDER IN HIS CHURCH, MARRIED WITH TWO CHILDREN. SHOT WHILE RESPONDING TO GUNFIRE AT A PLANNED PARENTHOOD OFFICE IN COLORADO SPRINGS, COLORADO.

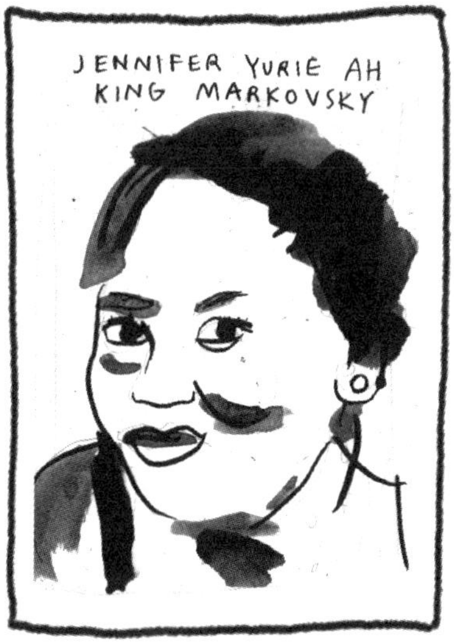
JENNIFER YURIE AH KING MARKOVSKY

JENNIFER YURIE AH KING MARKOVSKY
DECEMBER 22, 1979 – NOVEMBER 27, 2015

ORIGINALLY FROM HAWAII, MARRIED WITH TWO CHILDREN. SHE LOVED COOKING AND THE OUTDOORS. SHE WAS ACCOMPANYING A FRIEND TO THE PLANNED PARENTHOOD CLINIC, HER FRIEND WAS ALSO WOUNDED. SHE WAS SHOT IN COLORADO SPRINGS, COLORADO.

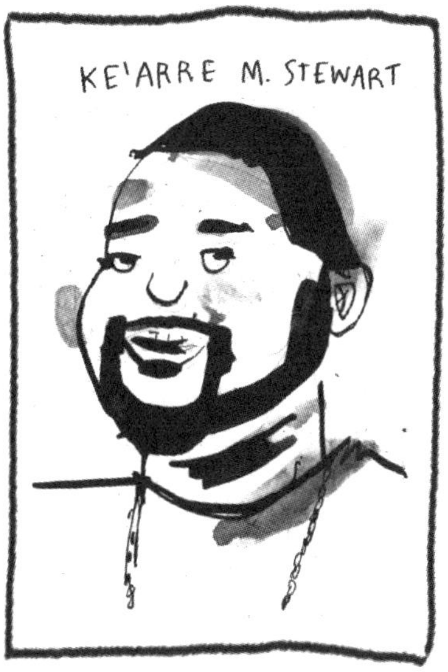
KE'ARRE M. STEWART

KE'ARRE M. STEWART
FEBRUARY 9, 1986 – NOVEMBER 28TH, 2015

AN ARMY VETERAN, AND INSURANCE WORKER, HE WAS MARRIED WITH TWO CHILDREN. HE WAS OUTSIDE THE PLANNED PARENTHOOD CLINIC MAKING A PHONE CALL WHEN HE WAS SHOT. DESPITE HIS INJURY, HE RAN INSIDE THE BUILDING TO WARN PEOPLE, AND CALLED 911. HE WAS SHOT IN COLORADO SPRINGS, COLORADO.

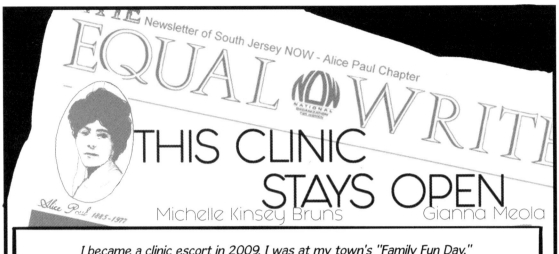

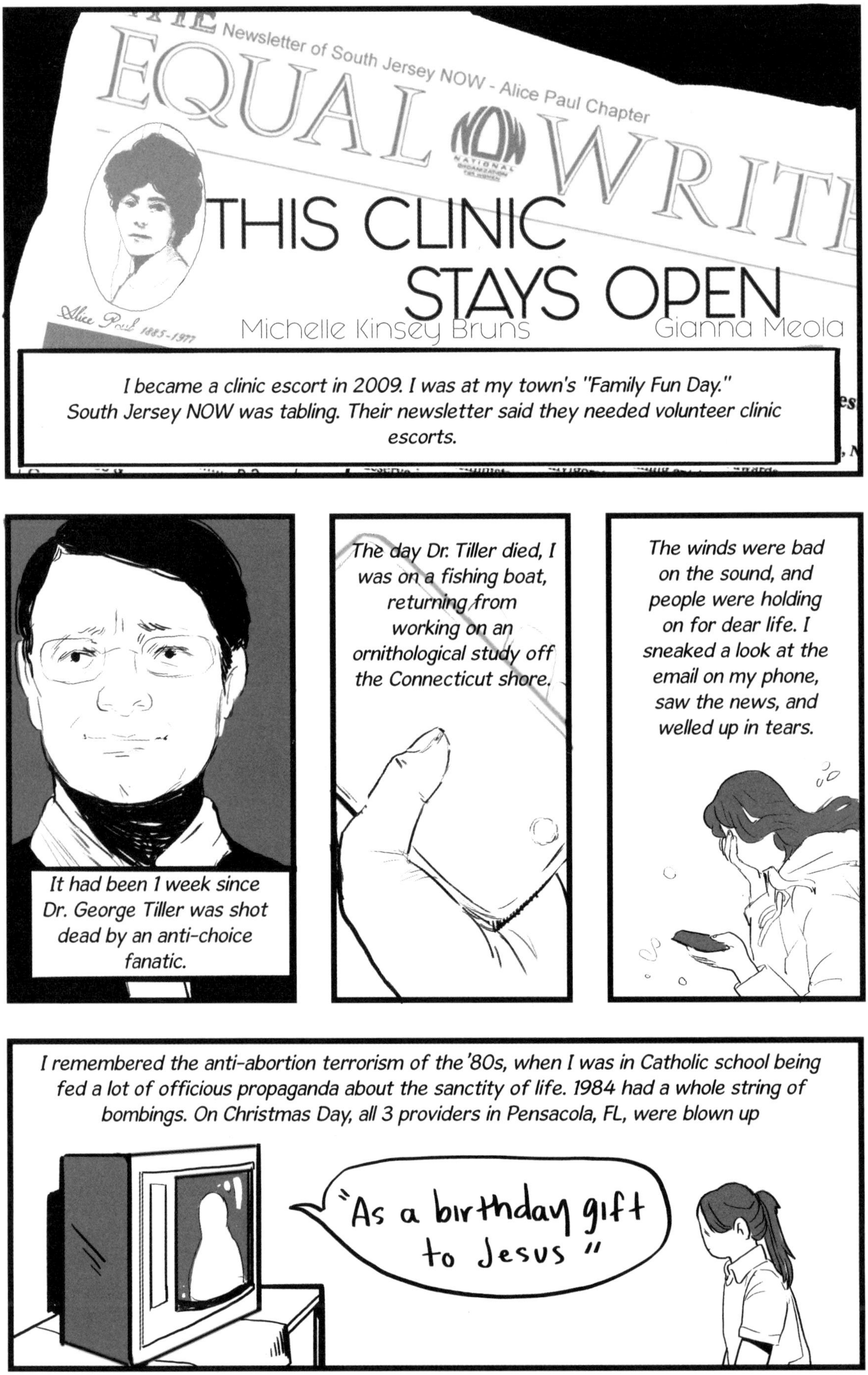

THE EQUAL WRITE
Newsletter of South Jersey NOW - Alice Paul Chapter
NOW NATIONAL ORGANIZATION FOR WOMEN
Alice Paul 1885-1977
THIS CLINIC STAYS OPEN
Michelle Kinsey Bruns
Gianna Meola
I became a clinic escort in 2009. I was at my town's "Family Fun Day." South Jersey NOW was tabling. Their newsletter said they needed volunteer clinic escorts.
It had been 1 week since Dr. George Tiller was shot dead by an anti-choice fanatic.
The day Dr. Tiller died, I was on a fishing boat, returning from working on an ornithological study off the Connecticut shore.
The winds were bad on the sound, and people were holding on for dear life. I sneaked a look at the email on my phone, saw the news, and welled up in tears.
I remembered the anti-abortion terrorism of the '80s, when I was in Catholic school being fed a lot of officious propaganda about the sanctity of life. 1984 had a whole string of bombings. On Christmas Day, all 3 providers in Pensacola, FL, were blown up
"As a birthday gift to Jesus"

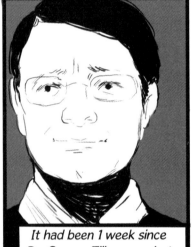

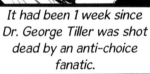

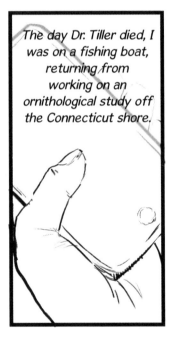

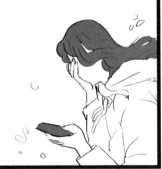

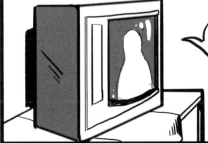

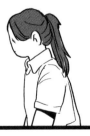

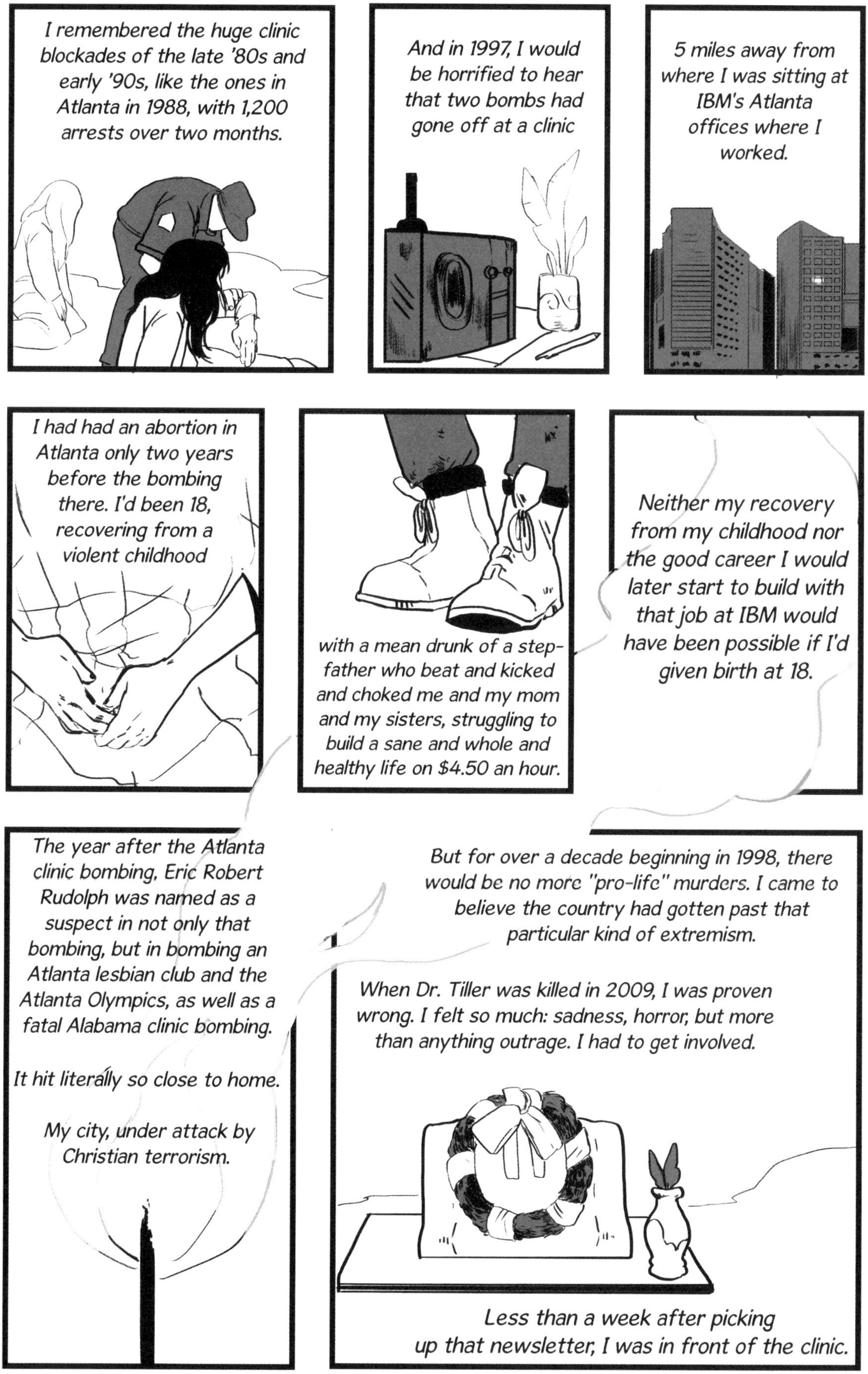

I remembered the huge clinic blockades of the late '80s and early '90s, like the ones in Atlanta in 1988, with 1,200 arrests over two months.

And in 1997, I would be horrified to hear that two bombs had gone off at a clinic

5 miles away from where I was sitting at IBM's Atlanta offices where I worked.

I had had an abortion in Atlanta only two years before the bombing there. I'd been 18, recovering from a violent childhood

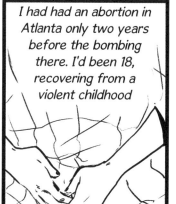

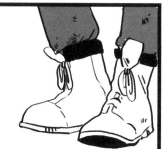

with a mean drunk of a step-father who beat and kicked and choked me and my mom and my sisters, struggling to build a sane and whole and healthy life on $4.50 an hour.

Neither my recovery from my childhood nor the good career I would later start to build with that job at IBM would have been possible if I'd given birth at 18.

The year after the Atlanta clinic bombing, Eric Robert Rudolph was named as a suspect in not only that bombing, but in bombing an Atlanta lesbian club and the Atlanta Olympics, as well as a fatal Alabama clinic bombing.

It hit literally so close to home.

My city, under attack by Christian terrorism.

But for over a decade beginning in 1998, there would be no more "pro-life" murders. I came to believe the country had gotten past that particular kind of extremism.

When Dr. Tiller was killed in 2009, I was proven wrong. I felt so much: sadness, horror, but more than anything outrage. I had to get involved.

Less than a week after picking up that newsletter, I was in front of the clinic.

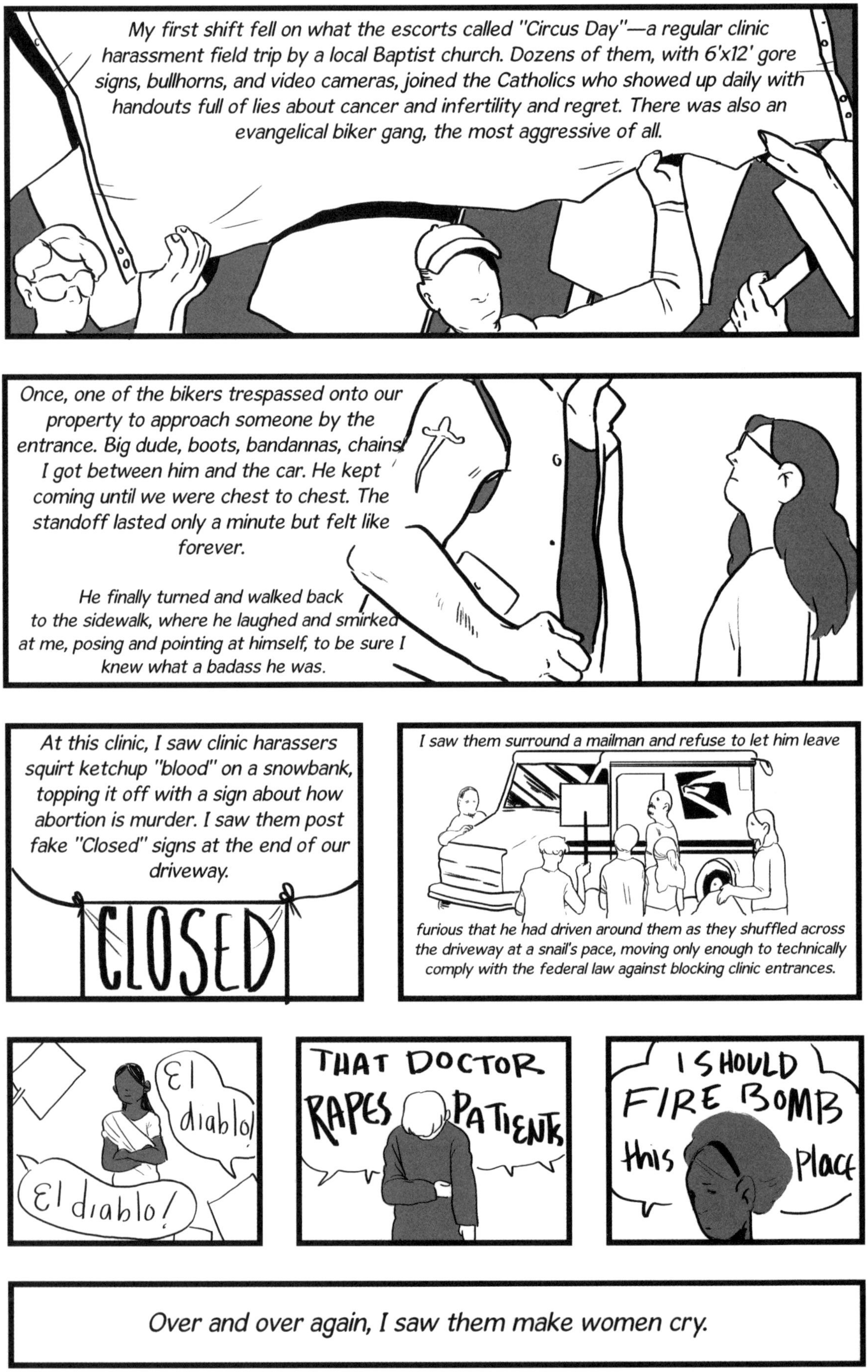
My first shift fell on what the escorts called "Circus Day"—a regular clinic harassment field trip by a local Baptist church. Dozens of them, with 6'x12' gore signs, bullhorns, and video cameras, joined the Catholics who showed up daily with handouts full of lies about cancer and infertility and regret. There was also an evangelical biker gang, the most aggressive of all.
Once, one of the bikers trespassed onto our property to approach someone by the entrance. Big dude, boots, bandannas, chains! I got between him and the car. He kept coming until we were chest to chest. The standoff lasted only a minute but felt like forever.
He finally turned and walked back to the sidewalk, where he laughed and smirked at me, posing and pointing at himself, to be sure I knew what a badass he was.
At this clinic, I saw clinic harassers squirt ketchup "blood" on a snowbank, topping it off with a sign about how abortion is murder. I saw them post fake "Closed" signs at the end of our driveway.
CLOSED
I saw them surround a mailman and refuse to let him leave
furious that he had driven around them as they shuffled across the driveway at a snail's pace, moving only enough to technically comply with the federal law against blocking clinic entrances.
El diablo!
El diablo!
THAT DOCTOR RAPES PATIENTS
I SHOULD FIRE BOMB this Place
Over and over again, I saw them make women cry.

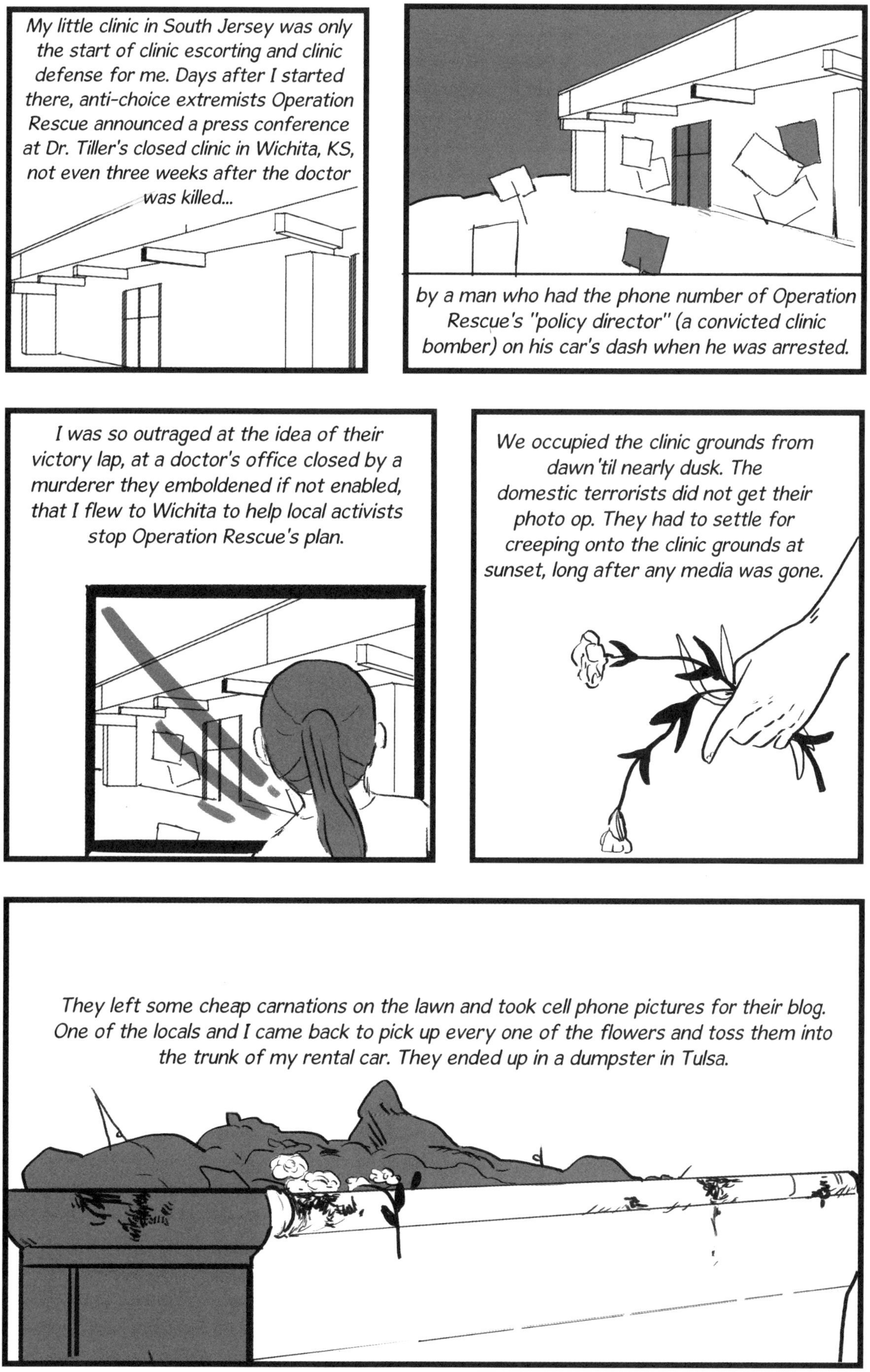

My little clinic in South Jersey was only the start of clinic escorting and clinic defense for me. Days after I started there, anti-choice extremists Operation Rescue announced a press conference at Dr. Tiller's closed clinic in Wichita, KS, not even three weeks after the doctor was killed...

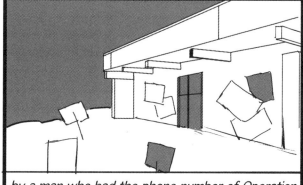

by a man who had the phone number of Operation Rescue's "policy director" (a convicted clinic bomber) on his car's dash when he was arrested.

I was so outraged at the idea of their victory lap, at a doctor's office closed by a murderer they emboldened if not enabled, that I flew to Wichita to help local activists stop Operation Rescue's plan.

We occupied the clinic grounds from dawn 'til nearly dusk. The domestic terrorists did not get their photo op. They had to settle for creeping onto the clinic grounds at sunset, long after any media was gone.

They left some cheap carnations on the lawn and took cell phone pictures for their blog. One of the locals and I came back to pick up every one of the flowers and toss them into the trunk of my rental car. They ended up in a dumpster in Tulsa.

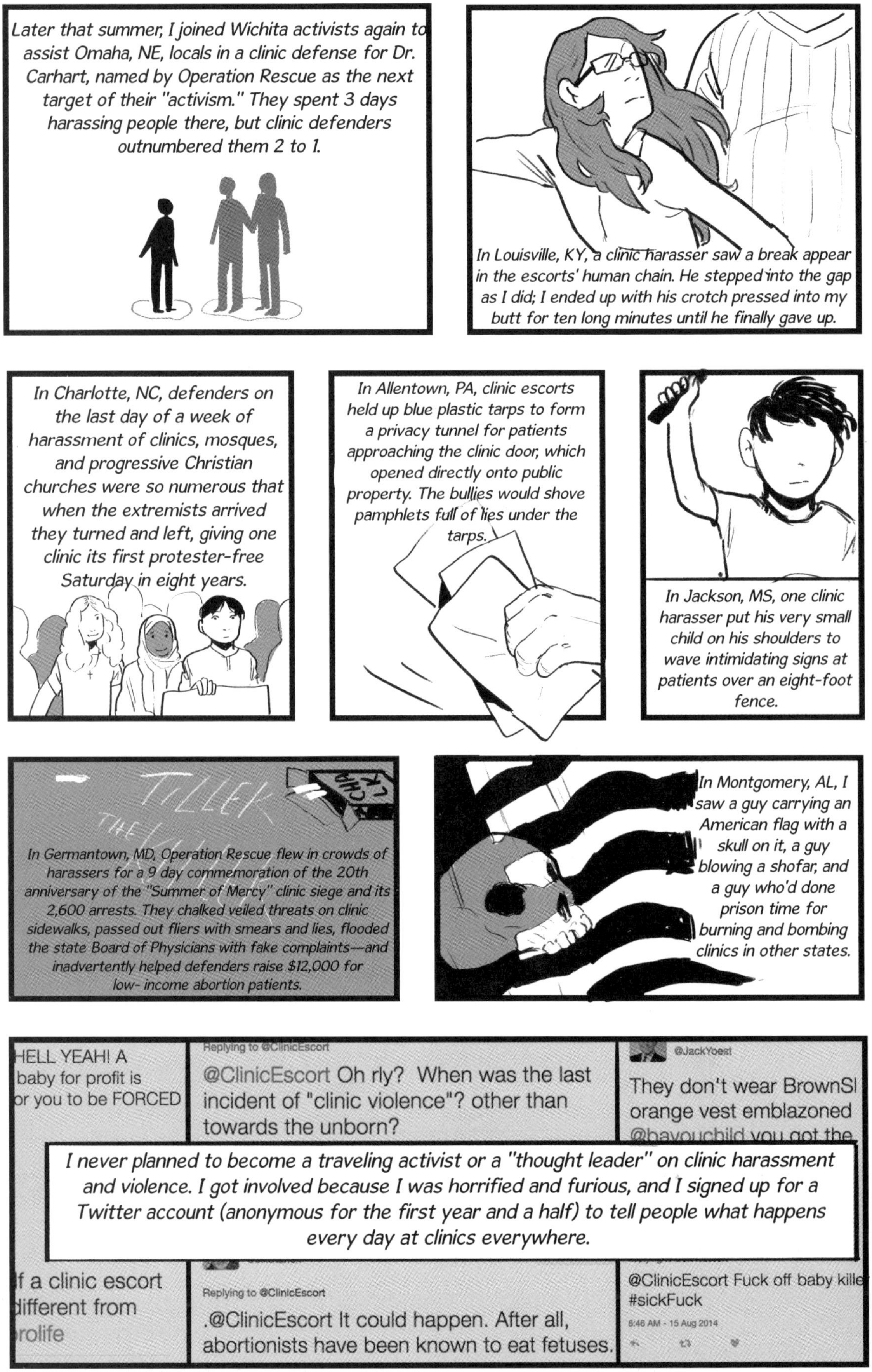
Later that summer, I joined Wichita activists again to assist Omaha, NE, locals in a clinic defense for Dr. Carhart, named by Operation Rescue as the next target of their "activism." They spent 3 days harassing people there, but clinic defenders outnumbered them 2 to 1.
In Louisville, KY, a clinic harasser saw a break appear in the escorts' human chain. He stepped into the gap as I did; I ended up with his crotch pressed into my butt for ten long minutes until he finally gave up.
In Charlotte, NC, defenders on the last day of a week of harassment of clinics, mosques, and progressive Christian churches were so numerous that when the extremists arrived they turned and left, giving one clinic its first protester-free Saturday in eight years.
In Allentown, PA, clinic escorts held up blue plastic tarps to form a privacy tunnel for patients approaching the clinic door, which opened directly onto public property. The bullies would shove pamphlets full of lies under the tarps.
In Jackson, MS, one clinic harasser put his very small child on his shoulders to wave intimidating signs at patients over an eight-foot fence.
TILLER
THE
In Germantown, MD, Operation Rescue flew in crowds of harassers for a 9 day commemoration of the 20th anniversary of the "Summer of Mercy" clinic siege and its 2,600 arrests. They chalked veiled threats on clinic sidewalks, passed out fliers with smears and lies, flooded the state Board of Physicians with fake complaints—and inadvertently helped defenders raise $12,000 for low- income abortion patients.
In Montgomery, AL, I saw a guy carrying an American flag with a skull on it, a guy blowing a shofar, and a guy who'd done prison time for burning and bombing clinics in other states.
HELL YEAH! A
baby for profit is
or you to be FORCED
Replying to @ClinicEscort
@ClinicEscort Oh rly? When was the last incident of "clinic violence"? other than towards the unborn?
@JackYoest
They don't wear BrownSl
orange vest emblazoned
I never planned to become a traveling activist or a "thought leader" on clinic harassment and violence. I got involved because I was horrified and furious, and I signed up for a Twitter account (anonymous for the first year and a half) to tell people what happens every day at clinics everywhere.
f a clinic escort
different from
rolife
Replying to @ClinicEscort
.@ClinicEscort It could happen. After all, abortionists have been known to eat fetuses.
@ClinicEscort Fuck off baby kille
#sickFuck
8:46 AM - 15 Aug 2014

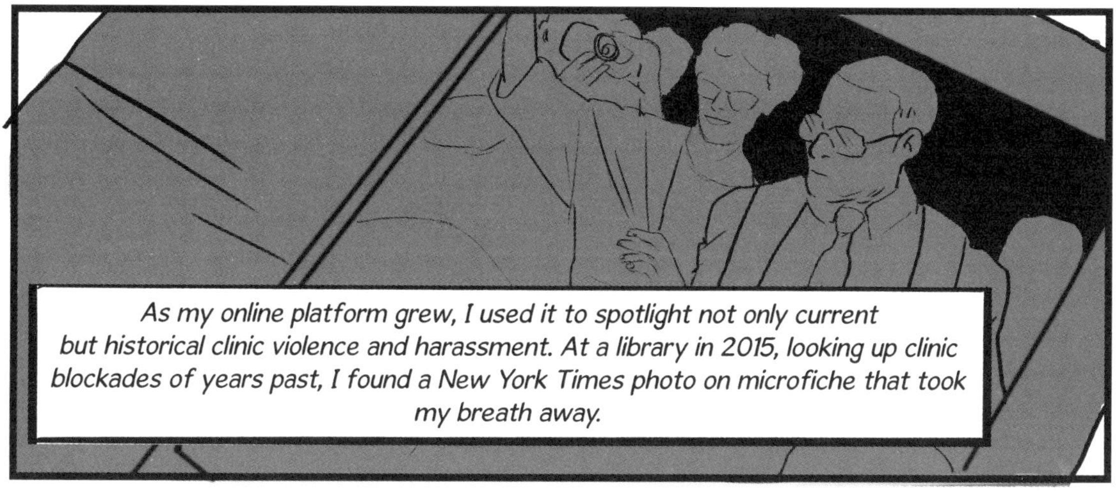
As my online platform grew, I used it to spotlight not only current but historical clinic violence and harassment. At a library in 2015, looking up clinic blockades of years past, I found a New York Times photo on microfiche that took my breath away.

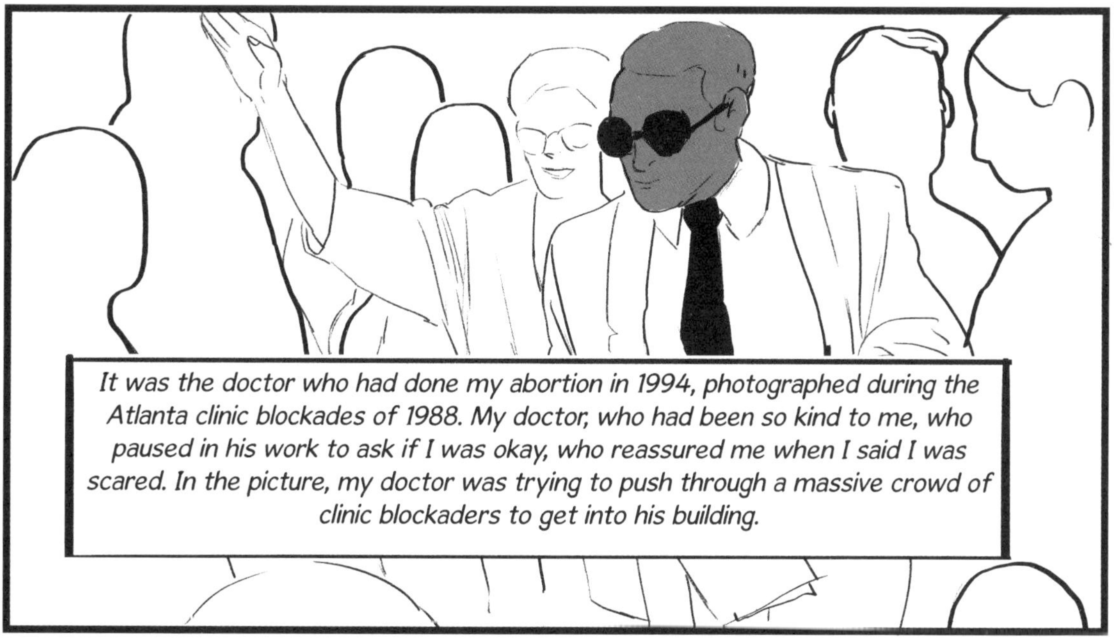
It was the doctor who had done my abortion in 1994, photographed during the Atlanta clinic blockades of 1988. My doctor, who had been so kind to me, who paused in his work to ask if I was okay, who reassured me when I said I was scared. In the picture, my doctor was trying to push through a massive crowd of clinic blockaders to get into his building.

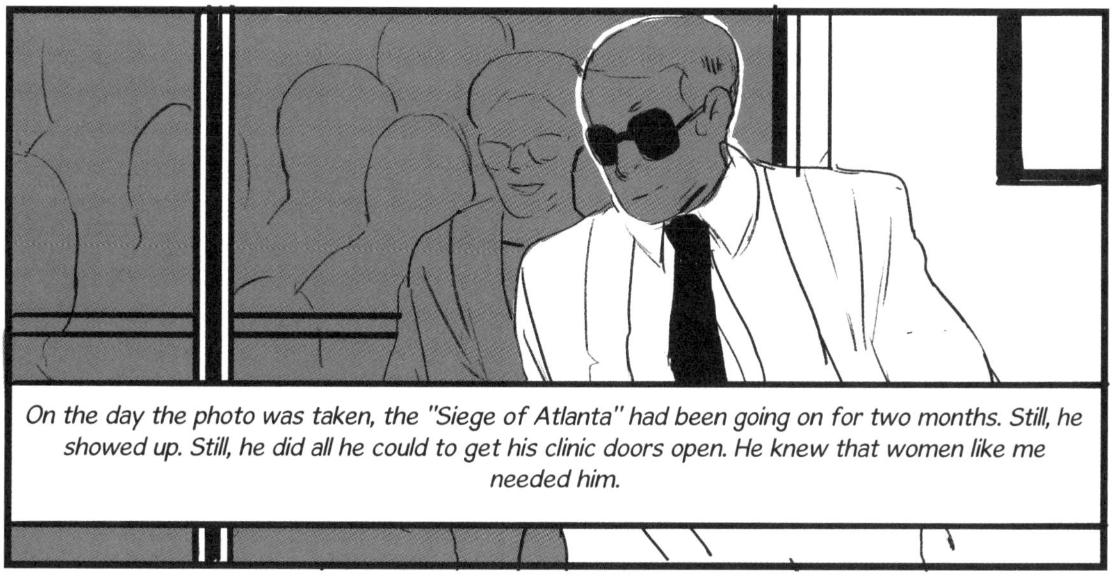
On the day the photo was taken, the "Siege of Atlanta" had been going on for two months. Still, he showed up. Still, he did all he could to get his clinic doors open. He knew that women like me needed him.

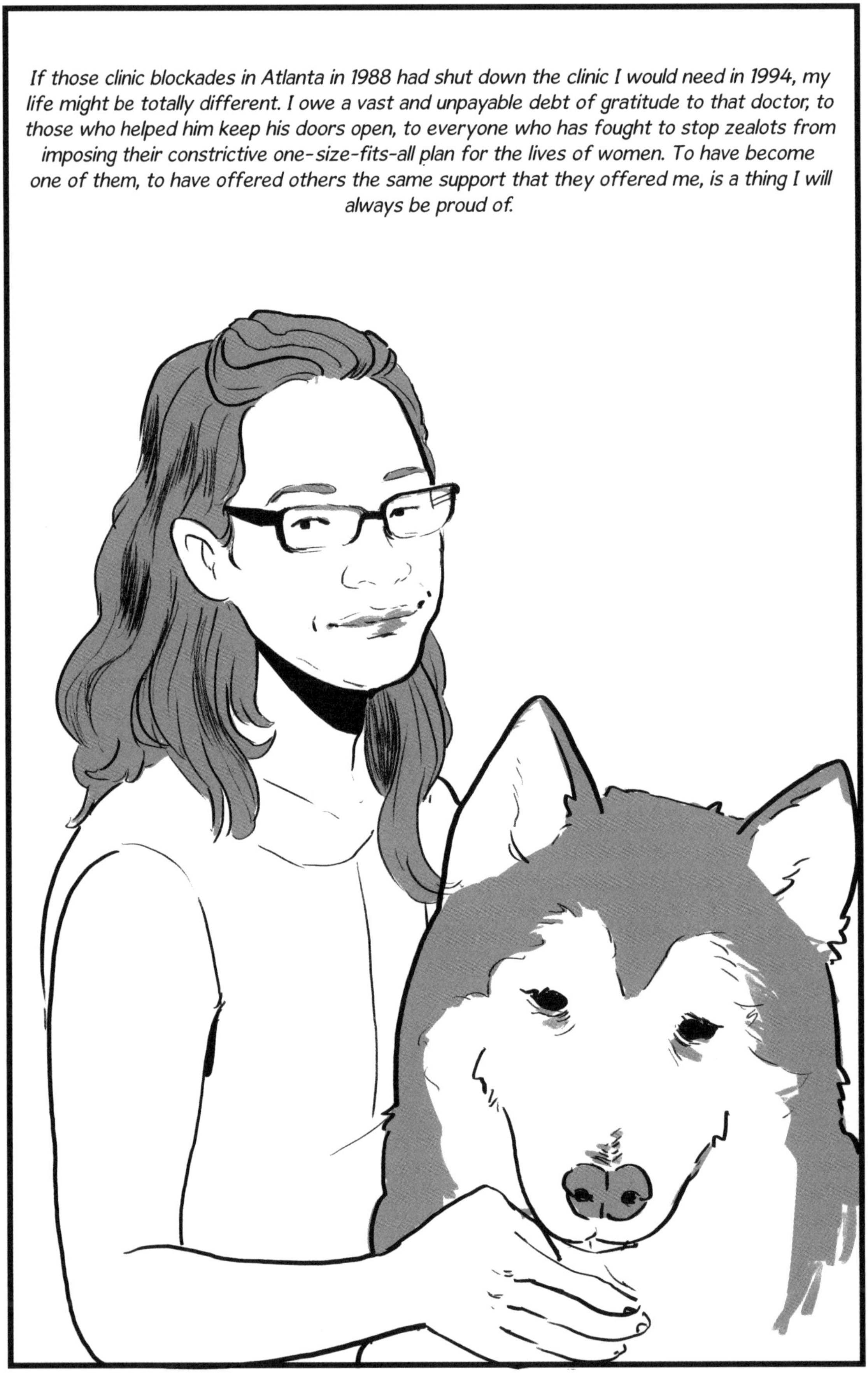
If those clinic blockades in Atlanta in 1988 had shut down the clinic I would need in 1994, my life might be totally different. I owe a vast and unpayable debt of gratitude to that doctor, to those who helped him keep his doors open, to everyone who has fought to stop zealots from imposing their constrictive one-size-fits-all plan for the lives of women. To have become one of them, to have offered others the same support that they offered me, is a thing I will always be proud of.

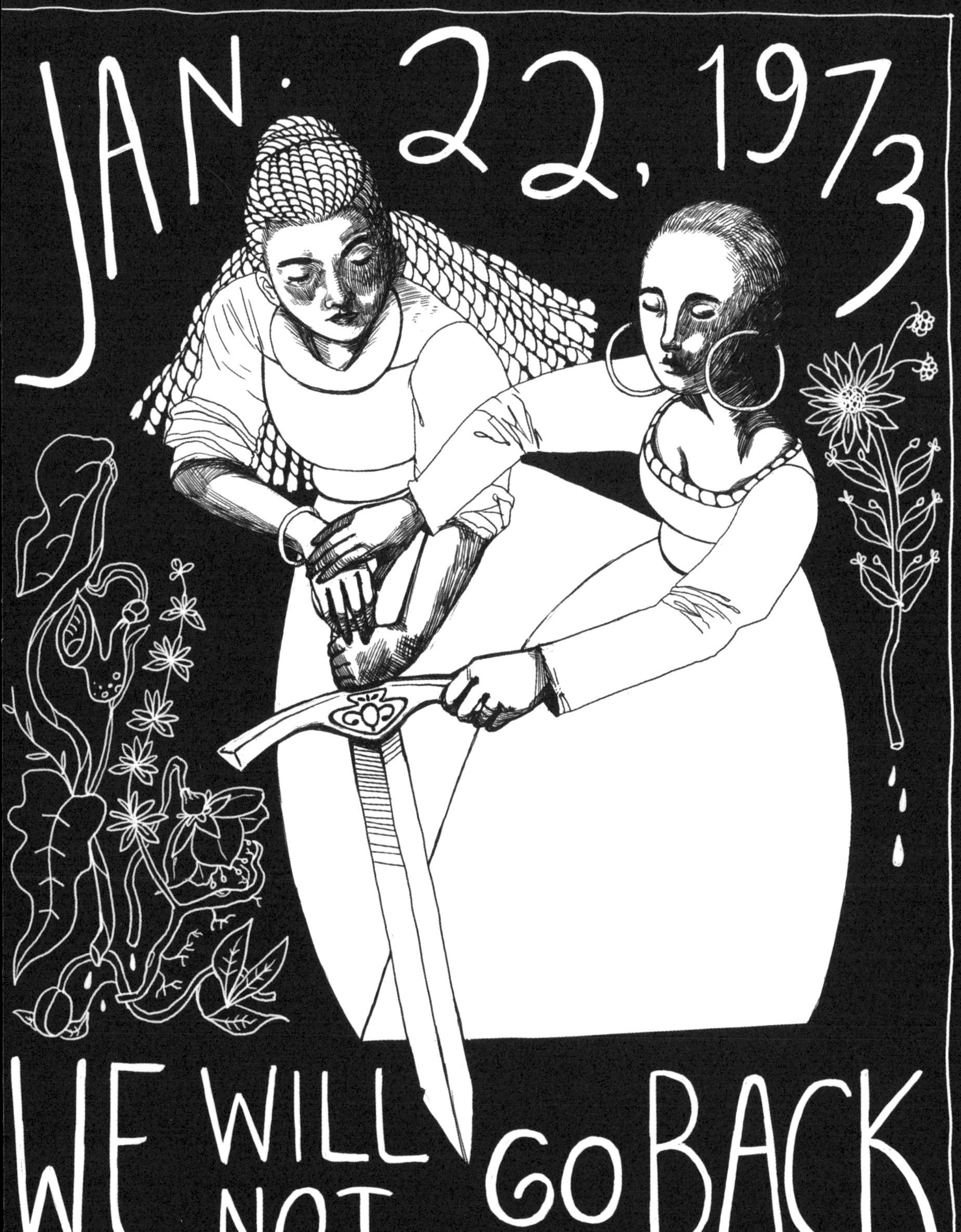
JAN. 22, 1973
WE WILL NOT GO BACK

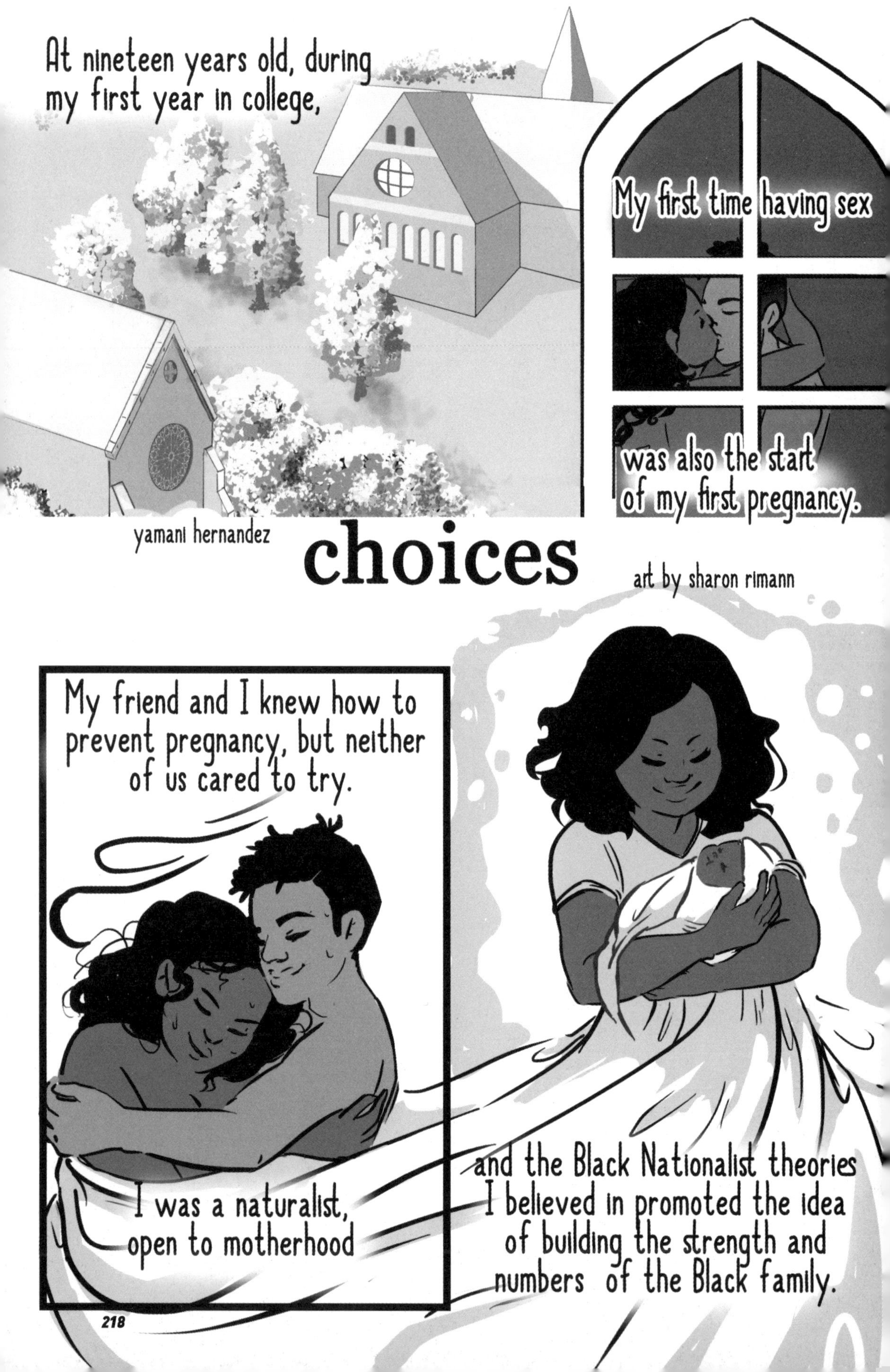

At nineteen years old, during my first year in college,
My first time having sex
was also the start of my first pregnancy.
yamani hernandez
choices
art by sharon rimann
My friend and I knew how to prevent pregnancy, but neither of us cared to try.
I was a naturalist, open to motherhood
and the Black Nationalist theories I believed in promoted the idea of building the strength and numbers of the Black family.

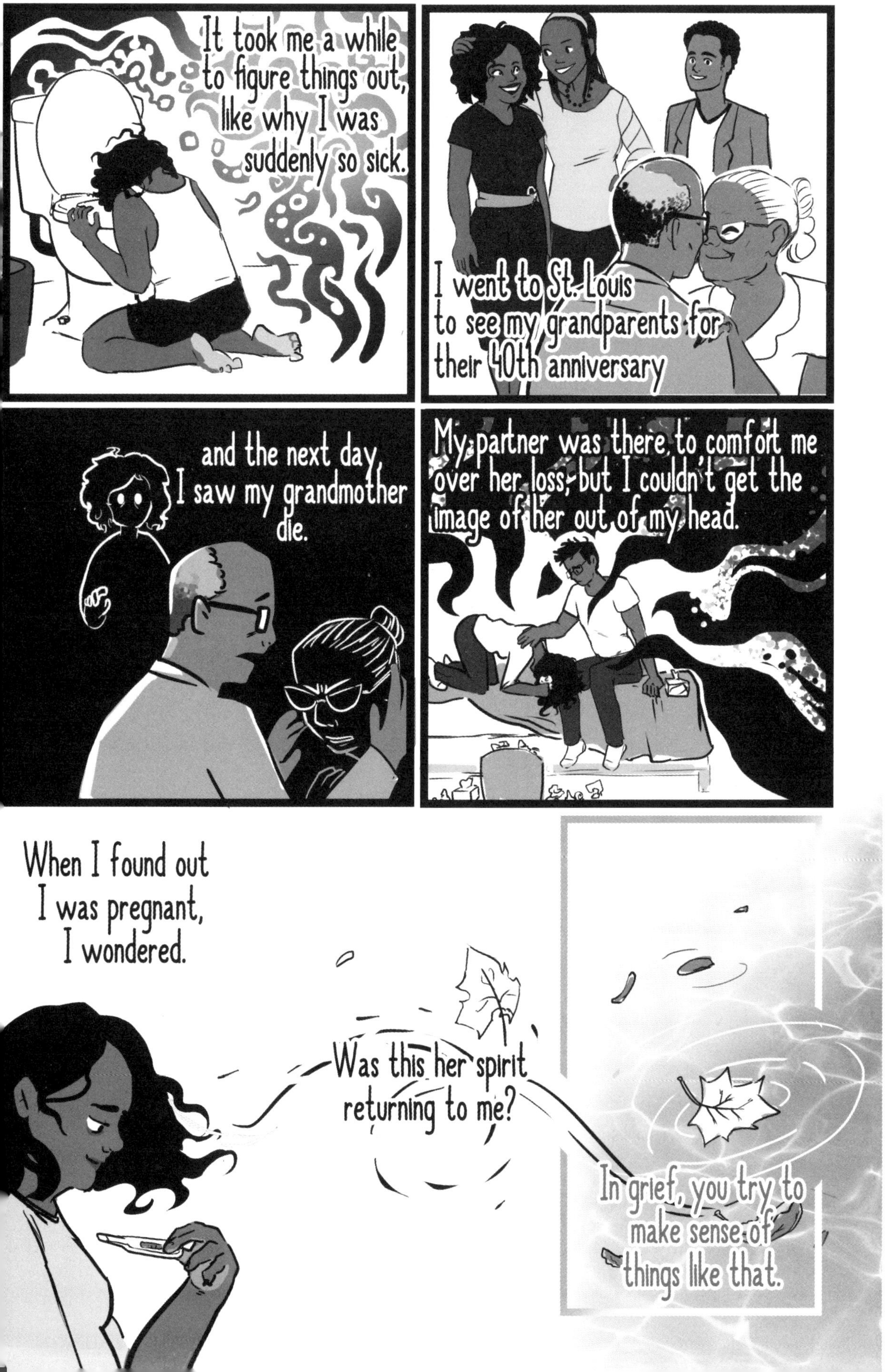
It took me a while to figure things out, like why I was suddenly so sick.
I went to St. Louis to see my grandparents for their 40th anniversary
and the next day, I saw my grandmother die.
My partner was there to comfort me over her loss, but I couldn't get the image of her out of my head.
When I found out I was pregnant, I wondered.
Was this her spirit returning to me?
In grief, you try to make sense of things like that.

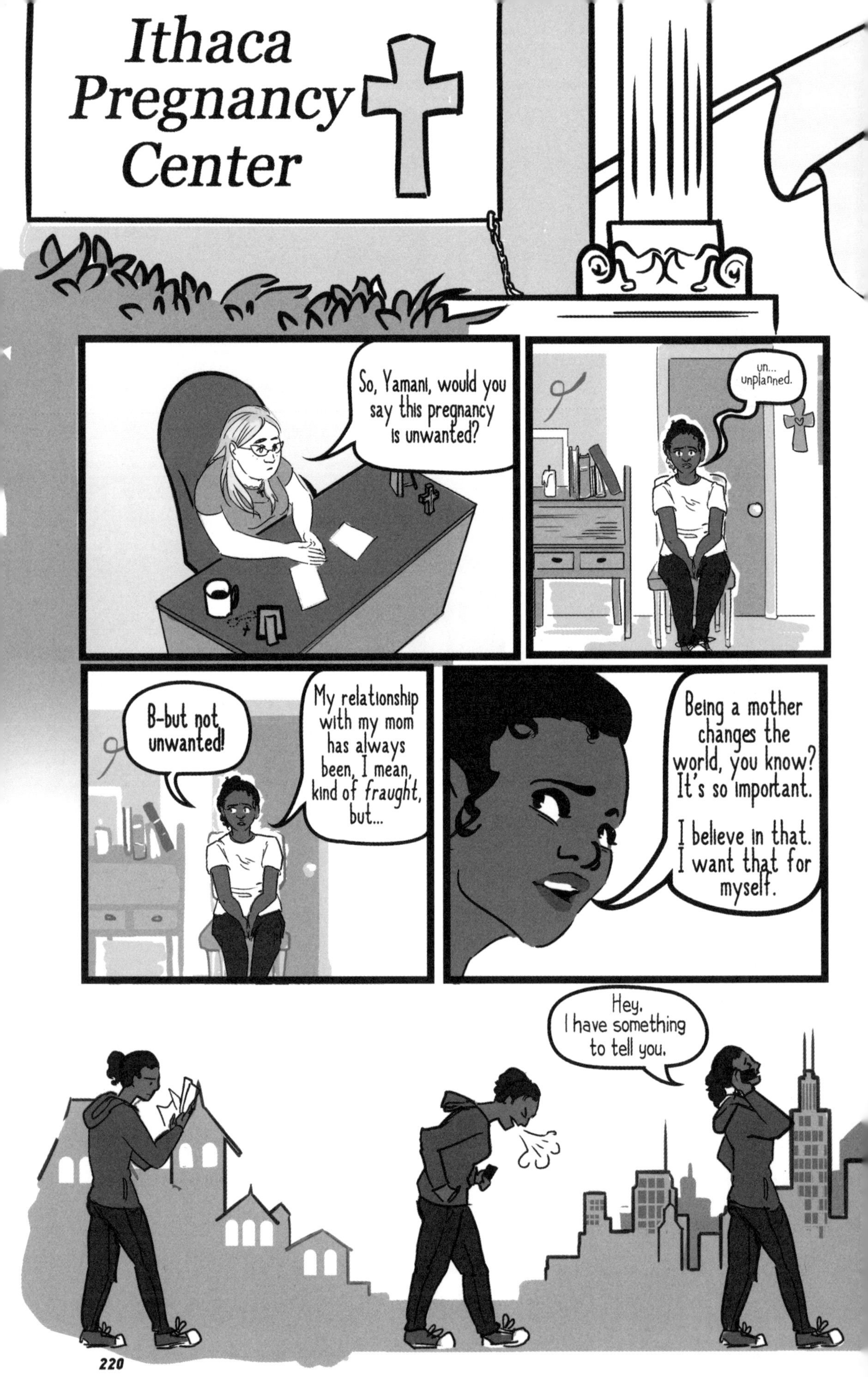
Ithaca Pregnancy Center
So, Yamani, would you say this pregnancy is unwanted?
un... unplanned.
B-but not unwanted!
My relationship with my mom has always been, I mean, kind of *fraught*, but...
Being a mother changes the world, you know? It's so important.
I believe in that. I want that for myself.
Hey. I have something to tell you.

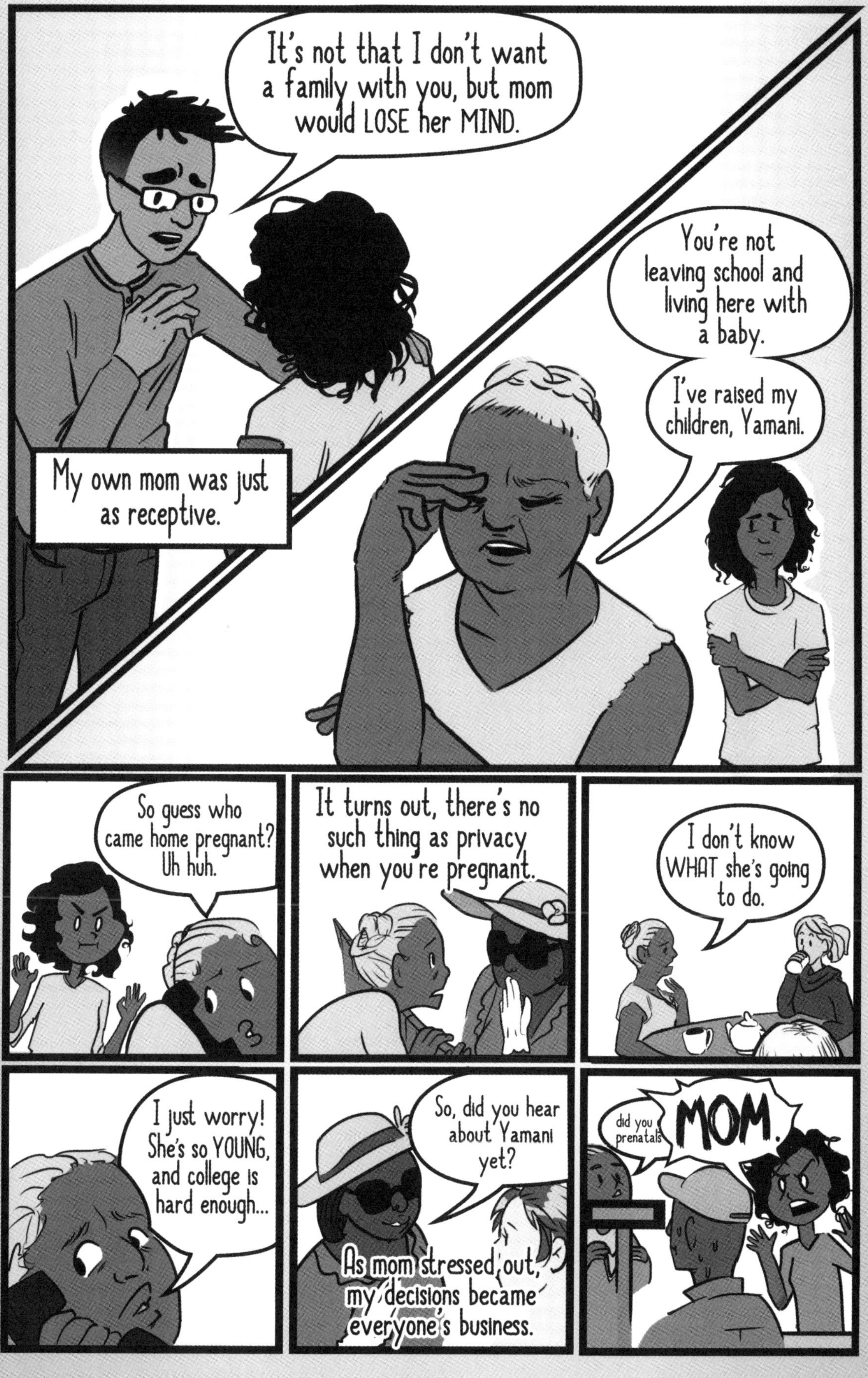
It's not that I don't want a family with you, but mom would LOSE her MIND.
My own mom was just as receptive.
You're not leaving school and living here with a baby.
I've raised my children, Yamani.
So guess who came home pregnant? Uh huh.
It turns out, there's no such thing as privacy when you're pregnant.
I don't know WHAT she's going to do.
I just worry! She's so YOUNG, and college is hard enough...
So, did you hear about Yamani yet?
As mom stressed out, my decisions became everyone's business.
did you prenatals
MOM.

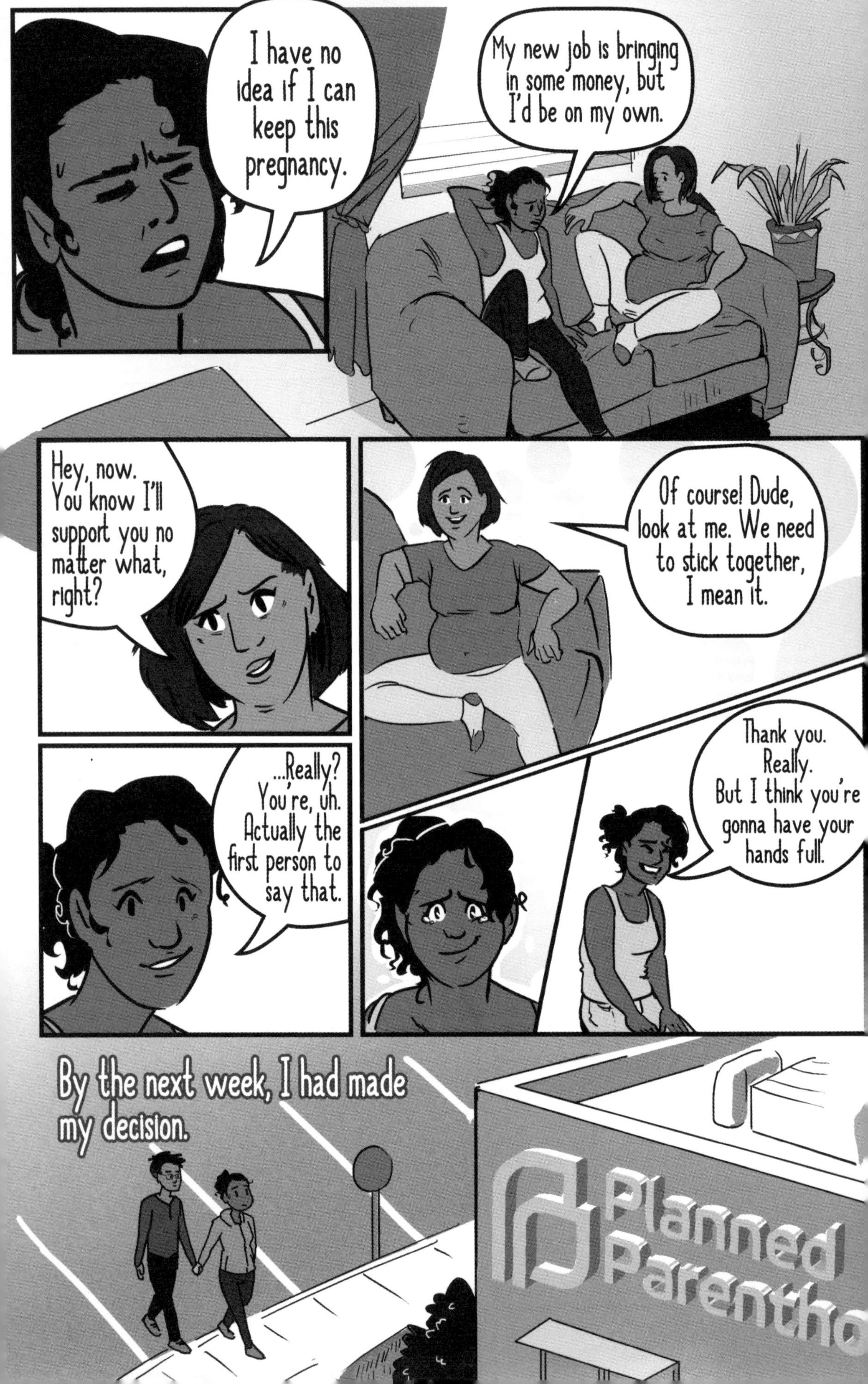
I have no idea if I can keep this pregnancy.
My new job is bringing in some money, but I'd be on my own.
Hey, now. You know I'll support you no matter what, right?
Of course! Dude, look at me. We need to stick together, I mean it.
...Really? You're, uh. Actually the first person to say that.
Thank you. Really. But I think you're gonna have your hands full.
By the next week, I had made my decision.
Planned Parentho

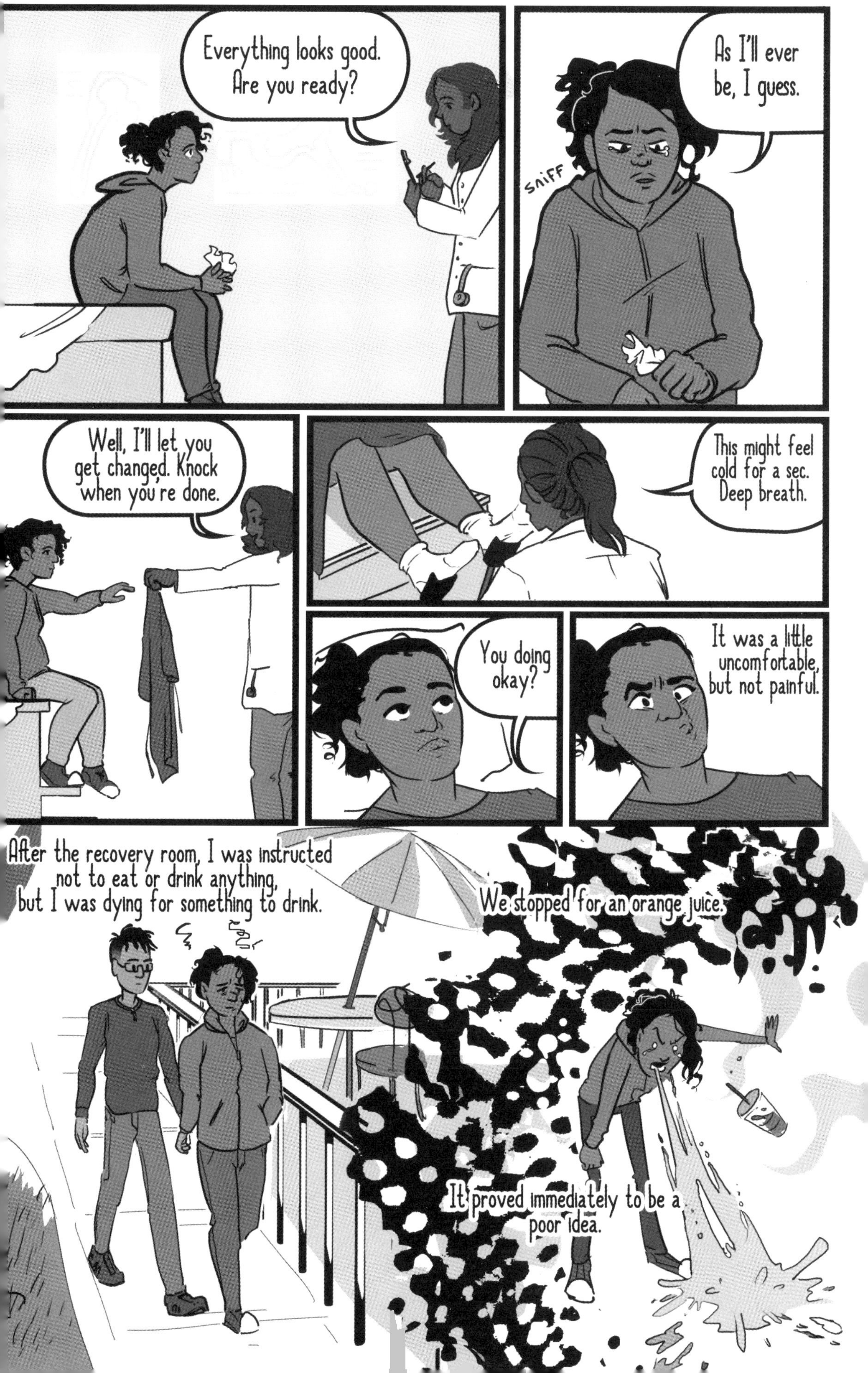
Everything looks good. Are you ready?
As I'll ever be, I guess.
SNIFF
Well, I'll let you get changed. Knock when you're done.
This might feel cold for a sec. Deep breath.
You doing okay?
It was a little uncomfortable, but not painful.
After the recovery room, I was instructed not to eat or drink anything, but I was dying for something to drink.
We stopped for an orange juice.
It proved immediately to be a poor idea.

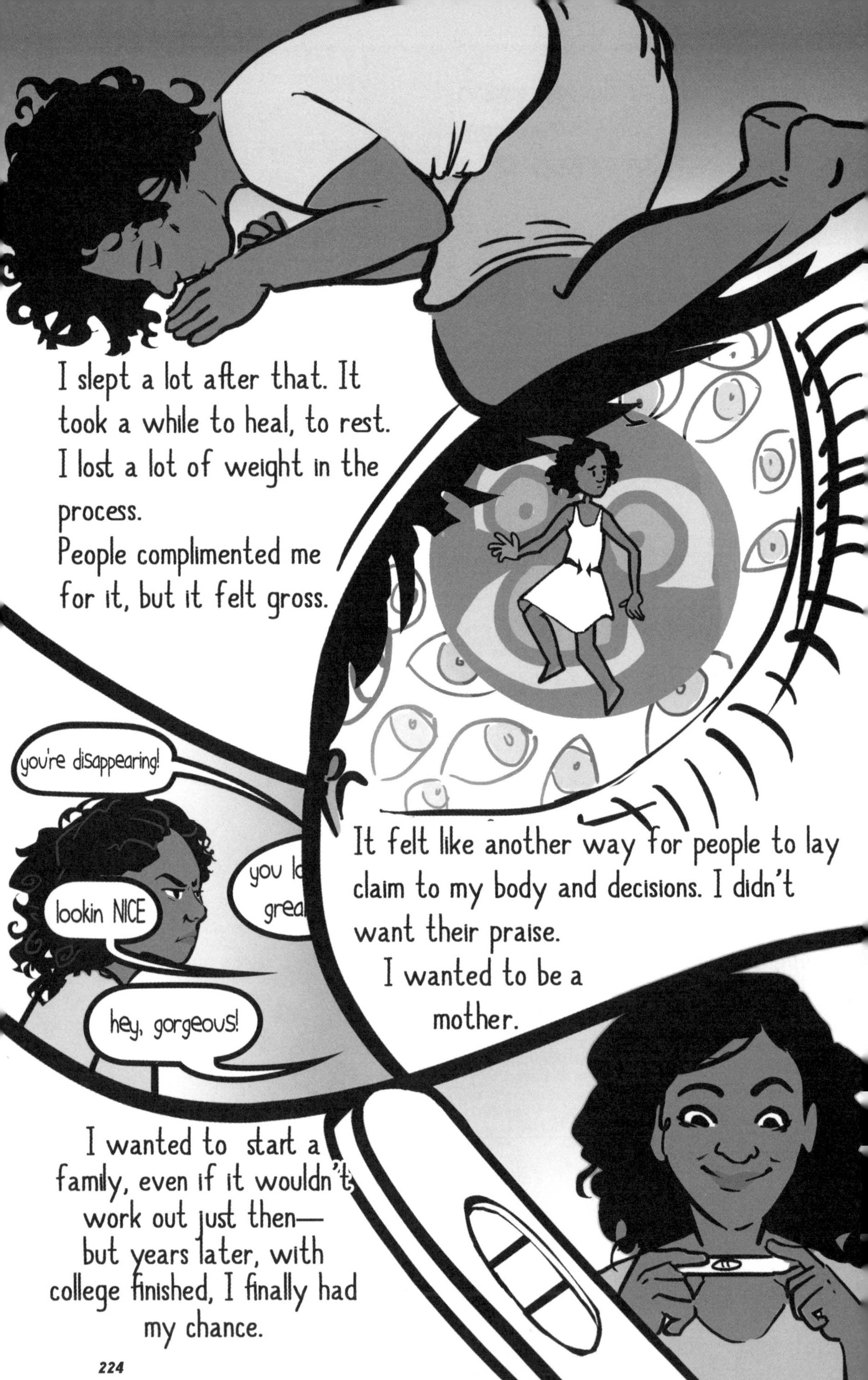
I slept a lot after that. It took a while to heal, to rest. I lost a lot of weight in the process.
People complimented me for it, but it felt gross.
you're disappearing!
lookin NICE
you lo
grea
hey, gorgeous!
It felt like another way for people to lay claim to my body and decisions. I didn't want their praise.
I wanted to be a mother.
I wanted to start a family, even if it wouldn't work out just then—but years later, with college finished, I finally had my chance.

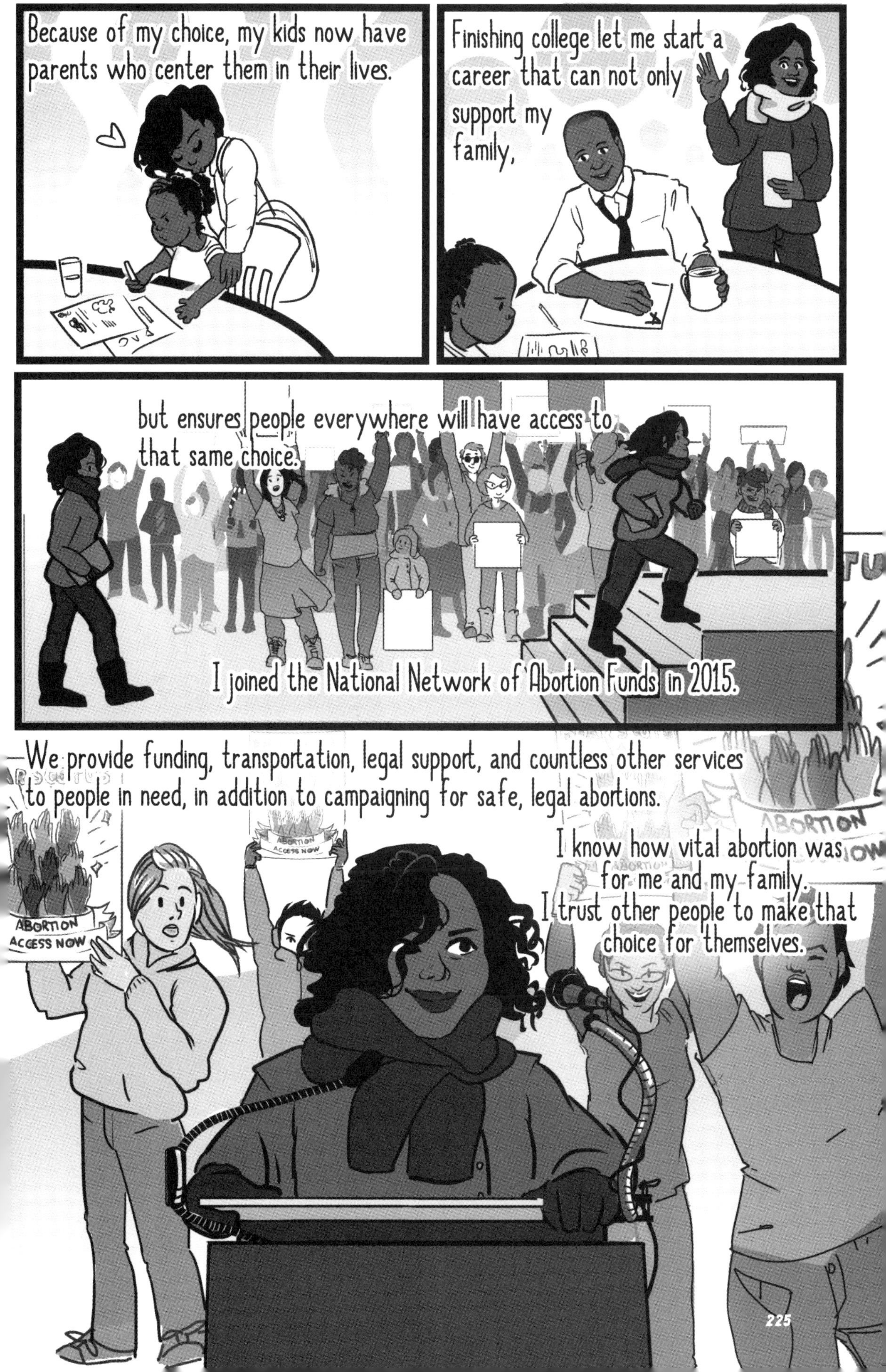
Because of my choice, my kids now have parents who center them in their lives.
Finishing college let me start a career that can not only support my family,
but ensures people everywhere will have access to that same choice.
I joined the National Network of Abortion Funds in 2015.
We provide funding, transportation, legal support, and countless other services to people in need, in addition to campaigning for safe, legal abortions.
ABORTION ACCESS NOW
ABORTION ACCESS NOW
ABORTION
I know how vital abortion was for me and my family.
I trust other people to make that choice for themselves.

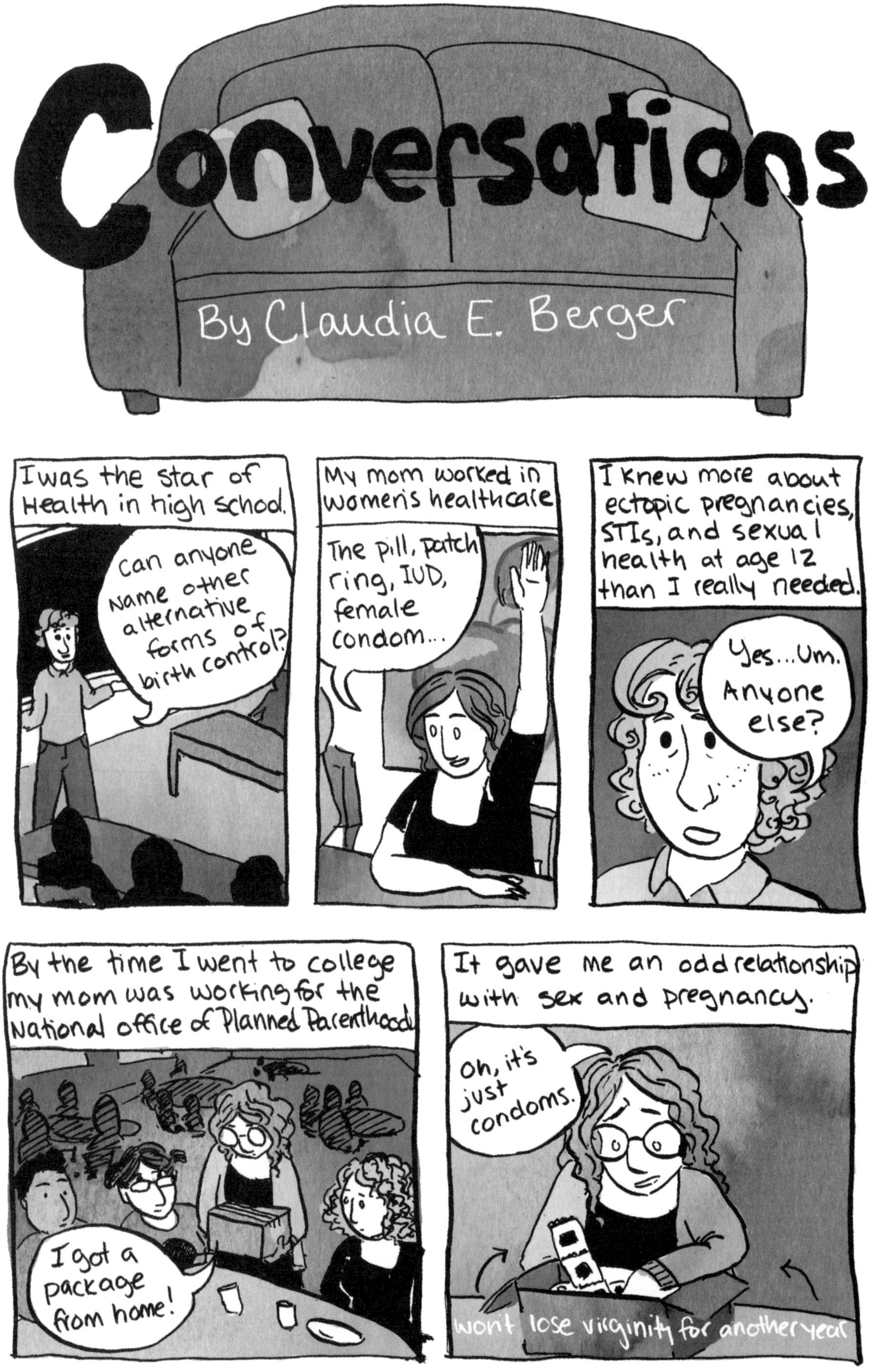
Conversations
By Claudia E. Berger
I was the star of Health in high school.
Can anyone name other alternative forms of birth control?
My mom worked in women's healthcare
The pill, patch ring, IUD, female condom...
I knew more about ectopic pregnancies, STIs, and sexual health at age 12 than I really needed.
Yes... Um. Anyone else?
By the time I went to college my mom was working for the National office of Planned Parenthood.
I got a package from home!
It gave me an odd relationship with sex and pregnancy.
Oh, it's just condoms.
won't lose virginity for another year

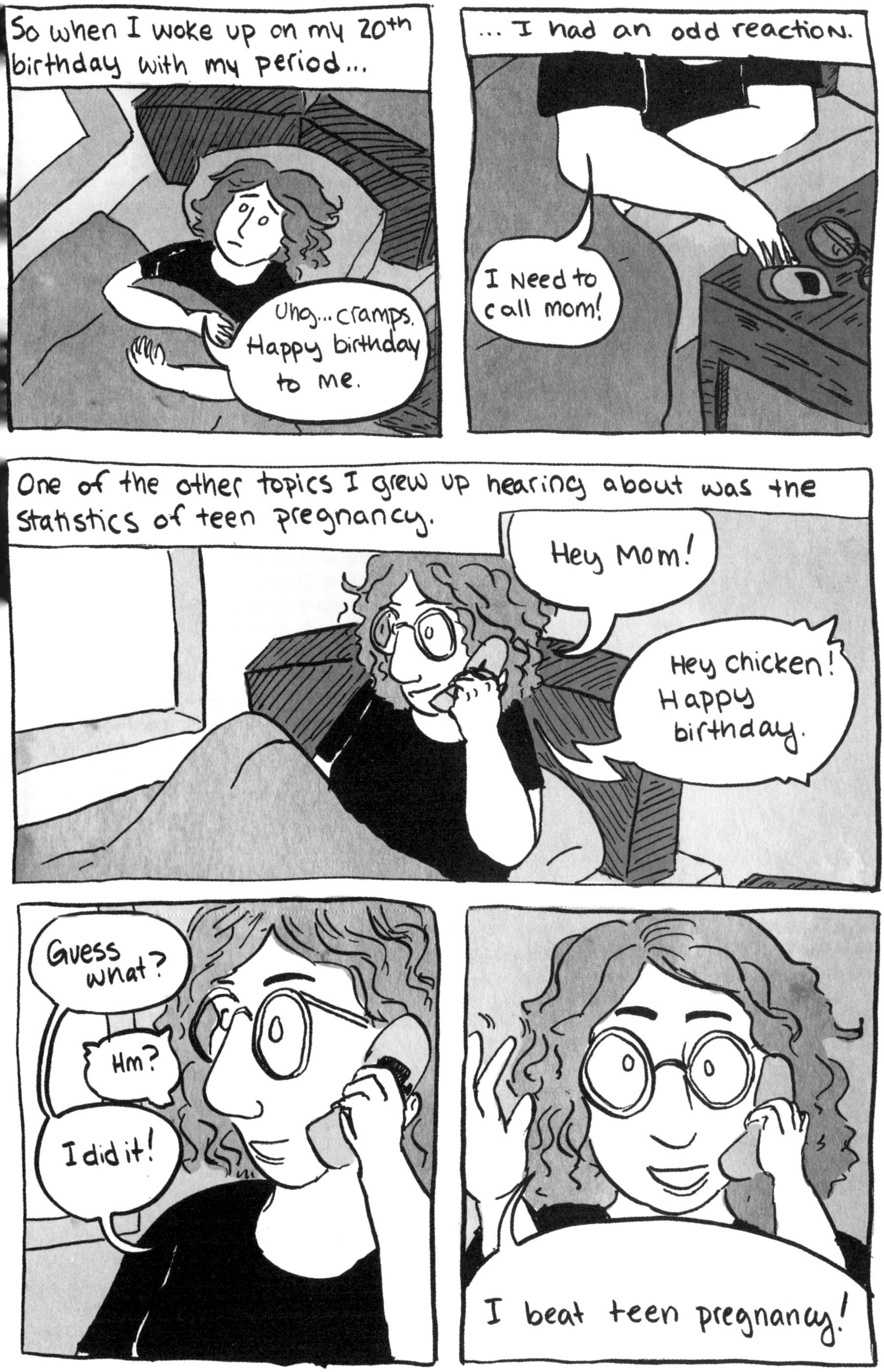
So when I woke up on my 20th birthday with my period...
Uhg... cramps. Happy birthday to me.
... I had an odd reaction.
I Need to call mom!
One of the other topics I grew up hearing about was the statistics of teen pregnancy.
Hey Mom!
Hey chicken! Happy birthday.
Guess what?
Hm?
I did it!
I beat teen pregnancy!

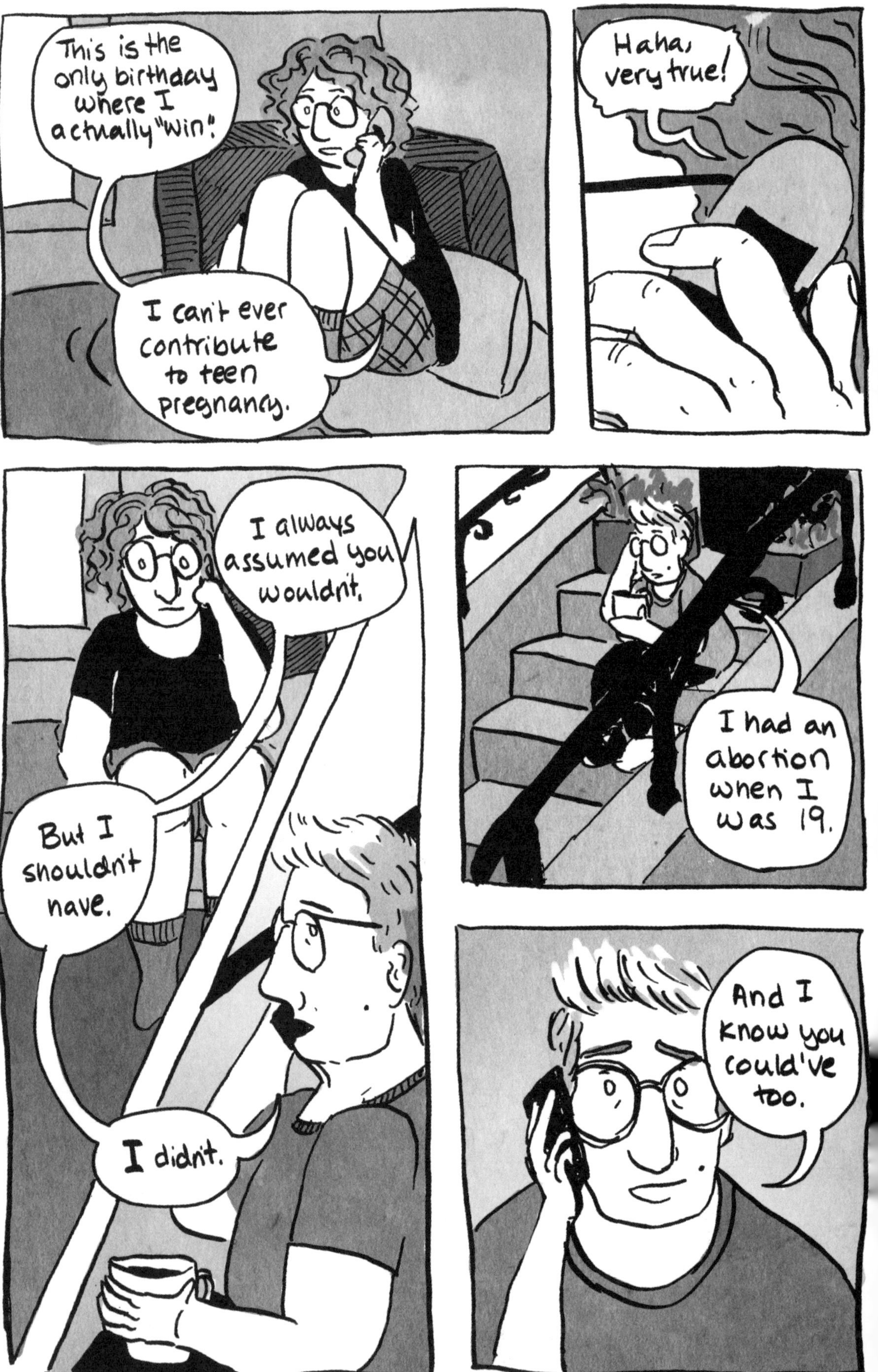
This is the only birthday where I actually "win".
I can't ever contribute to teen pregnancy.
Haha, very true!
I always assumed you wouldn't.
But I shouldn't have.
I didn't.
I had an abortion when I was 19.
And I know you could've too.

A few years later, I finally talked to her about what it was like; how it felt.

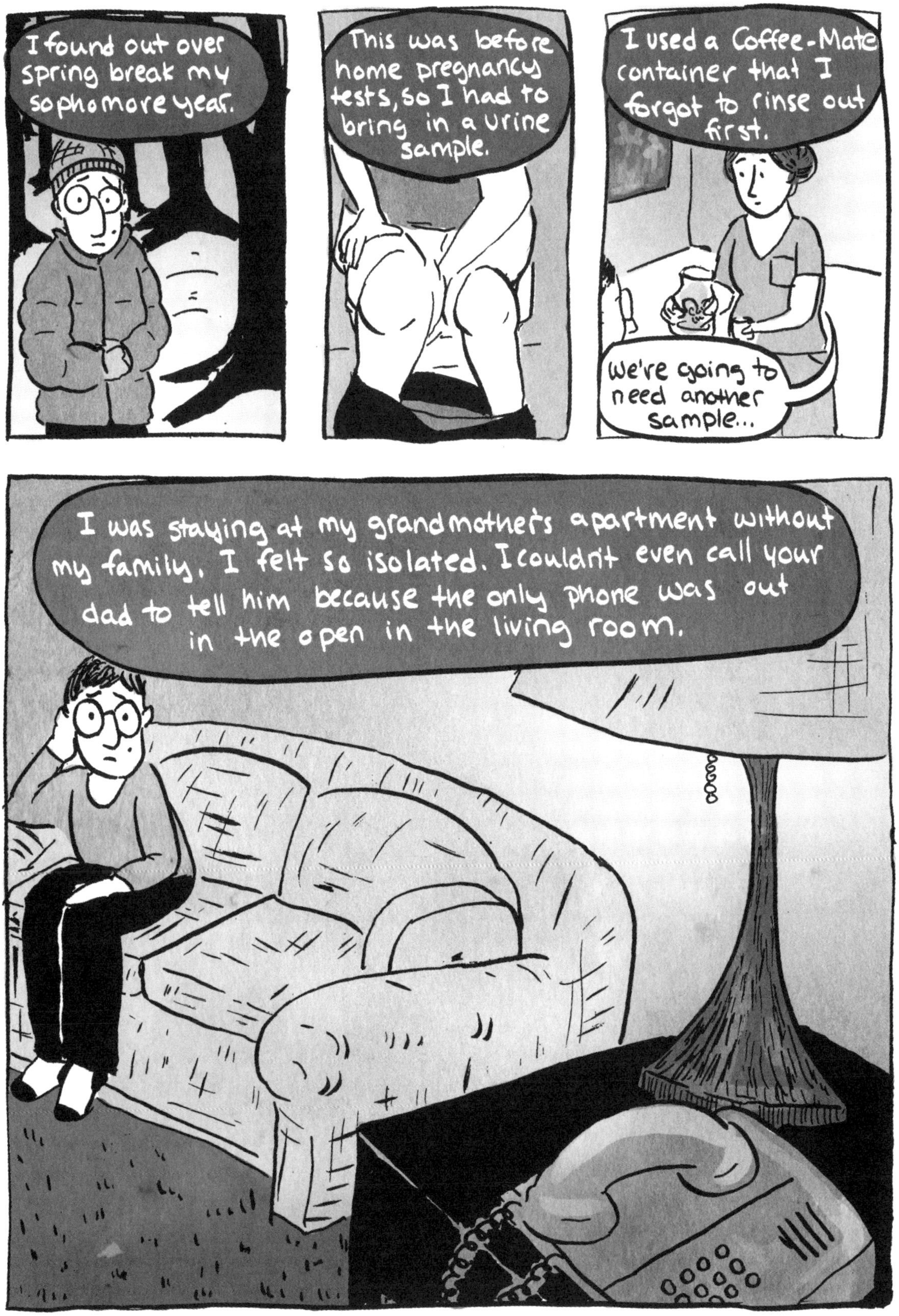
I found out over spring break my sophomore year.
This was before home pregnancy tests, so I had to bring in a urine sample.
I used a Coffee-Mate container that I forgot to rinse out first.
We're going to need another sample...
I was staying at my grandmother's apartment without my family. I felt so isolated. I couldn't even call your dad to tell him because the only phone was out in the open in the living room.

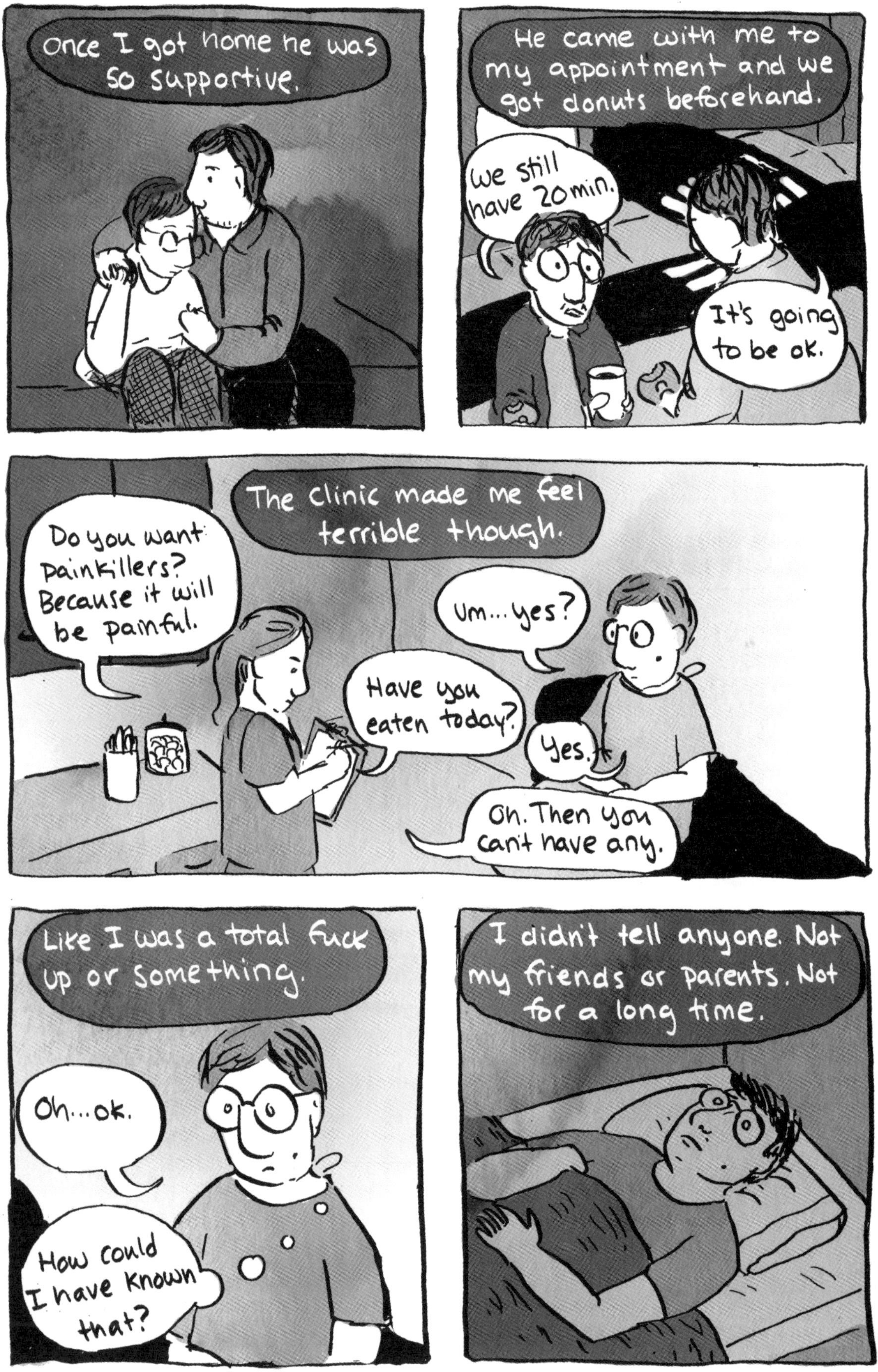
Once I got home he was so supportive.
He came with me to my appointment and we got donuts beforehand.
We still have 20 min.
It's going to be ok.
The clinic made me feel terrible though.
Do you want painkillers? Because it will be painful.
Um... yes?
Have you eaten today?
Yes.
Oh. Then you can't have any.
Like I was a total fuck up or something.
Oh... ok.
How could I have known that?
I didn't tell anyone. Not my friends or parents. Not for a long time.

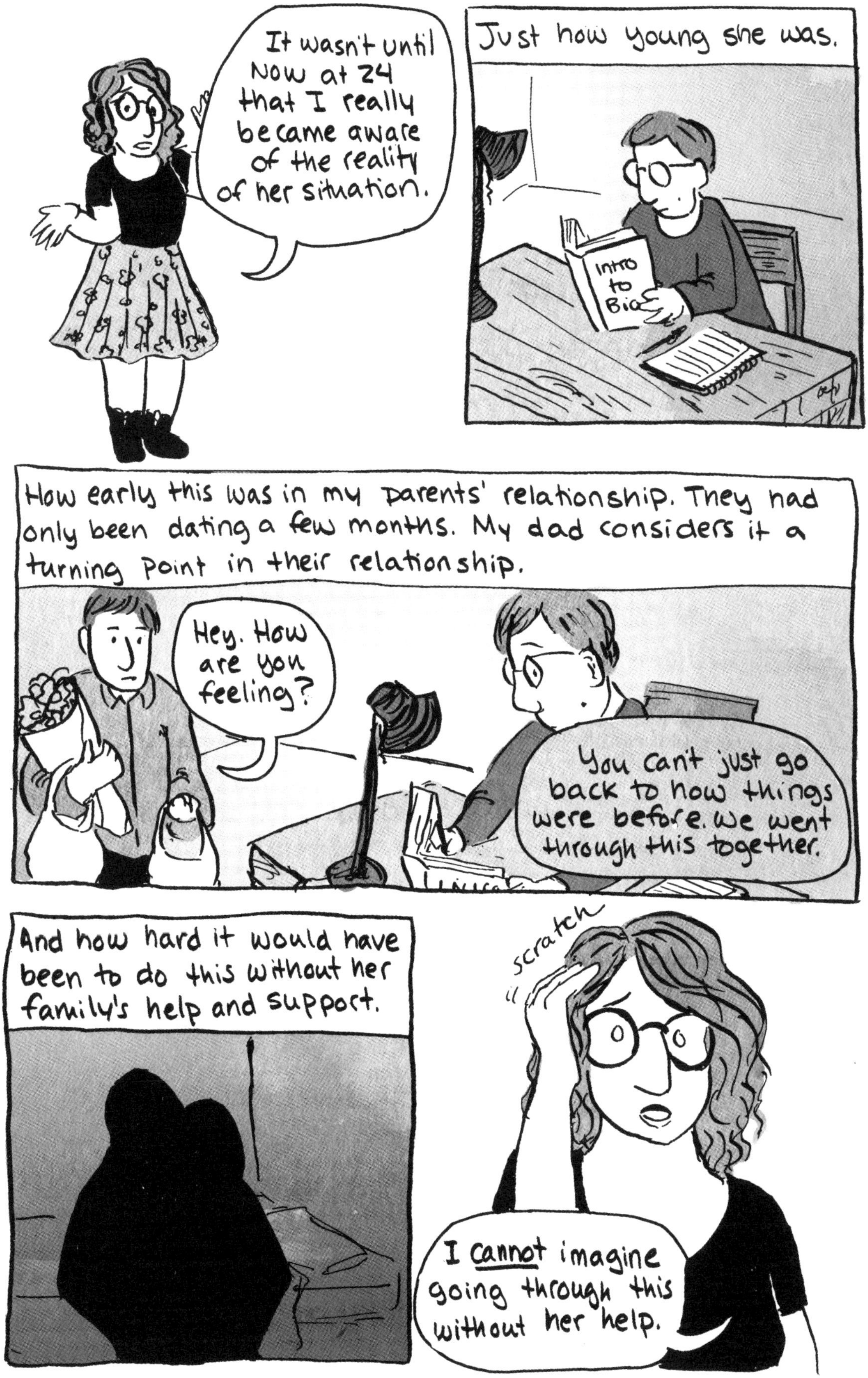

It wasn't until Now at 24 that I really became aware of the reality of her situation.
Just how young she was.
Intro to Bio
How early this was in my parents' relationship. They had only been dating a few months. My dad considers it a turning point in their relationship.
Hey. How are you feeling?
You can't just go back to how things were before. We went through this together.
And how hard it would have been to do this without her family's help and support.
scratch
I cannot imagine going through this without her help.

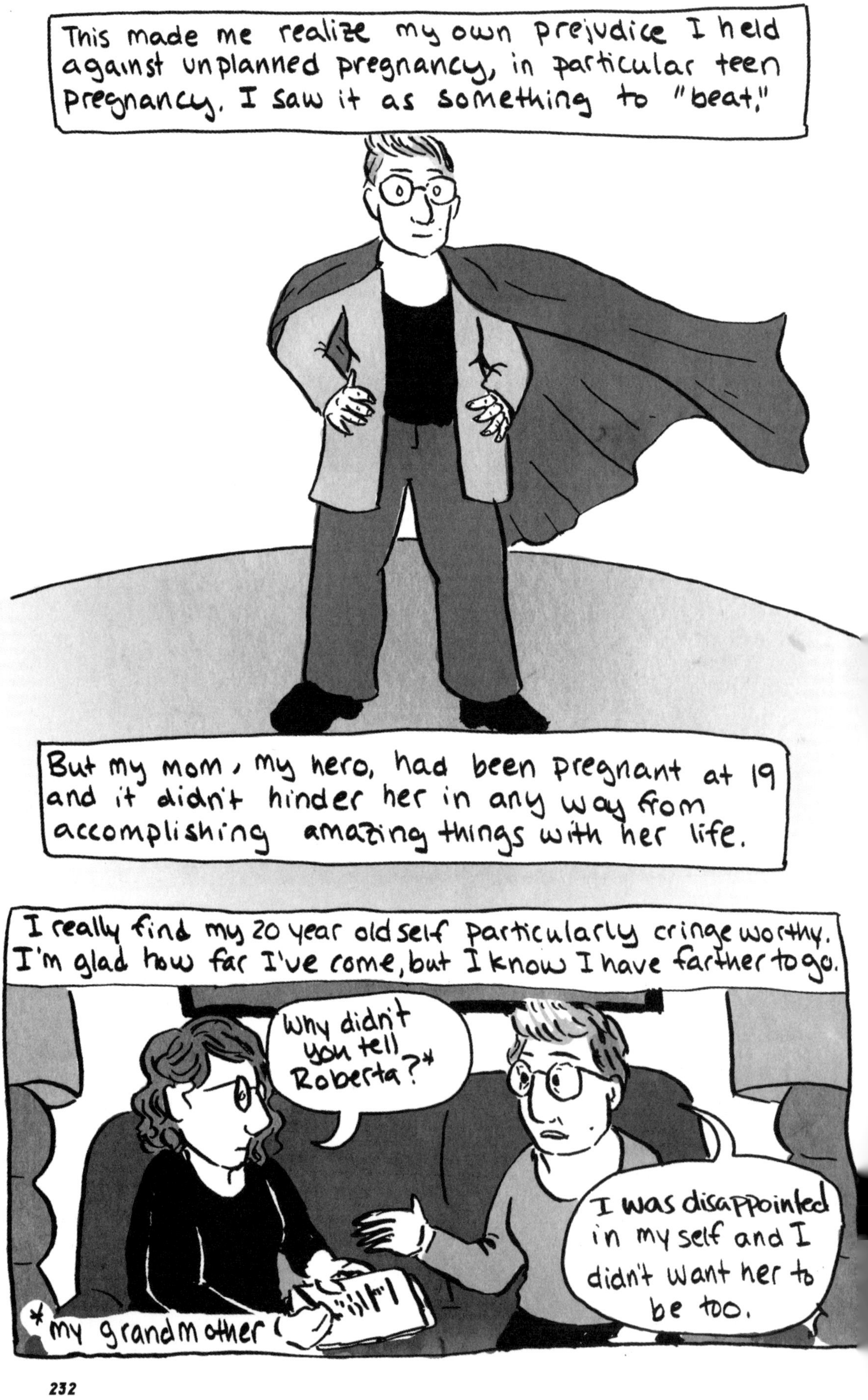

This made me realize my own prejudice I held against unplanned pregnancy, in particular teen pregnancy. I saw it as something to "beat."
But my mom, my hero, had been pregnant at 19 and it didn't hinder her in any way from accomplishing amazing things with her life.
I really find my 20 year old self particularly cringe worthy. I'm glad how far I've come, but I know I have farther to go.
Why didn't you tell Roberta?*
I was disappointed in my self and I didn't want her to be too.
*my grandmother!

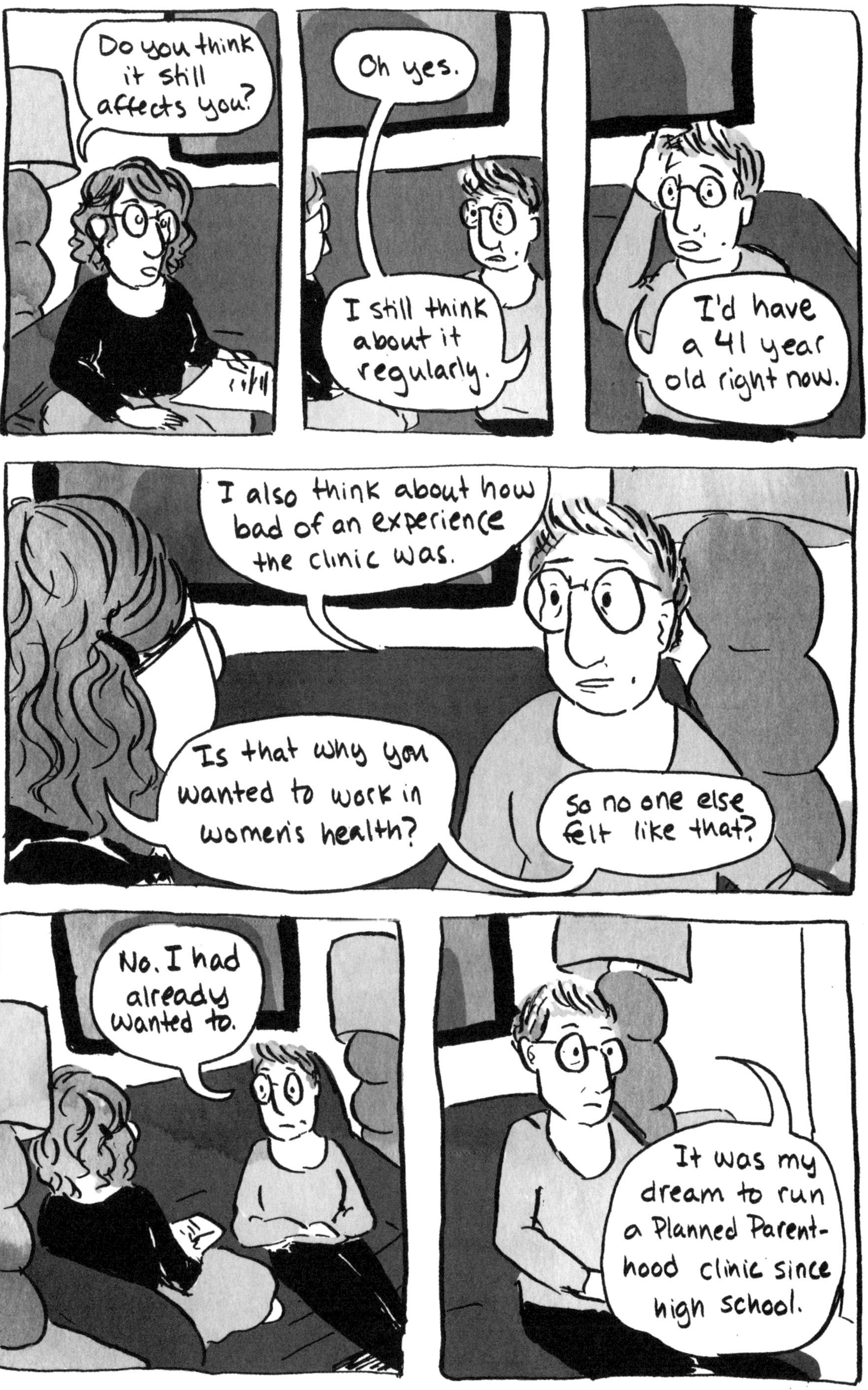
Do you think it still affects you?
Oh yes.
I still think about it regularly.
I'd have a 41 year old right now.
I also think about how bad of an experience the clinic was.
Is that why you wanted to work in women's health?
So no one else felt like that?
No. I had already wanted to.
It was my dream to run a Planned Parenthood clinic since high school.

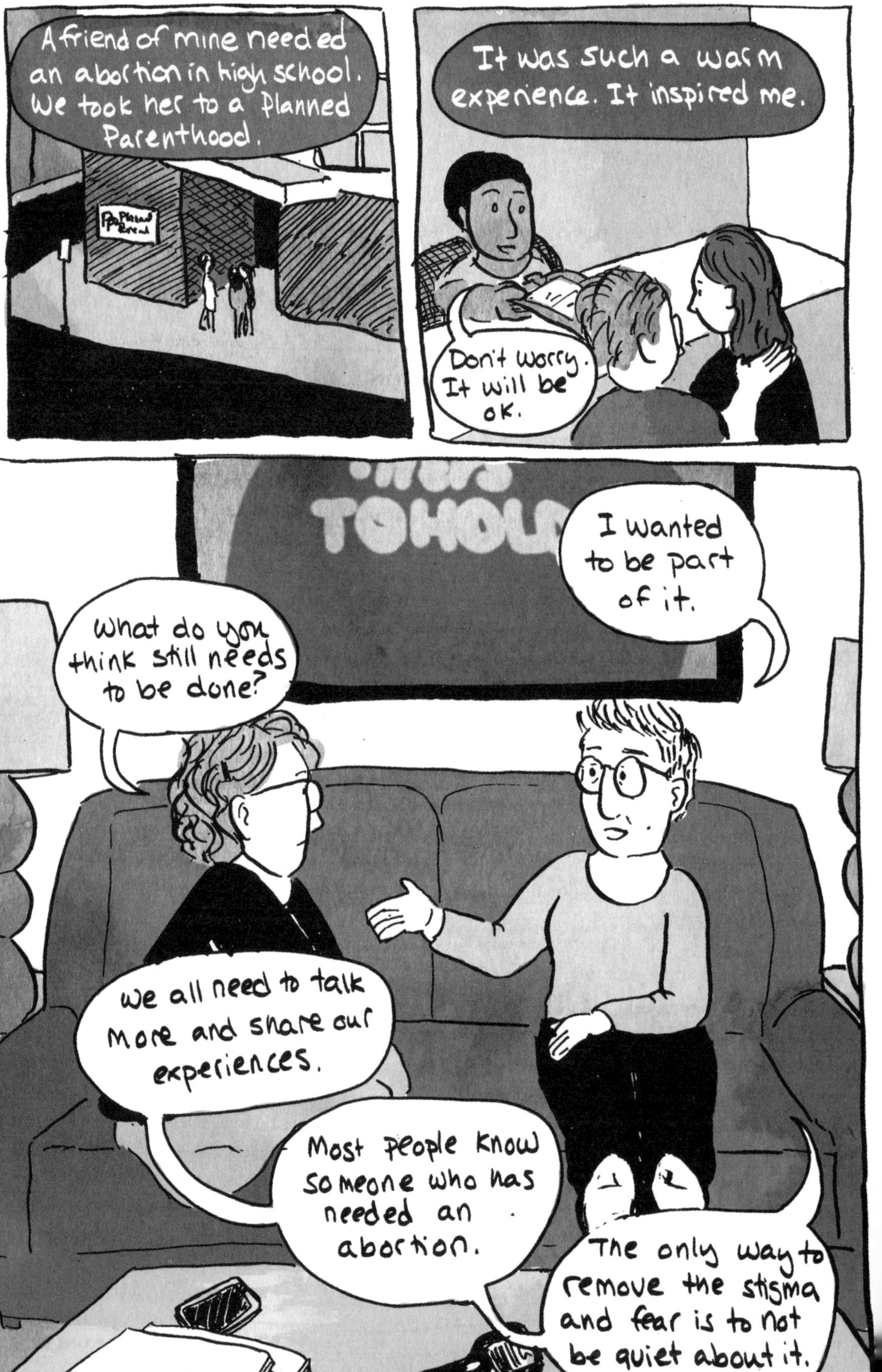
A friend of mine needed an abortion in high school. We took her to a Planned Parenthood.
It was such a warm experience. It inspired me.
Don't worry. It will be ok.
I wanted to be part of it.
What do you think still needs to be done?
We all need to talk more and share our experiences.
Most people know someone who has needed an abortion.
The only way to remove the stigma and fear is to not be quiet about it.

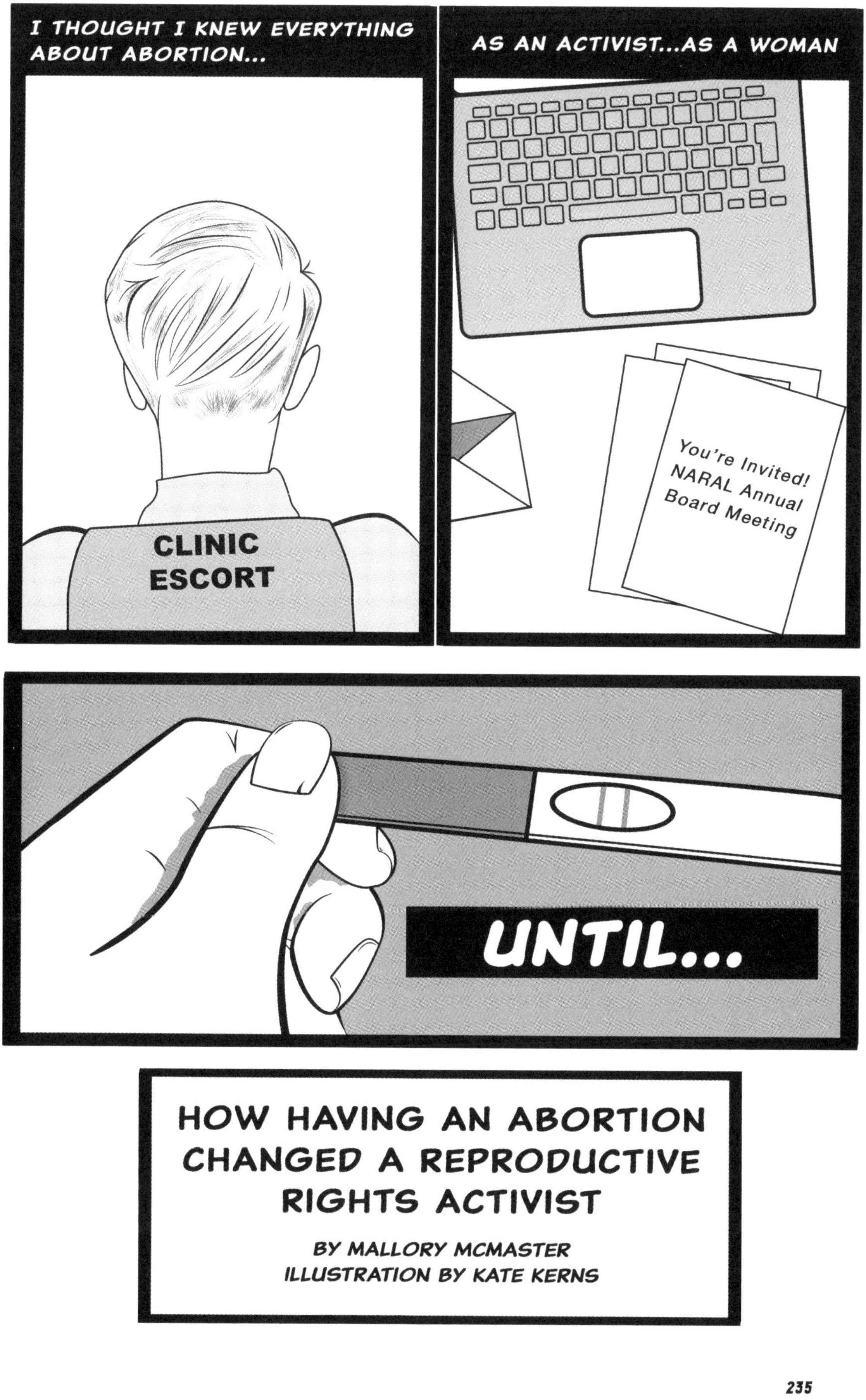
I THOUGHT I KNEW EVERYTHING ABOUT ABORTION...
CLINIC ESCORT
AS AN ACTIVIST...AS A WOMAN
You're Invited! NARAL Annual Board Meeting
UNTIL...

HOW HAVING AN ABORTION CHANGED A REPRODUCTIVE RIGHTS ACTIVIST

BY MALLORY MCMASTER
ILLUSTRATION BY KATE KERNS

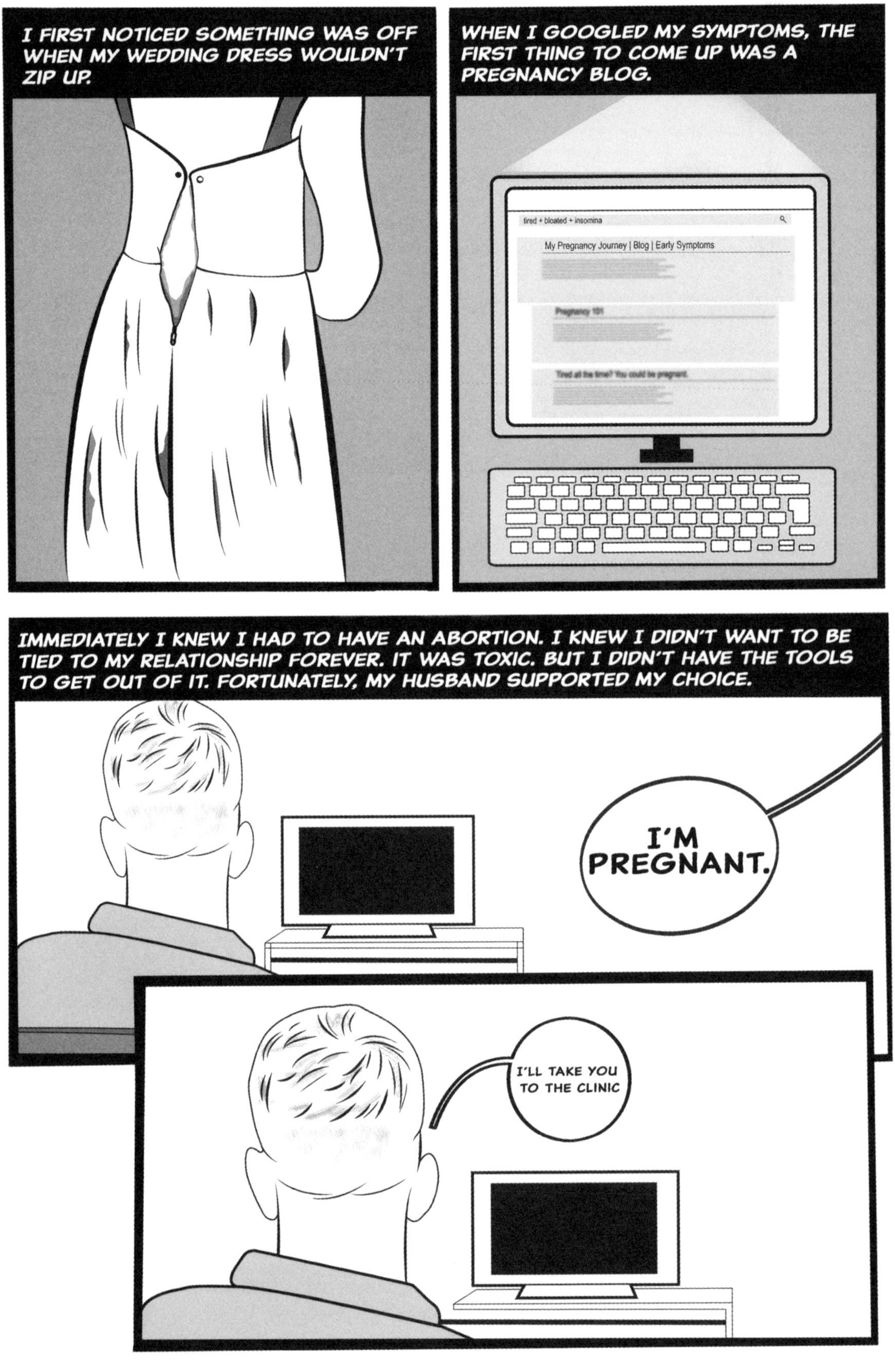
I FIRST NOTICED SOMETHING WAS OFF WHEN MY WEDDING DRESS WOULDN'T ZIP UP.
WHEN I GOOGLED MY SYMPTOMS, THE FIRST THING TO COME UP WAS A PREGNANCY BLOG.
tired + bloated + insomina
My Pregnancy Journey | Blog | Early Symptoms
IMMEDIATELY I KNEW I HAD TO HAVE AN ABORTION. I KNEW I DIDN'T WANT TO BE TIED TO MY RELATIONSHIP FOREVER. IT WAS TOXIC. BUT I DIDN'T HAVE THE TOOLS TO GET OUT OF IT. FORTUNATELY, MY HUSBAND SUPPORTED MY CHOICE.
I'M PREGNANT.
I'LL TAKE YOU TO THE CLINIC

THE CLINIC WAS CLOSED FOR NEW YEARS AND WAITING FOR IT TO REOPEN WAS PAINFUL. I WAS MISERABLE BEING PREGNANT. I DIDN'T FEEL LIKE MYSELF AND I HAD TO WAIT, AND WAIT, AND WAIT.

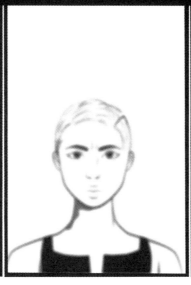

I WAS NEWLY MARRIED WHEN I FOUND OUT I WAS PREGNANT. BUT I KNEW I DIDN'T WANT TO HAVE KIDS WITH HIM, BE TIED TO HIM FOREVER. THE RELATIONSHIP WAS AWFUL AND ABUSIVE.

THE ABORTION WOULD HELP ME END THE RELATIONSHIP.

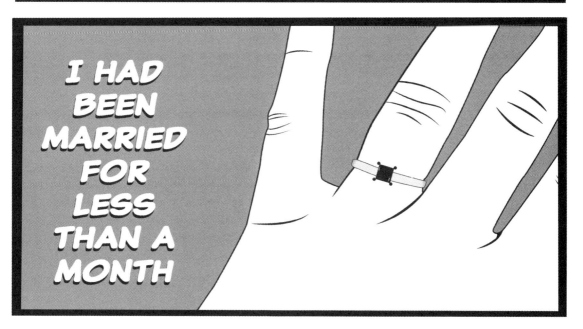

I HAD BEEN MARRIED FOR LESS THAN A MONTH

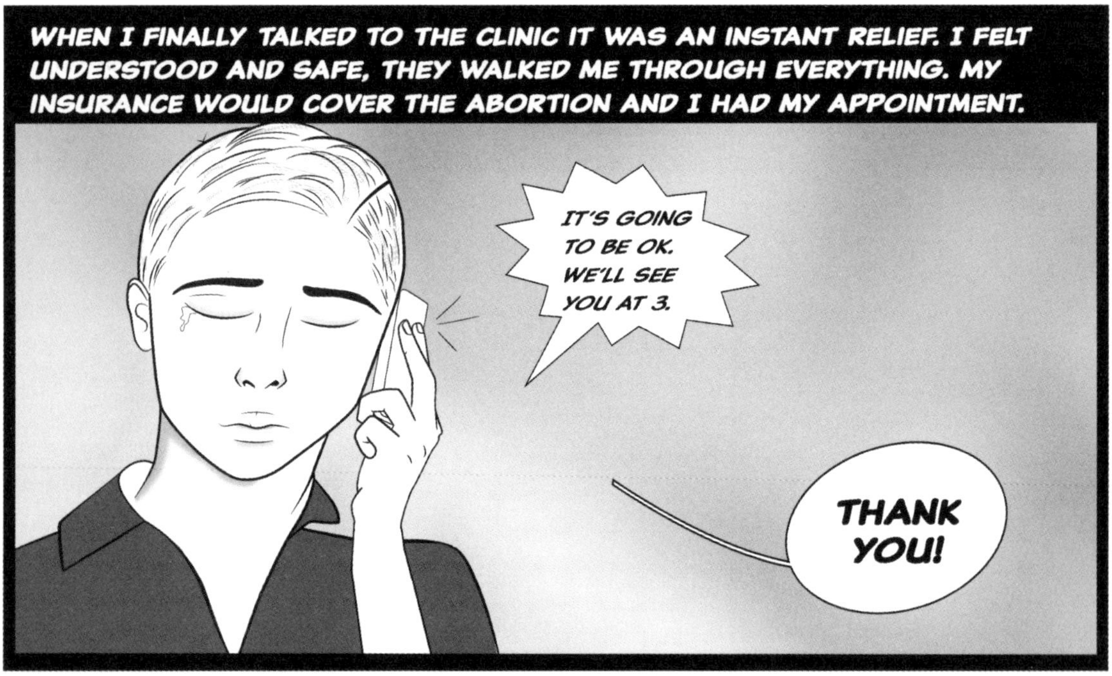
WHEN I FINALLY TALKED TO THE CLINIC IT WAS AN INSTANT RELIEF. I FELT UNDERSTOOD AND SAFE, THEY WALKED ME THROUGH EVERYTHING. MY INSURANCE WOULD COVER THE ABORTION AND I HAD MY APPOINTMENT.
IT'S GOING TO BE OK. WE'LL SEE YOU AT 3.
THANK YOU!

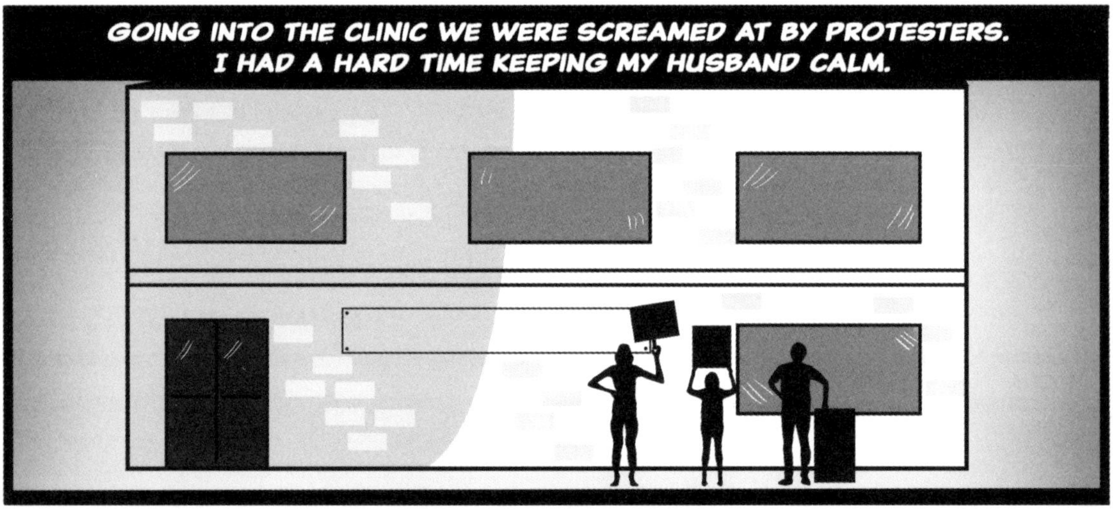
GOING INTO THE CLINIC WE WERE SCREAMED AT BY PROTESTERS. I HAD A HARD TIME KEEPING MY HUSBAND CALM.

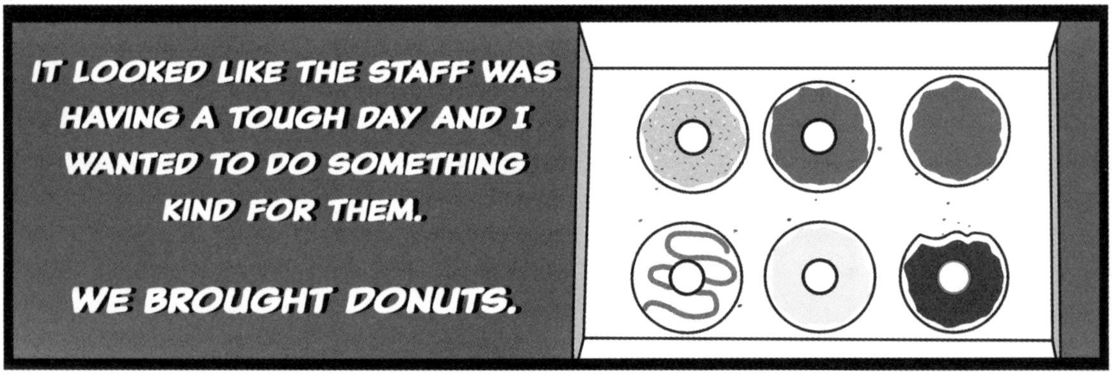
IT LOOKED LIKE THE STAFF WAS HAVING A TOUGH DAY AND I WANTED TO DO SOMETHING KIND FOR THEM.
WE BROUGHT DONUTS.

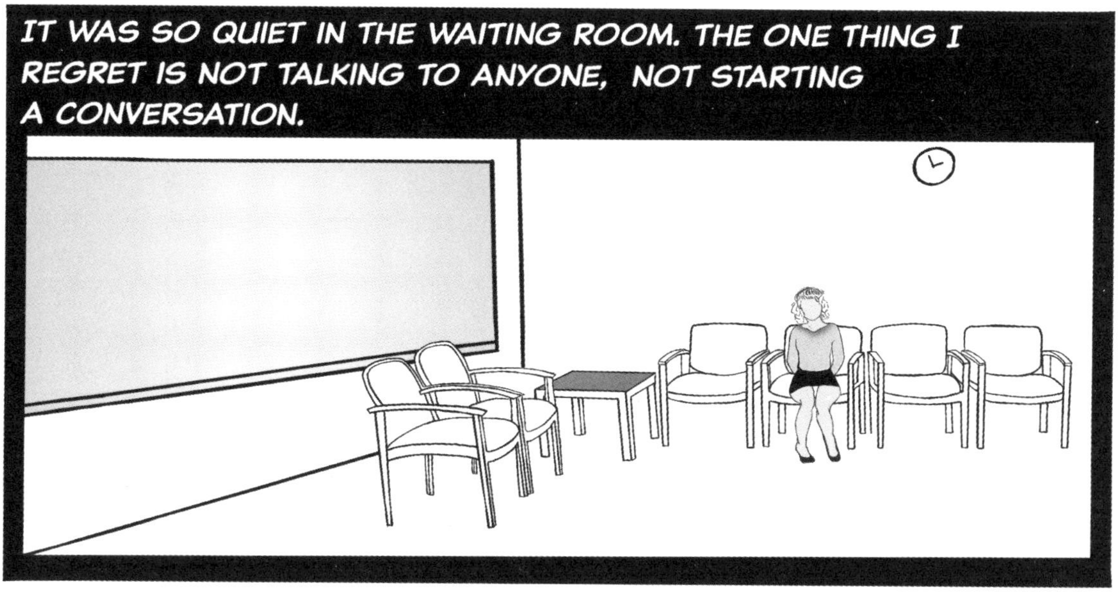
IT WAS SO QUIET IN THE WAITING ROOM. THE ONE THING I REGRET IS NOT TALKING TO ANYONE, NOT STARTING A CONVERSATION.

THE PROCEDURE

THE DAY OF I WAS FEELING AWFUL, BLOATED AND NAUSEOUS. THE PROCEDURE WAS REALLY QUICK AND I DON'T REMEMBER MUCH. WHEN I WOKE UP I FELT THE NAUSEA SETTLE.

I FELT LIKE MYSELF AGAIN.

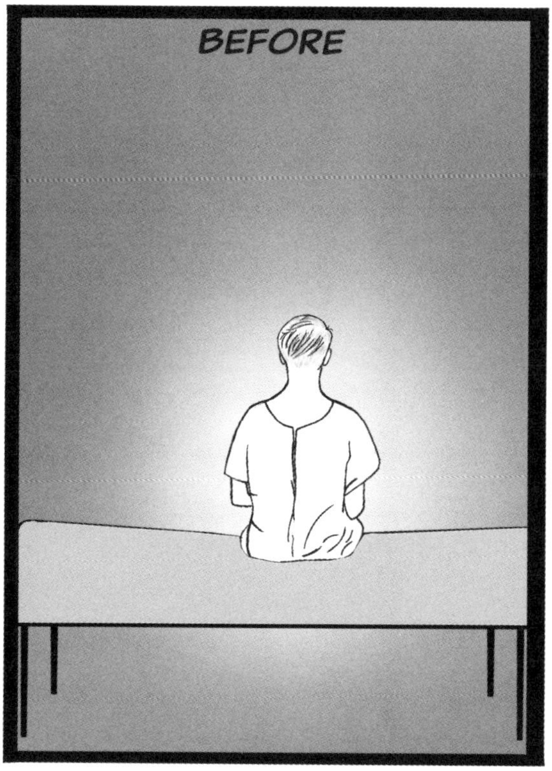
BEFORE

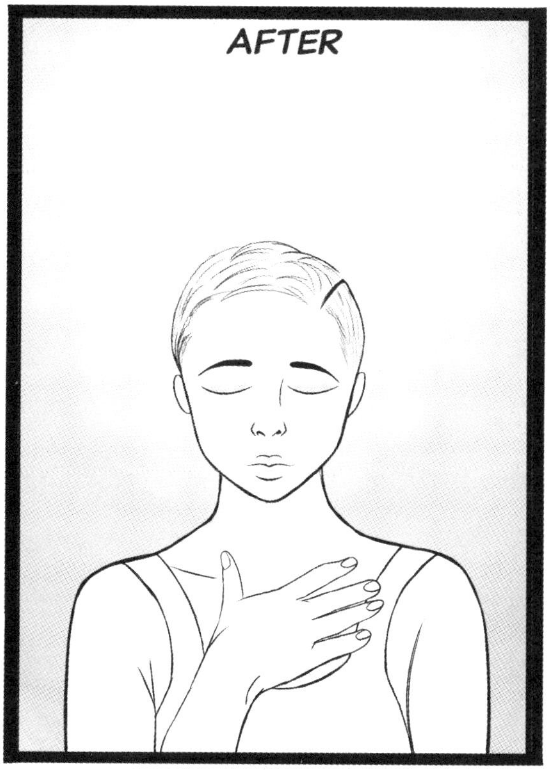
AFTER

WE DROVE HOME SOON AFTER. I WAS ABLE TO EAT. I STAYED HOME WITH NETFLIX AND THE NEXT DAY I WENT TO WORK. I FELT HUMAN AGAIN.

HAVING AN ABORTION CHANGED THE PATH MY LIFE WAS ON. THIS WAS THE FIRST STEP IN INVESTING IN MY FUTURE. IT GAVE ME CONFIDENCE IN MYSELF AND PERSPECTIVE ON MY ABUSIVE MARRIAGE. OVER THE NEXT FOUR YEARS I ENDED THE MARRIAGE, WENT BACK TO SCHOOL, BOUGHT A HOUSE, STARTED A CAREER I LOVE, RE-MARRIED, AND NOW WE'RE STARTING A FAMILY.

4 YEARS LATER

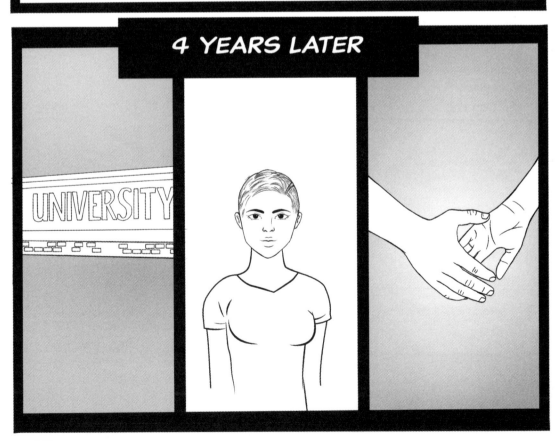

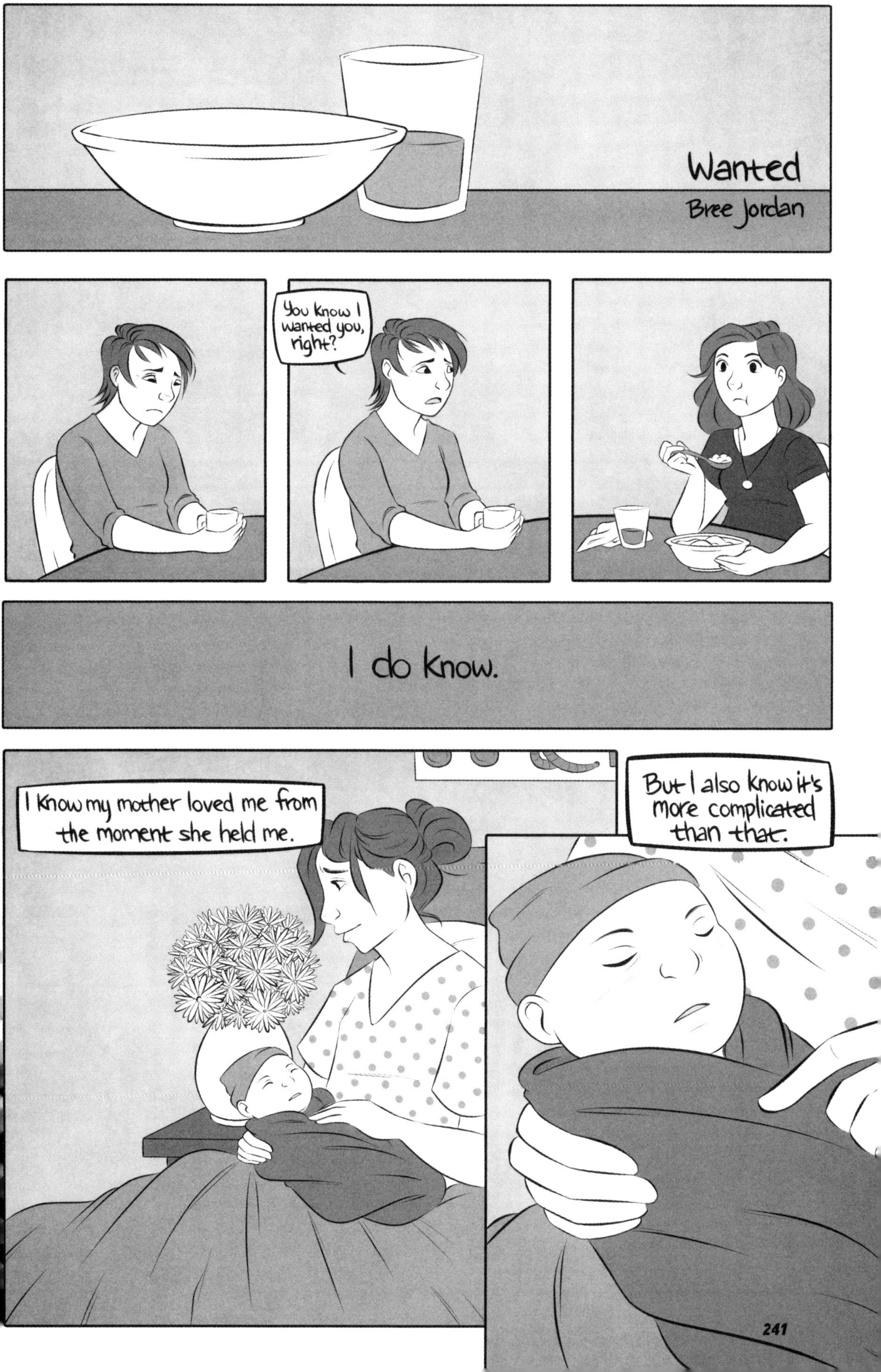
Wanted
Bree Jordan
You know I wanted you, right?
I do know.
I know my mother loved me from the moment she held me.
But I also know it's more complicated than that.

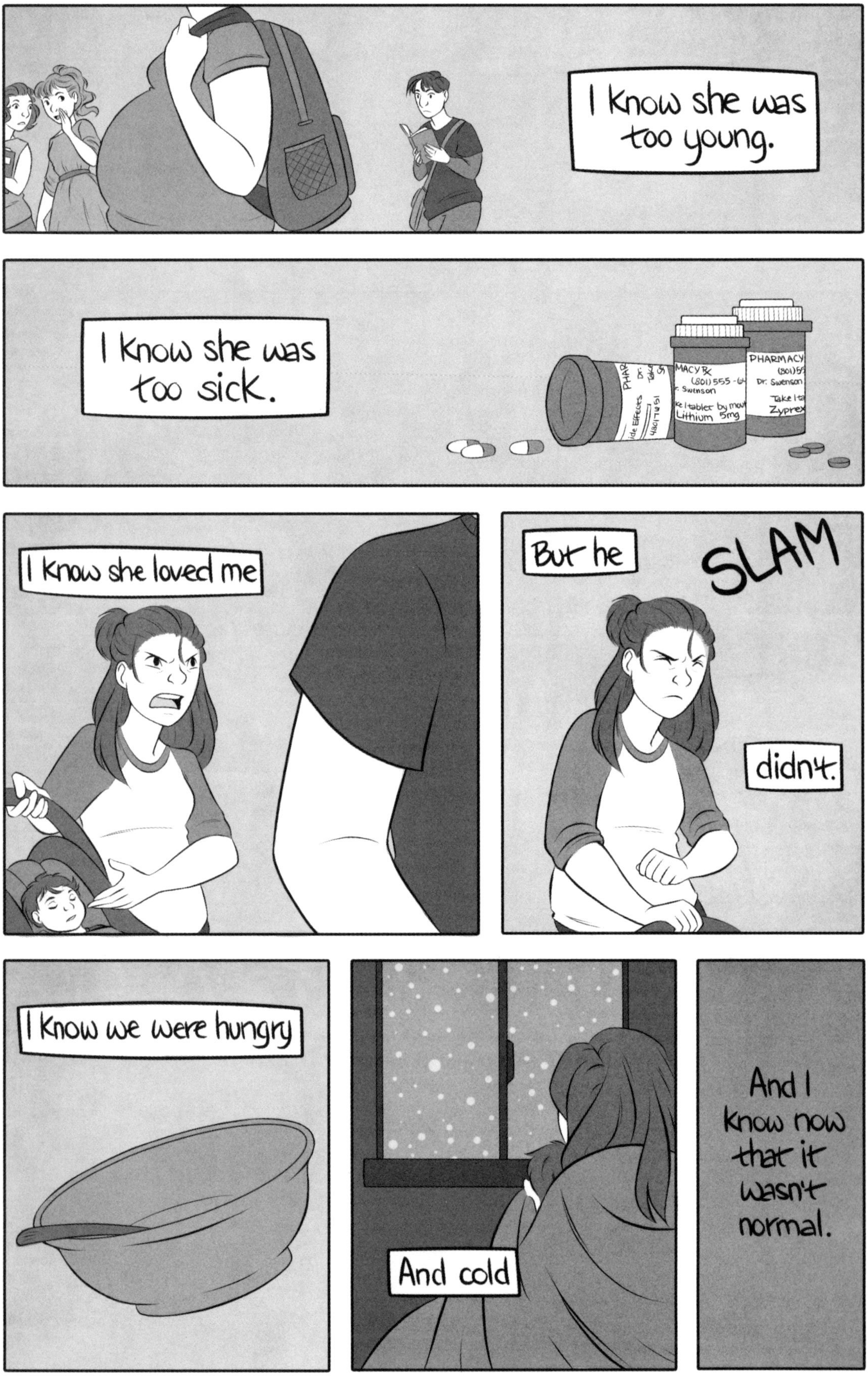
I know she was too young.
I know she was too sick.
PHARMACY
Dr. Swenson
Lithium 5mg
I know she loved me
But he
SLAM
didn't.
I know we were hungry
And cold
And I know now that it wasn't normal.

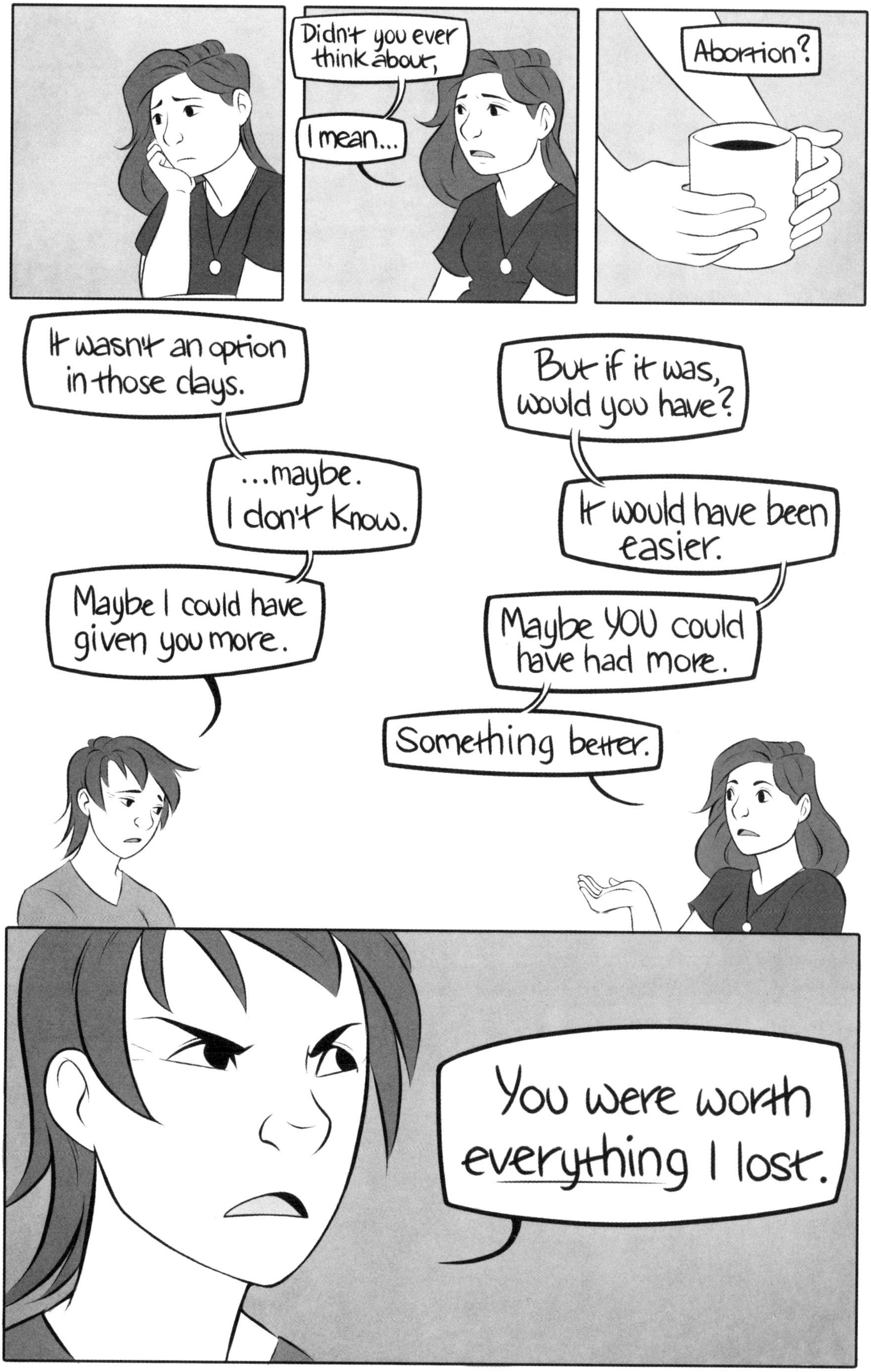
Didn't you ever think about,
I mean...
Abortion?
It wasn't an option in those days.
...maybe. I don't know.
Maybe I could have given you more.
But if it was, would you have?
It would have been easier.
Maybe YOU could have had more.
Something better.
You were worth everything I lost.

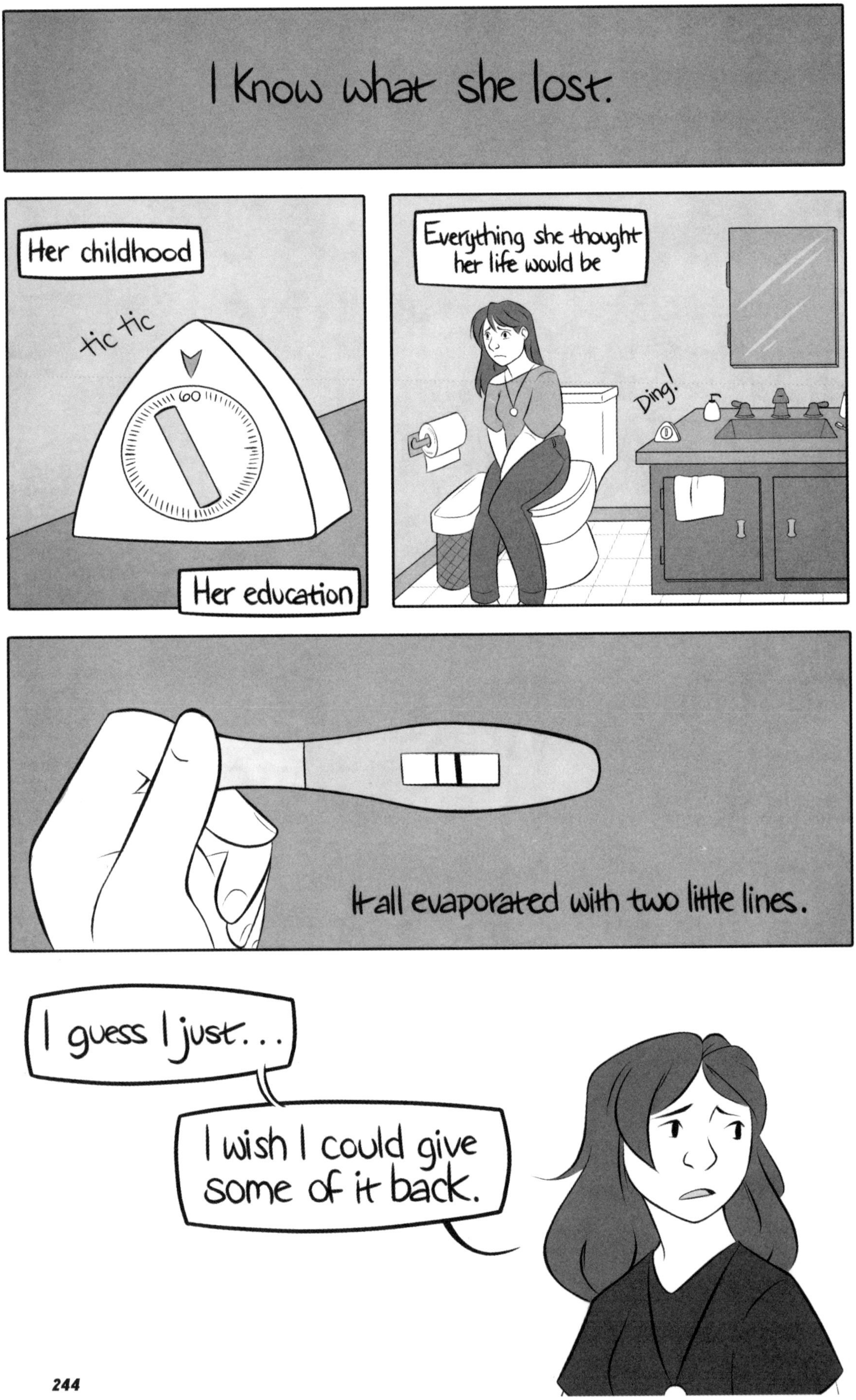
I Know what she lost.
Her childhood
tic tic
60
Her education
Everything she thought her life would be
Ding!
It all evaporated with two little lines.
I guess I just...
I wish I could give some of it back.

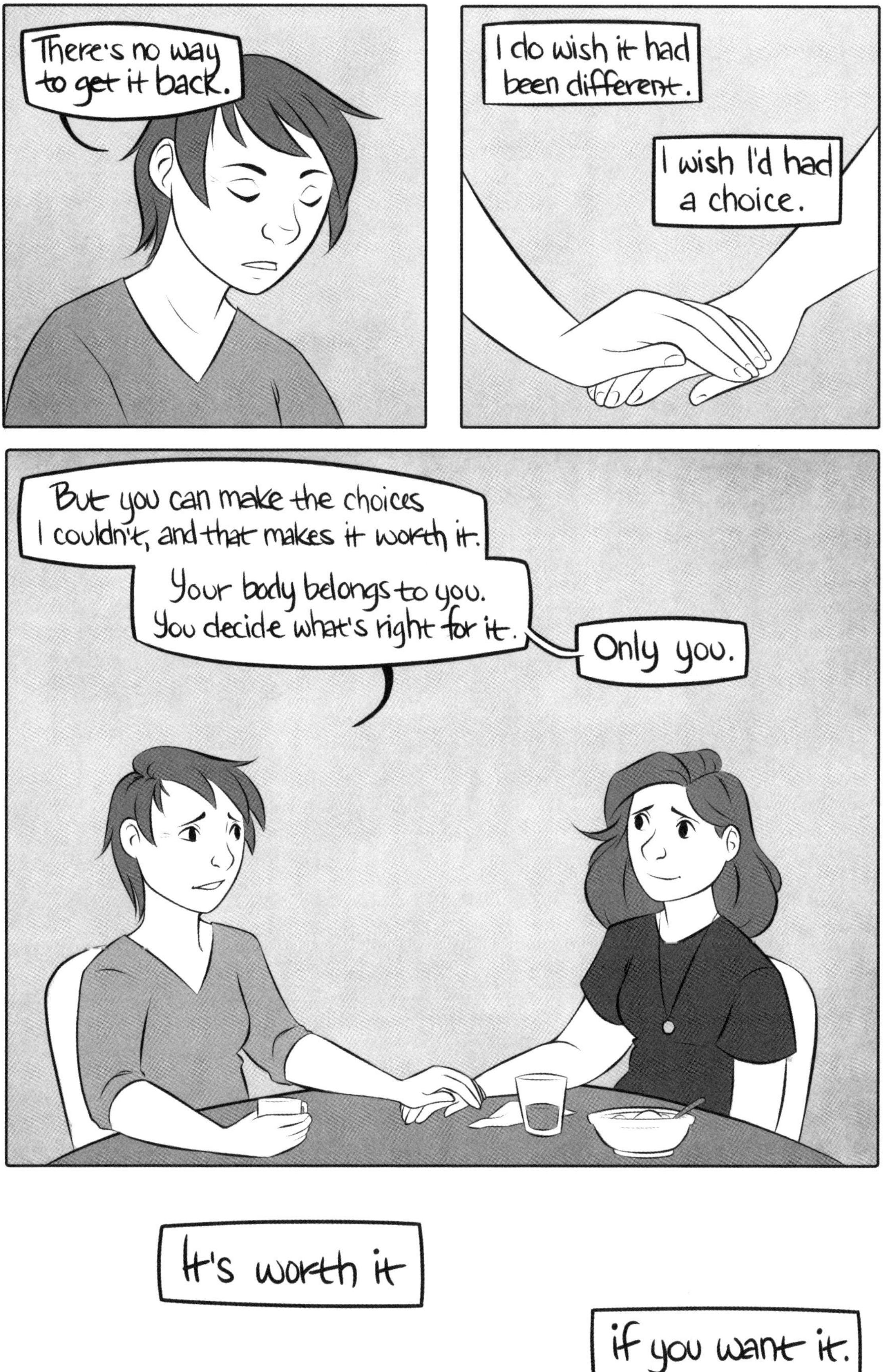
There's no way to get it back.
I do wish it had been different.
I wish I'd had a choice.
But you can make the choices I couldn't, and that makes it worth it.
Your body belongs to you. You decide what's right for it.
Only you.
It's worth it
if you want it.

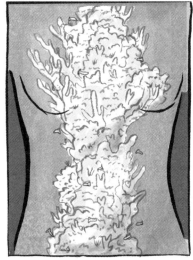
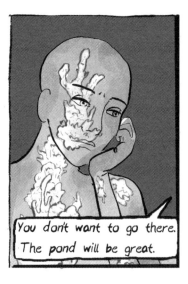

"Underwater" - CB Hart

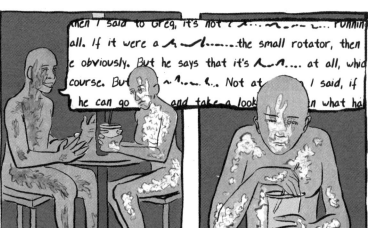

...hen I said to Greg, it's not .... running all. If it were a ~~~~......the small rotator, then e obviously. But he says that it's ~~......at all, whic course. But ~~...... ...... Not at ...... I said, if he can go ...... and take a look ...... n what ha...

Want to hop by the pond? I have a half hour to kill.

What's wrong with your place? We never go there, and it's closer.

You don't want to go there. The pond will be great.

Perfect, right?
I knew you'd like it.

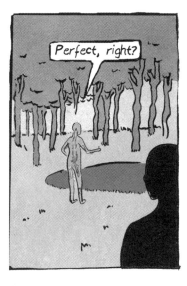

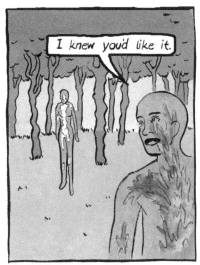

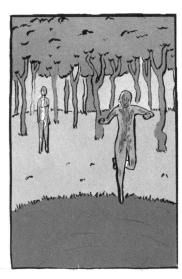

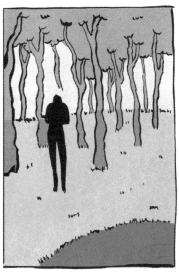

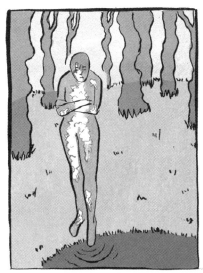

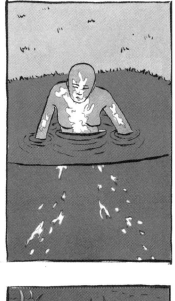

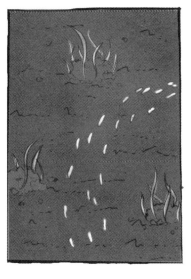

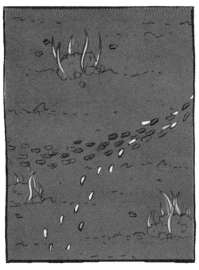

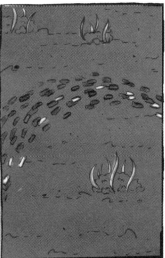

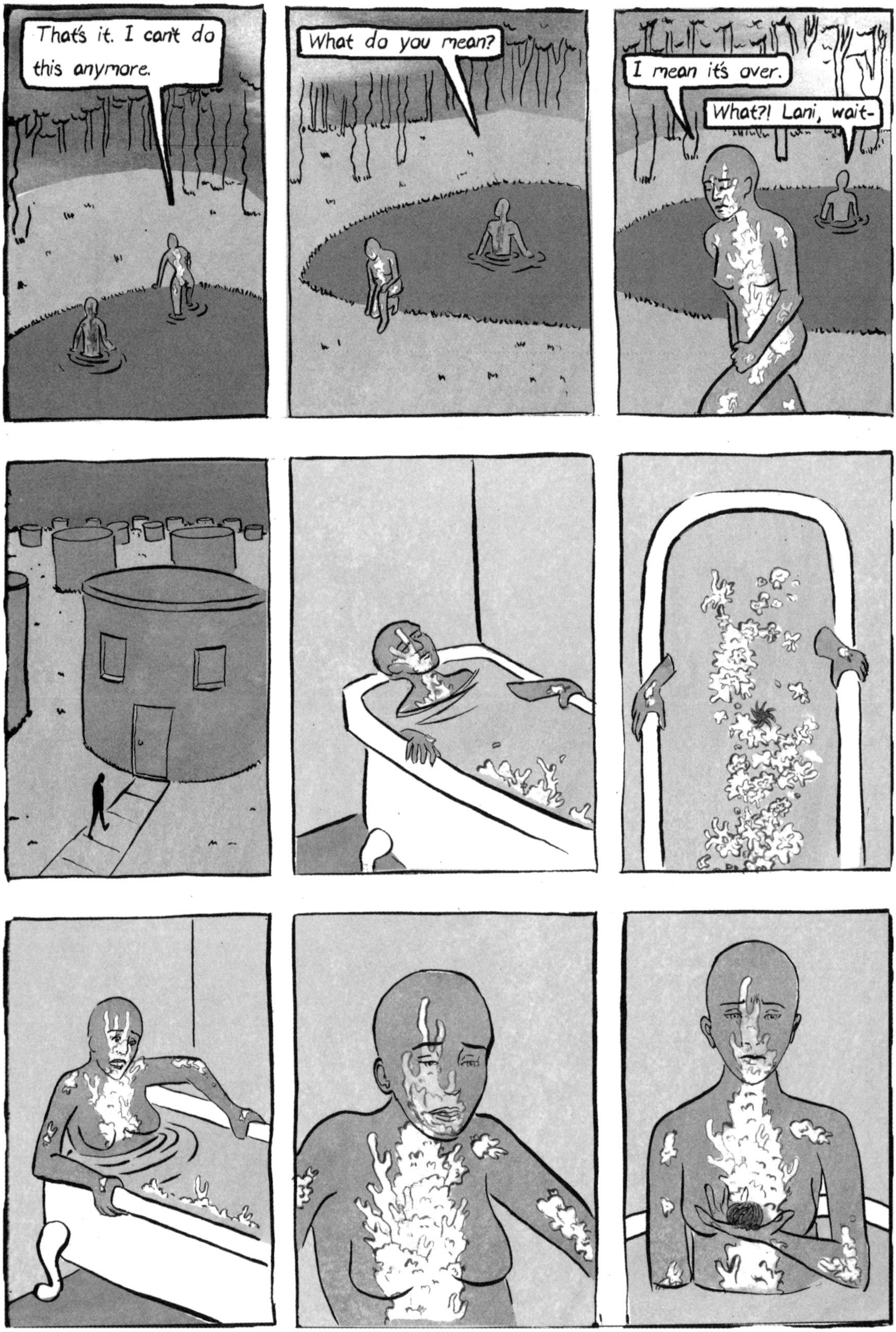
That's it. I can't do this anymore.
What do you mean?
I mean it's over.
What?! Lani, wait-

1
2
3
4
5
7
8
9
0
Turn on your screen.
What is it?
Turn on your screen.
Kinda busy.
I'm pregnant.
What?
I'm. . I'm pregnant. Turn on your screen.
Who's that, babe?
Is that why we couldn't go to your house?
I--I can explain.
Goodbye, Justin.

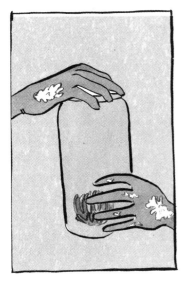

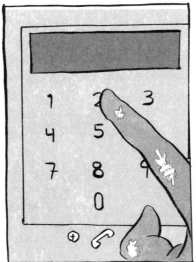

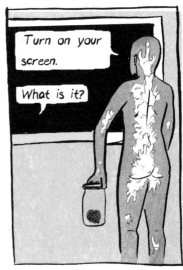

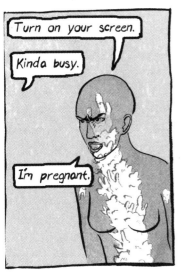

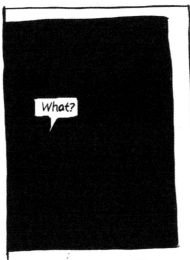

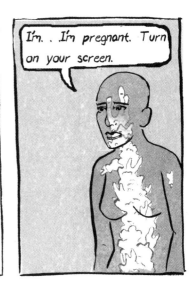

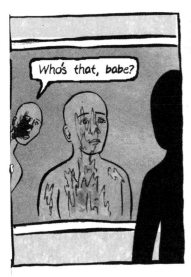

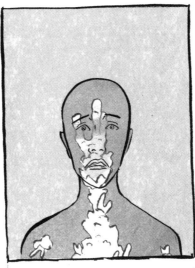

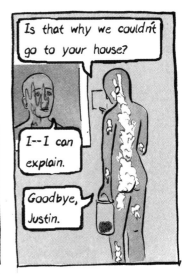

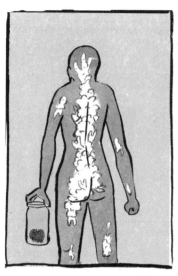

Hey, Kath. Are you free? I need to talk.

Hey Lani! Come in!

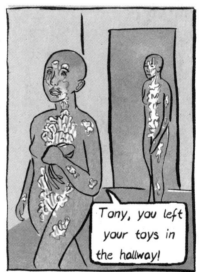

Tony, you left your toys in the hallway!

Hey Danny, Aunt Lani and I are going to talk. Can you go play in your room?

Do you want something to drink? I have fresh or brine.

Brine's fine.

Here you go.

Thanks.

How's Cecilia?

Good! I just put her to nap. Want to go peek?

She's getting so big now!
I think she looks just like Chris.
She's got your eyes.
It's funny. I never thought I'd be Mrs. Mom.
Chris and I thought we'd stop at one. But, look at us now. I was even showing off anemone pics at the canal station yesterday.
Can I ask you something?
Shoot.
Did you. . . Did you ever have any, before Chris?
Of course.
Would you like to see them?

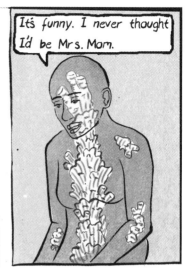

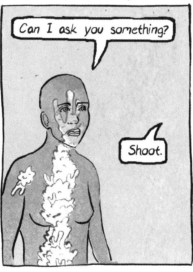

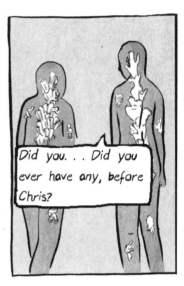

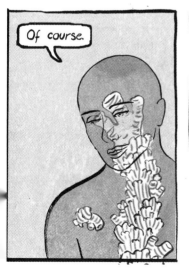

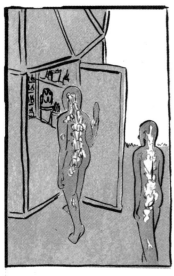

Here they are.

Go ahead and take a look.

They won't grow any bigger like this. But all they need is a little sunlight and they're fine on their own.

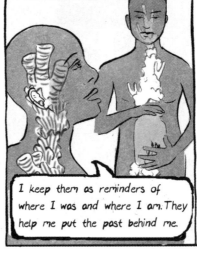

I keep them as reminders of where I was and where I am. They help me put the past behind me.

Without forgetting it's created who I've become.

You should go see mom and dad. They're only just over the hill.
I'm going to go check on the kids, but say hi to them for me, will you?
Don't forget, they're celebrating their 50th in two weeks! No skipping!
Hi, mom and dad.
Kath says hi.
I know it's been a while. It's just been busy.
Nothing major. My dissertation's going fine, it's just getting everything together, you know how it is.

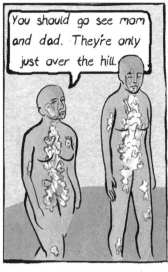

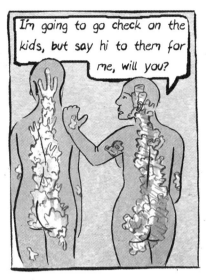

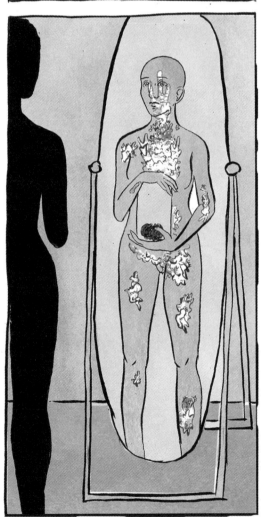

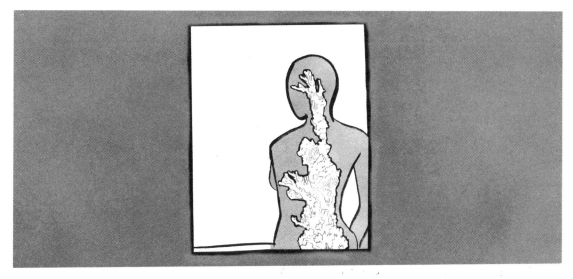

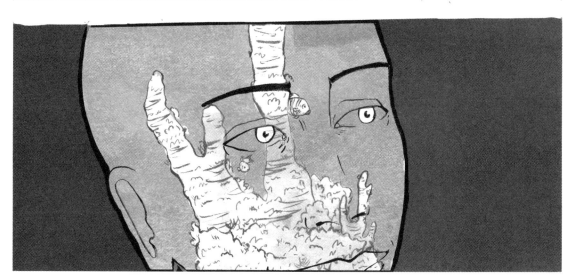

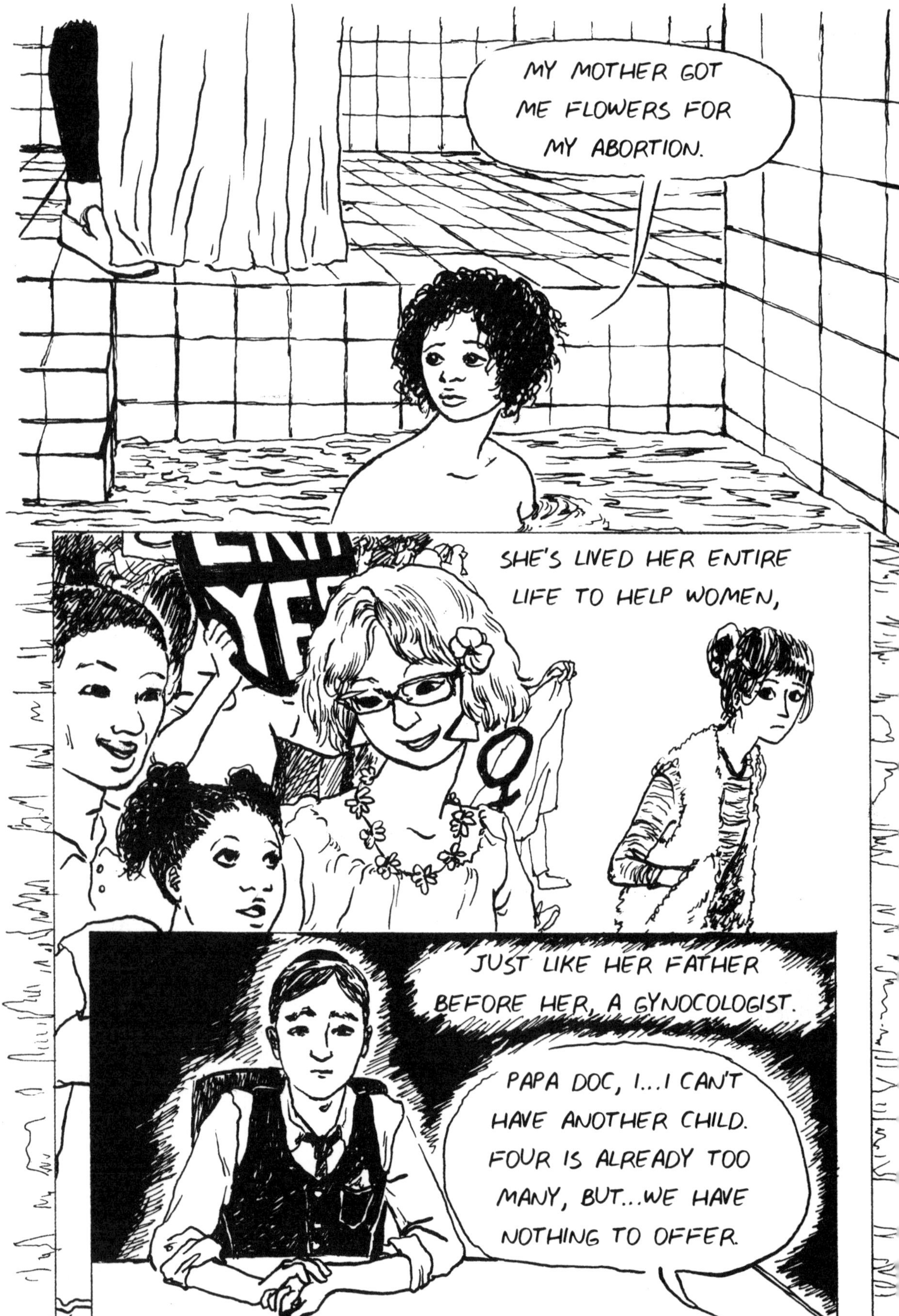
MY MOTHER GOT ME FLOWERS FOR MY ABORTION.
SHE'S LIVED HER ENTIRE LIFE TO HELP WOMEN,
JUST LIKE HER FATHER BEFORE HER, A GYNOCOLOGIST.
PAPA DOC, I...I CAN'T HAVE ANOTHER CHILD. FOUR IS ALREADY TOO MANY, BUT...WE HAVE NOTHING TO OFFER.
"TIKKUN OLAM" BY ANISE SIMON AND SARAH CROWE

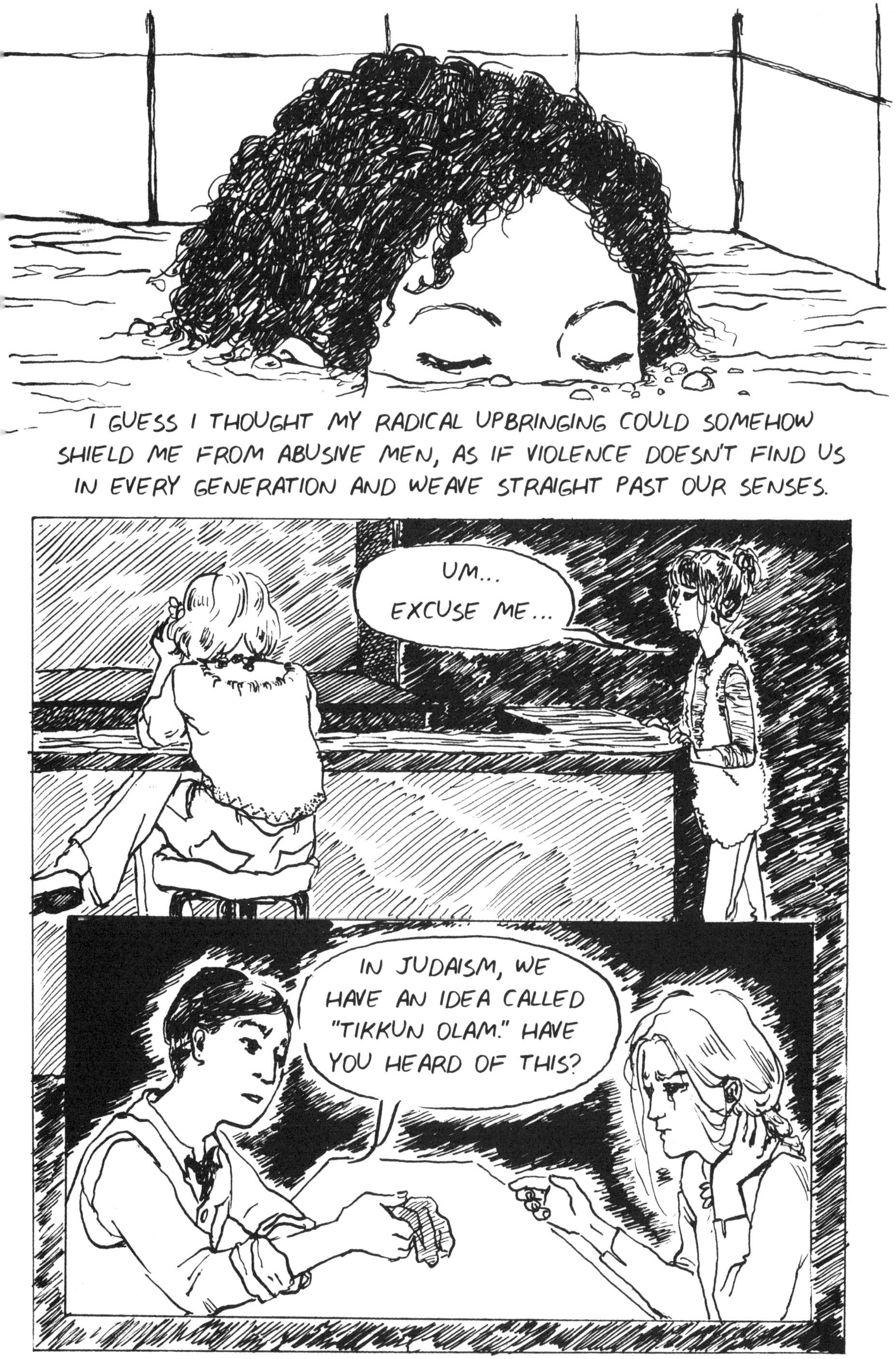
I GUESS I THOUGHT MY RADICAL UPBRINGING COULD SOMEHOW SHIELD ME FROM ABUSIVE MEN, AS IF VIOLENCE DOESN'T FIND US IN EVERY GENERATION AND WEAVE STRAIGHT PAST OUR SENSES.
UM... EXCUSE ME...
IN JUDAISM, WE HAVE AN IDEA CALLED "TIKKUN OLAM." HAVE YOU HEARD OF THIS?

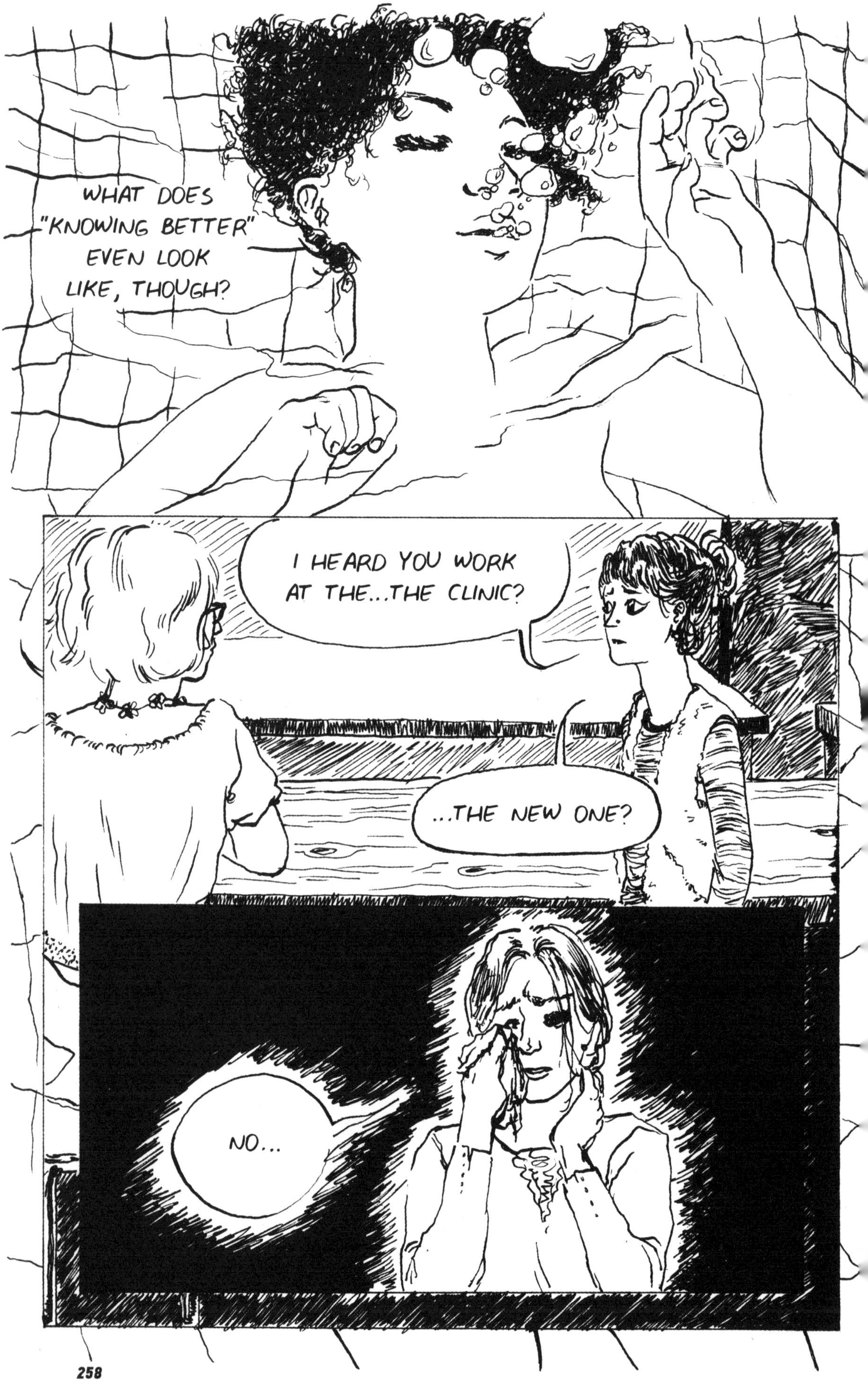
WHAT DOES "KNOWING BETTER" EVEN LOOK LIKE, THOUGH?
I HEARD YOU WORK AT THE...THE CLINIC?
...THE NEW ONE?
NO...

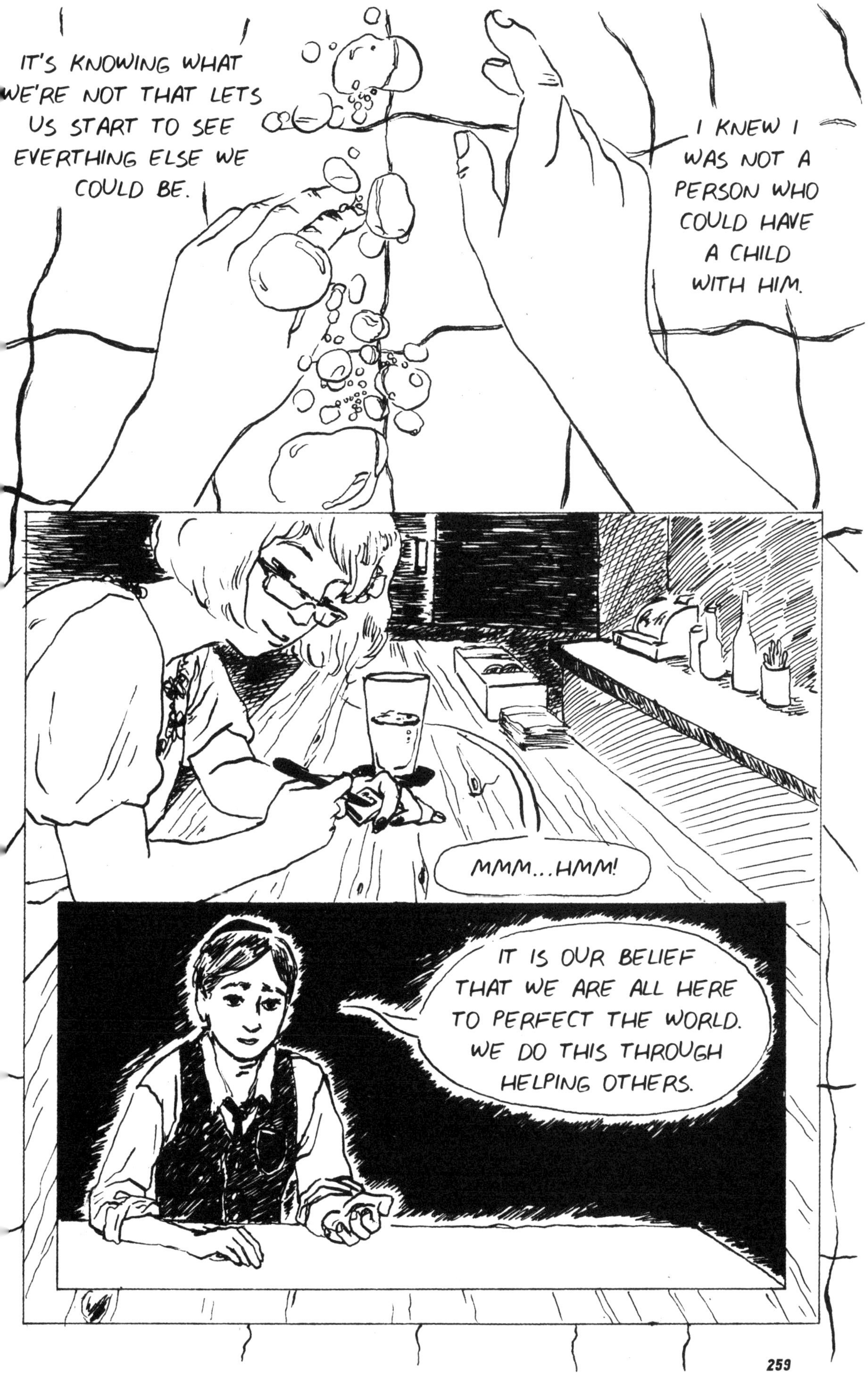
IT'S KNOWING WHAT WE'RE NOT THAT LETS US START TO SEE EVERTHING ELSE WE COULD BE.
I KNEW I WAS NOT A PERSON WHO COULD HAVE A CHILD WITH HIM.
MMM...HMM!
IT IS OUR BELIEF THAT WE ARE ALL HERE TO PERFECT THE WORLD. WE DO THIS THROUGH HELPING OTHERS.

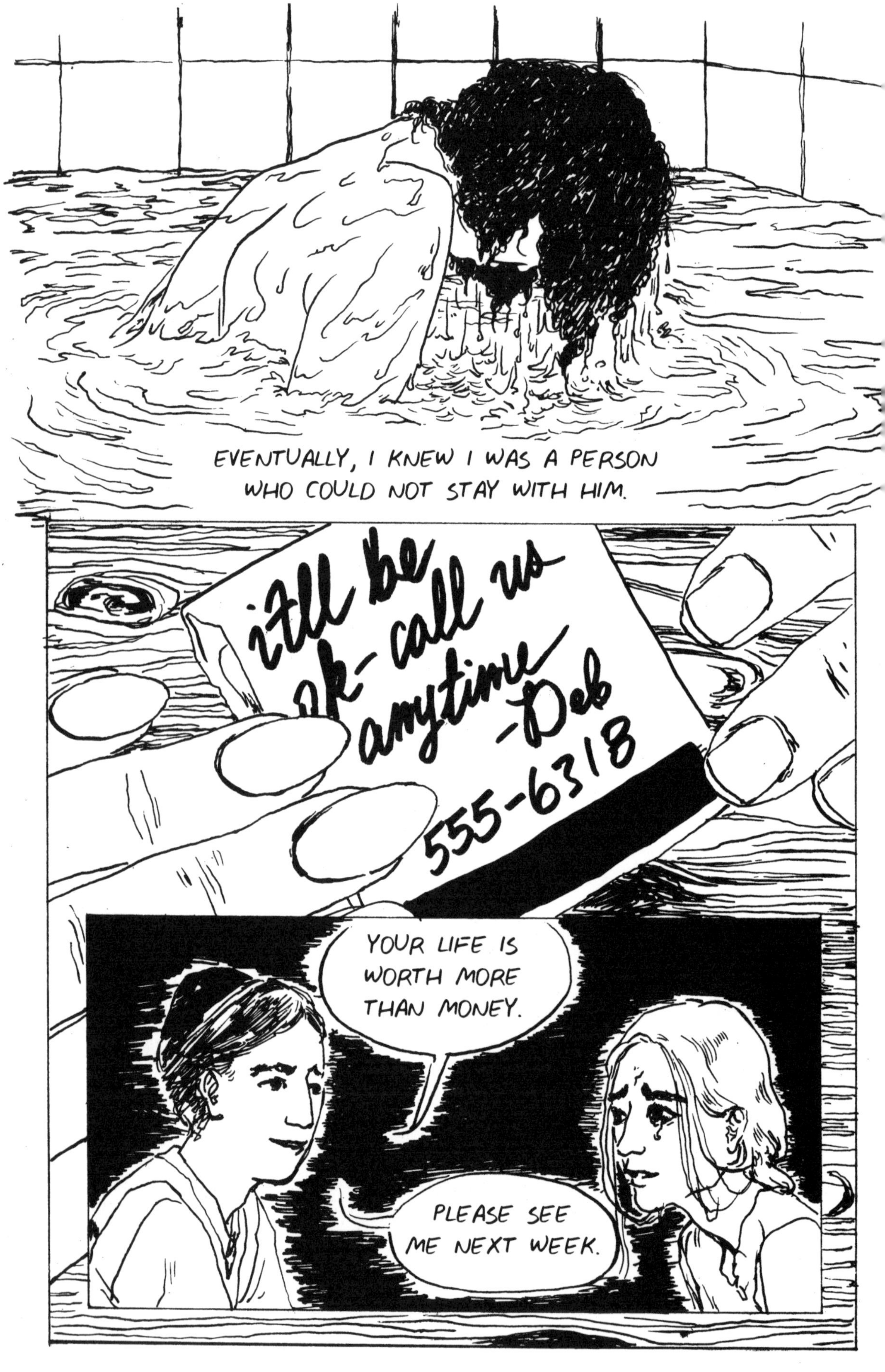
EVENTUALLY, I KNEW I WAS A PERSON WHO COULD NOT STAY WITH HIM.
it'll be ok- call us anytime -Deb 555-6318
YOUR LIFE IS WORTH MORE THAN MONEY.
PLEASE SEE ME NEXT WEEK.

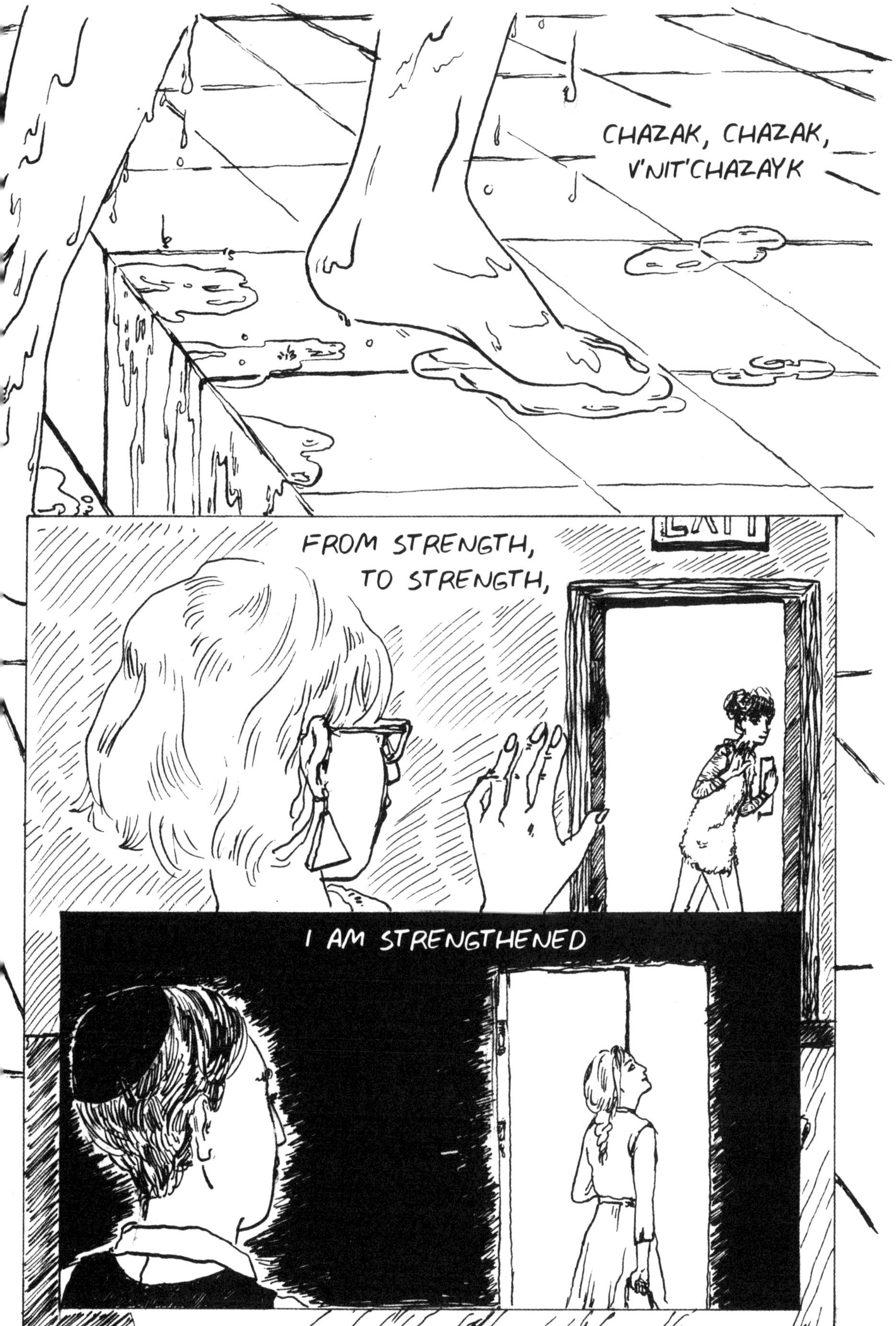
CHAZAK, CHAZAK, V'NIT'CHAZAYK
FROM STRENGTH, TO STRENGTH,
I AM STRENGTHENED

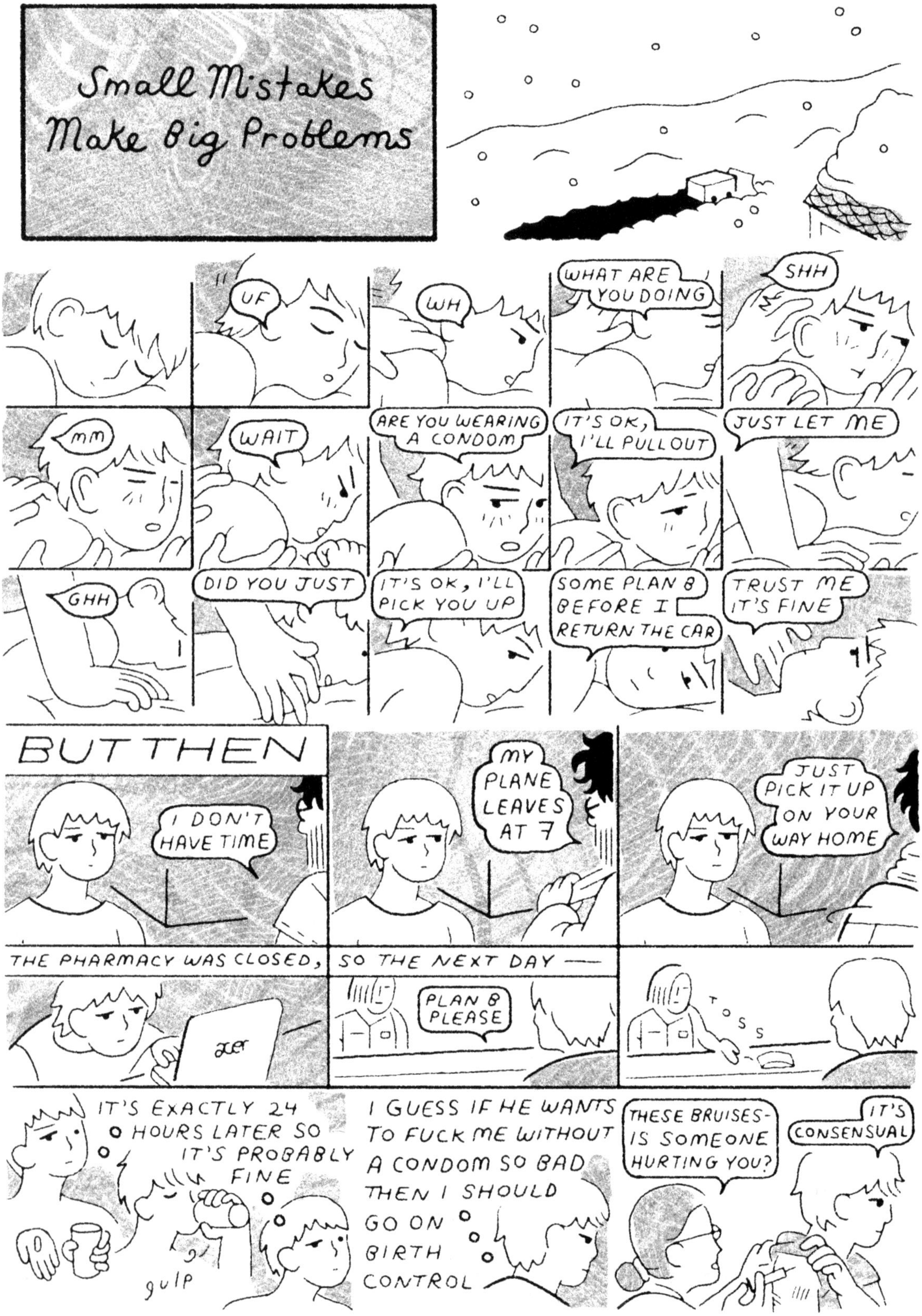

Small Mistakes Make Big Problems
UF
WH
WHAT ARE YOU DOING
SHH
mm
WAIT
ARE YOU WEARING A CONDOM
IT'S OK, I'LL PULL OUT
JUST LET ME
GHH
DID YOU JUST
IT'S OK, I'LL PICK YOU UP
SOME PLAN B BEFORE I RETURN THE CAR
TRUST ME IT'S FINE
BUT THEN
I DON'T HAVE TIME
MY PLANE LEAVES AT 7
JUST PICK IT UP ON YOUR WAY HOME
THE PHARMACY WAS CLOSED,
SO THE NEXT DAY —
PLAN B PLEASE
TOSS
IT'S EXACTLY 24 HOURS LATER SO IT'S PROBABLY FINE
gulp
I GUESS IF HE WANTS TO FUCK ME WITHOUT A CONDOM SO BAD THEN I SHOULD GO ON BIRTH CONTROL
THESE BRUISES- IS SOMEONE HURTING YOU?
IT'S CONSENSUAL

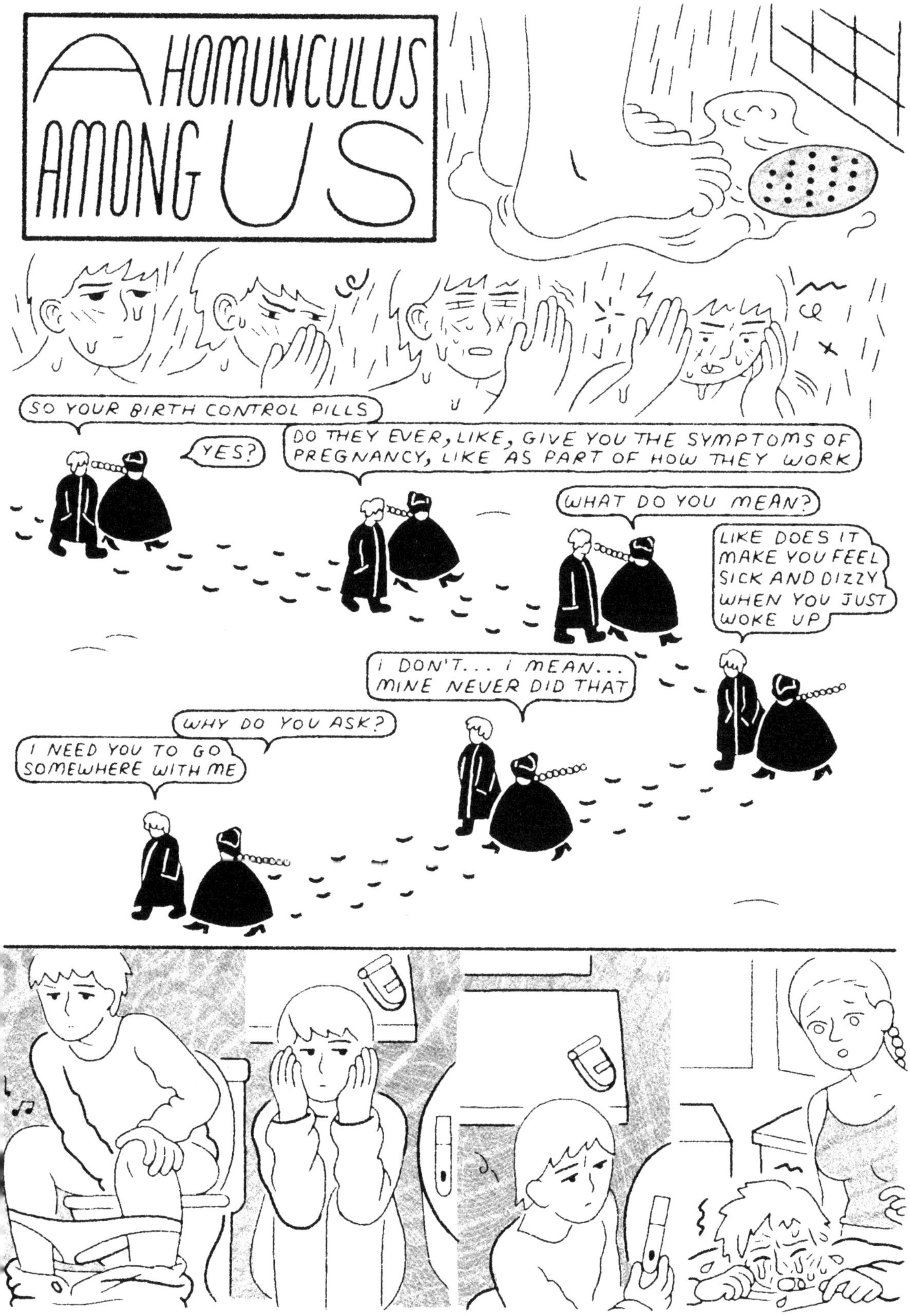
A HOMUNCULUS AMONG US
SO YOUR BIRTH CONTROL PILLS
YES?
DO THEY EVER, LIKE, GIVE YOU THE SYMPTOMS OF PREGNANCY, LIKE AS PART OF HOW THEY WORK
WHAT DO YOU MEAN?
LIKE DOES IT MAKE YOU FEEL SICK AND DIZZY WHEN YOU JUST WOKE UP
I DON'T... I MEAN... MINE NEVER DID THAT
WHY DO YOU ASK?
I NEED YOU TO GO SOMEWHERE WITH ME

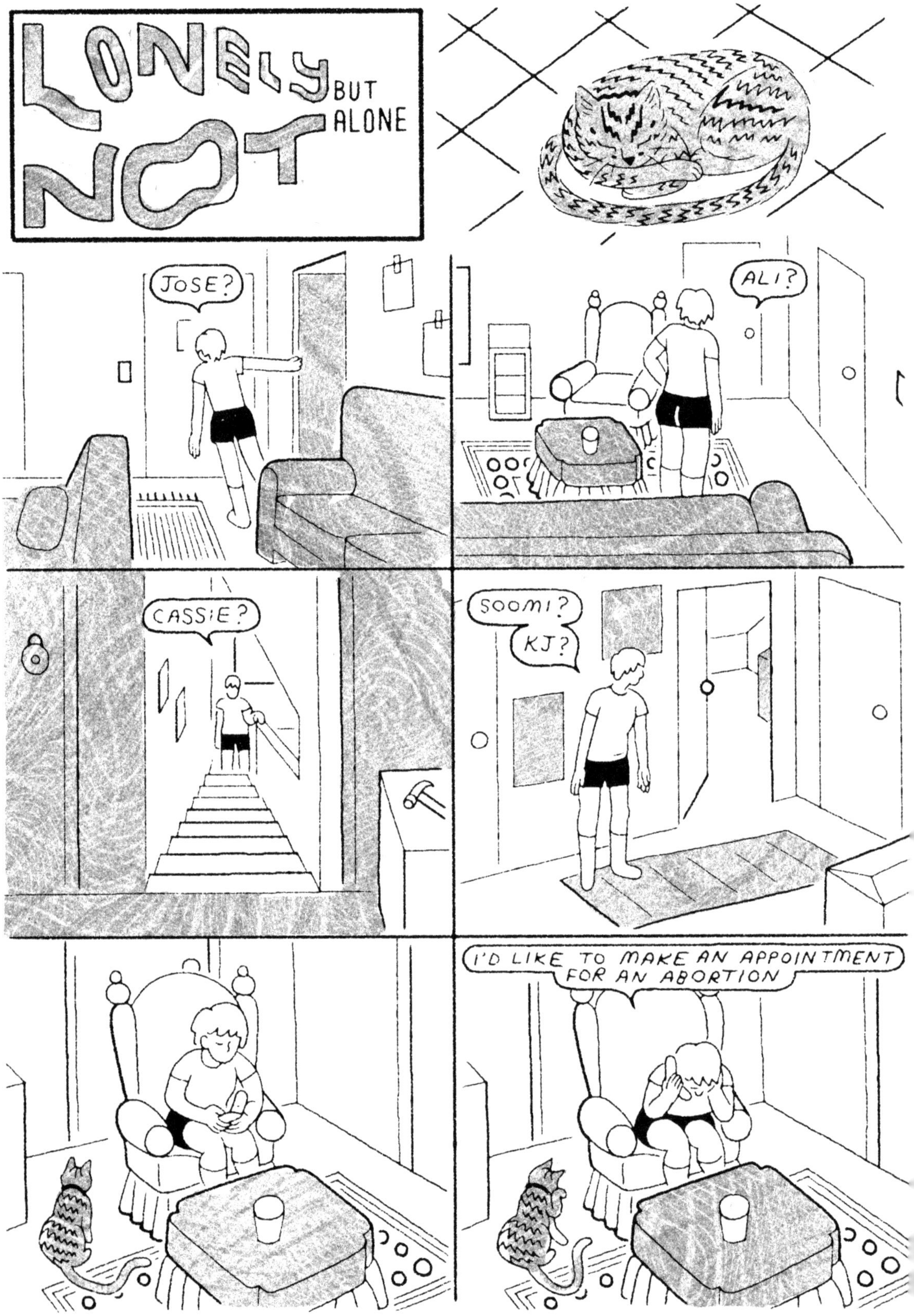
LONELY BUT NOT ALONE
JOSE?
ALI?
CASSIE?
SOOMI?
KJ?
I'D LIKE TO MAKE AN APPOINTMENT FOR AN ABORTION

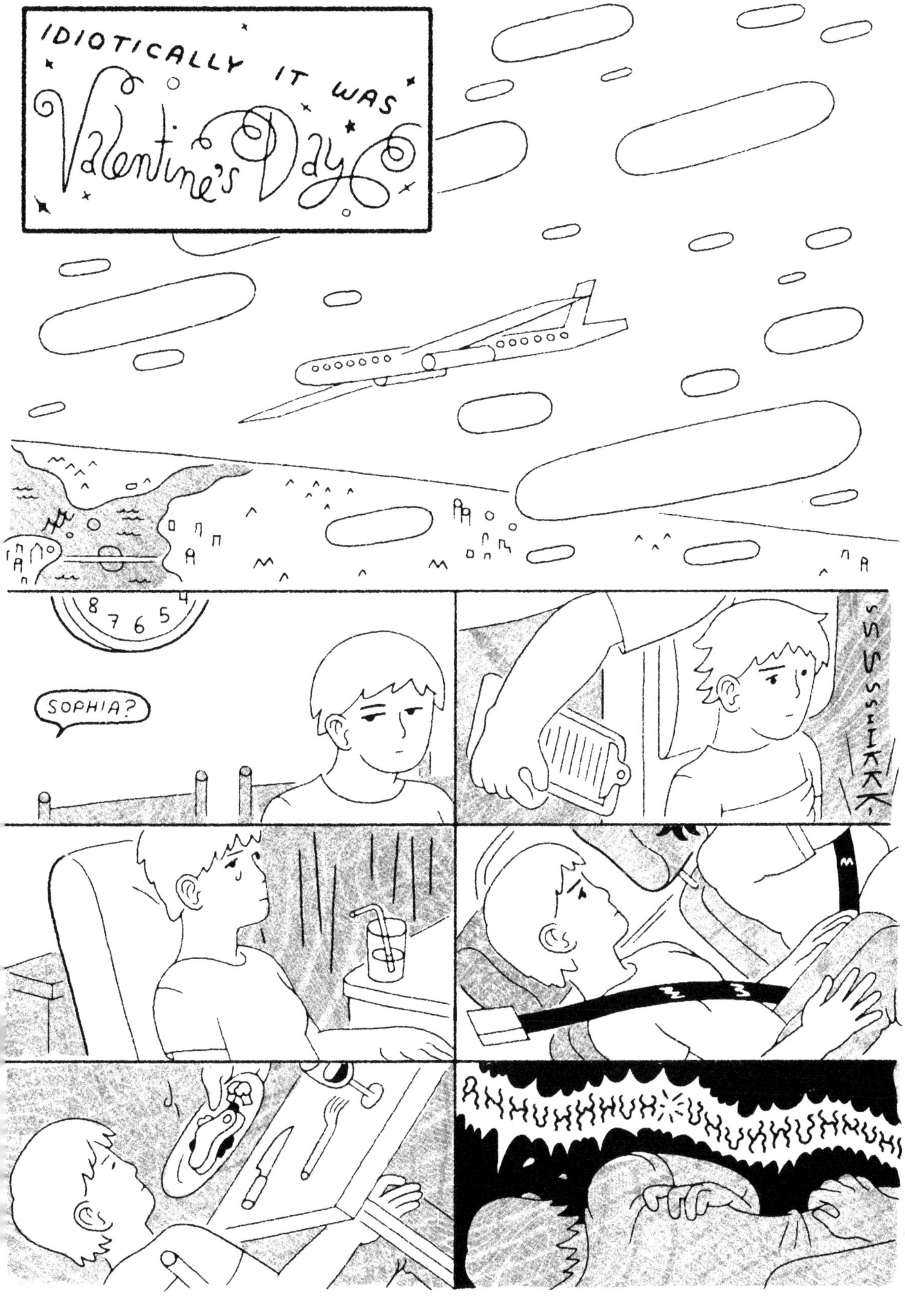
IDIOTICALLY IT WAS Valentine's Day
SOPHIA?
SSSSSIKKK-
ANHUHHHUH UHUHHUHNUHI

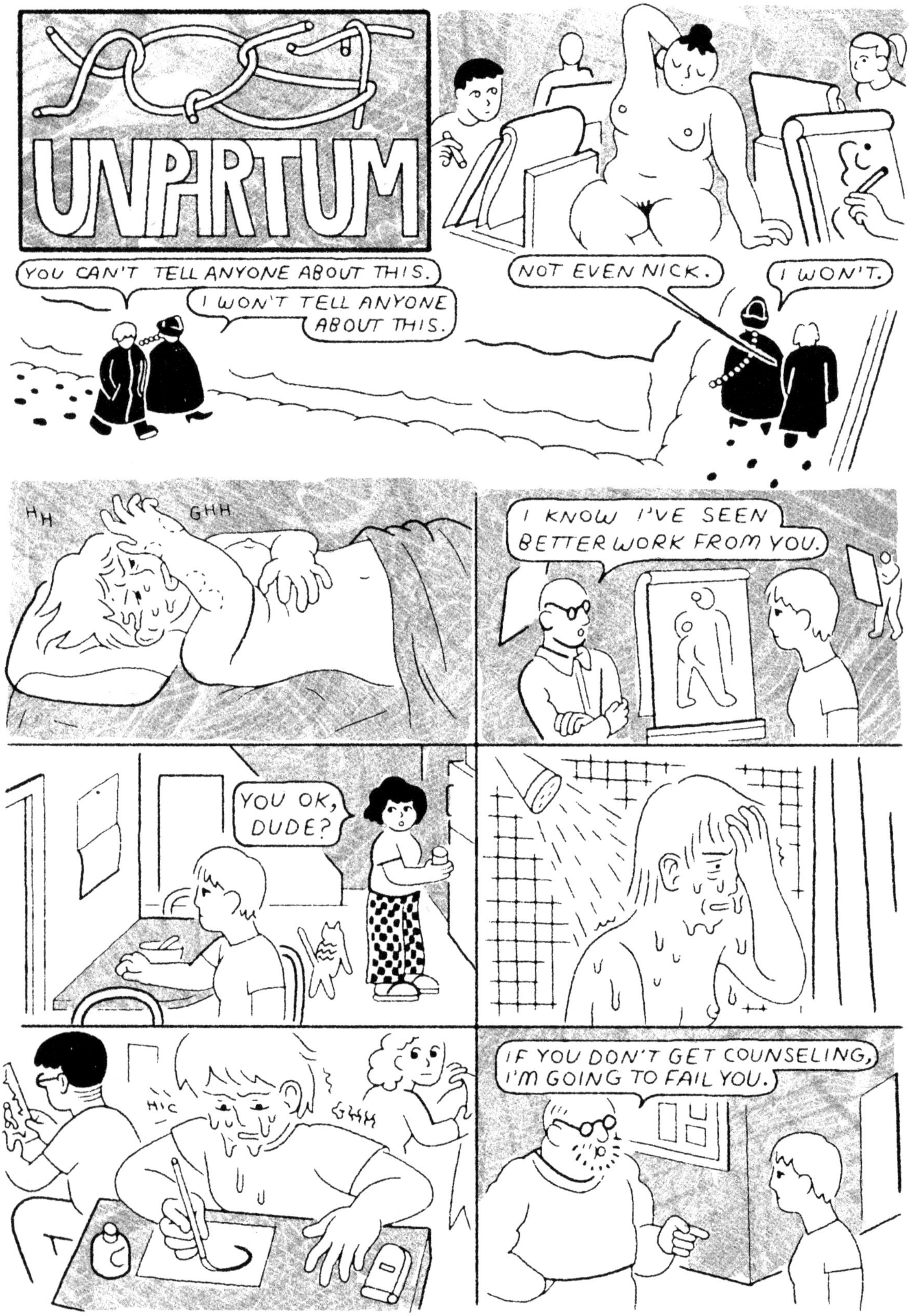
UNPARTUM
YOU CAN'T TELL ANYONE ABOUT THIS.
I WON'T TELL ANYONE ABOUT THIS.
NOT EVEN NICK.
I WON'T.
HH
GHH
I KNOW I'VE SEEN BETTER WORK FROM YOU.
YOU OK, DUDE?
HIC
GHH
IF YOU DON'T GET COUNSELING, I'M GOING TO FAIL YOU.

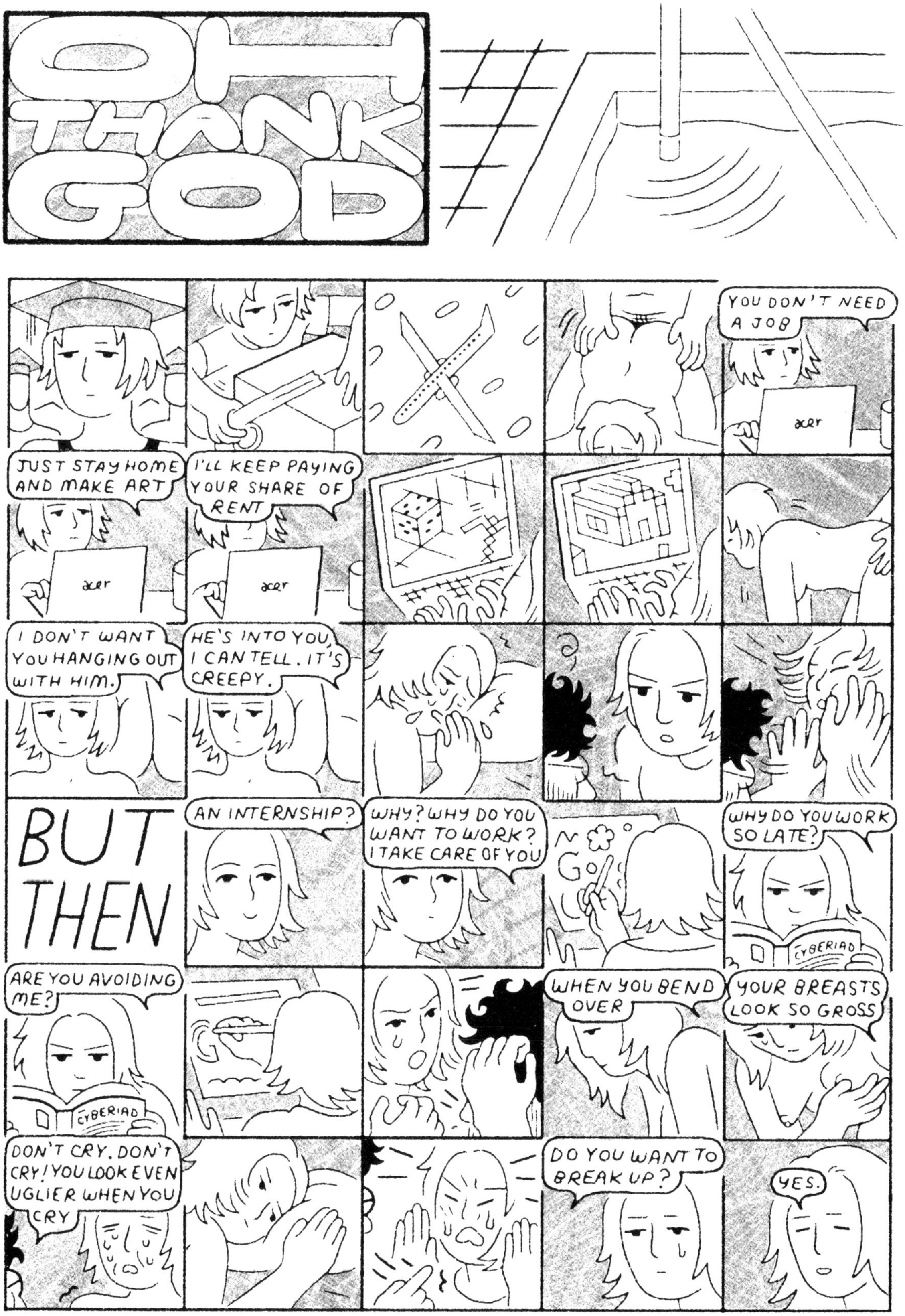
OH THANK GOD
YOU DON'T NEED A JOB
acer
JUST STAY HOME AND MAKE ART
acer
I'LL KEEP PAYING YOUR SHARE OF RENT
acer
I DON'T WANT YOU HANGING OUT WITH HIM.
HE'S INTO YOU, I CAN TELL. IT'S CREEPY.
BUT THEN
AN INTERNSHIP?
WHY? WHY DO YOU WANT TO WORK? I TAKE CARE OF YOU
WHY DO YOU WORK SO LATE?
CYBERIAD
ARE YOU AVOIDING ME?
CYBERIAD
WHEN YOU BEND OVER
YOUR BREASTS LOOK SO GROSS
DON'T CRY. DON'T CRY! YOU LOOK EVEN UGLIER WHEN YOU CRY
DO YOU WANT TO BREAK UP?
YES.

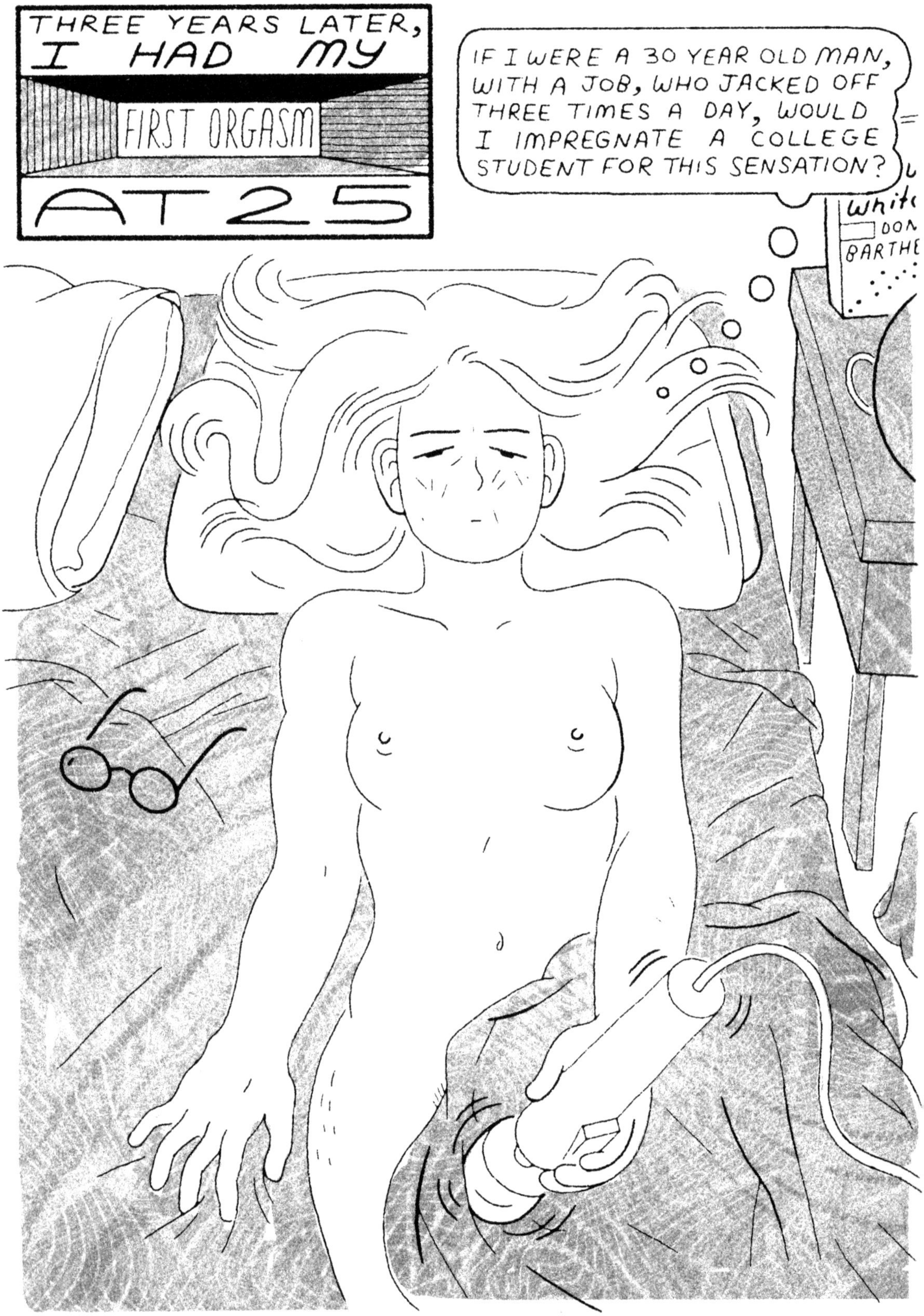
THREE YEARS LATER, I HAD MY
FIRST ORGASM
AT 25
IF I WERE A 30 YEAR OLD MAN, WITH A JOB, WHO JACKED OFF THREE TIMES A DAY, WOULD I IMPREGNATE A COLLEGE STUDENT FOR THIS SENSATION?

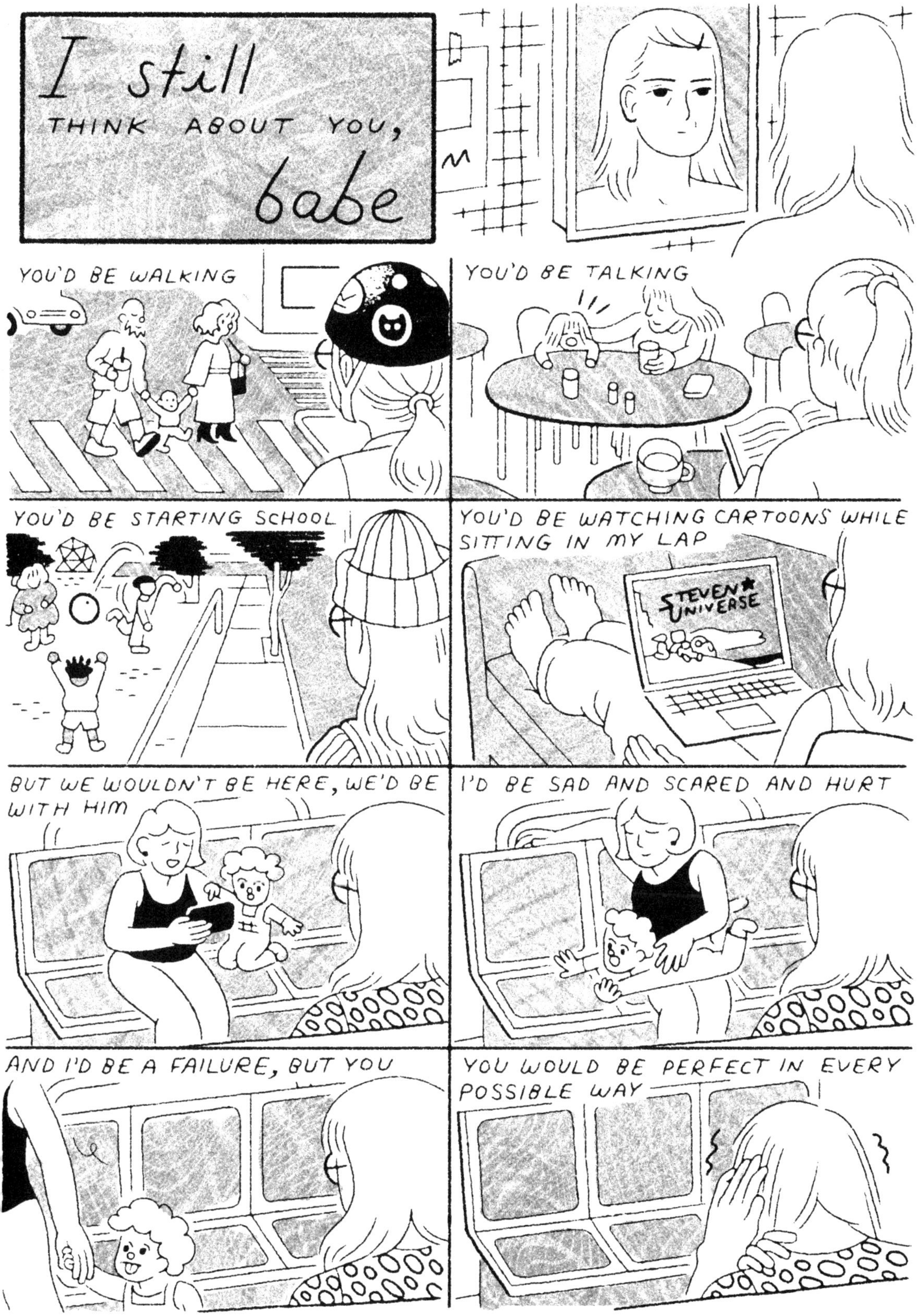
I still THINK ABOUT YOU, babe
YOU'D BE WALKING
YOU'D BE TALKING
YOU'D BE STARTING SCHOOL
YOU'D BE WATCHING CARTOONS WHILE SITTING IN MY LAP
STEVEN UNIVERSE
BUT WE WOULDN'T BE HERE, WE'D BE WITH HIM
I'D BE SAD AND SCARED AND HURT
AND I'D BE A FAILURE, BUT YOU
YOU WOULD BE PERFECT IN EVERY POSSIBLE WAY

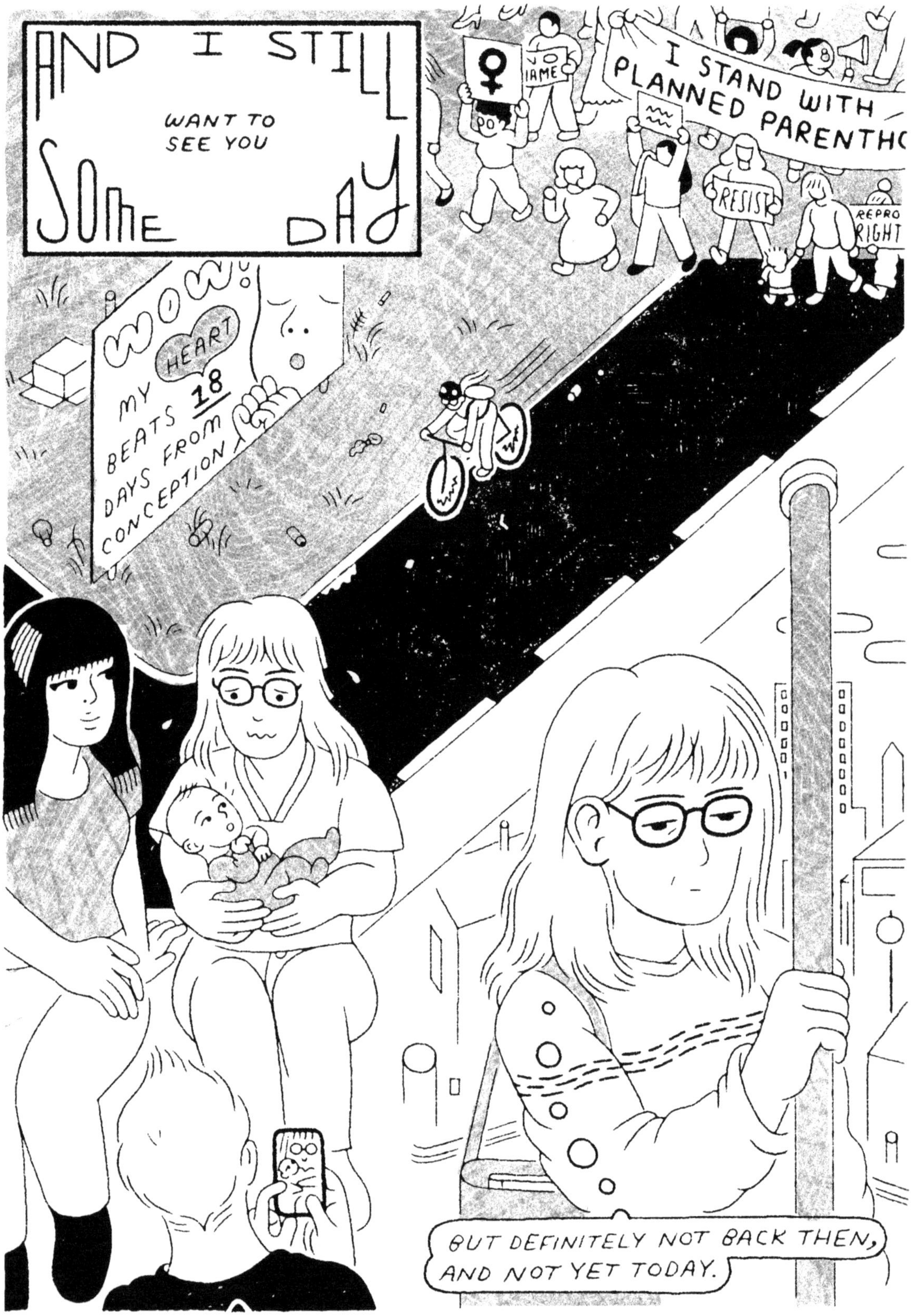
AND I STILL WANT TO SEE YOU SOME DAY
I STAND WITH PLANNED PARENTHO
RESIST
REPRO RIGHT
WOW MY HEART BEATS 18 DAYS FROM CONCEPTION
BUT DEFINITELY NOT BACK THEN, AND NOT YET TODAY.

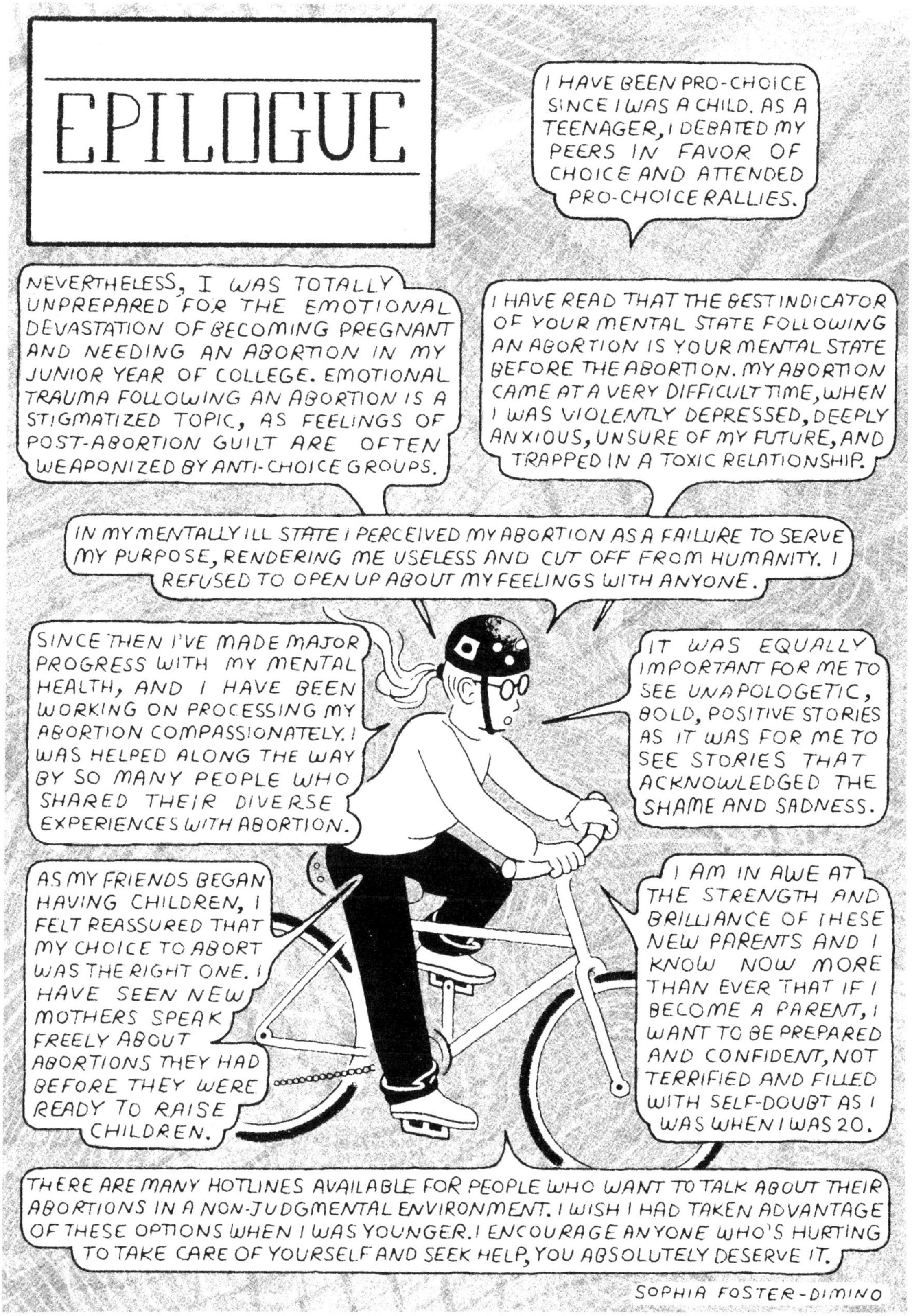
EPILOGUE
I HAVE BEEN PRO-CHOICE SINCE I WAS A CHILD. AS A TEENAGER, I DEBATED MY PEERS IN FAVOR OF CHOICE AND ATTENDED PRO-CHOICE RALLIES.
NEVERTHELESS, I WAS TOTALLY UNPREPARED FOR THE EMOTIONAL DEVASTATION OF BECOMING PREGNANT AND NEEDING AN ABORTION IN MY JUNIOR YEAR OF COLLEGE. EMOTIONAL TRAUMA FOLLOWING AN ABORTION IS A STIGMATIZED TOPIC, AS FEELINGS OF POST-ABORTION GUILT ARE OFTEN WEAPONIZED BY ANTI-CHOICE GROUPS.
I HAVE READ THAT THE BEST INDICATOR OF YOUR MENTAL STATE FOLLOWING AN ABORTION IS YOUR MENTAL STATE BEFORE THE ABORTION. MY ABORTION CAME AT A VERY DIFFICULT TIME, WHEN I WAS VIOLENTLY DEPRESSED, DEEPLY ANXIOUS, UNSURE OF MY FUTURE, AND TRAPPED IN A TOXIC RELATIONSHIP.
IN MY MENTALLY ILL STATE I PERCEIVED MY ABORTION AS A FAILURE TO SERVE MY PURPOSE, RENDERING ME USELESS AND CUT OFF FROM HUMANITY. I REFUSED TO OPEN UP ABOUT MY FEELINGS WITH ANYONE.
SINCE THEN I'VE MADE MAJOR PROGRESS WITH MY MENTAL HEALTH, AND I HAVE BEEN WORKING ON PROCESSING MY ABORTION COMPASSIONATELY. I WAS HELPED ALONG THE WAY BY SO MANY PEOPLE WHO SHARED THEIR DIVERSE EXPERIENCES WITH ABORTION.
IT WAS EQUALLY IMPORTANT FOR ME TO SEE UNAPOLOGETIC, BOLD, POSITIVE STORIES AS IT WAS FOR ME TO SEE STORIES THAT ACKNOWLEDGED THE SHAME AND SADNESS.
AS MY FRIENDS BEGAN HAVING CHILDREN, I FELT REASSURED THAT MY CHOICE TO ABORT WAS THE RIGHT ONE. I HAVE SEEN NEW MOTHERS SPEAK FREELY ABOUT ABORTIONS THEY HAD BEFORE THEY WERE READY TO RAISE CHILDREN.
I AM IN AWE AT THE STRENGTH AND BRILLIANCE OF THESE NEW PARENTS AND I KNOW NOW MORE THAN EVER THAT IF I BECOME A PARENT, I WANT TO BE PREPARED AND CONFIDENT, NOT TERRIFIED AND FILLED WITH SELF-DOUBT AS I WAS WHEN I WAS 20.
THERE ARE MANY HOTLINES AVAILABLE FOR PEOPLE WHO WANT TO TALK ABOUT THEIR ABORTIONS IN A NON-JUDGMENTAL ENVIRONMENT. I WISH I HAD TAKEN ADVANTAGE OF THESE OPTIONS WHEN I WAS YOUNGER. I ENCOURAGE ANYONE WHO'S HURTING TO TAKE CARE OF YOURSELF AND SEEK HELP, YOU ABSOLUTELY DESERVE IT.
SOPHIA FOSTER-DIMINO

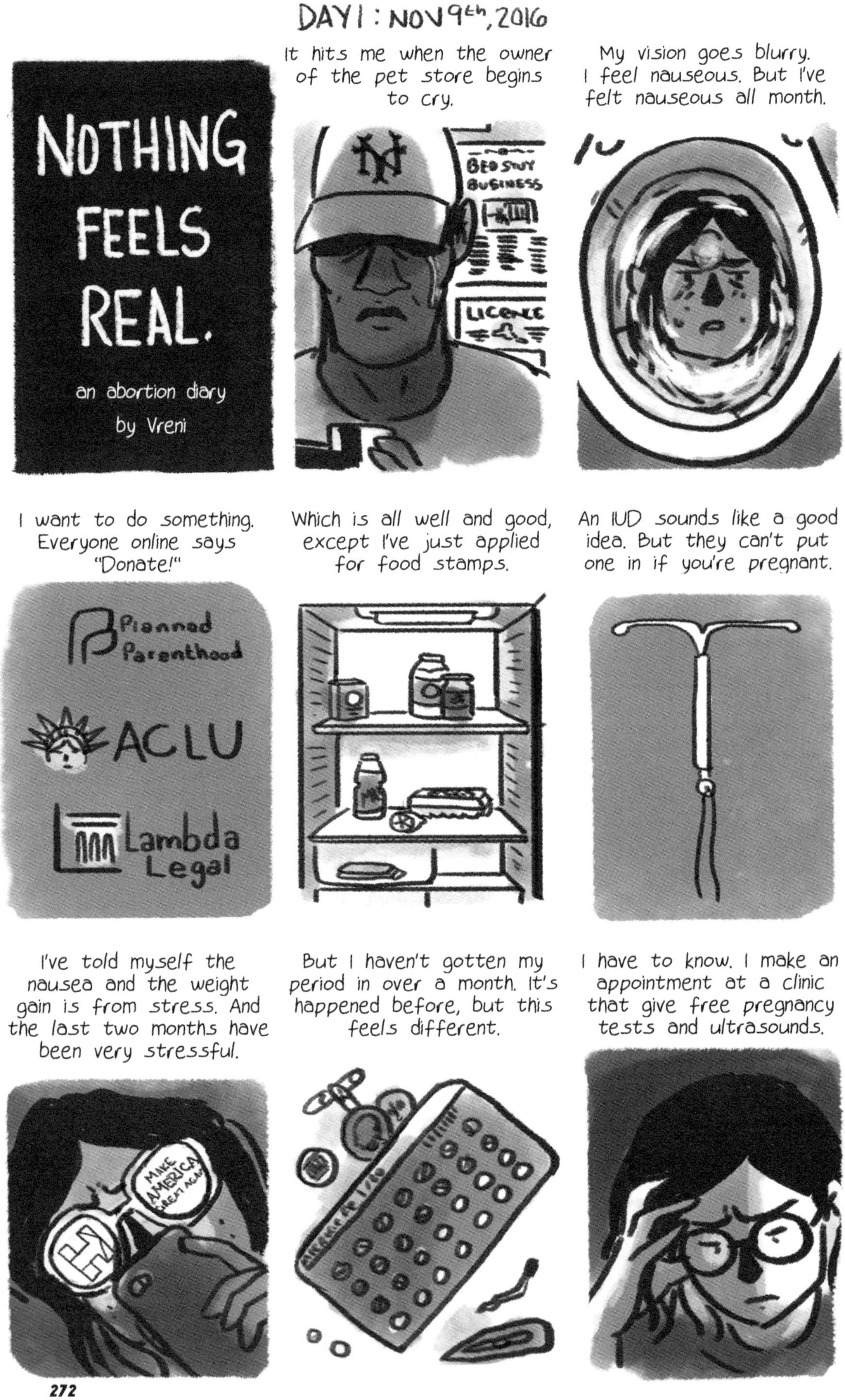
DAY 1 : NOV 9th, 2016
NOTHING FEELS REAL.
an abortion diary
by Vreni
It hits me when the owner of the pet store begins to cry.
BED STUY BUSINESS
LICENCE
My vision goes blurry. I feel nauseous. But I've felt nauseous all month.
I want to do something. Everyone online says "Donate!"
Planned Parenthood
ACLU
Lambda Legal
Which is all well and good, except I've just applied for food stamps.
An IUD sounds like a good idea. But they can't put one in if you're pregnant.
I've told myself the nausea and the weight gain is from stress. And the last two months have been very stressful.
MAKE AMERICA
But I haven't gotten my period in over a month. It's happened before, but this feels different.
I have to know. I make an appointment at a clinic that give free pregnancy tests and ultrasounds.

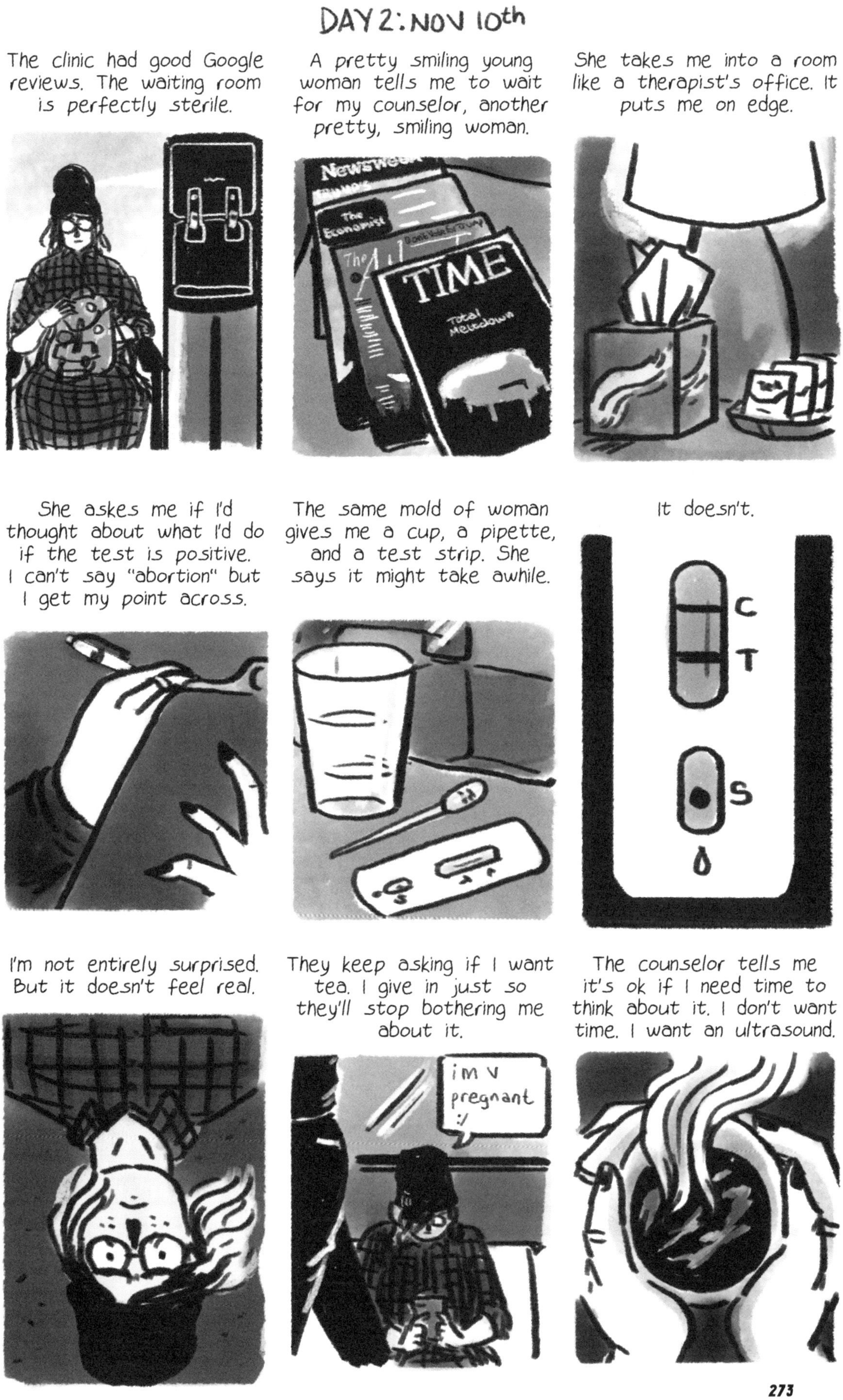

DAY 2: NOV 10th
The clinic had good Google reviews. The waiting room is perfectly sterile.
A pretty smiling young woman tells me to wait for my counselor, another pretty, smiling woman.
TIME
Total Meltdown
The Economist
She takes me into a room like a therapist's office. It puts me on edge.
She askes me if I'd thought about what I'd do if the test is positive. I can't say "abortion" but I get my point across.
The same mold of woman gives me a cup, a pipette, and a test strip. She says it might take awhile.
It doesn't.
C
T
S
I'm not entirely surprised. But it doesn't feel real.
They keep asking if I want tea. I give in just so they'll stop bothering me about it.
im v pregnant :/
The counselor tells me it's ok if I need time to think about it. I don't want time. I want an ultrasound.

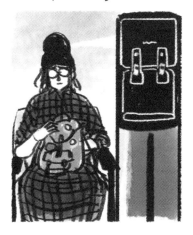

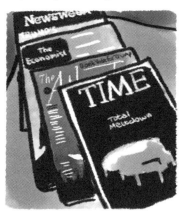

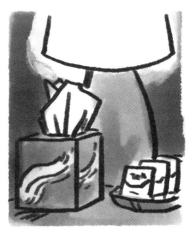

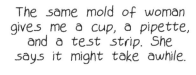

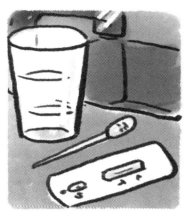

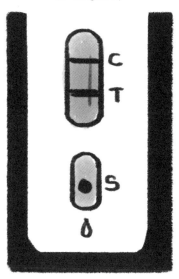

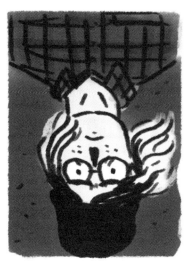

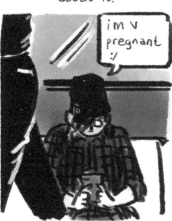

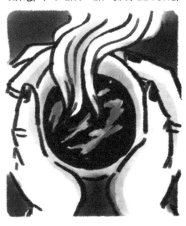

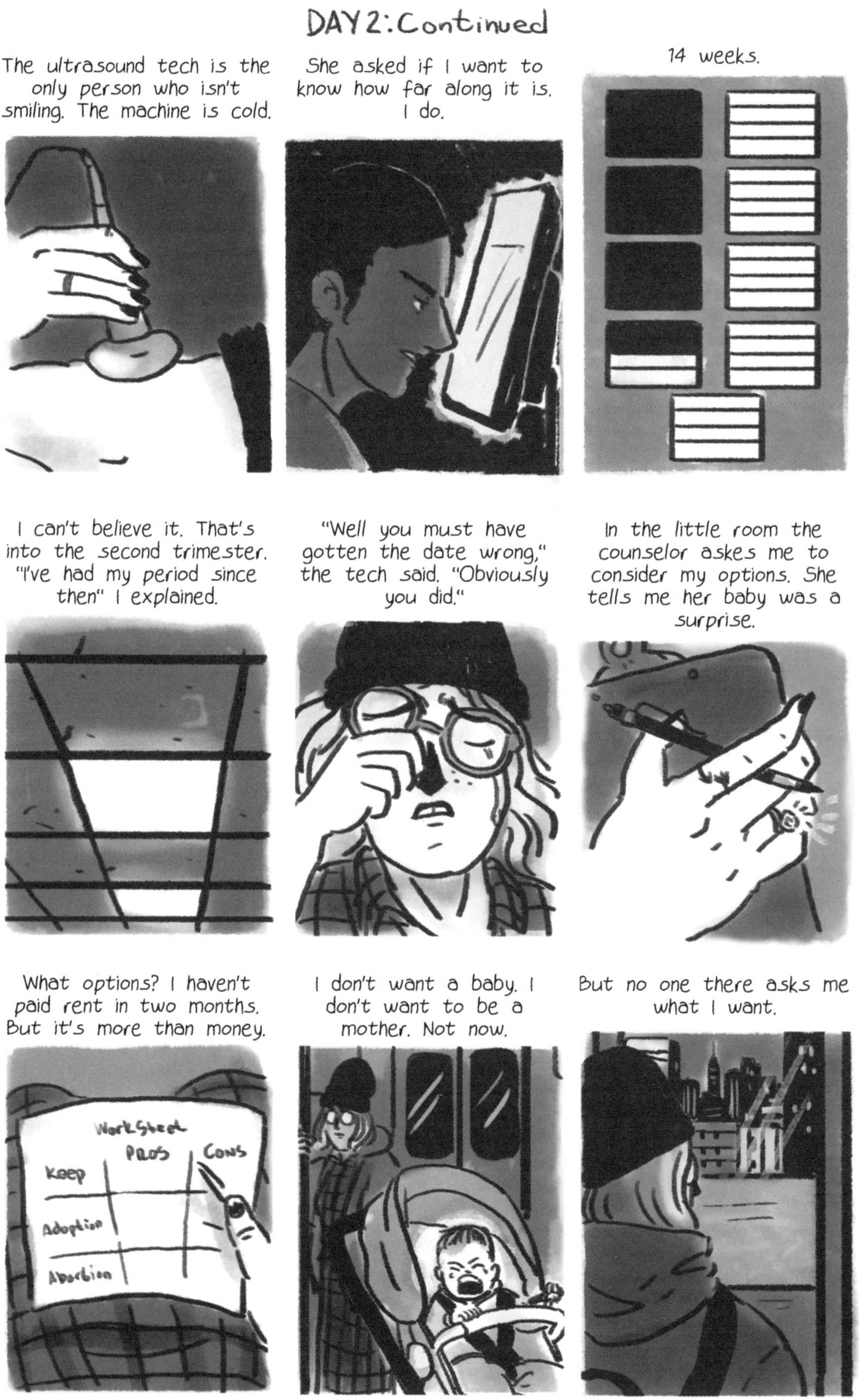
DAY 2: Continued
The ultrasound tech is the only person who isn't smiling. The machine is cold.
She asked if I want to know how far along it is. I do.
14 weeks.
I can't believe it. That's into the second trimester. "I've had my period since then" I explained.
"Well you must have gotten the date wrong," the tech said. "Obviously you did."
In the little room the counselor askes me to consider my options. She tells me her baby was a surprise.
What options? I haven't paid rent in two months. But it's more than money.
WorkSheet
PROS
CONS
Keep
Adoption
Abortion
I don't want a baby. I don't want to be a mother. Not now.
But no one there asks me what I want.

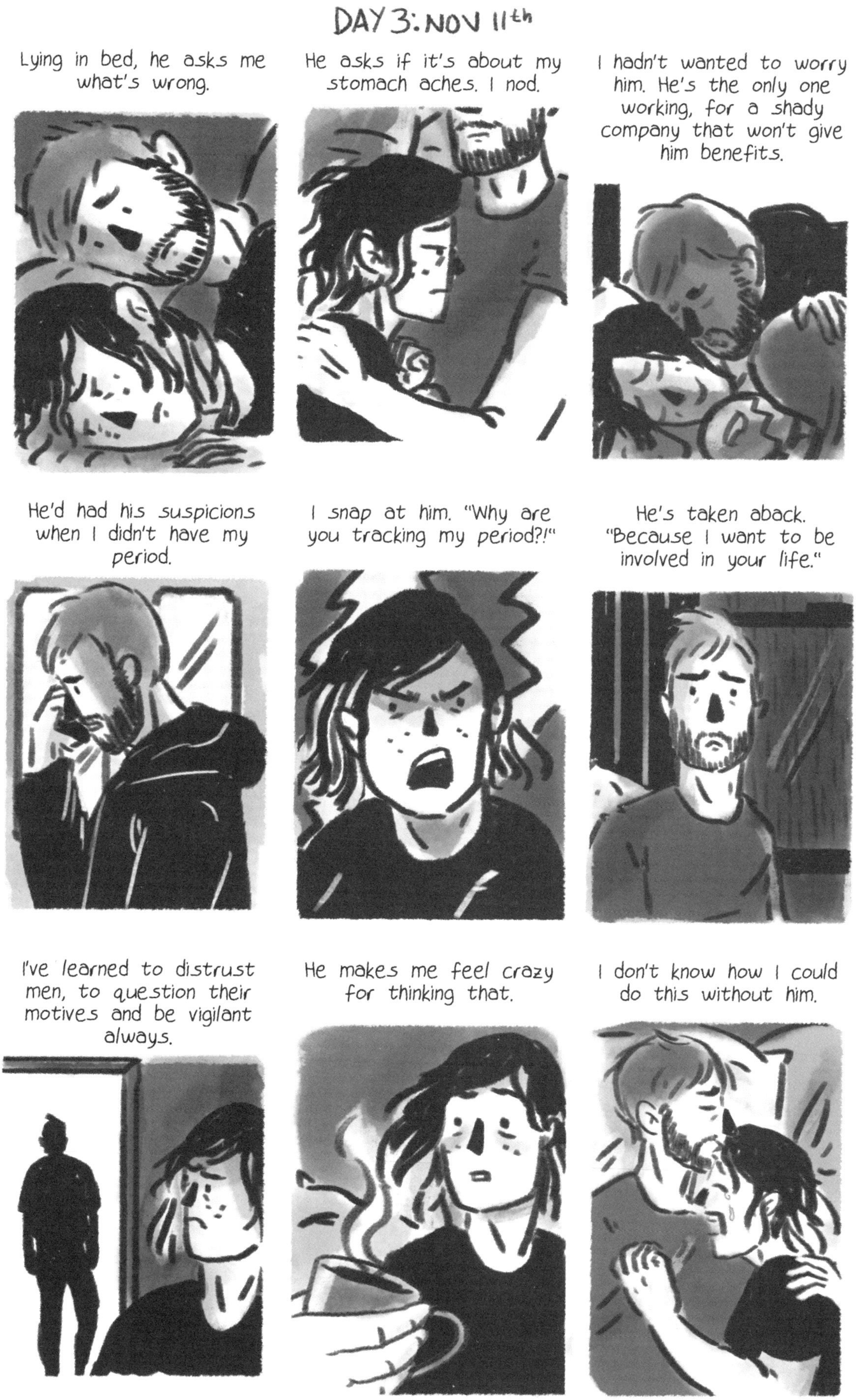
DAY 3: NOV 11th
Lying in bed, he asks me what's wrong.
He asks if it's about my stomach aches. I nod.
I hadn't wanted to worry him. He's the only one working, for a shady company that won't give him benefits.
He'd had his suspicions when I didn't have my period.
I snap at him. "Why are you tracking my period?!"
He's taken aback. "Because I want to be involved in your life."
I've learned to distrust men, to question their motives and be vigilant always.
He makes me feel crazy for thinking that.
I don't know how I could do this without him.

DAY 4: NOV 12th

I'm too far along to take the abortion pill, which is safe up to 10 weeks.

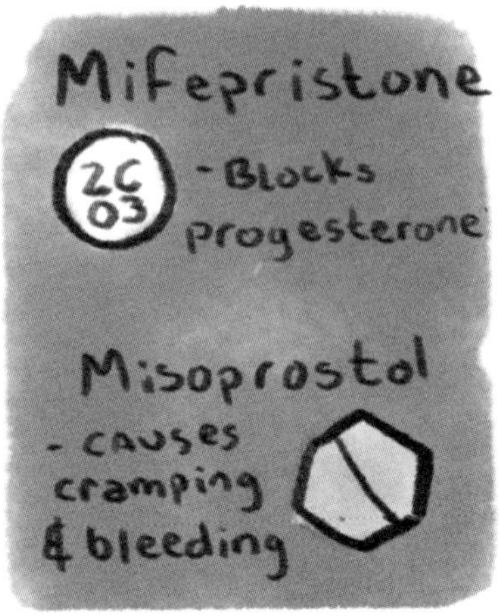
Mifepristone
2C 03
- Blocks progesterone
Misoprostol
- causes cramping & bleeding

From 10 to 16 weeks vacuum aspiration is used. It's a surgical procedure and I'm terrified.

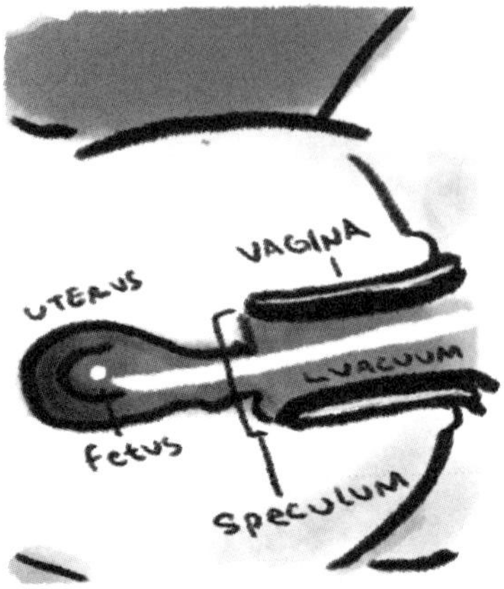
VAGINA
UTERUS
VACUUM
Fetus
SPECULUM

I'm also worried about the cost. I don't want to empty our savings account over this.

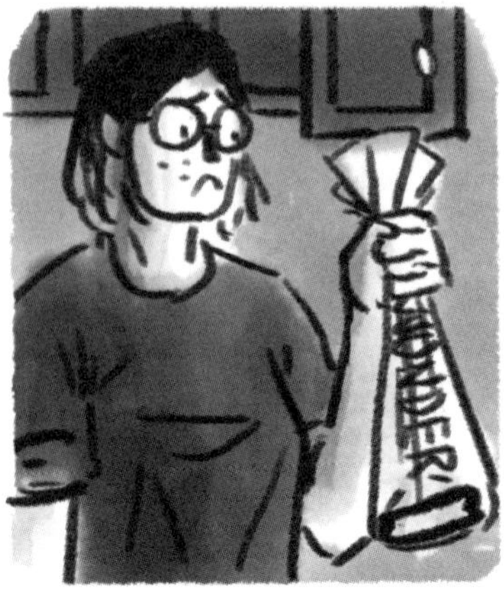

By the third clinic I call I can say "I'm calling about an abortion" without stumbling.

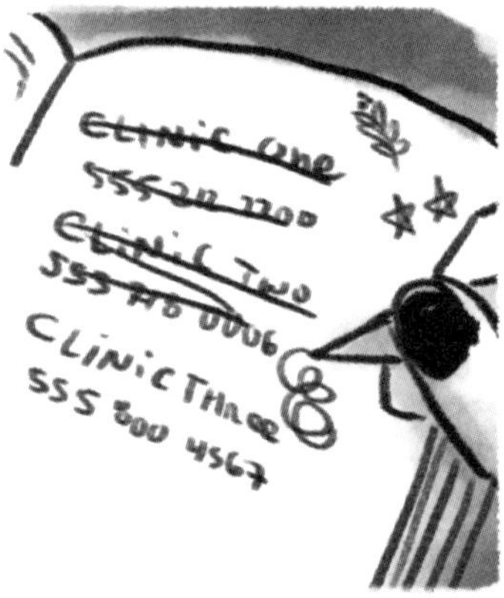
Clinic One
Clinic Two
CLINIC THREE
555 800 4567

One clinic is $420 "plus labwork" (she can't tell me how much labwork is), another is $650 "for everything", another was $720.

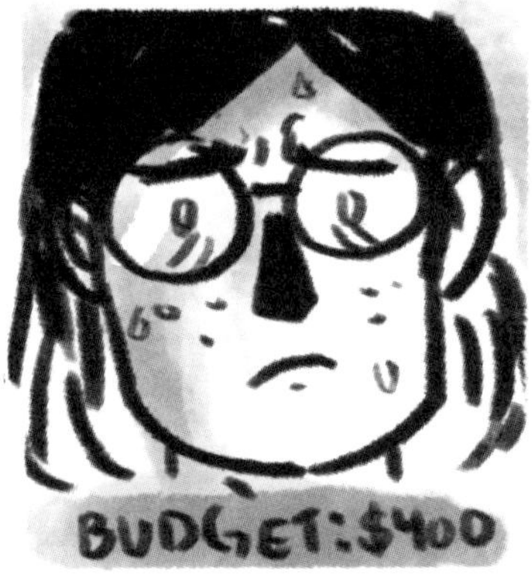
BUDGET: $400

I google "how to pay for an abortion" and find helpful information on the National Network of Abortion Funds site.

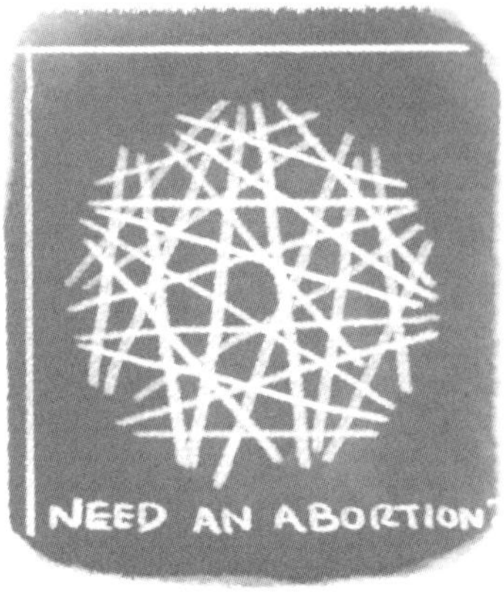
NEED AN ABORTION?

I end up calling Planned Parenthood and when I explain my situation they set me up with a financial counselor.

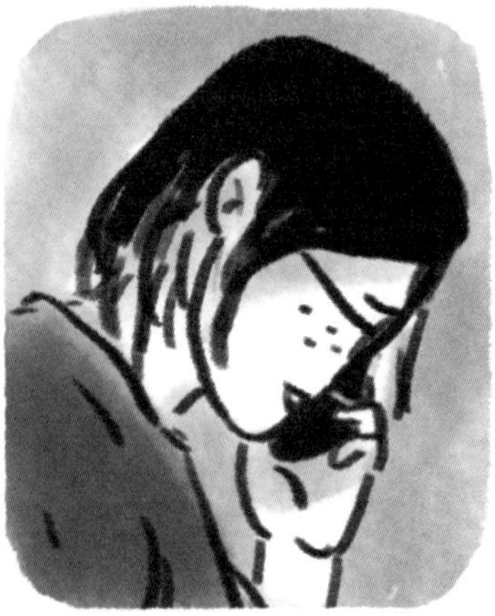

I tell the counselor how much I make ($0 currently) how much my boyfriend makes, and our rent.

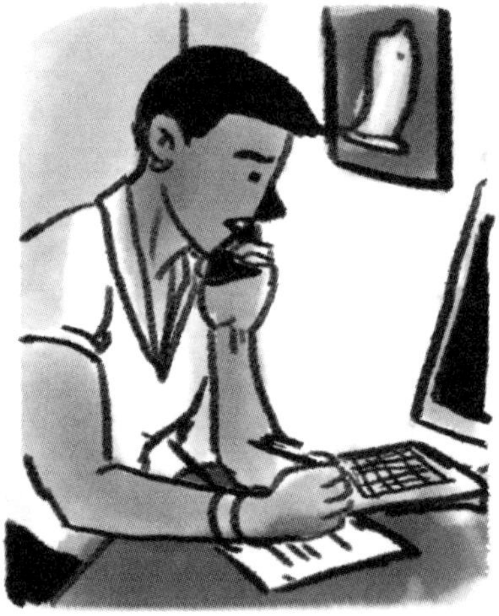

She says I qualify for emergency Medicaid and the whole procedure will be covered. I'm so relieved I cry.

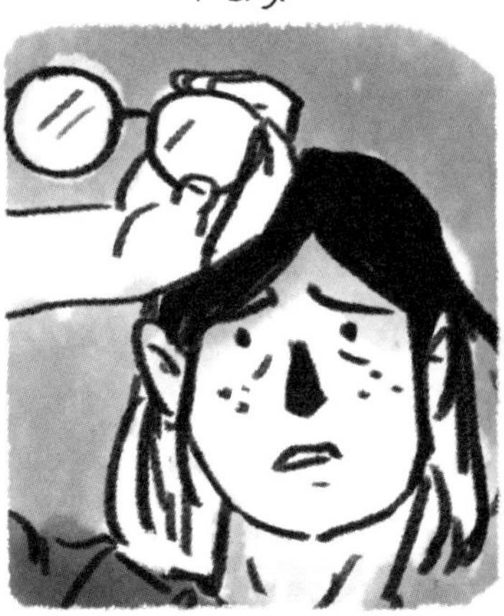

DAY 5: NOV 13th

The abortion is scheduled. It's actually happening. I thought I'd feel relieved.

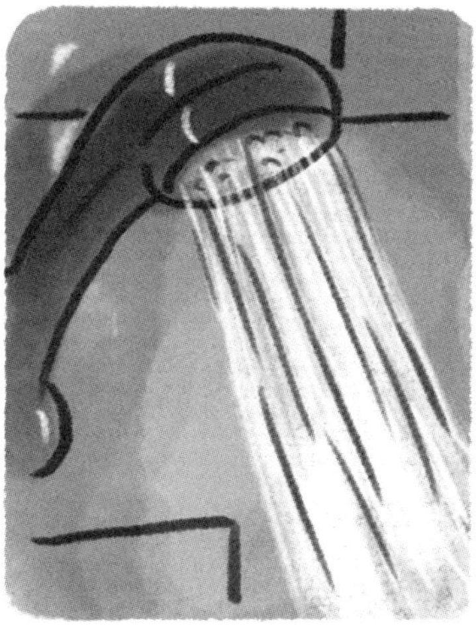

I've been throwing up for months, have heartburn constantly, and my breasts are huge and super sensitive.

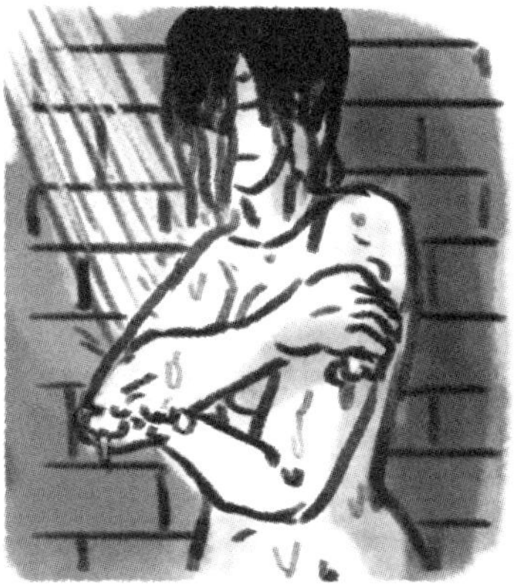

I don't feel relieved. I feel weirdly guilty.

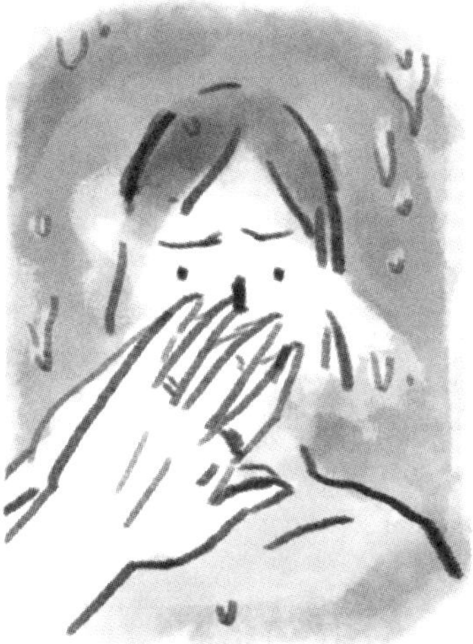

It's hard not to think about the fetus as a baby. As my baby.

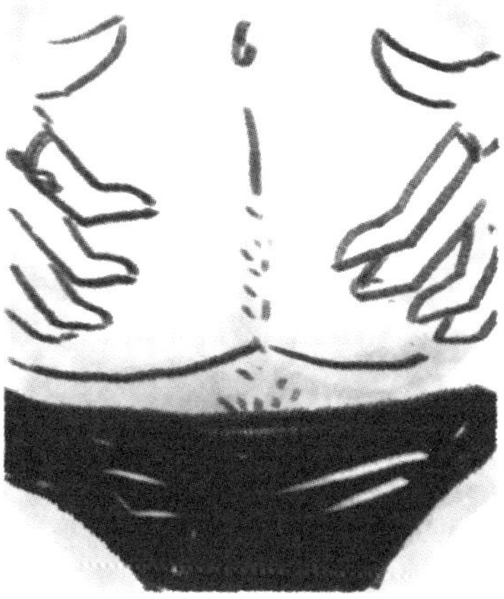

Back when I had a salary I had the "baby madness." For two months I couldn't stop thinking about babies.

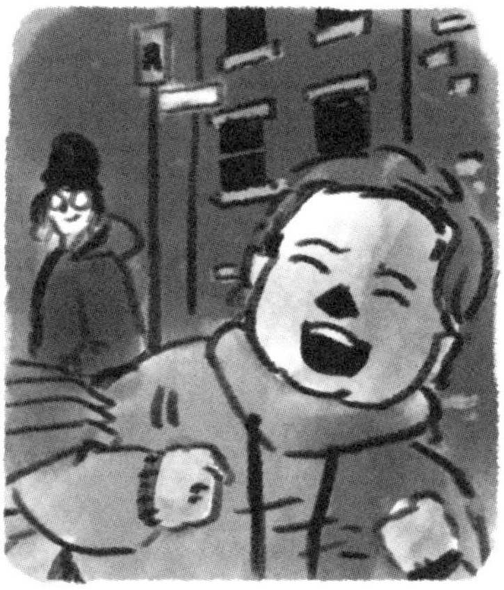

But the thoughts never felt like mine. It was like someone was inside my head, telling my how great life would be with a baby.

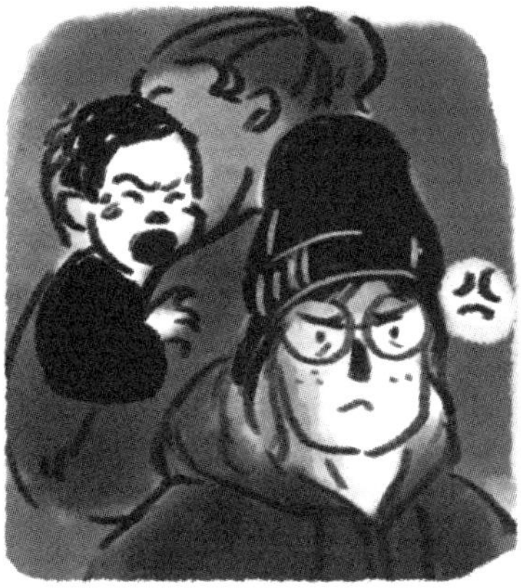

This felt the same way. These thoughts were outside my logical mind, but that didn't stop them.

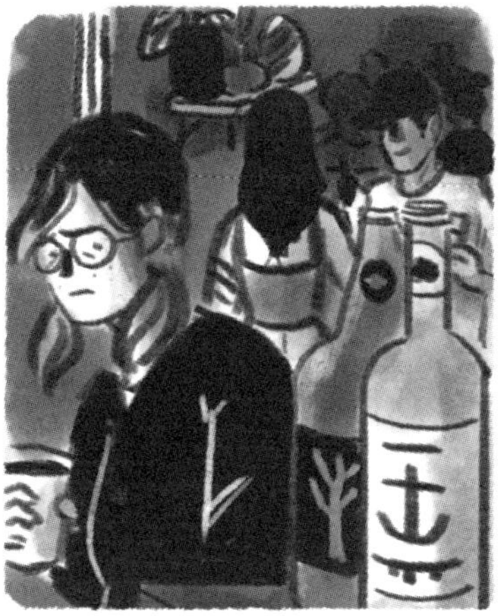

Maybe it's some internalized version of every hallmark abortion story: the poor, tragic mother, the baby she wants but can't have.

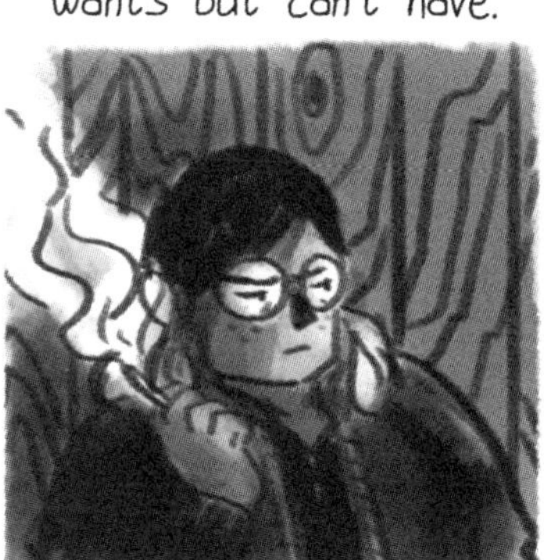

Or maybe I'm just scared that if I do this now the door to motherhood will be closed forever. I don't know if I want that.

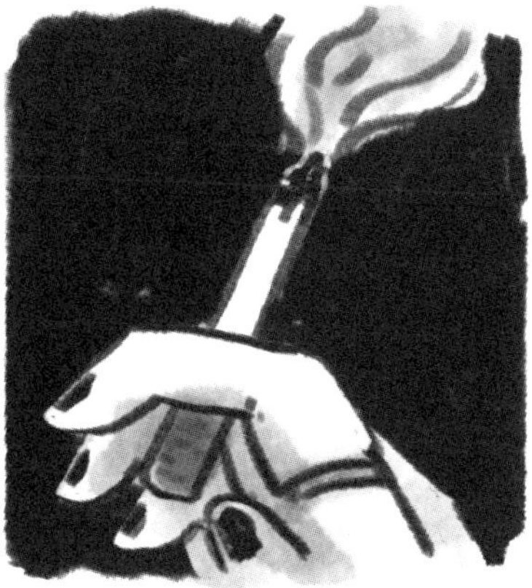

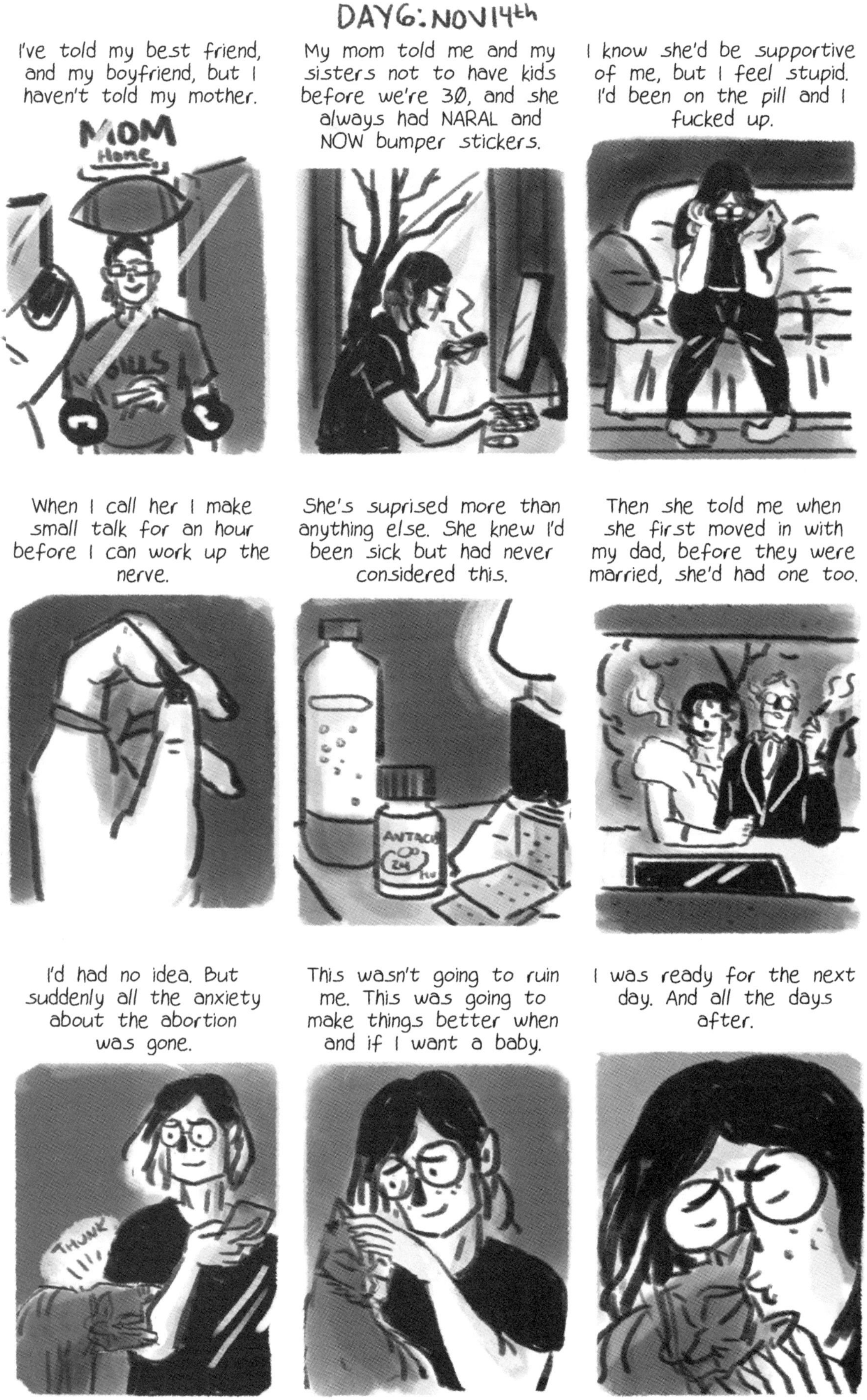
DAY 6: NOV 14th
I've told my best friend, and my boyfriend, but I haven't told my mother.
MOM
Home
BILLS
My mom told me and my sisters not to have kids before we're 30, and she always had NARAL and NOW bumper stickers.
I know she'd be supportive of me, but I feel stupid. I'd been on the pill and I fucked up.
When I call her I make small talk for an hour before I can work up the nerve.
She's suprised more than anything else. She knew I'd been sick but had never considered this.
Then she told me when she first moved in with my dad, before they were married, she'd had one too.
I'd had no idea. But suddenly all the anxiety about the abortion was gone.
THUNK
This wasn't going to ruin me. This was going to make things better when and if I want a baby.
I was ready for the next day. And all the days after.

DAY 7: NOV 15th

My best friend and my boyfriend come with me. I leave them in the waiting room, past the metal detectors.

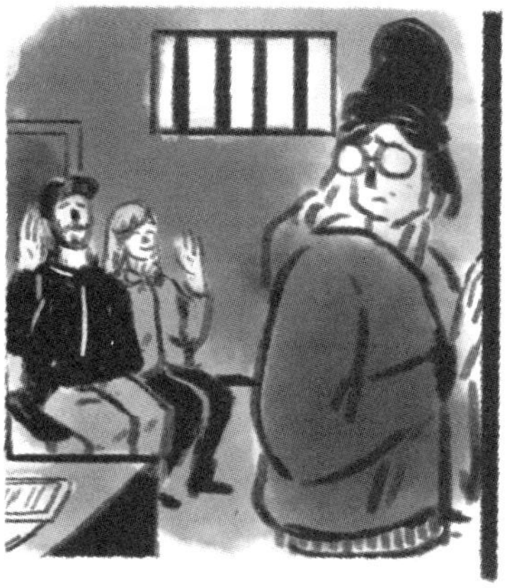

I wasn't allowed to eat or drink after midnight but I don't feel nauseous. I don't feel anything.

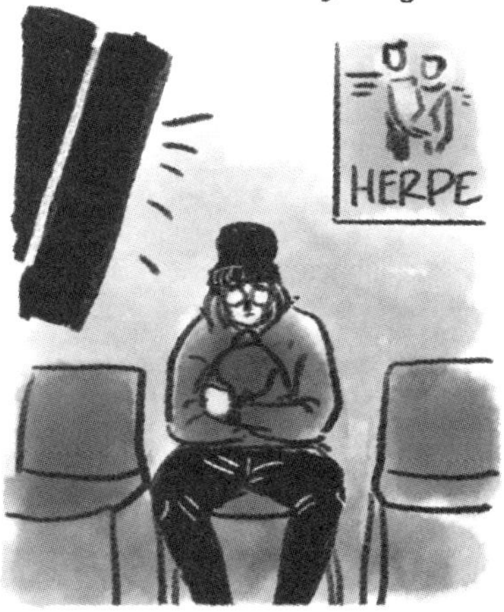
HERPE

There's one last counseling session. She asks if I want birth control. I've decided on Mirena, an IUD that lasts 5 years.

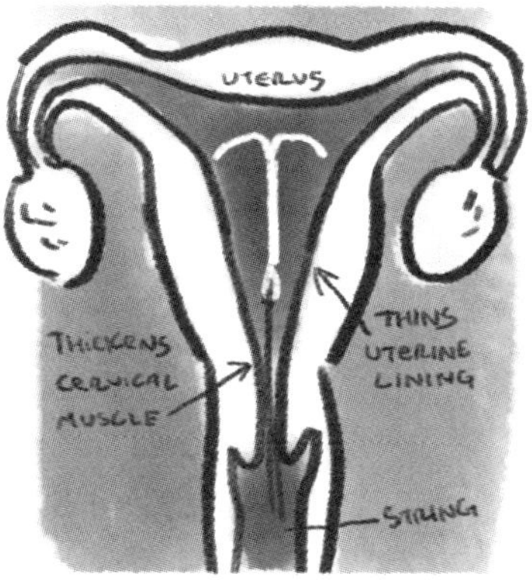
UTERUS
THICKENS CERVICAL MUSCLE
THINS UTERINE LINING
STRING

She asks if I want to see the ultrasounds they took. I say yes this time. I'm curious.

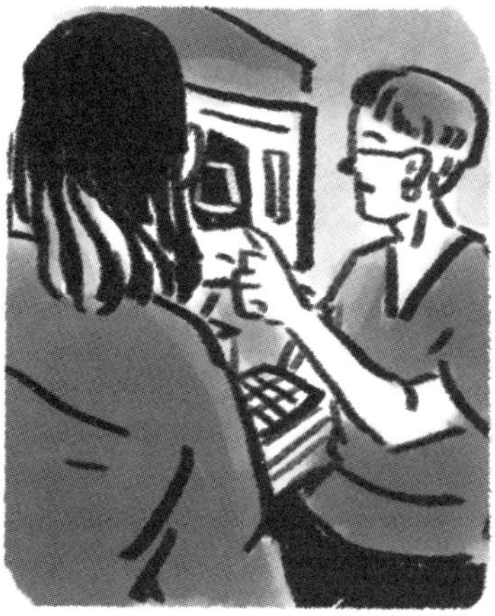

The first picture is a lump. She tells me the lump is fourteen weeks and three days old.

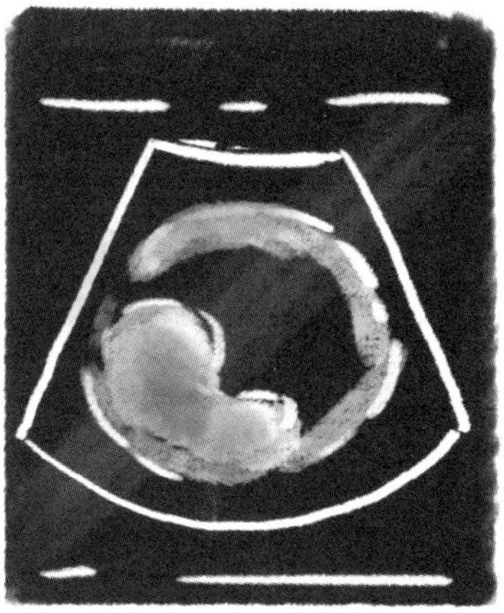

The second is a human skull. A tiny human skull, growing inside my body.

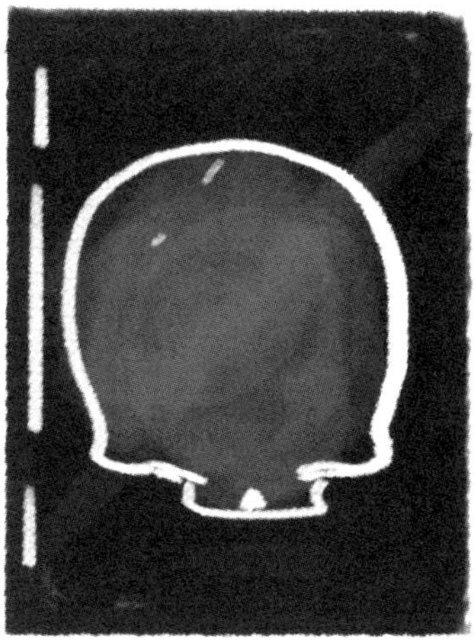

I put on a very awkward robe and some slippers. I try to keep myself covered as a nurse explains the next step.

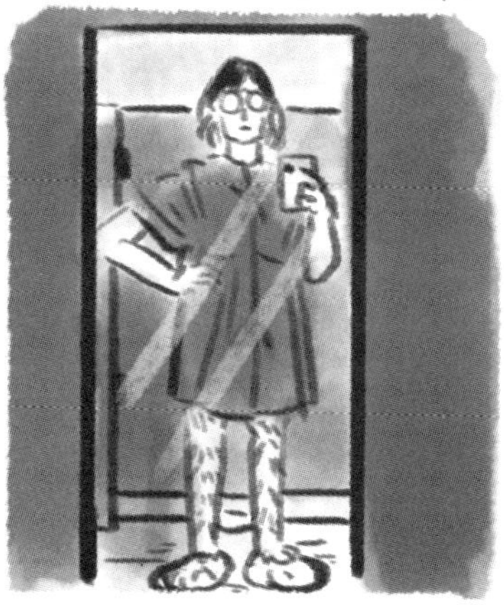

They'll give my some pills to help soften my cervix so the fetus can be removed without tearing anything.

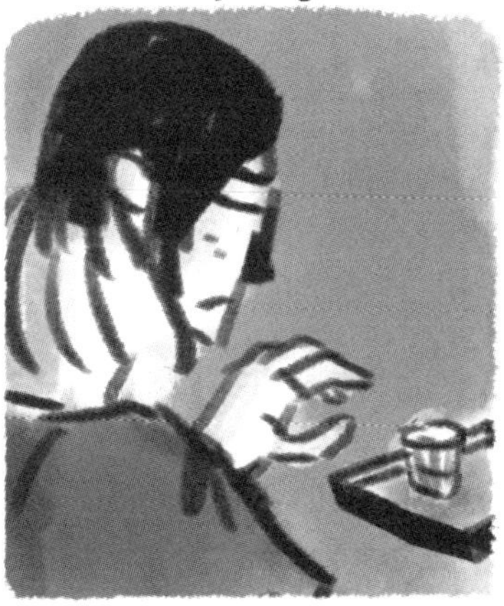

They sit me in a nice recliner with the pills in my lip. I have to wait 90 minutes for them to dissolve.

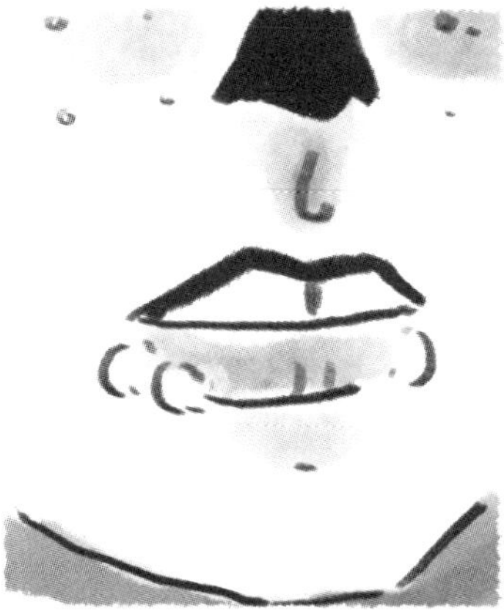

Dazed women hobble back to the recovery area, robes open, leaking blood.

I try to read a magazine but the words are fuzzy. I wish there was a tv. I feel so cold.

A nurse sees me shivering and tucks a blanket around me, just like my mom used to.

They call my name. The operating room is small. The doctors are kind and calm.

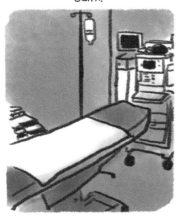

I start crying as the anesthesiologist puts a needle in my hand. I'm thinking about the skull.

They look concerned. "I'm ok," I tell them, "I just hate needles."

I'm still crying when I wake up in the chair. My insides are screaming.

The nurse from before holds my hand and tells me about her plans for Thanksgiving. By the time she's done describing the feast, the pain is gone.

My closest friends are waiting for me outside. I feel free, almost euphoric. I can't wait to eat my weight in rice balls and bubble tea.

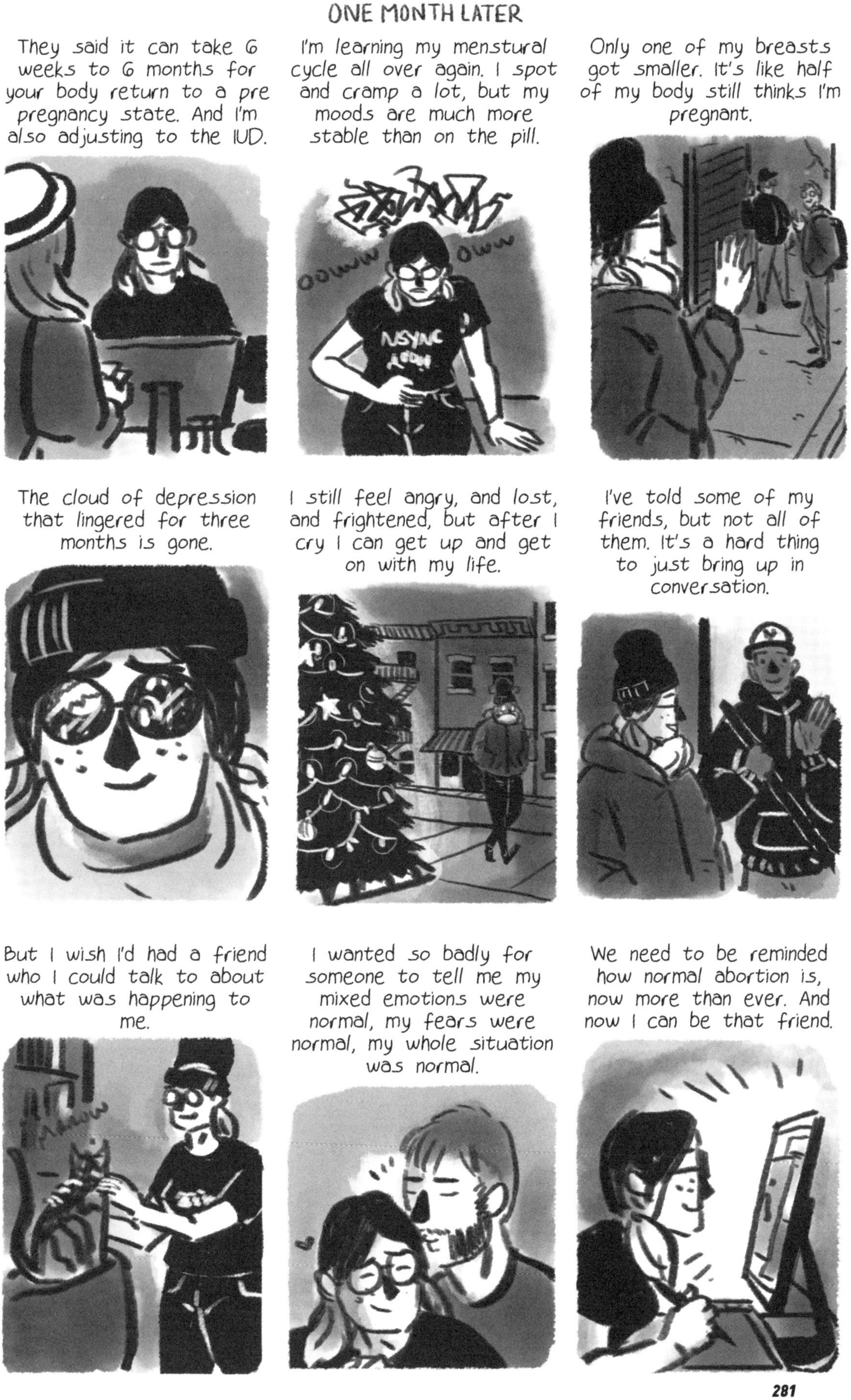
ONE MONTH LATER
They said it can take 6 weeks to 6 months for your body return to a pre pregnancy state. And I'm also adjusting to the IUD.
I'm learning my menstural cycle all over again. I spot and cramp a lot, but my moods are much more stable than on the pill.
NSYNC
Only one of my breasts got smaller. It's like half of my body still thinks I'm pregnant.
The cloud of depression that lingered for three months is gone.
I still feel angry, and lost, and frightened, but after I cry I can get up and get on with my life.
I've told some of my friends, but not all of them. It's a hard thing to just bring up in conversation.
But I wish I'd had a friend who I could talk to about what was happening to me.
I wanted so badly for someone to tell me my mixed emotions were normal, my fears were normal, my whole situation was normal.
We need to be reminded how normal abortion is, now more than ever. And now I can be that friend.

MJ Flores
wetestify.org/author/mj-flores

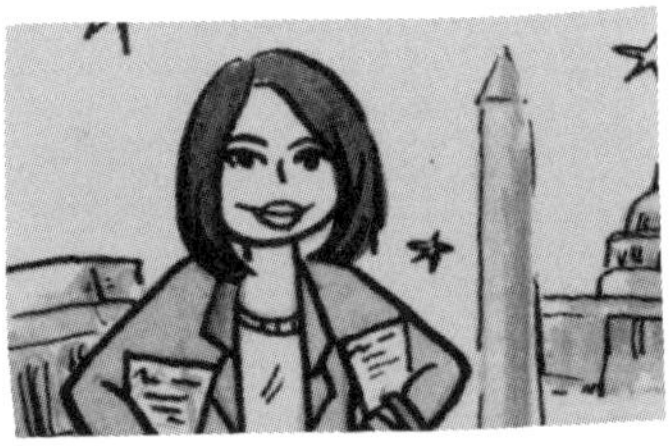

MJ Flores is a storyteller with We Testify, a program of the National Network of Abortion Funds, and shares her story to confront abortion stigma and challenge anti-abortion legislation.

Kat Fajardo
katfajardo.com

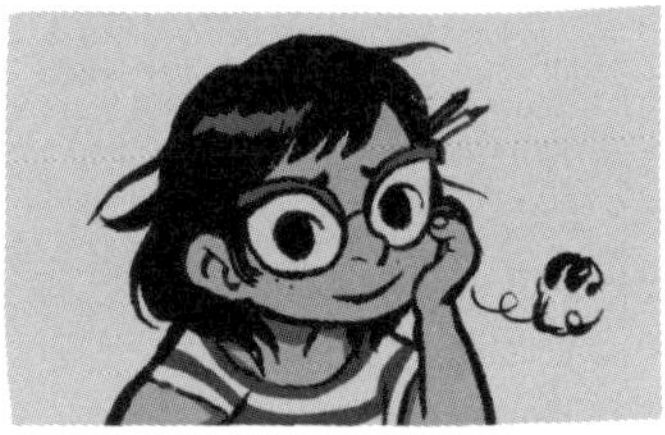

Kat Fajardo is a freelance comic artist, illustrator, and editor of *La Raza Anthology*. She creates playful and colorful work about self-acceptance and Latinx culture.

Kendra Josie Kirkpatrick
kendrajosiekirkpatrick.com

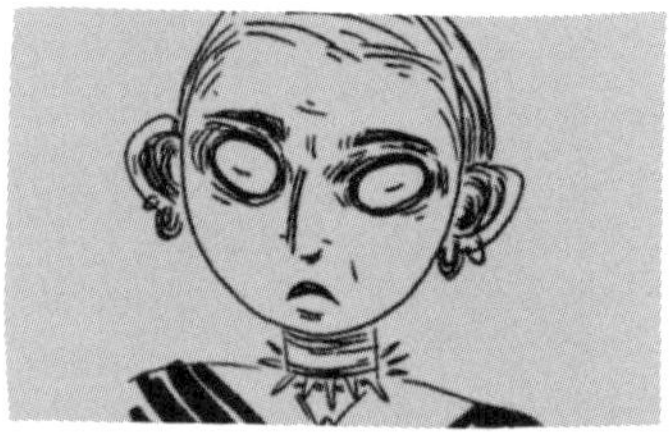

Kendra Josie Kirkpatrick enjoys large amounts of black on both her comic pages and her clothes, and has a passion for music that features people screaming. BFA Cartooning, SVA '16.

Jennifer Camper
jennifercamper.com

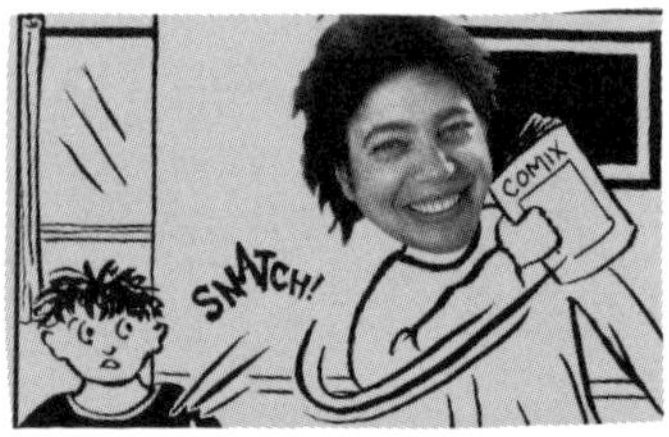
SNATCH!
COMIX

Jennifer Camper's books include *Rude Girls and Dangerous Women* and *subGURLZ*, and she edits the anthology *Juicy Mother*. She is the founding director of the Queers & Comics Conference.

Dr. Cynthia Greenlee
twitter.com/CynthiaGreenlee

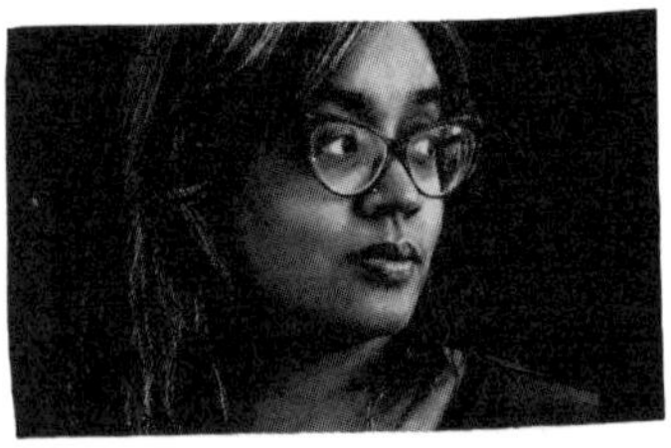

Dr. Cynthia Greenlee is a North Carolina-based journalist and historian. She's the senior editor at *Rewire*, the go-to website about reproductive justice, health, and rights in the United States.

Jaz Malone
jazimated.com

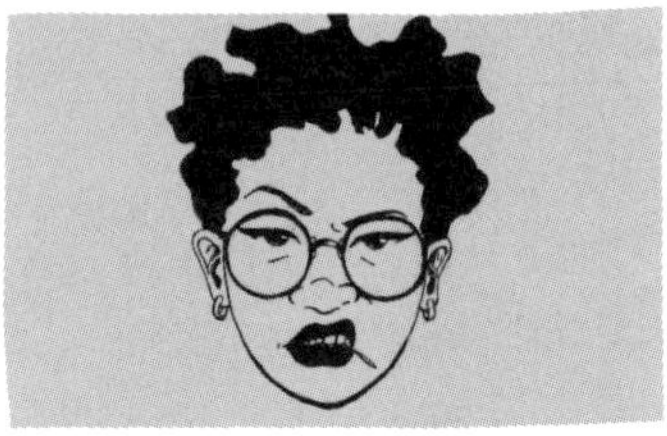

Jaz Malone received her BFA in Animation from The University of The Arts. She currently works in the tri-state area as an illustrator, digital arts instructor, and tea enthusiast.

Rickie Solinger

Rickie Solinger is a curator and a historian. She is the author or editor of eleven books about reproductive politics and satellite issues.

Rachel Merrill
rachelmerrill.net

Rachel Merrill was born and raised in Baton Rouge, Louisiana and now lives in the much colder Astoria, Queens. She enjoys beer and donuts, but not together.

Rachel Wilson
rachelwilson.contently.com

Rachel Wilson is a writer from the UK whose work has appeared on *i-D*, *The Guardian*, *Broadly*, *Noisey*, and more. She also grapples with her hand-me-down film camera sometimes.

Ally Shwed
allyshwed.com

Ally Shwed has worked with The Nib, BOOM! Studios, and IDW Publishing. She is a professor of sequential art, scriptwriting, and art direction at Tecnológico de Monterrey in Querétaro, México.

Hallie Jay Pope
graphicadvocacy.org

Hallie Jay Pope is a lawyer/cartoonist living in Washington, DC. She runs the Graphic Advocacy Project, a nonprofit that uses visual communication tools to explain legal concepts.

Anna Sellheim
annasellheim.com

Anna Sellheim graduated from the Center For Cartoon Studies in 2016. She has had her work featured on *The Nib*, *Upworthy*, and a bunch of cool anthologies. She moves around a lot.

Brittany Mostiller

Brittany Mostiller is the executive director of the Chicago Abortion Fund, a nonprofit that promotes reproductive justice through funding abortion and organizing for racial, economic, and gender justice.

Lilly Taing
lillytaingart.wixsite.com/portfolio

Lilly Taing is a LA-born seedling who illustrates and makes comics. She hopes to combine her passion for medicine and art to help patients and healthcare providers share their stories.

Lindsay Rodriguez
abortionfunds.org

Lindsay Rodriguez is the Communications Manager for the National Network of Abortion Funds. She joined NNAF after serving as Board President for the Lilith Fund for Reproductive Equity.

Lucy Haslam
lucyhaslam.com

Lucy Haslam graduated from Falmouth University, UK and now specialises in editorial work and comics. Some of these comics are made as part of the group Froglump.

Samantha Romero
wetestify.org/author/samantha-romero

Samantha Romero was an organizer for the Wendy Davis Campaign, which sparked her passion for reproductive justice. She is the President of the West Fund, and a member of We Testify.

Erin Lux
erin-lux.com

Erin Lux is a Brooklyn-based illustrator and cartoonist. She's the creator of the webcomic *Fascist Friends*, and many other short irreverent comics.

Candice Russell
wetestify.org/author/candice-russell

Candice Russell is a writer and abortion story-teller whose work has been featured in *Teen Vogue*, *ELLE*, *Glamour*, and *The Huffington Post*. She serves on the board of NARAL Pro-Choice Texas.

Laura Lannes
lauralannes.com

Laura Lannes is a cartoonist and illustrator from Brazil living in New York City. She is the editor of the *Bad Boyfriends* anthology.

Heidi Williamson

Heidi Williamson is the Senior Policy Analyst for the Women's Health and Rights program at the Center for American Progress and the Center for American Progress Action Fund. She is an avid comic book reader.

Julia Krase
wasteofpaint.net

Julia Krase is currently scribbling and petting dogs in Portland, Oregon. Her work is usually a product of pent-up emotion that can't be said with words.

Cathy Camper
cathycamper.com

Cathy Camper is the author the *Lowriders in Space* series, *Ten Ways to Hear Snow*, and more. She also writes zines and is a founding member of the Portland Women of Color zine collective.

Kriota Willberg
kriotawelt.blogspot.com

Kriota Willberg is the inaugural Artist-In-Residence at the New York Academy of Medicine. She is best known for her comics about injury prevention for cartoonists and artists.

Katie Brown

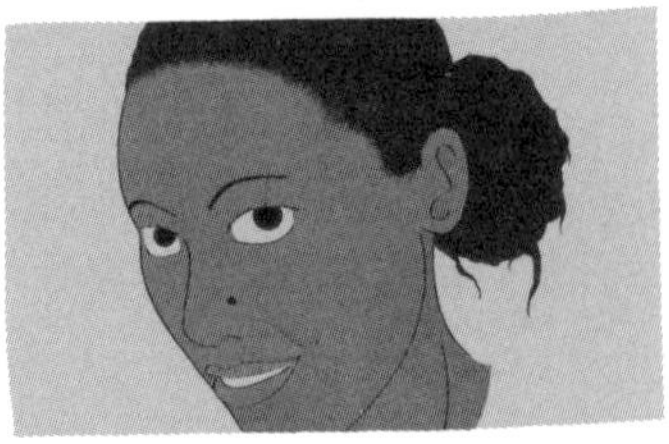

Katie Brown is an OBGYN resident and abortion provider. She lives in San Francisco with her husband, Andrew. This is her first work in comics, but hopefully not her last!

Andrew Carl

twitter.com/andrewthecarl

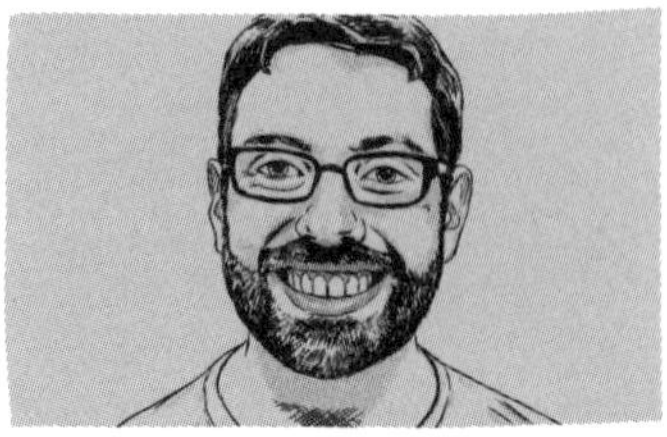

Andrew Carl is a writer, editor, husband, and cat-owner based in San Francisco. He's been honored with Eisner and Harvey Awards for his work and a doctor for a wife.

Ahmara Smith

ahmarasmithart.com

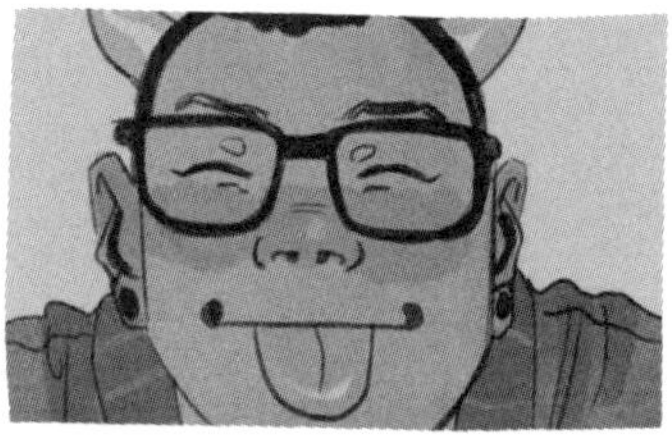

Ahmara Smith is currently pursuing a BFA in Sequential Art at Savannah College of Art and Design. They were born and raised in Atlanta, and they love drawing and writing comics!

Benita Ulisano

clinicvestproject.org

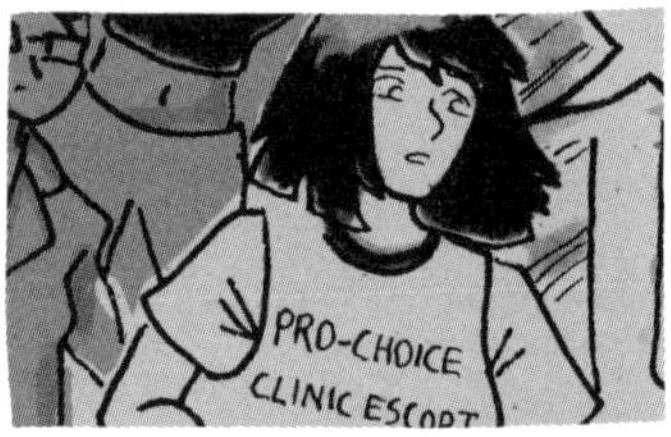
PRO-CHOICE
CLINIC

Benita Ulisano is a longtime abortion rights activist, clinic escort and founder of The Clinic Vest Project.

Laura Martin

lauramartinartist.tumblr.com

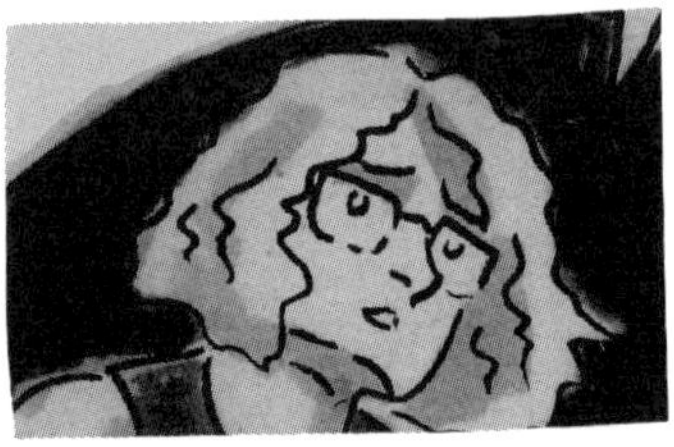

Laura Martin is an artist currently enrolled at the Center for Cartoon Studies in White River Junction, VT. When she's not drawing comics, she likes reading, playing video games, and jumping into very deep, cold bodies of water.

Steph Kraft Sheley

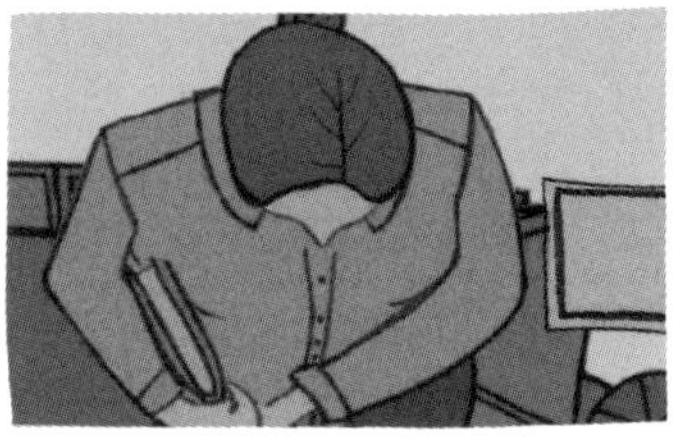

Steph Kraft Sheley is a lawyer and advocate for reproductive justice. She holds Juris Doctor and Master of Health Administration degrees from the University of Iowa, where she recieved the ABA/BNA award for Excellence in the Study of Health Law.

Plan C

plancpills.org

Plan C is a non-profit alliance of advocates who believe everyone has a right to know about the technology of medication abortion, including women in the United States.

Nomi Kane

nomikane.com

Nomi Kane is an alumnus of The Center for Cartoon Studies who draws editorial cartoons and short fiction comics whenever she can. By day, she works as a Staff Artist at the Schulz Studio.

Sarah Mirk
twitter.com/sarahmirk

Sarah Mirk is a journalist who covers politics, gender, and sexuality. She hosts Bitch Media's feminism and pop culture podcast *Popaganda*, and is a contributing editor at *The Nib*.

Kris Louis

dropr.com/krislouis

Kris Louis is an illustrator, cartoonist, graphic designer, and character designer originally from Long Island, New York. They have a cat named Charlie and they love fun facts and dad jokes.

Emily Lady

emilylady.com

Emily Lady lives with their cat/wife and a thousand hungry ghosts. Check out their weekly, much funnier, semi-autobiographical comic at emilylady.com

Sage Coffey

sagecoffey.tumblr.com

Sage Coffey is a nervous little cartoonist gremlin. They like to make comics that make them laugh and then cry and if they're lucky, laugh again.

Rachel Hays

Rachel Hays is a comic artist living in the Bronx, originally from Idaho. She's been hooked on DIY publishing since gluing her first story to a wallpaper swatch as a kindergartener.

Leah Hayes
leahhayes.com

Leah Hayes is an illustrator, musician, song-writer, and producer. She is the creator of the graphic novel *Not Funny Ha-Ha*. She works out of New York City and Los Angeles.

Tanya DePass
ineeddiversegames.org

Tanya DePass is the founder and Director of I Need Diverse Games, a not-for-profit foundation based in Chicago dedicated to better diversification of all aspects of gaming.

Wren Chavers
notcathi.com

Wren Chavers a recent graduate of the School of Visual Arts, and they're working to make all the comics they can! When they aren't making comics, they're making memes or bread.

Tatiana Gill
tatianagill.com

Tatiana Gill is a Seattle-based cartoonist whose art includes themes of body-positivity, feminism, mental health and recovery. She has created dozens of self-published comics.

Mick Moran
meetmickmoran.com

Mick Moran is a radical full-spectrum doula and the editor of The Doula Project's zine, *DIY Doula: Self-Care for Before, During, & After Your Abortion*.

Anna Bongiovanni
annabongiovanni.com

Anna Bongiovanni is queer cartoonist living in Minneapolis. They are the creator of *The Grease Bats*, a monthly webcomic for *Autostraddle*, as well as a contributing cartoonist to *Everyday Feminism*.

Daniela Diaz

Daniela Diaz is a We Testify abortion storyteller. Her advocacy and activism focuses strongly on the intersection of reproductive justice, HIV/AIDS and immigration from a global perspective.

Stephanie Rodriguez
stephguez.com

Stephanie Rodriguez hails from the Bronx, NY, and holds a BFA in Illustration from the School of Visual Arts. Her comics cross the line between comedic and tragic nostalgia.

Renee Bracey Sherman
wetestify.org

Renee Bracey Sherman serves as the Senior Public Affairs Manager at the National Network of Abortion Funds, where she runs We Testify, an abortion storyteller leadership program.

Kennedy Tarrell
kennedraw.tumblr.com

Kennedy Tarrell is a Storyboard Revisionist at DreamWorks Animation Television on *Spirit Riding Free*. They draw horses during the day and comics at night.

Katie Fricas
klongua.com

Katie Fricas is a cartoonist and illustrator in New York City. She has published political comics in *The Guardian* and is the creator of the pop culture zine *Fashionique*.

Michelle Kinsey Bruns
michellekinseybruns.com

Michelle Kinsey Bruns is an advocate for safety and privacy of abortion clinic patients and staff, and has been a clinic escort or clinic defender at anti-choice protests in nine states.

Gianna Meola
giannameola.com

Gianna Meola graduated from the School of Visual Arts with a BFA in Illustration. She enjoys traveling, sketching, and going on walks.

Jensine Eckwall
jensineeckwall.com

Jensine Eckwall is a Brooklyn-based illustrator whose work has been honored by the Society of Illustrators, American Illustration, Spectrum Fantastic Art, and 3x3.

Yamani Hernandez
abortionfunds.org

Yamani Hernandez is the Executive Director of the National Network of Abortion Funds, which works with member organizations to remove barriers to abortion access.

Sharon Rimann
phlegmmefatale.tumblr.com

Sharon Rimann was born in Missouri in 1993, and started drawing soon after. They are mostly self-taught, but will concede some credit to Bob Ross, Mike Mignola, and the devil.

Claudia E. Berger
claudiaeberger.com

Claudia E. Berger is a New York City-based cartoonist. She makes comics about mental health, mythology, and houseplants, and spends way too much time thinking about science fiction.

Mallory McMaster
twitter.com/malloryinpink

Mallory McMaster is an abortion activist, dog mom, terrible cook, and cleaning enthusiast hailing from Cleveland, OH.

Kate Kerns
katekerns.com

Kate Kerns is a graphic designer and illustrator from Kansas, now living in Austin, TX. She has worked as a victim advocate for the National Domestic Violence Hotline.

Bree Jordan
bree-jordan.weebly.com

Bree Jordan is a Salt Lake City-based comic artist and health care professional. Her work is frequently concerned with bodily autonomy, patient advocacy, and end of life planning.

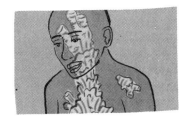

CB Hart
explodinglobster.com

CB Hart is a cartoonist living in San Mateo and graduate of the Sequential Artist Workshop.

Anise Simon
wetestify.org/author/anise-simon

Anise Simon works as the Southern Funds Coordinator at the National Network of Abortion Funds, where she provides support to grassroots abortion funds in the South.

Sarah Crowe
eworcharas.com

Sarah Crowe is a sculptor and cartoonist made in Austin, but made for New York.

Sophia Foster-Dimino
hellophia.com

Sophia Foster-Dimino is an illustrator and cartoonist, and teaches conceptual illustration at California College of the Arts. Her Ignatz-winning series *Sex Fantasy* is collected by Koyama Press.

Vreni
stillvreni.com

Vreni started writing and drawing her own stories as a child so she could be on Reading Rainbow. Her stories have more swearing now, but about the same amount of kissing.

Pam Wishbow
pamwishbow.com

Pam Wishbow went to school for illustration, and bounced a few times on her way from her childhood home in NJ to her new home in Seattle. She lives with her cats, Earthling and Guy.

Undue Burdens
by Hallie Jay Pope

Access Denied: Origins of the Hyde Amendment and Other Restrictions on Public Funding for Abortion. Retrieved from https://www.aclu.org/other/access-denied-origins-hyde-amendment-and-other-restrictions-public-funding-abortion

Arons, J. (2013, May 10). How the Hyde Amendment Discriminates Against Poor Women and Women of Color. Retrieved from https://www.americanprogress.org/issues/women/news/2013/05/10/62875/how-the-hyde-amendment-discriminates-against-poor-women-and-women-of-color/

—. (2016, September 23). Opinion: The Hyde Amendment Hurts Poor Women of Color the Most. *Newsweek*. Retrieved from http://www.newsweek.com/hyde-amendment-hurts-poor-women-color-most-501763

Fact Sheet: The Hyde Amendment. Retrieved from http://allaboveall.org/wp/wp-content/uploads/2015/06/Hyde-Amendment-Fact-Sheet-011717.pdf

Talbot, M. (2017, January 25). Daily Comment: Trump Makes the Global Gag Rule on Abortion Even Worse. *The New Yorker*. Retrieved from http://www.newyorker.com/news/daily-comment/trump-makes-the-global-gag-rule-on-abortion-even-worse

Urban Institute analysis of DYNASIM for the Kaiser Family Foundation. (2013, July 15). Median Income Among Medicare Beneficiaries, Overall and by Race/Ethnicity, Age, and Gender, 2012. Retrieved from http://kff.org/medicare/slide/median-income-among-medicare-beneficiaries-overall-and-by-raceethnicity-age-gender-2012/

Horror Stories
by Jennifer Camper

Blanchard, K., et al. (2010, November 24). Self-induction of abortion among women in the United States. *Reproductive Health Matters*, *18*(36), 136-146.

No Child Left Behind. (2017, February). *Harper's Magazine*,

Abortion Trials
written by Rickie Solinger
art by Rachel Merrill

Solinger, R. (1994). *The Abortionist: A Woman Against the Law*. New York, NY: The Free Press,

Jane
written by Rachel Wilson
art by Ally Shwed

Bart, P. B. (1987). Seizing the Means of Reproduction: An Illegal Feminist Abortion Collective—How and Why it Worked. *Qualitative Sociology*, *10*(4), Retrieved from https://automaticwriting1.files.wordpress.com/2013/07/seizing-the-means-of-reproduction.pdf

Kaplan, L. (1995). *The Story of Jane: The Legendary Underground Feminist Abortion Service*. Chicago, IL: UChicago Press,

Ross, L. J. (1998). African-American Women and Abortion. In R. Solinger (Ed.), *Abortion Wars: A Half-Century of Struggle* (pp.161-207), Berkeley and Los Angeles, CA: University of California Press. Retrieved from http://www.trustblackwomen.org/2011-05-10-03-28-12/publications-a-articles/african-americans-and-abortion-articles/31-african-american-women-and-abortion

Body & Soul, Science & Religion:
All Crowded Into One Uterus
by Kriota Willberg

Baday, A. B. Khitamy. (2013). Divergent Views on Abortion and The Period of Ensoulment. *Sultan Oaboos University Medical Journal*, *13*(1), 26-31.

Brind'Amour, K. (2007, October 30). Quickening. Retrieved from https://embryo.asu.edu/pages/quickening

Buklijas, T., Hopwood, T. Unborn 1300-1800s. Retrieved from http://www.sites.hps.cam.ac.uk/visibleembryos/s1_3.html

Gatrad, R., et al. (2005). Sikh Birth Customs. *Archives of Disease in Childhood*, *90*(6), 560-563.

Hill, M. A. (2017, July 25). Embryology. Retrieved from https://embryology.med.unsw.edu.au/embryology/index.php/Main_Page

Himma, K. E. (2005). A dualist analysis of abortion: personhood and the concept of self *qua* experiential subject. *Journal of Medical Ethics*, *31*(1), 48-55.

Mayo Clinic. (2017, July 8). Healthy Lifestyle/Pregnancy Week By Week. Retrieved from http://www.mayoclinic.org/healthy-lifestyle/pregnancy-week-by-week/in-depth/fetal-development/art-20046151?pg=2

Office on Women's Health. (2010, September 27). Stages of pregnancy. Retrieved from https://www.womenshealth.gov/pregnancy/you-are-pregnant/stages-of-pregnancy.html

Rothstein, P. Lung Development. PDF. Prod. Columbia University.

The Baby Center. (2015, August). Fetal Development Week by Week. Retrieved from http://www.babycenter.com/fetal-development-week-by-week

Tsimis, M. E., et al. (2015). Prematurity: present and future. *Mierva Ginecologica*, *67*(1), 35-46.

Wikipedia. Ensoulment. Retrieved January 28, 2017 from URL https://en.wikipedia.org/wiki/Ensoulment

Born and Forgotten
written by Katie Brown & Andrew Carl,
art by Ahmara Smith

Biggs, M. A., Upadhyay, U. D., McCulloch, C. E., et al. (2017, February). Women's Mental Health and Wellbeing 5 Years After Receiving or Being Denied an Abortion: A Prospective, Longitudinal Cohort Study. *JAMA Psychiatry*, *74*(2), 169-178. doi: 10.1001/jamapsychiatry.2016.3478

Committee on Gynecologic Practice. (2009, June). ACOG Committee Opinion No. 434: induced abortion and breast cancer risk. *Obstetrics & Gynecology*, *113*(6), 1417-8. doi: 10.1097/AOG.0b013e3181ac067d

Guttmacher Institute. http://guttmacher.org

Lee, S.J., Ralston, H.J., Drey, E.A., Partridge, J.C., Rosen, M.A. (2005, August). Fetal pain: a systematic multidisciplinary review of the evidence. *JAMA*, *294*(8), 947-54. doi: 10.1001/jama.294.8.947

National Center for Environmental Health, Division of Emergency and Environmental Health Services. (2016, September). Childhood Lead Poisoning Data, Statistics, and Surveillance. Retrieved from http://www.cdc.gov/nceh/Lead/data/index.htm

Texas Department of State Health Services. (2016, December). A Woman's Right to Know. Retrieved from http://dshs.texas.gov/wrtk/

—. (2016, September). A Woman's Right to Know Resource Directory. Retrieved from http://dshs.texas.gov/wrtk/

They Can't Get That From Us
by Steph Kraft Sheley

Alazri, M., Heywood, P., Neal, R.D., et al. (2007). How important is continuity of care? *Sultan Qaboos Univ Med J.*, *7*(3), 197-206.

Biggs, M.A., Upadhyay, U.D., McCulloch, C.E. et al. (2016). Women's Mental Health and Well-being 5 Years After Receiving or Being Denied an Abortion: A Prospective, Longitudinal Cohort Study. *JAMA Psychiatry*, *74*(2), 169-178.

Boodman, S.G. (2009, September 1). Abortion stigma affects doctors' training and choices. *Washington Post*. Retrieved from http://www.washingtonpost.com/wp-dyn/content/article/2009/08/28/AR2009082802785.html

Center for Reproductive Rights & Ibis Reproductive Health. (2014). Evaluating priorities: measuring women's and children's health and well-being against abortion restrictions in the states. Retrieved from https://www.ibisreproductivehealth.org/sites/default/files/files/publications/Ibis%20and%20CRR_Priorities_Project_FINAL_2014.pdf

Dunn, L. (2011, July 29). 5 tips to improve a hospital's brand. *Becker Hospital Review*. Retrieved from http://www.beckershospitalreview.com/hospital-management-administration/5-tips-to-improve-a-hospitals-brand.html

Flanagan, N. (2016, January). Reputation is everything: how 2 hospitals are weathering PR firestorms. *Healthcare Dive*. Retrieved from http://www.healthcaredive.com/news/reputation-is-everything-how-2-hospitals-are-weathering-pr-firestorms/412982/

Gulliford, M., Nathani, S. & Morgan, M. (2006). What is "continuity of care"? *J. Health Serv. Res. Policy*, *11*(4), 248-250.

Induced Abortion in the United States. (2017, January). Retrieved from https://www.guttmacher.org/fact-sheet/induced-abortion-united-states

Jerman, J., Jones, R. K. & Onda, T. (2016, May). Characteristics of U.S. abortion patients in 2014 and changes since 2008. Guttmacher. Retrieved from https://www.guttmacher.org/report/characteristics-us-abortion-patients-2014

Jones, R. K., Jerman, J. (2017). Abortion incidence and service availability in the United States, 2014. *Perspectives on Sexual and Reproductive Health*, *49*(1), 17-27.

Kaye, J., Amiri, B., Melling, L. (2016, May). Health care denied: patients and physicians speak out about Catholic hospitals and the threat to women's health and lives. ACLU. Retrieved from https://www.aclu.org/sites/default/files/field_document/healthcaredenied.pdf

Logsdon, M. B., Handler, A., Godfrey, E. M. (2012). Women's preferences for the location of abortion services: a pilot study in two Chicago clinics. *Mat. Child Health J.*, *16*(1), 212-216.

Martin, L. A., Debbink, M., Hassinger, J., (2014). Measuring stigma among abortion providers: assessing the abortion provider stigma survey instrument. *Women Health*, *54*(7), 641-661.

Memo on private insurance coverage of abortion. (2011, January 19). Guttmacher. Retrieved from https://www.guttmacher.org/article/2011/01/memo-private-insurance-coverage-abortion

"No Margin, No Mission" is too simplistic. (2013). *AMA J. Ethics*, *15*(2), 101-103.

Norris, A., Bessett, D., Steinberg, J. R., et al (2011). Abortion stigma: a reconceptualization of constitutents, causes and consequences. *Womens Health Issues*, *21*(3 Supp), S49-54.

Raymond, E. G., Grimes, D. A., (2012). The comparative safety of legal induced abortion and childbirth in the United States. *Obstet Gynecol*, *119*(2 Pt 1), 215-219.

Rodak, S. (2012, July 26). 8 best practices for managing a hospital's reputation. *Beckers Hospital Review*. Retrieved from http://www.beckershospitalreview.com/hospital-management-administration/8-best-practices-for-managing-a-hospitals-reputation.html

Schoen, J. (2013). Living through some giant changes: the establishment of abortion services. *Am. J. Public Health*, *103*(3), pp. 416-20.

Sudhakar-Krishan, V., Rudolf, M. C. J. (2007). *Arch Dis Child*, *92*(2), 381-383.

United States Conference of Catholic Bishops (2009). Ethical and religious directives for Catholic health care services, fifth edition. Retrieved from http://www.usccb.org/issues-and-action/human-life-and-dignity/health-care/upload/Ethical-Religious-Directives-Catholic-Health-Care-Services-fifth-edition-2009.pdf

University of Chicago. Accessing abortion in Illinois: a guide for health and social service providers: understanding abortion stigma and shame. https://abguide.uchicago.edu/page/understanding-abortion-stigma-and-shame

Upadhyay, U. D., Weitz, T. A., Jones, R. K. (2014). Denial of abortion because of provider gestational age limits in the United States. *Am. J. Public Health*, *104*(9), 1687-1694. doi: 10.2105/AJPH.2013.301378

U.S. abortion rate continues to decline, hits historic low. (2017, January 17). Guttmacher. Retrieved from https://www.guttmacher.org/news-release/2017/us-abortion-rate-continues-decline-hits-historic-low

Uttley, L., Reynerston, S., Kenny, L. (2013, December). Miscarriage of medicine: the growth of Catholic hospitals and the threat to reproductive health care. Retrieved from http://static1.1.sqspcdn.com/static/f/816571/24079922/1387381601667/Growth-of-Catholic-Hospitals-2013.pdf?token=pSDxeBBlXrRZOx%2BPE%2FJwWUkTuD4%3D

Uttley, L., Reynerston, S., Pawelko, R. (n.d.). Merging Catholic and non-sectarian hospitals: NYS Models for addressing ethical challenges. Retrieved from http://static1.1.sqspcdn.com/static/f/816571/23042588/1372882137057/Models+of+Catholic-secular+hospitals+mergers+in+NYS.pdf?token=pSDxeBBlXrRZOx%2BPE%2FJwWUkTuD4%3D

Weitz, T. A., Taylor, D. Desai, S., et al. (2013). Safety of a̲  ̲formed by nurse p̲ ̲dwives, and ̲ia legal w̲ ̲61.

C̲ ̲ ̲c-
c̲ ̲ ̲m-
at̲ ̲21,
Faúndes, ̲ ̲. for the
termination ̲ ̲.2 completed weeks of pregnancy. *International Journal of Gynecology & Obstetrics, 99*(Supplement 2). S172-S177.

Finer, L. B., Zolna, M. R. (2006), Declines in unintended pregnancy in the United States, 2008-2011. *New England Journal of Medicine, 374*(9), 843-852.

Grossman, D., et al. (2015, November 17). Knowledge, opinion and experience related to abortion self-induction in Texas. Texas Policy Evaluation Project. Retrieved from https://utexas.app.box.com/v/KOESelfInductionResearchBrief

Office of Population Research at Princeton University & Association of Reproductive Health Professionals (2017, January 24). History of Plan B OTC. Retrieved from http://ec.princeton.edu/pills/planbhistory.html

The Right to Remain Unpregnant
by Sarah Mirk

Mirk, S. (2010, February 18). Let's Talk about Sex: Planned Parenthood's President Talks About the New Center. *The Portland Mercury*. Retrieved from http://www.portlandmercury.com/portland/lets-talk-about-sex/Content?oid=2178071

—. (2016, October 31). The Political Power of Telling Abortion Stories. *Bitch Media*. Retrieved from https://bitchmedia.org/article/how-we-talk-about-abortion-election

Popovich, N. (2015, May 6). Colorado contraception program was a huge success—but the GOP is scrapping it. *The Guardian*. Retrieved from https://www.theguardian.com/us-news/2015/may/06/colorado-contraception-family-planning-republicans

Ramsey, L. (2016, December 4). Here's how much an IUD costs with Obamacare—and without. *Business Insider*. Retrieved from http://www.businessinsider.com/how-much-iud-procedures-would-cost-without-obamacare-2016-12

Schencker, L. (2016, December 1). After Trump's win, Planned Parenthood of Illinois reports big spike in IUD appointments. *Chicago Tribune*. Retrieved from http://www.chicagotribune.com/business/ct-trump-birth-control-demand-spike-1202-biz-20161201-story.html

Tabernise, S. (2015, July 5). Colorado's Effort Against Teenage Pregnancies Is a Startling Success. *The New York Times*. Retrieved from https://www.nytimes.com/2015/07/06/science/colorados-push-against-teenage-pregnancies-is-a-startling-success.html

Self Care After Your Abortion
by Rachel Hays

Abortion Aftercare. *Our Bodies, Ourselves* (2014, March 27). Retrieved from http://www.ourbodiesourselves.org/health-info/aftercare/

After the Abortion. Every Woman's Health Centre. Retrieved from http://everywomanshealthcentre.ca/after-the-abortion/

Aftercare Instructions. Feminist Women's Health Center. Retrieved from http://www.feministcenter.org/en/abortion-care/after-care-instructions

Caring for Yourself After an Abortion. Planned Parenthood. Retrieved from https://www.plannedparenthood.org/planned-parenthood-michigan/patient/abortion-services/caring-for-yourself-after-an-abortion

Tips to Speed Recovery After Aborition. Marie Stopes UK. Retrieved from https://mariestopes.org.uk/women/abortion/abortion-aftercare/tips-speed-recovery-after-abortion

ABORTION BASICS: ACCESS, FUNDING, & HEALTH EDUCATION

Abortion Care Network (abortioncarenetwork.org). An organization that ensures abortion access, supports providers, and fights stigma.

Center for Reproductive Rights (reproduciverights.org). A global legal advocacy organization dedicated to protecting reproductive rights, with a specialization in U.S. constitutional and international human rights law.

Guttmacher Institute (guttmacher.org). A research and policy organization with a focus on sexual and reproductive rights.

National Abortion Federation (prochoice.org). An organization with a mission to ensure safe, legal, and accessible abortions.

National Network of Abortion Funds (abortionfunds.org). A reproductive justice oriented organization that works to provide abortion funds to those in need.

Planned Parenthood (plannedparenthood.org). A national healthcare provider, women's health advocate, and resource for sex education and professional development.

Women's Reproductive Rights Assitance Project (wrrap.org). An organization that provides financial assistance for safe legal abortion and emergency contraception.

HISTORY

"African-American Women and Abortion," Loretta J. Ross, Originally printed in *Abortion Wars: A Half-Century of Struggle*, edited by Rickie Solinger. (http://www.trustblackwomen.org/2011-05-10-03-28-12/publications-a-articles/african-americans-and-abortion-articles/31-african-american-women-and-abortion). A comprehensive and powerful history by Loretta J. Ross, the groundbreaking reproductive rights advocate and originator of the concept of reproductive justice. Ross makes connections from white America's ownership of the Black body through slavery to the contemporary challenges disproportionately faced by women of color.

"History of Abortion in the U.S.," *Our Bodies Ourselves*. (http://www.ourbodiesourselves.org/health-info/u-s-abortion-history/). This 2014 article from *Our Bodies, Ourselves* provides a concise yet thorough introductory history of abortion access in the United States, covering legislative landmarks as well as grassroots initiatives. The piece is supplemented by links to primary sources and collected data as well as quotes from abortion seekers' personal experiences.

"Jane: An Abortion Service," CWLU Herstory Project, 2016. (https://www.cwluherstory.org/jane-abortion-service/?rq=jane%20abortion%20service). An introduction and thorough archive of The Abortion Counseling Service of Women's Liberation, a pre-*Roe v. Wade* network of illegal abortion providers better known as "Jane." The archive, hosted by the Chicago Women's Liberation Union Herstory Project, collects narratives of participants, original documents disseminated by Jane, academic research about Jane, and contemprary art created as a celebration of Jane's legacy.

"Women, Midwives, and Nurses: A History of Women Healers," Barbara Ehrenreich & Deidre English, 1973. (http://www.feministes-radicales.org/wp-content/uploads/2012/06/Barbara-Ehrenreich-and-Deirdre-English-Witches-Midwives-and-Nurses-A-History-of-Women-Healers.-Introduction..pdf). Before *Nickel and Dimed* and *Mother Jones*, Barbara Ehrenreich and Deidre English collaborated on this history of the persectution of women healers in the western world. A well-known feminist text advocating for women to know and trust their own bodies in the face of a patriarchal health system, but its completely Eurocentric approach hasn't aged well.

INTERSECTIONALITY

Philadephia Black Women's Health Project (http://www.blackwomenshealthproject.org/aaabortion.htm). The Philadelphia Black Women's Health Project presents a consice collection of facts about abortion, focusing on the demographic of abortion seekers and factors impacting access. Data is largely sourced from the Guttmacher Institute, Planned Parenthood and the National Abortion Federation. Part of a series of BWHP factsheets on health and reproductive justice written for Black women and families.

Healthcare Bill of Rights (healthcarebillofrights.org). A brief but powerful affirmation of the right to comprehensive health services created for an LGBTQ audience by the Network of Health Equity. The Healthcare Bill of Rights can be printed out and carried in one's wallet. The website also includes information about finding inclusive care providers, contacting Lambda Legal, and filing a complaint with the DHS.

"Abortion Access for LGBTQ People," National LGBTQ Task Force (http://www.thetaskforce.org/wp-content/uploads/2016/06/TF_FactSheet_Abortion-Final.pdf). A 2016 factsheet with a focus on Texas queer and trans populations in the face of proposed drastic cuts to abortion access. Exposes sites of structural violence at the intersections of gender and sexual identity, race, and class. Affirms the core concepts of reproductive justice: "the LGBTQ and repro* movements are inseparable: we are all working for the right to live our lives with dignity and the right to choose how we use our bodies—without government intrusion."

"Lesbians and Abortions," *New York University Review of Law & Social Change*. Volume 35, No.1, p. 274, 2011. (https://papers.ssrn.com/sol3/papers.cfm?abstract_id=1822502). Academic article with a legal lens notes that "the arguments for women's freedom to be a lesbian or to have an abortion are usually articulated independently from each other" and explores how assault, identity, and stigma affect abortion access for gay women.

"Informed Consent in the Medical Care of Transgender and Gender-Non Conforming Patients," *AMA Journal of Ethics*. November 2016, Volume 18, Number 11: 1147-1155.

REPRODUCTIVE JUSTICE & ADVOCACY

The Sea Change Program (seachangeprogram.org). The Sea Change Program is a Berkeley-based initiative "dedicated to transforming the stigma around abortion and other stigmatized reproductive experiences." They are largely research-based, creating resources based on analysis of personal accounts of abortion access. Their work is written and presented accessibly and is often interactive in form.

Exhale After-Abortion Talkline (exhaleprovoice.org). Exhale has provided dedicated post-abortion support in a myriad of forms since its inception in 2000. The organization coined the term "pro-voice" to refer to a movement centering the voices of personal abortion experiences. They have partnered with media organizations such as MTV and TED to promote abortion destigmatization and illuminate the power of personal narrative.

SisterSong Women of Color Reproductive Justice Collaborative (sistersong.net). The SisterSong Women of Color Reproductive Justice Collaborative is a decentralized network of Southern health workers and advocates founded in 1997. They are the originators of the "reproductive justice" framework, illuminating the unique experiences and challenges of indigenous women and women of color. SisterSong is primarily an advocacy organization, passionately illuminating the complexity and power of women's lived experience.

We Testify (wetestify.org). The National Network of Abortion Funds' We Testify program seeks to amplify the voices of those underrepresented in abortion storytelling. We Testify is women of color-led and has intersectionality at the heart of its mission statement. We Testify is a fairly young program, but it is already taking an approach both bold and compassionate: "We testify as experts to our experiences. We testify that our spirituality and abortion are one. When we speak out and share our stories, we demand to be counted." Currently their website hosts a diverse collection of personal narratives and a small but incisive reproductive justice factsheet.

COMICS & GRAPHIC NOVELS

Abortion Eve, Lyn Chevli and Joyce Farmer, 1973. Published mere months after the Supreme Court's *Roe v. Wade* ruling in January 1973, *Abortion Eve* is an early underground comic with a positive, conversational approach to abortion access.

My Most Secret Desire, Julie Doucet, 1995. Embodiment and its discontents are often the focus of Julie Doucet's comics. In this collection, she uses dream narrative to approach her complicated relationship with sexuality and childbirth. Though most work collected is from the '90s, Doucet's neurotic, even violent approach to womanhood is still an outlier in a medium dominated by men.

Not Funny Ha-Ha, Leah Hayes, 2015. Leah Hayes' graphic novel chronicles two women's abortion experiences (one surgical, one medical) without questioning or passing judgement. Hayes does not dwell on events leading up to the abortions, instead focusing on the experience of accessing a provider and going through the abortion process. Hayes' drawings are refreshingly absent of pathos, even when expressing anxiety and discomfort.

"Medical Abortion," Oh Joy Sex Toy, Erika Moen & Matthew Nolan, 2015. (http://www.ohjoysextoy.com/medical-abortion/). A short comic about stages of pregnancy, how medical abortion works, and what to expect.

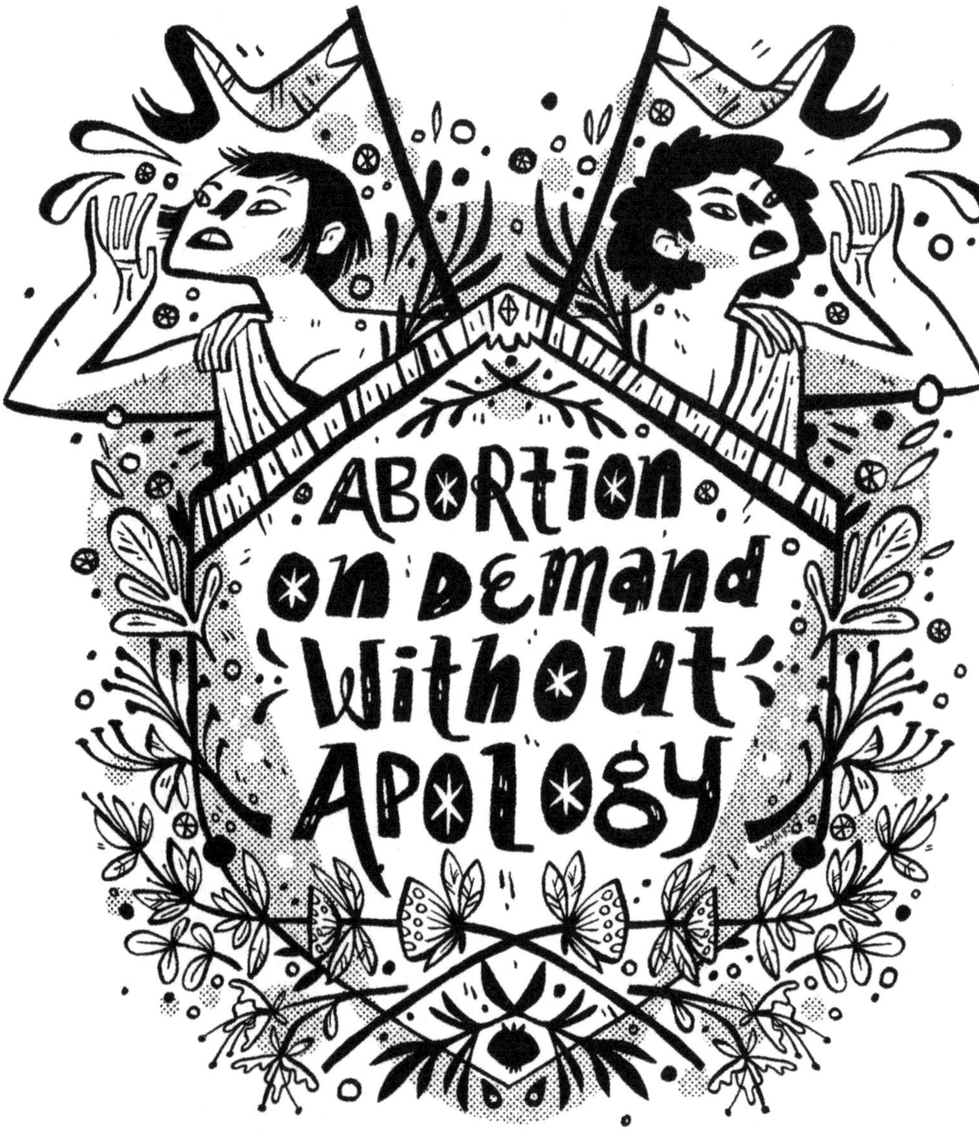
ABORTION
ON DEMAND
WITHOUT
APOLOGY

Pam Wishbow

Special thanks to everyone at the National Network of Abortion Funds and We Testify, especially Debasri Ghosh and Renee Bracey Sherman, for their incredible help with this project and for enriching and expanding our original vision. Thanks to O. Horvath for creating the resources list and to Francesca Lyn for editing the bibliographies. Lastly, thanks to everyone who donated to our IndieGoGo fundraiser for NNAF and made this book possible.